FEMINISM,
MEDIA,
AND
THE
LAW

FEMINISM,
MEDIA,
AND
THE
LAW

EDITED BY
MARTHA A. FINEMAN &
MARTHA T. MCCLUSKEY

New York   Oxford   •   Oxford University Press   1997

Oxford University Press

Oxford   New York

Athens   Auckland   Bangkok   Bogota   Bombay   Buenos Aires
Calcutta   Cape Town   Ear es Salaam   Delhi   Florence   Hong Kong
Istanbul   Karachi   Kuala Lumpur   Madras   Madrid   Melbourne
Mexico City   Nairobi   Paris   Singapore   Taipei   Tokyo   Toronto   Warsaw

and associated companies in
Berlin   Ibadan

Library of Congress Cataloging-in-Publication Data
Feminism, media, and the law / edited by Martha A. Fineman and Martha T. McCluskey.
p.   cm.
Includes bibliographical references.
ISBN 0-19-509628-2; ISBN 0-19-509629-0 (pbk.)
1. Women—Legal status, laws, etc.—United States.   2. Sex and law—United States.
3. Women in mass media—United States.   4. Sexism in mass media—United States.   5. Feminism—United States.
I. Fineman, Martha.   II. McCluskey, Martha T.
KF478.A5F456   1997
305.42'0973—dc20   96-9457

"Media Images/Feminist Issues" by Deborah L. Rhode, Signs, 20:3 reprinted by permission of
the University of Chicago Press, copyright © 1995.

"Hate Radio" was originally published in slightly different form in Ms. magazine, March/April 1994.
Copyright © 1994. "Hate Radio" is included in The Rooster's Egg by Patricia Williams.
Copyright © 1995 by The President and Fellows of Harvard College.
Reprinted by permission of the author, Harvard University Press, and Ms. magazine.

"Transforming Victimization" was reprinted in part from Tikkun Magazine, vol. 9, no. 2
a bi-monthly Jewish critique of politics, culture, and society.

"Blindfolded: Rape, and the Press's Fear of Feminism" is partly based on material from Virgin or Vamp:
How the Press Covers Sex Crimes by Helen Benedict. Copyright © 1992 by Helen Benedict.
Used by permission of Oxford University Press, Inc.

9 8 7 6 5 4 3 2 1

Printed in the United States of America
on acid-free paper

Preface

This volume includes the works of feminist scholars from a variety of disciplines. The authors are interested in how feminism as a methodology exploring the day-to-day "reality" of women's lives has been received and represented by legal institutions and the media. Consideration of these three subjects—feminism, law, and the media—reveals tensions among the respective articulated goals of the disciplines that are seemingly inevitable at this time in our culture. Objectivity and neutrality, the standards of both media and law, are called into question by feminist epistemology, which asserts that all "reporters" have perspectives that affect interpretation and selection. In this regard, feminism holds a historic antipathy to the media and has been critical of the legal system and its role in perpetuating inequality.

The media has traditionally been skeptical and dismissive of feminist critiques of society. Crude tactics, such as the marginalizing labeling of early feminists as "bra-burners," have given way to the more complex phenomena that makes neophyte antifeminists, such as Katie Roiphe, worthy of extensive media coverage while serious feminist scholarship is misrepresented and/or ignored. As the chapters in this volume indicate, the hostility directed at feminism and feminists remains a constant even as its form varies with the medium or the context of a specific message.

Law, secure in its position as a dominant normative system, need not (and, to a great extent, does not) take either the media or feminists very seriously. Legal institutions and the doctrines they produce meander along cultural chasms isolated from popular rumblings as well as "partisan" critiques by the neutrality and impartiality they profess to embody. Yet the law is a product of culture also, and it seems clear that law responds to public opinion. And public opinion, while perhaps not actually "shaped" by the media, is often guided in certain directions by what the media chooses to emphasize and address. In fact, media selection of the issues that are brought to public attention is an important step in defining what winds up on political and cultural (and hence, eventually, legal) agendas.

Most of the interdisciplinary work in this volume could be labeled "cultural studies." The authors look at society and culture and attempt to understand how and why certain negative explanations and representations of feminism have gained dominance in public and legal discourses. In exploring this question, the authors focus not so much on the origins of cultural anxiety about feminism and feminists as on the ways in which such anxieties are transformed into specific attacks, particularly as manifested in law or social institutions mediated by law.

The anxiety that feminism provokes in society as it is implicated in both the law and the media does not seem to be directed at the notion of gender equality per se. Even the more "radical" notion that there are some life events that might present distinctly "women's experiences" is no longer the source of general and widespread derision. In fact, much of the media seems obsessed with the idea of differences between men and women, generation mounds of analyses about the gender gap in political campaigns, as well as providing space for those who write about differences in language and perceptions. It is the feminist work that focuses in a critical way on the structure of our basic institutions, demanding the reconsideration (perhaps even the restructuring) of the social and economic locations of power that provoke the backlash and the attacks. This feminist work is correctly perceived as potentially threatening to the status quo and, hence, to mainstream institutions such as the law and the media.

The work in this collection considers the techniques that our society has adapted to cope with the anxiety generated by the feminist project. One significant technique has been the attempt to forcibly impose the "Rule of Law" on the shifting and unstable universe that feminism has helped to reveal. One strength of this volume is in the way the various chapters reveal how the everyday fits into the abstract tenets of theory, revealing the relevancy of a feminist approach to understanding hidden assumptions and biases harmful to women.

From the opposite perspective, it is evident that feminism and feminists must tap into the forces of popular culture and the media if they wish to affect the status and position of women in society. Law does respond to societal forces, and feminists must participate in the representations of women if they are to be able to have an effect on the direction of law and policy.

This collection begins an inquiry that must continue. We must understand and attempt to explain how the powerful forces shaping our realities work. We must not only note but also understand and debunk the conservative backlash. As many of the chapters here illustrate, feminist theory can serve as a source of hope.

This collection is a product of the ongoing work of the Feminism and Legal Theory Project at Columbia University School of Law. The project, which has been in operation since 1984, is committed to interdisciplinary work. This is the project's fourth published collection that considers issues involving law and legal regulation that are of particular interest to women. The other volumes are *At the Boundaries of Law* (Routledge 1991), *The Public Nature of Private Violence* (Routledge 1994), and *Mothers in Law* (Columbia University Press 1995).

New York   Martha Albertson Fineman

Contents

Contributors

MARIE ASHE is a Professor of Law at Suffolk University Law School in Boston, where she teaches criminal law, constitutional law, and jurisprudence. She has written and lectured extensively on topics relating to gender and law.

HELEN BENEDICT, an Associate Professor at Columbia University's Graduate School of Journalism, is the author of two novels and several books on sexual assault, including *Virgin or Vamp: How the Press Covers Sex Crimes* (1992) and *Recovery: How to Survive Sexual Assault* (1994).

SUSAN BISOM-RAPP is an Assistant Professor at Thomas Jefferson School of Law in San Diego, where she teaches employment discrimination, labor law, and torts. In February 1997 she received her J.S.D. from Columbia University School of Law. A recipient of the Woodrow Wilson National Fellowship Foundation Dissertation Grant in Women's Studies, her published scholarship focuses on feminist theory, critical race theory, and discrimination law. She holds a B.S. from Cornell University, a J.D. from the University of California, Berkeley (Boalt Hall), and an LL.M. from Columbia University School of Law.

DIANNE L. BROOKS is an Associate Professor of Legal Studies at the University of Massachusetts at Amherst. Brooks' chapter is part of a forthcoming book titled *The Law of Daytime: Soap Operas, Issue Plots and Law Narratives.*

KRISTIN BUMILLER is an Assistant Professor of both Political Science and Women's and Gender Studies at Amherst College. She is the author of *The Civil Rights Society: The Social Construction of Victims* (1988).

LYNN S. CHANCER is an Assistant Professor in the Department of Sociology at Barnard College. She is the author of *Sadomasochism in Everyday Life* (Rutgers University Press, 1992), a forthcoming set of essays on contemporary feminist debates (University of California Press, 1997), and is completing a project on high-profile crime cases involving biases of gender, race, and class.

AMY CHASTEEN is an Assistant Professor of Sociology at the University of Southern Mississippi. Her interests center on violence, gender, and race in law and popular culture. She has recently completed her dissertation, which analyzes representations of rape in the media, the law, and feminist theory, and explores how women negotiate and interpret these representations in their everyday lives.

MARY COOMBS is a Professor of Law at the University of Miami. She teaches and writes in the areas of family law, criminal law, and feminist theory, and is the coauthor of a forthcoming casebook on criminal law and the family. She is particularly and increasingly interested in the intersection of law and cultural/ideological images of family.

KATHLEEN DALY She has written on the ways that gender and race structure patterns of law-breaking and criminal court sentencing, formal and informal responses to violence against women, and the relationship of feminist theory to criminology, law, and justice. Her book, Gender, Crime, and Punishment (1994), is an empirical study of men and women defendants in the New Haven felony court.

JOYCE DAVIS teaches Legal Methods and a seminar on Family Law at Widener University School of Law, in Wilmington, Delaware. She received her LL.M. from Columbia University School of Law in 1995, where she was awarded the Finkelstein Fellowship and continues to be a J.S.D. candidate. She previously taught legal research and writing and Legal Services Orientation at Florida State University College of Law, and she helped to establish and develop an Alternative Conflict-Resolution Center at Florida State University. Other legal experience includes work as a staff attorney for the Florida legislature and for Legal Services of North Florida and private practice as both a solo practitioner and a founding member of a feminist law firm in Tallahassee, Florida.

MARTHA A. FINEMAN is Maurice T. Moore Professor of Law at Columbia University. Her research interests include the topics of divorce law, child custody law, and feminist theory. She is the author of The Illusion of Equality: The Rhetoric and Reality of Divorce Reform (1991) and, most recently, The Neutered Mother, the Sexual Family, and Other Twentieth Century Tragedies (1994). The founder and chair of the annual Feminism and Legal Theory conference since 1984, Professor Fineman has also coedited several works collected from these meetings, including At the Boundaries of Law: Feminism and Legal Theory (1990), The Public Nature of Private Violence (1994), and Mothers in Law: Feminist Theory and the Legal Regulation of Motherhood (1995).

JULIA E. HANIGSBERG is a J.S.D. candidate at Columbia University School of Law. A former Associate in Law at Columbia, and law clerk at the Supreme Court of Canada, her current research focus is the legal regulation of motherhood and the connection between ideologies of motherhood and procreative rights. She received her B.C.L. and LL.B. from McGill University Faculty of Law and her LL.M. from Columbia University School of Law.

TRACY E. HIGGINS is an Associate Professor of Law at Fordham University School of Law, where she teaches courses in Feminist Jurisprudence, Civil Rights, and International Human Rights. She received her A.B. in economics from Princeton University in 1986 and her J.D. from Harvard Law School in 1990. Professor Higgins has published in the areas of feminist political theory and jurisprudence and women's international human rights. She is currently interested in theories of social construction and their implications for theorizing women's sexual agency in law and democratic theory.

LISA CHIYEMI IKEMOTO is a Professor of Law at Loyola Law School, Los Angeles. Her current research focuses on two areas: gender, race, and class norms attached to procreation, and identity politics between and within communities of color. She teaches in the areas of bioethics, property, and family law.

E. ANN KAPLAN is Professor of English and Comparative Studies at the State University of New York at Stony Brook, where she founded and directs the Humanities Institute. She has written widely on literary and film theory, psychoanalysis, feminism, and postmodernism. Her books include Women and Film: Both Sides of the Camera, Rocking Around the Clock: Music Television, Postmodernism, and Consumer Culture, and Motherhood and Representation: The Mother in Popular Culture *and Melodrama*. Part of her new work in cultural studies and multiculturalism appeared in her new book titled *Looking for the Other: Feminism, Film, and the Imperial Gaze* (1997). Kaplan's many edited volumes include *Postmodernism and Its Discontents* and, most recently, *Generations: Academic Feminists in Dialogue* (with D. Looser) and *The Politics of Research* (with George Levine).

ISABEL KARPIN is a lecturer in the Faculty of Law at the University of Sydney in Australia where she teaches courses in feminist jurisprudence, legal institutions, constitutional law, and health law. Isabel received her LL.B. from Sydney University in 1987 and in 1991 she obtained a Masters of Law from Harvard University. She is currently in the process of completing her J.S.D. at Columbia University in New York. Her research interests include feminist legal theory, reproductive technology, and law and cultural production.

LAUREL LEFF is an Assistant Professor in the School of Journalism at Northeastern University. Previously, she was specialties editor of the *Hartford Courant*, national legal editor at American Lawyer Media, and a reporter for the *Wall Street Journal* and the *Miami Herald*. She holds a masters in the study of law from Yale Law School. Her chapter is an expanded version of remarks delivered at Columbia Law School during the Feminism and Legal Theory workshop.

CYNTHIA LUCIA is completing her dissertation on Hollywood's female lawyers in the Cinema Studies Department of New York University. She is a writer and editor at *Cineaste* magazine and teaches English and film at Horace Greeley High School in Chappaqua, New York.

MARTHA T. MCCLUSKEY is an Associate Professor of Law at the State University of New York at Buffalo. She is a J.S.D. candidate at Columbia University School of Law, where she was an Associate in Law from 1993 to 1995. Her current research focuses on workers' compensation insurance and critical perspectives on economic analysis of law. She has worked as an attorney for the Maine Public Advocate's Office on public utility and insurance regulatory issues, and she has also written essays on feminism and law for Maine news media. She received her J.D. from Yale Law School and an LL.M. from Columbia Law School.

ELAYNE RAPPING, a media theorist and critic, is a Professor of Communications at Adelphi University. Her work has appeared in numerous scholarly and mainstream publications. She writes regular columns on culture for *The Progressive* and *On the Issues: The Progressive Women's Quarterly*. Her books include *The Movie of the Week: Private Stories/Public Events, Media-tions: Forays into the Culture and Gender Wars*, and *The Culture of Recovery: Women, Addiction, and the 12-step Movement*.

DEBORAH L. RHODE is a Professor of Law and the Director of the Center on Legal Ethics and the Legal Profession at Stanford University. She is president elect of the Association of American Law Schools and a former director of Stanford's Institute for Research on Women and Gender. She writes primarily in the area of gender, law, and public policy. Her publications include *Speaking of Sex* (1997), *Justice and Gender* (1989), and two edited volumes, *The Politics of Pregnancy: Adolescent Sexuality and Public Policy* (1993), with Annette Lawson, and *Theoretical Perspectives on Sexual Difference* (1990).

MARGARET M. RUSSELL is an Associate Professor of Law at Santa Clara University in Santa Clara, California, where she teaches courses in constitutional law, civil procedure, and civil rights. She received an A.B. degree in history from Princeton University in 1979, a J.D. from Stanford Law School in 1984, and a J.S.M. degree from Stanford Law School in 1990.

ANN RUSSO is an Assistant Professor in the Women's Studies Program at DePaul University. She is a writer and activist involved in feminist and antiracist struggles against interpersonal and institutionalized violence. She is coeditor with Chandra Mohanty and Lourdes Torres of *Third World Women and the Politics of Feminism* and with Cheris Kramarae of *The Radical Women's Press of the 1850s*.

DEBORAH L. TOLMAN, Ed.D., is a Research Scientist and Director of the Adolescent Sexuality Project at the Center for Research on Women at Wellesley College. A developmental psychologist, she is currently studying how femininity ideology relates to a range of risks and resiliences embedded in sexual and intimate relationships for culturally and socioeconomically diverse girls as they move through adolescence. She is also

writing a book based on her research about adolescent girls' experience of their own sexuality,
entitled *Dilemma of Desire*, to be published by
Harvard University Press.

PATRICIA J. WILLIAMS is a Professor of Law at
Columbia University. Writing primarily in the
areas of race, gender, and law, Professor Williams
is also a member of the Board of Scholars at *Ms.*
magazine and a columnist for *The Nation*. She is
the author of *The Alchemy of Race and Rights*
(1991), *The Rooster's Egg* (1996), and *On Seeing
a Colourblind Future* (1997).

DONNA E. YOUNG is an Assistant Professor of
Law at the Albany Law School of Union University where she teaches courses in labor and
employment law, civil rights law, and civil procedure. She is a J.S.D. candidate at Columbia
University School of Law. She received an
LL.B. from Osgoode Hall Law School of York
University in Toronto and an LL.M from Columbia University School of Law. Her research
is in domestic and international labor regula
tion, feminist legal theory, and critical race
theory.

I

PORTRAYALS
OF FEMINISM
IN THE MEDIA

Introduction

DONNA E. YOUNG

In reflecting on the commercial media coverage of progressive social movements, one comes to appreciate the media's immense power to alter popular opinion on matters of public policy. Clearly, the media has the potential to advance the objectives of progressive movements. Too often, however, the media exercises its interpretive authority, sometimes deliberately and sometimes carelessly, to obstruct progressive social change. Therefore, feminists and others interested in using the media to promote social change must try to expose weaknesses in journalistic theory and practice while at the same time exploiting the media's transformative potential.

The chapters in part I, "Portrayals of Feminism in the Media," offer insightful analyses of the ways in which the commercial media has advanced or hindered feminist and other social movements. The authors examine newspapers and newsrooms, books, radio and television talk shows, and popular news and women's magazines to explore how the media presents feminism and feminist issues to the public. Different degrees of pessimism about the media's ability to accurately

address contemporary feminist concerns are reflected in the chapters. Each author concentrates on a different critique of the means by which the media constructs and shapes the theory and politics of feminism. Has the media been effective in bringing public attention to feminist concerns? How does journalism's method and theory of "objectivity" perpetuate sex and race discrimination? What are/should be the feminist responses to media-generated messages of hate and intolerance toward women, gays, lesbians, and people of color? What can feminists learn from the press-mediated appropriation of feminist methodology by those who are critical of feminism? And finally, does the media have the transformative potential to advance feminist objectives? In responding to these and other questions, the readings in this section make clear that despite being the target of vitriolic media coverage, feminism has proven to be a resilient vehicle for social change.

In chapter 2, "Media Images/Feminist Issues," Deborah Rhode examines the evolution of media practice from a time when women and women's issues were unrepresented in newsrooms and on editorial boards to a time when the discussion of women's issues in the media is commonplace, albeit often problematic. Although there have been significant improvements in the quality and quantity of media representations of feminism, feminists, and gender-related issues, there is still much room for improvement. Rhode demonstrates that we have moved from a period of "not-so-benign neglect" of women's issues to one in which press coverage too often caricatures and mischaracterizes feminist struggles. Rather than neutrally reporting on feminist issues, the media caricatures, personalizes, trivializes, and polarizes them. Rhode's comprehensive overview of the media's treatment of feminist issues provides a valuable context in which to scrutinize the commercial media's availability as a forum for attacks on feminism. Rhode exposes the connection between this media hostility to feminism and the tendency of many women to distance themselves from the feminist label. Alienation from feminism is not uncommon, nor is it surprising, given the general unpopularity of movements that espouse a fundamental restructuring of society. Rhode finds that the media's rather serious shortcomings are at least partially responsible for the alienation from feminism that many women experience.

Fueling alienation from feminism and other movements for social change, a small but powerful cadre of right-wing media figures openly pander to the fears and insecurities of their audience. Behind much of the mainstream media debates about race and gender are the rantings of popular radio and television demagogues who promote an open and crude form of intolerance in the guise of full and fair discussion. Their talk shows have enormous mass appeal. Witness the popularity of Howard Stern and Rush Limbaugh, who have become the pundits and policy-makers in a new era of hate.

Patricia Williams reminds us in chapter 3, "Hate Radio: Why We Need to Tune into Limbaugh and Stern," that this attack on women and people of color is not new. Pointing to past popular figures, like Morton Downey Jr. and Joe McCarthy, Williams argues that Stern, Limbaugh, and others are only their most recent incarnations. The views expressed by Stern and Limbaugh are not idiosyncratic. Indeed, in listening to them, Williams asserts, we are "listening to a

large segment of white America think aloud."[1] Most of Stern's and Limbaugh's listeners are white men. "Radio Racism," Williams proclaims, gives voice to that segment of the audience who believe and are encouraged to believe that they are a dispossessed, oppressed, powerless minority. Lesbians and gays, disabled people, women, and people of color become the villainous "other," competitors for scarce resources in a contracting marketplace. The struggle becomes "us" against "them." Those who identify with Stern or Limbaugh, those who belong to the "us" group, are seen to represent the "triumph of the individual." It is "them," those not part of the target audience, those who have been made the "other," who lose the authority to assert any claim to individuality. It is this outcome that so worries Williams. This essay is particularly timely given the recent debate about talk radio's role in providing the sort of environment from which right-wing, antigovernment militia groups can draw ideological support. Williams's essay functions as an especially valuable warning of the destruction that "hate radio" encourages.

While Limbaugh and Stern embrace bigotry and intolerance, most mainstream journalists claim to keep their own values and political beliefs in check in order to be neutral and objective. However, as Laurel Leff points out in chapter 4, "The Making of a 'Quota Queen': News Media and the Bias of Objectivity," "objectivity" as a journalistic method and philosophical framework offers the public subjective, value-laden opinion in the guise of objective journalistic discourse. Leff's articulation of the problems with journalistic objectivity fits within a wider critique of liberalism's adherence to principles of neutrality. Leff demonstrates how the "objective" press coverage of Lani Guinier's nomination to head the Justice Department's Civil Rights Division shaped the debate that eventually led to the defeat of her nomination. Leff argues that as a method, "objectivity" gives journalists undeserved authority and insulates them from the consequences of what they report. The objective method merely disguises individual judgment. As a philosophy, journalistic objectivity, like liberalism, tends to be hostile toward complexity, originality, and minority perspectives. It reinforces the status quo by embracing a conventional, not neutral, interpretive framework. New ways of thinking must struggle to be introduced into the public discourse. Through the objective method, Leff argues, the press was able to turn Guinier into a "radical extremist intent upon subverting American democracy." And through the interpretive framework of objectivity, the press "turned the legal scholar into a quota queen."

The Clarence Thomas confirmation hearings provide another opportunity to evaluate the journalistic ideal of objectivity. The hearings prompted a popular discussion of sexual harassment and of feminism itself. Sexual harassment has been an important issue in feminist legal literature for a long time. However, only in 1986, after years of feminist struggle, did the U.S. Supreme Court recognize that sexual harassment was a form of sex discrimination;[2] and it was not until the Thomas confirmation hearing in 1991 that the topic was discussed seriously and at length in the mainstream media. To some, the hearing marked the turning point at which sexual harassment finally became understood as a serious hindrance to women's full participation in the paid labor force. The hearings helped to raise the consciousness of the American public. However, not all the press coverage was accurate or helpful.

Several books have since been written about the controversy. In her discussion of David Brock's best-selling book *The Real Anita Hill: The Untold Story*, Mary Coombs exposes the techniques used by the media to vilify feminism while professing neutrality. In chapter 5, "The Real *Real Anita Hill* or the Making of a Backlash Best-Seller," Coombs uncovers the cynicism behind Brock's skewed and partisan reporting of events. Coombs shows that Brock's book is poorly researched and poorly written and offers convoluted and incoherent explanations of Anita Hill's testimony. Nonetheless, the book has received positive reviews and has become a best-seller. Coombs examines the patterns of thought in the commentary and reviews of Brock's book and offers a "socially rooted" explanation for the book's popularity. She suggests that the book's deployment of stereotypes and prejudices appeals to public sentiments. Coombs asserts that journalists approve of the book because of its professed neutrality and objective analysis: an assertion that coincides with Leff's critique of the journalistic ideal of objectivity. Despite the book's supposed adherence to this journalistic ideal, feminist analysis is depicted as biased and lacking in credibility. In fact, as Coombs aptly demonstrates, it is Brock's book that lacks credibility and has effectively fueled the backlash against feminism, racial justice, and affirmative action, paralleling wider patterns of intolerance in the mainstream media.

In addition to its importance as a test of journalistic objectivity, the Clarence Thomas/Anita Hill episode is a powerful example of how the invocation of "victimhood" by men often obscures the oppression of women. In an effort to lure the senators away from any meaningful evaluation of his qualifications, Thomas evoked powerful images of victimization, using his lynching metaphor to deflect attention from his shortcomings. Once Thomas became the victim, Anita Hill became his most powerful victimizer. Thomas's strategy helped him to secure a seat on the Supreme Court. In contrast, Anita Hill's allegations that she was a victim of Thomas's harassment were unsuccessful. What accounts for the success of Thomas's reliance on his status as victim, and Hill's failure?

Consider the recent attack against "victim feminists" who, it is argued, wrongly base their theories on women's status as victims rather than as agents. Critics, who are often self-proclaimed feminists, declare that "victim feminists" are responsible for alienating women and perpetuating male dominance over women. The media tends to record the debate between these different strands of feminism in the context of college campus discussions of date rape and sexual harassment. However, the media's representation of the debate does not capture the scope and complexity of the problem. How does one discuss women's subordination without magnifying women's vulnerability? This is a question that feminists have struggled with for some time. In attempting to answer this question, it is interesting to note the absence in the "victim/agent" controversy of a sustained critique of those who claim to be victims of feminists.

In chapter 6, "Fear of Feminism: Media Stories of Feminist Victims and Victims of Feminism on College Campuses," Martha McCluskey suggests that in responding to the victim/agent dilemma, we should examine not only the arguments against feminist victim narratives recorded in the media but also the victim narratives used by white, heterosexual, class-privileged men. McCluskey argues that stories of victimhood and harm can actually bolster one's power and autonomy, depending on one's position as authoritative subject. For example, men privileged by race, class, and sexual orientation are able to invoke narratives of harm with a negligible loss of power and authority. While providing background against which to evaluate the victim/agent dilemma, McCluskey urges us to reposition the discussion to consider how privileged men's use of the language of disempowerment has been successful in the media-mediated debate over gender oppression.

While it is apparent from the chapters in this section that the media is capable of distorting feminist messages, the media does not always reflect or inspire reactionary viewpoints. For example, some feminist issues have appeared in the pages of an unlikely forum of feminist intelligence: the popular women's magazine. In contrast to Limbaugh, Stern, and others, with their vicious attack against feminism, popular women's magazines—long considered to be antithetical to feminist ideals—may actually embrace and widely disseminate feminist teachings.

Julia Hanigsberg argues in chapter 7, "Glamour Law: Feminism through the Looking Glass of Popular Women's Magazines," that the popular women's magazine is a vibrant source of feminist thought that reaches many women who would not otherwise identify with feminism. Rhode's view of the popular women's magazine is more cautious. She suggests that women's magazines have the potential to undermine feminist objectives by focusing on self-transformation rather than on social transformation. Because of the spotlight on the individual, Rhode warns, women's magazines may de-emphasize feminists' call for collective action. However, in an era in which fewer than half of all women identify feminism as responding to their concerns, Hanigsberg argues that women's "popmags" are more feminist and intelligent than is generally believed. Hanigsberg stresses that feminists must capitalize on popular magazines' large circulation. She urges us to recognize that these magazines are more in touch with women's needs than other forms of literature are and that feminism in general would benefit from exposure to the magazines' diverse audience. Therefore, although the commercial media frequently distorts stories in order to appeal to majority interests, it can also make material with a progressive feminist message available to a large, otherwise unreached audience.

The chapters in part I provide a thoughtful examination of feminism's portrayal in the media. Rhode offers a historical background to the subsequent commentaries and demonstrates that the media has come a long way from its early treatment of feminism and feminists. Hanigsberg shows, for example, that women's magazines, although not always transformative, are evidence that feminism survives outside academic circles and that the media is at least partially responsible for this. However, feminism is still too often distorted by inaccurate media accounts. Much of the problem stems from journalists' inclination to see themselves as detached observers, disinclined to promote any particular political agenda. Leff and Coombs demonstrate, however, that the media is not free from bias or prejudice. In fact, it is the media's embrace of objectivity that makes it most apt to misrepresent important and complex social issues. Williams alerts us to another factor that undermines feminism and other progressive social movements: media bigotry, as displayed in the "hate radio" phenomenon. Williams and McCluskey encourage us to study the techniques used by those who have fueled the antifeminist backlash.

In reading the essays in part I, it is important to keep in mind that most commercial media enterprises cater to mainstream markets that respond more favorably to liberal, status-quo-oriented messages than to reformist, critical messages. The media relies on a liberal claim to objectivity and neutrality which I believe limits its ability to confront normative assumptions about gender, race, and class and distorts feminist theories that employ structural or systemic, rather than individualist, explanations of male domination. Each of the essays in this section explicitly or implicitly addresses the ways in which the commercial media's reliance on liberal notions of individual responsibility and autonomy overlooks the forces (i.e., patriarchy, white supremacy) that act upon individuals as members of groups.[1] The media's focus on individual achievement or failure, and its corresponding misrepresentation of feminist messages that call for a restructuring of social relationships, conceals feminism's principle strength: its insistence on the *collective* empowerment of all women. Because in most instances the mass media frustrates the goals of feminism, we ought to take seriously Coombs's warning not to trust the media. However, must feminists not also support Rhode's demand for a greater voice in shaping the media's portrayal of feminism?

This raises an important question, one that is at the center of feminist engagement with the commercial media. How are feminists to demand a greater voice in an enterprise that is structurally and ideologically hostile to feminism's message? Each author has discussed the magnitude of the commercial media's assault on feminist theory and practice. But it is important to keep in mind that not all feminist theories share the same ideological roots; therefore, not all are subject to the same media attack. Within feminism, there are competing and contradictory theories of women's oppression. I believe that the media is receptive to feminist and other theories to the extent that they are based on a liberal paradigm and coincide with market needs. For example, in the victim/agent debate, Roiphe, Paglia, Sommers, and other "antifeminist" feminists have enjoyed media support arguably because of their liberal assessment of individual autonomy and agency and their refusal to address the structural context in which patterns of inequality (i.e., patriarchy, white supremacy) have developed. Their work fits neatly within the existing social order without challenging that order and appeals to mainstream markets. In getting their points across, these authors and others such as David Brock employ rhetorical devices that appear to correspond to the media's liberal ideals of neutrality and objectivity. Likewise, some popular women's magazines may entertain feminist messages so long as the messages respond to the specific demands of their readership and conform to the liberal ideal of individual achievement. Because the media is not hostile to all feminist demands, we must be careful not to present the feminist critique of the media as being a debate between all feminists on the one hand and all media on the other, because the possible complicity between the two will be obscured.

Those feminist theories that challenge the possibility of an "objective" evaluation of the interaction between autonomous agents, and those that do not suit the tastes of a largely nonfeminist mainstream audience, are not readily translated into a language that the commercial media is ideologically equipped to understand and communicate. The forms of feminist theory and practice that most challenge the liberal status quo are the most likely to be misunderstood and/or mistreated by the media because of the media's own reliance on a liberal paradigm. We must therefore question whether the media is capable of understanding and fairly representing theories that threaten to undermine the liberal paradigm. This presents a significant challenge for those feminists who attempt to work with or within the commercial media. Rhode, Williams, Leff, Coombs, McCluskey, and Hanigsberg have addressed this challenge and have made important contributions to the debate over feminist engagement with the media by offering unique insights into the commercial media's obstruction of social change.

Notes

1. Interestingly, Robin Quivers, Stern's cohost, would probably agree. In a recent *New Yorker* article, Quivers says, "Howard is the voice of things people think about but don't say. I'm more the moral conscience of the show" (Als 1995).

2. See *Meritor Sav. Bank v. Vinson*, 477 U.S. 57 (1986).

3. Note that the media's dichotomization of the individual and the group is not applied consistently. For example, as Williams and McCluskey demonstrate, individualism is routinely denied to some people on the basis of their race, gender, and sexual orientation.

Media Images/Feminist Issues

DEBORAH L. RHODE

For those committed to feminism, a central concern has always been how the media reflect and recast feminist issues. For those committed to feminist research, media studies offer a particularly useful perspective on the social construction of a political movement. Indeed, even formulating this topic as a research question yields unexpected insights. In the *Readers' Guide to Periodical Literature*, "feminism" traditionally was not considered significant enough to warrant a separate entry. In the 1950s, the feminist heading had only a cross-reference to "Women, social and moral questions." This entry listed a handful of articles and a "see also" reference to alcoholism, divorce, harem, and prostitution. Over the next two decades, these cross-references expanded and eventually came to include "Women, equal rights." But not until the early 1980s did feminism become a topic heading in its own right.

The following discussion chronicles this evolution and certain persistent limitations in media texts and subtexts. The basic story is one of partial progress. Over the last quarter century, much has improved in press portraits of feminism, femi-

nists, and gender-related issues. Yet much still needs improvement. This essay suggests what and why. At issue is what the media choose to present (or not to present) as news about women and how they characterize (or caricature) the women's movement. This issue deserves greater attention from those interested in social movements in general and the women's movement in particular. The press is increasingly responsible for supplying the information and images through which we understand our lives (Hall 1977, pp. 340–42). For any social movement, the media play a crucial role in shaping public consciousness and public policy. Journalists' standard framing devices of selection, exclusion, emphasis, and tone can profoundly affect cultural perceptions (Gitlin 1980, pp. 3–7; Goffman 1974, pp. 10–11).

For the women's movement, mass-communication networks have done much both to frustrate and to advance feminist objectives. As subsequent discussion suggests, the mainstream press appeared largely uninterested or unsympathetic during the early years of the contemporary women's movement. And female journalists often lacked the critical mass and professional leverage to ensure systematic, evenhanded treatment of gender-related issues. That has changed dramatically, in part because of women's increasing involvement in the media and in part because of broader cultural changes in gender roles. As media theorists remind us, audiences always exert some control over the message they receive, and the public's growing concern about women's issues has reshaped popular discourse (Rapping 1994a; Rapping 1994b, pp. 10–12, 284). The press is increasingly an ally in making those issues into political priorities.

However, despite substantial improvements, we still remain stuck in some familiar places. The following discussion identifies persistent feminist concerns. Analysis begins with the absence of women in the media: their underrepresentation in positions of influence; the not-so-benign neglect of women's issues; the premature postmortems of the women's movement; and journalists' own contribution to the "demise" that they claim only to describe. Discussion then turns to the way that press coverage can demonize, trivialize, and unduly personalize feminist struggles. A final section offers consoling thoughts and proposals for collective action. After reviewing the forces that have increased sensitivity to gender-related concerns, the discussion suggests further strategies to that end. Only by gaining a better understanding of how media images construct and constrain feminist objectives can we come closer to realizing them.

Out of Sight, Out of Mind

The frequent absence of women in, on, and behind the news has been chronicled at length elsewhere and does not require extended treatment here. Longstanding gaps persist in women's representation and in the coverage of women's issues, and the problems are related. In the late 1940s, only one female journalist appeared on any television news program. By 1960, the number had increased to one per network. These female reporters handled only "women's" stories, such as those involving political wives, and sometimes filled in as weather girls (Marzolf 1993, pp. 33, 36–44). In the print media, the small group of female journalists generally had a separate, and anything but equal, status. Most were relegated to work as researchers rather than writers or to positions on the women's page, traditionally limited to food, fashion, furnishings, and society "do's and doings" (Beasley and Gibbons 1993, p. 16; see I. Ross 1974; F. Davis 1991, pp. 110–11; Robertson 1992; Kay Mills 1993; Quindlen 1993b, p. 2). The absence of women on news staffs typified broader patterns in media coverage; female underrepresentation was pervasive in everything from prime-time drama to children's cartoons (Tuchman 1978a, pp. 8–10; Robertson 1992, pp. 7, 181).

During the 1960s, the situation began to improve, in response both to the feminist movement and to the broader socioeconomic changes that the movement reflected and reinforced. Between the mid-1960s and the early 1990s, women's representation among television network news reporters and print journalists more than doubled (Marzolf 1993, p. 43). Over two-thirds of journalism school graduates are now women (Marzolf 1993, p. 43). Yet women also continue to be grossly underrepresented in media positions of greatest status and power and dramatically overrepresented in the lowest. Women account for less than 10 percent of editors in chief, news publishers, and deans or directors of journalism programs (Otto 1993, pp. 157–8; Kay Mills 1993, pp. 19, 25). A recent survey of newspapers and network news programs found that men wrote about two-thirds of the front-page stories and provided 85 percent of the television reporting (Bridge 1993). Women of color are even less visible. They account for only about 7 percent of the newspaper workforce, and 3 percent of its executives and managers. In the broadcast media, representative studies have found that women of color filed only 2 percent of the total surveyed stories and that no nonwhite women appeared in an annual survey of the fifty most prominent reporters (Beasley and Gibbons 1993, pp. 307, 317).

Once again, these gender imbalances in journalism are symptomatic of broader media patterns. Men hold 90 percent of upper level Hollywood executive positions, play two-thirds of the leads in prime-time television, supply 90 percent of the narrator's voices in television commercials, and monopolize 90 percent of televised sporting events (J. Carmody 1993, p. B12; Dutka 1990, p. 8; Lovdal 1989, p. 716; Messner, Duncan, and

Jensen 1993). Rarely do women of color exceed what is commonly described as a "sprinkling of minorities" (Women, Men and Media 1993; Minnesota Advisory Committee 1993, pp. 5–7; Edwards 1993, pp. 215–18).

The inadequate representation of women in media decision-making is mirrored in the media's inadequate representation of women's perspectives and concerns. According to recent surveys, men provided 85 percent of newspaper quotes or references, accounted for 75 percent of the television interviewees, and constituted 90 percent of the most frequently cited pundits (Bridge 1993; O'Reilly 1993, pp. 127, 129). This proportionality, or lack thereof, held up across subject matter areas, even on issues that centrally involved women, such as single motherhood and breast implants (S. Douglas 1992; Bridge 1993; O'Reilly 1993, pp. 125, 127; Pollitt 1994b). During the much-fabled "Year of the Woman" in politics, not one representative of a major women's policy organization appeared on any leading TV talk show (Wolf 1993a, p. 80). When female commentators do appear, it is often on explicitly "women's issues." How often, asks Katha Pollitt, do women show up on *Nightline* or *Crossfire* when the subject is not "Hillary Clinton: Does Whitewater Stigmatize All Women?" or "Is the Wonderbra Sexist?" (Pollitt 1994b, p. 409). The result is much as Kirk Anderson portrays it in his cartoon of a talk-show anchor previewing his program: "In the next half-hour, my wealthy white conservative male friends and I will discuss the annoyingly persistent black underclass, and why women get so emotional about abortion" (Ward 1993, p. 92).

Women's issues are also underrepresented in the mainstream media (Kahn and Goldenberg 1991, pp. 105–7). To be sure, the situation has improved dramatically since the 1960s and early 1970s, when leading papers rarely discussed matters such as child care and domestic violence or did so only in the "style" section (Quindlen 1993b, p. 3). Coverage has steadily increased, and dramatic events like the Hill/Thomas hearings or the O. J. Simpson trial can create a sudden cottage industry of commentary on problems that for centuries went unchallenged and unchanged. But on a day-to-day basis, gender biases remain. Subjects that are of greater interest to male than female readers have greater priority among largely male editors. Topics with the most

appeal to men but the least to women, such as local sports, obtain substantially greater newspaper resources than topics for which the relative interest levels are reversed, such as family/lifestyle issues (S. Miller 1993, pp. 167–68).

Particular concerns for women of color are often ignored, as are the women themselves. "How Can 29 Million People Be Invisible to Democrats?" asked a recent *Los Angeles Times* headline, referring to the Latino population. The same question could have been asked about the author's own profession, which rarely focuses on that constituency (Rogovin 1992, pp. 51, 55–58; Women, Men and the Media 1993; Minnesota Advisory Committee 1993, pp. 5–7).

What limited coverage does occur often presents biased images. The mainstream media prefer to center stories on deviance rather than on achievements or victimization among people of color, and to explain such deviance in terms of race rather than other, more complicated, factors (Minnesota Advisory Committee 1993, pp. 5–7). For example, rapes of white women by black men receive a grossly disproportionate amount of media attention, although they account for only a small minority of reported rapes. Sexual assaults against black women are largely overlooked, even though they constitute the group likeliest to be victims of such brutality (Benedict 1992, p. 9). During the week of the highly publicized rape of a white investment banker in Central Park by a nonwhite gang, twenty-eight other women in New York also reported rapes. Nearly all of these assaults involved women of color, and their rapes, including at least one of comparable brutality, went largely unreported by the press (Terry 1993, p. 160; Benedict 1992, p. 219).

Moreover, despite the enormous volume of commentary attempting to account for the Central Park assault, the most obvious gender-related explanations were notable for their absence. Almost all the coverage focused on race and poverty; almost none surveyed the research on gang rape, which reveals that such crimes are frequently committed by white middle-class athletes and fraternity members. As sociologist Jane Hood put it, "Like the proverbial fish who cannot describe water, Americans see everything but gender at work in the [New York] assault. Given more than 30 years of research on rape, that myopia is hard to explain" (quoted in Benedict 1992, p. 210).

Any adequate explanation would have to consider the media's own selective vision. In Helen Benedict's recent survey, only one of some thirty reporters who routinely covered sex crimes had ever read a book on rape, and few had made any effort to consult experts (see Benedict 1996). Indeed, many defended their inattention to issues of gender inequality. According to one *Newsday* editor, attempts to analyze rape as a sex crime are "thumbsucking journalism. . . . Once you write a piece about rape experts talking about why people do gang rape, there's no follow-up" (Benedict 1996). In explaining the *New York Times*'s selective coverage of the Central Park rape, the metropolitan editor acknowledged, "I can't imagine the range of reaction to the sexual aspect of the crime would be very strong. I may be wrong but I can't think right off what questions one ought to ask about that" (quoted in Benedict 1996).

Similar patterns are apparent in the news media's highly selective soundbites on prostitution. On the rare occasions when the press toys with the issue, almost all the coverage goes to sexy celebrity cases. Hugh Grant's escapade is the most prominent example. As Hollywood scripts go, this one had considerable sex appeal and a surprisingly happy ending. Here, the proverbial "hooker with a heart of gold" ended up with a small pot of it as well. Before her retirement, streetwalker Divine Brown earned a modest fortune from selling her story to a British tabloid. Even Hugh Grant found that lack of virtue is sometimes its own reward. In a single month he became the subject of some 2,800 press stories and pulled some of the highest ratings in talk-show history.

Yet what remained missing in almost all of this coverage is what for women should be the most significant issue. The relevant question is not the one Jay Leno put to Grant: "What the hell were you thinking?" (Kronke, 1995, F4). It is rather what we as a society are thinking when we choose to invest scarce law enforcement resources in futile, dehumanizing, and gender-biased responses to prostitution.

Many of the commentators who rose to Grant's defense denied or ignored this broader problem. Some falsely portrayed prostitution as a totally victimless crime. Yet an estimated two-thirds to three-forths of streetwalkers are raped and beaten an average of four to fifteen times a year. Substance abuse, sexually transmitted diseases, severe depression, and suicide also are common (Liedholdt, 1993, pp. 136–41).

For the men involved in commercial sex, adverse consequences are far less likely. According to recent surveys, about one in six men have employed a prostitute in the last five years ("Legalised Prostitution," 1991, p. 28). Rarely do these customers face significant penalties, a fact that almost never surfaces in media coverage of cases like Grant's. Nor do press accounts acknowledge the intersecting gender and racial inequalities of law enforcement. Women account for about 90 percent of all prostitution arrests, and 85 percent of those who serve jail time are women of color. (Nelson, 1993, p. 85). The United States spends upwards of $10 million annually on enforcement strategies that largely target streetwalkers rather than the main profiteers—men who are pimps or who operate brothels, massage parlors, and escort services.

The real sex scandal in West Hollywood should not have been about Hugh Grant. It should have been about neighborhood residents who opposed a facility for local prostitutes that would provide food, HIV testing, and drug counseling ("Westside Neighbors," 1995, B1). The money we currently devote to futile criminal strategies could much more profitably be spent on services for prostitutes, such as education, employment, health, and drug treatment programs, as well as more protection from coercion and abuse. So too, the stories the press highlights on prostitution are not the stories Americans most need to hear. The questions we should be asking are not why celebrities buy sex, but why the law offers such an ineffectual and inhumane response to sexual sales. And why do so many women find it more profitable to sell their bodies than anything else?

Efforts to increase the coverage of women's perspectives are often met with other strategies of confession and avoidance. One standard response, reflected in a recent interview with a *New Republic* editor, is that "it's really hard to get women; regrettably, writers of opinion pieces tend to be men" (Wolf 1993a, p. 84). If so, the media are in part responsible. Female journalists frequently bump up against what former columnist Anna Quindlen describes as the "quota of one" (Quindlen 1993b, p. 12). In explaining their unwillingness to carry a column by a woman who writes about women, editors will note that they "already have one" (Quindlen 1993b, p. 12; O'Reilly 1993, p. 125). This somehow turns out not to be a problem for columns by and about white men.

The marginalization of women occurs not only through failure to represent their perspectives but also through failure to recognize them as independent agents, apart from their relation to men. This symbolic erasure was apparent in television descriptions of ethnic cleansing in Bosnia, in which the targets of gang rape figured as wives and daughters (Ward 1993, p. 190). Like early English common law, which treated rape as a crime against men's property interest, some contemporary media accounts carry similar subtexts: "Five [males] broke into the home of a . . . school teacher, beat him, raped his wife, and looted everything they could find" (Beasley and Gibbons 1993, p. 34). Similarly, a recent newspaper headline—"Widow, 70, Dies after Beating by Intruder"—reflects the significance of women's marital status even after death (Ward 1993, p. 191). Other information, such as the victim's work as a crime prevention volunteer, is of less apparent importance.

Such persistent value hierarchies are aptly captured in a recent Cath Jackson cartoon. It features a male editor lecturing a female staffer on the obvious problems with an article titled "Wheelchair Woman Climbs Mt. Everest": "You've missed the main points: WHO is her husband? WHAT does he do? WHERE would she be without him and WHY isn't she at home looking after the kids?" (Jackson 1993, p. 4).

Marginalizing the Women's Movement

Given the media's long-standing inattention to women's voices, its marginalization of the women's movement should come as no surprise. During the late 1960s and early 1970s, the situation was much as one study titled it: "Blackout as Social Control" (Morris 1973, p. 3; Ceulemans and Fauconnier 1979). The *Washington Post* ran no story on the formation of the National Organization for Women (NOW), and the *New York Times* placed its brief account beneath recipes for a traditional Thanksgiving (Beasley and Gibbons 1993, p. 7). Gloria Steinem recalls that her colleagues at *New York Magazine* warned her against writing on feminism: "You've worked so hard to be taken seriously, Gloria. You must not get involved with those crazy women" (quoted in Thom 1993, pp. 223, 225). After presenting an initial cover story or television news profile, many media leaders felt that they had done their bit. Reporters who wanted to reach mainstream audiences were told, "We've already done a feminist story this year" (Thom 1993, p. 225). At the *Ladies' Home Journal*, it took an invasion by activists "wearing no makeup" to prompt any coverage of the women's movement (F. Davis 1991, pp. 111–14). The directive of one male editor captured widespread attitudes: "Find an authority who'll say this is all a crock of shit" (F. Davis 1991, p. 109). Such instructions turned into self-fulfilling prophecies. The frequent refusal to present feminists as anything other than "braless bubbleheads" justified decision-makers' refusal to present them at all (quoted in Rivers, 1996, p. 103).

Despite media leaders' reluctance to chronicle the rebirth of feminism in the 1960s and early 1970s, they had no such hesitation in reporting its demise. Beginning in the early 1970s, before many journalists had turned any serious attention to the women's movement, others were declaring it dead, dying, or permanently disabled (Faludi 1991, pp. 75–76). Despite periodic reprieves, press postmortems have continued with stunning regularity. "The women's movement is over," announced a 1981 cover story in the *New York Times* magazine (Friedan 1981, p. 14; Faludi 1991, p. 76). Anyone who missed that obituary did not lack for further opportunities to mourn. Indeed, as Ellen Goodman observes, the death and resurrection of feminism has become a "media staple like the monthly makeover in fashion magazines" (1992, p. 3D).

In these autopsies of the women's movement, most authors come to bury their subject, not to praise it. The diagnoses vary slightly, but movement leaders are almost always to blame. Their problem is either hating men or wanting to be just like them. Sally Quinn captures the prevailing wisdom in a 1992 column titled "Feminists Have Killed Feminism." Although this presumed death has often encouraged journalistic neglect, the causes of the movement's demise have also attracted some attention. According to one common story line, feminism's emphasis on equality has grown out of touch with women's essential identity and has propelled them into a workplace unresponsive to their needs. In these morality plays of sorts, the heroine is generally fertile and frantic or single and sullen. In either case, the solution lies with individual women rather than with social transformation. The happy ending often comes only when the would-be supermom realizes that no one has it all and then exchanges her self-seeking career for hearth and home (Mansfield 1985, p. C1; Fischer 1986, p. 96; Lawson 1986, p. 48; Faludi 1991, pp. 81–89). Thus, *Esquire*'s cover story about the ideal American wife pictures a former executive cheerfully scrubbing a toilet bowl (Finkel 1990, p. 2; Faludi 1991, pp. 88–89).

In an alternative script, the soulless spinster contemplates her rapidly declining marriage prospects with alarm but fails to make the necessary adjustments. Under *Newsweek*'s projections, the unmarried woman of forty has about as much chance of snaring a spouse as of being killed by a terrorist. Women presumably want to marry but apparently just "may not want it enough" (Salholz et al. 1986). The not-so-subtle implication is that uppity feminists get what they deserve. Women who put priority on their professions should not expect to live happily ever after.

As Susan Faludi has noted, these media narratives construct much of the trend that they claim only to describe (1991, pp. 80–88). The demographic doom projected for single women in their thirties and forties turned out to be grossly overstated, and the saga of mothers' return to full-time motherhood ignored a more significant statistical pattern (Faludi 1991, pp. 80–88). By the early 1990s, a majority of women with young children were in the paid labor force, a dramatic increase over earlier decades (Institute for Women's Policy Research 1993). Moreover, a close reading of the texts as well as subtexts of the happy homemaker sagas often suggests a different moral than the one the author draws. Some of these heroines would have preferred to keep working part-time if the option had been available (Faludi 1991, p. 88). Even more might have preferred an equitable division of household responsibilities, if the journalist had thought to ask that question. But these aspects of feminism's aspiration to equality seldom figure in conventional accounts.

Rather, the not-so-subtle message is that feminists' aspirations are somehow askew. Christina Hoff Sommers and Katie Roiphe receive exten-sive coverage for their complaints that feminists exaggerate sexual violence and inequality (Sommers 1994a; K. Roiphe 1993b). In Sally Quinn's diagnosis, women are "falling away from 'feminism' because it doesn't represent them . . . or their problems"; the concept of motherhood "unbelievably ha[s] gotten lost on many of the feminists who felt having babies [is] not the politically correct thing to do." As a result, she adds, many women see the women's movement as a "fringe cause"—anti-male, anti-child, anti-family, and anti-feminine" (Quinn 1992).

"Unbelievably" may be the key word here, although not in the sense that Quinn intends. Who are these mother-bashing, man-hating harpies she has in mind? Here, one of the main joys of journalists is apparent: the blissful freedom from footnoting. Of course, a few of the usual suspects could always be rounded up. But the most plentiful source of such "anti-family" bias is not leading feminists but, rather, the press coverage that disfigured them.

Caricatures and Characterizations

If, as leading commentators repeatedly maintain, women are alienated from feminism, the media's own caricatures are at least partly responsible. Much early coverage of the women's movement focused exclusively or disproportionately on "extremist" tactics and rhetoric. Such selective profiles are, of course, by no means unique to feminism. For obvious reasons, the "radical fringes" of social movements often receive undue attention; they play to the press's perennial search for dramatic events, startling sound bites, and "good visuals" (Gitlin 1980, pp. 283–84; Bennett 1988, pp. 26–44). Focusing on the fringes is also a way of undermining challenges that some journalists find threatening to their own group status and worldview (Hall 1977, pp. 344–46; Gerbner 1978, pp. 16–18). However, the women's movement has been particularly vulnerable to such adverse coverage because what gains attention for feminist issues often runs counter to what passes as appropriate feminine behavior. For much of the last century, the press has contributed to popular caricatures of "unsexed" harpies with deviant lifestyles and unfounded fantasies of male domination.

Some of this deviance was the media's own invention. The most celebrated example is, of course, bra-burning, a term coined by a journalist to describe feminists' protest at the 1968 Miss America Pageant. No undergarments were in fact charred; they were ceremoniously deposited in a trash receptacle. The problem with the reporter's poetic license was less its inaccuracy than its linkage of feminism to other protests that mainstream America found highly threatening: burning draft cards, burning crosses, and burning buildings in urban riots. And among many women, the lingerie bonfire has now moved from fiction to fact. A recent example surfaced in a National Public Radio poll, when a middle-aged woman linked her distaste for feminism with an earlier protest. She could still remember when a movement leader "took off her bra and burned it downtown . . . in public." And as this interviewee made clear, "I'm not burning my bra. I'm keeping my bra on" (quoted in C. Page 1991).

Time magazine's coverage of the women's movement during the 1970s and 1980s offers a representative sample of common media characterizations: "strident," "humorless," "extremist," "lesbian," and, of course, "hairy legged" ("Who's Come a Long Way, Baby?" 1970; "Liberating Women" 1970; Wallis 1989; S. Douglas 1992). In *Time*'s rendering, the leaders of "women's lib" had a "penchant for oddball causes—from ban-the-bras to communal childrearing—that leave many women cold" ("Who's Come a Long Way, Baby?" 1970). In what purported to be a later "Second Look," *Time* offered samplings of shrillness, failed to mention any substantive achievements, and capped it all with a ludicrous cartoon of Kate Millett. She appeared braless in a lacy pinafore, waving the ostensibly offending undergarment in a militant gesture of protest (P. Kamen 1991, p. 64). A decade later, in a cover story on women facing the 1990s, *Time* reported that "hairy legs haunt the feminist movement as do images of being strident and lesbian" (Wallis 1989; S. Douglas 1994, p. 275). Do tell.

Other public renderings of the movement were scarcely more flattering. Betty Friedan, the "Mother Superior" of the movement, came across as a "double-chinned," "badgering eccentric," whose theories reflected her own unhappy marriage and interpersonal failings (S. Douglas 1994, p. 229). In some instances, indictments were solicited from presumptively normal women. A

representative 1970 *New York Times* account featured reactions to "women's lib" from "traditional" groups that reportedly "had for decades championed women's rights," such as the Daughters of the American Revolution, the Women's Christian Temperance Union, and the Junior League. According to traditionalist leaders, feminists were "ridiculous exhibitionists"—"a band of wild lesbians," and many of them were "just so unattractive. . . . [Perhaps they weren't] completely well" (Fosburgh 1970).

Even when the press purported to be more positive, its compliments typically were backhanded. Thus, Germaine Greer was a "rare feminist who likes men" ("Sex and the Super-Groupie" 1971, p. 75; Kahn and Goldenberg 1991, p. 106). This kind of coverage remains common. A typical description appears in the *New York Times Magazine*'s 1994 profile of Shannon Faulkner, the woman who challenged her exclusion from an all-male military college: "She is not a crusader, activist, earthshaker, cantankerous man-hater, lesbian, or ugly duckling out to find a mate" (Manegold 1994, p. 59). So too, a 1993 *Boston Globe* story about Clare Dalton, a professor who settled a sex discrimination suit against Harvard Law School, reports with evident relief that she does not sound like some "crazed feminist spouting anti-male . . . jargon" (Doten 1993, p. 36).

Hillary Clinton has experienced constant variations on similar themes. In an effort to combat characterizations as a "bossy, humorless, radical feminist" or an "overbearing yuppie wife from hell," she has kept her distance from the "f-word" (Dowd 1992; P. Morrison 1992; Rutten 1992). When pressed during the 1992 presidential campaign, Clinton responded that she believed in equality but rejected some of what the term feminism has "come to mean today;" she did not wish to dismiss "maternal values" or "cease caring about the men in [her] life" (Dowd 1992; see Rutten 1992; P. Morrison 1992). When polls suggested that about 70 percent of the American public preferred a "traditional first lady," Clinton strategists attempted to cast Hillary in that image (Walsh 1993, p. 46). She got a kinder, gentler hairdo, more mother-child photo ops, and lower-profile public appearances, standing by her man but not opening her mouth. As First Lady, Clinton has still had to maintain her distance from feminism's "fringe associations," including rumors of lesbianism (Blumenfeld 1994, p. 213). "Feminism," as her press secretary doggedly insisted, "is a misplaced angle. It's not an accurate theme for [Clinton]. She represents today's modern woman," who, by (press) definition, is not a feminist (Blumenfeld 1994, p. 213).

As Clinton's experience suggests, a common form of demonization occurs through the linkage of lesbianism and feminism. Media coverage of this connection has proven especially problematic, not only because it trades on homophobic stereotypes but also because it implicitly legitimates them. Ever since Betty Friedan's widely publicized expression of concern about feminism's "lavender menace," the organized women's movement has struggled with the trade-off between principles and pragmatism in its public image. A major watershed for the National Organization for Women occurred in the early 1970s, after a *Time* magazine article announced: "Ironically, Kate Millett herself contributed to the growing skepticism about the movement by acknowledging at a recent meeting that she is bisexual. The disclosure is bound to discredit her as a spokeswoman for her cause, cast further doubt on her theories and reinforce the views of those skeptics who routinely dismiss all liberationists as lesbians" (quoted in F. Davis 1991, p. 268). Feminist leaders united in an angry response, and the following year a NOW conference passed its first unequivocal prolesbian resolution (F. Davis 1991, p. 268). As those leaders generally recognized, the role of lesbians within feminist organizations could not be denied; it could only be embraced. Activists would always be vulnerable to homophobic uses of the lesbian label, as was Friedan herself (F. Davis 1991, p. 268). The only way to counteract adverse public reactions was to combat the prejudices on which they rested.

This was not, however, the mainstream media's prescription. Some two decades after the Millett incident, NOW president Patricia Ireland received much the same treatment. Following public disclosures that Ireland had both a husband and a female companion, Sally Quinn summarized a common view: "What kind of standards is she espousing? It is impossible to read the Ireland declaration and argue that the movement she leads is in touch with the majority of women" (Quinn 1992). Despite strong protest, other columnists took a similar position, and Quinn herself added the following justification

for her view: "The perception that NOW is a lesbian-dominated organization is the reason why we have a backlash against feminism. Most women are turned off by having a lesbian presence in the movement. That's not my feeling. I'm just reporting on it. I agree with everything that gay rights supporters think. I'm just saying you should keep it to yourself, if you're a lesbian" (quoted in Schwartz 1992, p. 21; see Safire 1992, p. 17).

It is also impossible to read this quote and argue that media spokespersons such as Quinn are "in touch" with the real interests of American women. Prejudice against "effeminate" gays and "unfeminine" lesbians builds on the same gender stereotypes that restrict opportunities for all individuals, whatever their sexual orientation. Fear of the lesbian label also discourages activism on women's issues. For leaders like Ireland, silence on sexuality is not a solution, it is part of the problem. The more that lesbians and gays feel unable to escape the closet, the greater their difficulties in challenging its constraints. By condemning those who are open about their sexual orientation, commentators like Quinn compound the prejudices they claim merely to describe.

Personalization and Trivialization

After a point, of course, stories of stridency begin to grate, so coverage of feminism has often included a lighter touch. A favorite strategy is to personalize women's political struggle. Although this technique is common for all public figures, the profiles of feminists often carry a special edge. One approach is to treat activists challenging the sexual objectification of women in objectified terms, by focusing on their appearance. Ti-Grace Atkinson had a "dreamy, softly sexy style," and Germaine Greer had "lean good looks," while Kate Millett did not "wash her hair" ("Sex and the Super-Groupie" 1971, p. 75; "Who's Come a Long Way, Baby?" 1970, p. 75; F. Davis 1991, p. 96; S. Douglas 1992, p. 5).

This focus on appearance leaves feminists in a long-standing double bind. Those who defy cultural standards of femininity are subject to ridicule, and their cause acquires guilt by association. Feminism appears as the last refuge of homely harpies and confirms claims like Rush Limbaugh's: "Feminism was established to allow unattractive women access to mainstream society" (quoted in Rohlena, 1993, p. 57). Commentator Christina Hoff Sommers doesn't go that far, but she does point out that "[t]here are a lot of homely women in women's studies" (quoted in Quindlen, 1994, p. A21).

Yet feminists who take pains to look attractive are equally vulnerable; they risk seeming vain, petty, or hypocritical for pandering to sexist values. The media have long delighted in catching activists in such seeming contradictions. When reporting the first mass rally for equal rights by the contemporary women's movement, the *New York Times* chose as a headline, "Leading Feminist Puts Hairdo Before Strike" (1970). Betty Friedan apparently had been delayed by her hairdresser.

Similar problems confront women in other settings. Female political leaders have long risked appearing too feminine or not feminine enough. The result for aspiring candidates has often been media profiles like the one of Barbara Boxer while she was a congressional aide. Picturing her in a "cook's corner," the article noted that "Julia Child she's not." However, although her schedule left "little time for fancy cuisine," Boxer was still capable of whipping up an "inventive" peach cobbler between political conversations (quoted in Witt, Paget, and Mathews 1994, p. 206).

Such gender stereotypes have declined in frequency, but they have by no means vanished from media landscapes. During the 1992 "Year of the Woman" political campaigns, many female candidates found themselves described in sexually freighted terms. Lynn Yeakel was "an unlikely standard bearer, a former full-time mother," and Carol Moseley-Braun was a "den-mother with a cheerleader's smile" (quoted in Witt, Paget, and Mathews 1994, p. 206). In the profile on Braun, not until the twenty-second paragraph did persistent readers learn that she was also a lawyer, former prosecutor, and veteran state senator (Witt, Paget, and Mathews 1994, p. 206). This kind of coverage not only diminishes women's credibility but also marginalizes their substantive message. And the targets of such accounts can do little without compounding the problem. The double bind is well captured by the cartoon of a TV newscaster offering a campaign update: "When asked her dress size, the president lost her womanly virtues and became stern, even hectoring" (Haines 1993).

Worse yet, the media's frequent preference for style over substance has lured feminists into other no-win situations. The campaign for a constitutional Equal Rights Amendment provides ample illustrations. To counteract assertions that supporters of the amendment were all radical harpies rather than "normal" homemakers, pro-ERA groups planned a series of culinary gestures. In one celebrated instance, seventy-five housewives assembled to serve Eggs Benedict to Illinois representatives and senators. Neither opponents nor the press let the event pass unnoticed. The day before the brunch, Phyllis Schlafly and other anti-ERA activists sent legislators small loaves of home-baked bread labeled, "Let us stay in the kitchen" (Rhode 1983, pp. 1, 57; Rhode 1989, p. 74). Unsurprisingly, reporters presented this sequence as a playful contest among rival hausfraus. "Rights Battle Booms from Kitchens," chortled a *Chicago Daily News* headline (quoted in Rhode 1989, p. 74). The *Chicago Tribune*'s narrative, "Women Try to Cook up Votes," began: "Women on both sides of the fight over ratification of the Equal Rights Amendment appear to have decided that the way to a legislator's vote is through his stomach" (quoted in Rhode 1989, p. 74). Responding to one reporter's question, an irate ERA proponent observed icily that "this brunch was planned a month ago and was not an attempt to show that liberated women can cook as well as unliberated ones" (quoted in Rhode 1989, p. 74). What the event was originally designed to show—the breadth of mainstream support for equal rights—was lost in translation. Such coverage continued as ERA supporters and proponents squared off across the nation in a struggle for the minds and palates of state legislators. Yet the inevitable consequence of this quiche-and-cookie crusade was to trivialize the real issues and to divert attention from serious questions of sex-based discrimination.

Two decades later, a similar culinary confrontation, with similar results, occurred during the Bush/Clinton presidential race. Here, the rival contestants were the incumbent First Lady and her challenger. Hillary Clinton backed into the bake-off following an ill-considered comment. In response to repeated questions about conflicts of interest in her legal career while her husband was governor, Clinton observed that the problem was hardly avoidable, although perhaps she could have "stayed home, baked cookies, and had teas" (quoted in Dowd 1992).

The press reports that followed lambasted Clinton from all points on the political spectrum. Moderate and conservative commentators accused her of devaluing a homemaking role that society as a whole had also undervalued. Critics from the left pointed out that Clinton herself was able to escape baking only because she could hire less privileged women to do it for her. Columnist Julianne Malveaux, in a column titled "Wise Up Hillary: Women Bake Cookies," deplored Clinton's "patrician" insensitivity:

> Most women work, not because they want to, but because they must. . . . In nearly half of all black married couple families, a woman's wage makes the difference between poverty and middle income. These women may not have the choice that Hillary Clinton implied she had, to work or to stay home. . . . In other words, Hillary Clinton, if you don't bake the cookies you munch at the governor's mansion, some other woman did. If you aren't cleaning your house, some other woman is. If you aren't providing child care, some other woman is. All of this women's work, from your lawyering to her cooking, is connected. (Malveaux 1992)

These were, of course, fair points. What was less fair was how some commentators lifted Clinton's statement out of context or gave it disproportionate attention even after her public apology.[1] Worse still was the media coverage that she received after *Family Circle* invited her and Barbara Bush to submit their favorite chocolate chip cookies for competition. In expiation for her prior sins, Clinton apparently had to enter the fray, but her gesture did little to appease media critics. "What next?" wondered Anna Quindlen. "Eleanor Roosevelt fudge?" (Quindlen 1992). Here was an accomplished professional who had "already changed her name, her hair, her clothes, and her comments[,] . . . [now] reduced to hawking her chocolate chip cookie entry" (Quindlen 1992). In many press accounts, the not-so-subtle subtext was that this is a woman who willingly trades principles for political gain. According to one *Boston Herald* commentator, "if she thought it would help get Bill elected, [Hillary] would show up at the next rally in four-inch heels and a peek-a-boo bra. If she had gone back

to her own life with an occasional campaign appearance, she would not have so grated on one's nerves, barking all over CNN about baking brownies and giving teas. It may be hard for Hillary to accept, but she is not the candidate. And America's not ready for a his and her presidency" (Eagan 1992).

Yet when First Lady Clinton attempted a more traditional feminine image, these efforts prompted no less derision. Her appearance in a high-necked designer evening gown in *Vogue* earned commentary on her "pussycat" look, under newspaper headlines such as "Come up and Vote for Me Sometime" (quoted in Dowd 1993). Ridiculed first as "frumpy," Clinton did no better when she posed as seductive; as one commentator noted, she might as well be selling moisturizing cream (quoted in Dowd 1993). Clinton's fashion forays during a 1994 trip abroad prompted widespread criticism from the European and American press. "Fashion stayed home" was the apparent consensus, but the First Lady also earned ridicule for trying to bring it along (Dowd 1994a, p. 17). Not only was she denounced for wearing "absurdly" styled accessories; she was also mocked for press releases that sounded like fashion promotions: "Mrs. Clinton wore a two-piece fuchsia Noviello Bloom suit of a linen blend. . . . Bone shoes and a matching purse finish[ed] the suit" (Dowd 1994a, p. 17; "Hillary Pillory!" 1994, p. 42).

Of course, the problems surrounding Clinton's public image are not all of the media's making. Much of this coverage reinforces popular prejudices but does not create them. What is missing in most press accounts, however, is any acknowledgment of the double bind confronting women like Clinton. Given the strong public preference for "traditional" First Ladies, she could hardly abandon the effort to resemble one. Yet once the debate was framed in terms of "policymaking [versus] cookie baking," feminine versus feminist, she could not avoid alienating some substantial constituency, whatever her response (Blumenfeld 1994, p. 213). On the battleground of symbolic politics, cookies serve as an important metaphor—a stand-in for a broader set of societal values.[2] Ambivalence over gender roles plays out in sexual sound bites and culinary contests. On this terrain, feminists are at a decided disadvantage. But neither can they refuse to compete. What Clinton most needed was not a different image but a different debate, one that focused less on personal style and more on political substance. At issue were deeper questions about the role of candidates' wives and the dilemmas of professional women. Yet most media coverage, even when it spotted such questions, did little to advance the search for answers.

Personalizing issues is a problem both because it diverts attention from more substantive discussion and because the choice of persons to cover is frequently skewed by class, race, ethnicity, and gender. Abortion is another case in point. According to recent surveys, the press produces more articles on how the abortion question affects various political candidacies and parties than on how women with unwanted pregnancies are affected by growing restrictions on abortion services (Devitt 1992, p. 19). Articles on Medicaid funding are typically cast in terms of political skirmishes among elected officials or contests between prolife and prochoice activists (Devitt 1992, p. 19). Seldom do we hear anything from or about the women, particularly low-income women of color, whose lives are permanently marred by the absence of birth control or prenatal services.

There are other biases in the choice of whose problems receive coverage. The outpouring of interest in the case of Lorena and John Bobbitt is a recent illustration. The media's fascination with such an ostensible confirmation of male fantasies of feminist revenge was perhaps understandable (Tannen 1994). What was less forgivable was the astounding absence of coverage concerning the far more common patterns of domestic violence in which men routinely brutalize women.[3]

A cottage industry of commentary focused on the details of the Bobbitt case. The *New Yorker*, not known for its coverage of gender-related topics, ran three cartoons on the subject in a single issue. One featured three blind and tailless mice listening to a radio account; the caption read, "She cut off his *what* with a carving knife?"[4] Another pictured what appeared to be a mild-mannered middle-aged couple seated at the breakfast table peacefully reading the newspaper. The wife, looking placidly at her spouse, demands, "Pass the cream or I'll cut off your penis."[5] The media spin on this event tapped into both public and private dimensions of gender re-

lations. For many commentators, the incident offered an all-purpose metaphor for individuals' personal experience of sex-based inequality and the broader societal patterns underlying it.

Yet where is that attention when women's bodies, including their sexual organs, are mutilated? Such abuse is scarcely an aberrational event in contemporary America. An estimated four million women are battered annually, and half of all female murder victims are killed by a spouse or lover. Domestic violence is by far the largest cause of injury for women, and sexual mutilation of their bodies is a staple of coroners' (although typically not press) reports (Rhode 1994, pp. 1193–94; United States Department of Justice 1994; Women's Action Coalition 1993).

The Bobbitt case inspired substantial coverage of a problem reportedly "far more widespread than people think"—women's abuse of men (Brott 1993; Simon and Young 1994). What it could and should also have done was to direct comparable attention to another problem that is substantially more widespread than the first—men's abuse of women and the inadequacy of governmental responses. The Bobbitt prosecution also would have been an ideal occasion for focusing public attention on many states' failure to criminalize marital rape except under limited circumstances.

When informed press coverage occurs, it can promote substantial changes in public consciousness and social policy. As subsequent discussion indicates, the media's treatment of battered women following Nicole Simpson's murder is a case in point. A responsible press also could have made more and less of the Bobbitts—less on the prurient details of their interaction, more on its cultural context and the need for effective societal responses.

Polarization of Issues

A related problem in media coverage involves the polarization of feminist issues. All too often, the press achieves "balance" by presenting extreme positions on both sides of a complicated question. What drops out of that debate is anything sensible in between. This kind of polarized coverage is not, of course, unique to feminist issues. Simplified spectacle and sensationalist rhetoric win out on many subjects (Gitlin 1980, pp. 27–29; Bennett 1988, p. 40; Tannen 1994). But the women's movement consistently attracts more than the customary share of skewed sound bites.

For example, in covering public protests, reporters commonly offer a sampling of the most radical comments and then make special efforts to interview hostile onlookers or "regular" women on the street who are alienated by such rhetoric. One consequence of this juxtaposition is that feminists appear in highly charged circumstances likely to yield polemics, while their opponents appear in more contemplative settings, conducive to more "reasoned" responses (Gerbner 1978, p. 48; P. Kamen 1991, pp. 64–65). Another result is that debates among women are cast as catfights. Men remain above the fray as seemingly objective onlookers, never opponents, in the feminist struggle (S. Douglas 1994, pp. 185, 221). Such coverage undercuts claims to sisterhood while masking male resistance to gender equality.

On policy issues, the tendency to present only extreme positions often ends up misdescribing the problem and miscasting the solution, (Wolf 1993a, pp. 97–101). The mid 1990s "rape hype" controversy offers a representative case. Beginning with Katie Roiphe's highly publicized polemics on campus rape, the media have served up endless accounts of feminist exaggerations (K. Roiphe, 1993b). Much of this coverage of "rape hype" has itself been hype. Even when reporters attempt to present both sides, the captions for their stories often undercut any pretense to objectivity. Most titles raise a doubting eyebrow: "Date Rape Hysteria"; "Rape Hype Betrays Feminism"; "Crying Rape"; "Stop Whining"; "Women, Sex and Rape: Have Some Feminists Exaggerated the Problem?" (Faludi 1993, p. 61; McCluskey 1996).

The debate, such as it is, appears largely defined by spokespersons at the extremes, such as Catharine MacKinnon or Andrea Dworkin as the radical feminists and Katie Roiphe or Camille Paglia as the radical skeptics. Common quotes from MacKinnon include: "Compare victims' reports of rape with women's reports of sex. They look a lot alike" (quoted in K. Roiphe 1993b, p. 81; see Sommers 1991, p. A14). From Dworkin, we learn: "The hurting of women is . . . basic to

the sexual pleasure of men" (quoted in Crichton 1993, p. 54). That these are not exactly mainstream feminist positions is rarely acknowledged, and then only as an afterthought.

At the other end of the spectrum, Roiphe's largely fact-free efforts to debunk rape statistics are paraded as facts. Roiphe dismisses a widely credited estimate that one in four women has experienced a forcible sexual assault or attempted assault on the grounds that "if I was really standing in the middle of an epidemic, a crisis, if 25% of my female friends were really being raped, wouldn't I know it?" (1993b, p. 52). That question hardly seems rhetorical, given Roiphe's lack of sympathy toward allegations of acquaintance rape. Missing from her accounts, as well as from most press coverage of them, is any systematic review of recent research. A vast range of studies leaves no doubt as to the high frequency of rape and the low frequency of victims willing to report it (Rhode 1994, pp. 1194–95). Even the Federal Bureau of Investigation and Senate Judiciary Committee, hardly fanatical feminist institutions, have identified rape as one of the most underreported felonies (Federal Bureau of Investigation 1984, p. 14; Committee of the Judiciary 1993, p. 8; Brenner 1993).

To detail all of Roiphe's omissions and distortions would be an enterprise unto itself and enough commentators have done so that no repetition is required here (Faludi 1993; Pollitt 1994a). But in the places where careful critical review would be most helpful—the mass circulation press—Roiphe's anecdotal analysis has often gone unchallenged. Even magazines that include some critical commentary leave the impression that hers is the voice of reason amid an otherwise lunatic fringe. The caption under her 1993 *Newsweek* photograph reads, "Roiphe condemns feminist hysteria" (Crichton 1993, p. 54).

Blurring the Focus

A final sense in which the media's coverage of feminist issues undermines feminist objectives involves the focus on self-transformation rather than social transformation. In much of the popular press, particularly women's magazines, readers get a steady stream of advice about how to make it in a man's world—how to be a successful manager and a supermom. "We assume our readers are feminists with a small f," explained one editor of a women's magazine (Kaminer 1993a, p. 53). These readers reportedly are interested in feminism as a lifestyle but not as a political commitment. Magazines for teenagers set the stage for such worldviews. Over 60 percent of surveyed articles focus on beauty, fashion, diets, and food, leaving no doubt that how young women look is more important than what they think (Peirce 1990, p. 491).

Some contemporary coverage of "lifestyle" issues does, of course, represent an obvious advance over what used to be standard fare in these magazines, such as how to create a "poet's kitchen" or have a baby in a bomb shelter (Friedan 1974, pp. 34–37). But the current focus has equally obvious limitations. As Barbara Ehrenreich notes, the women's movement in such settings appears to be less a movement than a "self-improvement program for the upwardly mobile woman" (1981, p. 97). The radical potential of feminism, like other left political challenges, is often defused and deflected" (Gitlin 1980, p. 291). Such media coverage encourages individuals to believe that they can meet all challenges individually—by choosing the right accessories, the right degree of assertiveness, the right time-management skills, and so forth. In this journalistic universe, feminism's aspirations to equality are widely shared, but its call for collective action is widely ignored.

Consoling Thoughts and Collective Action

This narrative should not, however, end on a purely negative note. Although the preceding comments have focused on what has been wrong in media coverage, there has also been an increasing amount that has been right. The growing number of feminist journalists, critics, and consumers has made a demonstrable difference in how feminist issues are presented.

The Hill/Thomas hearings are an obvious illustration. To be sure, there was much to dislike in some media coverage of African American women in general and Anita Hill in particular. Yet the insistence by many members of the press that allegations of sexual harassment be taken seriously marked a turning point. And the follow-up coverage on the scope of the problem offered an extraordinary occasion for collective consciousness raising. Women have long been harassed, but only their livelihoods have been at risk. Now men realize that *their* futures may be affected as well. Moreover, the ways in which the media stereotyped and silenced black women during these hearings did not pass unnoticed, as it might have during earlier decades. After a black sociologist's editorial in the Sunday *New York Times* attempted to legitimate Thomas's actions as a form of "down-home courtin'" among southern blacks (O. Patterson 1991), a coalition of African American women formed to publish their protest. Fifteen hundred women signed the coalition's statement, which ran as an advertisement in the *Times* and other newspapers. And at least some mainstream media coverage explored other responses in the African American community, not only to the Thomas nomination but also to racist coverage of it.

Similarly, the media's treatment of the murders of Nicole Simpson and Ron Goldman marked a watershed concerning domestic violence. Although it took an extraordinarily dramatic script with a celebrity star to gain attention, the first wave of reporting was thorough and thoughtful. The press turned a much-needed floodlight on the nature of family violence, the limitations in law enforcement responses, and the inadequacies of social services. Equally significant was the media's coverage of their own prior coverage. The press questioned its previous silence about battering, its lionization of athletes, and its focus on the "tragedy of O. J. Simpson" rather than on his murdered wife and her friend ("The Editorialists" 1994; Goodman 1994b). Nor did commentators let pass unnoticed that it took a white victim and black batterer to catapult issues of domestic violence to center stage (Adams 1994, p. 36; Pasternak and Seymour 1994, p. 26).

Of course, some of the coverage was a mixed blessing. There were the obligatory "alternative" angles—the inaccurate or misleading assertions that women "hit men more often than men hit women" and that domestic violence is a "dance of mutual destructiveness" for which both sexes are equally responsible (Dunn 1994; Farrell 1994; Sherven and Sniechowski 1994). Some publications' glancing coverage of domestic violence appeared little more than protective coloration for a titillating saga. As with the "thought pieces" in

Playboy, reporters and their audience could reassure themselves that they were not really interested in lurid details but only in "this Very Important Issue" (M. Boot 1994; Kolbert 1994). But whatever its limitations, the media blitz left in its wake significant positive results: a new body of legislation; a heightened sense of judicial, prosecutorial, and police accountability; and an increased demand for prevention and support services.

As the preceding discussion indicates, the coverage of many gender-related topics, including sexual violence, still leaves much to be desired. But the fact that there *is* substantial coverage, which generally includes feminist perspectives, represents substantial progress. These perspectives have dramatically altered the ways in which the public understands gender relations (Rapping 1994a, p. 27; Rapping 1994b, pp. 10–12). Similarly, the formation of media groups such as Women, Men, and Media and the growth of gender-related media research have heightened awareness of how the press reflects and refracts feminism.

The challenge remaining is to respond to the inadequacies that we can increasingly identify. Much more could and should be done to monitor biases, organize protests, and expand coverage of women's perspectives and concerns (Women's Institute for Freedom of the Press 1993, pp. 8–9; Beasley and Gibbons 1993, pp. 295–96). Many individuals have access to the women's movement only on the terms that the press provides. If we are to realize feminism's potential, feminists need a greater voice in shaping its public image.

Notes

A version of this essay also appeared in *Signs: Journal of Women in Culture and Society* 1995, vol. 20, no. 3, © 1995, The University of Chicago, and in Rhode, 1997.

1. Clinton stated: "I deeply regret that my comment about baking cookies and having teas was taken out of context. There is nothing in my life or work that could be construed as disparaging women who choose to stay home and raise a family. I honor them. Those are the choices my own mother made" (Carroll et al. 1992, p. 31).

2. For discussion of the importance of such metaphors in political life, see Howell 1990, pp. 26–27, and Rhode 1989, pp. 74–76.

3. A review of some two hundred articles between June 1993 and May 1994 revealed pervasive gender biases in media treatment, as well as ethnic stereotypes suggesting that female brutality comparable to Lorena Bobbitt's was common in Latina culture (Groll 1994).

4. The cartoon by Arnie Levin appeared in the *New Yorker,* November 19, 1993, p. 91.

5. The cartoon by J. B. Handelsman appeared in the *New Yorker,* November 19, 1993, p. 102.

3

Hate Radio

Why We Need to Tune In to Limbaugh and Stern

PATRICIA J. WILLIAMS

Three years ago I stood at my sink, washing the dishes and listening to the radio. I was tuned to rock and roll so I could avoid thinking about the big news from the day before—George Bush had just nominated Clarence Thomas to replace Thurgood Marshall on the Supreme Court. I was squeezing a dot of lemon Joy into each of the wineglasses when I realized that two smoothly radio-cultured voices, a man's and a woman's, had replaced the music.

"I think it's a stroke of genius on the president's part," said the female voice.

"Yeah," said the male voice. "Then those blacks, those African Americans, those Negroes—hey, 'Negro' is good enough for Thurgood Marshall— whatever, they can't make up their minds [what] they want to be called. I'm gonna call them Blafricans. Black Africans. Yeah, I like it. Blafricans. Then they can get all upset because now the president appointed a Blafrican."

"Yeah, well, that's the way those liberals think. It's just crazy."

"And then after they turn down his nomination the president can say he tried to please 'em, and then he can appoint someone with some intelligence."

Back then this conversation seemed so horrendously unusual, so singularly hateful, that I picked up a pencil and wrote it down. I was certain that a firestorm of protest was going to engulf the station and purge those foul radio mouths with the good clean soap of social outrage.

I am so naive. When I finally turned on the radio and rolled my dial to where everyone else had been tuned while I was busy watching Cosby reruns, it took me a while to understand that there's a firestorm all right, but not of protest. In the two and a half years since Thomas has assumed his post on the Supreme Court, the underlying assumptions of the conversation I heard as uniquely outrageous have become commonplace, popularly expressed, and louder in volume. I hear the style of that snide polemicism everywhere, among acquaintances, on the street, on television in toned-down versions. It is a crude demagoguery that makes me heartsick. I feel more and more surrounded by that point of view, the assumptions of being without intelligence, the coded epithets, the "Blafrican"-like stand-ins for "nigger," the mocking angry glee, the endless tirades filled with nonspecific, nonempirically based slurs against "these people" or "those minorities" or "feminazis" or "liberals" or "scumbags" or "pansies" or "jerks" or "sleazeballs" or "loonies" or "animals" or "foreigners."

At the same time I am not so naive as to suppose that this is something new. In clearheaded moments I realize that I am not listening to the radio anymore; I am listening to a large segment of white America think aloud in ever-louder resurgent thoughts that have generations of historical precedent. It's as though the radio has split open like an egg, Morton Downey Jr.'s clones and Joe McCarthy's ghost spilling out, broken yolks, a great collective of sometimes clever, sometimes small, but uniformly threatened brains—they have all come gushing out. Just as they were about to pass into oblivion, Jack Benny and his humble black sidekick Rochester get resurrected in the ungainly bodies of Howard Stern and his faithful black henchwoman, Robin Quivers. The culture of Amos and Andy has been revived and reassembled in Bob Grant's radio ministrelry and radio newcomer Daryl Gates's sanctimonious imprecations on behalf of decent white people. And in striking imitation of Jesse Helms's nearly forgotten days as a radio host, the far right has found its undisputed king in the personage of Rush Limbaugh—a polished demagogue with a weekly radio audience of at least twenty million, a television show that vies for ratings with the likes of Jay Leno, a newsletter with a circulation of 380,000, and two best-selling books whose combined sales are closing in on six million copies.

From Churchill to Hitler to the old Soviet Union, it's clear that radio and television have the power to change the course of history, to proselytize, and to coalesce not merely the good and the noble, but the very worst in human nature as well. Likewise, when Orson Welles made his famous radio broadcast "witnessing" the landing of a spaceship full of hostile Martians, the United States ought to have learned a lesson about the power of radio to appeal to mass instincts and incite mass hysteria. Radio remains a peculiarly powerful medium even today, its visual emptiness in a world of six trillion flashing images allowing one of the few remaining play-

grounds for the aural subconscious. Perhaps its power is attributable to our need for an oral tradition after all, some conveying of stories, feelings, myths of ancestors, epics of alienation, and the need to rejoin ancestral roots, even ignorant bigoted roots. Perhaps the visual quiescence of radio is related to the popularity of e-mail or electronic networking. Only the voice is made manifest, unmasking worlds that cannot—or dare not?—be seen. Just yet. Nostalgia crystalizing into a dangerous future. The preconscious voice erupting into the expressed, the prime time.

What comes out of the modern radio mouth could be the *Iliad*, the *Rubaiyat*, the griot's song of our times. If radio indeed is a vessel for the American "Song of Songs," then what does it mean that a manic, adolescent Howard Stern is so popular among radio listeners, that Rush Limbaugh's wittily smooth sadism has gone the way of prime-time television, and that both vie for the number one slot on all the best-selling book lists? What to make of the stories being told by our modern radio evangelists and their tragic unloved chorus of callers? Is it really just a collapsing economy that spawns this drama of grown people sitting around scaring themselves to death with fantasies of black feminist Mexican ablebodied gay soldiers, earning $100,000 a year on welfare, who are so criminally depraved that Hillary Clinton or the Antichrist-of-the-moment had no choice but to invite them onto the government payroll so they can run the country? The panicky exaggeration reminds me of a child's fear: . . . *And then, and then, a huge lion jumped out of the shadows and was about to gobble me up, and I can't ever sleep again for a whole week.*

As I spin the dial on my radio, I can't help thinking that this stuff must be related to that most poignant of fiber-optic phenomena, phone sex. Aural sex. Radio racism with a touch of S&M. High-priest hosts with the power and runamok ego to discipline listeners, to smack with the verbal back of the hand, to smash the button that shuts you up once and for all. "Idiot!" shouts New York City radio demagogue Bob Grant, and then the sound of droning telephone emptiness, the voice of dissent dumped out some trapdoor in aural space.

As I listened to a range of such programs, what struck me as the most unifying theme was not merely the specific intolerance on such hot topics as race and gender, but a much more general contempt for the world, a verbal stoning of anything different. It is like some unusually violent game of "Simon Says," this mockery and shouting down of callers, this roar of incantations, the insistence on agreement.

But, ah, if you *will* but only agree, what sweet and safe reward, what soft enfolding by a stern and angry radio god. And as an added bonus, the invisible shield of an AM community, a family of fans who are Exactly Like You, to whom you can express, in anonymity, all the filthy stuff you imagine "them" doing to you. The comfort and relief of being able to ejaculate, to those who understand, about the dark imagined excess overtaking, robbing, needing to be held down and taught a good lesson, needing to put it in its place before the ravenous demon enervates all that is true and good and pure in this life.

The audience for this genre of radio flagellation is mostly young, white, and male. Two-thirds of Rush Limbaugh's audience is male. According to *Time* magazine, 75 percent of Howard Stern's listeners are white men (Andersen 1993). Most of the callers have spent their lives walling themselves off from any real experience with blacks, feminists, lesbians, or gays. In this regard, it is probably true, as former Secretary of Education William Bennett says, that Rush Limbaugh "tells his audience that what you believe inside, you can talk about in the marketplace" (Bowman 1993). Unfortunately, what's "inside" is then mistaken for what's outside, treated as empirical and political reality. The *National Review* extols Limbaugh's conservative leadership as no less than that of Ronald Reagan, and the Republican Party provides Limbaugh with books to discuss, stories, angles, and public support (Bowman 1993). "People were afraid of censure by gay activists, feminists, environmentalists—now they are not because Rush takes them on," says Bennett (Bowman 1993).

The history of the United states has been marked by cycles in which brands of this or that hatred come into fashion and go out, are unleashed and then restrained. If racism, homophobia, jingoism, and woman-hating have been features of national life in pretty much all of modern history, it rather begs the question to spend a lot of time wondering whether right-wing radio is a symptom or a cause. For at least four-hundred years, prevailing attitudes in the West have considered African Americans less intelligent. Recent statistics show that 53 percent of people in the United States agree that blacks and Latinos are less intelligent than whites, and a majority believe that blacks are lazy, violent, welfare-dependent, and unpatriotic.

I think that what has made life more or less tolerable for "out" groups have been those moments in history when those "inside" feelings were relatively restrained. In fact, if I could believe that right-wing radio were only about idiosyncratic, singular, rough-hewn individuals thinking those inside thoughts, I'd be much more inclined to agree with Columbia University media expert Everette Dennis, who says that Stern's and Limbaugh's popularity represents the "triumph of the individual" (Andersen 1993) or with *Time* magazine's bottom line that "the fact that either is seriously considered a threat . . . is more worrisome than Stern or Limbaugh will ever be" (Andersen 1993). If what I were hearing had even a tad more to do with real oppression, with real white *and* black levels of joblessness and homelessness, or with the real problems of real white men, then I wouldn't have bothered to slog my way through hours of Howard Stern's miserable obsessions.

Yet at the heart of my anxiety is the worry that Stern, Limbaugh, Grant, and others represent the very antithesis of individualism's triumph. As the *National Review* said of Limbaugh's ascent, "It was a feat not only of the loudest voice but also of a keen political brain to round up, as Rush did, the media herd and drive them into the conservative corral" (Bowman 1993). When asked about his political aspirations, Bob Grant gloated to the *Washington Post,* "I think I would make rather a good dictator" (Dobbs 1987).

The polemics of right-wing radio are putting nothing less than hate onto the airwaves and into the marketplace, electing it to office, teaching it in schools, and exalting it as freedom. What worries me is the increasing-to-constant commerce of retribution, control, and lashing out, fed not by fact but by fantasy. What worries me is the reemergence, more powerfully than at any time since the institution of Jim Crow, of a sociocentered self that excludes "the likes of," well, me, for example, from the civic circle and that would rob me of my worth and claim and identity as a citizen. As the *Economist* (1993) rightly observes, "Mr. Limbaugh takes a mass market—white, mainly male, middle-class, ordinary America—and talks to it as an endangered minority."

I worry about this identity whose external reference is a set of beliefs, ethics, and practices that excludes, restricts, and acts in the world on me, or mine, as the perceived, if not real, enemy. I am acutely aware of losing *my* mythic individualism to the surface shapes of my mythic group fearsomeness as black, as female, as left-wing. "I" merge not fluidly but irretrievably into a category of "them." I become a suspect self, a moving target of loathsome properties, not merely different but dangerous. And that worries me a lot.

What happens in my life with all this translated license, this permission to be uncivil? What happens to the social space that was supposedly at the sweet mountaintop of the civil rights movement's trail? Can I get a seat on the bus without having to be reminded that I should be standing? Did the civil rights movement guarantee us nothing more than the right to use public accommodations while surrounded by raving lunatic bigots? "They didn't beat this idiot [Rodney King] enough," says Howard Stern.

Not long ago I had the misfortune to hail a taxicab in which the driver was listening to Howard Stern undress some woman. After some blocks, I had to get out. I was, frankly, afraid to ask the driver to turn it off—not because I was afraid of "censoring" him, which seems to be the only thing people will talk about anymore, but because the driver was stripping me too, as he leered through the rearview mirror. "Something the matter?" he demanded, as I asked him to pull over and let me out well short of my destination. (I'll spare you the full story of what happened from there—trying to get another cab, as the cabbies stopped for all the white businessmen who so much as scratched their heads near the curb; a nice young white man, seeing my plight, giving me his cab, having to thank him, he the hero, me saved but humiliated, the cabdriver pissed and surly. I fight my way to my destination, finally arriving in a bad mood, militant black woman, cranky feminazi.)

When Yeltsin blared rock music at his opponents holed up in the parliament building in Moscow, in imitation of the U.S. Marines trying to torture Manuel Noriega in Panama, all I could think of was that it must be like being trapped in a crowded subway car when all the portable stereos are tuned to Bob Grant or Howard Stern. With Howard Stern's voice a tinny, screeching backdrop, with all the faces growing dreamily mean as though some soporifically evil hallucinogen were gushing into their bloodstreams, I'd start begging to surrender.

Surrender to what? Surrender to the laissez-faire resegregation that is the metaphoric significance of the hundreds of "Rush rooms" that have cropped up in restaurants around the country; rooms broadcasting Limbaugh's words, rooms for your listening pleasure, rooms where bigots can capture the purity of a Rush-only lunch counter, rooms where all those unpleasant others just "choose" not to eat? Surrender to the naughty luxury of a room in which a Ku Klux Klan meeting could take place in orderly, First Amendment fashion? Everyone's "free" to come in (and a few of you outsiders do), but mostly the undesirable nonconformists are gently repulsed away. It's a high-tech world of enhanced choice. Whites choose mostly to sit in the Rush room. Feminists, blacks, lesbians, and gays "choose" to sit elsewhere. No need to buy black votes, you just pay them not to vote; no need to insist on white-only schools, you just sell the desirability of black-only schools. Just sit back and watch it work, like those invisible shock shields that keep dogs cowering in their own backyards.

How real is the driving perception behind all the Sturm und Drang of this genre of radio-harangue—the perception that white men are an oppressed minority, with no power and no opportunity in the land that they made great? While it is true that power and opportunity are shrinking for all but the very wealthy in this country (and would that Limbaugh would take that issue on), the fact remains that white men are still this country's most privileged citizens and market actors. To give just a small example, according to the *Wall Street Journal*, blacks were the only racial group to suffer a net job loss during the 1990–91 economic downturn at the companies reporting to the Equal Employment Opportunity Commission (Sharpe 1993). Whites, Latinos, and Asians, meanwhile, gained thousands of jobs. While whites gained 71,144 jobs at these companies, Latinos gained 60,040, Asians gained 55,104, and blacks lost 59,479 (Sharpe 1993). If every black in the United States were hired tomorrow, the numbers would not be sufficient to account for white men's expanding balloon of fear that they have been specifically dispossessed by African Americans.

Given deep patterns of social segregation and general ignorance of history, particularly racial history, the media remains the principal source of most Americans' knowledge of each other. The media can provoke violence or induce passivity. In San Francisco, for example, a radio show on KMEL called "Street Soldiers" has taken this power as a responsibility with great consequence: "Unquestionably," writes Ken Auletta (1993) in the *New Yorker*, "the show has helped avert violence. When a Samoan teenager was slain, apparently by Filipino gang members, in a drive-by shooting, the phones lit up with calls from Samoans wanting to tell [the hosts] they would not rest until they had exacted revenge. Threats filled the air for a couple of weeks. Then the dead Samoan's father called in, and, in a poignant exchange, the father said he couldn't tolerate the thought of more young men senselessly slaughtered. There would be no retaliation, he vowed. And there was none." In contrast, we must wonder at the phenomenon of the very powerful leadership of the Republican Party, from Ronald Reagan to Robert Dole to William Bennett, giving advice, counsel, and friendship to Rush Limbaugh's passionate divisiveness.

The outright denial of the material crisis at every level of U.S. society, most urgently in black inner-city neighborhoods but facing us all, is a kind of political circus, dissembling as it feeds the frustrations of the moment. We as a nation can no longer afford to deal with such crises by *imagining* an excess of bodies, of babies, of job-stealers, of welfare mothers, of overreaching immigrants, of too-powerful (Jewish, in whispers) liberal Hollywood, of lesbians and gays, of gang members ("gangsters" remain white and, no matter what the atrocity, less vilified than "gang members," who are black), of Arab terrorists and uppity women. The reality of our social poverty far exceeds these scapegoats. In form if not substance, this right-wing backlash resembles phenomena like anti-Semitism in Poland: There aren't but a handful of Jews left in that whole country, but the giant balloon of heated anti-Semitism flourishes apace, Jews blamed for the world's evils.

The overwhelming response to right-wing excesses in the United States has been to seek an odd sort of comfort in the fact that the First Amendment is working so well that you can't suppress this sort of thing. Look what's happened in Eastern Europe. Granted. So let's not talk about censorship or the First Amendment for the next ten minutes. But in Western Europe, where fascism is rising at an appalling rate, suppression is hardly the problem. In Eastern and Western Europe as well as the United States, we must begin to think just a little bit about the fiercely coalescing power of media to spark mistrust, to fan it into forest fires of fear and revenge. We must begin to think about the levels of national and social complacence in the face of such resolute ignorance. We must ask ourselves what the expected result is, not of censorship or suppression but of so much encouragement, so much support, so much investment in the fashionability of hate. What future is it that we are designing with the devotion of such tremendous resources to the disgraceful propaganda of bigotry?

Notes

4

The Making of a "Quota Queen"

News Media and the Bias of Objectivity

LAUREL LEFF

Three days after President Clinton withdrew Lani Guinier's nomination to be head of the Justice Department's Civil Rights Division, the *Washington Post* published a postmortem that credited Clint Bolick of the "libertarian-oriented" Institute for Justice with defeating the nomination. *Post* reporter Michael Isikoff (1993c) wrote that the Institute of Justice "produced a drumbeat of press releases, reports, and op-ed articles that portrayed the University of Pennsylvania law professor as a proquota, left-wing 'extremist' bent on undermining democratic principles—labels that stuck and helped fuel the debate over the Guinier nomination in terms that made it difficult for her allies to recover."

Fifteen days earlier, Isikoff (1993a) himself had been part of that drumbeat. In the *Post's* first major article on the Guinier nomination, he had quoted conservatives' assessments of Guinier as a proquota, " 'extreme' left-wing activist." To explain her "controversial" views, he had used several direct quotes from two law review articles—every one of which had been cited by Bolick (1993) in a *Wall Street Journal* op-ed piece on

April 30, or by conservative *Journal* columnist Paul Gigot (1993) in a May 7 column.

In a subsequent interview, *Post* reporter Isikoff (1993d) defended his use of the quotations, saying he spent "about an hour" with the two law review articles, totaling 119 pages, to get "enough of a flavor" to make sure the "quotes were not twisted out of context." He conceded, however, that his article did not fairly summarize Guinier's complex views on achieving greater minority representation under the Voting Rights Act. That, he said, was not his job. "This is not a case where newspaper reporters set the agenda," Isikoff said. "What I was doing was reporting a controversy. My job was to explain to our readers what the controversy was about. The excerpts merely explain what it was she had written that had generated controversy."

In essence, Isikoff's "defense" was that he was being manipulated, and he knew he was being manipulated, but he was powerless to stop it. Once a controversy had been created and existed as an event in the world, Isikoff was saying, he had no choice but to report and thus reinforce it.

Stranger still is *Newsweek* reporter Bob Cohn's rationalization for the headline on his first Guinier article: "Crowning a 'Quota Queen'?" (Cohn 1993a). "Clinton's Quota Queens" (referring to another nominee, a Hispanic woman, as well) had been the headline on Clint Bolick's *Wall Street Journal* column, though the phrase never appeared in the article, and the conclusion that Guinier supports quotas—despite her repeated statements that in voting rights cases she does not—seems to be based on one confusing sentence in one article about the need for more women and minority judicial nominees (Guinier 1989). *Newsweek's* Cohn (1993c), however, expressed few qualms about including the racist and sexist term, saying its use was appropriate because "quota queen" "was not in *Newsweek's* voice" and because it "was around town; it was the way most people identified her." Of course the term was around town because it appeared in the *Los Angeles Times* (Broder 1993), *USA Today* ("House Approves Smaller Spending Bill" 1993), and the *Washington Post* (Isikoff 1993b), not to mention *Newsweek*. Yet Cohn, like Isikoff, defends his actions because the seemingly irresistible alliteration, like the "controversy," was an event in the external world that both reporters felt obligated to cover.

My purpose in this article is to explore where this sense of journalistic obligation and disconnection comes from and what impact it has on press coverage, particularly of ideas that might be considered unconventional. I think the answer can be found in objectivity, a concept that despite withering criticism continues to have a persistent and perverse hold on the journalistic imagination.[1] Objectivity's grip can be seen both in journalism's method, which purports to minimize reporters' subjective judgments through scientific techniques, and in its spirit, which demands seemingly neutral interpretive frameworks to make sense of controversial events.

The result, however, is anything but scientific and neutral. Like formalism in law, the objective method in journalism does not eliminate individual judgment, it merely disguises it. The result is news articles with an authority they do not deserve and reporters who can disassociate themselves from what they write. The objective spirit pushes journalism to embrace interpretive frameworks that seem the most neutral but are merely the most conventional. In the case of the press

coverage of Lani Guinier's nomination, objectivity steered the media toward familiar constructs about race and gender to make sense of the controversy over her appointment. Objectivity then enabled journalists to disclaim responsibility for the "quota queen" portrait they themselves had painted.

I will proceed in three stages. First, I will discuss journalists' understanding of objectivity. Second, I will show how the continuing reliance on the objective method manifested itself in the press coverage of Lani Guinier's nomination to head the Justice Department's Civil Rights Division.[2] And third, I will argue that the interpretive frameworks journalists applied to the Guinier nomination dictated the negative story lines.

The Meaning of Objectivity

Objectivity, as journalists understand it, encompasses the commonsense and philosophical uses of the term but also expresses something more. To be objective as a journalist—as to be objective in everyday language—means to be impartial, unbiased, without a personal stake in the outcome of the events being witnessed. And to believe in objectivity in journalism is also to embrace a philosophical framework in which facts can be separated from values, news can be distinguished from opinion. Objective journalism, however, refers to more than the need for impartiality and the belief in a divide between facts and opinions; it also refers to a method, a way of doing journalism.

To understand the relationship between objectivity as a method and objectivity as a professional orientation and philosophical framework, a bit of history is required.[3] At the turn of the century, journalists subscribed to what has been labeled "naive empiricism," the belief that "facts are not human statements about the world but aspects of the world itself" (Schudson 1978, p. 11). Turn-of-the-century journalists believed that facts, as tangible aspects of the external world, could and should be separated from opinions, which were personal, subjective judgments. The reporter's job, therefore, was to venture forth into the world, round up all the facts, deliver them unadulterated to the newspaper office, and finally steer them opinion-free into print. As long as journalists were not careless, lazy, or corrupt, the newspaper account would accurately reflect the world as it was. If ten reporters from ten different newspapers covered a fire, for example, the assumption was that in the absence of easily circumvented bias they would produce ten nearly identical stories. The newspapers of this era were commonly referred to as "mirrors" for events.

By the 1920s, however, cracks appeared in the mirror.[4] Journalists began to realize that subjective judgment was involved in almost every step of the reporting process. The facts that even a well-trained reporter perceived depended as much on the reporter's vantage point as on the facts themselves; the reporter might not view all the facts, or she would see the same facts but through her own unique prism. And even if the facts were clear, not all of them could find their way into a news account. A journalist had to decide which facts to seek, which facts to use, and the order in which to use them.

To assist the journalist in this undertaking and to make it as unbiased a process as possible, journalism turned to the emerging social sciences and the "scientific method." What evolved was a journalistic style known as objectivity (journalists had not used the term previously), which relies on four techniques: verification, qualification, attribution, and balance. Facts need to be verified, either through the "evidence of the senses" or by reliable secondary sources. The facts that cannot be verified in the time available or cannot be verified at all require the use of one or more of the other techniques. Information can be qualified, meaning the information is presented as carefully and noncommittally as possible. Use of such words as "seemingly," "apparently," or "suggests" implies that the reporter has some doubts about the veracity of the information presented and thus seeks to "qualify" it. Or the facts can be attributed to an authoritative source; as one editor explained, a news story could be made "authentic" by putting a "man of standing and importance behind it" (Bastian 1924, p. 59). Finally, if the truth is still illusory, news articles can be "balanced," with both sides of a story being presented. A 1935 journalism textbook provides an example of how pernicious the idea of balance can be. "Some types of news demands that both sides in a controversial matter be given a chance to have their position stated," the book explains. These stories "involve struggles between rival groups, each of which is strong

in its own right, and each of which is anxious to get as much propaganda across to the newspaper readers as is possible." The textbook's example of a story that demands balanced coverage: "the Jewish persecution by the German Nazi government" (Porter and Luxon 1935, p. 118).

By the 1930s, the objective method—verification, qualification, attribution, and balance—guided American journalism. In using this methodology, journalists no longer believed they could mirror events, but they thought they could at least paint a realistic portrait.

In the post–World War II era, however, objectivity has provoked a devastating critique from both inside and outside the profession. Verification of important facts is difficult; verification of all facts is impossible. Qualification is a temporary solution at best, an admission of defeat at worst. Attribution and balance enable sources to manipulate journalists and present a self-serving and distorted view of events. Even more fundamentally, post–World War II journalists no longer believed that even if they could present just the facts, those facts would necessarily best represent the truth. Isolated facts lack meaning; they need to be tied to other events and placed within a historical and sociological perspective. Journalists need to interpret events as well as report them. They need to make decisions about an event's importance, meaning, and impact. In other words, they need to rely on subjective value judgments to fashion an accurate news story. Rather than a mirror, or a realistic portrait, the metaphor for late-twentieth-century journalism might be more like an impressionistic or even abstract painting.

One example may provide a way to conceptualize this change in journalism's metaphoric role from that of a mirror to something more like a Miro. A turn-of-the-century journalism textbook instructed: "Do not . . . speak of people as 'prominent,' 'well known,' 'wealthy,' or 'beautiful,' unless they really are so" (Given 1907, p. 235). Prominence, wealth, and beauty were facts of the external world that either were or were not to the turn-of-the-century journalist. By the 1920s, however, a reporter could not just describe someone as prominent; she would need to supply verifiable facts, such as the person's occupation—bank president, say—or quote someone else saying the person was prominent. After World War II those facts would not be considered good modes of thought and norms of professionalism are discussed later. Insofar as book reviewers respond to a different set of norms and do not perceive themselves as part of the journalistic enterprise, my conclusions are problematic. Nonetheless, perhaps reflecting the idea that "fools rush in," let us proceed.

The positive reviews are the consequence of a series of decisions: the editor's decision to review this book, the choice of the reviewer, and the reviewer's assessment of the book. Both editor and reviewer presumably made a preliminary determination that the book was worth reviewing. Books that the editor or reviewer perceives as clearly bad are unlikely to merit any review unless the publication of the book is independently newsworthy, such as a sequel by a best-selling author (see, e.g., Kakutani 1994, reviewing Ellis 1994), or a book that attacks a journalistic icon like the First Amendment (see, e.g., Romano 1993 and Posner 1993, reviewing MacKinnon 1993). The extended, highly critical reviews of Brock by English and Sullivan may be further examples of the former phenomenon: the Brock book and the earlier response to it were news.

I suggest that there are three media-specific reasons for the appeal of the Brock book. First, the book benefits from being read quickly and superficially, and this is what reviewers in the daily and weekly press have time for. Second, the form of the book—a cross between the quest and the detective novel genres—would likely be particularly appealing to journalists. Finally, and most significantly, the book asserts a dichotomy between "us," believers in objectivity, rationality and fairness, and "them," feminists and racial progressives, who reject these values. Mainstream journalists are professionally inclined to Brock's side of the divide he creates.

Book reviewers for such outlets as the *New York Times* or the *Washington Post* may read several books a week. They do not have time for the reflective, critical process that reveals the deep flaws in Brock's book. Such a quick reading, for example, encourages acceptance of the author's framing of the issue. Those aspects on which he concentrates, such as Hoerchner's alleged error in identifying the harasser about whom Hill complained, or Hill's alleged pattern of sexual aggression and lack of professional achievement, are accepted as the central issues in the case. Facts that he ignores or barely alludes to, such as Clar-

ence Thomas's rhetorical mistreatment of his sister or the political views of Brock's key sources at Oklahoma, disappear from the reviewer's view as well. The author's pattern of highlight and shadow is simply accepted, rather than subjected to analysis.

Similarly, a quick reader is less likely to notice the book's incoherent pictures of Anita Hill. Rather, he will accept one of those pictures as "the" explanation. Compare the "dedicated liberal and feminist" of Lehmann-Haupt with the "dupe of the interest groups" version accepted by Groner. Only the later commentators, who had more time to examine the book, saw the conflict (see English 1993; Quindlen 1993a; K. Sullivan 1993). Deadline pressures also benefited Brock by making it harder to uncover his rhetorical traps or the thin and revealing content of many of the footnotes.

The book also embodies a genre likely to appeal to writers and journalists. It begins with the author as disinterested observer. He is puzzled by an apparent inconsistency, by the fact that somebody lied, and decides to get to the bottom of it. The remainder of the book is the result of his investigation. Sources are uncovered and quoted; tiny details are disclosed and placed in context; by the end, the conclusion is irresistible. The form is rather like that of a detective novel, with Brock as the detective—and the end of a detective novel is always the revelation of the truth, hidden beneath lies and obfuscations. Alternatively, the book echoes the quest for truth of the classic investigative reporter. The investigative journalist, Woodward and Bernstein or Edward R. Murrow, serves as the hero of the quest, uncovering corruption and restoring the body politic to health. Reviewers, even more than the general public, may be seduced by such a genre story.

Finally and most significantly, the reception of the book may reflect the complex relationship between journalistic self-understanding and both the book and its target. In assessing the reviewer's response to the book, as in assessing the book itself, we should remember that "it takes willful ignorance to deny that journalists tend to give more favorable coverage to the ideas and opinions that comport with their personal beliefs" (Goodrich 1993). In summary, journalists believe in an ideal of objectivity. The book manages both to appear superficially to fit within that enough either. Describing someone as a bank president did not necessarily establish prominence without additional context. The president of a $10 million bank would be prominent in small-town U.S.A. but not necessarily in Manhattan. So journalists might have to return to describing someone as prominent, as long as they had a neutral framework to back that judgment up.

To this point, it might seem as if the transformation of American journalism in the twentieth century is a tale of a profession's coming of age and growing enlightenment, from a naive belief in facts to a sophisticated understanding of the importance of the subjective. But it is not. At the end of the century, most journalists still cling to objectivity as both a method and philosophy. As Theodore Glasser (1992, p. 183) explains:

> What remains fundamentally unchanged is the journalist's naively empirical view of the world, a belief in the separation of facts and values, a belief in the existence of a reality—the reality of empirical facts. Nowhere is this belief more evident than when news is defined as something external to—and independent of—the journalist. The very vocabulary used by journalists when they talk about news underscores their belief that the news is "out there," presumably waiting to be *explored* or *uncovered* or at least *gathered*.

The reasons for this persistence involve a complex interaction of professional norms with market imperatives.[5] The persistence of objectivity, however, is not harmless. As a method, it enables journalists to create the appearance of an authority they lack and frees journalists from taking full responsibility for what they write. And as a philosophy, it leads journalists to rely on interpretive frameworks that seem neutral but are more accurately described as reinforcement of the status quo. The last two sections of this article will illustrate those propositions through an examination of the press coverage of Lani Guinier's nomination.

The Persistence of the Objective Method

The news media did a dreadful job of explaining Professor Guinier's scholarship. The news media did a dreadful job of assessing whether that scholarship was relevant to the post for which she was nominated. For my purposes here, however, that will be taken as a given.[6] In this section I will focus instead on how the press used the objective method to depict Guinier as a radical extremist intent upon subverting American democracy, without feeling as if they were responsible for that portrait. And in the last section I will explore how three seemingly neutral interpretive frameworks ultimately turned the legal scholar into a quota queen.

The press coverage of the Guinier nomination exhibited all four of the objective method's techniques—verification, qualification, attribution, and balance. As the following examples will illustrate, the use of these techniques did not free reporters from the need to make judgments; at best they merely disguised the judgments being made from the public, and seemingly even from the reporter. As an example of the latter, take *Washington Post* reporter Isikoff's rationale for using the exact same quotes in his May 21 article that Clint Bolick, an avowed conservative activist, had used in his *Wall Street Journal* editorial-page attack. In an interview Isikoff (1993d) justified his quoting of the same two sentences and four phrases from two-hundred pages of academic writing by noting that he had *verified* that they actually appeared in Guinier's article. Isikoff did not have to *read* Guinier's articles; ensuring that the words appeared was enough. Relying on verification, one of the techniques of objectivity, freed Isikoff from the work of reading Guinier's articles and from feeling guilty about not having bothered to find out if those selected quotes reflected Guinier's overall meaning. And Isikoff was not alone.[7] While some reporters actually read Guinier's work, including David Savage (1993b) of the *Los Angeles Times* and Michael Tackett and Linda Campbell (1993, pp. 1142, 1255) of the *Chicago Tribune*, most did not. To some reporters, "verifying" what Guinier wrote did not even require looking at the articles themselves; all they needed was another reporter telling them what the articles said. American Lawyer Media columnist Stuart Taylor Jr. (1993b) said in an interview that he received several frantic calls from reporters asking for a quick summary of Guinier's view, to be used in articles due later that day. Or as *New York Times* reporter David Margolick (1993) wrote: "Mr. Taylor is surely one of the few people in Washington or any-where else to actually wade through her [Guinier's] articles. Instead, almost everyone is relying on reconstructions by journalists and partisans, injecting further distortion into the debate." What Margolick did not say is that most of the journalists' "reconstructions" were based on accounts by partisans or other journalists.

Journalists also used qualification to blunt the impact of statements they were not quite sure about. In fact, the *Post*'s Isikoff (1993a) seems to want to "qualify" his own method of quoting from Guinier's scholarship, noting that her controversial writings "involve heavily footnoted law review articles that both supporters and opponents acknowledge are not easily summarized." He then, of course, proceeded to summarize them. At least one reporter thought that a statement frequently used by the press to illustrate Guinier's radicalism—that she had described Virginia governor Douglas Wilder as not an "authentic" black representative—needed to be qualified. In an interview, the *New York Times*'s Neil Lewis (1993a) put great stock on the fact that he had written that Guinier "suggests" that Wilder "could be" an example of an inauthentic black leader. But these qualifications probably did not serve their stated function; most readers of Lewis's carefully phrased claim were as likely to zero in on the racially loaded subtext—that Lani Guinier called Doug Wilder an Uncle Tom—as were the readers of less careful publications. Perhaps the best example of the journalistic pretense that qualification insulates journalists from the charges they levy is Bob Cohn's defense of *Newsweek*'s "Crowning a 'Quota Queen'?" headline. That "quota queen" was in single quotes and followed by a question mark was enough for Cohn to conclude that the term was "not in *Newsweek*'s voice." In most instances, qualification does not so much warn the reader that a journalist is unsure of a conclusion as legitimize the journalist's use of a shaky conclusion.

Attribution is used even more frequently to distance a journalist from the opinions expressed in her article. None of the news articles stated directly that Guinier was an extremist; instead, they all quoted named or unnamed sources to that effect. Tony Mauro (1993), writing in *USA Today*, said Guinier "was labeled by one conservative critic as 'breathtakingly radical' on issues of race." Guinier "has been described by oppo-

nents as a 'quota queen' and advocate of reverse racial discrimination," wrote the *Los Angeles Times*'s John M. Broder (1993). In another *Los Angeles Times* article (Lauter 1993a), Guinier is described as having "been accused by opponents of advocating views that amount to racial separatism." The *Post*'s Isikoff (1993a) wrote that "conservative activists" say that passages from Guinier's writings "reveal her as an 'extreme' left-wing activist with a far-reaching social agenda."

The "activists" and "opponents" were not all anonymous. Senator Orrin Hatch was quoted in the *New York Times* (N. Lewis 1993b) as saying: "She is an architect of a theory of racial preferences that if enacted would push America down the road of racial balkanization." The same article quoted Senator Alan Simpson: "Her writings are very disturbing and suggest a kind of racism in reverse." To Senator Robert Dole, Guinier is a "consistent supporter not only of quotas but of vote-rigging schemes that make quotas look mild." That such labels were attributed to others, however, did not blunt the cumulative impact of reading charge after charge of extremism, radicalism, separatism, and reverse racism.

Finally, journalists used "balance" to demonstrate that their articles about Lani Guinier were fair. None of the articles is unremittingly negative. In the *Post* article, reporter Isikoff (1993a) noted that "civil rights groups and lawyers across the country . . . hailed Guinier as the ideal candidate to fulfill the president's pledge to restore civil rights activism to the department's front burner." He also mentioned two colleagues' observation that Guinier was "far from radical," that she was "thoughtful, balanced and intelligent." Ronald Brownstein (1993) of the *Los Angeles Times* quotes a colleague of Guinier's from the NAACP Legal Defense and Educational Fund crediting Guinier with "creating more opportunities to build 'cross-racial' bridges." But that's one paragraph in a twenty-seven-paragraph story. These comments come across as minor counterpoints to an already-established, overpowering theme. They seem, in fact, to be just what they are: dissenting perspectives thrown in to prove the fairness and impartiality of the journalist.

Journalists' attempts to be balanced also manifested themselves in a more subtle way. For reasons that will be discussed later, virtually every article written about Guinier compared her confirmation battle to that of failed Supreme Court nominee Robert Bork. Donald Baer (1993) of *U.S. News & World Report* wrote, "Liberal Guinier is looking just like conservative 1987 Supreme Court nominee Robert Bork." *Newsweek* said, "Conservatives laid the groundwork for 'Borking' Guinier with her own words" (Cohn 1993b). "C. Lani Guinier . . . is quickly becoming the Robert H. Bork of the left," wrote David Savage (1993a) in the *Los Angeles Times*.

A particularly interesting example appeared in *Post* reporter Isikoff's (1993a) article: "Insisting that many of Guinier's writing have been twisted 'out of context,' they [White House aides and civil rights lawyers] also have sought to play down some of her articles in much the same way that, years earlier, Bork's defenders tried to minimize the importance of some of his writings." This sentence accomplishes two things. First, it reasserts the accuracy of Isikoff's quoting of Guinier's article by noting that a nominee's "defenders" will always attack the way scholarly articles are used in political fights, the implication being that such attacks are to be expected and are not to be taken seriously. Second, the continual Bork references remind the reader that journalists are not ideologically biased; they are as likely to attack scholars of the right, such as Bork, as scholars of the left, such as Guinier. The implied message: Journalists' conclusions are implicitly trustworthy. Balance, like the other three objective techniques, serves to establish the legitimacy of the journalistic enterprise rather than further the cause of impartial journalism.

The crucial point about the objective method in journalism is that just like formalism in law (Fischl 1987; Singer 1984), it produces indeterminate results. It does not lead to unbiased stories; nor does it lead to stories that are necessarily biased in favor of the right. It could be argued that the objective method's reliance on "authoritative sources" implies a bias toward established authorities. There is certainly evidence for that proposition, and that may be how the method has in fact worked (Reese 1990, p. 395; Glasser 1992, p. 176). A 1959 journalism textbook, for example, offers this advice: "If you must report something out of your presence go directly to the most responsible person concerned and ask him or her for information. Usually a line from the manager is worth a column from the janitor (C. Warren 1959, p. 52)." Harvey L. Molotch (1978,

p. 182) argues that the reliance on authoritative sources has been particularly detrimental to women. "Traditional dependence by the media for spokesmen from the top of such institutions means that the sexism which blocks women's mobility in other realms accumulates to block women from even knowing they exist as a public phenomenon." Scholars have suggested that the nonhierarchical structure of the women's movement, combined with hostility toward the media, made it difficult for journalists to find "authoritative sources" in the movement. This, in turn, inhibited coverage of the movement, particularly in its initial stages (Freeman 1993; Kahn and Goldenberg 1991; Cancian and Ross 1981).

But the terms "authoritative" and "source" in and of themselves are open-ended. A reporter could decide that the janitors are the best authorities on how a company treats its workers. A reporter could seek out the voices of many women to express the views of the movement. Those decisions are made by journalists, not by a method. A reporter using the exact same techniques—verification, qualification, attribution, and balance—could just as easily have written a story concluding that Guinier was a thoughtful, moderate scholar and experienced civil rights litigator who would have made an outstanding assistant attorney general. The danger of the objective method is not that it leads to certain outcomes but that it masks the pervasive subjective judgments implicit in all news stories, lending them unwarranted authority. It also makes it easier for reporters to distance themselves from the contents of their articles: I did not call Lani Guinier a quota queen, Bob Cohn can say, I just related what was around town; I did not create the controversy over Lani Guinier, Michael Isikoff can say, I just reported on it. That distancing makes it more likely that a journalist will not read all of a scholar's articles before she writes about them or will not think through the implications of using a sexist, racist term. "Objective reporting virtually precludes responsible reporting if by responsible reporting we mean a willingness on the part of the reporter to be accountable for what is reported," wrote Theodore L. Glasser. "Objectivity requires only that reporters be accountable for *how* they report, not what they report" (Glasser 1992, p. 180).

Of course, there are institutional pressures that constrain individual reporters. The most frequently cited constraint in this situation, and in many others, is time. Many reporters claimed that they did not read Guinier's admittedly lengthy law review articles, and thus had to depend on others' accounts of them, because they were under deadline pressure; they simply did not have the time. It is important to recognize, however, that this "pressure" was self-imposed, if not by the journalist herself then by the organization she worked for. It didn't have anything to do with any external time-bound reference points, such as the date of Guinier's nomination or confirmation hearings. The news stories on her law review articles were not rushed to coincide with Guinier's nomination. Only the *Wall Street Journal* column by Clint Bolick appeared right after her nomination. Most of the news stories on her law review articles did not appear until several weeks later—plenty of time to read and digest even complicated articles. Nor were reporters hustling to write stories in anticipation of impending confirmation hearings; in fact, hearings were never scheduled. Instead, reporters were responding to perceived competitive pressures: because articles about Guinier's troubled nomination appeared in some publications, similar articles had to appear in all publications immediately. Pressure to have the story first or at the same time is a self-serving media construct. As Michael Schudson (1986, p. 81) points out, "The journalist's interest in immediacy hangs on an anachronistic ritual of the media tribe. Getting the story first is a matter of journalistic pride, but one that has little to do with journalistic quality or public service. It is a fetishism of the present, an occupational perversion, and one peculiarly American."

Similarly, for an individual reporter to write an article that discussed Guinier's views rather than dwelling on the controversy would have required her to buck the overwhelming journalistic ethos. Reporters imposed a negative spin on the Guinier story because other reporters imposed a negative spin. Once the first stories, queued off of Bolick's *Wall Street Journal* article, focused on the Guinier "controversy," other stories followed suit. "Lacking an objective standard for evaluating what are often highly ambiguous situations, journalists find it useful to agree among themselves," wrote Stephen D. Reese (1990, p. 393). Or as Leon V. Sigal (1973, pp. 180–81) explained: "So long as newsmen follow the same routines, espousing the same professional values and using each other as their standard of comparison, newsmaking will tend to be insular and self-reinforcing. But that insularity is precisely what newsmen need. It provides them with a modicum of certitude that enables them to act in an otherwise uncertain environment." More concretely, reporters often find it easier to agree with other reporters because then they do not have to justify their different positions to their editors. Success in large, bureaucratic organizations, especially ones devoted to serving a mass audience, rarely comes from taking iconoclastic stances. To understand these constraints, however, is not to minimize the choices involved for reporters, editors, or organizations. Again, the danger of objectivity is that it masks choices.

The Search for Neutral Frameworks

If the objective method did not dictate the uniformly negative and almost uniform press treatment of Lani Guinier's scholarship, what did? I think the answer lies not in the method but in the spirit of objectivity. Despite a devastating critique, objectivity has retained its hold on journalists. At the same time, journalists have increasingly recognized the importance of interpretation. Both of these phenomena—the persistence of objectivity and the rise of interpretation—have been well documented. What has received much less attention is how these two seemingly contradictory impulses coexist and affect news coverage. Theodore Glasser and James S. Ethena (1989) indirectly explored the interaction of objective and interpretive journalism in their study of investigative reporters. Investigative reporting involves an implicit moral claim—that something is wrong which needs to be uncovered and corrected. But the imperatives of objectivity prevent a reporter from directly making a moral judgment about what is wrong. Instead, investigative reporters must identify a source of moral authority outside themselves to justify their investigation. Glasser and Ethena (1989, p. 10) identified five ways that the "task of objectifying a moral claim is accomplished through an appeal to some self-evidently credible moral authority." They include: "1) appeal to the law 2) appeal to formalized code or guidelines 3) appeal to recognized expertise 4) appeal to morality as evidenced in statistical or other comparisons and 5) appeal to common decency." By relying on these seemingly objective yardsticks, reporters can identify and assess the wrongdoing without sacrificing their neutrality. Glasser and Ethena conclude that "these appeals . . . serve to insulate reporters from responsibility for their own judgments." Daniel C. Hallin (1992b) found a similar unwillingness on the part of the television journalists covering political campaigns to make value judgments. To avoid such judgments and yet retain their essential role as interpreters, the journalists concentrated on technical issues.[8]

> The mediated, journalist-centered form of modern TV news places journalists in a difficult position. They are expected to take center stage as interpreters of the campaign; yet "no one elected the media," as the phrase goes, and their role can easily become a focus of political controversy. Hence, television journalists feel more comfortable making essentially technical judgments about campaign performance, judgments that can be presented as nonpartisan and verified by polls and the judgments of other political professionals. (For the same reason, when TV journalists do turn their attention to policy issues, they tend to focus on questions of fact rather than value: "Did Reagan in fact cut Medicare?" rather than "Should Medicare have been cut?") (Hallin 1992b, p. 21)

For both the investigative and political reporters studied, the impulse is the same—to choose the most neutral framework for analyzing events, whether it is a violation of the law to justify an investigation or slipping poll results to explain a poor political campaign. The need for objective interpretation, however, is not limited to political campaigns or investigative projects. Certainly any complex story—and perhaps *any* story—requires a framework to make sense of the event being described. The third part of this article will explore the three frameworks journalists constructed to assess Lani Guinier's nomination: I will call these frameworks market, social consensus, and preexisting practices. Although further work is required in this area, my assumption is that these "neutral" frameworks are used in most news coverage, whether the ones I identify here or those based on technical expertise, as identified by Hallin, or on external moral author-

ities, as identified by Glasser and Ethena.[9] In the case of Guinier's nomination, they had particularly pernicious results. The tone of the coverage, which I will argue was dictated by the choice of frameworks, "managed to kill off this nomination," as *Los Angeles Times* reporter David Savage (1993b) said in an interview. But the danger of the press's reliance on these seemingly neutral frameworks extends beyond the Guinier nomination. Unlike the objective method, which produces indeterminate results, these frameworks tend to reinforce already-established ways of thinking. What is taken to be neutrality is actually conventionality. The press's preferred interpretive modes tend to be hostile to complexity, to originality, and to minority perspectives. Guinier's scholarship, a complex and original minority perspective, did not receive a sympathetic reading from the news media, and according to this analysis, neither would most feminist theories. To understand why, it is necessary to discuss each framework in relation to the media's coverage of the Guinier nomination.

The market framework refers to the construction of a news narrative around the perceived ability of an idea, policy, or politician to gain approval from the general public. These stories are often referred to in political campaigns as "horse race" stories, tales of who's ahead and why. That approach, however, does not end with campaigns, nor is it limited to the electoral process. When journalists score a president's week good or bad, their judgment is not based on whether he introduced important legislation, made morally compelling speeches, or helped negotiate peace with feuding foreign countries. Instead, they measure a presidency based on the president's ability to score points on some amorphous Geiger counter of public sentiment. Even public figures or ideas that do not face electoral tests are judged on their ability to woo the public. Michael Jackson's fortunes, both literal and figurative, rise and fall in the journalistic narrative based on his ability to persuade the public that he is or is not a child molester. Journalists are more comfortable with these quantitative, thus seemingly objective, measures than with what seem to be more subjective judgments about the worth of legislation, the importance of the moral message, or the justness of the peace.

So when Clint Bolick created a "controversy" over Guinier's nomination in the *Wall Street Jour-*

nal, the press jumped. First, the controversy transformed a story about a nomination into a story about a fight. That not only made the story more dramatic but also provided a ready-made framework for analyzing it: who's winning, who's losing. And that's precisely the way most of the press framed the story. "Ms. Guinier has suddenly become President Clinton's next confirmation battle," wrote Neil A. Lewis (1993b) in the *New York Times*. "Those charges have sent Democrats scurrying for cover and have put Guinier's nomination in trouble just three weeks after it was announced," wrote David Savage (1993a) in the *Los Angeles Times*. Second, the controversy over Guinier's nomination fed into a preexisting story line on the Clinton presidency. Guinier's nomination came in the midst of several "bad" presidential weeks, from the press's point of view. The controversy over her appointment fed into the interpretive framework of a president losing favor with the public because of too-liberal policies. As Leslie Phillips (1993) wrote in *USA Today*: "As President Clinton attempts to steer his administration to the middle of the political spectrum, he is re-evaluating his controversial choice for the Justice Department's chief guardian of civil rights laws." Or as the *Los Angeles Times*'s David Lauter (1993b) wrote, in anticipation of the nomination's withdrawal: "The Guinier nomination and a decision to withdraw it, coming on top of a series of other missteps that have shaken the Clinton White House in recent weeks, could inflict damage on the already beleaguered Administration."

Given that the stories about Guinier were framed as a fight over her nomination—and it seemed to be a fight she and the president were losing—the next logical step in developing the story was to explain why she was losing.[10] And there was a ready explanation put forward by Bolick and other Republicans: Guinier was a radical, an extremist, a separatist. So it is not surprising that those charges were given greater prominence and more play than the alternative view. That Guinier was a talented litigator and thoughtful scholar would not have explained why she was losing in the market of public opinion.

It could be argued that the market framework does not evidence bias. Had the Clinton presidency been viewed as winning in the market, then the Guinier stories would have reflected that. In this case I think the other two interpretive frameworks, which are discussed later, still would have led the press to shape the story negatively. But the more important response is that the bias of the market framework is not in who wins and who loses but in the fact that winning or losing is the most important measure and that it is determined based on perceived popularity. First, the "objectivity" of this approach is irredeemably compromised by the tools used to gauge public sentiment. Especially for fast-breaking stories, the press relies on little more than the off-the-cuff comments of a small group of pundits or the equally ill-considered opinions expressed in a small number of "man-in-the-street" interviews.[11] And even if journalists rely on more "scientific" public opinion polls, the polls only measure the opinions of people who know little more about the subject than what the media has told them. The process is thus completely circular. The press concludes that certain ideas will be unpopular, presents those ideas anticipating a negative reaction and therefore highlights their controversial nature, and then measures their popularity by interviewing or polling people who have read primarily negative things. Even assuming that the tools could be perfected, however, journalists' reliance on the market framework ensures that original ideas will be poorly received. By definition, these ideas are not those of a majority. But if popularity is the basis for judging ideas, only the most comfortable and conventional ideas will be welcomed by the press.

The social consensus framework is a variant of the market framework. Here the emphasis is not on winning in the market but on conforming to an unstated social agreement. The assumption is that this consensus exists, can be identified (although how is never explained), and accurately reflects reality. Deviation from the consensus marks one as an outsider and, even more important, as wrong. Underlying the news coverage of Guinier's nomination is the press's image of a social consensus on race issues that goes something like this: While race was once a determinative factor in electoral politics, it no longer is, as evidenced by the election of blacks to important positions. To continue to worry about race is a sign that the worrier perceives the world exclusively from a racial perspective.

The press's primary mission in reading Guinier's scholarship was to determine whether her views confirmed this consensus. They did not. In fact, Guinier's articles explicitly challenge these assumptions about race and electoral politics. But rather than weigh the merits of her challenge, examine her documentation, assess her arguments—in other words, evaluate her scholarship as scholarship—the press would not be diverted from its already-adopted framework. The only question was whether Guinier fit within this "mainstream." As Samuel Issacharoff (1993) of the University of Texas said in an interview after Guinier's defeat: "Is Guinier outside the mainstream? This was the main question I was asked by all the reporters who called me. What I tried to say—before I gave up on it and answered the way they wanted me to answer, yes or no—was that it was very hard to speak of a mainstream in this area. There are only a handful of people writing about this." To most reporters, however, there was no ambiguity either about the existence of a "mainstream" or the fact that it was bad to be outside it.[12] Steven V. Roberts (1993), writing in U.S. News & World Report, encapsulates this view:

> And what alarmed so many about Guinier's views is that she describes America as if it were South Africa, as if race were the dominant definition of American political identity and motive. The gap between white and blacks seems so irreconcilable to her that extraordinary measures are needed to buttress black power. There is no room for trust, no possibility of tolerance. Her nomination failed because so many Americans think her views fail democracy's critical test: striking a fair balance between majority and minority rights.

The social consensus framework is useful for journalists both because it seems to be an impartial standard (the journalist is reflecting not *her* views but those of the society at large) and because it is by definition unlikely to offend the majority of a journalist's audience. As Daniel Hallin (1992a, p. 20) points out, journalists are "constrained by the need to avoid offense to any major political faction, or more powerfully, to the majority sentiments of the moment."

But in its wholesale and unthinking adoption of the social consensus framework, the press ignores three critical questions: Is there such a thing as social consensus, particularly on deeply divisive issues such as racial politics? And if there is, how do you determine what that social consensus is? And finally, even if there is a social consensus and it can be identified, is that necessarily the best way to measure the worth of an idea? These questions, which should make any journalist pause before blithely assuming an understanding of a social consensus, become particularly disturbing in the context of Guinier's nomination. In this case, more than others, there were red flags to signal the dangers of assuming, without evidence or analysis, the existence of a social consensus. For one thing, in her scholarship Guinier acknowledges the "social consensus" that journalists take for granted and then demonstrates in a meticulous fashion how and why it is false. Presumably her arguments should have led journalists to consider and at least directly address the question of how much of a consensus there really is on the role of race relations in electoral politics. Instead, journalists used her attack to brand her outside the mainstream without reflecting on the arguments themselves. Perhaps that can be explained by the fact that most journalists did not read her articles but instead relied on others' accounts of them. Or maybe they concluded that her arguments were not persuasive, though it is likely that that level of engagement would have generated a deeper dialogue on race relations. Or perhaps the allure of a supposedly neutral and inoffensive framework overpowered any serious consideration of her argument. As it was, she was defeated by a claim about race relations that she had devoted a scholarly career to rebutting.

Still more disturbing than that irony is the ease with which journalists assumed a social consensus on the issue of race. That a perceived social consensus might be no more than the majority's view would seem to be a self-evident danger. That danger would seem to be particularly acute when the consensus is supposed to be over issues of race. And it would seem to be overwhelming when those identifying the consensus—in this case, reporters—are for the most part themselves members of the majority group. Yet the press expressed no such reticence in declaring a social consensus on the role of race in electoral politics. If journalists are willing to assume a social consensus in an area so marked by division, then they would surely presume one in murkier areas. If being outside the social consensus becomes the framework for evaluating the worth of an idea—as it did in Guinier's case—then the press inevitably will judge harshly any perspectives, including those of minorities and feminists, that diverge from the so-called mainstream.

The last interpretive framework is that of preexisting practices, or the application of frameworks used in previous controversies to a current one. It is the journalistic equivalent of fighting the last war. In Guinier's case, it meant that the press applied two existing models, derived from similar recent controversies, to her nomination. The Guinier story was seen as a combination of the "divisive race battle" story and the "controversial judicial nominee with a paper record" story. That meant the conventions developed in reporting those controversies were applied to the Guinier nomination whether they fit or not.

In recent years, "divisive race battle" stories have been about quotas, so applying the preexisting practices framework, the Guinier story was about quotas too. It did not matter that Guinier's scholarship—purportedly the reason for the controversy—barely mentions quotas, except to say that she does not support them in voting rights cases. "A lot of my colleagues had the reaction, 'We know what this is about, we know this is about quotas,'" David Savage (1993b) of the Los Angeles Times said in an interview. What mattered was that journalists knew how to assess public figures based on their stance on quotas: Support for quotas made someone liberal (maybe even radical), elitist, and probably unpopular; denunciation of quotas placed a person in the coveted mainstream. Since the actual evidence for Guinier's support of quotas could not be found in her scholarship, it was *assumed* from her race and gender. She was a black, left-leaning woman, so she just had to be a quota queen.

How that phrase became the defining description of Guinier is instructive, revealing both the lengths to which conservatives would go to mischaracterize her writings and reporters' dependence on a preexisting framework no matter how inapposite. In his *Wall Street Journal* article, Clint Bolick (1993) offered two pieces of evidence that Guinier supported quotas. First, in a single paragraph in a forty-one-page article, she discussed the importance of "diversity in the appointment process" for judicial nominees, concluding that "the Senate Judicial Committee should begin evaluating federal judicial nominations with reference to specific goals for increasing non-white nominees" (Guinier 1989, p. 432). And second, Bolick wrote that Guinier "proclaims that antidiscrimination laws mandate a 'result-oriented inquiry in which roughly equal outcomes, not merely an apparently fair process, are the goal.'" Bolick made much of the quote, even though the statement appeared in a footnote and Guinier was quoting another author (Guinier 1989, p. 461). He and those who regurgitated his analysis ignored her comment in the *Virginia Law Review* that while she could be accused of "outcome-oriented jurisprudence," her "focus on legislative *rules,* not decisional *outcomes,* adequately answers this criticism." And Guinier never proclaimed (authors rarely proclaim in footnotes) that the law *mandates* "roughly equal results." When read in conjunction with the sentence that follows, Guinier seemed to be claiming that "substantive equality" should be measured both by "the process," which "must be equal," and "the results," which "must also reflect the effort to remedy the effects of a century of official discrimination." This complex idea was reduced to "Lani Guinier does not believe in equal opportunity" in articles in the *Washington Post* (Isikoff 1993a), the *Los Angeles Times* (Brownstein 1993), *Legal Times* (S. Taylor 1993a), and *Newsweek* (Cohn 1993b). For example, Steven V. Roberts, Ted Gest, and Thomas Toch (1993) wrote in *U.S. News & World Report:* Guinier "says she does not believe in quotas. But she has written that civil-rights enforcement should be a 'result-oriented inquiry in which roughly equal outcomes, not merely an apparently fair process are the goal.'" So even though Guinier barely mentions the issue of quotas in her work, they became the focus of most news articles about her.

The second preexisting model that journalists applied to Guinier's nomination was that of the "controversial judicial nominee with a paper record." Hence the repeated and near-universal comparisons with Robert Bork's failed Supreme Court nomination. For most reporters, the last time they were forced to read law review articles was for a controversial-judicial-nominee-with-a-paper-record story. Because Clint Bolick made Guinier's law review articles the subject of controversy, the fight over her nomination became that kind of story too. It did not matter that she was not a judicial nominee; that she, unlike Supreme Court candidates, would be constrained by the need to persuade a conservative judiciary; or that she would be subject to control by the president and the attorney general. While most of the news articles mentioned the similarities with Bork's failed nomination, few mentioned the dissimilarities. In fact, when Bork was nominated to be solicitor general in the Nixon administration, he was never questioned about his law review articles, law professors Leon Friedman and Burt Neuborne (1993) noted in a letter to the *New York Times*. A *New York Times* article did note that as assistant attorney general Guinier would not make policy on civil rights, but that idea was expressed in one sentence in the eighteenth and last paragraph of the story (N. Lewis 1993b). Most coverage devoted only a paragraph or two to Guinier's career, and only one article, a profile by the *Washington Post*'s David Von Drehle (1993), included extensive information on her litigation background—and that appeared after Clinton had withdrawn her nomination. Only the *Chicago Tribune* ("No Grounds" 1993), in an editorial, suggested that the focus of the press coverage might be askew. After criticizing some of Guinier's views, as expressed in her law review articles, the paper endorsed her nomination: "The error here—as in the case of Bork—is to assume what a scholar suggests in an academic article is also what she will pursue in public office. . . . No one is about to give the civil rights division the green light to try and get a court to demand a minority veto on legislation. Guinier, even if she were so inclined, will not be allowed to push any radical agenda in litigation." But because the controversial-judicial-nominee-with-a-paper record framework was applied, her views as expressed in law review articles became the decisive factors in determining her suitability to be an assistant attorney general. Professor Derek Bell noted in an interview the irony that the most common complaint about affirmative action is the difficulty of finding "qualified" blacks, but in this case "you can't imagine anybody being more qualified than Lani Guinier[,] . . . and suddenly, qualifications mean nothing" (Bell 1993).

The danger of the preexisting practices framework, like that of the two previous frameworks, is that it limits public discourse to what is already familiar. Had news reports actually focused on the subject of Guinier's scholarship—the ineffectiveness of current judicial and legislative remedies in increasing blacks' influence on electoral politics—it may have opened up discussions on race and politics. But by insisting that the subject of her scholarship was quotas, the press merely rehashed an old argument among basically the same participants. Had the press examined her record as a litigator, along with her scholarship, it might have led to a wide-ranging conversation on the qualifications of the nation's chief enforcer of the civil rights laws. Instead, the public learned little about what the assistant attorney general for civil rights does and a great deal (though warped almost beyond recognition) about a few law review articles.

If the market, social consensus, and preexisting practices frameworks seem to be different ways of describing the same phenomenon, there's a good reason. A long-standing, deep-seated professional ethic makes journalists reluctant to make value judgments, yet most journalists recognize that such judgments are an unavoidable part of the profession. So they settle for the next best thing to real objectivity—the appearance of objectivity, whether in pseudoscientific methodology or in seemingly neutral interpretive frameworks. The attempt to assume neutral perspectives inevitably leads to modes that presume that "what is" is neutral, whether one is talking about existing popular sentiments, perceived social consensus, or established professional practices. These frameworks also all suffer from the same defect—they tend to make it harder to introduce new ways of thinking into the public discourse. That is not to say that new ideas never find their way into the mass media; they do, despite the press's inherent antipathy for them. Identifying how and why this occurs would be an interesting subject of scholarly attention. But what this article has shown through the press coverage of Lani Guinier's nomination is just how hard it is for that to happen.

The implications for feminist and other nontraditional scholarship are obvious. The press savaged Lani Guinier's scholarship, which is straightforward, analytical, and for the most part extremely clear. Rather than radical or extremist, her articles reflect a liberal-reformist orientation.[13] And look what the press did to her.

Notes

1. For a thorough recounting of the general attack on objectivity, see Hackett 1984.

2. I read all articles referring to Guinier that appeared between April 29 and June 16, 1993, in seven newspapers (the *Chicago Tribune*, *Legal Times*, the *Los Angeles Times*, the *New York Times*, the *Wall Street Journal*, the *Washington Post*, and *USA Today*) and four magazines (*New Republic*, *Newsweek*, *Time*, and *U.S. News & World Report*).

3. I will focus here on *how* the concept of objectivity has changed, not *why* it changed. There is a vast and conflicting literature attempting to explain the transformation of American newspapers from partisan journals, in which all information was presented from a particular political or moral viewpoint, to seemingly impartial publications, in which news stories reported the facts and opinions were relegated to the editorial page. Some scholars have pointed to material factors, such as the rise of the Associated Press and the decline of multinewspaper towns, to explain the dominance of the objective ideal. See Shaw 1967; Roschco 1975. While taking note of market conditions, Michael Schudson (1978) persuasively argues that the rise of objectivity was as much a function of the change in the culture of journalists as any change in the material conditions of journalism. Sorting out the complex social, economic, and theoretical movements that gave rise to objectivity, however, is not as important for the purposes of this paper as recognizing objectivity's enduring hold on modern journalism.

4. For a detailed discussion of these changes in journalism, see Leff 1986, based on a study of 121 journalism textbooks published between 1879 and 1985.

5. Exploring why objectivity has persisted in the face of both a devastating critique and the growth of interpretation is beyond the scope of the paper. There may be interesting parallels, however, in the persistence of formalism in law. Even though the realist attack on formalism is over sixty years old and law has a much more developed scholarly tradition than journalism, legal scholars have just recently begun to grapple with the reasons for formalism's continuing power. See R. Gordon 1984; Sarat and Kearns 1991.

If, as Michael Schudson (1978, p. 159) suggests, journalists came to believe in objectivity to "seek escape from their own deep conviction of doubt and drift," then paradoxically, the need for objectivity in journalism and formalism in law would only grow more intense as faith in them waned. The failure of what Schudson identifies as the "critical culture" in journalism and reform movements in law, such as critical legal studies, may have compounded the disillusionment and thus, again paradoxically, deepened the need for what they so profoundly criticized. Or objectivity in journalism and formalism in law may persist for more pragmatic reasons, from the bureaucratic imperatives involved in news coverage, as described by Gaye Tuchman (1978b), to the need to deflect criticism and libel suits, as posed by Herbert J. Gans (1979) (see also Tuchman 1972). Or it may be, at least for journalism, that the need to reach a mass audience and be supported by mass-market advertisers requires that the

news media at least appear not to offend anyone. All of these possible explanations shape the way in which objectivity continue to influence journalism. For the purposes of this paper, however, the focus will be on the microdecisions that journalists make, apart from the macro-influences of the for-profit corporations that employ them.

6. For a discussion of exactly what the press got wrong and how it got it wrong, see Leff 1993.

7. The reluctance to read documents isn't unique to press coverage of Guinier's nomination. Stephen Hess's (1981) study of Washington reporters found that only in one-quarter of the articles he studied did the reporter rely on documents, and most of those documents were previously published news articles.

8. This phenomenon has been well documented, particularly in studies demonstrating the press's overwhelming interest in the "horse race" aspects of political campaigns rather than issues. See, for example, T. Patterson 1980; Robinson and Sheehan 1983.

9. A potentially fruitful avenue of research would be to explore the ways in which these neutral frameworks are applied over a variety of news stories and how they affect news coverage.

10. The story line that emerged after Guinier lost the nomination was, "What went wrong?" Here again, the press focused almost exclusively on technical problems. To Gwen Ifill (1993), writing in the *New York Times*, the problem was inadequate staff work: Clinton's staff was unwilling to inform the president about Guinier's radical views because she was a friend of the president. To David Lauter and Sam Fulwood III (1993), writing in the *Los Angeles Times*, the problem was White House incompetence: The president and his staff had "put Guinier's name forward without understanding her positions on some of the most politically sensitive issues in American life—the issues her office would oversee." To Donald Baer (1993) of *U.S. News & World Report*, the president's people should have known better. "The White House had no reason to be caught off guard. *U.S. News* has learned that Senate Democrats warned a Clinton aide before the nomination about Guinier's articles."

11. It is interesting to note that in Guinier's case, the press's attempts to gauge public sentiment did not extend beyond the Beltway. The only quotes to appear were those of senators or lobbyists in Washington, D.C. The press assumed that the general public had a negative reaction to her appointment but did nothing to measure it.

12. Most of the attempts to portray Guinier as outside the mainstream focused on her political approach, as expressed in her law review articles. Because her articles focused on race, not on gender, that was the basis for branding her outside the mainstream. But there were some indications that her status as a woman, particularly a woman of color, also led to the press depiction of her as an outsider. The repeated references to her as a "quota queen" conjured up images of welfare queens. In addition, *U.S. News & World Report*'s pejo-

rative description of her—"strange name, strange hair, strange ideas"—also highlighted her race and gender (Baer 1993).

13. Truly radical ideas are likely to be dismissed before they even find their way into print. The few studies of press coverage of the early women's liberation movement show that the media basically ignored it (see Morris 1973). Feminist ideas that did find their way into the mass media were ridiculed (see Tuchman 1978b).

5

The Real *Real Anita Hill,*
or the Making of a Backlash Best-Seller

MARY COOMBS

In April 1993, the Free Press published David Brock's *The Real Anita Hill*. The book purported both to expose a variety of inconsistencies and inaccuracies in the testimony of Professor Hill and her key witnesses and to show that she was a left-wing feminist with one or more of a number of character flaws. The inevitable conclusion, if one accepted the accuracy of Brock's research and conclusions, was that Professor Hill's charges against Judge Thomas were baseless and that he had been the innocent victim of a vendetta engaged in by Hill and by the "Shadow Senate" of liberal senators, staffers, and lobbyists.

This heavily footnoted screed quickly became a best-seller. It first appeared on the *New York Times* best-seller list on May 16, 1993, rising as high as number three, and remained on the list for eleven weeks (Maryles 1994). Acclaim for the book was not limited to some "great unwashed" mass public; it received respectful to enthusiastic early reviews, including reviews in such mainstream media as the *New York Times* and the *Washington Post.*

The simplest explanation for a book's positive reviews and popularity is that it is a good book. In part 1 of this essay, I refute that contention with a brief review of the book. Part 2 demonstrates the extent of positive responses to the book by reviewers and the general public. Part 3 explores alternative explanations for those responses, both in the book's linkage to public perceptions of issues of race, gender, and political power and in Brock's evocation of the mantle of journalistic objectivity. Finally, I speculate briefly about the lessons we might learn from those responses: What can we do either to structure the popular and media responses to our issues or at least to mitigate the damage to our causes from media hostility?

The Book: A Brief Review

A nonfiction book can receive good reviews and be popular because it presents a compelling and apparently accurate account of an interesting event. The assessment of the book's value necessarily turns in large part on how well, in the opinion of the reader/reviewer, the author has captured the truth of the event. Yet ordinarily neither the reviewer nor the reader has any direct knowledge of the event described; frequently, they have little grounding in the prior literature dealing with the event. The assessment of the book's "truth," then, reflects one or both of two sources. First, the book may be perceived as true because its conclusions are consistent with the reader's preexisting understandings of how the event must have occurred; that is, it confirms the reader's prejudices. Second, the book may be internally consistent and coherent, providing a narrative that makes sense as a story.

The high level of credibility granted Brock's book, I suggest, reflects its feeding of stereotypes and cultural fears and desires. Viewed apart from this cultural framing, it is simply a very bad book. It is poorly written; its research is weak; its arguments are often bizarrely convoluted; and its explanations for Professor Hill's behavior are logically incoherent. It is bad science and it is a bad story: Unless one comes to the book with the same stereotypes about race and gender on which the book relies, the behavior of the "characters" is incoherent. Since these defects in the book are apparent from a moderately careful reading of the book itself, without the need to check Mr. Brock's research or examine other materials, the popularity of the book and the positive tone of the reviews calls for a socially rooted explanation.

The first and perhaps most obvious flaw in Mr. Brock's book is its claim to embody neutral reportage. Brock opens the book with the statement, "Like most Americans, I tuned into the Thomas-Hill hearings with an open mind" (1993a, p. vii). This claimed objectivity rapidly disappears, buried under an avalanche of rhetorical games and gratuitous nastiness. Let me give two examples of the rhetorical trick and two of the snide aside.

One frequently used ploy is to present an allegedly ambiguous fact and then ask a series of rhetorical questions, always ending with the one that places Hill and her supporters in the worst possible light. For example, the chapter presenting the testimony of her four supporting witnesses ends with a set of such questions: "Why

did she specifically tell the FBI that she had not told her boyfriend John Carr, only to have Carr later appear as a witness? . . . Why would Hill say she had told only her closest friends of the harassment, when in fact she told at least one person she barely knew? . . . Were these contradictions simply the inevitable consequence of reconstructing events ten years past, or were they the inevitable loose threads of a fabricated story?" (Brock 1993a, pp. 202–3). Similarly, Brock notes that Hill completed the polygraph exam (which she passed) at 1:15 on Sunday but that her attorney, Charles Ogletree, was not told of the results until late that afternoon. Ignoring the possibility that Ogletree was busy with other matters, Brock speculates, "Why the four-hour gap? Did Hill keep taking the test until she passed it?" (p. 284, footnote omitted).

Brock frequently takes what would seem to be discomfiting facts and uses them in unnatural and therefore superficially helpful ways. For example, Clarence Thomas's inaccurate and prejudice-feeding attack on his sister for welfare dependency is ignored in Brock's discussion of Thomas's qualifications and history. It appears, rather, as evidence for the claim that the (allegedly) liberal Anita Hill would have had a political motive to defame him (p. 368). Attacks by others on Hill are repeated with only the mildest distancing, making comprehensible the legal rule that republishing a libel is a form of libel. Consider, for example, the following: " 'Anita Hill and her friends turned [University of Oklahoma law school] into a politically correct sleaze pit,' said William Michael Roberts, perhaps overstating the case somewhat" (p. 349).

Other comments are not only nasty but gratuitously so. Denigrating comments about Hill or her key witnesses are at least marginally defensible as part of a slow building of a prosecutorial case. But what legitimate purpose is served by relaying this unsourced story?: "On one of Thomas's first days at the Supreme Court, some of the cleaning women there approached him . . . and wished him well on the court. They also told Thomas they could never have approached Thurgood Marshall that way" (p. 279).

The pretensions to scholarship fare no better, on examination, than the pretensions to neutrality. True, there are over forty pages of notes. Reviewers and careful readers who read as well as count, however, will realize how often significant assertions are unsourced. Consider, for examples, the statements (1) that Hill's stress "may well have been . . . compounded by harassment from Chris Roggerson, who had recently become Thomas's executive assistant" (p. 316); (2) that Hill had to leave the Wald Harkrader firm and "simply accepted the first job that Gil Hardy could procure for her" rather than choosing to work for Thomas at the Department of Education (p. 291); or (3) that James Brudney, one of the alleged leakers, was close to Hill (itself an inference from thin and false evidence) and that "[p]resumably, therefore, he knew something about Hill's true feelings toward Thomas" (p. 115). All these assertions are central to one or another aspect of Brock's indictment of Hill; none are supported.

Surprisingly often, Brock's footnotes cite to anonymous sources, despite his angry criticism of Hill and her supporter Susan Hoerchner for seeking to make their charges against Thomas anonymously. Indeed, in a quite breathtaking display of chutzpah, Brock uses the unwillingness of his sources to be named as evidence that they are telling the truth. A professor's demand for anonymity "is a measure of how politically correct supporting Hill has become in university and legal sources" (p. 421, n. 2), while Washington lawyers' claims for anonymity reflect their "fear of jeopardizing their current legal practices" (p. 413, n. 13). Whatever liberalism may have crept into academia, the notion that Washington lawyers are more concerned with offending a University of Oklahoma law professor than ingratiating themselves with a sitting Supreme Court justice borders on the absurd.

Similarly, Brock devotes much of chapter 4 to excoriating the Shadow Senate (Brock's epithet for those opposing Thomas) for leaking documents. He asserts that Senate staffer James Brudney's actions in allegedly leaking the FBI report on Hill to the media constituted "a grave ethical lapse" that, except for a legal technicality, "would have been a federal crime . . . . far more blatant . . . than anything prosecuted in the Iran-Contra affair" (p. 161). Yet Brock uses confidential sources for many of his most critical points. His sources include the background investigatory material from the FBI file on Clarence Thomas and the transcripts of the Judiciary Committee

interviews with Susan Hoerchner and Gary Phillips. The left "leaks"; Brock, on the other hand, shows his journalistic skill by independently obtaining such sealed documents (pp. 391–92, nn. 11–13). This means either that some member of the conservative equivalent of the Shadow Senate leaked them to David Brock or that he stole them. In any event, their uncheckability means that the text that they "support" must be taken on faith, as much as if no footnote reference existed.

The clearest demonstration of the politics behind Brock's book and the positive response to it is in his stretched and implausible chains of inference from the particular "facts" asserted to his conclusion about "the real Anita Hill." A story is internally credible when it is simple: A few basic points account for essentially all the evidence. In contrast, Brock frequently rejects the most simple and obvious explanation for events in favor of more convoluted ones, linked only by their consistent placing of Hill and her supporters in a negative light. One might call it Brock's "reverse Occam's razor." For example, he suggests that Susan Hoerchner "may or may not have had" contacts with the Shadow Senate that permitted her to bring Hill's claim to their attention (p. 122). What is his evidence for the possibility (segued into an inferred likelihood) of such contacts? She had (presumably) been acquainted with Brudney since he and Hoerchner's brother were classmates at Yale Law School (p. 122). She had also worked for several months in 1980 at the Center for Law and Social Policy, a group that was, eleven years later, a member organization of the Alliance for Justice, which led the fight against the Thomas nomination (p. 207). Such attenuated connections sound like the work of Kennedy conspiracy buffs.

The most blatant example of Brock's choosing the more convenient over the more plausible explanation involves Hoerchner's claim, first to the FBI and then at the Senate committee hearings, that Anita Hill had told her in the spring of 1981 that "her boss, Clarence" had sexually harassed her. This statement cannot be wholly true: Hill did not begin to work for Thomas until the fall of 1981. Hoerchner thus misremembered either the date or the name. The name "Clarence" seems more memorable than the specific date of a conversation approximately ten years earlier. In her testimony, Hoerchner made clear which she was more certain about. "I remember in particular one telephone conversation I had with Anita. I should say, before telling you about this conversation, that I cannot pin down its date with certainty. I am sure that it was after she started working with Clarence Thomas, because in that conversation she referred to him as her boss, Clarence" (U.S. Senate Committee on the Judiciary 1991, part 4, p. 276). The only significant counter-evidence is that Hill and Hoerchner were in more frequent contact in 1981 than in 1982.

Brock, however, assumes that Hill's story is false and that Hoerchner misidentifies the harasser about whom Hill complained. To make this version hold together, Brock has to create a melange of possible explanations, none wholly coherent, for why Hill might have complained that she was being harassed at the Wald Harkrader law firm in the spring of 1981. Furthermore, reports by her other supporters must refer to another true claim (of harassment by someone else while she worked for Thomas), or (another) false claim, or a misunderstanding of a complaint by Hill that she was insufficiently appreciated. One wonders whether these complexities are "the inevitable loose threads of a fabricated story" (p. 203).

Perhaps the most striking defect in the book is the logical inconsistency of his explanations for people's behavior and motivations. John Carr and Joel Paul both testified in support of Hill. Carr, he asserts, "may have had a hidden motive" to claim that Hill had complained of Thomas because one of the partners in his firm was on record opposing the nomination (p. 246). By contrast, Paul's testimony is subject to question because he had declined to sign a petition opposing the nomination—if he knew that Hill had complained of such harassment, "why *didn't* he sign it?" (p. 248).

Similarly, Brock suggests that Thomas's refusal to withdraw his name from nomination supports his thesis. Brock's logic is that if Thomas were guilty, he would not risk a hearing and would resign; therefore, his refusal to resign supports his claim of innocence. Brock also insists that Hill had hoped to induce Thomas quietly to withdraw; she was only reluctant to be identified or required to tell her story publicly. But if Thomas were wholly innocent—if the alleged harassing

comments had never been made—Hill would have no reason to think he would withdraw. An anonymous, invented charge has no power. And though Brock attacks Hill's competence as a lawyer and as a professor, he portrays her as quite clever in her actions and choices in regard to the Thomas nomination.

Finally, Brock realizes that he needs some explanation for Hill's actions (other than the simple one that she was telling the truth). No single explanation holds up. Instead, Brock provides a smorgasbord of explanations, apparently untroubled by their logical incoherence. Hill was a would-be lover scorned, or she was a disappointed disciple, or she was a liberal mole from the beginning. She was a nearly innocent dupe induced to come forward by the mistaken identification of Thomas by Susan Hoerchner and/or by the unrelenting pressure of the Shadow Senate, or she was a radical feminist wholly implicated in the wicked plot. She had been sexually harassed, although never by Thomas, or she concocted stories of harassment to cover up her inadequacies at work. She deliberately perjured herself, or she lived in a fantasy world (and thus could pass a lie detector test). Brock sees no reason to choose among these explanations. He isn't interested in the "real Anita Hill." Rather, his book is designed to defend Clarence Thomas and to attack all the invented Anita Hills, in their black, female, liberal "political correctness."

This critique is wholly internal. Any moderately careful reader or reviewer could have, and should have, seen these flaws in the book. (I should confess that I do have a scintilla of inside knowledge; I was an associate at Wald Harkrader and Ross at the same time as Anita Hill and found Brock's portrait of her wholly inconsistent with the woman I knew. See Mayer and Abramson 1994, p. 89.) Two sources that might have been easily consulted by reviewers, however, would have confirmed the unreliability of the book. First and most obvious is the *American Spectator* article in which Brock first floated the story that became this book (Brock 1992). Writing there to an audience of the converted, without the limits of footnotes and, perhaps, without the review of the Free Press's libel lawyers, Brock is still more vitriolic and one-sided. Among the assertions that did not make the transition to the book were that "the word around the [Wald] office was that Hill had leveled a charge of sexual harassment to deflect attention from serious professional difficulties" (Brock 1992, p. 21); that "one Wald attorney—who did not provide any documentary proof—says that Hill was caught falsifying time sheets" (Brock 1992, pp. 21–22); "that Hill often spoke of going out with Brudney, and of having spent weekends at his apartment" (Brock 1992, p. 23); and that Education Secretary Bell "received several allegations of sexual harassment from Anita Hill during the time she worked at the department" (Brock 1992, p. 25).

In the article, Brock concluded that Hill was "a bit nutty, and a bit slutty" (1992, p. 27) and that "[b]ased on what we know of her attitude toward Thomas, her uneven temperament, her underwhelming intellect, her political and sexual prejudices, her weird relations with men, her history of frivolously charging sexual harassment, and finally her petty dishonesty," it is natural to conclude that she was part of a conspiracy against Thomas (1992, p. 27). His apparent willingness to publish any slander for which he had any anonymous source should have raised high a red flag regarding the validity of his conclusions in the book.

One other readily available external source, regarding Brock's picture of Anita Hill as "part of the self-described radical vanguard" in the Oklahoma law faculty (1993a, p. 342) is irresistible (at least to a law professor). A check of the Lexis law review database shows the following publications by Professor Hill prior to the hearings: "Bankruptcy, Contracts and Utilitarianism," *Missouri Law Review*, vol. 56, p. 571 (1991); "Prairie Production Inc. v. Agchem-Division Pennwalt Corp. and Rothe v. Maloney Cadillac: Old and New Approaches to Manufacturer Liability for Economic Loss," *Consumer Finance Law Quarterly Report*, vol. 44, p. 42 (1990); "A Comparative Study of the United Nations Convention on the Limitation Period in the International Sale of Goods and Section 2-725 of the U.C.C.," *Texas International Law Journal*, vol. 25, p. 1 (1989); "The Relative Nature of Property in the Context of Bankruptcy: Resolution of a Conflict between Federal Pension Law and Bankruptcy law," *University of Kansas Law Review*, vol. 40, p. 643 (1992); and "A Drawee's Right to Restitution of Mistaken Payments under Articles 3 and 4 of the U.C.C.: A Plea for Clarification," *Journal of Law*

and Commerce, vol. 7, p. 293 (1987). Hardly the life work of a "self-described radical"!

Reviewers' Responses

As I noted earlier, the mainstream press reviews were quite positive. Because they are the most generally influential among the book-buying public and, indirectly, the public at large, I focus first on the reviews in the *New York Times*, daily and Sunday, and the *Washington Post*. Each accepts the book largely on its own terms and balances criticism with a basic acceptance of Brock's claim to have shown that Professor Hill's claims were not credible. I then briefly examine the more openly polemical reviews and commentaries.

The first review to appear was that by *New York Times* senior book review editor, Christopher Lehmann-Haupt, two weeks after publication (Lehmann-Haupt 1993a). He opened by calling the book an "impressive investigative study" and closed with the claim that the book "is well-written, carefully reasoned and powerful in its logic. It is must reading for anyone who feels remotely touched by the case." Lehmann-Haupt accepted uncritically Brock's claim that he had "closely scrutinized" the sworn testimony of both protagonists and "found Judge Thomas's to be valid on every point while Professor Hill's was shot through with 'false statement.'" He found persuasive the political explanation for Hill's [assumed] perjury. She had "become a dedicated liberal and feminist by the time of Judge Thomas's appointment," and her political disillusionment with Thomas and "her evident sense of historical mission allowed her to suspend normal personal ethics and justified in her mind whatever means were necessary in order to achieve her noble ends." Such lavish praise was scarcely balanced by Lehmann-Haupt's recital of three minor flaws in the book and his suggestion that Brock's focus on Hill "inevitably lends his case the thinnest veneer of bias."

Next to weigh in was the reviewer for the *Washington Post*, Jonathan Groner (1993). His review was a little more cautious; he concluded that the book wasn't the "last word" but "the first salvo in a long and salutary search for the truth . . . of one of the nation's unsolved political mysteries." On the whole, however, the review was quite positive. Brock's book wasn't "a rabid right-wing smear" but "a serious work of investigative journalism that builds a case quietly and incrementally." Groner agreed with another alternative from the multiple negative portrayals of Hill that Brock provides; here she is a victim of media leaks and liberal interest groups that used her, a villain only in causing delay by her insistence on anonymity. Groner's apparent desire to praise the book led him to ignore his own insights. In regard to the issue of whether Hoerchner had misremembered the date or the identity of the harasser in the crucial call from Hill, Groner recognized that "the confusion is understandable; which of us can precisely recall the month in which a 10-year-old event occurred?" Yet elsewhere he found the alleged error in the date of the call "perhaps the most telling point in the book." In a comment on the controversy over the Brock book and its reception, Groner said, "There are some people out there who feel personally threatened by a challenge to the liberal orthodoxy. . . . Hill has been elevated to the status of an icon" (Kurtz 1993). (Groner's positive reaction was unsurprising, given the eerie parallels between *The Real Anita Hill* and the reviewer's own earlier book, *Hillary's Trial* [Groner 1991]. In that book, Groner concluded that Eric Foretich was falsely accused of abusing his daughter and excoriated the child's mother and the feminist forces that supported her in her attempt to wrest custody from him.)

The *New York Times Book Review* found a woman, Signe Wilkinson, who gave a similar "positive with reservations" review (Wilkinson 1993). Wilkinson created the appearance of balance by largely accepting Brock's criticisms of Anita Hill (noting, for example, his "systematic destruction of the slim evidence corroborating her testimony") while condemning his attack on the liberal Shadow Senate as a transparent attempt to make something out of ordinary political alliances. Wilkinson, like Groner, noted inconsistencies between the composed and graceful woman we saw testify and Brock's portrait of her as "so inept in the classroom that she can't convince her students she knows the law." Those criticisms, however, did not undermine her basic acceptance of the book's thesis. Although she found that "his reporting is not beyond suspicion and his speculations leave nagging questions unanswered," she asserted that we must "grappl[e]

with the problems that Ms. Hill's testimony raises." She conceded that Brock "fails to drive a stake through the heart of Anita Hill's accusations, though he badly damages her case." (One can only hope that Wilkinson was consciously ironic in her "Hill as vampire" metaphor.) Like Brock and her colleague Lehmann-Haupt, she suggested that the hearings were a mistake. "Even staunch Hill supporters ought to consider whether publicly airing last-minute charges against a nominee is wise, even if it serves what might be seen as the greater good."

Other reviews in the mainstream press tended to repeat the patterns exhibited in these three: mild to high praise balanced with some criticism, an acceptance of the book's self-definition as serious scholarship or investigative journalism, and the uncritical use of Brock's frame for viewing the controversy (see, e.g., Garrow 1993). Thus, reviewers and critics generally accepted Brock's proposition that Thomas must be viewed as innocent unless the charges were indisputably shown true—in effect, holding Hill and her supporters to the standard of proof beyond a reasonable doubt. (This proposition originated not with Brock, but in the Senate itself, as critically noted by, for example, E. C. Jordan 1992, pp. 4–5.) In assessing Brock's charges against Hill, however, the paradigm applied by reviewers (and readers) appeared to be "where there's smoke, there's fire." There are so many charges that some of them must be true, and any gap or inconsistency in her story is sufficient to condemn her.

Not surprisingly, conservative commentators in both mainstream and right-wing media seized on the book and praised it effusively, using it as a weapon against perceived enemies on the left and center. Syndicated columnist and religious fundamentalist Cal Thomas said the book "takes every charge leveled by Hill . . . and destroys them (and her credibility) one by one. . . . Those who believed Anita Hill based on her testimony need to read this book and then offer Clarence Thomas an apology" (Thomas 1993). William F. Buckley Jr., columnist and founder of the conservative journal *National Review*, asserted that Hill has become a cause for "certain people" who hope to force Thomas to "rescue himself from disrepute" by "joining the gang to remake the Constitution into the ideological pointillism that suits political correctness" (Buckley 1993).

Thomas Sowell, a well-known conservative

economist and commentator, also used the book as a weapon against political enemies (Sowell 1993a). Those who "used Hill for their own political purposes do not care in the slightest whether she was lying or not." They want "to turn sexual harassment into a charge where an accusation is the same as proof. . . . [T]hese new revelations about Anita Hill only underscore how dangerous such a policy would be." A few days later, he returned to this theme. Hill's supporters, rather than Thomas's, were deemed unable to accept ambiguity: "Why was it so important for the anointed to believe one side in a situation where no evidence could possibly be conclusive? A whole vision of the world was at stake. To admit that the other side might be right . . . would be to open the door to the shattering possibility that you had been a fool to believe in the vision . . . that gave you your own special moral standing" (Sowell 1993b).

The conservative pundits also used the Brock book, as Brock himself did, to excoriate the allegedly liberal media. Brock would not get the Pulitzer he deserved, one complained, because "practically every newsroom and studio in the country harbors an incensed feminist or career minority member who scares hell out of her colleagues" (Tyrrell 1993).

Strident right-wing attacks on Hill and use of the book to demonize progressives and feminists in the media and elsewhere were not limited to the United States. Barbara Amiel launched a similar salvo in the *London Times* (Amiel 1993). She repeated Brock's claim that "to believe Anita Hill, you have to find that dozens of responsible people with no axe to grind have told lies." The book's publication was used to attack the presumed "grip that feminism has on the American media with a power equivalent to Nazism before it took over Germany." The proof of this power? Though the book was climbing the best-seller charts, after three weeks Brock was only making his first television appearance and would likely be forced to appear with a "representative of politically correct thinking." Amiel asserted that a book that came out the other way would have its author "on every channel." Yet none of the other books on the Hill/Thomas controversy—Phelps and Winternitz 1992, T. Morrison 1992b, or Mayer and Abramson 1994—received as wide attention as that by Brock; Brock's eleven-week residence on the best-seller lists dwarfs the three-

week stay of the far more thorough and subtle, but less strident, *Strange Justice* (Mayer and Abramson 1994).

The conservative columnist with perhaps the best access to the mainstream public is George Will. In his *Newsweek* column, one of the earliest published reactions to the book, he concluded that "Brock assembles an avalanche of evidence that Hill lied" (Will 1993a). He accepted and regurgitated all of Brock's key claims—the timing of the call from Hoerchner, the reason for leaving Wald Harkrader, the inconsistency of the alleged corroboration, and Hill's political motives for harming Thomas (evidenced by her role "in the shrill but conventional campus leftism of racial and sexual politics" at The University of Oklahoma Law School). He found it telling that "no one could be found to testify to ever having seen her exhibit the demeanor of a harassment victim" and that she didn't avoid Thomas as (Will asserts) most victims do. He attempted to preempt any disagreement: "Brock's book will be persuasive to minds not sealed by the caulking of ideology." Finally, he embedded the attack on Hill in a wider attack on "the system of racial preferences that put her on a track too fast for her abilities, that taught her to think of herself as a victim and made her fluent in the rhetoric of victimization."

Liberal commentary on the book and the responses to it were largely confined to identifiably liberal and left-wing media. The primary critical responses to Brock in the mainstream media were by columnists Anna Quindlen and Anthony Lewis. Quindlen attacked Brock for his excessive reliance on Thomas supporters and anonymous detractors of Hill, for his false claim of neutrality, and for his nasty attacks on the Shadow Senate and on Hill's supporters. Applying a mind not obviously sealed by the "caulking of ideology," she concluded that the Hill/Thomas dispute is "one of the enduring socio-political mysteries," and one for which the Brock book doesn't provide an answer (Quindlen 1993a).

Lewis's response to the previous reviewers, as well as the book itself, was considerably more slashing (A. Lewis 1993). He excoriated reviewers for describing a book by a "partisan ideologue" as an "impressive investigative study" and for accepting the author's "factual assertions without checking." He asserted that Mayer and Abramson (1993) "show that the claims are based on alleged anonymous sources or are easily disproved. What is left in the book is a farrago of the preposterous and the vicious."

More extensive reviews and commentaries from a progressive perspective appeared in *The Nation*, the *New York Review of Books*, and the *New Yorker*. Dierdre English, in *The Nation* (English 1993), described Brock's book as "a far-fetched attempt to prove that Hill built her charges on a case of mistaken identity" and then "brazenly carried out the most shameless and vengeful lie in modern political history." She highlighted the inconsistency in Brock's depictions of Hill: "He shifts from one vision of Hill— the cold-blooded strategist—to another: the malleable dupe of archfeminist Catharine MacKinnon." She concluded that the book is "a sham and a scandal, marking a journalistic standard so low that no reputable publishing house should have touched it," and that the earlier reviewers should have recognized Brock's "evident ill will." Like English, Kathleen Sullivan (1993) stressed Brock's vacillating explanation for Hill's behavior as "fantasy or perjury." The former, she notes, echoes the common defense strategy in rape or sexual harassment cases of "labeling women accusers crazy or delusional." The latter requires an explanation for the perjury; none that he proposes are persuasive, including the implicit claim that Anita Hill was "a liberal feminist Democrat who fabricated her charges against Thomas as part of an elaborate political conspiracy to block his appointment."

The most widely known response was a lengthy article by Jane Mayer and Jill Abramson in the *New Yorker* (Mayer and Abramson 1993) which detailed their own research on the Hill/ Thomas controversy and provided a series of point-by-point rebuttals to Brock's research, to the facts presented and ignored or undiscovered, and to the uses Brock made of those facts. (Much of the material therein also appears in their later book on the Hill/Thomas events [Mayer and Abramson 1994]). The article evoked a lengthy response by Brock which he published in the *American Spectator* after the *New Yorker* refused to print it (Brock 1993c). He defended some of his claims, conceded others but dismissed them as insignificant, and challenged some of Mayer and Abramson's facts and sources. He reprised his technique of the suggestive, rhetorical question. In responding to Mayer and Abramson's claim

that there may be other corroborating witnesses to whom Anita Hill spoke of harassment, he said, "Could it be that memories are being enhanced even now, as Anita Hill's credibility is being undermined in a best selling book?" (Brock 1993b, p. 28). The nit-picking duel is less than fascinating reading. While I found that Mayer and Abramson emerged, overall, with far more superficial wounds, book sales suggest that they inflicted little damage.

Explaining the Responses of the Mainstream (Media)

The largely positive responses to the Brock book, I suggest, reflect both general cultural patterns and the effect of ideologies and structures particular to the media. By "media" I refer here to print media, particularly newspapers, in part because I am exploring the responses to a book. Book buyers are by definition a relatively literate group who read and respond to print media, though the effects of the print media are likely to spread outward to a larger public. Furthermore, I explain the response in part by a discussion of journalistic culture and collective self-understandings. These beliefs were developed in the context of print media and may not be held by, or appropriate to, the electronic media (see, generally, Bollinger 1991, Levi 1993). (In other contexts, of course, such as analyses of wider political movements, a study of media must include and perhaps focus on electronic media, such as the radio talk shows of Rush Limbaugh and his local clones.) I explore first the media-specific explanations and then the more general cultural causes, in search of both explanation and of lessons we might draw from the Thomas/Hill/Brock story for limiting the damage that the media might inflict on feminists and other progressives in the future.

Before I begin examining the "media" response, two caveats are necessary. First, I do not have direct access to the minds of the relevant decision-makers. Thus, like Mr. Brock, I necessarily engage in, at best, informed speculation: I suggest certain patterns of thought and/or organizational structure that might lead to the result to be explained. Second, my "data" here is book reviews and political commentary. Neither of these belongs to the core "news reporting" whose

ideal and to demonize feminist ideology as a dangerous attack on it.

The journalistic conception of objectivity is a complex one and has changed over time (see generally Leff 1997). In its most simplistic variant, it is a form of correspondence epistemology: There are facts in the universe that any careful, unbiased observer would find and could report. News, then, is simply the facts (Schudson 1977, pp. 4–5). If a story opens with a "news" paragraph, this "proclaims that what follows is factual and hard-nosed, a veridical account of events in the world" (Tuchman 1978b, p. 5).

Journalists who reflect on their experience know that this naive empiricism is false. Henry Luce of *Time* has been quoted as saying, "Show me a man who thinks he is objective . . . and I'll show you a man who's deceiving himself" (Manoff 1986b, pp. 259–60). Such self-deception, of course, is not unknown. "In the absence of authoritative standards for journalistic concepts, the old-fashioned view that 'news' is simply a mirror placed before reality still lives" (Romano 1986, p. 39).

The more dominant contemporary understanding of objectivity, however, is as a matter of method. A reporter, like a social scientist, is being objective if she follows the procedures demanded by her profession. These journalistic procedures include investigating claims and seeking confirmation, presenting conflicting possibilities, relying on and quoting appropriate sources, avoiding extreme and therefore incredible claims, and following journalistic rules for organizing a story (Tuchman 1972, pp. 665–70). The story is what the sources say about the newsworthy event, with the sources chosen for credibility and balance. On one view, applying these institutionalized methods of news-gathering is designed as the means for achieving objectivity (Tuchman 1978b, p. 179). Viewed another way, objectivity simply *is* what results from applying appropriate methodology (Manoff 1986a, p. 4). On this latter view, objectivity is quite distinct from discovering "objective" facts. "Objectivity in journalism denotes a set of rhetorical devices and procedures used in composing a news story. Objectivity, in this sense, has no bearing whatsoever on the truthfulness or validity of a story" (Sigal 1986, p. 15). (The notion of balance that inheres in this concept of objectivity can be applied across the contents of a newspaper as well as

within a particular story. Thus an additional possible explanation for the favorable coverage of the Brock book may be a conscious or unconscious response to criticisms by the right that the media had been too favorable in its original coverage of Anita Hill and, in general, too "politically correct" [W. Boot 1992, p. 26].)

In order to follow these procedures, however, the journalist must adopt a particular attitude of "detachment, disinterestedness, maturity" (Schudson 1977, p. 266). The journalistic method of objectivity means being "free from values and ideology" (Gans 1979, p. 182). "Every reporter [should] gather and structure 'facts,' in a detached, unbiased, impersonal manner" (Tuchman 1972, p. 664). This stance, reporters realize, is not natural. It is, however, an essential component of objectivity. "If one is to make statements about what the world is that others can take as trustworthy, one needs to stand outside oneself and so separate them from one's own subjective preference about what the world should be" (Schudson 1977, pp. 3–4). On this understanding, then, both method and disinterestedness are professional necessities. Together they constitute objectivity and form the bedrock for journalistic credibility (Schudson 1977, p. 262).

All this is not to say, of course, that journalists have necessarily examined the concept of objectivity and adopted it in a thoughtful and serious way. This would be improbable if for no other reason than that "objectivity" comprises a set of not wholly compatible ideas, such as a lingering belief in fact as truth and a belief that objectivity requires balance between competing and contradictory views of the truth. Furthermore, journalists recognize that even objectivity as method or disinterested detachment is not descriptive of what they do every day but is at best a set of norms regarding what they *should* do.

> Objectivity might be a professional ideal, but it is one that seemed to disintegrate as soon as it was formulated. It became an ideal, after all, precisely when the impossibility of overcoming the subjectivity of presenting the news was widely accepted. . . . Objectivity in journalism seems to have been destined to be more a scapegoat than a belief and more an awkward defense than a forthright affirmation. (Schudson 1977, p. 269)

Nonetheless, working journalists at least sometimes articulate a set of beliefs that sound much like "objectivity as truth." *New York Times* columnist Frank Rich, for example, recently criticized Brock's approach for threatening "the reporter's traditional calling of objectively seeking and writing the truth" (Rich 1994). In her participant-observer study of journalists, Gaye Tuchman discovered that "news workers found the 'intuitively obvious' distinctions between fact and value judgment difficult to explain" (Tuchman 1978b, p. 99). Objectivity as ideal becomes a justificatory belief, a way of legitimating what would be a highly problematic enterprise. Journalists must gather and write "news" on tight deadlines, satisfy editors and readers, and avoid libel suits from the subjects of stories. All these goals are furthered by presuming that news reporting is in some way objective. "The term 'objectivity' stands as a bulwark between [journalists] and their critics" (Tuchman 1972, p. 660).

Maintaining such a belief, however tenuously, also helps quell internal questions about the enterprise. In his study of the rise of the concept of objectivity, Michael Schudson concludes that "objectivity was understood as an ideal counter to the reality of the reporter's own subjectivity; . . . [it allowed him] to seek escape from deep convictions of doubt and drift" (Schudson 1977, pp. 269, 295). The belief in objectivity, then, appears to be rather akin to some people's belief in God—one cannot defend it with rational arguments; it is essential to one's sense of oneself; and though one's behavior may often seem to belie the belief, the belief helps structure and justify one's life. That such a belief cannot withstand scrutiny does not mean that an attack on it by others will be taken lightly.

The journalistic belief in objectivity could have led to an undeservedly positive assessment of Brock's book through two channels. First, the book itself seems to demonstrate the methodology of objectivity. (Brock's claim of objectivity is, of course, utterly without basis. He was a fellow at the Heritage Foundation with extensive bona fides in the conservative movement, and a regular contributor to the right-wing *American Spectator* and *Washington Times*. As his own acknowledgments section states [p. ix], the book was funded in part by the Bradley Foundation and the Olin Foundation, the latter headed by William Simon, a leader of the Citizen's Committee to Confirm Clarence Thomas.) If it were seen as neutral and objective, this would make it attrac-

tive to those for whom this is the right way to present a factual story. After placing himself and his quest as the frame of the book in the author's note, Brock disappears. As in journalism, his own actions in discovering the facts and organizing their presentation is obscured. He "couch[es] his bias in passive, legalistic form, thus intimating a neutrality that doesn't exist" (Goodrich 1993). He relies heavily on sources and quotations. "Quotations of other people's opinions are presented to create a web of mutually self-validating facts" (Tuchman 1978b, p. 95). What he wants the reader to believe is set off by either quotation marks or question marks. The latter, too, is a journalist's technique. Objectivity does not permit the writer to present his own views as such. Irony, however, is a legitimate form of rhetoric, though it is neither necessary to the task of presenting the "facts" nor neutral in its impact on the reader. "Although explicit judgments are suppressed, ironic narrative seeks to establish a bond between writer and reader in order to persuade the latter that he has discovered judgments for himself" (Manoff 1986b, p. 228).

A belief in the ideal of objectivity could also lead to a positive assessment of Brock because of his target. In the epilogue, Brock makes clear that he sees the support for and belief in Anita Hill as part of a larger and dangerous movement—feminism. (Feminism is his explicit target and the primary base for the critiques of traditional "objective" epistemologies. Brock's "neutral" political stance also conflicts with the positions of racial progressives. This issue is explored later.) Feminists, he says, believe "that American society is a patriarchal system that enshrines a male perspective. . . . Notions of logic, objectivity, equality under law and the common good are all regarded as reflections of this patriarchal bias" (1993a, p. 383). He claims that feminism, taken to its logical conclusion, would "undermine the fundamental premise of legal reasoning that truth can be objectively determined by logical analysis" (1993a, p. 384).

This view of feminist epistemology is exaggerated but not wholly invented (see, e.g., Bartlett 1991; Harding 1991). Such perspectivity is in deep tension with the possibility of journalistic objectivity. Feminism would posit that there is *no* possibility of getting (entirely) outside one's own perspective, of being disinterested, and that it is a mistake to purport or attempt to do so. The reporter cannot avoid seeing the world through particular eyes and judging it through particular values and thus cannot make the claim to believability that objectivity seems to provide.

The inevitability of perspective is, of course, a truism. Walter Lippman said in 1922 that "the facts we see depend on where we are placed and the habits of our eyes" (quoted in Gans 1979, p. 310). This truism, however, has not eliminated a complex, continued belief in some form of objectivity. Ideology exists but can, with effort, be avoided. One can be adequately aperspectival and disinterested if one remains in the moderate, nonideological center (Gans 1979, p. 191). "Common sense" can be used to determine which statements by which informants can be accepted as "fact" (Tuchman 1972, p. 674).

Feminism, however, proposes a much more pervasive perspectivity. For example, feminists criticize the "reasonable person" standard, suggesting that at least in certain contexts, men and women have such different views that there is no such creature as the ungendered "reasonable person." Even more problematically for an objectivist, they draw the normative conclusion that that concept is a dangerous legal fiction. They call for recognizing that the "reasonable person" is really the "reasonable man," with all his prejudices and limitations, and suggest that in certain contexts the appropriate standard is the reasonable woman (Scheppele 1992; N. Ehrenreich 1990; Abrams 1989). In his overheated fashion, Brock reads this as a rejection of any standard of proof, of the presumption of innocence and of reasoned analysis (1993a, pp. 385–86). Even in a less hyperbolic version, however, the feminist insistence on perspective and its rejection of objectivity are deeply threatening to traditional ways of doing business in journalism, as in law. Insofar as Brock succeeds in presenting himself as the defender of this "Western liberal tradition" (1993a, p. 386), journalists might be inclined to be generous in their reviews and commentaries.

Brock and the Backlash against Feminism and Racial Justice

Brock's book sold very well. Its popularity is, in part, a reaction to the positive media coverage I have already discussed. Positive reviews generate book sales, as do teaser excerpts like that in the *Wall Street Journal* (Brock 1993b). George Will's column practically commanded the open-minded reader to purchase the book. The popularity of this and more recent conservative books also reflects a new social phenomenon. The book was touted by Rush Limbaugh, and its author was invited onto Pat Robertson's 700 Club, a venue that reaches an audience that, I suspect, rarely reads, and even more rarely is influenced by, anything in the *New York Times* or the *Washington Post*. Brock's publisher, the Free Press, under the editorship of Adam Bellow, has become the new book publishing arm of this expanding right-wing movement (Streitfeld 1994).

The *Real Anita Hill* also had certain characteristics that would attract many readers. I first note those that are less explicitly political and then focus on the book's appeal as a validation of anti-political-correctness backlash.

First, the book purports to solve a mystery. If one believes its arguments, it replaces doubt and confusion with a relatively straightforward, coherent story. Both narrative theorists and lawyers recognize the appeal of such stories (see, e.g., Abrams 1991; Coombs 1993; Pennington and Hastie 1991). Brock tells both the story of Thomas and Hill and, framing it, the story of his uncovering the truth and redeeming a man's falsely besmirched reputation. Both resonate with classic story lines, going back at least to the biblical tale of Joseph and Potiphar's wife (Genesis 38–39). In addition, readers, like journalists, may be deeply disturbed by the amoral, radically postmodern vision of feminism in Brock's book. The world may, in fact, be totally socially constructed and filled with incommensurate epistemologies divided along such axes as race and gender, so that conflicting stories like Hill's and Thomas's are mediated by a framework of "dominant narratives" which "reflect a gendered zero-sum equation of credibility" (Crenshaw 1992b, p. 408–9). Epistemological truths, however, are not subject to simple physical proofs. And radical perspectivity is not a philosophy likely to appeal to the man in the street. He prefers a simple story of justice and truth triumphant, thank you very much.

The desire for a coherent story, in which one side is shown to have told the truth and the other to have lied, could equally well have been met by a book that showed that Anita Hill told the truth and Clarence Thomas did what she claimed and perjured himself in denying it. The recent book by Jane Mayer and Jill Abramson, *Strange Justice* (1994), nearly does that. They uncover still more confirmation of Hill's story and independent witnesses of Thomas's vulgarity and interest in pornography (see, e.g., Mayer and Abramson 1994, pp. 55–58). (Intriguingly, their story also appears to confirm the vision of a world that not only appears to be but is different depending on the situation of the viewer, for it suggests that Thomas behaved differently when in white and African American worlds, confining his display of the more earthy and vulgar aspects of his personality to the latter.)

That alternative, however, would lack one of the appeals of Brock's tale—it exonerates Thomas. Thomas was a judge and is a justice; he is bright and articulate, serious, and openly religious. He is a protégé of the well-respected Senator Danforth. It is hard for many people to believe a man like that could have done the things charged. Sexual harassment is vile and disgusting; thus, only an obviously vulgar man could be believed to have engaged in it (see S. D. Ross 1992, discussing the similarly incredible but true case of American University president Richard Berenzden). It is not only hard to believe Thomas guilty; it is better not to believe it. The man will be on the Supreme Court for the next forty years, helping to decide major legal and moral issues for us. Since he will be on the Court, it is more comfortable to believe he did not get there wrongly. Brock evokes this concern in his very last sentence, arguing, "The American people were . . . harmed [by Hill's totally unsubstantiated charge], since . . . the public's faith and trust in the integrity of the . . . Supreme Court have been perhaps irreparably tarnished" (1993a, p. 387).

The explanation for the book's popularity that seems both truest and most disturbing, however, is that it affirmed a series of antifeminist, racist stereotypes and created a safe harbor for believing that political correctness is the major problem in American society today. (Although Brock's explicit target, particularly in the epilogue, is feminism, the book also readily supports an attack on racial justice and affirmative action, both in its portrait of Anita Hill and in its defense of a version of the "Western liberal tradition" that affirms the status quo and rejects any race- or gender-conscious political change.) It provided evidence, for those already inclined to believe such canards, that Anita Hill was a sexually voracious black Jezebel and/or an undeserving, ungrateful beneficiary of affirmative action.

The hearings themselves had presented both of these images, largely thanks to the questioning by Senators Spector and Hatch. Hill, they implied, fantasized that Thomas had said these things because, deep down, she wanted his sexual attentions and had been denied them (see Crenshaw 1992b). The image is a powerful one, for it "placed Professor Hill in the traditions of the promiscuous, lascivious black woman" (Freedman 1992, p. 1363). It was hard to believe that story, however, when you saw Professor Hill; her demeanor was so utterly in conflict with it. Indeed, I suspect, the shift in public opinion over time reflected in part the greater staying power of that image of a strong, reserved, brave, and anguished woman than of the particularities of any of the attacks on her.[1] Brock, however, provides, if you believe him, a context that would make the picture of Hill as a promiscuous, lascivious, vengeful woman more credible. He suggests that she had claimed sexual harassment before. He recounts allegations that she engaged in sexually explicit talk with colleagues and behaved in an inappropriately sexualized manner toward her male students. He "reconstruct[s] Hill's image into that of a wanton sexual tease, coming on to her students in bizarre ways and engaging in kinky sexual conversations" (Mayer and Abramson 1993, p. 92). She is described as simultaneously a radical feminist who oppressed her students and a sex fiend who put pubic hairs in their exam papers. The person who had difficulty comprehending "Hill's identity as a highly educated, ambitious, black female Republican" (Painter 1992, p. 204) who also was a fantasizing, sex-crazed Jezebel could now ignore or dismiss the first picture and see only the second—one of the classic stereotypes of black women (Wilkins 1992, p. 1519).

Brock places much of his emphasis, however, on explanations for Hill's actions that were less prominent at the hearings. She was a radical, race-conscious feminist who consciously opposed Thomas because he was a conservative. She was a beneficiary of affirmative action whom Thomas had refused, finally, to promote to a job for which she was unqualified. Thus, from a mix of personal anger and political strategy, she perjured herself to harm him. Brock rejects the label many had applied to Thomas—the undeserving beneficiary of affirmative action (1993a, pp. 27, 39)—and applies it instead to Hill. He presents a story in which she is an incompetent lawyer at her first job and leaves when told that "it would be in her best interests to consider seeking employment elsewhere" (1993a, p. 223). Indeed, she only was offered such a high-powered job because of misguided affirmative action (1993a, p. 220). Brock asserts a similar pattern of incompetence in teaching, quoting students and former colleagues to the effect that she did not know the law and could not teach it. The job at Oral Roberts "thrust her into a situation for which she was ill-prepared. . . . She was not knowledgeable enough to teach any particular field" (p. 339). Again, she only obtained a job because the school was trying to placate the A.B.A. and exploited "her protected position as a black woman in an era of affirmative action" (1993a, p. 341). (Brock seems untroubled about relying for proof of Hill's incompetence, and thus the harm of affirmative action, on the statements of two white men with axes to grind: Each visited at Oklahoma, apparently did not receive a permanent offer, and either left law teaching or moved to an unaccredited school.)

This picture of Hill serves both a narrative purpose and a political purpose: It provides a motive for her to lie and a reason to applaud the outcome of the hearings and the installation of an opponent of affirmative action on the Court. Hill's motive to lie, if lie she did, was always one of the mysteries of the hearings. Senator Heflin asked her a series of rhetorical questions that might provide such a reason. "Are you a scorned woman?" "Are you a zealoting civil rights believer?" "Do you have a militant attitude relative to the area of civil rights?" "Do you see that . . . you can be a hero in the civil rights movement?" "Are you interested in writing a book?" She denied them all (U.S. Senate Committee on the Judiciary 1991, part 4, pp. 87–88). Brock provides different answers to Senator Heflin's questions: Hill *was* a civil rights militant; she *was* a scorned woman; she *did* want to be "a hero in the civil rights movement"; and she wanted to preserve the affirmative action programs that she so desperately needed. She is no longer conservative, but liberal or radical; she is no longer a

competent and ambitious Yale Law School graduate, but a failed product of failed policies.

Many people are uncomfortable with affirmative action and see it as a way in which blacks and women rise above the place they deserve in our alleged meritocracy. Attacks on racial and gender justice, recharacterized as special rights, political correctness, and false claims of victimhood, are an increasing part of our cultural and political dialogue. (see, e.g., D'Souza 1991; K. Roiphe 1993b; Sommers 1994a; Herrnstein and Murray 1994). Brock's "desire to demonize Hill pluck[ed] a cultural chord that lies deeper than we would like to believe" (English 1993). Both English (1993) and Kathleen Sullivan (1993) note that *The Real Anita Hill*, and its reception, are skirmishes in a culture war. George Will makes this clear in his use of the book to attack "racial preferences" and "the rhetoric of victimization" (Will 1993a). The book's success, then, is in part the result of its partaking in and feeding the backlash against feminism and other progressive movements.

The worldview in which Anita Hill is a symbol of the evils of feminism, affirmative action, postmodernism, and the counterculture, in some unholy alliance, has the marvelously self-protective property that contradictory evidence, such as the increased belief in Hill since the hearings, simply becomes further proof of the dangerous power of the enemy. Consider the story exemplified by Brock's version of Anita Hill: She sought to ambush Thomas with anonymous charges and made them public only when the Shadow Senate and their media henchpersons forced her to do so. Yet she has since become a hero, "the Rosa Parks of sexual harassment" (1993a, p. 13). Her supporters praise her lavishly (see, e.g., Crenshaw 1992a, p. 1467; Leibman 1992, p. 1441). She was a poor teacher, yet there was a move to provide her with a named chair. She claimed to be uninterested in public attention, yet she spent much of the year after the hearings, while on sabbatical, receiving awards and giving speeches (pp. 11–12). Anita Hill becomes, for the right, a symbol of the loss of the innocence and meritocracy that once characterized America. Her accomplishments and the shifting public perception in her favor do not prove, as a less politically charged reading might suggest, that she was and is a competent professional woman without a motive to lie. Rather, each becomes additional proof of the undeserved triumph of affirmative action and political correctness.

The book in a sense recapitulates the hearings themselves. Both turn political events inside out, painting the disenfranchised as politically powerful and the politically powerful as victims. The most extraordinary instance was Clarence Thomas's description of himself as the victim of a "high-tech lynching." By evoking that trope, he forced the Senate to prove its bona fides as nonracist by voting for him. He simultaneously erased Anita Hill. "She became a part of the white racist conspiracy. . . . [Thomas] had gained exclusive control over the content of the symbol race, giving it a gender that allowed Professor Hill no place within it" (Davis and Wildman 1992, p. 1382; see also A. Ross 1992, p. 44).

This rhetorical move carried particular weight in the black community, evoking memories of attacks on other black men for their alleged sexual behavior (Burnham 1992, p. 310). Orlando Patterson expanded on this theme in his widely discussed commentary on the controversy. In Patterson's version, Thomas did make the comments Anita Hill reported, but they were simply a form of "down-home courting," recognizable as such in the black community. Hill must have known how they would be misread by the white community, thus her public reporting was a form of race treason, justifying Thomas's denial that they were made at all (O. Patterson 1991).

Perhaps Brock's most powerful rhetorical move is his suggestion that acceptance of his conclusions is a litmus test of honesty. Those who believe and want to believe are reassured; any who would still dare to support Professor Hill are condemned. He begins with an author's note describing himself as having an open mind when the hearings began; two pages later he becomes the hero who has refused to be silenced by politically motivated attacks. His previous article on the topic (Brock 1992), he notes, had been criticized as appealing to " 'popular stereotypes of black people as sensually obsessed, and women as vindictive and of black women as both.' Only silence could inoculate an author against such unmerited attacks, and, I believe, it is precisely the fear of such attacks that best explains the deafening silence from my colleagues in the press

on the facts of this case" (1993a, pp. vii, ix). Throughout, he refers to his anonymous sources as forced into silence by the fear of attack by the politically correct. He concludes with this "challenge" to his readers: "Many people will be tempted to . . . continue to assert Hill's veracity. . . . For readers such as these, no amount of evidence is likely to be persuasive. The will to believe her account will outweigh whatever facts have been presented here. For open-minded readers, on the other hand, the evidence presented must weigh heavily against her credibility. . . . [N]o reasonable person could believe that sexual harassment occurred in this case" (1993a, p. 381).

The epilogue identifies these ideologically blinded readers—feminists. Any reader not already hopelessly identified with that outcast group will be tempted to align herself as open-minded and, therefore, nonfeminist. Feminists are dangerous and crazy. Their very claimed belief in Hill demonstrates their contempt for the value of truth. Since no one could honestly believe her claims (at least after reading Brock's book), her supporters must be engaged in promoting a useful lie. They think the value of her story for highlighting the issue of sexual harassment "is finally more important than whether or not she was in fact harassed by Thomas," so "Hill's testimony may be justified . . . on the utilitarian moral grounds that govern public affairs" (1993a, p. 22).

The attack on feminism in the book is explicit as well as implicit. Brock "warns of an encroaching feminism in which 'all men are seen as rapists,' " so that "it does not matter whether Hill actually proved her case against Thomas or not" (1993a, p. 385). If his view is accepted, evolving commitments to improve gender relations and eradicate sexual harassment are delegitimated, for they are "born in sin" (K. Sullivan 1993). This myth of "political correctness" versus "truth," though most directly targeted at feminists, is a weapon against racial progressives as well, for from this perspective, affirmative action is another example of substituting politics for the honest assessment of merit. The racial politics, however, are somewhat more subtle. Brock and his cohorts can present themselves as protecting a good black man from a high-tech lynching by feminists and the unscrupulous, left-wing Shadow

Senate. What happened to Thomas was not a lynching, however, and Anita Hill was not the leader or the dupe of a lynch mob. Rather, Thomas was a symbol of retrenchment in racial politics, made palatable by his blackness. As presented in Brock's book, his race becomes irrelevant to his life story, and racial policies become the illegitimate means by which the unqualified Anita Hill was in a position to harm him.

The book, I suggest, is what a common-law lawyer might call an attractive nuisance. It is dangerous, and seductively so. Thousands of readers have had their fears confirmed and their prejudices fostered. If these broader cultural backlash phenomena explain at least part of the book's appeal, does this provide any lessons for progressives? The lessons are not encouraging ones. The right, through its adoption of the concept of political correctness, has rather successfully turned the notion of silencing developed by radical feminists and critical race theorists on its head. Now, "femi-Nazis" are in control and (white, male) voices of reason are silenced. Their sources need not be named, for fear of political correctness explains the desire for anonymity and vouches for the truth of the charges. Readers, too, are implicated in this process; failure to agree with Brock and his ilk is evidence of cowardice or worse. It is really quite extraordinary, in a time when Rush Limbaugh, David Brock, How-ard Stern, and Katie Roiphe make the best-seller, list, that anyone can, with a straight face, charge that some "political correctness police" has silenced its opponents.

We must, first, not let ourselves be silenced. We must tell our own stories, in a variety of fora to a variety of audiences, so that they become familiar and thus credible (Coombs 1993). In order to get those stories placed in the mass media, we need to continue the struggle for adequate representation in that media. The *New York Times*, which published two of the more obsequious reviews, also has a long history of sex discrimination in its newsroom (Robertson 1992). We need to counter the smears of our activities and beliefs. In particular, we need to do the arduous and meticulous work of establishing the facts, as Mayer and Abramson (1994) have done. Finally, we need to recognize that the media has its own agenda. We can sometimes use it to reach the public, but we must never, never trust it.

Notes

1. See S. Patterson 1994: The percentage of Americans believing Anita Hill climbed from 29 percent in October 1991 to 43 percent in December 1992; the percentage believing Thomas declined from 48 percent to 39 percent.

6

Fear of Feminism

Media Stories of Feminist Victims and Victims of Feminism on College Campuses

MARTHA T. MCCLUSKEY

"Victim Feminism" in the Media

A profusion of mainstream media reports have declared that one of the biggest problems facing U.S. women in the 1990s is that feminists talk too much about women as victims. "Has sisterhood become victimhood?" ask ads for Katie Roiphe's book *The Morning After: Sex, Fear and Feminism on Campus* (1993b). Roiphe (1991) argues that college feminists' emphasis on the problem of date rape has served to reinforce what she claims are traditional ideas of women as victims and men as aggressors: "Let's not chase the same stereotypes our mothers have spent so much energy running away from. Let's not reinforce the images that oppress us, that label us victims, and deny our own agency and intelligence, as strong and sensual, as autonomous, pleasure-seeking, sexual beings." Hundreds of newspaper stories, magazine articles, and talk shows across the United States (and beyond) have featured Roiphe's book as a focal point of a controversy, describing the book with headlines such as "The

Victim Trap" (B. Sullivan 1993) or "Stop Whining . . ." (Picker 1993).

Conservative critics have long denounced feminism (and other civil rights movements) for promoting victimization (e.g., A. Miller 1990). The recent controversy over Roiphe's book has stressed similar criticisms from many who identify themselves as liberals and feminists, though these critics of victimization differ widely in their overall views of feminism. In a *Glamour* article previewing her book *Fire with Fire*, Naomi Wolf (1993b) argues that "victim feminism . . . has dominated public debate for the last twenty years," portraying women "as silenced and helpless rather than as potent agents for change"; she asserts that feminism's recent successes mean that this attitude is now obsolete or even destructive. In an *Atlantic Monthly* cover story on "Feminism's Identity Crisis," Wendy Kaminer (1993b) warns that feminists' emphasis on women's sexual victimization threatens feminist political gains. A *Newsweek* cover story discussing the issues raised in Roiphe's book quotes Betty Friedan as saying,

"I'm sick of women wallowing in the victim state. . . . We have empowered ourselves" (Crichton 1993).

Many of those who have received the most publicity in this debate over "victim feminism" are self-proclaimed feminists whose "feminist" activism and scholarship appear to be limited to attacks on feminism, as Susan Faludi notes (1995). Camille Paglia declares: "Let's get rid of Infirmary Feminism, with its bedlam of belly-achers, anorexics, bulimics, depressives, rape victims, and incest survivors. Feminism has become a catch-all vegetable drawer where bunches of clingy sob sisters can store their moldy neuroses" (quoted in Stoffman 1994). In an essay titled "Keeping Women Weak," Cathy Young says that feminism went wrong when it told women "that we were victims, with little control over our lives and our choices" (1994, p. 219). Discussing her book *Who Stole Feminism?* on the talk-show circuit, Christina Hoff Sommers (1994c) complained that "the orthodox feminists are so carried away with victimology, with a rhetoric of male-bashing," that the most important task remaining in order to achieve gender equality is to "save young women from the feminists."

The mainstream media often points to U.S. college campuses as the nucleus of these problems with feminism. Mona Charen (1994) warns that "gender feminists, triumphant on the American campus and highly influential in the society at large, believe that women are victims of something called the 'sex/gender system,' which perpetuates male dominance over females." *Newsweek* sums up feminism's influence by saying, "If it's chilly in the workplace, it's downright freezing on campus" (Crichton 1993). In particular, the media discussion of "victim feminism" highlights efforts at elite schools to confront acquaintance rape and sexual harassment with "Take Back the Night" marches, date rape education programs, and new rules governing sexual conduct.

Difference to Dominance in Feminist Legal Theory

This media fascination with feminism's so-called victim problem both reflects and distorts struggles within feminist legal theory and practice. One of feminism's strengths has been its ability to reveal

barriers to women's full and equal participation in society. As Sommers (1994b) notes, "In the bad old days, a lot of women's victimization was invisible." But feminist efforts to expose the pervasiveness of restraints on women's lives sometimes appear to contradict feminist visions of women as self-determining agents capable of creatively shaping the world.

This victim/agent dilemma echoes another dilemma confronting feminist struggles for equality: the apparent choice between equal treatment and special treatment. If equality laws require that women be treated the same as men, then women risk being penalized when they appear different from men (when women seek legal protections against pregnancy discrimination in employment, for example) (Law 1984; Finley 1986). In response to that dilemma, many feminists noted that women are disadvantaged under the law not only because the law too often falsely assumes that women are different from men but also because the law unjustly privileges men's "differences" (Finley 1986, pp. 1152–59; MacKinnon 1987, pp. 32–45; Minow 1990, p. 58). Feminists working on a variety of legal issues have argued that apparently neutral legal rules and policies can disadvantage women if women's particular needs are denied legal recognition or if harm to many women is perceived as trivial or natural compared to harms that primarily affect privileged men (see, e.g., Rhode 1991; Fineman 1991a). In response to the failures of formal equality law, some feminists attempted to shift the question of gender equality from whether women are different to whether men are dominant and women subordinate under the law (MacKinnon 1987, pp. 40–45; Colker 1986).

But if legal and societal recognition of harm depends as much on gender privilege as on neutral principles, then challenging gender subordination is not necessarily any easier than challenging gender difference. Kathryn Abrams has discussed the parallels between the "victimization" controversy sparked by Roiphe's book and the long-standing feminist debates over the "dominance" approach to equality (Abrams 1994, p. 1549), which many fear may reinforce women's subordination by stressing women's vulnerability in the face of male power. Furthermore, if harm is a political construction as well as a discoverable fact, those with the most power will be best able to define themselves as victims under the law. Prominent versions of feminism have often recognized harms faced by economically privileged white heterosexual women to the exclusion of the particular problems faced by women of color, lesbians, and working-class and poor women (hooks 1984; A. Harris 1990). And if the law tends to more easily recognize and redress harm to certain groups of men than to most women, then those men may be more successful at claiming that their gender differences are deserving of the most protection. Ironically, those who suffer loss of privileges as a result of feminism may be able to make the most credible claims of victimization.

The theme of male dominance and female victimization has been particularly important in feminist discussions of issues of violence against women (Schneider 1986, pp. 220–21; M. Mahoney 1994, p. 59). Male violence against women is a widespread problem that historically has tended to be suppressed from public view in law and media (Marcus 1994), except when characterized as interracial violence against white women. Many feminists have emphasized women's experiences as victims of male violence and male sexual abuse in part in an attempt to demonstrate that those harms are serious problems deserving of legal protection. At the same time, many feminists have expressed concerns about how the legal system can be used to recognize and redress these previously hidden injuries to women without contributing to old stories that cast women as inevitably damaged and vulnerable to male control (Schneider 1986; M. Mahoney 1994). How can we name and challenge the ways in which many women are victims of gender-related harms without denying that most (if not all) women also share in a complex reality of power, pleasure, and privilege?

My thesis is that we can learn how to better respond to this apparent victim/agent dilemma by looking at another side of the story—at media representations of some who claim to be victims of feminism. After all, those who identify with privileged white male authority often have had it both ways: Our legal system is testament to the successes some have had at positioning themselves as both vulnerable victims and authoritative agents. For example, Oliver North's teary-eyed stories of obedient suffering in the Iran-contra hearings[1] not only helped protect him from criminal charges but also propelled him

to a U.S. Senate nomination. Victimization linked to gender politics, in particular, can frequently inscribe potency as well as passivity. From Robert Bly[2] to Rush Limbaugh,[3] the airwaves and print media are saturated with the voices of heterosexual white men whose fame and fortunes have been secured in part through stories of suffering due to feminist power.

It is not simply the subject matter of one's story—victimization—but also one's position as authoritative subject that determines whether or not narratives of harm bolster or undermine one's power and autonomy. Victimhood can work both to confirm the inauthenticity and inadequacy of subordinated groups and to support the authenticity and strength of those with relative privilege. By comparing feminist narratives of sexual victimization with victim narratives of those whose privileged position is threatened by feminist reforms, we can better understand how authority and agency is constructed in the popular media and how that authority can be subverted and extended to "others."

Feminist Victim Narratives

In 1990, I wrote some essays for the local media commenting on a civil liberties union lawsuit that challenged my undergraduate college's right to ban fraternities. The college had decided to prohibit its students from belonging to fraternities after many years of disciplinary problems related to fraternity activities; among other problems, several all-male and predominantly white fraternities at that private college had long been a focus of complaints of sexual harassment and abusive behavior toward women (McCluskey 1992, pp. 267–68). The lawsuit challenging the ban on fraternities was a test case[4] under a new state law[5] aimed at providing remedies for civil rights violations from private parties, particularly hate groups like the Ku Klux Klan. The state civil liberties union argued that the college's decision to discipline some students for participating in fraternity activities violated those students' rights to freedom of association.

My commentaries on the fraternity lawsuit included a narrative about my college experiences of harassment and assault by previous members of the fraternity at issue in the lawsuit. In the dispute about the fraternity ban, the local media had widely discussed the harm to students' rights from the college's prohibition on fraternities, without including discussion of the continuing history of harm to women and other students caused by those fraternities (see McCluskey 1992, pp. 282–87).

Like many feminist legal scholars (Coombs 1993, pp. 313–14; Estrich 1987, pp. 1–3), I attempted to use personal stories in order to explore biased assumptions underlying the law's response to the sexual victimization of women. By publishing our own victim narratives, feminist scholars have personified the victim/agent dilemma underlying the controversy over Roiphe's book. In my essays about the fraternity case, I positioned myself both as silenced victim acted upon by others and as speaking author attempting to reconstruct the framework within which those others act. But according to the critics of feminist victim stories, my victim narrative risks failure on two grounds: First, it demonstrates that I am an emotional, vulnerable female who needs protection from responsible, rigorous debate. Second, it shows that my exercise of power in speaking out about harms from fraternities is misleading and unprincipled—a result of emotional manipulation.

For example, Roiphe (1993b) criticizes "rape-crisis" techniques such as campus Take Back the Night marches and speak-outs protesting violence against women. Though such activities may be "intended to celebrate and bolster women's strength, [they seem] instead to celebrate their vulnerability" (K. Roiphe 1993b, p. 44). "As the speakers describe every fear, every possible horror suffered at the hands of men, the image they project is one of helplessness and passivity" (K. Roiphe 1993b, p. 44). Furthermore, Roiphe complains that the use of confessional stories of sexual abuse is "a natural trump card" that unfairly turns rational discussion into "the teary province of trauma and crisis" (1993b, p. 56). "By blocking analysis with its claims to unique pandemic suffering, the rape crisis becomes a powerful source of authority" (K. Roiphe 1993b, p. 57). Following that view, the very fact that my story of victimization may have been a compelling story of harm added proof to my inauthenticity. Victim narratives like mine are likely to be suspect both for demonstrating excessive weakness (victimizing women) and for exhibiting excessive power (victimizing men).

Indeed, casting the problem in terms of the old equal treatment/special treatment dilemma, some critics suggest that feminist complaints about sexual victimization are illegitimate attempts to retain protection in the face of growing power and equality. One conservative critic complains, "Do they want to push equity or do they want to push the victim status?"; she insists that "you can't have it both ways" (Fields 1994). Roiphe suggests that some painful experiences which many feminists attribute to date rape and sexual harassment are simply the necessary price of sexual freedom and equality. She warns that stories presenting women as victims of sexual violence risk putting women back on a restrictive pedestal, which she depicts by opening her book with an image of her grandmother spending her days of protected boredom going shopping, playing cards, and getting manicures (K. Roiphe 1993b, p. 3).

But as many activists and scholars have described at length (e.g., hooks 1984, pp. 1–3), this stereotype of a protected woman on a pedestal takes a grossly incomplete and distorted view of the problem of gender inequality by making the experience of a small group of economically privileged women stand for the problems of women with vastly different experiences. The media tends to ignore that this stereotype of the privileged woman on the pedestal coexists with (and reinforces) a corresponding stereotype of the "fallen" women—a stereotype that is tied to race, class, and sexuality (Benedict 1992).

In the traditional story, to be authentic victims, women generally need to establish sexual "innocence" (Higgins and Tolman 1997) and to affirm the authority of economically privileged white men. But women who take action to testify about their injuries from middle- or upper-class men of the same race may risk losing their status as authentic victims because their speaking against such men denies their innocence and dependence. "As Roiphe dryly notes, being 'silenced' is an experience of the articulate, whose tone is often self-congratulatory: I have survived victimization, so I am very brave" (Will 1993b). When women demonstrate agency, they often risk losing credibility. From Eve in the Garden of Eden to Anita Hill in the U.S. Senate hearings, the exercise of power by a female subject is frequently told as a sign of weakness; women's assertiveness is frequently interpreted to be motivated by emotional or sexual excess, personal greed, or whim. In other words, our resistance is constructed as our victimization as instruments (or pawns) of internal or external diabolical forces.

But asserting claims to both victimization and equality can be a means of escaping a double bind rather than an attempt to "have it both ways." What this mainstream media debate constructs as a choice between protection and powerlessness on the one hand and risk and responsibility on the other may be more usefully interpreted as a contest over whose struggle for security is construed as a sign of individual responsibility and autonomy and whose is a sign of pathology and dependence.

Stories of Victims of Feminism

Media victim narratives starring men who are economically privileged, white, and heterosexual are often central to establishing the rationality and authority of their demands for protection. The mainstream media prominently features stories about male victimization from ambiguous or false claims of sexual harassment or date rape. A common theme of the media discussion of Roiphe's book was the image of fearful, confused, and powerless heterosexual males faced with threatening college feminists.

For example, *Newsweek*'s cover story on college feminists' activism against date rape and sexual harassment opened by saying that the women at Brown University "play hardball" and create a "siege mentality" among college men through techniques such as listing the names of men accused of rape on bathroom walls (Crichton 1993). Numerous news stories tell about college men victimized by antirape flyers or posters (Manning 1993; Kranhold and Farrish 1993; Morrow 1994). Others describe the suffering of college men who have been subject to disciplinary proceedings for engaging in sexual actions without adequate consent (Adler and Picker 1990; D. Sullivan 1994). Some stories described college men's feelings of confusion and shock while attending mandatory date-rape workshops (Reidy 1993; Kranhold and Farrish 1993).

One newspaper's analysis of the date-rape issue opened by asking readers to imagine themselves as heterosexual men unable to approach women to ask them out for fear of being accused of sexual harassment; the article goes on to discuss stories of men accused of rape or sexual harassment by young women (Chunn 1993). A *Washington Times* editorial ("Date Rape 101" 1993) warned that fraternity parties and football games are in danger of being replaced by a tyranny of "Political Correctness gestapos on campuses" who threaten to "ruin the lives of those students unfortunate enough to fall within their grasp." *New York* magazine's cover story on date rape contrasted one anecdote about a woman's experience of being raped by a date with two anecdotes about college men who had been victimized by false accusations of campus rape (Hellman 1993). A British newspaper began its story on date rape by raising the specter of a male student "scraping a living waiting at tables," having lost his professional career as a result of feminist extremists, who have spread "a new, draconian sexual code . . . like a malevolent fungus" through U.S. universities (Driscoll 1993). But despite their prominence in the media, these victim narratives about those who fear the effects of campus feminism have not faced the same kinds of controversy and criticism as have victim stories about college women who claim to have been harmed by rape or sexual harassment.

Victims Create Epidemics of Fear

Mainstream media commentators have widely discussed the danger that "rape-crisis" feminism may create an "epidemic" of fear among women. Roiphe warns that blue security lights installed on college campus walkways as part of antirape programs will make women "learn vulnerability and lurking dangers in the bushes" and will teach women "to be on your guard with every man" (1993b, p. 28). She chides date-rape educational pamphlets dramatizing female students' fears of sexual harassment, complaining that if colleges encourage such feelings of vulnerability among female students, "their hothouse flowers are going to wilt in the light of postcollege day" (K. Roiphe 1993b, p. 109). Roiphe fears that even if male victimization of women is a real problem, acting as if male dominance exists is "a dangerous train of thought" because it "carries us someplace we don't want to be" (1993b, p. 89)—back to the stereotypical pedestal which Roiphe imagines as the central feminist problem.

Yet media discussions of feminist "totalitarianism" (Sommers 1994c) and "gender war" (Leo 1994) on college campuses generally have not raised comparable concerns that such dramatic warnings will make male students wilt when they face bigger dangers after graduation. Far from scolding men for getting caught up in a crisis atmosphere and for dwelling on their vulnerability, Roiphe is proud that her publicity has brought her "hundreds of letters from men saying, 'I'm grateful to you for saying that all men are not rapists'" (C. May 1994). Some prominent critics of "victim feminism" have promoted apocalyptic stories of men as victims of campus feminism. According to Sommers (1994b), "charges of harassment are made so carelessly and on such slight grounds that we now have a genuine witch hunt on many of your campuses. . . . Every man is now—stands to be accused if he's ever been alone in a room with a woman." Columnist John Leo (1994) quotes a former prosecutor who says that she is "'very frightened' for men on campus" and that "the pendulum has really swung" so that "young men are now the victims." Indeed, the Heritage Foundation reports that feminist arguments about women's victimization "are nothing less than an assault on our very existence as a nation and a society" (A. Miller 1990).

Victims Exaggerate Their Injuries

The media controversy over "victim feminism" has given substantial publicity to claims that feminism tends to exaggerate harm to women. Sommers has gained media fame for purporting to expose many feminist claims as inconsistent with statistical evidence. One report about her book quotes Sommers as saying that "in every case that I looked into of women's victimization—of information produced by a feminist research center or a feminist researcher—it was unreliable" (Romano 1994). The media has also given widespread attention to Roiphe's criticisms of a survey used to suggest that one in four women in college may have experienced rape.

In contrast, the image of the fateful "morning after" which titles Roiphe's book and which underlies many male victim stories has not been accompanied by popular media discussions of the lack of solid empirical evidence supporting the fears of false accusation it represents. Roiphe's book offers no evidence of male college students

or professors who have suffered physical or material harm or prosecution from being falsely accused of date rape due to women who have a change of heart following consensual sexual encounters (though she does tell two anecdotes of false accusations of rape in other contexts; see K. Roiphe 1993b, pp. 39–42). Sommers disparages feminists for making claims about the prevalence of rape without adequate statistical support (1994a, pp. 210–26) but offers no statistical support whatsoever for her repeated claims of feminist "witch-hunts" against men on college campuses (Sommers 1994a, p. 116; 1994b).

Similarly, no statistics accompany the media's frequent warnings of feminist "male-bashing" (Hinds 1993; Carlson 1994). Nor do such warnings acknowledge the diversity or complexity of feminist views on men. For example, few if any of the mainstream media commentators on Roiphe's book appear to have considered bell hooks's years of prolific writings on the importance to feminism of treating men as allies, not enemies (hooks 1984, pp. 67–81; hooks 1994, p. 81) or the major trends in feminist theory and activism critical of identity politics and essentialist notions of gender (Danielsen and Engle 1995; Butler and Scott 1992; A. Harris 1990).

Feminism is particularly under fire in the media for attempting to stretch the meaning of "rape" and "sexual harassment." According to Roiphe (1991), "certain feminists are busy turning rape into fiction. Every time one Henry James character seizes the hand of another Henry James character, someone is calling it rape." Paglia (1994a) derides feminists for "this broadening of the idea of rape, which is an atrocity, to those things that go wrong on a date—acquaintances, you know, little things, miscommunications—on pampered elite college campuses." Naomi Wolf (1994) warns that "feminism has to start being so scrupulously fair" in order to avoid representing the problem of gender injustice as a gender war which casts "all men as brutal, rapacious beasts."

But the proliferation of stories about male victims has not yet sparked a hot market for books like Naomi Wolf's, Katie Roiphe's, or Christina Hoff Sommers's, books urging a heterosexual white male audience to be scrupulously accurate when they talk about their fears of feminist power. The media rarely feature cautionary tales about the danger to elite men of a comparable loss of authority for their tendency to expand the terms "crime" and "violence" to cover virtually any exercise of power that potentially limits elite nongay male sexual freedom.

A *Newsweek* article criticizes Antioch College's student conduct guidelines (which require students to receive explicit consent for every step of sexual activity) on the ground that this policy "criminalizes the delicious unexpectedness of sex" (Crichton 1993). In fact, such student conduct codes are private disciplinary proceedings with no criminal penalties. Nonetheless, columnist John Leo (1994) gravely quotes Cathy Young's warning that feminists are "trying to dictate the curriculum and write campus codes that would turn 90 percent of the men into rapists." In the dispute over my college's ban on fraternities, a local newspaper quoted a national fraternity leader's statement that the college president "and his hand-picked thought police regiment have advanced repression to new heights" and complained that the college administration "has essentially made it a crime punishable by expulsion to be a heterosexual male who chooses to formalize his friendship with other like-minded friends" ("Colby Defends Crackdown on Underground Fraternities" 1991). In fact, the college had temporarily suspended, not expelled, the students in an internal disciplinary proceeding with no criminal consequences and had not prohibited students from associating in other kinds of exclusively heterosexual male organizations.

Feminist-inspired restrictions on male behavior may even count as crimes of historic proportions. In response to my college's ban on fraternities, one fraternity member wrote a letter printed in the campus newspaper declaring that the college's ban on fraternities was a form of "genocide" comparable to the Holocaust and the Cambodian killing fields. Discussing his book *The Myth of Male Power* (1993a), Warren Farrell warns that the current plight of men is comparable to the historical status of enslaved African Americans. Farrell (1993b) explains that "the difference between slaves and males is that . . . men are taught to think of their slavery as power."

Victims Are Unpopular

Even though many suggest that feminists tend to sway the public too easily with unsupported stories of victimization, prominent critics of "victim

feminism" also tend to blame feminists for driving the majority of women away from feminism. A common argument is that many women shrink from identifying with feminism because of the indignity of the victim role that feminists present.

Roiphe explains that women are "loath to call themselves feminists" because "being a feminist has come to mean being a victim of one form or another of oppression" (quoted in Picker 1993). Sommers (1994c) reports that few women on college campuses will admit to being feminists: "Young women don't want to be associated with [feminism] anymore because they know it means male-bashing, it means being a victim, and it means being bitter and angry. And young women are not naturally bitter and angry." Mary Matalin (1993) declares that "[feminist] extremists have tragically transmuted the energizing battle cry 'I am woman, I am strong' to the neurotic 'I am woman, I am oppressed, victimized, powerless.' These women do not represent people like us." In a more conciliatory tone, Naomi Wolf argues that women in the mainstream have gone further in embracing feminist power than the "victim feminism" expressed in the organized movement (1993a, p. 142).

Yet antifeminist media spokespeople thrive on using stories of victimization to encourage popular identification with masculinist interests. Few are warning radio talk-show host Rush Limbaugh that he will lose his audience—which Limbaugh (1994) claims totaled 20 million listeners a week—if he doesn't stop talking about white male helplessness in the face of totalitarian feminist control over government and academia. Instead, commentators cite the theme of white male fear of feminism as a ticket to popular media success (Nyhan 1994; Nethaway 1995). Michael Crichton's novel *Disclosure*, a story of an angry white man victimized by sexual harassment from a female superior, was on the *New York Times* best-seller list for twenty-two weeks before becoming a major Hollywood movie (James 1994). Indeed, victim stories by white heterosexual males are sometimes credited with being a major force behind the Republican landslide in the 1994 elections (Estrich 1994; Farney 1994).

Victims Are Weak and Cowardly

The media have widely reported concerns that feminists who talk about women as victims represent women as whiny and weak rather than strong and brave. Writing for the *New York Times Book Review*, Wendy Kaminer says Roiphe is persuasive when she warns that feminist stories of elite college women as victims will contribute to what Kaminer disturbingly terms the "effemination of feminism" (1993a, p. 41). Similarly, Roiphe approvingly quotes Betty Friedan's use of the words "impotent" and "sterile" to describe feminist antirape activism (1993b, p. 44). But neither Kaminer nor Roiphe nor other prominent mainstream media commentators have shown comparable concern that a strategy that focuses on the victimization of men will contribute to the so-called effemination or impotence of masculinity.

To the contrary, in the debate over President Clinton's proposed changes to federal prohibitions against lesbians and gay men in the military, those straight male soldiers who confessed fears of shared showers and same-sex sexual advances were not widely scolded or scoffed at for talking like prudes. Instead, such concerns about imagined male sexual victimization deserved extensive hearings and sober recognition for raising tough problems of national defense.

For heterosexual white men, apparently, complaining about gender oppression demonstrates resistance to weakness (Keith 1993). A leader of a men's rights organization explains that "instead of being wimps . . . men are finally speaking up and they're getting tough about it" (DeMarco 1994). For women, however, complaining about gender oppression shows capitulation to weakness. Camille Paglia declares that men are weak because they are "emasculated by feminism's stern dictates" (quoted in Corliss 1994), while she suggests that women are weak because they are too prim, pampered, and infantile to accept what she claims is natural male aggression (Paglia 1994b, pp. 30–35). Indeed, the common choice of words like "effeminate" and "impotence" to describe feminism's victim problem suggests that women act like victims not because of anything they do or say but because they are not virile heterosexual men.

While those women who speak out about white male abuses of power risk perpetuating images of female weakness and whininess, those who speak out against abuses of feminist power frequently use their tales of victimization to establish themselves as models of strength and

honor. Reporting that she has been "pilloried and picketed, in a torrent of abuse and defamation," Paglia explains that she is "an ornery outsider" who has "helped restore free speech to America" (1994b, p. xv). Sommers complains that feminists have attacked her and called her names but that her husband "calms her down" (quoted in Carton 1994); her husband says he worries about her because "she attracts so much hostility from these women," though he insists that Sommers still "stands up very well" (quoted in Romano 1994).

The media has particularly portrayed Roiphe as a victim of feminist "attack": She "feels misunderstood" (Worrell 1993), "pilloried and excommunicated by some feminists" (Noble 1993) and faced with "name-calling," "threatening letters," and "people who really hate" her (Picker 1993). Yet Roiphe's experiences of verbal victimization at the hands of feminists confirm her status as someone who is "courageous" and willing "to speak out against the herd" (Lehmann-Haupt 1993b).

It is not only Roiphe's victimhood that is heroic: Her irresponsibility is also evidence of her bravery. Kaminer's review applauds Roiphe's book for showing that college feminists' injudicious use of the terms "sexual harassment" and "date rape" is evidence of their "fashionable emptiness" and of the students' "sheer mindlessness" (1993a, p. 41). At the same time, Kaminer decides that Roiphe's "injudiciousness" in criticizing feminists in her book is "part of its charm" and is what makes the book "nervy" and "brave" (1993a, pp. 1, 41).

Victims Need Protective Rules

Prominent critics of feminist activism against date rape and sexual harassment frequently point to feminists' demands for legal or political change as a particular sign of weakness. In their view, many feminists tend to contribute to images of women as helpless victims when they seek institutional rather than individual solutions to problems of sexual victimization.

Roiphe denounces new college codes that aim to set higher standards of consent for student sexual conduct: "The implication is that women are too gullible or too weak, or too innocent, too fragile to communicate on a very basic level" (quoted in D. Sullivan 1994). "The idea that women can't withstand verbal or emotional pressure infantilizes them" (K. Roiphe 1993b, p. 67). Cathy Young (1992) criticizes feminist efforts to strengthen campus policies on date rape: "The law is not there to ensure we have trauma-free relationships." According to Roiphe, "there would never be a rule or a law, or even a pamphlet or peer counseling group, for men who claimed to have been emotionally raped or verbally pressured into sex" (1993b, p. 69).

Yet this concern that legal protection leads to victimization did not get much attention in the mainstream media discussion of President Clinton's short-lived attempt to lift prohibitions against gay men and lesbians in the military. In that situation, heterosexual military men sought not just a pamphlet or a counseling session but congressional hearings and federal legal protection—and not from verbal coercion or emotional pressure but simply from the merest mention of their comrades' same-sex desires.

Stories that portray heterosexual white men as uniquely prone to emotional domination may establish their demands for institutional support as reasonable and natural rather than as irrational or infantilizing. For example, in the Glen Ridge rape case, a group of white male high school students were accused of using a baseball bat, a broomhandle, and a stick to rape a young woman who had a mental disability. A news story about the case reported that attorneys for the accused students argued that "the young woman wasn't vulnerable to the young men, so much as the young men—and their raging hormones—were vulnerable to her" (Dreyfous 1993). Though the argument in that case was unsuccessful (the jury found the students guilty), many still assume that laws against sexual harassment and rape should accommodate heterosexual men's supposedly natural weakness in the face of women's sexuality—without concern that such protection will make men into victims.

The more common fear expressed in the media is that men become victims when feminists *remove* legal protections that excuse men for nonconsensual heterosexual behavior. A *Playboy* interview reports that men "respond naturally" to women who dress in certain ways, so that as a result of sexual harassment laws, "we have men absolutely terrified in the office" (Kammer 1994). Similarly, in a 1994 *New Republic* cover story titled "Feminists, Meet Mr. Darwin," Robert

Wright argues that "victim feminists" fail to understand that the sexual double standard is a matter of "nature," not politics; he claims that laws which attempt to control what he sees as natural male heterosexual aggression risk victimizing both men and women (though he adds that such laws nevertheless may sometimes be justifiable on "higher" grounds).

Victims Are Oversensitive to Speech

Critics frequently charge that some feminist legal protections against date rape and sexual harassment are misguided attempts to protect women from the effects of offensive speech. According to Paglia (1994a), "if someone offends you by speech, we must train women to defend themselves by speech. You cannot be always running to tribunals." Roiphe writes, "Instead of learning that men have no right to do these terrible things to us, we should be learning to deal with individuals with strength and confidence. If someone bothers us, we should be able to put him in his place without crying into our pillow or screaming for help or counseling" (1993b, p. 101). Cathy Young (1993) says, "What I find demeaning is the portrayal of women as helpless victims who can't put a jerk in his place without running to Big Brother—or Big Sister—for help." Paglia (1994a) admonishes feminists to follow her example: "I express my anger to men directly. I don't get in a group and whine about men." (Of course, she doesn't hesitate to get on national TV to complain about feminists.)

But media stories about those who are victims of feminist speech frequently assume that feminist verbal criticism is too harmful to be left to private individual rebuttals. Media stories warn of college graffiti or posters accusing male students of date rape or harassment, but such stories do not tend to ask why those male students cannot simply respond to such speech with more speech of their own. Without discussing why college males are so vulnerable to verbal persuasion, columnist John Leo (1994) quotes Cathy Young's claim that campus educational workshops on date rape and sexual harassment leave male students "sometimes essentially badgered into conceding that they may have raped some of their seemingly willing sexual partners."

Narratives of male victimization through feminist speech often describe men's fear not of violence or physical coercion but of being called names or feeling embarrassed. A local newspaper columnist protested my undergraduate college's punishment of student football players who violated the college's fraternity ban; he argued that making the football team a laughingstock by removing some of the players is "more offensive than any amount of hazing, beer drinking, or wolf whistles," since "losing is bad for a young man's soul" (Hanrahan 1990). But rather than demonstrating that college men are thick-skinned and able to chalk disappointing setbacks up to experience (as Roiphe insists that women must do when hurt by some forms of sexual harassment or date rape), this columnist declares that male college football players' sensibilities are so delicate that they need more protection from laughter than women do from sexual harassment.

Leo (1994) fears that few men will speak up about gender issues "out of fear of being identified as huggers and drummers in the woods." Sommers reports that male professors and administrators cannot stand up to what she claims is widespread feminist control of universities because many men have "lived in fear of being called sexist. A lot of men just run for cover" (Carton 1994). Some suggest that heterosexual men cling to the protections of the sexual double standard because they worry that they might have to face questions about their sexuality if women have equal authority to ask men for consensual sex (Chunn 1993; Hitchens 1993).

"Real" Victims Are "Others"

The mainstream media critics of campus-based "victim feminism" typically purport not to disparage all claims of victimization but instead to more sharply confine such claims to "real" victims and victimizers. Roiphe (1993b) explains that her criticisms of "rape-crisis feminism" are not meant to deny the seriousness of real sexual victimization. Instead, she objects to extending concern about rape to the "average man" (p. 100); she disparages suggestions "that we should subject all of our male friends to scrutiny" (p. 65). As a sympathetic Newsday reporter noted, "That's not to say that Roiphe thinks women are free to take a midnight stroll through Central Park" (Picker 1993). Roiphe explains, "I just don't think we need to teach every freshman woman that the average rapist might be the boy

next door" (quoted in Behrens 1993). Mary Matalin (1993) tells Newsweek readers that feminist "extremists" who complain about violence against women must be distinguished from "women like you and me," insisting, "Our sons are no brutes; our men are not monstrous pigs."

Newsweek's discussion of Roiphe's book acknowledges that even conservative statistics show that college women are at high risk of sexual assault but then comments: "You want to talk victimization? Talk to the mothers all over America whose children have been slaughtered in urban cross-fire" (Crichton 1993). Sommers (1994c) complains, "There's more services to protect these young [college] women from rape than for women in, you know, downtown Newark." In the media coverage of my college's fraternity ban, a local newspaper columnist imagined the situation of the young college men punished for joining a fraternity as "absurd" and went on to mock the idea that "a gang of bleeding heart liberals decided fraternities are akin to the Khmer Rouge and L.A. street gangs" (Hanrahan 1990). Right-wing activist Phyllis Schlafly (1994) writes, "The feminist ideology is based on the lie that American women are oppressed victims, whereas in fact American women are the most fortunate class of people who ever lived." Sommers (1994c) similarly scorns the idea "that contemporary American women are in the thrall to men, to male culture. . . . It's so silly. . . . No women have ever had more opportunities, more freedom, and more equality than contemporary American women."

Such comments by critics of "victim feminism" displace negative images of victims and victimizers from elite college students onto "others" who are supposedly distant in terms of race, class, nationality, ethnicity, or disability, while reinforcing the identification of victims of oppression as marginalized, powerless, and pitiful. bell hooks notes that white fascination with black victimization through white supremacy silences more subversive representations of "loving blackness," though she cautions against a mere reversal of a white privilege/black victim paradigm (1992, pp. 10–12).

Concern about appropriating the pain of "real" victims is rarely discussed in the publicity over stories of victims of real or imagined excesses of feminism. The media coverage of Oleanna and Disclosure, two popular fictional narratives of heterosexual middle-class white men who are accused of sexual harassment, did not typically ask whether such stories are a form of privileged whining that ignores the more serious injustices faced by many young African American men who run a high risk not only of false accusations but of incarceration and physical violence at the hands of a discriminatory criminal justice system. When the University of New Hampshire temporarily suspended Professor J. Donald Silva from his teaching position because of student complaints about sexual comments he made in class, the press did not debate whether the widespread publicity he received would detract attention from the many blue-collar workers who face the more common risk of losing their jobs because of a global political economy that encourages labor restraints and capital mobility.

Indeed, popular victim narratives of those who claim victimization from feminism sometimes draw legitimacy from identification across class and race lines. *Disclosure*—a story about corporate executives—appears to tap into the anger and economic insecurity of working-class white men: The lead character complains, "Why don't I just be that guy, that evil white guy you're always complaining about. . . . When did I have the power, when?" (James 1994). In his 1995 *Village Voice* essay titled "Save the Males: The Making of the Butch Backlash," Richard Goldstein notes that "the Angry White Male wears a blue collar even when he's a millionaire." Rush Limbaugh (1994) claims that his popularity stems from his "rejection of the elites." In fact, Limbaugh's audience tends to be well-educated white men, and his annual income is estimated at $25 million (Boyer 1995). In addition, the stories of white men concerned about being victimized by false accusations of sexual offenses sometimes gain credibility from association with an all-too-real and appalling history of oppression of African American men on false charges of sexual assault of white women.

Furthermore, the mainstream media frequently obscures the fact that prominent women who complain about "victim feminism" appear to have race and class interests in common with the relatively privileged men who are frequently targeted as victimizers by campus feminists. Some of the most widely publicized complaints about campus "victim feminism" come from women (for instance, Roiphe, Sommers, Paglia, and Young). By emphasizing those critics' shared gender identity with the feminist college women they criticize, the mainstream media gives the critics an impartial position from which to reveal feminist antirape activism as self-serving.

This superficial appearance of impartiality, however, depends on making gender eclipse considerations of race, class, and sexuality. In fact, the mainstream media discussion of Roiphe's book generally excluded any comments from women of color. When *Newsday* published an essay by bell hooks (1993), it was titled "Color Roiphe Privileged, Says Black Feminist." In contrast, Roiphe was typically denominated "author" or "young author," not "white author" (see, e.g., Worrell 1993). And Mary Matalin's *Newsweek* essay praising Roiphe's book was titled "Stop Whining!" without the qualification "Says White Wealthy Conservative."

By portraying both elite college feminists and inner-city or foreign "others" as victims (legitimate or not), the mainstream media tends to construct the illusion of a white American middle class of strong, autonomous individuals. In this view, elite college women do not deserve legal protection from certain kinds of sexual victimization because of their relatively powerful socioeconomic position. Their claims of victimization are represented as evidence of a desire to stay on a protected pedestal. But "other" women, with less socioeconomic privilege, may not deserve legal protection, because their victimhood is evidence of their failure to exercise responsible agency, or because legal protection will reinforce their victim status. This media picture means that feminist activism becomes either the elite asking for privilege, or the poor asking for handouts—and therefore supposedly irrelevant or threatening to the presumed majority of women.

"Real" Victims Need to Be Controlled

"Real" victims, whose injuries deserve redress and protection, apparently are those who are unable to effectively assert autonomous agency. But the dependency those victims must establish to prove they deserve institutional protection also makes their claims for protection suspect in a culture that idealizes individual autonomy. Writers for the conservative press sometimes contrast the "culture of victimization" (often attributed to feminists and to "black leaders") with "personal responsibility" (Karl 1992). The Personal Responsibility and Work Opportunity Reconciliation Act of 1996 (H.R. 4), which aims to reform welfare by penalizing poor women and children, shows that women who might appear more likely than elite college feminists to fit the stereotypes of "real" victims are also more likely to receive less sympathy, more criticism, and additional injury.

But some victim stories can serve to confer a double benefit instead of a double bind. Victim narratives by those with privilege can work to deny the social agency that results from that privilege, cleverly making the most privileged deserving of the greatest legal protection. If less privileged "others" offer opposing victim narratives, they merely confirm their subjective self-interest and failure to take responsibility for their own actions—thereby proving the illegitimacy of demands for "special" legal protection above and beyond the norm. In contrast, those who claim to be harmed by feminism often succeed in invoking their personal victimization as evidence of their impartiality and responsibility.

When I told my stories about fraternity violence against women, some responses suggested that I was talking about emotional personal experience with little relevance to the issue of fraternity members' civil liberties (see McCluskey 1992, p. 276, n. 73). In contrast, media stories described the fraternity members' feelings of victimization by the fraternity ban as a problem raising questions of universal rational principles, such as freedom of association rights. Similarly, media reports frequently presented Professor Silva's claims of victimization by charges of sexual harassment as a defense not of personal ambition or class privilege but of free speech (A. Lewis 1994; Kilpatrick 1994). Reporters and editorial writers typically did not ask why Silva did not simply quit (or move to another university) if he was annoyed by feminist challenges to his teaching style (in contrast to questions asked of Professor Anita Hill when she testified about sexual harassment by Supreme Court nominee Clarence Thomas).

When those who traditionally have had access to public authority complain about their own fear and suffering from charges of harming others, their complaints often are presented as evidence of their sensitivity and as occasions for public sympathy and generosity. A New Republic article titled "Defining Deviancy Up" protested the extent to which "normal" and "ordinary" middle-class heterosexual men are now accused of deviancy, while "others" who were previously widely seen as deviant (criminals, people with mental illnesses, and single mothers) now may be portrayed as "normal" (Krauthammer 1993). The author criticized feminists for expanding the concept of rape to include date rape by college students, suggesting that these victimizers are particularly prone to being victimized: This "higher class of offender" is "more malleable" (Krauthammer 1993). He worries that "the guilt-ridden bourgeois, the vulnerable college student, is a far easier object of social control than the hardened criminal or the raving lunatic" (Krauthammer 1993). The heterosexual male college student, in this view, demonstrates his responsibility and credibility as a victim through his greater dependence on social approval from others than those with less privilege.

Similarly, when several female senators unsuccessfully sought to withhold full retirement honors to Admiral Frank B. Kelso 2d because of his wrongdoing in the investigation of the Tailhook sexual harassment scandal, supporters won sufficient votes to protect Kelso's full pension by using sentimental testimony about his family's potential suffering (Dowd 1994b). Senator Sam Nunn claimed that to deny the admiral his four stars would be to scapegoat him (Dowd 1994b; "So Little Leadership" 1994). This view implies that Kelso's position of authority (Chief of Naval Operations) excused his irresponsibility, while his suffering as a result of his irresponsibility in turn justified continued protection of his authority.

When those with a tradition of authority are held accountable for their actions, they may be represented as victims; restrictions on their independence are seen as frustrating their ability to act as free and responsible agents. But when those with less authority are held accountable for their actions, restrictions are commonly seen as necessary for free and responsible agency. Newsweek's cover story on feminist activism against date rape and sexual harassment on college campuses was titled "Sexual Correctness" and contained numerous stories warning of the problems caused when society turns away from liberal standards of tolerance (Crichton 1993). That issue emphasized the harms to young people of enforcing rules establishing "correct" sexual conduct on college campuses. Another *Newsweek* issue with a cover titled "Shame" featured an article stressing the need to *reject* liberal standards of tolerance and the importance of a societal return to strict rules of morality—particularly regarding sexual conduct (Alter and Wingert 1995). This time, however, the magazine concentrated on stories about the success of using shame and punishment to force "correct" sexual conduct on welfare recipients, inner-city youth, and single parents—with no mention of the merits of feminists' attempts to impose stricter standards of sexual conduct on college campuses.

Beyond Campus Victims

Feminists may be tempted to dismiss the media's fascination with "victim feminism" as a trivial matter. When asked for a comment on Sommers's book, a spokesperson for National Organization of Women responded, "Because we're working on pressing issues like health care reform and the Violence Against Women bill in Congress, we do not have the time to comment on the latest critique of feminism" (Carton 1994). The mainstream media's identification of feminism with activism on date rape at elite U.S. colleges contributes to constructions of feminism as a movement outside the purview of the majority of women, or, as bell hooks (1993) suggests, a sport for privileged white girls. The diversity of women's experiences of sexual and intimate violence (see, e.g., Russo 1996; Crenshaw 1994; Eaton 1994; Lundy 1993) tends to be excluded from this media debate. Furthermore, this media attention to campus "victim feminism" contrasts sharply with the lack of media attention to feminist activism (on and off campus) on other issues, such as welfare, tax policy, health care, labor organizing, and economic development—issues where feminism might more readily be viewed as relevant to women and men of many races, nationalities, and economic classes.

Yet the "victim feminism" debate also provides an occasion to challenge and reconstruct the popular assumptions about power and individualism, assumptions that underlie many other public policy debates. The mainstream media often constructs the controversy over "victim feminism" as an intergenerational split: young feminists who want to celebrate sexuality and

independence are suppo. dly rebelling against certain feminist foremothers who have advocated sexual protection. This construction of the "victim feminism" debate repeats and reinforces coinciding narratives in popular media that blame mothers, particularly single mothers and those who are women of color, for economic dependence and inequality (see Fineman 1995, pp. 107–10).

In addition, critics of campus activism against date rape and sexual harassment may have captured media attention because this activism appears to pose a particular threat to particularly privileged men—the putative authoritative "fathers" of traditional legal discourse. Some of the most generous publicity for Roiphe's views, for example, has come from news media particularly aimed at highly educated and wealthy white men. For example, the *New York Times* originally published Roiphe's views on college date rape as an op-ed essay (K. Roiphe 1991), then published a chapter of her book in the magazine section (K. Roiphe 1993a), followed by two generally favorable book reviews (Lehmann-Haupt 1993b; Kaminer 1993a), one gushing interview (Noble 1993), and a second op-ed essay (K. Roiphe 1993c)—with only some short letters from critics in response. In comparison, the less upscale and less prestigious *USA Today* published one generally approving article about Roiphe's book (DeCrow 1993) and one that balanced Roiphe's views with the views of those who believe campus date rape is a serious problem (Manning 1993).

Richard Goldstein (1995) notes that the backlash of "angry white men" has substantial appeal among prosperous white male professionals, who fear that their authority to make the rules is no longer taken for granted—despite their success in maintaining disproportionate economic power. Nonetheless, traditionally misogyny has been more likely to be a subject of sustained mainstream media criticism when it is associated with, for example, construction workers, teenage black male rappers, or Arab fundamentalists rather than white American corporate executives or elite U.S. college students. Feminism, on the other hand, tends to be represented in the mainstream media as a concern of white women in professional career paths. Within that framework, feminist claims to victimization appear to be little other than elitist whining. Feminists must confront the ways in which elite white men are particularly implicated in male supremacy, yet such efforts must not be grounded solely in a concern for remedying harm to elite white women.

Using Victim Stories to Challenge Inequality

Feminist victim narratives are not necessarily transformative, just as they are not necessarily regressive. My point in contrasting victim narratives about harm from feminism with victim narratives challenging male violence against women is not to suggest that feminist stories of gender-based harm are necessarily more authentic or credible than others. Instead, I hope that this examination of the double standard in victim stories can help us move from contests of competing victimizations to more complex understandings of the relationship between exercising power and experiencing injury.

Narratives from both feminist victims and those who feel victimized by feminism demonstrate that telling stories of suffering is an act of power as well as a confession of powerlessness. Though the preexisting social and political context influences whether a narrator's stories of harm are interpreted as heroic or victimizing, those victim stories can also contribute to reshaping the narrator's authority and the broader political context in which the narratives are interpreted. The claims of victimization made by those who feel harm from feminism reflect not just feminist weakness and antifeminist power but also feminism's real power in changing law and public opinion. Clearly it can be effective, as well as rational and responsible, to give voice to personal pain and to respond to expressions of others' pain.

Yet not all claims of suffering deserve relief. It is necessary to decide which declarations of injury simply express the hurt feelings that may result from giving up the privilege to hurt others with impunity. Victim stories need to be told and evaluated with awareness of their power and potential impact on others, not dismissed or venerated on the assumption that they are beyond criticism and rational debate. Nor should victim narratives be assumed to be rebellious assertions of individual identity in resistance to societal dictates. Victim narratives get their power and

meaning from a social and political context that may exceed their author's intentions. White women who carelessly level accusations of male sexual violence without examining and challenging the relationships between narratives of sexual victimization and racial oppression can fuel a climate of racism that harms men of color, just as promoting epithets that link prochoice feminists with Nazis can help fuel a climate of misogynist violence against abortion clinic workers.

If women tell victim stories as an assertion of our own problems without considering others' pain, we may simply reinforce a model that grounds strength and autonomy in a demonstration of the ability to push away others' concerns. That model of autonomy underlies Rush Limbaugh's claim that his version of promoting group fear and blame constitutes "rugged individualism," while the Democratic Party's efforts to build coalitions that recognize the needs and contributions of a diverse society are merely examples of a "constituency of victimhood" (Limbaugh 1994).

The mainstream media often presents the "victim problem" in feminism as an issue of feminism going too far beyond individual opportunity and equality for women (for example, Wattenberg 1994). But the problem is more that the mainstream media tends to construct a version of feminism that does not go far enough. What makes women appear to be victims is not women who talk about how they are harmed by gendered privilege and power, but the media's frequent presentation of feminism as a movement that simply purports to allow individual universalized "women" to compete on the same terms as individual unspecified "men," without challenging the underlying double standards and intersecting forms of oppression and power which structure that competition.

Stories of victimization may have limited value for ending oppression, not because they make the oppressed seem too dependent and lacking in autonomous agency but because they may make oppression seem too individualized.[6] Feminists should strive to use expressions of personal harm not simply as individual catharsis but to question and change the political institutions—like law and media—in which that harm is interpreted. We need to tell stories that help to undermine the dichotomy between those seen as strong and responsible individuals on the one hand and those needing social support on the other. Autonomous agency is a product of social and political support as well as individual pluck. If power and victimhood are seen as mutually exclusive, many women may be alienated by feminism both because they feel both too victimized and too powerful—neither sufficiently free and strong to succeed without social support and male authority nor sufficiently powerless and oppressed to forego claims to independence, creativity, and pleasure.

Furthermore, feminists should strive to make the media and the law attend to the ways in which race, class, sexuality, physical ability, and other factors combine with gender to harm women. Kimberlé Crenshaw (1995) explains that feminist efforts to politicize violence and sexual harassment must include attention to problems of concern to many black women, such as harassment of recipients of public benefit programs. To "take back the night" for all women, feminists will have to address other forms of violence than date rape.

Finally, the problems of powerlessness in women's victim narratives are not automatically converted into power in men's victim narratives. The extent to which stories of personal victimization bring their narrators power and powerlessness depends in part on a complex interaction of identifying factors that include race, class, and sexuality as well as gender. Justice Clarence Thomas's victim narrative claiming that his televised congressional hearings on sexual harassment charges represented a "high-tech lynching" helped him secure his nomination to a position of highest legal authority in the U.S. Supreme Court; yet, unlike many white male public figures facing comparable charges, he could not escape being the focus of a public spectacle fraught with anxiety over race and gender which left his credibility damaged. But being a victim does not necessarily prevent one from also being an oppressor; responsibility does not require complete autonomy and perfect power.

Comparing the authenticity of competing victim stories in a contest for the "most oppressed" risks taking our attention away from the underlying structures that make too many of us victims. Male victim stories have gained so much power recently not simply because of male privilege but because so many men—and women—in the United States have become real victims of our misguided economy and inadequate social support systems. The media's construction of a struggle for power between "angry white men" and feminists deflects attention from the growing economic inequality between a relatively small group of highly educated white men in skilled professions and the majority of white men in the United States. We need to expose the class differences between white men and to emphasize the common benefits to many women and men that can come from looking at victimization and power as an issue of race, class, and sexuality, together with gender. Though feminists should continue to speak out about gendered oppression, and though we should question many of those who claim to be victimized by feminist reforms, we should strive for solutions that will create fewer victims.

Notes

This chapter draws in part on my essay "Transforming Victimization" (McCluskey 1994). Reprinted in part from *Tikkun* magazine, a bi-monthly Jewish critique of politics, culture, and society. Subscriptions are $31.00 per year from Tikkun, 251 West 100th Street, 5th floor, New York, NY 10025.

Particular thanks are due to Lisa Brush, Lynn Chancer, Samantha Dulaney, Martha Fineman, Sarah Herbert, Carl Nightingale, Joanna Piepgrass, and Robert Thomas for their comments on earlier versions.

1. Eve Kosofsky Sedgwick presents the image of Oliver North's tears to note that "straight male self-pity . . . is associated with, or appealed to in justification of, acts of violence, especially against women" (E. K. Sedgwick 1990, p. 145).

2. Robert Bly's book *Iron John* (1990) was on the *New York Times* hard-cover best-seller list for sixty-two weeks (see Johnston 1992). In contrast, Gloria Steinem's *Revolution from Within* (1992) was on the best-seller list for thirty-four weeks, and *Backlash* by Susan Faludi (1991) for thirty-nine weeks (Kakutani 1993).

3. Rush Limbaugh (1994) claims that he has sold six million copies of his books and that his programs are broadcast on 659 radio stations and 250 TV stations.

4. *Phelps v. President & Trustees of Colby College*, 595 A.2d 403 (Me. 1991).

5. Maine Civil Rights Act, Public Law 1989, chapter 582; codified as amended in *Maine Revised Statutes Annotated* (West), title 5, sections 4681–83.

6. For an astute discussion of how the "woman as victim" model in the context of divorce law leads to individualized solutions that fail to address the political problems faced by custodial mothers, see Martha Fineman 1991a, pp. 145–46.

7

Glamour Law

Feminism through the Looking Glass of Popular Women's Magazines

JULIA E. HANIGSBERG

Who reads women's magazines? . . . Millions of American women do, of every class, background, religion, race, and age. Who reads Ms. and the *Village Voice?* A few hundred thousand people, mostly urban, white, middle class, and college educated.

—Naomi Wolf, *Fire with Fire*

Just twenty years ago, who would have believed it? The United States Attorney General—top lawyer in the land—is named Janet. And sitting on the lofty bench of the U.S. Supreme Court are two women. Yes, we (women) still have a long (long) road ahead, but in arenas as public as the U.S. Senate and as private as the home front, we have indeed made stunning moves forward!

—Andre Peyser, "We've Come a Long Way Baby!",
Cosmopolitan

Academic feminism is alive and well, albeit full of controversy and occasionally a bit self-pitying.[1] Feminist theory is being written, taught, and thought about in all disciplines in the university. Courses on feminist legal theory are standard in law schools today. Yet only 41 percent of women say that feminism reflects their concerns (Doner 1993, p. 41; Kaminer 1993b; S. Douglas 1994, pp. 7–8), although they embrace much of what the women's movement has made possible for them (procreative freedom; equal access to the same educational, professional, and economic opportunities as men; more humane maternity and paternity leave policies, recognition of the

epidemic of violence against women) (Yost 1994; S. Douglas 1994, p. 272).[2] The premier issue of the American edition of the popular European women's magazine *Marie Claire* proclaims, in an article titled "The Feminist Mistake" (1994), that "real women" do not align themselves with feminist viewpoints. The ominous subtitle to the article reads, "Women are jumping off the feminist bandwagon in droves."[3] Katie Roiphe, in a book that received extraordinary media attention,[4] has suggested that in its incarnation on college campuses, feminism bears no relationship to real women's lives and aspirations (K. Roiphe 1993b). Roiphe is part of a larger movement attempting to discredit feminism for its alleged failure to represent women's interests (e.g., Sommers 1994; Patai and Koertge 1994). The conclusion often drawn is that feminism has failed women, that women outside academe do not espouse feminism as a worldview, and that feminism has no relevance to their lives.

Though this evidence may give us reason to fear that some women are at least eschewing the *label* "feminist," it does *not* prove that feminism is dead outside academic circles. Rather, a dynamic and exciting feminism is ubiquitous in one of the most mainstream forums—the popular women's magazine.

In this chapter I want to suggest that popular women's magazines, a genre not generally known for radical thought, are in fact a repository for a significant amount of feminist thinking, although not always under that name.[5] The importance of these women's popmags is in fact heightened by the alienation from the label "feminist" that many women seem to feel. If women do not want to label themselves feminists, they may not seek out reading material that would implicitly mark them as such. In short, they might not read *Ms.* But they will and do read *Glamour, Mirabella, Mademoiselle, Vogue, Essence, Harper's Bazaar,* and other popmags—magazines that, I contend, are "smarter" than they may be perceived to be. For example, *Glamour* won the 1992 National Magazine Award for public interest for two articles on teenage pregnancy and abortion and the 1991 award for general excellence for a magazine with a circulation exceeding one million, beating out other finalists, including *Time* (D. Carmody 1992). These magazines disseminate important feminist ideas and allow women an access to feminism that they might not otherwise have (Doner 1993; S. Page 1991; Rapping 1994c; Wolf 1990, pp. 71–72).[6] *Glamour* magazine's editor in chief, Ruth Whitney, has gone so far as to call *Glamour* "a mainstream feminist magazine," and *Mirabella's* editor, Grace Mirabella, says that she assumes her readership to be feminist (Kaminer 1993b). If feminism is to survive, and if law is to continue to be informed by feminist visions of justice, then it cannot merely be—or, perhaps more important, be perceived to be—the domain of a certain "radical fringe" within academic settings, as some current media portrayals seem to want to suggest (Wolf 1993a).

The significance of popmags to feminists is connected to the reasons that legal scholars (and others) are beginning to recognize the importance of popular culture more generally (Chase 1986; hooks 1994; Radway 1984; Mayne 1984; McClary 1991). First, and perhaps most important, is the very fact of the popularity of this material. Popmags have huge circulations; their contents are read by millions of women (Doner 1993; D. Carmody 1995; Schlosberg 1992).[7] The feminist messages these magazines send are worth thinking about for this reason alone. But second, these magazines may be more in touch with the needs and desires of women than other forms of literature ("The Feminist Mistake" 1994) (even if in some respects these are "desires" that they and their advertisers work hard to cultivate and expand). Thus, if academics, lawyers, and people who care deeply about bettering women's lives want to reach women, popmags may be able to give them important clues to what must be done to address women's needs and concerns. Women's magazines are worthy of study for the same reason that they can be dangerous: They serve to socialize women and girls in this society (Guddiero and Weston 1985; S. Douglas 1994; Wolf 1990). By recognizing that there is a role for feminism in these magazines, feminists can get access to an extraordinarily diverse audience of women readers.

However, this is not to underestimate the degree to which these magazines produce and reflect antifeminist messages as well (Doner 1993; S. Douglas 1994; M. Goldstein 1994; McCracken 1993; Wolf 1990; Rapping 1994c).[8] While the purpose of this chapter is to provoke thought about the feminism in popmags, these magazines also consistently impose negative stereotypes and imagery upon their readers. For each article decrying the omnipresence of eating disorders is an advertisement or editorial layout featuring an underweight model; for each article that calls attention to the dangers of plastic surgery is a picture of a figure beyond most women's dreams; for each article challenging African American women to love their beauty, there is a model with light skin and eyes, straight hair, and Anglo-Saxon features (Women, Men, and the Media 1994; Roan 1992; Bordo 1993b). Studying visual representations in popular women's magazines, "Women, Men, and the Media" (1994) found that while the content of articles in women's magazines is both more responsible than and superior to what it was twenty years ago, photos in advertising and editorial pages have not changed. They continue to show images of "overwhelmingly slim, occasionally skeletal models." In addition, the number of African American women portrayed is extremely low in all but *Essence*, a magazine that explicitly targets African American women (Gregory and Jacobs 1993). Portrayal of non-able-bodied women is almost nonexistent. However, the study praised *Essence* for showing the greatest variety of body shapes and sizes and for portraying more realistic images of women (Women, Men, and the Media 1994).[9]

It is this juxtaposition of messages that makes women's popular magazines much more complex than they initially appear and, I would suggest, explain in part why "smart" women still read them. Thinking about the relationship between these texts and their audiences as more than a passive one, but rather as a site in which readers play an active role in producing meanings, suggests that women see around the negative imagery produced in advertisements and photo editorials in subtle ways. Women may realize that the images they see are unreal and unrealistic and nonetheless adopt these images as emblematic of cultural norms. Accordingly, women can to a certain extent respond to these images by calculating the risk and worth of adopting them. Thus, women adopt the norm, for example, by having silicone breast implants even once they know them to be dangerous, not because they do not understand that the implants have serious side effects or because they are passive cultural dupes, but rather because they have rationally gauged large breasts to be "worth the risk" in order to be desired, loved, and successful in our sexist culture (Bordo 1993b, p. 20). As feminist philosopher Susan Bordo (1993b, p. 30) has pointed out:

> Although many people *are* mystified (insisting, for example, that the current fitness craze is only about health or that plastic surgery to "correct" a "Jewish" or "black" nose is just an individual preference), often there will be a high degree of consciousness involved in the decision to diet or to have cosmetic surgery. People *know* the routes to success in this culture—they are advertised widely enough—and they are not "dopes" to pursue them. Often, given the racism, sexism, and narcissism of the culture, their personal happiness and economic security may depend on it.

It is in this context that meaning in popular women's magazines is produced (S. Douglas 1994, p. 16). But arguing that meaning is manufactured through a relationship between text and reader is not to ignore the inequality of power between the producers and receivers of information (McCracken 1993, p. 73), nor is it to underestimate the danger to women that the portrayal of unrealistic images presents. There is, indeed, evidence to suggest that there is a correlation between reading women's popmags and poor self-image (Hiscock 1994; Sanders 1994).[10]

It is within this tangled framework that I examine the feminism of popular women's magazines. I contend that despite some protestations to the contrary, feminism is very much in the mainstream. To discuss this hypothesis I have looked at popular women's magazines—mainstream publications if ever there were such a thing. I will show that even in these bastions of femininity, feminism has found a home, and that its existence there demonstrates that women outside of academe, of different backgrounds, ages, and interests, have access to and may crave feminist approaches to important issues.

I should say a word about methodology. In writing this chapter, I have not attempted a comprehensive survey of the content of popular women's magazines. Rather, I have taken a look at a variety of magazines over a period of about one year. Specifically, I have looked at *Allure*, *Elle*, *Essence*, *Glamour*, *Harper's Bazaar*, *Mademoiselle*, *Mirabella*, *Self*, and *Vogue*. Augmented by a history of falling prey to the "vice" of reading popmags, this cursory survey has given me an overview of certain of their contents both feminist and otherwise. The choice of these magazines is subjective. They all, however, fall roughly into the category of beauty/fashion magazines designed to reach an audience of adult women, in contrast to teen magazines, such as *Seventeen* and *Sassy*, and service magazines (known in the industry as the "seven sisters"), such as *Ladies' Home Journal* and *Good Housekeeping*.

Women's magazines have covered most of the critical feminist issues of recent years. All have emphasized that women who are battered are never at fault, that the glass ceiling should be fought, that women should earn equal pay for equal work, that "no means no," that women have a right to fight unwelcome sexual advances, that men should be equal participants in housework and childcare responsibilities, and that the criminal and judicial system are prejudiced against rape victims (Doner 1993, p. 39). In the following pages, I want to take a brief look at some of the topics that women's magazines feature. As I hope to illustrate, there is definitely more in these pages than tips on applying mascara and losing weight.

Feminism

Some popmags discuss important issues within feminism on virtually a monthly basis, examining everything from gender discrimination faced by Muslim women (Goodwin 1994) to Betty Friedan on women and aging (J. Stone 1993).

For example, excerpts from feminist Naomi Wolf's book *Fire with Fire* (Wolf 1993a) first saw print in two articles in the pages of *Glamour* (Wolf 1993b; Wolf 1993c). While this book has been the subject of criticism and controversy among feminists (e.g., hooks 1994), it is clearly a work that defines itself as feminist and discusses feminist authors and issues. At the same time, these two Wolf articles provide a message that is highly palatable to the majority of readers of popmags. First, these excerpts adopt a self-esteem-boosting tone consistent with the pop psychology that is a staple of the women's magazine.[11] Wolf argues that women already have the power to achieve what they want if they can only learn how to use it. She urges women to throw off the mantle of "victim feminism" and to become "power feminists." While using the "f-word" and thus promoting the discussion of feminism (France 1993), Wolf's pieces also suggest a feminism geared toward the middle class. This version of feminism does not seek to profoundly shake up the status quo (hooks 1994). The economic order is not being challenged. This is a feminism that embraces, and suggests that all women learn from, their Republican sisters. While nonpartisan approaches are important for effective political action and bridge building (as exemplified, for example, by *Glamour*'s bipartisan "Women in Washington: What Have They Done for Us Lately?" feature), they also convey a feminism packaged for an audience perceived as requiring a nonthreatening message. Wolf herself is a nonthreatening messenger who "fits" in the pages of a popmag: She is conventionally attractive, wears makeup, and vigorously professes her

heterosexuality. Nevertheless, discussions of power feminism send out to women the clear statement that not only is feminism alive and well but that there is at least a version of feminism out there which they can embrace. Voices such as Wolf's in mainstream magazines allow stereotypes to be broken down. Do people really fear that being a feminist means being a lesbian? If the answer is yes, and that scares them away, then Wolf speaks to them. Not a profound message by most standards of feminist theory, but clearly one that some women reading popmags need for reassurance.

Popmags have also featured articles suggesting a reasonably nuanced critique of the encroachment of the public sphere on individual private lives. In her "think piece" on this issue in *Mirabella*, Wendy Kaminer (1994) discusses the pros and cons of the privacy rationale for *Roe v. Wade*, which has succeeded in protecting women's right to abortion but has also entitled government to withhold funding for abortion services. Kaminer brings in various issues that challenge the public/private dichotomy, such as the Supreme Court's decision upholding a Georgia sodomy law in *Bowers v. Hardwick*. She also discusses the feminist positions for and against restricting access to pornographic material. This essay brings up important legal issues and discusses them from a variety of perspectives. Although she uses the explosive and unfortunate Rush Limbaugh epithet "feminazi" to give her headline some additional punch ("Feminazis, Nous?"), Kaminer's piece is intelligent and portrays feminist visions of privacy, and law's place in regulating it, as multiple and complex. Immediately following Kaminer's piece is another thoughtful feminist essay by Ellen Willis decrying the media's portrayal of feminists as puritans and the likes of Katie Roiphe and Camille Paglia as the great prosex mavericks (Willis 1994). Instead, Willis focuses on the "pro-pleasure" stance that she argues was at the inception of the women's movement, exemplified by feminist activist Germaine Greer. She puts the blame for the antisex strain portrayed in the media not on feminism itself but, rather, on the overall social climate, characterized by its antiabortion terrorism, fear of AIDS, and hysteria over teenage sex and pregnancy.

Another example discusses issues of race and gender. In "From the Valley of the Chador," Jan

Goodwin (1994) discusses "gender apartheid" in Saudi Arabia, unmasking a phenomenon that, she argues, has long been thought of as a "personal problem" and revealing it to be a political issue that deserves attention from the international human rights community. The article takes the position that gender persecution should be a qualification for refugee status under international law and analyzes current immigration policy in Canada and the United States.

Even *Glamour*'s annual "Women of the Year" feature has an important feminist component. In that segment a diverse group of women are featured not for their looks but for their achievements. The section has an important role-modeling function and often shows women who have chosen nontraditional career paths.[12] Among the women who have been included in recent years are Supreme Court Justice Ruth Bader Ginsburg; Attorney General Janet Reno; then Surgeon General Joycelyn Elders; author and playwright Anna Deveare Smith;[13] New York sex crimes prosecutor Linda Fairstein; Mary-Claire Kind, a scientist researching genetic links to breast cancer; jockey Julie Krone; civil rights and children's rights activist Marian Wright Edelman; gun-control lobbyist Sarah Brady; author and columnist Anna Quindlen; law professor Anita Hill; politician Carol Moseley-Braun; and author Susan Faludi (Stern 1993; "Women of the Year" 1994).

This is not to say that all the discussion of feminism in women's magazines is hard-hitting and thought-provoking. For example, jumping on the Katie-mania bandwagon, *Mirabella* featured an interview with the young author by *her mother* (A. Roiphe 1993). While Roiphe the elder cautions, "Catharine MacKinnon is going to get you" and, later, "Catharine MacKinnon is definitely going to get you" (A. Roiphe 1993, p. 55) in response to some of her daughter's ideas, and wonders out loud, "Is it possible that from my liberal hearth I bred a reactionary? Have you turned into a neoconservative?" (A. Roiphe 1993, p. 54), the interview, not surprisingly, fails to seriously challenge Roiphe's argument that the prevalence of date rape and sexual harassment are both exaggerated by feminists, with the result that women are being forced back into the sexual stereotyping of the 1950s and being turned into victims. The *Mirabella* interview skirts the real problems with Katie Roiphe's book (hooks 1994,

p. 101; McCluskey 1997; Pollitt 1994a; Abrams 1994). It appears, on the whole, that popmags reflect current controversies within feminism rather than consciously choosing sides.

Thus, women's popmags do take on feminist issues and situate them in context for their readers. While not every piece on feminism published is nuanced or sophisticated, all of the pieces are serious, and the magazines do provide a place for feminist ideas to be aired and debated in front of a mainstream audience.[14]

Politics

Popmags have begun to develop a more sophisticated vision of what women are interested in reading. No longer simply providing information on "beauty" products, they have also begun to provide concrete data about the actions of federal and state governments on issues of interest to women. They have also begun to highlight the contributions of women in government all along the political spectrum. Not only are popmags talking about politics; they are also doing a great job. As Pat Reilly, director of communications of the National Women's Political Caucus, notes, "Women who aren't in publishing think that publications such as *Vogue* and *Glamour* that feature articles about fashion and beauty aren't geared to an audience who cares about politics or issues. That's not true. . . . *Vogue*'s political coverage was excellent and *Glamour*'s editorials were stupendous" (Doner 1993, pp. 39–40).

A few examples will serve to illustrate the kind of political reporting that is present in women's magazines. A monthly feature in *Glamour* entitled "Women in Washington: What Have They Done for Us Lately" chronicles the records of female politicians on issues of importance to women. A nonpartisan feature, this column is an up-to-date assessment of the importance of women in the political life of this country. A recent sample cited a study by the Capitol Hill Women's Political Caucus which found that while women made up just 11 percent of all members of the House of Representatives between August 1993 and June 1994, they introduced 42 percent of the bills concerning women and families (Marmon and Rubin 1995). The same column discussed the passage of Senator Carol Moseley-Braun's amendment promoting equity in college sports. *Mirabella* featured a story on the first female Prime Minister of Canada, labeling her a feminist (Swan 1993). *Glamour* has featured articles on Sarah Brady's antigun lobbying (Leive 1994a) and interviews with prominent female politicians (Britt 1993; Leive 1994b). *Mademoiselle* has also published state-by-state directories of the laws relating to issues of particular interest, from gun control to capital punishment to sodomy (Howard 1993).

These kinds of articles are feminist in several ways. First, they do not assume that women are only interested in reading about fashion, dieting, and makeup. They implicitly treat women as intelligent and multidimensional consumers who are well-informed and want to stay that way. In addition, they provide women with important role models—women who are featured for what they achieve rather than how they look. These magazines directly and indirectly promote the prochoice, antigun, "liberal-democratic" agenda that is largely consistent with many feminist political projects.[15] Finally, these articles are particularly useful to feminist lawyers, since they keep women abreast of legal developments and empower them to become active in influencing lawmakers and exercising their rights.

Health and Safety

Women's health issues receive prominent coverage in popmags. All the magazines routinely cover medical breakthroughs of general interest, as well as those of particular interest to women. *Glamour* featured the first breast self-exam column to appear in the popular media (Warren 1993). Other examples of issues that have been covered include an analysis of the dangers of pesticide residues on fruits and vegetables (Howkins 1994), women and aging (J. Stone 1993), ob-gyn patient abuse (Lever and Schwartz 1993), premenstrual syndrome and its fallacies (Tavris 1993), research on genetic links to breast cancer (Angier 1993), AIDS, the female condom (Raeburn 1995), endometriosis (Drexler 1995), and sexually transmitted diseases (Keehn 1994; "Women and the Chlamydia Epidemic" 1994; Monson 1993). In October 1994 most women's popmags featured lengthy and informative articles on breast cancer in recognition of breast cancer awareness month (Women, Men, and the Media 1994). Most of the magazines have monthly health columns that feature news about

recent medical breakthroughs. This style of reporting is exemplified by *Self*'s "Medical Flash!" monthly feature. In one month it reported the following eight medical news stories: the isolation of the gene that causes a rare form of breast cancer; the possibility that garlic fights colds; the heightened risk of ovarian cancer for women who take the fertility drug clomiphene; music's effectiveness in reducing the stress of operating surgeons; the addition of offices of women's health to the Food and Drug Administration (FDA) and the Centers for Disease Control; the increased risk of contracting AIDS for women suffering from a common vaginal infection; the availability of free reconstructive surgery to women who have been physically disfigured due to domestic violence; and the FDA requirement of certification for mammography clinics. All of this information is culled from reputable scientific sources, such as *Science*, *The New England Journal of Medicine*, and the *Journal of the American Medical Association* ("Medical Flash!" 1995).

Popmags took a particularly prominent position during the 1994 national debate over the future of health care in the United States. *Mirabella* sponsored symposia in Washington and New York on the health care question; these symposia featured Hillary Rodham Clinton (Hodge 1992). They also fully covered the issue and Clinton's contribution to it within the magazine (Mirabella 1993a; Mirabella 1993b). *Self* also sponsored a nine-city satellite question-and-answer forum on the Clinton administration's health care proposal; again, Clinton herself participated. *Glamour* also adopted an editorial position in favor of health care reform ("When It Comes to the New Health-Care System" 1994).

Women's magazines play a very important role in keeping women informed about the health of their own bodies. They provide unabashedly frank advice and information enabling women to take an active role in their medical care and choice. A recent example is a *Glamour* piece on the female condom. Not only did the article talk about FDA research; it also interviewed women and men who had used the female condom. Finally, the article came with an *illustrated* guide to the insertion and use of the female condom (Raeburn 1995). Throughout the article, emphasis was put on the importance of women's having control over the means to protect themselves from sexually transmitted diseases. The female condom was clearly seen as a way for women to assert greater responsibility and achieve greater autonomy over their sexuality and sexual health.

Eating disorders are also covered extensively in popmags (Douglass 1993; Anderson 1994; J. Sedgwick 1995; Gregory 1994). There is, of course, an irony to this coverage. While the articles decry American women's fixation on dieting and the dangers of eating disorders such as anorexia, bulimia, and the newly coined "body dysmorphic disorder" (Sanders 1994), they are surrounded by photographic representations of women ranging from "waif-like" to skeletal (Women, Men, and the Media 1994) and features on the latest diet (albeit likely a critique of anything about the diet that is unhealthy or lacks nutritional balance). Women are thus constantly being pulled in two directions at once—being held up to a bodily ideal that is probably impossible to realize, while being told that trying to achieve it can itself be detrimental to their health.[16]

Procreative Freedoms

Both legal and health issues related to procreative freedoms figure prominently in popmags. The abortion issue, for example, has been discussed within the pages of most popmags, including Glamour, New Woman, Ladies' Home Journal, Cosmopolitan, Vogue, Essence, and Mademoiselle (Doner 1993, p. 41). A national study showed that since Roe v. Wade, Glamour has run the most articles of any popmag on abortion and that it has consistently had a prochoice editorial stance (Ballenger 1992; Kaminer 1993b, p. 53), as well as maintaining a vocal editorial presence on procreative freedoms more generally (e.g., "Clinton's Reproductive Rights Report Card" 1994). At the same time, interestingly and provocatively, popmags have attempted to discuss a variety of perspectives on procreative choices, including those of men (Sturz 1993) and Christian women (Cunningham 1994). The ability to stray from feminist orthodoxy because of their mainstream readership may in fact allow popmags to publish a diversity of views, which can foster dialogue along the different sides of the abortion debate.

Women's mags are also one of the only places to which women can turn for information on innovative sources of birth control and conception inhibition. For example, popmags have documented the use of RU 486 (the so-called abortion pill) and the troubles getting the FDA to approve it for use in the United States even though it is widely, and safely, used in Europe (Christiano 1994). Similarly, popmags have provided information on the morning-after pill (Laird 1994; Benshoof 1995) and the woman's condom (Raeburn 1995).

Sexuality

Popmags also cover important issues to do with women's sexuality. For example, Glamour has a monthly column titled "Sex and Health." It has also featured articles on the Antioch College sex code, delving into the debate about sex and rape on college campuses (Wolff 1994), and on lesbians coming out at work (Sloan 1994). The latter is, I think, a particularly important article to appear in a mainstream women's magazine. Not only does it acknowledge diversity of sexual orientation, providing a more welcoming atmosphere for lesbian readers; it can also serve the important function of sensitizing women who may not knowingly have contact with lesbians in their day-to-day lives. By featuring an article on one aspect of lesbian experience in a heterosexist culture, the magazine can serve to normalize diversity. A similar effect is achieved by Glamour's making tennis star Martina Navratilova one of its 1994 "Women of the Year" and specifically calling attention to her gay rights activism ("Women of the Year" 1994). This point should however, not be overstated. The overwhelming assumption in popular women's magazines is of a heterosexual readership that is particularly concerned with their relationships with men. Thus, even an article in Essence suggesting that not everyone must marry is provocative in this context (Jones 1994).

Popular Culture

The media is also approached from a pro-women perspective in popmags. They make a point of featuring women prominently and critically examining popular culture for the way it portrays women. For example, Glamour has conducted end-of-the-year surveys of the portrayal of women in movies (A. Thompson 1994), and it approached the much-publicized David Letterman vs. Jay Leno "talk-show wars" of 1994 by asking when a *woman* was going to have a late-night talk show (Krupp 1994). Recently, *Essence* featured two articles with contrasting opinions on whether gangsta rap is anti-woman (T. Roberts 1994; Coker 1994).

Girls

When a study came out exploring the ways that girls are ill-served by the education system, women's magazines gave it prominent play. The magazines demonstrated an interest and concern over the way that girls are being harmed. Even *Elle*, a very fashion-focused monthly with relatively little coverage of politics or feminist issues, addressed this concern (E. Richardson 1994). *Mirabella* and *Glamour* both featured articles on how to prevent girls from losing their self-esteem as they reach puberty and on the role of traditional education in perpetuating this vicious cycle (S. Campbell 1994; O'Reilly 1994).

Another issue popmags frequently tackle is teen pregnancy. *Essence* featured an article rejecting the conventional media posture that teen mothers are inevitably doomed. Rather, the feature showed how teen mothers can nonetheless have full lives and explore their potential (De Witt 1994). It is significant, and perhaps not surprising, that *Essence*, a magazine aimed at an African American readership, would take this posture on the issue. Teen pregnancy in America has been constructed by much of the mainstream media as a problem with the African American community. By taking a contrasting approach, Deborah Gregory opens this issue up to further and less bipolar debate. This article also provides positive role models for young readers who are single moms. For women who see themselves portrayed in the media most often as social problems rather than individuals who still can play a valuable part in society, articles of this sort serve an important function.

Essence also featured a piece on the phenomenon of girls joining gangs, an article exploring the dimensions of racism and violence that confront adolescent girls in urban areas (Abner 1994). The article not only documents the problem but also suggests concrete measures that

women can follow in order to stem the tide of girls joining gangs.

Law

Articles about law and justice play a prominent role in these magazines, for which they rarely receive credit in the feminist community. For example, I mentioned earlier an important piece in *Mirabella* on the treatment of women persecuted because of their gender in Muslim countries under international law (Goodwin 1994), and the regular political coverage that is featured in many popmags. In addition, *Essence* has confronted the complicated issues of the intersection of gender and race in prison (J. Nelson 1994). *Glamour* has frequently discussed legal issues. For example, the magazine has featured an editorial on gender bias in the prison system ("Even in Prison, Men Get Better Treatment" 1994); it called attention to Clare Dalton's out-of-court settlement with Harvard University following Harvard Law School's decision to deny her tenure (Schillinger 1994); and it also featured an editorial on *Harris v. Forklift Systems* before the Supreme Court handed down its decision in that case ("The Sexual-Harassment Controversy" 1994). The editorial argued that the Supreme Court should overturn the decision of the Sixth Circuit and reject the severe psychological injury formula, which the Court went on to do in a 9–0 decision (*Harris v. Forklift Systems*).

Violence against women and its relation to gender bias is a topic that has been frequently discussed in popmags (Benderly 1994). In a recent article, *Self* examined whether courts are biased against women who kill their batterers (Hurt 1995). The article is accompanied by photographs by Donna Ferrato, a well-known chronicler of abused women (1991). The article discusses evidence that women who kill men are charged with more serious crimes and given longer sentences than men who kill women, despite the fact that the female defendants generally come to court with either no or many fewer prior convictions than their male counterparts. The article attributes this difference to the context of gender bias through which the justice system still sees women. The point is made that the difference in treatment between men and women is ironic, given that the vast majority of women who commit homicide are themselves victims of violence at the hands of men. The article cites U.S. government statistics showing that women commit only 10 percent of the homicides in the United States but that roughly 80 percent of those women convicted of killing a man claim to have been physically and/or sexually abused by their murder victims. As the author of the article puts it, "Gender bias in America's justice system is inextricably linked to how that system views domestic violence" (Hurt 1995, p. 120).

This same issue was the subject of a *Glamour* essay six months earlier written by Brenda Aris, a woman who had been convicted of shooting the husband who beat her and had been sentenced to fifteen years to life in prison (Aris 1994). That essay also includes a discussion of battered women's syndrome and the work of Dr. Lenore Walker, the psychologist who coined the term.

Another topic frequently addressed is rape and the reaction to it by the legal apparatus. For example, *Glamour's* article "Repeat Rapists: How Can We Stop Them?" discusses the legal responses to repeat sex offenders and the constitutionality of so-called predator laws (Draper 1994). Critical of these laws, the article suggests that they are at once too narrow and exaggerated, concentrating on the most sensational crimes, and that such laws fail to address the sex criminals who do not fit into the predator category, but who exist in much greater numbers, while shielded from the public spotlight (Draper 1994, p. 287; Jacoby 1994).

In "The Good News about Rape," Susan Bolotin, writing in *Elle*, interviews the head of the Sex Crimes Prosecution Unit of the New York County District Attorney's Office, Linda Fairstein (Bolotin 1993). The article reports on the positive changes in rape law—for example, the end to the requirement of corroboration of the rape victim's evidence and the passage of rape shield laws, generally forbidding cross-examination of victims on their prior sexual history. However, the article does not ignore the fact that not all the news is good—that rape continues to be the most underreported crime in the nation and that it has increased in frequency at a rate four times that of the general crime rate. In addition, the article reports the inadequacy of funding of both rape counseling services and

rape-crisis telephone help lines (Bolotin 1993, p. 91).

In popmags, violence against women is never trivialized.[17] Discussion of it is generally, thorough and provides an accurate representation of the state of the law. Features on the issues of domestic and sexual violence both enable women to be informed about some of the dangers they may face at the hands of criminals and warn them about gender bias within the justice system. At the same time, they encourage women to take an active role in combatting violence against women through alerting criminal prosecutors and their representatives in government to the importance of responding to violence (e.g., Bolotin 1993). Popmags thus provide a useful forum for feminist lawyers wanting to disseminate information about legal problems, developments in the law, and what women can do to more fully participate in the legal process. Lawyers like sex-crimes prosecutor Linda Fairstein clearly employ popmags to reach a broad cross section of women (e.g., Bolotin 1993; D. Carmody 1995).

Race

Essence consistently covers issues relating to women and race, which is not surprising, given its target audience and its mission to empower African American women (Doner 1993, p. 42; D. Carmody 1995). In the words of editor in chief Susan L. Taylor, "The mission of *Essence* . . . is to inspire, inform and uplift Black women, to help our sisters move their lives forward so that they can carry the word and thereby hopefully uplift our race" (D. Carmody 1995). The magazine has long had a decidedly feminist bent. Taylor's predecessor, longtime editor in chief Marcia Ann Gillespie (currently editor in chief of *Ms.*), describes herself as "a feminist who wears make-up and has high heels in her closet" (L. Wright 1994). *Essence* also serves the important function of providing a vehicle for cross-racial understanding. The magazine can give white women insight into the needs and interests of the African American community. This can be particularly useful to lawyers and judges. For example, Sarah Buel, a white assistant district attorney in Massachusetts and an adjunct professor at Boston College Law School, uses articles from *Essence* in her "Domestic Violence and the Law" course and other lectures. She advises whites to subscribe to the magazine. As she puts it, "There are tremendous stereotypes that even my colleagues make about African American women. *Essence* talks about issues in a way that would help white judges, police officers and prosecutors" (D. Carmody 1995).

One example of *Essence's* excellent coverage was in the wake of the Anita Hill/Clarence Thomas hearings, when it featured a twenty-one member roundtable of African Americans from academia, the arts, media, and politics discussing the topics "Should Blacks speak out against other Blacks?" and "Was a Black woman used to bring down a Black man?" (Doner 1993, p. 42).

While the other popmags are still insufficiently attentive to diversity among their readership, they are beginning to do a better job of confronting racism. While the photographic representations continue to be overwhelmingly of white women (Women, Men, and the Media 1994), features exploring issues related to race may be becoming more prominent. A notable example is a new monthly feature in *Glamour* called "Bridges," which deals specifically with women and race. The connection between body image and race was also explored in *Glamour's* pages in an article discussing a survey which found that black girls expressed more positive feelings about their bodies and overall looks than did white girls (Dominus 1995).

Concluding Thoughts

Popular women's magazines are not merely fluff and beauty "reporting." They *are* that, but they are also serious sources of hard news that report on issues of importance to women. Popmags allow women to be exceptionally well-informed on questions of health, violence against women, and the justice system, among other concerns. But as I have stated, popmags are far from ideal from a feminist perspective. The feminism contained within their pages is juxtaposed with visual portrayals of women which range from merely fantastical to dangerous. The magazines also contain countless articles on fashion and beauty, monthly diet and fitness advice, and the notorious "how to get and keep a man" features and "is he the man for you" multiple-choice quiz-

zes. This "nonfeminist" content is not an aside; it is why many women read these magazines. This stands to reason: If you want your feminism undiluted, you've got other alternatives, including *Ms.* But I suspect that there are many readers like myself: subscribers to *both* Ms. and *Glamour.*

Ms. is different. It has no advertisements at all—a decision made in order to evade the pressure with respect to content put on popmags by advertisers (Steinem 1994). It is unconcerned with exercise, diet, and fashion. What it does do is excellent advocacy journalism on a range of issues of concern to women in this country and around the world. Its coverage of most issues is much longer and deeper than the typical popmag's. It has made a noticeable effort to increase its coverage of international events. It has also increased its efforts to represent a plurality of women's voices in the wake of criticism of its white, middle-class bias. For example, it featured a roundtable discussion on the nature of feminism with bell hooks, Gloria Steinem, Urvashi Vaid, and Naomi Wolf ("Let's Get Real about Feminism" 1993). Ms. is an excellent source of feminist news and cultural reporting, and I faithfully devour each issue.

But feminists can have interests other than feminism. Some feminists work out and want information about new exercise trends and equipment. Some feminists cook and want new recipes. Some feminists work in office jobs and want tips on managing the boss. Some feminists dress up to go out and want to see the latest in the little black dress. Some feminists even have "boyfriend" trouble and don't mind getting a little free advice (even if they probably take what they find in popmags with a grain of salt).

At the same time, women who might not label themselves feminists in a million years still want to know if a "harmless" treatment they are being given by their doctor causes cancer. They want to know if there is a new birth control method out there which is safe and effective but which is being stalled by right-wing prolife forces. They want to know if the spouse who beats them is going to be privileged by judges and courts. They want to know if their mother, who has been raped, stands a fair chance of seeing justice done in court.

Popular women's magazines do not meet every woman's need. Yet they do serve an important role and should not be dismissed by feminists. "Serious" authors and journalists do not hesitate to cover important issues in a magazine like *Playboy*, or introduce their fiction in *Esquire*. They do not seem to fear that because, for example, those readers pay to look at pictures of naked women, they are unable to understand or are not interested in weighty topics. But I fear that feminists write off popmags because their work would have to share space with mascara ads and fashion features.

It is critical that women doing and writing feminism find forums to disseminate their ideas that will reach women who are not necessarily already the "converted." Feminism must reach over the walls of academe, past the specialty left-leaning repositories, such as *Ms.*, *Lillith*, *Tikkun*, and *The Nation*, to a wider audience. Popmag readers are this audience. They are reading, voting, writing their representatives in Washington. Feminists need to be speaking and listening to them.

Notes

I wish to thank Lorne Sossin for his invaluable insights, and Martha McCluskey and Marcia Sells for their helpful comments. I would also like to thank Marlene Sanders of the Columbia Journalism School for providing me with the Women, Men, and the Media study cited herein. In addition, I gratefully acknowledge the financial support of the Social Sciences and Humanities Research Council of Canada, the Canada-U.S. Fulbright Program, and the Columbia University School of Law.

1. For a lively discussion of controversies within feminist theory, see Hirsch and Fox Keller 1990. For an example of the more self-pitying dynamic in the context of a critique of women's studies programs, see Patai and Koertge 1994. For an interesting discussion of this latter trend, see Sternhell 1994.

2. Susan Douglas (1994, p. 272) describes this phenomenon as the "I'm not a feminist but . . ." cliché, meaning that such women espouse all of the benefits reaped by the women's movement while still shaving their legs, wearing makeup, and not wanting to be thought of as a man-hater—that is, while not wanting to take on the baggage of the "feminist stereotype."

3. See also the *Time* cover story "Women Face the '90s: In the '80s they tried to have it all. Now they've just plain had it. Is there a future for feminism?" (Wallis 1989). Clearly, this is not a new discussion.

The irony of the *Marie Claire* survey is that in the same issue of the magazine are several articles that have feminist content. See Laver 1994 (the story of a Canadian member of the British Columbia legislature who lost custody of her children because the judge found that she was too ambitious); Ball 1994 (profiling successful women); Walt 1994 (discussion of the role of women in South Africa); Hinton 1994 (first-person account of surviving ovarian cancer).

4. A Lexis search of major papers and magazines performed on February 2, 1995, came up with 345 references to Katie Roiphe.

5. I should point out that for the purposes of this article I am adopting a rather generous definition of "feminist." Thus, I think discussions that are undermined, for example, because they are insufficiently attentive to differences among women or among feminists themselves, are still important contributions to the mainstream media offerings to women.

6. As Naomi Wolf (1990, pp. 71–72) points out, "What is seldom acknowledged is that [women's magazines] have popularized feminist ideas more widely than any other medium—certainly more widely than explicitly feminist journals. It was through these glossies that issues from the women's movement swept out from the barricades and down from the academic ivory towers to blow into the lives of working-class women, rural women, women without higher education. Seen in this light they are very potent instruments of social change."

7. Kalia Doner (1993) cites the following circulation figures: *Glamour*, 2.1 million; *Vogue*, 1.2 million; *Mademoiselle*, 1.2 million; *Elle*, 900,000; *Harper's Bazaar*, 770,000; *Mirabella*, 600,000; *Cosmopolitan*, 2.7 million; *Self*, 1.4 million. *Essence's* circulation topped 1 million for the first time in 1993 (D. Carmody 1995). By contrast, *Ms.* has a circulation of only approximately 100,000 to 200,000 (Schlosberg 1992 quotes the 100,000 figure. In a telephone conversation with the *Ms.* circulation department I was quoted the 200,000 figure as an approximation, since the magazine is not audited).

8. What Kalia Doner (1993, p. 37) calls "a confusing hodgepodge of self-loathing attitudes and empowering opinion," Susan Douglas (1994, pp. 271–72) describes as the "schizophrenic landscape" of women's popmags, "in which editorials, advice columns, and articles urge us to be assertive, strong, no-nonsense feminists while the fashion and beauty layouts insist that we be passive, anorexic spectacles whose only function is to attract a man and who should spend our leisure time mastering the art of the pedicure." Douglas has also been quoted as saying, "We're getting mixed messages. . . . In the front [of women's magazines] there are pieces on feminist artists, how to ask for a pay raise, how to fix a transmission. But in the back it's how to develop thighs the size of a 12-year-old boy" (M. Goldstein 1994).

9. The Women, Men, and the Media study (1994) looked at nine popmags (*Allure*, *Harper's Bazaar*, *Cosmopolitan*, *Elle*, *Essence*, *Glamour*, *Ladies' Home Journal*, *Mirabella*, and *Vogue*) during the month of October

1994 to determine how women are portrayed in advertising and editorial photos.

Susan Bordo (1993b, pp. 263–65) points out that while *Essence* consistently tries to promote diverse images of African American beauty in its pages, its efforts are thwarted by its advertisers, who insist on using images of straight-haired, light-eyed, and light-skinned models: "This ongoing battle over the black woman's body and the power of its 'differences' ('differences' which actual black women embody to widely varying degrees, of course) is made manifest in the twentieth-anniversary issue, where a feature celebrating 'The Beauty of Black' faced an advertisement visually legislating virtually the opposite (and offering, significantly, 'escape' [at Casual Corner, a clothing store]). . . . This invitation to cognitive dissonance reveals what *Essence* must grapple with, in every issue, as it tries to keep its message of African American self-acceptance clear and dominant, while submitting to economic necessities on which its survival depends. Let me make it clear here that such self-acceptance, not the reverse tyranny that constructs light-skinned and Anglo-featured African Americans as 'not black enough,' is the message *Essence* is trying to convey, against a culture that *denies* 'the Beauty of Black' at every turn. This terrain, clearly, is not a playground but a minefield that constantly threatens to deconstruct 'difference' *literally* and not merely literarily."

10. A study published in the *Journal of Social and Clinical Psychology* found that women who spent a lot of time watching television and reading women's magazines were more likely to develop eating disorders and to be dissatisfied with their appearance than women who did not. (Hiscock 1994).

11. For example, "It doesn't matter anymore if 'society is ready' for women to attain equal status. Ready or not, society no longer has the power to stop us. The question is not whether society is ready to yield gender equality, but whether women themselves are ready to take possession of it" (Wolf 1993c, p. 223).

12. Portraying women in nontraditional careers and encouraging women to surmount barriers based on their gender is an important feature of popmags. See, for example, Cain 1994 (photo spread of African American women who are successful in business); S. Mahoney 1994; Pinkney 1994; Dominus 1994 (describing successful American Airlines flight attendant strike); "Women Crime-Fighters" 1994 (describing the first women Texas Rangers elite firefighters).

13. Who has also been profiled in *Essence* ("People: . . . Anna Deveare Smith" 1994).

14. Contrast the now-notorious mocking coverage of the so-called 'new feminism' in a well-respected men's magazine, *Esquire* (Friend 1994; E. J. Carroll 1994; Goodman 1994a). The article pitted feminists against each other, portrayed (with obvious approval) the "new" "do-me feminists" as prosex and promen, and distorted the words of many of the feminists it quoted (hooks 1994, pp. 73–81).

15. Of course, this is not to imply that a "liberal-democratic" agenda is the only feminist agenda, nor that this agenda itself is not subject to feminist criticism.

Victoria Sackett (1984, p. 47) pays *Glamour* a backhanded complement by criticizing the editorial stance of the magazine as anti-Reagan and anti-Republican: "The magazine has come to believe that its readers are interested in no policies other than those loosely defined as 'women's issues,' and that they are of one mind about them. Several editorials have been directed against Reagan and his job performance, one a letter to be mailed to the magazine, that would be forwarded to the president. Readers were asked to check items from 'the list of concerns that *I* consider most urgent' [emphasis in the original]. There followed a series of those things *Glamour* considered most urgent: "legal—therefore safe—abortions for all women, and increased federal funding for rape victims, victims of domestic violence, day care, and women in business."

16. Women, Men, and the Media (1994) found that of 243 images it studied, only fourteen depicted women over forty, while the vast majority (211) showed women in their twenties. Similarly, while *Glamour* can feature Betty Friedan critiquing the way that our society deals with women and aging, the visual representations in popmags are overwhelmingly of very young women.

Neither my study nor Women, Men, and the Media distinguishes between photographic representations in editorials and advertisements. In their effect on women's sensibilities there is little difference. Nor is there any real difference in their content. Editorial photographs are in essence advertisements meant to create hospitable environments for the paying advertisers: they include credits with information on where to buy every element of the representation, including makeup and clothing.

17. However, the coverage of violence may be relatively partial. For example, violence within same-sex relationships is not given the same coverage that violence within heterosexual couples is.

II

FEMINISM, LAW, AND POPULAR CULTURE

8

Introduction

SUSAN BISOM-RAPP

Popular culture is a fertile analytical site for feminist legal theory. Reaching an audience of millions, mass media both reflects and shapes social attitudes and increasingly provides a forum for political and cultural debates, particularly those that implicate law. It alternately functions as an instrument for social change and a tool for restabilizing or reconfiguring the status quo. As such, its analysis can provide feminists working in law with a barometer for gauging the impact of their ideas and with a point from which strategy can be formulated.

The essays in part II focus on the representation of law, legal issues, and lawyers in visual media, specifically television and Hollywood movies. Central to this inquiry is whether and how these media articulate feminist concerns about law. The answers given are diverse and complex, contingent to a great extent on the genre and topic each scholar explores. Indeed, the essays validate the feminist precept that one's perspective changes what one sees.

Arguing against the grain of "backlash" the-

ory, Elayne Rapping and Dianne Brooks offer relatively optimistic assessments of feminism's impact on televised legal narratives. Rapping examines the television docudrama and argues that it provides space for feminist ideas about law to enter public discourse and gain authority. Focusing on *The Burning Bed*, the dramatization of the precedent-setting Francine Hughes case, which established the battered women's syndrome defense, she exposes the strengths and weaknesses of the genre as a vehicle for feminist ideology. Brooks analyzes the evolution of the rape narrative on daytime television soap operas and finds that feminist themes and issues are significantly present in current rape plots.

Isabel Karpin is less sanguine about television's representation of law. Analyzing coverage of three recent child custody and visitation cases on news programs, on talk shows, and in docudrama, she observes that feminist insight on the construction of the "natural" family was almost entirely absent. Instead, societal trauma over the breakdown of the biologically based, patriarchal

87

nuclear family was stabilized by reconfiguring the "natural" family paradigm into one that is paternally governed and based on psychological bonds.

Margaret Russell and Cynthia Lucia each provide troubling appraisals of Hollywood films. Russell looks at the role of African American women in movies about women and the legal system and finds their stories subject to absence, erasure, and distortion. Lucia surveys films about white women lawyers and concludes that these "heroines" are depicted as dangerously ambitious and professionally and personally deficient, in need of the instruction and heroic intervention of men in all aspects of their lives.

Representation of Feminist Concerns

Whether and how popular culture represents feminist concerns about law depends on who controls the medium, whose gaze is legitimated by it, and whose narratives are left out or distorted in the process. Interestingly, these essays indicate that it is in those genres traditionally maligned as feminine—the daytime soap opera and the TV movie—that feminist ideas have had the greatest impact. That women play a significant part in producing docudramas and soaps, and that both genres are aimed at a female audience, inform both Rapping's and Brooks's insights.

These factors influence more than the selection for dramatization of legal issues that are important to women; they affect the perspective from which the issues are presented. Francine Hughes's story is presented from the "female gaze." Current rape plots are depicted from the subject position of the victim.

In contrast, Russell connects the exclusion of African American women from Hollywood filmmaking to the marginality of black female characters in movies about women and the legal system. These stories are told from the dominant white gaze; the perspectives of minorities are peripheral; cultural myths about them proliferate; their narratives are invisible. Lucia similarly connects the lack of media control—of the films she reviews, only one was directed by a woman—to the negative portrayals of white women lawyers in mainstream movies.

Portrayal of the Legal System

Popular portrayal of the legal system is also a concern of these scholars. The authors conceptualize law as a dominant ideology which is masculine, preoccupied with finding truth, protecting society from disruption, and ensuring that justice is done. Rapping argues that despite its feminist bent, *The Burning Bed* validates and valorizes this ideology through Francine Hughes's white male lawyer, a fictitious heroic character who leads the audience to a feminist understanding of his client's story. Lucia observes a similar ideological embrace in female lawyer films, contending that these movies are vehicles for restoring law and patriarchy to uncontested positions. Brooks, in contrast, notes that soaps represent law in a way that is consonant with feminist teachings: as a system that often misfunctions and fails to protect women. All three scholars imply that challenges to the legal system and its animating ideology are an advance for feminism.

Karpin makes the issue complex by demonstrating that destabilizing patriarchal ideology and institutions does not necessarily lead to feminist outcomes. For example, the return of two-year-old Baby Jessica by her adoptive parents to her biological father was represented on television as a misfunctioning of the rigid, uncaring, rule-bound legal system. Yet in endorsing a different legal outcome—that the child should have remained with her adoptive parents—television ratified a psychologically based nuclear family that is structurally identical to the old patriarchal one.

Karpin explains that by weighing in against biological distinctions, televised coverage of the three cases suppressed the birth mothers' narratives and their bodily connection to their children. These missing stories, like the invisible narratives of African American women noted by Russell, precluded feminist ideas from entering the virtual debate.

Ironically, the logic informing popular representation of these cases is the formal equality paradigm, which in most cases precludes legal distinctions based on sex and, by extension, biology; the very model endorsed by some liberal legal feminists. Thus, what appears to be a liberal feminist position ends up privileging men and disadvantaging birth mothers.

The Resilience of Patriarchal Norms

Karpin's observations demonstrate that patriarchal norms and values are ubiquitous in popular culture, a recurrent theme in these essays. Lucia for example, explains that while women lawyer films seem at first blush feminist in character—white women are portrayed as active, powerful professionals—the movies mask a deep, conservative patriarchal ideology. This ideology is expressed in a number of ways: In some movies the attorneys' biological fathers are central to the plots; in others a male lover or potential lover instructs the female lawyer, even though he has no legal training; often a powerful, older male lawyer initiates the female lawyer into legal culture; "thinking like a lawyer" is often equated with "thinking like a man"; the female lawyer advances her career at great personal cost; many times order is restored when the lawyer, through the legal process and often due to male intervention, discovers the "truth" about her client or case; and perhaps most tellingly, in some films the lawyer's ambitions are quelled when she falls in love with a good man.

Rapping, too, is attentive to the resilience of patriarchal values, which she recognizes may compromise the feminist messages she discerns in *The Burning Bed*. While the docudrama effectively challenges the norms that proscribe female violence under any circumstances, this is accomplished by reinforcing norms about the family, motherhood, and middle-class values. Hughes is depicted as a perfect mother, acting to protect her children and to further her aspirations to a middle-class existence, characterizations that track with the sponsors' goal of selling consumer products during commercial breaks, though not with the real Francine Hughes.

Brooks similarly finds that soap opera rape plots simultaneously disrupt traditional patriarchal orthodoxy and reinforce it. Although the fraternity gang rape of a drunken college student may be portrayed from the victim's perspective, soap opera's stylistic conventions undermine potential feminist insights. Rape victims are usually represented at trial and through the forensic investigatory process by men, giving males a heroic stature. Victims and assailants are white, perpetrating the myth that women of color are not or cannot be raped. Convicted rapists are ultimately reintegrated into the community, eclipsing the reality of recidivism and the systemic nature of violence against women. Nevertheless, she and Rapping admonish that while the messages transmitted may be mixed, soaps and docudramas can play a significant role in changing popular understanding of and disseminating feminist ideas about law.

A skeptic might wonder whether this optimism is warranted. Patriarchal values do appear intractable, if not insuperable, potentially diluting, if not negating, feminist ideas. Yet even Karpin, whose analysis of television is much less encouraging, offers a glimmer of hope that television can become a space for floating alternative feminist narratives. She argues that television is an especially powerful medium for interrogating legal outcomes because it can reveal and comment on the effects of legal decision-making.

Karpin demonstrates that this property of television actually enabled an advocate for birth mothers to give voice to their legal concerns about the Baby Jessica case. Karpin locates this rupture in the patriarchal-versus-paternal-family construct in a few moments of dialog on the CNN issue program *Crossfire*.

Increasing Feminist Access and the Role of Viewer Agency

All of the essays suggest a vital question: How can feminists gain greater influence over the messages deployed in popular culture? In part I, Julia Hanigsberg suggested that they engage with it directly by, for example, writing articles for women's fashion magazines. Whether the editors of those publications would accept such articles is unclear, although ironically, the fact that fashion magazines, like soaps and docudramas, are devalued as feminine offers reason for hope.

It is more certain that access to elite genres like Hollywood filmmaking is extremely limited. Feminists hoping to influence moviemaking probably need to rely on less direct strategies.

One possible strategy is to focus on viewers. The promise of visual media to provide space for feminist counternarratives depends as much on viewer reception as it does on the construction and presentation of the narratives themselves. None of the authors see viewers as passive recipients of popular culture; rather, viewers are considered active interpretive agents. Russell advocates critical spectatorship as a way to surmount and "talk back to" the sexist and racist assumptions undergirding Hollywood films, noting that this can be a powerful pedagogical tool.

Rapping, too, recommends oppositional viewing, arguing for a shift in the producer/viewer paradigm so that feminist activists, teachers, and writers who interpret media texts are considered part of text construction.

Lucia's focus is somewhat different. She wonders what, exactly, different viewers make of the predictable outcomes in many of the female lawyer films. Recall, for example, that order is restored when the lawyer, through the legal process and often due to male intervention, discovers the "truth" about her client or case; and quite frequently, the film ends when the lawyer's ambitions are quelled because she falls in love with a good man. Does the gap between such uncomplicated closure and the viewer's own experience alter interpretation of the film? Or is the viewer's need for reassurance paramount? And is that need for reassurance not disruptive of itself?

Such questions point to issues that might be explored further. First, in the active process of interpreting popular culture, what are viewers getting? Karpin provides a partial answer, noting that a CNN–USA *Today* Gallup poll found that eight out of ten people believed that Baby Jessica should have been left with her adoptive parents, indicating that they accepted the predominant view presented by the media. One wonders whether the results would have been as overwhelming if the narrative of the birth mother had been extensively aired.

Next, how do viewers negotiate meaning? Brooks sheds light on how soap opera fans make sense of these media texts. She notes that fans discuss the programs extensively, a process that merits further examination.

Finally, how does interpretation change based on gender, race, and class? Brooks posits that women of color may be able to read the "double text" of soap opera plots. Is this so? Russell advocates teaching students the art of critical reading so that they can engage in the process themselves. As effective as this approach may be, is it too limited? What is the best way to teach a broad and diverse audience alternative ways to read media texts? Hanigsberg, with her suggestion that academic feminists find new vehicles for their messages, may be on to something important.

Conclusion

The essays in this section, in varying forms, advocate releasing feminist and antiracist narratives into popular culture. Of course, deploying counternarratives in no way guarantees their embrace. Indeed, I would argue that consumers of popular culture are adept at discounting ideas they deem too progressive. The common signal for dismissal of such ideas is assigning to them the derisive label "politically correct." Yet the power of mass media is undeniable. If feminists hope to influence the structure of our political and cultural debates, they must turn their attention to and engage with it.

9

The Movie of the Week

Law, Narrativity, and Gender on Prime Time

ELAYNE RAPPING

When *The Burning Bed* aired on prime time in October 1984, it drew 75 million viewers, becoming one of the highest-rated movies (theatrical or made-for-TV) in TV history, a distinction it still holds. This made-for-TV movie dramatized the precedent-setting case of Francine Hughes, the battered wife who set her husband's bed on fire after seventeen years of abuse and was acquitted of murder by reason of temporary insanity. In the decade since its original airing, *The Burning Bed* has taken its place among the ranks of TV texts which have come to be considered "major media events." In their original airing and through subsequent media circulations in reruns, classroom and community screenings, video rentals, and the endless use of selected clips and references in contexts too numerous and diverse to count, these TV texts have entered the public sphere (now largely constituted within the televisual frame, which is our common symbolic "home") and have permanently affected public consciousness and discourse around key public issues.

In the brief time—less than a decade—since *The Burning Bed*'s first airing, of course, the growth of cable and narrow-casting has exponentially increased the number and power of such publicly significant media events, as well as the confusion over their nature and role in public life. Not only are we now experiencing major political and legal events—the Hill-Thomas hearings, the William Kennedy Smith rape trial, the Rachel Kingsley parental "divorce" trial, the Menendez parricide trial, and the O. J. Simpson murder trial are only the most dramatically obvious examples—through commercially mediated structures; we are also exposed to endless streams of commercially mediated representational and discursive "takes" on such important events and issues, after the fact, through endless news, talk and public affairs programs, and soap operas, sitcoms, and dramatic series.[1]

Amid this welter of material, the made-for-TV movie, or docudrama, I will argue, continues to maintain a central place among representational genres that deal with key social issues—

especially issues of gender and the law. Moreover, for a variety of economic, political, and dramatic reasons, it is within the docudrama form that feminist positions have most often, and most interestingly (although always within hegemonic limits and with serious contradictions) been put forth on commercial television. Indeed, I will argue against the grain of certain aspects of "backlash" theory, which see the media, especially television, as a monolithically misogynist force working against the ideas and gains of feminism. Instead, in many significant cases the docudrama has opened up space within which oppositional feminist ideas and values have been able to intervene in public debates and gain a certain amount of authority. Indeed, in many cases the efforts of feminist legal activists to intervene in courtroom procedures, in the interest of gender justice, have been furthered, intertextually, by the efforts of feminist-influenced TV movie producers who have taken their courtroom arguments (watered down and dramatized in problematic ways I will explore) to a broader audience.

In this sense, TV movies and the many people who participate in their construction—from the actual actors in the "real" events on which they are based, to the producers, writers and directors, even to the millions of viewers whose opinions are "consulted" in various direct and indirect ways—become participants in the complex processes by which social change takes place.

In saying this, I am employing a model of media power relations and dynamics that needs to be at least briefly explained. The common "spectacle/spectator" model assumes a binary, static "them/us" relationship between (active, intentional) media producers and (passive, unaware) viewers, to whom media texts "happen" or "are done." Instead, I am conceptualizing the media in terms of a far more dynamic and complex relationship between texts and reality in which the production process itself is understood as a complex set of power relationships, crossing many social, ideological lines and affecting and being affected by many differently constituted, but always gendered, subjects and agents.

My model of media power relations comes largely from Foucault's conception of power: that "power's condition of possibility . . . must not be sought in the primary existence of a central point, in a unique source of sovereignty" but, rather, that it must be understood as "the multi-

plicity of force relations imminent in the sphere in which they operate . . . as the process which through ceaseless struggles and confrontations, transforms, strengthens or reverses; as the support which these force relations find in one another, thus forming a chain or system, or, on the contrary, the disjunctions and contradictions; and lastly as the strategies in which they take effect." Thus, he has written, "power is exercised from innumerable points in the interplay of nonegalitarian and mobile relations" (Foucault 1978, pp. 16, 92–93; see also Grossberg 1992, pp. 37–67).

If we apply this dynamic model of power relations to commercial media relations—and it is, I believe, a particularly apt model for the current media situation—we can begin to see the docudrama of gender justice as a form in which feminists do indeed participate at many levels and points in time. Nor would I limit my understanding of feminist participation in the construction of gendered legal docudramas to the real-life actors in the original cases and the network production personnel. On the contrary, feminists as activists, teachers, writers, and so on, during the course of time in which ideas and strategies relating to certain legal issues are constructed and circulated throughout society generally, do participate in the process of textual construction in ways too diverse and diffuse to be recognized and counted.

If we add to this formulation of media relations certain feminist political theories of how oppositional forces come to be constituted and to enter public life, the political role of docudramas, as interventions into public discourse, becomes clearer. Teresa de Lauretis speaks of "women," for example, as "empirical/historical subjects" who participate in the construction of "the fictional construct 'woman'" through discursive practices, of which television is surely a central one (de Lauretis 1984, p. 5). And Nancy Fraser speaks of television as a central element of the "public sphere," within which feminists, as oppositional voices, do indeed intervene and work to revise and reconstruct hegemonic discourses, as part and parcel of their other agitational and discursive activities, in the classroom, the courtroom, the streets, wherever. "However limited a public may be in its empirical manifestation at any given time," she writes, "its members understand themselves as part of a potentially wider public," whose goal it is to enter the "structured setting where cultural and ideological contest or negotiation among a variety of publics takes place" in the interest of realizing their "emancipatory potential" for "agitational activity" (Fraser 1991, pp. 67–68). Docudramas about gendered legal issues clearly exist in such a setting.[2]

In fact, because of its history and nature, the docudrama is a particularly interesting textual intervention within which various power struggles are played out, with varying results, depending on the conditions of each case. And for reasons I shall trace, it has often allowed far more leeway to feminists than most. TV movies about trials involving rape, date rape, surrogacy, sexual harassment, incest, abortion, unequal working conditions, and more are staples of the form. Indeed, more than 50 percent of all TV movies feature female protagonists dealing with a (usually gendered) social issue, broadly defined (Rapping 1992). Moreover, by its very nature and position within the hierarchy of media texts, the docudrama has come (again, in its best moments) to carry more authority and influence in the larger social world than such forms as soap opera, sitcoms, and talk shows, because of its scheduling position, promotional machinery, star power, and claim to social or historical "seriousness."

To demonstrate all of this and evaluate its significance, I have chosen to focus on a single case, that of *The Burning Bed* and its portrayal of domestic violence. In its construction, and in its complex aftermath, it has most obviously played a role in the changing debates and assumptions about domestic violence over the last decade and in the changing conditions—in the courts, the social service institutions, and the criminal justice agencies—within which acts of domestic violence and retaliations against them are now understood and dealt with.

Contested Narratives: Gender and Genre on Network Television

It is no accident that gender issues seem to be figuring more and more prominently in courtrooms and on TV screens these days. We are living in a "postfeminist" era, by which I mean only that many of the most explosive and oppositional ideas put forth by Second Wave feminists in the 1960s and 1970s, relating to sex, gender, and family relations, have dramatically altered the

terms on which public debate and political and legal negotiations now are conducted. Though we feminists have not, certainly, overturned the dominant patriarchal discourses and narratives that construct our common social lives, we have most certainly altered them. That is, we have successfully challenged the patriarchal assumptions and norms of gender relations at least to the extent that traditional masculinist rules and customs are no longer unquestionably allowed to prevail. Rather, in courtrooms, on TV screens, and in boardrooms, bedrooms, and most other sites of gender negotiation, feminist challenges to male hegemony are in play, sometimes successfully so.

From this perspective, feminism—even when the "backlash" is at its most powerful and vicious—has changed the terms on which major discussions of gender issues take place, for now and forever. No more can the male power structure blithely assume that its "business as usual" approach to gender issues will go unchallenged. The 1993 unanimous Supreme Court ruling on sexual harassment, *Harris v. Forklift Systems, Inc.*[3]—intriguingly concurred with by the two most recent appointees at the time, Thomas and Ginsburg—reveal, for example, that in the matter of workplace gender relations, feminist theorists and agitators have indeed changed at least some of the terms informing constitutional legal proceedings.

The strategies of trial lawyers and TV producers have much in common in cases in which foundational, patriarchal assumptions about gender (and class) are at stake. The cases of such women as Francine Hughes, Mary Beth Whitehead, Nancy Ziegenthaler, and others—all of which have been represented in docudramas—make these commonalities clear. In both arenas, we have what amounts to a battling out of competing narratives about gender (and class) relations, each based on a particular set of cultural and political assumptions about men and women and power and desire.

Again and again, in these cases, whether mediated through legal or televisual constructs—and in both arenas, the Hughes case was typical—we have two opposing versions of reality, one based on traditional patriarchal master narratives, the other on feminist efforts to amend or replace those narratives with oppositional, feminist versions of what the facts and incidents might really signify. (The number and import of actual factual disagreements may differ from case to case, but in every instance, such cases will feature arguments involving interpretation of even the most undeniable facts, in accordance with the different, gendered, assumptions about their import.) And it is within the public arenas of the actual courtroom and its popularly mediated film and TV representations that we, as a public, come to learn and (in cases where feminism makes inroads) relearn the gender lessons that regulate our common lives.

In the Hughes case, the issue at stake was violence—where and when violence is appropriate and acceptable; where and when it should be punished or given social sanction—a matter on which the rules are always heavily gendered within patriarchy for obvious reasons involving the social control of women. In the actual courtroom, and on screen, what was enacted was a (feminist) challenge to the master narratives by which men, within patriarchy, have been given permission to violate women, while women, under no circumstances, have been allowed to exercise similarly violent impulses, even in self-defense. In all our master narratives, whether legal or dramatic, women who kill or maim are demonized and purged, while men, in all but a few circumstances, are naturalized and authorized. But with the advent of feminist legal challenges to these norms in the courts, and the related advent of representational versions of such cases—most often through docudrama—we have begun to see these narrative models challenged, more and more often and successfully.[4]

It may be objected, at this point, that my analogy between television and courtroom drama breaks down at the point of production, so to speak. Feminist legal theorists and attorneys, after all, act intentionally and politically in the construction of their oppositional narratives and assumptions when they challenge patriarchal legal precepts. Television producers, by contrast, it is usually assumed, act blindly in the interest of the capitalist, patriarchal media, seen as a misogynist monolith.

But this is the very assumption I am challenging in this analysis. I want to argue, rather, that both the legal system and the media are dominantly and pervasively sexist, by virtue of the dominant texts and narratives and ideologies which inform them and upon which they are built. Nonetheless, in complex ways, feminist and other oppositional forces—in *both* areas—do indeed intervene and challenge dominant precepts, texts, and narratives at every turn, and in parallel ways. Just as there are feminists, and those influenced by feminism (by choice or force) working within media, so there are such people working within the legal system as well. Every judge who is forced to assent to newly declared, feminist-informed laws and precepts regulating sexual harassment (Clarence Thomas's vote on the 1993 sexual harassment decision, again, is the most dramatic example of this), no matter what his or her own personal feeling, has been forced, in effect, to act in the interest of feminist ideas of gender justice. And by the same token, every corporation or network executive who is convinced, on financial grounds—as so many are in the wake of successful ventures like *The Burning Bed*—to sponsor or fund feminist-inspired dramas because women audiences and consumers watch them, has been similarly coerced. And if this is not always, or even usually, the case, it is nonetheless the case often enough (once is often enough) to make a difference. In Nancy Fraser's formulation of feminist opposition within the public sphere, such textual and legal interventions are a form of political agitation.

It is worth noting briefly at this point that the participation of women, many of whom are feminists, or at least influenced by feminist ideas, in the media workforce—as a direct result of feminist agitation and propaganda in the last decade—has grown enormously. And it is television, far more than the movie industry, that has opened its doors to women, especially in high positions. This is because, first, TV is less prestigious and therefore less likely to be tied to an Old Boys' Network mentality; and second, TV, as I've said, pays more attention to women viewers because of its commercial nature and therefore seeks out women staff more often.

To be sure, feminist victories in any sphere are exceptional cases in the sense that the dominant narratives and ideologies and laws *remain* dominant and stand, against the impact of such oppositional texts and rulings, as symbols of the ultimate power of patriarchy. Nonetheless, the struggle continues, legally and textually, as power is continuously challenged and hegemony chipped away at. This is true even within the context of a powerful backlash. The Foucaultian formulation of power struggles allows for setbacks and defeats without giving up the game, since the game is so complex and internally varied.

The Feminization of Prime Time/The Prime-Timing of Feminism

Feminists, then, and those who are influenced by or represent feminist ideas, do indeed participate in subtle and dramatic ways in the construction of TV movies, at every stage of the process by which they come into being, are aired, and then intervene in subsequent public events and discourse. As my case study will show, feminist activists, feminist and feminist-influenced creative staff, feminist-influenced viewers and consumers, and—not least—feminist-influenced women whose lives become textualized all participate indirectly or directly in the decisions by which such movies are produced. This participation may take place at every level, including conception, the pitch, the actual production, the marketing, the promotional strategy, and the framing structures that surround and identify such movies.

Nor is it accidental that the docudrama so often presents such cases. Dramatically and commercially, the TV movie was in fact developed expressly for this purpose. It is, at its best at least, the form the networks most often choose when they decide to do the kind of "classy," "serious" television program that allows them to put forth their most heartfelt, "good guy," "public service" face. It is the one dramatic form (I don't include here major live public events like elections and wars, which are done not within entertainment divisions but within news divisions) in which the networks often invest, in the interest of political rather than commercial capital. In other words, the networks need a certain amount of "social responsibility" and "dignity" in every season, and the docudrama (with all the intriguing contradictions the form contains) often fills that bill. It is a "long form" that allows more depth than most; it attracts serious creative talent hungry for socially meaningful work; and it is a one-shot deal that can be far grimmer and more serious than the traditional series forms, which need to play to regularly returning audiences (see Rapping 1992).

But even if this explains why the networks spring for a few serious TV movies a year (often at a commercial loss), it does not explain why the movies they make tend—and they do—to feature woman-oriented and even feminist-oriented stories told from the point of view of the female gaze. The reason for this—as I've suggested already—is that the networks know that women, a majority of the prime-time audience, like social-issue movies. Women buy most sponsored consumer products (that is why television, generally, worries more about female audiences than do theatrical movie producers today); and women—again, marketing and demographic researchers know this—tend to view social issues, especially gender issues, from a more progressive, feminist-tinged slant than do men.[5]

TV movies, then, have developed along certain conventional lines that work in ways which inevitably tend to present more oppositionally feminist-inspired narratives of gender issues than do theatrical films or other, more male-oriented TV forms. They tend to feature female heroines and present their experiences from *their* perspectives, as other cultural forms do not. And they tend to privilege the woman's arguments and experiences, in the interest of audience identification.

Some of this is not political but simply inevitable, given the dramatic conventions of this form and of all TV narrative. Once a female protagonist is designated, the needs of dramatic and narrative convention dictate that *her* interests and feelings will be privileged. The controversial movie *Roe v. Wade,* as a matter of fact, went through seventeen nervous rewrites under pressure from right-to-life and other right-wing forces so that there was no chance that the antiabortion position was not *at least* as strongly presented, discursively, as the prochoice. Even so, in its ultimate form the movie was decidedly sympathetic to Weddington and "Roe" (as the antiabortion forces accurately complained). This is because it is in the nature of dramatic narrative to sway audiences to the positions of those from whose viewpoint we see the action. When you have a well-told story of two female protagonists, underdogs within the legal profession and the social world, both played by major movie stars (Holly Hunter and Amy Madigan), who go against the patriarchal power structure, you have a classic David and Goliath saga, with all that implies for audiences. And when both protagonists' actions are seen from *their* points of view, and in terms of issues that many women (as the demographics had already shown) will relate to—struggles with unsympathetic husbands, colleagues, bosses, and so on—you have a clearly biased presentation in which facts and rational arguments, while always a factor, are inevitably colored by the power of emotional factors.

In this, the TV movie is again in some ways similar to the courtroom drama. While facts and proof are obviously important, in cases in which gender and family norms are being challenged, an overarching need is to persuade juries (the courtroom audiences) to sympathize with the plaintiff's or defendant's personal perspective through the use of emotional factors. Since the force of tradition and common sense will inevitably be with the party representing institutional power, it is necessary for the oppositional challengers to hegemonic norms to be especially good at raising consciousness of inequality through emotional and dramatic ploys.

I was most dramatically made aware of this kind of narrative battleground, within courtroom cases involving sex and gender and family dynamics, in the televised proceedings of the first Menendez parricide case. The prosecution, using a classic "patriarchal" (and capitalist) model of narrative convention in which essentially "evil" children were seen to act violently out of ingratitude, disrespect, and greed—the typical "bad seed" scenario—made a compelling case for the death penalty. Nor did there seem much to challenge in the prosecution case, since the media, and popular sentiment, made this analysis easily persuasive. Fear and hostility toward youth is, after all, a commonly held attitude these days. And when the youths involved wear Armani clothes and stand to inherit $14 million, the public is even more likely to dislike them and assume their guilt.

But the defense—in the persons of two impressive female attorneys—managed, without really challenging "the facts" of the prosecution case, to present a wholly different narrative, this one based on a whole *different* set of relevant facts (the evidence of child abuse) and an oppositional set of ideas about gender and generational violence within the patriarchal family, culled largely from concepts developed and em-

ployed by feminists in recent years. So effective was the emotional and narrative power of their efforts that they changed the entire thrust of the case, managing—and this seemed impossible at trial's start—to get two hung juries, thoroughly split and polarized (in one case along clear gender lines) over the issue of patriarchal power abuse, both emotional and sexual.

The defense did this by masterfully reorganizing jury *perceptions* not only of what facts might be in question in the case but of what narratives and assumptions about the patriarchal family the jury should be using to gauge the guilt of the defendants. By offering an antipatriarchal, implicitly feminist counternarrative in which the father, not his sons, is the evil wrongdoer, they—as the Court TV commentators continuously noted—nearly "nullified" the jury. From the viewpoint of a feminist analysis of patriarchal abuses of power within the nuclear family, the case was so turned on its head that many commentators considered *acquittal* a possibility, until the judge's instructions to the juries eliminated that possibility. This story, like that of *The Burning Bed* and *Roe v. Wade*, contains in its very transcripts the kind of "dueling narratives" of gender and patriarchy on which these movies are so often based. And as in these cases, the defense, by managing to keep their clients from death, successfully employed a feminist counternarrative to challenge the unquestioned power and authority of the patriarchy.

Versions of Insanity, Temporary and Otherwise

Let us turn now to the actual events of the Hughes case and the process by which the story was transformed into media text. In 1963, when Francine Hughes married Mickey Hughes, many of us were just beginning to think about the conditions under which we lived as women and to struggle to change them. Nearly two decades later, when she finally killed Mickey, we had successfully built a feminist movement and developed many ideas and projects devoted to helping victims of domestic violence and changing the ways in which institutions treated them.

During this period, Francine Hughes, unaware of feminism or its ideas, suffered endless beatings and threats from her husband and sought help, unsuccessfully, from every institution and agency she could think of. For the most part, she accepted his violence because every authority and institution she came into contact with told her that 1) she had no choice and 2) it was "right" for her to do so.

It was after the killing that Hughes's path first crossed that of the organized women's movement. Her case was taken up by a local feminist group that publicized the trial as a political event and helped to construct the legal defense—temporary insanity—which was used to acquit her.[6] The importance of the case, for women, was obvious. It depended on convincing the jury—against the grain of sexist assumptions about female and male violence and against legal tradition, which would view the crime, quite clearly, as "premeditated," since she waited for Mickey to pass out and then deliberately set him on fire and ran—not only that years of physical and sexual abuse was *not* "normal" and "all right" within the marriage but also that Hughes's own acts of violence were not hopelessly "unnatural" for a woman but were in fact justified. With Hughes's acquittal, a precedent was set that significantly furthered the cause of women forced to defend themselves against chronic domestic abuse. It remained for the verdict and its implications to reach a wider audience of women than might be expected to read about, or be personally affected by, the case itself.

Several years after the acquittal, Robert Greenwald, an independent TV producer with a history as a student activist in the 1960s and as an off-off-Broadway theater director, read about the case and decided to option it for TV. The salient facts of this part of the story, filled with contradiction and irony as they are, nonetheless reveal the often byzantine ways in which feminist ideas and voices do sometimes insert themselves into mass media. Feminists took the Hughes case to the public sphere and politicized it. Greenwald (and later a number of other men and women involved in the production) heard about her story and found it moving and also—most important—packageable for network TV. (Farrah Fawcett, whose starring role necessitated her stay in a women's shelter for about a month, was among those involved whose participation was most dramatically influenced by feminism.) They

persuaded a major network, who then persuaded corporate sponsors to fund it—under certain conditions we will explore—because they were aware, through marketing studies, of the appeal of just this kind of story to post-1960s women viewers and consumers. This is a very general, oversimplified description of the indirect ways in which feminists clearly participated in the construction of this movie, in ways that extend far, in time and space, beyond the actual location site in which it was taped.

Greenwald himself was not necessarily a feminist when he decided to do this story, although he was a socially concerned progressive. He had, in fact, come to L.A. to make serious movies but had soon learned that movies about social issues were not being made theatrically but only for television. He then set out to learn how to produce TV dramas and to chalk up some credits, wherever he could, in order to give himself credibility and bankability in the industry. The list of TV movies he directed in order to gain the money and power to do what he actually wanted is embarrassing to him today (*Portrait of a Stripper* and *Portrait of a Centerfold* are typical titles), but such are the contradictions of trying to do serious work within the belly of the beast.

When Greenwald was ready to pitch his first serious, independent production effort, he had learned enough about the business to realize that his best bet was a woman's story because networks, for reasons just mentioned, knew that such stories were bankable. (He went on to make several other feminist-inspired hit TV movies, including *Lois Gibbs and the Love Canal* and *A Deadly Silence* [about the trial of Cheryl Pierson], for the same complex reasons.) In order to pitch the Hughes story, Greenwald, by then a smooth operator, snagged Farrah Fawcett—then the country's major sex symbol because of the "jiggle" crime series *Charlie's Angels*—for the lead. This is a typically contradictory angle to TV producing. Actresses, especially as they age and grow professionally, long for meaty, meaningful roles and find almost none in Hollywood. Therefore, they do TV movies. And networks, worrying about the appeal of "serious" and "downbeat" social issue stories, will only consider them if—as Greenwald learned—they can pin them to a glamorous star.[7]

Greenwald's next contradictory step was to play the violence angle—again, a necessity for promoting such "unsexy" movies—although in fact the violent scenes in the movie are relatively minimal and very far from glamorous. Nonetheless, in pitching his idea he agreed to allow the network to publicize it as a violent, sensational movie, using the most distressing clips in the film, out of narrative and thematic context, and in ways which are arguably quite offensive. This, again, is standard with TV movies. They hook viewers, as one-shot deals, only by being extensively promoted in dramatic, attention-getting ways, usually exploiting sex and/or violence. (At this point it is perhaps worth commenting on the common argument, from feminists, that such tales of "victimization" are part of the backlash. In fact, even the worst of these movies—at least in their TV versions—always stress heroism and female triumph, never victimization. One reason is that these movies—unlike the standard "woman in danger" movie—present a female viewpoint, because they are made for a female audience.) Finally (and less problematically), Greenwald promised a vivid courtroom drama, which, he knew, was a particularly popular narrative conceit well suited to the docudrama form. In fact, as in most such movies, the second half of *The Burning Bed* is devoted entirely to the trial.

As this very abbreviated sketch of what happened reveals, such, are the contradictory paths by which, regularly, feminist-inspired narratives of gender justice are packaged and produced, by creative and business staffs, representing, or influenced by the power of, feminist ideas as they circulate in public realms of all kinds. But while the compromises involved in going this route—more of which will be documented below—are problematic, it would be too easy to argue that they negate whatever good may have come of Greenwald's own (admittedly mixed) intentions. I will argue, in describing the actual film and its effects, that this is not the case. On the contrary, for all its problems, *The Burning Bed* managed to put forth several important feminist ideas, ideas that effectively challenged the dominant master narratives about gender violence usually acted out in popular culture. Moreover, in its aftermath, it has served feminist ends even more broadly, as it has entered the public realm as a compromised, but still clearly feminist, version of the ideas at issue in cases in which sexual and domestic violence figure.

Blood, Soap, and Family Values

The Burning Bed, from its inception in legal and feminist history to its production as a media text, had many progressive midwives and godmothers and godfathers working to get its feminist message across. Nonetheless, when it finally aired, it had inevitably undergone a series of transformations that sharply altered and compromised its original potential.

The Burning Bed was made more carefully, intelligently, and slowly than most docudramas are today.[8] To its credit, it did not simplify, glamorize, or demonize male violence as most movies do (think of the much-praised *Silence of the Lambs* or *Cape Fear*, for example). Nor did it rely on an essentialist argument for male violence, as do many movies and even many feminist theorists. Because of Greenwald's interest in the social causes of male violence, he managed to commission a script which—implicitly—suggested a "social constructionist" take on the issue of family violence. It portrayed the Hughes situation in a fairly sophisticated (for TV) way in which, at each stage of the narrative, Hughes was shown to confront some very powerful institutional force or ideology against which she was powerless to prevail, either because she had no personal power or support or because she had no alternative ideology to help her see her situation. Her encounters with social service agencies, which offer endless rounds of red tape in response to her pleas that she is about to be murdered, and her similar dealings with police officers, who refuse to help her because her husband has not abused her in their presence, are only two examples.

Indeed, the movie itself—again, for television—had a rather complex structure that involved flashbacks of her story interspersed with framing and containing scenes involving her meetings with her attorney and, later, her actual trial. In these framing scenes, set in the jail, the audience sees Hughes learning—along with the viewer—to "renarrativize" the events of her life according to a new set of assumptions, provided by the filmmakers (through the device of the lawyer/narrator), about what was actually happening to her and why.

It is in the scenes with the lawyer that the contradictions of this movie are most intriguing and contradictory. On the one hand, it is only by providing this flashback mechanism and, in effect, showing the Hughes story from the view of her (male) lawyer, that the filmmakers lead the audience to what is (and Greenwald was aware of this) a feminist version of the story and its moral. On the other hand, the lawyer himself represents some very conservatizing gender and class assumptions, built into the hegemonic norms of network TV, by which the feminist message of the case was dramatically compromised. In other words, the movie did present a feminist counternarrative to the traditional patriarchal view of domestic violence. But it did not allow women—as activists, lawyers, or victims— to be seen as agents of their own liberatory thoughts and deeds. Rather, it presented another man, a "good" man, as Francine Hughes's savior. In this way, feminist ideas were seriously contained, watered down, and "declawed", so to speak, as they were put in the hands and mind of another, reformist version of middle-class, white, straight male authority.

The lawyer, of course, is a fiction, an invented character created to fulfill the norms of network courtroom drama, which demanded a white, professional male hero to act as savior/mentor to the working-class, confused, and uneducated Francine Hughes. The actual defense, of course, was developed by activist feminists and publicized as a political case with implications for all women whose lives are organized around patriarchal assumptions about marriage and gender violence. This is the most obvious "demand" made upon Greenwald by his funders.[9] The other two major generic conventions by which the Hughes story was subtly altered to fit—or at least not entirely destroy—the basic tenets of commercial male-dominated media genres concern class and family representation. In ways that diverged far from the (less sunny) facts of the case, Hughes was portrayed as 1) a perfect mother acting, finally, to protect her children; and 2) an upwardly mobile aspirant to middle-class respectability, for whom her attorney serves, most emphatically, as a role model and perhaps even a romantic alternative to the working-class, economically unsuccessful husband she has finally managed to leave.

These two issues, like the importance of individualistic, male heroism, are largely non-negotiable on network drama—especially in movies as ideologically dangerous as this one potentially was—for obvious reasons. Sponsors sell women viewers the image of perfect middle-class

family comfort and luxury at each commercial break. A heroine like Francine Hughes would have had to be portrayed as someone who, like the women in the ads for soap and floor wax and Diet Pepsi, was driven primarily by a desire for better things and a better, richer man. The idea that she might be driven by a desire for freedom, independence, or empowerment was no more acceptable to network norms than was the dramatic portrayal of feminist agitation.[10]

As for family values (as we now call them), they too are built into TV dramatic codes, especially those which define gendered narratives meant for female audiences, such as the docudrama. The final freeze frame of the movie shows—predictably—the acquitted mother embracing her children. Indeed, much of the power of the piece comes from Greenwald's low-key, riveting presentation of most of the violence from the point of view of the terrified children, huddled against walls, hunkered under bedclothes, or running for their lives. The idea that a woman might leave an abusive marriage, even one this abusive, in her own self-interest still made the networks nervous. The "profamily," "good mother" line that TV supports at every turn had to be maintained here by insisting that Francine acted, primarily, as a mother protecting her young.[11]

The importance of such "pro-family" ideology on television cannot be overestimated. Not only must the ending be implicitly happy; the narrative closure must also heavy-handedly reinforce hegemonic norms about family and motherhood, even when, in other places, it is allowed to put forth more liberatory messages. The truth about Francine Hughes's future for example, was quite different from what the movie's freeze frame implies. She did not go on to a better man or a higher-class position. She didn't even maintain custody of her oldest daughter. Not surprisingly, after years of degradation and abuse, she did not easily "move on up" to a better life, filled with commodities and pleasures from the set of *Let's Make a Deal*. Indeed, her actual life, as far as I have followed it, did not diverge as radically from her former life as one would have hoped. Nor should that be all that surprising, given the very limited opportunities and supports for such women, even today.

Nonetheless, for all its limits and compromises, the movie had a profound effect on public consciousness and debate, largely because of its dramatic power and realism, its highly unglamorized view of male violence, and its success in presenting, to an audience not yet widely aware of this on any level, a fairly radical counternarrative to the "woman in danger" master version then showing at most malls and drive-ins.

From the first scene, actually, the film sets itself up in terms of a battle of versions, or narratives, about cases like Hughes's. On first meeting her, for example, the attorney tells her, "It's sort of ironic. I used to work in the prosecutor's office. A few months ago, I would have been prosecuting this case." It is as if the writers were signaling us, at the start, that there are two ways to tell this story, and the one we are going to hear is a new one. The lawyer himself announces to us that he has—just recently—changed his own position in such cases. A few months ago he would have been calling for Hughes's conviction. Today, suddenly, his role calls for him to see things differently. In this, the movie echoes the position of the network itself, which until recently would most certainly have been presenting stories of gender violence from a patriarchal perspective but which "ironically" has come, by the mid-1980s, to take the other side, the woman's side. The attorney then proceeds to describe to us the new version of justice that he has suddenly found himself upholding, developing his narrative—his analysis, as it were—further in each recurring consultation scene with his client. She tells him more of her story; he develops (as indeed the real Hughes's lawyers did) a defense in which its elements are reorganized to fit into a newly gendered and politicized explanation of what happened, based on values and beliefs that are wholly different from the ones Francine had been taught to believe when the actual events were taking place.

After the first establishing encounter between Francine and her lawyer (and between the lawyer and the audience), for example, we see a flashback of the Hugheses' courtship in which all the assumptions of early 1960s gender relations are clearly (almost didactically; TV movies aim for a sixth-grade level of sophistication) spelled out. But already we have been instructed, through the establishing authority of the lawyer, in how we must view these details. The most salient aspect of this segment, seen in these terms, is the reason given for the Hughes marriage, a reason loaded

with prefeminist baggage about the sexual pressures placed on "good girls" to marry early: Mickey wants sex; Fran demurs until marriage; they marry, and so on.

After the wedding the couple moves into his parents' cramped home, and Mickey, already drinking and chronically unemployed, is seen to take his first swipe at his wife and to get no criticism from his parents or brothers. Again the lawyer's perspective colors this incident and we see it from the defense's viewpoint. Mickey's father and mother approve his actions, so it must be "normal." Then we return to the jailhouse meetings of Fran and her attorney, at the second of which, in desperation because she refuses to defend herself (she accepts the patriarchal view that she must "have deserved" her beatings), he gives her a letter from another battered woman, who, he tells her, has read of the Hughes case and has been inspired to leave her husband.

This is as close as the movie gets to making a generalization about domestic violence as a social issue of wider scope. The genre demands human-interest stories featuring a single protagonist, a single-family situation. No generalizations which might seem to accuse men, as a class, and which suggest that many men, even those watching the movie, might be included in the charges against Mickey Hughes, are ever included.[12]

The movie continues in this way, boldly and affectively dramatizing the many steps in Hughes's story, at each of which she is told by family members that Mickey is doing what husbands normally do and that she is somehow to blame and must accept it; or that there is simply nothing the laws, the courts, the police, or the social service agencies can do about it. And then, at midpoint in the tale, having seen the facts of the case as they occurred, the narrative shifts to the courtroom, where each of the actors who have so confused and oppressed Francine is called to account by her attorney, armed with his alternative version of things.

Very dramatically and effectively, the defense attorney brings all of these people to the stand and, in effect, turns their stories upside down with his authoritative, reasonable counterversion of the facts, in which the logic and morality of these relatives and bureaucrats are shown to be cruel and insane. Did the policeman who thought Mickey was "harmless" because he hadn't attempted to harm him (the policeman) "honestly believe" that Mickey would have "tried anything" in front of an armed police officer? Was Mickey's mother telling the truth about her son's peaceful, loving behavior to his wife, in light of the fact that police records reveal that Mickey had actually beaten his own mother to the point that she herself had been forced to call for help? And so on, the defense goes, through the list of prosecution witnesses. The counternarrative is thus employed in the final half of the film quite heavy-handedly, so that no viewer can miss the point of Francine's desperation and victimization.

But if the final version of the story is hammered home definitively by the male lawyer in actual courtroom scenes, there is, most interestingly, another narrative tack taken in this film which suggests, almost anachronistically, what might be a "prefeminist" point of view about even the very early events.

The narrative I refer to comes to us from yet another invented character in the film—this one too reflective of a tradition, or convention, of woman-oriented docudrama, but a more progressive one. Fran has a "best friend" who supports the heroine and speaks with the voice of empowerment throughout the movie, although her voice is muted and isolated. This friend, throughout, tells Francine to leave Mickey. And it is to this friend that Francine several times confides her own fragile but nonetheless existent impulses toward autonomy even from the start. This friend seems almost to reflect the growing consciousness of more privileged women in the 1960s, as she continuously urges Francine to act independently and with self-respect. One such incident comes when Francine expresses hesitancy about marriage, for example. "I don't know," she says, "I'd like to get out of here, I think, maybe work somewhere," and her friend nods in support of this somewhat radical (for this time and place) idea.

Throughout the movie, this friend, continues to contradict the more powerful ideas and pressures of family and state and to support Francine's better, healthier instincts. In fact, the final crisis comes—and this *is* factual—when Francine, encouraged by her friend, gets a grant to go to business school and Mickey, frightened and enraged by her newfound independence, tears her books up, page by page, and then beats and rapes her. The image of the book pages falling to the ground, as the desperate Francine watches helplessly, is among the film's most moving. While the (potentially) liberatory narrative suggested throughout by this friend is never more than a hint, it is nonetheless interesting from the point of view of my theme of contesting narratives of a woman's life.

In the end, of course, it is not this minor female character's voice but that of the network's representative—the male lawyer—that prevails and that places the final interpretation on the events in question. As the final scene of Mickey's cruelty and Francine's desperate act of violence and escape is shown, we also get the longest, most dramatic moments of the attorney's summation. Indeed, they are part and parcel of a single narrative move: The events of the fatal night—as he himself has told us—could be told from the view of the prosecution or the defense. But this time, we are going to hear the defense's spin on things, the voice of white, male authority more or less *giving* the battered women of the world permission and guidelines for escape. Again, the contradictions of the form are obvious. The traditional hero must present the new narrative and give it authority. You can have your verdict, the network seems to be telling us, but only if you let us present it, in a version we can live with, a version that doesn't do damage to commodity culture or traditional family values. Mickey Hughes, then, becomes a scapegoat, a bad boy who must be purged, and then replaced by a good man, one the networks prefer anyway because he represents respectability—the white, male legal system and, not least, disposable income.

And so a feminist story, a feminist case, has been constructed to fit the hegemonic norms of commercial television. Much has been lost in the translation, but much, I would argue, has been accomplished as well. It is no small thing for a TV movie to empower a crazed wife to kill her husband in cold blood and live happily ever after, happy, smiling children in her arms, schoolbooks leading her to a productive, middle-class future, reclaimed; think of *Fatal Attraction* and other such demonized representations of angry, aggressive women. This movie managed to create sympathy for what in most movies would be a heinous act, even if committed by a male against a female. It managed to say—albeit through the official voice of patriarchy and capital—that wife abuse is no longer OK in television or in reality and that men who are engaging in it should perhaps think again.

In the aftermath of the film, especially when viewed from the perspective of the near-decade since it first aired, much has changed in our "commonsense" views about domestic violence. Even the very next day, many women left their husbands and went to shelters they did not know about before they saw the news follow-ups that always follow such "special event" docudramas. And the movie—not on its own, of course, but surely as one small link in a chain of feminist-engendered moves to change laws and policies about domestic violence—has by now become part of a broad movement to empower and support battered women. The women who organized the original defense committee, as well as the many other men and women who directly and indirectly acted to get this movie made, have had an impact on the criminal justice procedures in domestic violence cases and on the general culture within which cases like this one are negotiated.

Not all TV movies are as good as this one. And even this one, as I've suggested, had more than its share of infuriating and embarrassing moments for feminists. Nonetheless, all things considered, the plight of women in the home and in the courtroom has probably been served more than hindered by movies of this kind about politicized legal cases involving gender justice.

Notes

1. See Garber, Matlock, and Walkowitz 1993 for an interesting and timely collection of essays on such events and their implications.

2. For an extended discussion of the theoretical bases for this approach, see Rapping 1994a.

3. The ruling, briefly summarized, stated that the proof of sexual harassment severe enough to warrant the court's finding in the woman's behalf need not include evidence of severe emotional distress. As Justice O'Connor nicely explained, a woman need not suffer a nervous breakdown to be justified in successfully claiming sexual harassment (*Harris v. Forklift Systems, Inc.*, 114 S.Ct. 367; 125 L. Ed. 2d 295, 302 [1993].

4. Because movies are so much more likely to be taken seriously and discussed publicly than television drama, we are far more aware of theatrical examples of this kind of thing, like *The Accused* and *Thelma and Louise*, than TV versions. Nonetheless, it is the docu-

drama that is the most common site for feminist interventions.

5. I was told much of this by network staff members and executives with whom I spoke.

6. I was marginally involved in the Francine Hughes case. I was then heading up the Feminist Task Force of the New American Movement, a national New Left organization. The East Lansing chapter of NAM was one of the groups that organized support for Hughes and helped to develop her defense strategy, so I was invited to speak at a rally for her.

After the movie was made, I spent some time interviewing Robert Greenwald, the producer/director. Much of my information about the movie is based on my personal conversations and experiences with Greenwald.

7. The list of female stars who agree to do TV movies, often against their agents' wishes, is lengthy. It includes Joanne Woodward, Anjelica Huston, Jane Fonda, Glenn Close, Holly Hunter, Amy Madigan, and many more.

8. Indeed, it is another irony of the form that the success of such movies as this one has led to the enormous popularity of the form and to the subsequent phenomenon of cheap, sleazy, mindless docudramas like the Amy Fisher films, which are made and promoted as quickly and cheaply as possible.

9. When I asked Greenwald why activism, generally, and feminism, specifically, were left out, he told me that such things "don't work" on TV. Such are the ways in which self-censorship seeps into the thinking of trained professionals.

10. Indeed, one reason we rarely see working-class subjects on TV is that sponsors do not want their ads for glamour and luxury to conflict with the images—and potential messages—of stories dealing with less glamorous characters who may, nonetheless, live happily ever after. Since the 1950s, actually, when ethnic and working-class sitcoms were the norm, sponsors have generally insisted on a stylistic "fit" between ads and programs in which the characters' stories may easily be seen to support the push toward glamour and consumption on which TV is built (Barnouw 1975). The story, while as grim and shabby in style as TV gets, nonetheless could be seen, subtextually, to suggest an "upwardly mobile" future for Francine, as represented by the ideas and values of her attorney.

11. Interestingly, *Roe v. Wade* had a similar "good mother" slant tagged onto it. The networks could not have simply sanctioned a woman's right to abort for her own reasons. "Roe"'s anguish at the thought of giving her baby up for adoption was stressed very heavily—to the point of using a labor-room scene in which she is not allowed to touch her child, followed by a scene in which she attempts suicide over the loss.

12. Similarly, in a movie like *Lois Gibbs and the Love Canal*, no generalizations about corporate pollution were permitted. Only the one (unnamed) company involved was mentioned, as if to say "Yes, we

have one or two bad apples, among men and corporations, but we take care of them, one case at a time, as is the way of a functioning democracy—at least on television drama." This is standard for TV movies and justified on grounds of "dramatic" criteria. Activism and collective implications, say the networks, do not "work" on the small screen, which in significant encounters can only accommodate close-ups and two-shots, individualized moments affecting individual characters.

10

Rape on Soaps

The Legal Angle

DIANNE L. BROOKS

> Why does a person watch *Dallas* and in my case, why does a serious intelligent feminist like watching *Dallas?* It releases primitive feelings in me, I go dizzy, hate, love, loathe, feel disgusted, condemn and often dash away a tear. . . . My leisure reading consists 90 percent of feminist books, but when I'm watching *Dallas* with my girl friend and Pamela comes down the stairs wearing a low-necked dress, then we shout wildly: just look at that slut, the way she prances around, she ought to be called Prancela. Bobby is a decent chap, like my eldest brother, and Jock is like my father, so I can hate them intensely too. . . . I like to let it all hang out, a sort of group therapy, mostly together with friends.

> —Ien Ang, *Watching* Dallas

I begin with this quote from Ien Ang's *Watching Dallas* in order to situate myself as a soap fan. I have been one since junior high school, although I don't really know how or exactly when it happened. My mother was not a television soap fan, but in the course of my work on this project she did admit to me that she was a radio soap fan. I inherited what I like to refer to as a melodramatic imagination,[1] which in turn served to assist me in understanding the nature of soap opera. This, added to my formal soap viewing instruction from my best friend's mother—who was the more typical homemaker soap fan—inspired what was to become a lifelong fascination. Soon I was looking forward to getting home in time to see the end of *One Life to Live* or *Days* and all of *General Hospital* or *Another World*. It is probably the advent of technology (VCRs, soap news groups) that has allowed me to continue to be a soap fan, something not available to those of earlier generations, like my mother, who worked outside the home. Over time, I have learned how to watch soaps and developed into what I consider to be a skilled soap reader, inventing plots and predicting outcomes, analyzing constantly.

In the process of educating myself, however, I have gone in and out of soap-watching phases. During the "Luke and Laura" era on *General Hospital*[2] I was attending a black women's college where a society had formed around the ABC soap lineup. After transferring to another college, I entered an "inactive phase," because I had neither the daytime flexibility nor the VCR technology to keep up with the soaps. But I guess I resigned myself to lifelong fandom during law school and the bar exam. As many know, and many more do not, law school is usually a hellish experience, intellectually and emotionally empty, thus requiring "escape" for consolation. Particularly during the miserable isolation of studying for the bar exam, I turned to soaps, taping them to savor during my evening dinner breaks.

When I began this project I was somewhat mystified and slightly tentative about my identity as a soap fan. As I worked, I realized the complexity of their attraction. They are filled with familiar faces and familiar plots, like old friends. The visual image activates my unconscious in complex ways. Fan culture, the society that forms around viewing and discussing these programs, attracts me as well. Although questions remain, I am no longer trying to hide my fascination (both pleasurable and academic) with these complex visual narratives. I have come out of the closet, so to speak, although I continue to find myself in the position of defending this most maligned genre. I have always been fascinated by culture, both "high" and "low," and taking an academic turn toward the domain of the undervalued is both natural and empowering. And to that end, I join those who have already begun to explore the mysteries, complexities, and power of the soap opera.

My aim in this chapter will be to examine the intersection of the law and soap opera through the consideration of "issue plots" generally and rape in particular. This analysis will not be comprehensive but will focus on specific plotlines from the ABC soap operas *All My Children* and *One Life to Live*. It is my intention to seriously consider the ways in which soap operas construct a legal culture that is aimed primarily at women and that is both realistic and melodramatic. I am also interested in considering issues of audience reception. As a person of color who is not proportionally represented in visual media, I am particularly interested in fan culture among differentiated viewing groups, a theme which I develop further elsewhere (Brooks forthcoming).

Soap Opera and "Relative Realism"

So then how does one come to study soap operas and the law? I will begin with a personal anecdote.

When I began law school in the fall of 1986, I turned on the television to find *L.A. Law*. *L.A. Law*'s existence as a hybrid crime drama (or law-and-order drama) and soap opera is important for

my discussion. Certainly, as I watched then I was delighted that a show had been created for "us"—that is, for the hundreds of first-year law students beginning our careers with a slick and glamorous image to sustain us through what turned out to be three dreary and horrifying years. One of the marks of the show's "soap-opera-ness" was that it drew us in, in a manner not so dissimilar from the way in which fans were drawn into other evening soap operas like *Dynasty* and from the way in which fans have been drawn to daytime soap operas for over half a century. And of course the beauty of this was that you didn't have to apologize or explain why you liked it or watched it because it was on at 10 P.M. and it was about THE LAW.

Of course, many of my colleagues who are *L.A. Law* fans would not be happy with its label, here, as a soap opera. However, it is sometimes discussed on the soap opera Internet newsgroup of which I am a devoted member. If we examine *L.A. Law* through the lens of several soap opera theorists, it becomes clear that the program does indeed contain many of soaps' generic characteristics or conventions. In his discussion of several aspects of soap operas' technical and narrative conventions, Robert C. Allen (1985) states that "soap opera style represents the crystallization of a set of stylistic conventions taken over from Hollywood filmmaking practice (called by film scholars the classical Hollywood narrative style)" (p. 64). This is true, on some level, of most television programming: It incorporates the practice of the "classical style" of Hollywood cinema (Bordwell, Thompson, and Staiger, 1985). Thus, for example, editing is invisible, space corresponds to narrative significance, and the types of shots are mainly the close-up and two-shot (medium-long-shot framings), which function to focus attention on facial expression and figure relationships. Even though *L.A. Law* is shot on film and soap operas are shot to tape, *L.A. Law* does rely on both stylistic and narrative techniques common to soaps. The program's visual effect is to maintain the illusion of the real and to focus the "action" around personal interaction. Narratively, *L.A. Law* contains more than the usual number of regularly appearing characters (more than ten), none of whom can be singled out as the weekly hero/heroine of the program. Another common characteristic is the comparative redundancy of the plotlines, which serves to emphasize that characters have histories and memories. So, for example, *L.A. Law* and other prime-time soaps "recap" previous episodes at the beginning of each weekly episode and then "preview" what is to follow at the close. With regard to their narrative, soap operas are texts that are virtually ungraspable as a whole at any given moment because of overlapping and drawn-out plots. Despite the "miniclosures" of certain internal narratives, as in, for example, the "trial" sequences of *L.A. Law*, the overall story does not move toward any eventual end.

In her essay "The Politics of Soaps: Pleasure and Feminine Empowerment," Mary Ellen Brown (1987) lists eight generic characteristics of soap opera texts. In this context, *L.A. Law* possesses most of these qualities, although sometimes to a lesser extent than daytime dramas do. First, it adopts a *moderately serialized form*, so that certain plotlines occur over a period of episodes and are continuous, like the question of whether Arnie Becker will ever settle down and be a committed lover. Second, as I have already discussed, the program has *multiple characters and plots*. Third, *L.A. Law* is *abruptly segmented* in a way that faithfully replicates the structure of daytime soap operas, so that the first segments of any show establish the three to four "plots" that will be played out in each program. Fourth, because it is a show about the "practice" of law, it necessarily relies on the verbal as opposed to the active, so that it *emphasizes dialogue, problem-solving, and intimate conversation*. Finally, although less so than in daytime soap operas, *L.A. Law* is peopled with sensitive, *idealized male characters* (the fifth characteristic) and *female professional characters* (the sixth characteristic). The last two characteristics (although in Brown's listing they are the third and eighth) deal with time and setting and may not seem to conform to the structure of *L.A. Law*. However, time does seem to pass between episodes, thus *paralleling actual time*, so that you could not necessarily show episodes out of sequence without noticing. Finally, although the home does not function as the setting, one can argue that the law firm is the *place that functions as the home and the setting for the show*.

In spite of all of this, I am not arguing that *L.A. Law* is a purely "feminine narrative" in exactly the same sense that daytime soap operas are (Modleski 1982; Fiske 1987). After all, daytime dramas have always been aimed at female audiences and therefore are structured to appeal, generally, to women. In prime-time soap, men tend to be more central or even to dominate plotlines more than would ever be allowed in daytime. For example, a former *L.A. Law* fan suggested that when the program chose to write out one of the only strong "bad" women characters by throwing her down an elevator shaft, this seemed to be much more indicative of male fantasy than of the desire to appease a daytime viewing audience. More significantly, the ideology of disruption is not allowed to dominate the narrative of *L.A. Law* as it is does in daytime, although it occurs. There is a "justice triumphs" requirement such that each trial has some sort of resolution, reinforcing the ideology that the system functions—even if with occasional mistakes. As I argue further and expand upon in the book from which this chapter is excerpted, soap operas are more likely to highlight the improper working of the institution, with eventual outside intervention perhaps reversing unjust legal outcomes.

Although earlier I discussed my own feeling of connection to *L.A. Law* in relation to its proximity to my situation as a first-year law student, I suggest that its equally significant and much broader appeal lies in its innate soap-opera-ness. Many more than my first-year classmates have succumbed to the combination appeal of this program, and others like it: law schools noted a phenomenal increase in applications in the years immediately following *L.A. Law*'s premiere (Gillers 1989).[3] Among my own undergraduate students, many of whom go off to pursue careers in law (as lawyers, paralegals, and law enforcement personnel), informal and formal surveys reveal that their primary knowledge of law is by way of television. But curiously, once I reduce *L.A. Law* to its barebones soap opera structure, many change their minds.

In spite of my attempt to break down the intellectual barriers between "high" and "low" culture when I teach, I still find that even in the discussion of television, which students in spite of their captivation have learned to intellectually disdain, there are gender and class barriers between daytime and prime-time television. For example, both male and female students applaud programs such as *NYPD Blue* and *Law and Order* as high-quality shows because of their realism. Each of these programs is a very conventionally structured crime drama, influenced by the

Bochco school of filmic stylization: Each incorporates hand-held camera work and other techniques that distance these programs from the more static "cops and robbers" techniques of earlier programming, like *Dragnet* and *Starsky and Hutch*. Certainly, when students are pressed about what exactly makes these programs so "realistic," they, as (in the technical sense) uncritical viewers, point not to their own experiences with the legal system but, rather, to other programming.

When asked to discuss soap operas, male students are almost universally dismissive of their value, although many admit to watching them, particularly the nighttime soaps—for example, *Beverly Hills 90210* and *Melrose Place*. Only the true daytime "fans," still primarily female students, will seriously discuss or compare daytime soap operas to anything on prime time. John Fiske discusses how television employs particular strategies in order to "cope with, and help produce, a crucial categorization of its viewers into masculine and feminine subjects" by structuring narratives around sex-role stereotypes and the anxieties that are produced therein (1987, p. 179). For example, daytime soaps rely on narratives of constant disruption of the status quo, because subordinated women viewers find pleasure in this: It is their fantasy. On the other hand, male viewers' pleasure derives more clearly from "masculine performance," demonstrated in an achievement of a clearly designated objective (Fiske 1987, p. 179), even though certain subgroups of men "negotiate" the dominant themes by, for example, identifying with action villains rather than heroes. But because the dominant ideology of this culture is white, middle-class, and male-centered, and in spite of the fact that networks rely on daytime revenues to fund prime-time programming, soap opera continues to face, as Agnes Nixon herself says, "the cliche of denigration"(Nixon 1994).[4]

Such devaluation of the feminine is usually articulated as being based on a question of realism: Daytime television is despised not because of its association with women per se but, rather, because it is far less "realistic" than most prime-time programming, particularly those programs within the crime drama genre. In the particular context of law, this gendering of television audiences works to reinforce the dominant ideology of the law, which is that the law is male and that it is mainly concerned with solving crime, thereby protecting society from disruption by alien others, including subordinated groups like women, ethnic minorities, the working class, and the poor. If a program were not recognizable as affirming this particular ideology of law and order, it would not appeal to male viewers because it would not then be seen as "realistic."

I recognize, however, that there are many ways in which subordinated groups read these dominant texts and negotiate their meanings in order to find pleasure "against the grain." For example, women, ethnic and racial minorities, and non-middle-class viewers may respond that these programs are "realistic" based on their ability to take on the subject position of the hero and accommodate themselves within the dominant ideology. Simultaneously, subordinated groups may be less likely to laud the "realism" of these programs over something that is directed at them because their reality is differently constructed. The law does not represent comfort and protection to women or African Americans, for example, to the same extent that it does to white males. Moreover, these viewers do not see themselves represented in prime-time crime drama as active subjects but, rather, as "objects" of rescue or pursuit or as token background members, and thus the texts are steps removed from their reality. Thus, subordinated group members may be able to read the *double text*: reading both with and against the grain and deriving pleasure from gendered, racialized, and class-situated texts that appear to be oppressive.

Within the particular context of gendered texts, the opposite does not appear to be the case. In other words, because most men are not generally skilled at "reading" the reality in daytime soap operas, they do not derive pleasure from them and consequently lambast them for being ridiculously unrealistic. Even male students who admitted watching soaps criticized them for being far more unrealistic than prime-time crime dramas, particularly with respect to the law. But the law that one sees in daytime soap operas is the law that does not protect women from sexual violence, that takes children away from the custody of their mothers, and that convicts the wrong person while letting the real killers get away, at least temporarily. Obviously, to most women these are the aspects of the law that matter most.

Technically, prime-time programming is more expensive and employs more "tricks" to give certain genres, particularly crime dramas, a heightened sense of "realism" (Gitlin 1983). For any number of reasons we have come to associate film image with a higher modality of "realism" than that associated with programming that is videotaped. Again, soap operas are filmed to tape, while prime-time programming is filmed and more heavily edited, thus more "constructed." Yet the perception remains among viewers that prime-time shows approximate the "real" to a greater extent than do daytime shows. This is because, as Fiske says, "the essence of realism is that it reproduces reality in such a form as to make it easily understandable. . . . [I]t is thus defined by the way it makes sense of the real, rather than by what it says the real consists of" (1987, p. 24). We have come to associate the filmic look or aesthetic with realism, whereas video seems more stagey. As an ideological project, this serves to construct viewers' dominant perceptions of institutions such as the law. Thus television reproduces the law as predominantly male, just, and powerful, narratively shoring that visual image up with techniques that draw on classic cinematic techniques. Soap operas, on the other hand, reproduce their own version of the real but are more ideologically open to alternative readings, which allows for a recognition of an alternative "reality."

Thus, this project is more than simply an exploration of how accurately daytime programming presents legal issues. An analysis of television as a project of cultural studies requires an investigation of the ideological construction of the legal institution for visual consumption. This investigation focuses on soap operas for a number of reasons. First, soap opera is persistent: The genre has an uninterrupted sixty-plus-year history (including radio). Second, it is a form that is targeted to, consumed by, and to a significant extent produced by women. The audience is currently estimated at around 6.7 million (C. Williams 1992),[5] even though many are heralding soap opera's demise because of cable competition and the even lower cost of producing talk shows. Although there are increasing numbers of male viewers, soap audiences continue to be primarily composed of women. But these women are by no means a uniform group: They include working-class women, women who work at home, highly educated professionals and college students from various cultural backgrounds. For example, there is a large African American female audience for daytime television in general, and soap operas in particular, and when these women are surveyed, they read soap opera somewhat differently than their white counterparts.

For feminist theorists seeking to understand legal issues and their effect on a multiplicity of women, examining soaps is a way of studying crosscultural reception. Soap operas are a "feminine narrative" (Fiske 1989) not only because of their target audience—women working in the home and caring for children—but also because women have always been an integral part of their production. There is some question as to who actually invented the soap opera. Yet the first radio serial, *Painted Dreams,* was arguably created by and definitely written and acted by a woman, Irna Phillips. After *Painted Dreams,* Phillips continued to exert an enormous influence on the creation of soaps and on other prominent soap creators, such as Agnes Nixon, creator of *All My Children* and *One Life to Live.* Women have continued to be an integral part of the production of soaps, as much as they continue to be the primary producers of romance fiction. So women are writing to women about what they know. And although they always have been situated in small towns and have been preoccupied with "domestic" concerns about family and relationships, soap operas have also always incorporated "public life" themes, such as crime, and have portrayed women as professionals; the earliest example is the radio soap about a woman lawyer entitled *Portia Faces Life.* This effort to deal with larger world issues has somewhat followed sociopolitical movements, particularly feminism, so that the influence of the women's movement can now be seen in the content and manner of presentation of soap operas in the 1990s (Rapping 1987).[6]

My third reason to focus on soap operas is that they depend on legal narratives. As a commercial vehicle that seeks as well to "commodify their audience," soaps do their part to reinforce the dominant ideology that constructs and supports all cultural institutions, of which the law is among the most powerful. However, soap operas are also open texts, allowing and encouraging alternative readings to a larger extent than other types of narratives aimed at male audiences, so that their construction of the law is perhaps alternative and enlightening.

"There is no pleasure in being a 'cultural dope'; there is, however, real pleasure to be found in, for example, soap operas that assert the legitimacy of feminine meanings and identities within and against patriarchy" (Fiske 1987, p. 19). If one accepts that argument, then the first leap of faith is taken toward a serious consideration of soaps, their contents and their readings.

It is not my project in this chapter to rescue from criticism the representation of rape in visual communication media. It is instead to shed some light on both the positive and negative, and to perhaps speculate on the negotiation processes of some audiences. In fact, I will attempt to "reread" rape.[7] Since sexual violence is so integral a part of society, it appears throughout cultural production. I am interested, particularly, in the manifestation of the rape narrative tradition in soap opera. It has been my contention all along that soap operas are more than simply visual vehicles by which the dominant forces of a capitalist, individualist, patriarchal, and racist society "teach" women how to be. Yet to some extent this *is* the function of soap opera. I am interested in exploring the extent to which soap opera texts disrupt the paradigm of the rape narrative *and* reinforce it—all in the context of the law. In order to do this I will discuss some history of rape narratives on ABC soap operas and then closely read a recent rape storyline on *One Life to Live*, the story line that in fact inspired this project.

Rape Narrative Tradition on Soap Operas

The history of sexual violence on soap opera is nothing if not problematic. Many people associate soap opera rape with the *Gone with the Wind* rapist-as-lover scenario, and it is true that very often soap operas have functioned to demean women characters by making them either fall in love with their rapists or become a better character as the result of the crime. These approaches to rape rely on and therefore serve to reinforce the mythology that informs rape discourse and the operation of rape law. Conventional sex-role stereotypes, such as the myth of the uncontrolla-

ble male sex drive, rapists as evil strangers/others, and false accusations, persist even in the most insightful plots. Yet the inherent openness of the soap opera text has always allowed a larger number of perspectives to be presented with respect to rape when compared to other cultural production, particularly television and film. Moreover, soap opera's existence as a feminine text (in the Modleski sense) allows for negotiation such that the tension that is apparent in the "classic" romanticization of rape scenario can be opened up for examination. For example, one immediate problem is female agency, which rape law tends to disallow. Particularly from the late 1960s, soap opera has always had to grapple with the dilemma of characterizing strong women while negotiating around their sexual agency; love, romance and, increasingly, sex are the focal point of much soap action. So how to construct a victim who has agency? The early answer may have been to recast the victim and perpetrator as lovers *or* make the perpetrator an evil stranger. But even the second solution presents problems. Due to the repetitious and drawn-out story lines of soaps, villains are never sufficiently marginalized and become popular integral figures—part of the soap family, so to speak.

The early choice in most non-issue-oriented soap operas, meaning all but *One Life to Live* and *All My Children*, was very often to romanticize rape. Although most soap operas currently incorporate social issues into their plotlines, the Agnes Nixon–created soap operas, *One Life to Live* (premiering in 1968) and *All My Children* (premiering in 1970), are recognized as having led the way. In an interview, Ms. Nixon explained that she felt that she had an obligation to educate and make her audiences aware while explaining both sides and making people understand each other. ABC approached her while she was writing for another soap, offering to give her leeway to create and push her soaps in the direction that she wanted.

But again rape mainly appeared not as an issue but as a melodramatic focal point for romance. This brings us to what has become to many the paradigm for disgraceful characterization of rape on soap operas: the "Luke and Laura" episodes of *General Hospital*, which occurred in 1978. Even though their initial sexual involvement occurred as the result of a rape, this soap opera couple and their extended plotline, which was primarily action and adventure, signifies a sort of turning point in soap opera insofar as the producer sought to capitalize on younger fans in order to expand the target audience beyond the housebound hausfrau. The particular story line goes that Luke and Laura had developed a sort of working relationship: He was the owner and she was an employee of the local disco. Overcome by desire on an occasion when they were dancing together, Luke raped Laura, the music swelling to a crescendo somewhat reminiscent (although not as passionately violent) of Rhett's sweeping of Scarlett up the stairs.

Many viewers were not pleased with the way in which the couple was brought together, despite the popularity of the principals. Nevertheless, many fans were so enamored of the actor (Tony Geary) that they later either forgot or were not troubled by the fact that Laura divorced her then-husband (a lawyer, by the way) to run away to adventure with her former rapist. Even though some writers attribute the reformation of Luke to audience response, the character was never initially written as totally *bad*: This ambiguity seems to have given the writers enough of an opening to reform the rapist, a soap opera convention dictated by the necessity of holding onto the most popular characters and actors who play them in spite of their villainy.

Martha Nochimson (1992) offers another explanation for the "reform" of Luke. Working from a psychoanalytic perspective, Nochimson argues that Laura (Genie Francis) represented a new narrative of feminine identity. Instead of threatening the coherence of a (male) narrative, as in conventional film and television, female sexuality redeemed the narrative and was the focal point for finally saving the community. Nochimson is arguing that Laura's erotic power emerges during that scene and in fact that "rape" is really a misnomer, because sex itself is an act in defiance of a submission to patriarchy: Luke's to his mob boss and Laura to her husband. To sum it up in Nochimson's words, "The so-called rape of Laura by Luke was not a rape at all, since it was almost completely free from association with dominance-subordination eroticism. The labeling of their sexual encounter as a rape originated with Laura's use of the term. But . . . she described her lovemaking with Luke in this way

only because she initially did not have the appropriate language" (1992, p. 81).

Later Nochimson explains that Laura does spend the night with Luke and returns home to Scotty and claims rape to explain her overnight absence. Nochimson concludes here that this is not an antifeminist sort of false rape-accusation scenario. Instead, in context it demonstrates the "failure of discourse" available to Laura, suggesting that we the audience know all along that the rape was not so.

This analysis of the Luke and Laura rape demonstrates the possibility of multiple readings. However, one troublesome aspect of the psychoanalytic reading of this rape as not a rape is that although it attempts to account for female viewer positioning on an unconscious level—that is, young women could identify and relate positively to this story line because they recognized that the sex was not rape—it may in fact ignore the most troubling aspects of this presentation. In fact, it reinforces the issue of violence present in sex by romanticizing it, without any explanation or attention paid to the *confusion*. Laura cried "rape" and later changed her mind, but it is never clear why. At least Margaret Mitchell immediately problematized Rhett and Scarlet's relationship: There were, in fact, some negative consequences.

Yet for all the popularity of that story line, there have been many changes in sexual violence story lines since the late 1970s: Many rapes that involved acquaintances have been more seriously developed as full-blown legal narratives, culminating in the trial and conviction of the guilty party. By examining two recent examples of rape narratives on both *All My Children* and *One Life to Live*, I would like to list and analyze the makeup of the "rape narrative." In this discussion I hope to highlight changes in the construction of the story line that correspond to changes in the larger society. I also hope to highlight some of the unique characteristics of soap opera rape narratives based on the specific dictates of the genre.

Rape narratives have always worked because they present an important opportunity for dramatic tension, as do all legal narratives. First and foremost of the characteristics of the rape narrative is the question of victim and assailant. For example, since the late 1970s soap operas have recognized that it is no longer acceptable to use rape as a romantic engine for the unification of two characters. The familial framework of soap operas has meant that it has always been more likely that when a character is raped, that character is a central figure (or is being developed into a central figure) and is raped by an antagonistic acquaintance of some type—for example, a jealous ex-lover who is a relative by marriage. There have been story lines involving "strangers," but since soap operas are primarily about relationships and community, there must always be the possibility of allowing the "bad" character to enter the "family" and therefore not remain a stranger. So the assailant and victim usually know each other and have some sort of prior relationship, many times a sexual history. The victim has many times been a primary character of previously or presently questionable virtue: The early approach was to use the rape to "transform" a somewhat bad character into a good character, but since the late 1970s and into the 1980s this approach has been used less and less. What remains, however, is the requirement that the victim have some sort of tainted past in order that dramatic tension be maintained throughout the course of the accusation, the investigation, and ultimately the trial. A "transformation" may also occur at the level of the victim's own coming to power, so to speak: Soap operas, like most other popular American mediums, offer a somewhat paradoxical individualist/familial tension. The victim triumphs through the support and aid of friends and family as well as through her own decision to reach down and find her "inner strength." In many cases this finding of inner strength can be read as signaling a transformation of sorts. Nonetheless, I would suggest that the true transformation of the victim remains only to the extent that rape narratives must, for maximum dramatic potential, provide a victim with a complicated past in order to make the actual case that much more difficult to prosecute.

Since in most cases the rapist is a member of the soap opera community, one of the almost insurmountable dilemmas involves what to do with him once he is convicted. The assailant is usually villainous, often marked as decidedly non-middle-class, perhaps upper-class with a bad work ethic. By the late 1970s, rapists do generally stand trial and are somehow or other brought to justice and jailed—and then? If the character/

actor is popular, which is often the result of the protracted story line, the writers are pressed to find a way to keep the story line going. There may be many scenes of the perpetrator in prison for a period, usually culminating in some heroic act meant to exonerate the character so that the action can at last be moved out of the prison setting. It is increasingly rare for criminal characters, particularly rapists, to die or be simultaneously replaced by a "twin" or "look-alike." Importantly, however, even when he is out of prison, the rapist is not usually reformed. He does not usually become a good pillar of the community but instead remains tainted and forever designated as a villainous character, which signals the changes in rape narratives on soap operas.

The second major characteristic of rape narratives flows from the first: The community's reaction must be divided. Again, since in most cases the rape involves two (or more) characters who are members of the soap opera's extended family, the opportunity arises for the other characters to line up or take sides, leading to even more interfamily, intercommunal tension and disputes. Again, the questionable character or past of the victim, or some act of the victim, is usually what precipitates this division, yet increasingly the division is broken down when the true character of the *rapist* is revealed.

Finally, the setting and progression of the narrative depend on the trial and its aftermath. There are, of course, cases of rape or rape accusations that do not culminate in trial, but I am focusing this discussion on those that do because of the increasing legal-issue orientation of a narrative that has been commonplace for some time. Before I center on the courtroom proceedings themselves, I would like to attend briefly to how the act itself is portrayed or not. As I mentioned earlier, it has become increasingly problematic, thanks mainly to the infusion of feminist perspectives, to simply show the act of violence. One would probably never see an enactment as graphic as the rape scene in the Hollywood film *The Accused*, mainly because of daytime television's restriction on violence. Nonetheless, soaps do dramatize the violent act to draw the viewer into the action. However, they now tend to situate the viewer on the side of the victim. Previously, little attention may have been paid to the camera perspective during the rape; for example, the scene may have been shot with the camera over the shoulder of the rapist or simply shooting at both victim and assailant. Now, more attention is given to actually using the shot-counter shot, *starting from the perspective of the victim*, with a much more disturbing but perhaps less "voyeuristic" effect.

The main characteristics of the rape trial are generally the same for all trial narratives on soap operas, with some particularities. First are the identities of the legal practitioners: the prosecutor, defense attorney, and judge. Second, rape trials literally tell the story through witness testimony and through opening and closing arguments. Third, rape-trial stories feature concurrent investigations outside of the trial and missing evidence. In most soap trials, the prosecutor and judge are secondary characters, while the defense attorney is a main character. To complicate the obvious woman's perspective of the rape narrative, this defense attorney is usually female, corresponding to the common legal strategy of having a woman defend an alleged rapist in order to present a sympathetic picture to the jury. Soap opera narratives pay much attention to conversations outside of the courtroom among those community members attending, usually reinforcing the divisions referred to above. The judge is seated, and the action usually begins with the opening statements of the prosecution and the defense. Increasingly, a prosecution expert will appear in sexual violence cases, serving the purpose of educating the audience about rape statistics and about victim behavior.

But the focal point of the trial narrative is the testimony of the victim, perhaps accompanied by flashbacks to the events in question. It is here, of course, that character questions are exposed publicly the victim often breaks down in some form or other during the testimony. The damning testimony is usually elicited during the cross-examination of the victim and periodically results in eruptions, followed by gasps and noise from the gallery followed by gaveling and warnings by the judge.

This pattern of argument between witness and lawyer/audience eruption/gaveling is again a common device in all dramatized trials, functioning to signal the direction of the proceeding. Inevitably, the word of the victim alone will still not convict the rapist: This is enunciated throughout, becoming increasingly clear at the narrative eruption points. Finally, it is the missing corroborative evidence that will ultimately convict the rapist. And it is the concurrent investigation that continues throughout the trial that will bring this evidence to light. This investigation, of course, is usually headed by the present or potential romantic interest of the victim. It is important during the entire course of the rape narrative that the good men be distinguished from the bad and that the victim not be portrayed as wholly distrustful of men. The outcome of the trial is protracted for as long as possible, but thanks to the heroics of those on the outside, those who are guilty will be convicted.

These characteristics of rape narratives support the contention that soap operas are ideologically complicated. Although on some level they function to reinforce dominant ideology about justice winning out and men coming to the rescue of women, they are open to much negotiation. Rape narratives also incorporate feminist ideology. Again, what they still fail to do is construct rape narratives from the perspective of women of color: Rape victims and their assailants are always white, perhaps defusing the mythology about interracial rape but not acknowledging the intraracial violence suffered by nonwhite women, who constitute a significant portion of the soap opera audience.

As I mentioned earlier, two examples of rape narratives demonstrate the generic quality of this type of story line. In 1979, *One Life to Live* constructed a rape narrative involving a character named Karen Woleck and her sinister brother-in-law, Brad Vernon. Because Karen had a tainted past (she had been involved in prostitution), she was the ideal character around which to build a story line involving rape. Her assailant, Brad Vernon, was the spoiled, wealthy (villainous) husband of Karen's angelically good sister Jenny, who was also sickly and pregnant at the time the rape occurred. The writers initially complicate the plot by delaying Karen's report to the police but ultimately try and convict the rapist.

Ideologically, Karen presents an interesting case (although not unique) because her character is complicated before, during, and after the rape; thus, the rape cannot be said to have a transformative or "sanitizing" effect on her. Karen's character caught on because of her inevitable lapses in judgment: She was never evil but was certainly not "good." Her initial failure to report the rape, although done for good reason, turned out to be yet another in a string of wrong choices for Karen that continued until she was written out of the show because of the departure of the actress. This rape narrative is less instructive in the overtly feminist sense (no dialogues about rape statistics), but it does signal a change in point of view regarding the victim: In spite of a checkered past she is vindicated legally but not altogether morally.

The 1987 *All My Children* rape narrative takes another step as a feminist-influenced rape narrative, while still retaining the classic rape narrative ambiguities. In that case Natalie is a character who was introduced as having questionable morals but who has, prior to the rape, been established as well on her way to being more good than bad. She is raped by an acquaintance, and one with whom she has had a previous relationship. Ross, the accused and ultimately convicted rapist, is also a well-established character with many interfamily connections in Pine Valley. For these reasons, the community lines up, even causing a rift between Ross's ex-wife and her husband; the ex-wife attends the trial just to see if the man she married could do such a thing.

The writers obviously construct this rape trial as a sort of instructional acquaintance-rape drama within the usual melodramatic framework. Ross's attorney is of course a women and a secondary character, there merely as a figure to complicate the plot. District Attorney Peter Ramsey begins the "realist" instructional aspect of the narrative in his opening statement: "Rape is a felony not withstanding 'acquaintance rape.' . . . [A] crime has been committed . . . regardless of the previous or present relationship of the two people involved."

He also asks the jury not to be influenced by the look and demeanor of the accused and not to think of rape as being limited to strangers leaping out of bushes. The informative aspects of the narrative also include the testimony of a rape-crisis counselor, who presents rape statistics as well as her opinions about the status of the victim—that "she fit the profile of the rape victim all too well."

So by 1987, the soap opera rape narrative evinces the influence of feminist discourse and legal discourse of rape. Although the melodramatic framework of soap opera has always yielded certain characteristic constructions of these narratives—for example, the complex relationship between the victim and rapist—public discourse informed mainly by feminist activism has resulted in additional characteristics that further ground the narrative by injecting it with its required dose of realism. The voices of friends counseling the victim as well as the attorney's remarks disclose statistical information on the prevalence of acquaintance rape. These are rapes by men you know, goes the instruction, not strangers or "others." Ultimately, the rapist in the 1987 *All My Children* story line is imprisoned based primarily on the introduction of the "missing witness," not because a woman's word is enough to deliver a conviction. Thus the soap provides a mediated utopian ending not only because the conviction is based on a "melodramatic" intervention but also because narrative dilemmas caused by the never-endingness of soap opera require that the rapist somehow be reintegrated into the soap opera community. In both of the examples described above, the characters are eventually imprisoned and later reintegrated into community by an exonerating act.

These characteristics of the rape narrative demonstrate the complexity of this type of story line, a complexity which is characteristic of soap opera in general and which defies reduction to a simple seduction of images theory. These social issue/law narratives act to shore up the melodramatic framework of soap operas by giving them the required base of "realism" that is demanded by contemporary television audiences. Pure melodrama, found in early Hollywood "women's films," for example, relied on exaggerated situations and fiercely moralistic outcomes. Contemporary drama is more "realistic" in the narrative sense across all genres—so that even contemporary Westerns are less purely fantastical when compared to earlier epics. Rape narratives on soap operas employ some realist style in their presentation of certain points and, especially by the late 1980s, invite viewers to not only negotiate around the standard ideologies of sex roles but to a limited extent actually instruct viewers who are less immersed in feminist discourse about the consequences and opportunities available to victims of sexual violence. What they do not do, of course, is articulate a true criticism of the gender, race, and class ideologies that create a haven for sexual violence; nor do they acknowledge violence against women other than white women. But what they do is a significant achievement beyond what is done elsewhere in popular film and television.

One Life to Live and the Campus Rape Story Line of Summer 1993

In May 1993 I turned on the ABC soap opera *One Life to Live*, which I had been watching off and on, during lunch, and I noticed that the program was building up to some sort of climactic point in a story line involving a character called Marti Saybrook. May is a network sweeps period, which of course influences the ebb and flow of soap opera story lines, so not surprisingly, soon thereafter the climactic event occurred: a rape. But this rape had some unique characteristics; significantly, it was a gang acquaintance rape, committed by three apparently well-educated, wealthy, "clean-cut" fraternity types.

What I intend to do in this section is to read this story line according to its structure as a rape narrative, drawing attention to its particular strengths and weaknesses as realist melodrama in the legal tradition. Let me begin my analysis with a brief synopsis of the story line up to the point of the rape. From that point on, I will discuss both those aspects of the story line which conform to the characteristics of the rape narrative and those which are distinctive. The story line cannot truly be "summarized," because it continues to some extent one year later; since its inception it has yielded several Emmy awards for writing and acting.

The Story Line

Marti, the rape victim, began her stint on *One Life to Live*, as a bad, minor character, as a part of a story line involving a gay character.[8] She represented the self-destructive, privileged, college girl, sexually promiscuous and with a serious drinking problem. Her main purpose early on seemed to be to thwart the career and romance of the Reverend Andrew Carpenter. Marti developed a crush on Reverend Carpenter, and when he did not respond, she became key in circulating a rumor that he was gay and therefore responsible for the fact that a teenage gay character had come out. Ultimately, the story line "ended," and

Marti began to make the transition from being primarily bad to primarily sympathetic. The writers complicated the character from the beginning by giving her lupus, but through further development they explained her cynicism and self-destructive behavior as the result of her being orphaned: Her parents had died when she was quite young, leaving her to be raised by a selfish aunt. So at a point soon after her initial introduction as a background annoyance, the writers, in response to both audience interest in the character and the talent of the actress, rehabilitated the character by emphasizing her displacement and her lack of family.

As Marti's redemption continues she gains enough self-confidence to embark on a fledgling romance with another "new" character, Suede. It was the hope of the producers to develop the Suede character into one of the "hotter" younger male characters by putting him in the center of a potentially romantic story line, according to the writer I interviewed. But in the midst of Marti's transition/new romance, she and Suede have the inevitable disruption which weakens her already shaky resolve to be totally good. (Soap opera convention always places obstacles in the way of any romance and creates disruptions once the romance is consummated.) Marti heads to the "Spring Fling," a fraternity end-of-semester party, with another main male character, drinks too much, dances wildly, and is taken to her friend Kevin's room to sleep it off. Todd Manning, the wealthy, fraternity-member football-player stereotype, introduced as a minor character, notes Marti's drunken state and concocts a plan for revenge. Todd and Marti had one sexual encounter during a tutoring session sometime in the past, and Todd now blames her because he failed an exam in that subject. Todd watches Kevin take Marti up to his room because she is "out of control." After Kevin leaves, Todd and two of his fraternity buddies, Zack and Powell, gang-rape Marti, tying her arms to the bed and gagging her with a sweatband.

Marti passes out and later awakens to find that Kevin has returned. She escapes and soon decides to report the rape, and in an extended scene she is examined and then interviewed by a policewoman. At this point the writers chose to complicate the plot by introducing an element of mistaken accusation by having Marti finger her friend Kevin in addition to the guilty three. All four are arrested, and the trial begins shortly thereafter. The wealthy defendants hire the best lawyer in town, Nora Gannon, the *woman* defense attorney whose ex-husband happens to be the prosecutor. As the trial progresses, people rally to the aid of Marti, attempting to help her find evidence, like the sweatband used to gag her during the rape. Marti realizes during her own testimony that she did in fact make a mistake in accusing Kevin; the charges are then dropped against him, further complicating the case against the real rapists. Simultaneously, Nora Gannon, the defense attorney, discovers that her clients are indeed guilty when another college student comes forward and tells the story of how Todd raped her. Nora attempts to be excused from the case and instead chooses to undermine her own clients' testimony, pressing the weak link, Powell, to try to get him to confess. After none of this succeeds, Nora botches her closing argument, causing the judge to declare a mistrial.

Soon thereafter, Todd threatens to rape Marti and another character, Luna. When Luna fights back and injures Todd in self-defense, he is hospitalized and is on the verge of being prosecuted for assault. But Powell, apparently the best of the bad rapists, comes forward stating that he witnessed the attempted rape incident. Despondent over his own guilt, he is on the verge of suicide when Marti "rescues" him by promising to forgive him if he confesses. Powell confesses, implicating the other two. Todd and Zack get eight years; Powell gets four. Note that this story line began in May 1993 and continued until mid-September, when the young men got convicted. Since then time has been telescoped: Powell has been released; Todd has escaped and is currently in the midst of his "reformation."

OLTL's Standard Rape Narrative

The *One Life to Live* story line I have described conforms to many of the conventions of the rape narrative as it is presented in soap operas. First, the characteristics of and relationship of the victim and assailant to each other quickly become central to the story line. Marti represents an ideal narrative victim because of the combination of her morally ambiguous past and her evolution into a more sympathetic character. The act of rape itself is not transformative, in that Marti does not become good and saintly as a direct re-

sult of a sexual assault; in fact, the writers were attentive to avoiding that slant. But the act is transformative in that the character comes into the "family" of Llanview: Although she initially causes the characteristic community rift, her defenders, including everyone but the rapists themselves, eventually pull close together. And the transformation from self-loathing cynic that began prior to the assault is further enunciated through Marti's continuous declarations, particularly after the mistrial, of no longer accepting her status as victim. Thus, in spite of the overt attempts of the writers, the structure of the narrative demands "transformation," although in the case of *One Life to Live* this previously "degrading" plot strategy is a bit more complex.

Todd, Zack, and Powell are a complicated alternative to the standard soap opera rapist, despite the obvious class stereotyping, because their relationship to the victim is somewhat different than in previous rape narratives and because they are *multiple*. Clearly, of the three, Todd is the leader and most recognizably villainous of the rapists. Yet he *and* his cohorts possess the standard rapist characteristics, in that they may represent other than "middle-class" values (here, upper-class villains) and they know, and in Todd's case have had a sexual relationship with, the victim. But while Todd may embody the evil "other," at the other end of the spectrum, Powell, who bows to peer pressure, does not. And although the victim knows the rapists, only Powell has the quasi-familial community relationship usually apparent in rape scenarios; they are all "peripheral" characters until well into the story line. So the fixed categorization of either "stranger" or "acquaintance" rape and the images that are associated with those two concepts is somewhat problematized. This is possible primarily because the rape is committed by a group composed of individuals that the soap opera can choose to develop. In fact, in the tradition of *One Life to Live*, the writers sought to generate an issue plot that had some social recognizability and relevance and chose a gang acquaintance rape at least partly because of the much-publicized gang rapes in the New York area at the time. Two incidents were cited as being particularly influential: the St. John's University rape case where a student unsuccessfully tried to prosecute several members of a fraternity and the Glen Ridge, New Jersey, incident in which a woman with mental retardation was raped by several high school students (Whitesell 1994).

The rapists' ambiguous status as members of the community also problematized the standard rape narrative's reliance on "the divided community." In order to resolve this problem and thus reopen the narrative, the false accusation of the well-established character was introduced. The writers also claimed that this complication was necessary because the three "real" rapists were until this point relatively minor characters, and thus involving a main character in the trial would guarantee viewer loyalty and interest (Whitesell 1994). In fact, though, that particular complication served to frustrate and annoy most viewers, according to discussions with fans. The unique attempts to problematize the standard characterizations of rapists was somewhat set back by this complication. It did conform to the soap necessities of extending the plot and complicating the predicted outcome; nonetheless, it did raise the specter of victim believability, an issue that is generally critiqued in feminist rape discourse.

The presentation of the act itself also represents a site of alternative possibilities. Again, a conscious effort was made to dramatize the rape from other than the usual voyeuristic perspective. There were no full-body shots of the assailants and the victim together during the assault; instead, most shots were close-ups from the perspective of the victim. There were relatively few shots of the victim in a pained expression; rather, there were shots of her wrist ties or the gag about to be used. These scenes were constructed to disturb rather than to excite or invite the audience to watch. My argument here is that the careful construction of these scenes signals another level of adaption of the rape narrative to the exigencies of rape discourse in the larger world.

Since *One Life to Live* is particularly suited to trial narratives for a number of reasons, the May 1993 rape trial served to ground the melodrama in a number of ways. The conventional requirements of soap opera melodrama inflected with realism factored into not only the very clear "informational aspects" of the trial but also into other dramatic elements. *One Life to Live* dispatched assistants to do research on rape and talk to rape counselors as well as relying on its law school–educated writer to write most of the trial scenes. So, for example, rape shield laws are fully explained in the course of defense attorney Nora Gannon's questioning of the victim. Nora explains that rape shield laws prevent her from asking Marti about past sexual relationships with anyone other than those who are accused of raping her.

The deployment of the female defense attorney as a standard plot complication seems justified yet truly becomes one of the most significant focal points of the trial. In fact, the writer Christopher Whitesell felt uncomfortable having Nora Gannon represent the rapists but could not prevail against genre convention. But because Nora is a primary character who is skillfully portrayed by the actress Hillary B. Smith, the "coming to truth" of the lawyer could be explored somewhat differently. It is fairly standard in popular film and television that defense attorneys defending guilty clients realize their mistake too late. Ideologically, this implies that even defense attorneys should not be defending guilty clients. Narratively, this allows the proper legal resolution of the trial to be achieved extralegally, emphasizing the extent to which the legal system actually does not work in the interests particularly of those who are "outside" because of race, class, gender, or sexual orientation. In the case of *One Life to Live*, however, in the midst of this awakening, the attorney explores and discusses all of the possible ways of not exonerating the rapists and not compromising her professional responsibility. Soap operas have the time to explore the personal dilemma caused by a conflict that the real law tries to dismiss (as personal) and that prime-time television tries to override.

An extralegal process usually resolves the rape-narrative dilemma with the appearance of a missing piece of evidence or a missing witness. This structure does not fundamentally change in the May 1993 story line; however, the gang-rape structure allows for this conventional approach to be somewhat altered. There is the promise of missing corroborative evidence throughout the trial: There is the sweatband used as a gag, and later there is a woman who was raped by Todd who comes forward too late. Both of these turn out to be "red herrings" that do not function to close the case; it is the good/bad rapist Powell who becomes the focal point of the resolution/conviction because of his overall weakness and remorsefulness. After Todd attempts to carry out a second assault against the victim, Powell's weakness turns into a questionable strength that will ultimately resolve the dilemma of how to continue to incorporate the character in the story line after he has committed a rape: He ultimately confesses to witnessing the second assault as well as participating in the initial rape.

New Developments in the Soap Opera Rape Narrative?

John Fiske, in his discussion of soap opera treatment of progressive subjects, argues that "all sides of an issue can be explored and evaluated from a variety of social points of view. . . . [N]o point of view is given clear hierarchical precedence over any other" (1987, p. 195). What is uniquely interesting about this plotline is that it so fully embodies the absolute complexity of the soap opera genre, a complexity that is often dismissed as confused, unsatisfying and insulting. To some extent this is true and troubling in the *One Life to Live* narrative, yet the story line does presume that some points of view are wrong: In Marti's case rape does not suggest or lead to romance. Although this commitment to the wrongness of rape may signal a certain firm position on an issue, factoring in the mistaken accusation, on the other hand, seems to undermine that commitment—signifying a retreat, perhaps, by calling attention to the specter of false accusation. Of course, this constant tension and frustration and the never-ending story are what characterize soap opera. The writers use this plot mechanism based on the popular mythology of "false accusation" to both draw out the plot, tell "another side" of the story, and generate the necessary frustration in the viewer.

But again, certain particularities of this story line make a commitment to some limited feminist ideology apparent. In spite of the mistaken accusation, the viewer occupies the subject position of the rape victim. Thus, the viewer knows that the victim was indeed both raped and mistaken, and skilled soap readers know that she will be vindicated: At this point the writers know that the fans would not stand for anything else. She was raped by a group of well-educated, upper-class men, counter to the stereotypical prime-time villains, who are normally associated with violent sex crimes, both historically and in contemporary society. The trial itself educates as well as explores on the level of both melodrama and realism the misfunctioning of a legal system that in reality frequently does not vindicate rape victims. Next I would like to point to two particularly innovative attempts to move the rape narrative beyond its standard construction.

One of the standout moments that carried this plotline beyond the standard soap opera rape narrative depicted Marti's postrape trauma and hospital examination. I point to this as a standout moment not only because of my own recognition of its impact but also because the viewers I interviewed and collected data from, who had not themselves been rape victims, felt that they learned something significant about victim trauma over the course of the development of the plotline; and I suggest that much of this has to do with this particular scene. Perhaps it is not good to "scare" women into submission by visualizing the horrors of sexual violence, but I would suggest that the reason that public discourse on rape has reached the much-improved level it has is due to open discussions and face-to-face encounters with victims. Earlier I discussed what I consider to be the positive, less voyeuristic way in which the rape itself was constructed. Everyone who watched that scene was forced into the victim/female point of view regardless of their own gender; and increasing numbers of men do watch soap operas. The traumatic effect on the victim is initially characterized first by Marti's inability to talk about or even consider reporting the crime. But as her "community" support comes forward, she is urged to at least go to the hospital and have an examination. She is ushered into the examination room by one of the main characters, who is a nurse and who pronounces that she is a rape counselor. The following shot is of a rape evidence kit. Once the examination begins, again, there is a proliferation of point-of-view shots from the victim's perspective. These shots predominate and are either extreme close-ups of both the nurse or doctor asking questions and dispensing information or close-ups of the actual evidence being gathered, such as hair and fingernails. The scene is temporally framed by two shots of the clock in the room, designating and signaling the slow passage of time. This "editing" of this scene, meaning the cuts from camera to camera, are unusually sharp, creating a kind of montage effect that emphasizes the disruptiveness of the examination process. By the time a final shot of the clock signals the end of the examination, with a voice announcing that it is indeed over, the viewer is drained. Not long after this scene, that day's episode ends with a culmination of this invasive, violated feeling. A picture of Marti and her dead parents fades to the victim in the shower scrubbing herself relentlessly with soap while experiencing intermittent flashbacks to the rape. The scene cuts to four brief flashbacks as Marti falls to the floor of the shower; it ends on a freeze frame of her silent scream, as emotionally forceful a visual image as seen on daytime television or anywhere. It is also an image almost unique in its focal point. So it is here, I contend, that daytime television realizes its social and political potential, as it presents the actual process of reporting a rape from the victim's perspective in an in-depth and emotionally powerful manner.

The second disruption of the conventional rape narrative occurs at the close of the rape trial. The writers chose the conventional approach to creating tension in the "one-sided" rape narrative by having the extraordinarily principled Nora Gannon defending the rapists. Initially, of course, she believes in their innocence mainly because of the fourth mistaken defendant, whom the victim eventually clears. But little by little Nora discovers that they are indeed guilty, thanks in part to the emergence of a previous victim. It is at this point that she struggles with the conflict between the ideal of the rule of law and her own moral reasoning. First articulating the more legalistic perspective, she states, "My entire life, entire life has been the law. I uphold it, I honor it, I love it. With every fibre of my being I believe everyone is entitled to a fair defense. . . . [I]t is my duty, my moral responsibility *as a lawyer* to stand by them and defend them zealously to the end" (*One Life to Live*, September 1993, emphasis added).

This pronouncement comes in the form of a sort of Socratic dialogue between Nora and her boyfriend, who is urging her to withdraw from the defense. And although her utterances about the rule of law seem firm, it is her morality that finally forces her to challenge the strict construction of the law. First Nora attempts to withdraw, then she tries to get the weakest link in the gang to confess during testimony. Nora's appearance and manner increasingly degenerate as the inter-

nal conflict manifests itself, culminating in her closing argument, where she asks the jury to be "blind justice"—to close their eyes and not be swayed by the appearance of her clients as nice, well-educated college men. Finally, at the peak of her plea to the jury, the main villain interrupts and the judge orders a mistrial, sanctioning Nora for her failure to uphold her professional responsibility.

It is in this way that the writers have raised the stakes of this text by not only significantly dramatizing the constraint of the formal legal process but even further problematizing the relationship of gendered and racial others to it. Neither the defense attorney Nora nor the African American prosecutor Hank Gannon are able to prevail within those rules. On some level this is a result of the requirement of all soap opera that plotlines be extended to the maximum. Yet this extension functions to draw attention to the inability of the legal process to find truth. Unlike narratives that must provide a resolution within an hour or two, the soap opera has the time to fully expose this fallacy and to focus on alternative methods of vindication. And rather than chastise the character for being a bad lawyer, this narrative presents the possibility of a different and richer "legal" morality, an issue that is much debated within the context of feminist legal theory and practice. For example, Katherine Bartlett (1991) argues that feminist lawyers should and do employ "feminist methods" in their practice and points to "practical moral reasoning" as an example. She states, "Disadvantaged by hidden bias, feminists see the value of modes of legal reasoning that expose and open up debate concerning the underlying political and moral considerations. . . . [F]eminists turn to contextualized methods of reasoning to allow greater understanding and exposure of injustice" (Bartlett 1991, p. 381).

I am not suggesting, however, that the *One Life to Live* plotline is calling for a radical restructuring of the legal system. Nora's moral dilemma, presented within the melodramatic/realistic framework of soap opera, does open this issue up for consideration in a manner that differs significantly from the predominant considerations of law and order. Hank Gannon, the African American prosecutor, signals a possibility as well, but one that is not developed in the same manner and may never be. Soap opera remains primarily a place that incorporates only some feminist concerns, not those of all "feminized" others, such as black men. On the other hand, this limitation may be slowly changing: *All My Children*'s Livia Frye is an African American woman attorney who may be said to employ "feminist" legal methods.

What, then, do we as fans and feminists do with the soap opera rape narrative? I have tried to demonstrate that soap operas do not deserve some of the merciless criticism they generate whenever one mentions "rape" and "soap opera" in the same breath. Rape narratives, at least those that culminate in trials and vindication, have changed and adapted to the demands of their viewers as well as to wider public discourse about sexual violence. This newer approach is by no means "feminist" in the radical sense—and it cannot be, because of the dictates of a commercial reactionary medium. Soap operas do retain some aspects that are in fact justifiably objectionable to feminists, but at the same time, they also incorporate aspects of feminism, perhaps in attempt to "inoculate" viewers against any real movement. Yet this attempt at control fails, and fails particularly in the area of soap opera, due to the particular requirements of the soap opera text itself. When the rigid yet dramatically pliable structure of the law meets this narrative form, the law itself becomes available to the same possibilities of negotiation that the television text does.

Notes

This chapter is based on material from the forthcoming *The Law of Daytime: Soap Operas, Issue Plots, and Law Narratives,* which will be published by Duke University Press.

1. The term "melodramatic imagination" is used in academic literature on film, as, for example, in Christine Gledhill's introduction to *Home Is Where the Heart Is* (1987b). In that discussion she refers to the "melodramatic imagination" as a dramatic concept or genre originating in novel and stage which cinema sought to fully realize. I borrow the term and give it a more personal definition here: that is, a way of recognizing, reading, and valuing a particular type of storytelling that is referred to as melodrama.

2. The "Luke and Laura" era of *General Hospital* is often heralded as a turning point in the development of soap opera. Luke and Laura, who will be discussed later in this chapter, began their relationship with a rape; but, more important, they became one of the most popular couples in soap opera history. It is at this point that legions of college students began being counted as a significant portion of soap opera fan culture, and this *General Hospital* plot was one of the first aimed specifically at this younger group.

3. See, for example, Gillers 1989.

4. Agnes Nixon is the creator of the three currently running soap operas—*One Life to Live, All My Children,* and *The City*—and has been writing for soap opera for over 30 years.

5. This figure is down from the all-time soap opera viewer high of twenty million in 1970.

6. Elayne Rapping discusses, generally, how issues that feminism brought to the public, such as rape and domestic violence, are now a staple of daytime television talk shows. I would argue that this phenomenon is also apparent in soap opera.

7. I take this suggestion from the introduction to Higgins and Silver 1991.

8. Most "new" characters are tested on soaps. The actors/actresses are given short-term contracts, and the characters are then developed depending on a number of factors, including the audience response to the actor and the story line. Of course, this depends as much on the actor's ability and general appeal as it does on the writer's skill.

11

Pop Justice

TV, Motherhood, and the Law

ISABEL KARPIN

Anyone who was a regular TV viewer in the United States from April to August 1993 would have to conclude that the American mass media was obsessed with circulating stories of familial breakdown.[1] If it wasn't reporting the story of the adopted child[2] returned to her biological parents after two years, it was telling of a child switched at birth who was now struggling to find a familial ground on which to rest her daughterhood.[3] Or the story of a woman locked in a battle over custody of a child conceived through sexual intercourse with a man who contracted her services under a surrogacy agreement.[4] Those five months were a turbulent time for the nuclear family, where new kinds of parents were floated and endlessly negotiated:

> We have a changing American family that's running out there, and it's not something that we all want, but we can't close our eyes to it either. In Michigan, for example, there are 200,000 children, according to the 1990 census, and I would wager more by 1993. The 200,000 chil-

dren that are living in third-party households, those are people other than their parents that are raising these children, and this is because of the epidemic of children born out of wedlock because of divorce, because of drug or alcohol dependency, problems of financial setbacks. The question now becomes, in our country, what do we do to protect those children if they are in established environments, and they look to people other than biological adults to be their parents? (Richard Victor, attorney for Baby Jessica 1993)

This chapter is about TV and its relation to law and the making of the modern family. Through an examination of three legal cases that were also media and cultural events, I analyze what constitutes the "natural" family and "natural" familial relationships. I look at how that "natural" family gets stabilized as natural and what kind of ideology informs that stabilization. Arguably, it is only in those moments when the "unnatural" or aberrant family is represented (on television, for example) that a "natural" or normal family form emerges as the absent referent. It is everything the family currently being discussed, criticized, and represented is not. It is Richard Victor's original American family—the one that is now subject to change.

Victor lays claim to this older notion of family and then asks us to start our project of familial reconstruction in a new place—a place where children can be protected despite the absence of biology. This potentially disruptive shift in the taxonomy of the family is not, however, a new idea. Mainstream liberal ideology, in tune with this shift, tends to support families constructed through psychological rather than physiological bonds. The reason for this is rather complex. Liberal feminism has tended to argue in favor of some kind of formal equality where distinctions based on biological sex are deemed irrelevant. Some legal liberal feminists have advocated allowing biological sex-based distinctions only, with respect to reproduction (Law 1984, p. 955). Only where "the law [in doing so] has no significant impact in perpetuating either the oppression of women or culturally imposed sex-role constraints on individual freedom." If the law has this impact, then according to these same feminists "it must be justified as the best means of serving a compelling state purpose" (Law 1984, p. 963). Legal liberal feminism and liberal feminism generally have been extremely successful at both the legislative level and in terms of changing the way people think.

But what does this mean for biological and nonbiological families? The same kind of logic is brought to bear on these arrangements. Distinctions based on biology are considered irrelevant and reactionary and driven by a desire to perpetuate sex-role stereotyping. What is perceived as relevant is how well the family functions—as if that were a neutral determination that could be made with no reference to values that reflect either a sexual hierarchy or a race or class-based hierarchy. It is then assumed by liberal feminists and others alike that because we have challenged the outward significance of the biological tie we have necessarily severed the tie that binds women to mothering and in so doing have loosened the masculine grip on power in the family. In other words, it is thought that with this shift away from biology, another shift follows—a freeing up of the rigid masculine hierarchization of

the family, where patriarchy reigns and women are subordinate.

I argue that this move away from biology is not necessarily liberatory but, rather, constitutes a shift from a patriarchal ideal of familial construction to a paternal ideal. The family has been transformed, if we can call it that, from a zone of authoritarianism to a zone of reconstructed masculinity. But nevertheless, the founding structure is still centered around the paternal figure. This move, from the patriarchal to the paternal, is one identified by feminist film theorist Vivian Sobchack in recent science fiction film (Sobchack 1991). My interest is in the way the medium of television effects this shift through its representation of certain legal cases dealing with maternal rights.[5]

Some of what I do here will be an analysis of just how the visual technologies of contemporary "Western" society are operative and crucial in the production of the natural family. In particular I will be looking at the way the "lived body" of the "birth mother"[6] gets made and unmade, regulated and deregulated, denied and fetishized.

I

Television seems to have a special relation to law. TV is littered with shows about the law. From cop shows to *Cops*, from shows about lawyers to shows about law cases, television in the United States, and to a lesser extent in Australia, is always doing law.[7]

In her article "Video/Television/Rodney King: Twelve Steps beyond *The Pleasure Principle*," Avital Ronell contends that "television has always been related to law, which it locates at the site of crucial trauma. Even when it is not performing metonymies of law it is producing some cognition around its traumatic diffusions: thus even the laugh track, programming the traumatic experience of laughter, can be understood to function as shock absorber" (Ronell 1992, p. 1). Ronell is here identifying two ways in which law is instantiated at the moment of "crucial trauma." The first is what she calls the "performance of metonymies of law," which I understand as the representation or dramatization (usually as narrativization) of parts (George Holliday's video recording of the Rodney King beating, for example) which stand in for the whole (the legal system, or justice—itself only metonymically representative of social culture). The second involves a more generalized encounter with the medium of television. I have called this encounter "pop justice" in my title, and it encompasses the whole stream of cultural images and forms that constitute the intersecting materials of legal and cultural practices. TV is never merely representative but is always engaged in a process of "cultural" production.

There are three aspects to the medium of television that are particularly important to this analysis. First, television is invested in a rhetoric of "liveness." It is touted as a medium of instantaneous mass electronic communication. This means there is a certain "being-there-ness" about television that makes it part of the representation and not just something which represents. Jane Feuer puts it this way: "TV exploits its assumed "live" ontology as ideology. In the concept of live television, flow and unity are emphasized, giving a sense of immediacy and wholeness, even though network practice belies such unity, even in—especially in—live coverage of events" (Feuer 1983, p. 16). Second, and inevitably connected to the first, time on television is discontinuous. It is broken up into episodes, serials (termed continuous narratives, although they are continually broken up), commercial breaks, news headlines, programs, and so on. Repetition is also a highly important mode on television. Sobchack considers this particularity to be the distinguishing mark of the electronic: "The primary value of electronic temporality is the *instant*, which (thanks to television and videotape) can be selected, combined and instantly replayed and re-run to such a degree that the previously irreversible stream of objective time seems overcome" (Sobchack 1990, p. 57). Finally, the third aspect, which again stems from the other two, is TV's relation to the world. It offers access to so many different modalities that it becomes impossible to argue for its distinctness from those modalities. When TV is reporting law, it is doing law.

One very obvious area in which the lines between TV and law are blurred is the area of testimony. Ronell, citing Anita Hill, Rodney King, and the Vietnam and Gulf Wars, claims that television "has become the locus of testimony" (Ronell 1992, p. 10). But it is testimony unfettered by the rules of evidence. Whereas, in law, testi-

mony must be of a certain quality before it can be proffered in court,[8] there is no such restriction on TV. Some feminist legal theorists have critiqued the way rules of evidence work to distort a narrative that is otherwise textured with social, emotional, and contextual detail. They claim it renders those very significant elements irrelevant (White 1990). Others have argued that the circumvention of the rules of evidence through these television forums makes it impossible to achieve justice. I want to argue that it is necessary to step outside this dichotomy of good and bad and explore what it means to discover that narratives such as these are contingent on the forums in which they operate.

The media frenzy surrounding the O. J. Simpson murder trial illustrates this problem. Programs like *Hard Copy* and *A Current Affair* pay big money for exclusive stories about major players. In one case a woman who claimed she saw O. J. at the crime scene (the conventional eyewitness) had been paid so much for her story that the prosecution decided not to call her, believing her testimony to be totally compromised. TV was doing law. Later, the prosecution turned to a witness and asked him whether his story had yet appeared on TV. The witness stated that it had not, to which the prosecutor replied, "Well I guess this is a scoop for us."[9] Law was doing TV.

Instead of seeing the media as a space that taints and distorts law, I want to explore how TV can operate as a dynamic space offering the possibility of public contestation and debate through forums such as the news, talk shows, reality TV, and docudramas. Raymond Williams has described TV as "at once an intention and an effect of a particular social order" (R. Williams 1975, p. 128), suggesting that TV is both the creation of a particular social order and an inevitable consequence of it. But I would go further and suggest that TV is also productive of that social order. Although TV is not yet directly interactive, it is nevertheless integrated in the circuit of social and cultural production, and the law is by no means immune from it or even, dare I suggest, distinct. Making this connection more vigorously, Avital Ronell has said that TV is "itself trying to tell us something about the status of legal and social fictions" (Ronell 1992, p. 1). TV is both an interpretive apparatus through which we view the world and itself an apparatus which must be interpreted.

The TV broadcast of the beating of Rodney King shows how Ronell's analysis is played out. TV and law have not just become embroiled, each referring to each other, but intermingled. In the case of the beating of Rodney King, TV was used as an apparatus of justice. People could see for themselves how law on the streets of L.A. was being administered, or so it was claimed. The video not only spoke for itself but was clear and convincing evidence: "You've got to see it to believe it." And you did! When Holliday's video was beamed into our living rooms we watched as sixteen white police officers surrounded and beat a single black man. Although only a portion of the video was ever broadcast, the scene looped endlessly. While we could turn our heads or change channels, the camera staunchly refused to lift its gaze away from the evidence of the beating. But that same videotape was used successfully in the defense of the police, broken down into a frame-by-frame evidentiary narrative that neutralized the power of TV. The video was converted into a series of stills that captured and contained a different narrative. According to Avital Ronell, the seemingly counterintuitive not-guilty verdict that resulted stemmed from the failure on the part of the prosecution (and presumably all of us who felt the video spoke for itself) to realize that the video required a reading. Having realized that, one can take the further step and recognize that reading a video as a photograph (as a series of stills) will change the way it is perceived (Ronell 1992, p. 16). It is with this mandate in mind that I make my venture here into the strange world of law and television.

While I want to hold out for the possibility of some kind of resistant space within the mass-media communications forum, primarily because it would seem to offer up some hope for the democratization of law, the examination that I bring to bear critiques the operations of popular cultural resettlements of the "natural" in the face of its destabilization. The cases I look at are chosen precisely because they concern institutions (families), practices (law), and ideals (motherhood) that both are undergoing destabilization and are operative in sustaining the existing cultural terrain. They seem to offer up a fetishized space crucially in need of restabilization. What I am specifically concentrating on is the trauma these cases provoke because they trouble the

meaning of "family" and "mother." I will argue that this trauma is fundamentally connected to the so-called contemporary crisis of patriarchy that I will map out more fully later in this chapter.

Before going any further it is necessary to fill in the stories that are the centerpoint of my discussion.

The Cases

The Baby Jessica Case   This case concerned a custody battle over a child named Jessica. Prior to giving birth, Jessica's birth mother, Cara Schmidt (then Kalusen), decided to put the child up for adoption. The lawyer for the prearranged adopting couple (the DeBoers) appeared at her bedside forty hours after the birth, secured her signature on a document in which she relinquished all her maternal rights, and took custody of the child. Although Iowa law specified a waiting period of seventy-two hours after the birth before signatures could be obtained, the period was waivable, and the lawyer for the DeBoers acted on the basis of that waiver. Either immediately upon the birth or very soon thereafter, Cara changed her mind. Within twenty days of the adoption she began making efforts to get her baby back. Prior to the birth Cara had falsely identified a certain person as the father. The consent to the adoption of that misidentified person was sought and obtained, and as a result the biological father had never actually relinquished his paternal rights. When it was revealed that the biological father had never consented, it was clear that the adoption would not be legal. The facts of this case reveal a legal system that failed at every juncture to act quickly and compassionately.

Cara, who was not married to the father prior to the birth, married him, and together they initiated court proceedings to get Jessica back. The legal battle began on March 21, 1992, when Judge Josala of the Iowa Juvenile Court said that she did not have jurisdiction to give Cara back her rights. Both Cara and Dan appealed to the Iowa Supreme Court and were successful. Over the two years there were some twenty court decisions, all of which, barring one, went against the DeBoers. The DeBoers, who had custody of Jessica, lived in Michigan and refused to give her up. Finally the Michigan Court of Appeals held that the Iowa decision stood and that the child should be returned to her biological parents on August 2, 1993. In coming to this conclusion, the Michigan Court of Appeals threw out a Michigan lower court decision finding that it was in the best interests of the child to remain with the DeBoers.

The Kimberly Mays Case   Kimberly Mays discovered at the age of ten that the people who had raised her from birth were not her biological parents. Due to a hospital mix-up (although there is some talk of deliberateness), Kimberly Mays was switched with another baby shortly after birth and went home with the "wrong" family. The other baby, Arlena Twigg, went home with Kimberly's biological family and lived as their biological child until the age of ten, when she died of a heart defect. At that time blood tests revealed that Arlena could not be the biological child of the Twiggs, so Regina Twigg and her husband initiated an investigation to find out what had happened that day at the hospital. They discovered that Kimberly (alive and living with Robert Mays as his biological child) was in fact their biological child. Over the years they attempted, and at times succeeded, to form a relationship with Kimberly. But by the age of fourteen Kimberly felt the strain of moving between two families to be too great and claimed that the Twiggs were tearing her family apart. With the help of the lawyer who represented Geoffrey K (George Russ) in his "divorce" action against his mother, Kimberly asked the court for an order that the Twiggs have no more to do with her. To make such an order the court had to find that the man Kimberly Mays had assumed was her biological parent was her legal father and that the Twiggs had no rights based on their biological connection. The court ordered that it was not necessary for Mr. Mays to adopt Kimberly, as he was indeed her legal father, and that Kimberly's stepmother was entitled, despite the lack of consent on the part of the Twiggs, to adopt Kimberly and become her legal mother. Kimberly's other mother, the mother whom she had assumed to be her biological mother, had died when Kimberly was still very young. Although Kimberly's court action was successful, in recent times she has reinstated her relationship with the Twiggs, deciding to live with them in 1994.

The Chamberlain/Kaplan Case   Susan Chamberlain agreed to act as a "surrogate" mother for Joseph and Jean Kaplan. The parties, anxious to get the process under way, determined to conceive the child through sexual intercourse as opposed to artificial insemination. Court testimony as to whose idea this was is contradictory. In any case, after a number of attempts a child was conceived. Before the birth, Susan Chamberlain changed her mind about the arrangement and initiated proceedings to retain custody of the child once it was born. Media coverage of the case focused incessantly on testimony concerning the sexual encounters between Susan Chamberlain and Joseph Kaplan. The court awarded custody of the baby to Joseph Kaplan and gave Chamberlain visitation rights. This case was almost always presented in the media alongside the other two. All three events occurred at much the same time, and media calls for comparisons between them were commonplace, although actual comparisons were hard to come by. For instance, in the lead-up to a general discussion on *Sonya Live* of the Baby Jessica case and the law of adoption, a clip of the Kimberly Mays case was included. In the Court TV version of the Chamberlain/Kaplan case, the scene of Baby Jessica being handed to her biological parents was replayed in the opening sequence. This was not unusual.

TV and the Law

The three cases I have described above are not simply stories about familial breakdown. On the contrary, at the same time that these stories were being circulated in the media, the possibility of familial stability and unity was both implicitly and explicitly realized. The struggles were always represented as if the stable nuclear family unit was the ground from which each of these cases represented a shocking aberration. In other words, the crisis of familial breakdown signaled the possibility for restabilizing the traditional "family" and its constituent parts: father, mother, and child.

Martha Fineman has developed a schema of the idealized family in which she critically describes the *legal* natural family as held together by a horizontal sexual tie between the father and the mother (Fineman 1992, p. 662). This legal version of the natural family is not a construct operating in isolation from its televisual or popular counterpart. In fact, it is within the context of TV that this "natural" legal formation comes under spectacular challenge. It becomes a site of "popular trauma" which is rendered in televisual rhetorics that both problematize and resolve the trauma as social knowledge. I am suggesting that in this instance, TV operates at several levels to reinscribe the traditional rhetorics and to resist them.

My argument is that the three legal events that captured the popular cultural imagination did so because they operated to legislate notions of the "natural" family *as* cultural production. In the moment in which the cases became a commodity for popular consumption, the trauma of their impact was both registered and managed through their representation.

Returning, then, to Avital Ronell's contention that TV operates as a shock absorber, it is clear that in the three cases I am discussing, the trauma that TV cushioned seems to settle on a primary dislocation—that of the "natural" and its relation to the "maternal."

Vivian Sobchack argues in her article "Child/ Alien/Father: Patriarchal Crisis and Generic Exchange" that American bourgeois patriarchy has experienced a crisis since the late 1960s. Related to the crisis is the

> disintegration and transfiguration of the "traditional" American bourgeois family—an ideological as well as interpersonal structure characterized, as Robin Wood so frequently points out, by its cellular construction, its institutionalization of capitalist and patriarchal relations and values (among them monogamy, heterosexuality, and consumerism), and its present state of disequilibrium and crisis. (Sobchack 1991, pp. 3–4)

The crisis over the dislocation of the natural in the realm of the maternal stands in for the larger crisis of patriarchy in the cases I am exploring. This crisis is expressed in the efforts to locate a more liberal settlement of the bourgeois family than its prior incarnation as a biologically connected and heterosexually governed unit. The "best interests of the child" rule, a liberal feminist construction (Fineman 1992, p. 656), has so permeated dominant culture that patriarchal lineage is no longer an answer to the question posed

in the title of the docudrama "Whose Child Is This?" (the story of the "war" for Baby Jessica). Patriarchal lineage (or biological relationship) continues to be an answer in law, particularly in the case of adoption, where the "best interests" rule is subordinated to the biological ties of the natural parent, requiring them to be rendered unfit before they can be displaced (Cahn 1994, p. 330). Nevertheless, each of the *media* presentations of the cases to which I refer operated within a framework in which that principle was paramount. The ascendancy of this precept, which emphasizes the helpless vulnerability and innocence of the child, enables a move from the patriarchal as a traditional, authoritarian, and antisentimental stance to the paternal as a reconstructed masculine space. In liberal feminist politics this shift represents a move toward the realm of equality.

I want to think about Sobchack's idea of the shift from the patriarchal to the paternal in the context of Fineman's emphasis on the sexualized family as a site of patriarchal control. The "natural" nuclear family in her schema does not depend on a biological link. It is resilient to liberal moves that demand its opening up, its inclusivity of new family forms. The structure of the patriarchal family remains intact in the face of these new traumas. Fineman says:

> Historically, in order to qualify as the foundational family relationship, a heterosexual union had to be legally privileged through marriage. There is a great deal of current agitation to eliminate this formality. "Liberals" seek to expand the traditional nuclear family model, urging the recognition of informal heterosexual unions within the definition of the family. There are also calls for the acceptance and legal legitimation of same-sex relationships in the form of proposed domestic partnership laws.
>
> Even in the context of the proposed liberalized definitions of family, the adult sexual affiliation remains central. . . .
>
> Formal, legal, heterosexual marriage continues to dominate our imagination when we confront possibilities of intimacy and family. (Fineman 1992, pp. 663–64)

Martha Fineman's analysis of the "natural" and idealized nuclear family as organized around a sexual tie keys into the cultural anxiety surrounding the destabilization of the "natural." That destabilization occurs when the natural is no longer coterminous with the biological. In order to restabilize the family, popular cultural forms offer a new "liberal" version of the natural family that is now independent of biological ties but still contained comfortably within the patriarchal paradigm of what Fineman calls the "sexualized family." To illustrate this point, it is instructive to listen to Roberta DeBoer's attempts to establish her family as a credible unit. In an interview on CNN's *Larry King Live* DeBoer said, "I'd like to clear up just the beginning of this program, which indicated that Jan and I are foster parents. We are Jessica's natural parents. If this little child can sing her 'A-B-C's,' she can clearly identify to you and the rest of the world that have asked a hundred times who her natural parents are, and that is about the purest form of a definition that I think anyone can find" (DeBoer 1993). One reason the Baby Jessica case produces so much public anxiety, therefore, is that the DeBoer family unit represents a liberal success story. The nuclear family, which for at least the last decade in American politics has been figured as a resource of social stability, is now under attack and trying to assert itself in a new liberalized form. Rather than being protected, however, it is depicted as being viciously torn apart by the old patriarchal form of family, which depends on blood lineage. The family unit neatly produced by a mother, a father, and a child is not respected. The media comments that Jessica will have to leave the only "home she has ever known" (Walters 1993b; C. Reed 1993, p. A7) and on the other hand that "Jessica will be taken into seclusion now to *try* to make a family" (B. Williams 1993) reinforce and quell these anxieties (consider the critique of this usage in O. Thompson 1993, p. 85).

The Techniques of TV

One specific way in which TV operates to effect these social reconfigurations of the natural is by taking us into a realm where the law cannot visit—the after-effects. TV effectively represents the consequences of legal decision-making. Defining "popular trials," Robert Hariman states, "They usually lack the key element of closure provided by the trial's verdict" (Hariman 1990,

p. 2). Law as it stands speaks in a discourse that is intolerant of uncertainty, demands the clear and definitive answer, and relies on the foundational and universal truth. News media, talk shows, and docudramas all offer a version of law that is not contained within the strict unifying boundaries of the law. There is a terrain of "serious" legal discourse that imagines itself as separate from and "superior to" political discourse.[10] TV troubles the edges of that terrain. Issues that are answered definitively by a court of law are torn asunder by an image after the law has decided.

Watching the news in the United States on August 3, 1993, it was impossible to miss just such an image—the image of Baby Jessica (as she was titled) being handed over from her adoptive to her biological parents. This reiterated and fetishized image forced a coming to terms with the consequences of the legal determination. It evoked a narrative that viewers, lawyers, and feminists had been struggling with for months. The cameras recorded the tearful and screaming toddler being carried from the arms of her adoptive mother and placed in a car. This image was, of course, masterfully replicated in the telemovie *Whose Child Is This?: The War for Baby Jessica*, provoking one news commentator to ask what the child actor had been told in order to elicit such a convincing performance. He states, "That final scene of Jessica being taken from her parents who loved and cared for her is nearly as agonizing to watch in reenactment as it was in news footage that aired last month when it happened" (Shales 1993, p. B1).

The most significant aspect of this image is not its intrinsic tear-jerking qualities but, rather, its positioning within the larger debate that I have been mapping—namely, what constitutes "family" in the face of the destabilization of the biological as coterminous with the natural. The image is offered as testimony to the naturalness of the psychological tie.

Between the news media and the courtroom is Court TV. Interestingly, the Court TV version of the Baby Jessica case (an hour-long condensed version, which can be purchased for $26.50) finishes with the judge's decision. Court TV offers an intermediate discourse between law and popular culture. It is a media form that is attentive to both the rhetorics of the law and the rhetorics of television. Court TV does make its textual interventions, explaining testimony and legal rules, having outside-court interviews, and opening telephone lines to the general public. Further, we know that the camera is no innocent in the process of representation, even in the case of the seemingly neutral presentation of the courtroom trial. The camera guides our understanding as it moves its focus from juror to defendant to witness to lawyer depending on where a hoped-for facial response will be registered. Court TV insists on the facility of the legal process, where tics, winces, and nods have evidentiary value. The image of Baby Jessica being taken from her adoptive mother, although not present in Court TV's edit of the Baby Jessica case, does appear, for instance, in Court TV's edit of the Chamberlain/Kaplan case—reminding us again that Court TV is also TV.

Having identified earlier the three key ways in which TV operates differently than other media, I want now to show how those differences affect social and cultural production. TV both transmits daily experience and is a part of it. In doing so it works to blur the edges of the private and public worlds. The separation of these two sectors through the ideology of patriarchy is systematically undermined by mass-communications technology. In this way we can read TV as a mode of resistance. I am not denying that mass-communications technologies such as TV are also implicated in the maintenance of the dominant ideology. What I am suggesting is that in at least one respect, by its conflation of public and private spheres, TV works against the production of dominant ideology at the same time that it represents it. It does so in the following way. Television is broadcast publicly, yet it most commonly is received privately. That reception occurs in the private space of the home. In this way the distinction between the public and the private is troubled. Television provides a bridge between the public and the private sphere, bringing that which is public into the private sphere for consumption. Sobchack puts it like this: "A man's home in bourgeois patriarchal culture is no longer his castle. In the age of television, the drawbridge is always down; the world intrudes" (Sobchack 1991, p. 4).

Ronell is similarly struck by TV as a connective apparatus: "If TV has taught us anything . . . this principally concerns, I think, the *impossibility of staying* at home. In fact, the more local

it gets, the more uncanny, not-at-home it appears. Television . . . is about being-not-at-home, telling you that you are chained to the deracinating grid of being-in-the-world" (Ronell 1992, p. 6). The radical potential of this blurring of public and private space was not something that more conservative commentators were immune to. Lynn Spigel reminds us of the words of Philip Wylie, who, in a widely read postwar tract called "Generation of Vipers," updated in 1955 to include the impact of TV, claimed that women and technology had formed an alliance to turn men into passive, "de-sexed, de-souled, decerebrated" mates (Spigel 1992, p. 213). Lynn Spigel argues that popular media of that time often suggested that television threatened to "rob men of their powers": "Here, television's blurring of private and public space was a powerful tool in the hands of the housewives who could use the technology to invert the sexist hierarchy at the heart of the separation of spheres. In this topsy turvy world, women policed men's access to the public sphere and confined them to the home through the clever manipulation of television technology" (Spigel 1992, p. 214).

Temporal discontinuity, discussed earlier also has a significant impact on this blurring of public/private worlds. Its narratives are always broken up, often repeated, and usually invested in the rhetoric of instantaneousness. Sobchack argues that the fractured and nonlinear temporal nature of TV results in a disinvestment in the lived body and an investment in the represented. She says "the electronic constructs a meta-world where ethical investment and value are located in *representation-in-itself*" (Sobchack 1990, p. 56). Like Sobchack, Jane Feuer views the medium of TV differently from either cinema or photography. For her, the difference lies in the rhetorical emphasis it places on "liveness." She argues that the ideology of liveness which TV constantly invokes is used to overcome the otherwise inevitable fragmentation and disunity of TV, thus enabling the construction of familial-type unity. Feuer posits the American breakfast show *Good Morning, America* as an example. Describing the compere as the "father" of the *Good Morning, America* family sitting in his fictional living room, Feuer argues that the electronic connecting and linking done through the compere operates to create a unity where there is none. "Television," Feuer concludes, "in its liveness, its immediacy, its reality, can create families where none exist" (Feuer 1983, p. 20).

Avital Ronell, on the other hand, theorizes the episodic discourse of TV somewhat differently. She agrees that "among the things that TV has insisted upon, little more is prevalent than interruption or the hiatus for which it speaks and of which it is a part" (Ronell 1992, p. 6), then goes on:

> Because of its transmission of ghostly figures, interruption, and seriature, television would be hard to assimilate to the Frankfurt School's vision of it, where the regime of the visual is associated with mass media and the threat of a culture of fascism. This threat always exists, but I would like to read the way television in its couple with video offers a picture of numbed resistance to the unlacerated regimes of fascist media as it mutates into forms of video and cybernetic technology, electronic reproduction and cybervisual technologies. (Ronell 1992, p. 9)

In contrast to Feuer, Ronell insists on the radical potential of a discourse that is constantly making sense out of a fractured and disunified view. Understanding mass-communications technology in this way offers us the potential for challenging foundational concepts of what represent "the natural" and "the real." Indeed, if the *Good Morning, America* family is really a family, what does that do to our understanding of families? The medium of TV, then, forces us to engage in a constant reworking of ethical constructs. Ultimately, this may offer us alternatives to dominant "naturalized" patriarchal constructions.

The breakdown of the family unit, its invasion from outside and constant reworking to find stable ground, is in part a function of the pervasiveness of mass-communications technology. Public interest and media concentration on legal cases involving contests between birth mothers and others signals a loss of deterministic rationality. A headline in the *San Francisco Chronicle* that reads "Birth Mothers: Pro and Con" (1993, p. A18) is a clear statement of this destabilization and represents a tremendous leap forward in perverse logic. Prior to recent liberalizations of the family form, the choice offered in the headline would have been unthinkable.

With that in mind, I want now to turn to the specific cases. I have deliberately not read the law

reports, as I want to deal with the cases as cultural artifacts.[11]

II

In "Child/Alien/Father: Patriarchal Crisis and Generic Exchange," Vivian Sobchack discusses the destabilization of the nuclear family as follows:

> At a time when the mythology of our dominant culture can no longer resolve the social contradiction exposed by experience, the nuclear family has found itself in nuclear crisis. Rather than serving bourgeois patriarchy as a place of refuge from the social upheavals of the last two decades (many of which have been initiated by organized groups of young people and women) the family has become the site of them—and now serves as a sign of their representation. Not only has the bourgeois distinction between family members and alien Others, between private home and public space, between personal microcosm and sociopolitical macrocosm, been exposed as a mythological distinction, but also the family itself has been exposed as a cultural construction—as a set of signifying practices, as well as significant, practices. The family and its members are seen, therefore, as subject to the frightening, but potentially liberating, semiotic processes of selection and combination—and their order, meaning and power are perceived as open to transformation, dissolution and redefinition. (Sobchack 1991, p. 5)

On November 8, 1993, it was reported on CBS news that "a Massachusetts woman was so moved by the Baby Jessica case that she has offered one of her unborn twins to the DeBoers for adoption." The power of the mass media is rendered awesome in this moving and momentous gesture. What is it about the Baby Jessica story that played on this woman's deepest sympathies? Could it be the effect of its media saturation? If that is so, then we might be compelled to ask whether she had seen the telemovie *A Child Too Many* (1993), in which a woman who agrees to be a surrogate mother refuses to hand over her baby when to do so would result in the separation of the twins to which she subsequently gives birth.

Or perhaps the Massachusetts woman who offered one of her twins to the DeBoers heard the radio-show host Nicki Reed proudly announce on public radio that she had put her baby up for adoption. Reed saw her announcement as a necessary corrective that had to take place on the public airwaves, as the Baby Jessica case had "cast a shadow over the adoptive process." Reed said, "I don't really feel like we birthmoms should be ashamed and should be hiding. I think we should come out of the closet and say this is what I've chosen to do and I feel good about it" (N. Reed 1993). Her use of the metaphor of "coming out of the closet" speaks volumes. It seems that the only available narrative to draw on is one of sexual shame, of hidden identity that is open to accusations of deviance.

The Baby Jessica, Kimberly Mays, and Susan Chamberlain cases have several things in common. They were all concerned with divvying up rights among competing parents over custody and visitation of their children. The Baby Jessica and the Kimberly Mays cases pitted biological parents against parents who were variously called "psychological," "social," and "emotional" parents. Although the Susan Chamberlain case concerned a custody battle between two biological parents, Chamberlain's status as a surrogate cast her biological connection, at least in the eyes of the public, into an unnatural frame. This case, like the other two, fundamentally troubled how we think about families and mothers. It is the troubling of these two key cultural concepts that has been both a part of and a response to the contemporary crisis of patriarchy described more fully in the first part of this chapter. The family as we once knew it is no longer a stable category. It is not insignificant, then, that in the aftermath of these three cases, TV talk-show host Phil Donahue showcased the most bizarre family formations he could find. He solicited the help of the Seegers, a couple who "looked" perfectly normal but had created their family by unorthodox means. Two years after they adopted their first child, the Seegers decided to have another child, who they wanted to be the biological sibling of the first child. They discovered that the birth parents of the first adopted child had separated, but the Seegers arranged to obtain egg and sperm from them. The only question that remained was where to gestate the embryo. This problem was solved when Mr. Seeger's adult daughter by a previous marriage stepped in and offered to have the embryo implanted in her womb and to carry it to term. The result, according to Donahue, was a child with six not unrelated parents.[12]

Media fixation on the construction of new family forms is evident. Apart from Susan Chamberlain's appearance on the daytime talk shows *Sally Jessy Raphael* and *Geraldo* and the Kaplans' appearance on *Sally Jessy Raphael* and the daytime talk show *Maury Povich*, talk-back TV shows like *Larry King Live* and *Sonya Live* and news feature shows like *Nightline* and *48 Hours* seem obsessed with sorting out the complicated forms. To assist the viewers, invited guests included psychologists, sociologists, feminist law professors, adoption advocates, and representatives of birth-mother organizations and birth-parent organizations. Of course, in the age of "equality" one frequently encounters representatives of birth-father organizations, too.[13]

In the media rendering of the Baby Jessica case, for instance, the debate very quickly organized itself along an axis that situated a biological father's rights at one end and the claim of the liberal family at the other. This debate can be summarized as the patriarchal versus the paternal—where the paternal represents a tolerable reconstruction of the patriarchal as a caring masculine domain. It was rare for Cara's birth-mother rights to be either articulated or supported.[14]

In the Kimberly Mays case, the issue primarily concerned the question, "What defines a family: biology or psychology?" The media focused on Kimberly Mays, Robert Mays (her legal father, as it was ruled), and Regina Twigg (Kimberly's biological mother). The absence of Mr. Twigg was noted and explained away by Mrs. Twigg as evidence of his incapacity to overcome his anger and hurt. However, whether or not Mr. Twigg was present (and he often was), the media focused on Mrs. Twigg as the primary combatant. Here is an excerpt from a Barbara Walters interview with the parties on the ABC news show *Turning Point* on July 27, 1993.

WALTERS [voice-over]: On one side is the biological family she's never lived with and barely knows, the Twiggs.

MS. TWIGG: It's beyond belief, the grief, because this was my flesh-and-blood baby I didn't tell anybody to take.

WALTERS [voice-over]: On the other side, Bob Mays, the father who raised her as his only child, and is fighting to keep her by his side.

MR. MAYS: I wouldn't care if they trace her heritage to Cabbage Patch, USA, she's mine. I'm her father, I always have been, and I always will be.

There is an obvious coalescence between the shift I have been describing from the patriarchal to the paternal and the structure of the debate as Walters sees it.

A little later on, the same dilemma—but this time, voiced-over, the words of Kimberly:

WALTERS [voice-over]: In the end, after all the theories and allegations, the real question raised by this troubling case comes down to what actually defines a family.

KIMBERLY [voice-over]: To me a family is something that loves each other, something that doesn't consist of biology, but just loves each other for who they are. 'Cause biology doesn't make a family.

WALTERS [voice-over]: And yet Regina Twigg feels robbed and deprived.

MS. TWIGG: I've many times imagined what it would have been like if she had grown up with us. That's only natural. She's my flesh and blood. But it didn't happen.

Here biology without patriarchy in the form of Mrs. Twigg is pitted against the liberal family. After Kimberly's comments that "biology doesn't make a family," Walters says, "And yet Regina Twigg feels robbed and deprived." The conundrum isn't how to make it possible for all parties to form relationships with those they love; rather, it is why, if biology doesn't make a family, Regina feels robbed and deprived.

Interestingly, in the Kimberly Mays case the psychology of Regina Twigg was the subject of speculation. Media commentators questioned the love of a woman who would persist in her claims despite the clear and definitive statement of her biological daughter that it was "tearing her apart." On Turning Point, a psychologist's report described Regina's mental state as "erratic," "paranoid," and "prone to distortion" and recommended termination of all parental rights. Regina Twigg, characterized as having all the traits of a

woman whose child had been mysteriously swapped at birth for another, represented the irrationality of biology.[15]

In the Susan Chamberlain case the normative definition of the family depended on its clinical technologization. The fact that the baby was produced not by artificial insemination but "the natural way," as it was described, undermined the "naturalness" of the birth mother's connection to this child, marking it instead as sexual deviance. In the May episode of the Sally Jessy Raphael program on which Susan Chamberlain appeared, an audience member railed against Chamberlain, saying, "I think it's an unusual situation. When the only really moral people or semi-moral people are the lawyers, you know that you're dealing with a bad situation. What we have here is a case of double adultery. We have essentially a situation where a prostitute or a woman was hired to do what a woman should only do with her husband" (Chamberlain 1993a).

In popular debate, family has become the site of social upheaval. The use of mass media to trouble distinctions between the real and the sensational, between surface effect and the "inner" truth, is, therefore, extremely valuable. However, the process must be subject to a constant critique, and there are several ways in which TV coverage of these cases acknowledges the fundamental shaking of the ground only to restabilize that ground in favor of the patriarchal hierarchy and against birth mothers. Make no mistake—in all three of these cases, birth mothers lost. Even in the Baby Jessica case, from a legal perspective it was the biological father (Dan Schmidt) whose claims were legitimated rather than the biological mother's. Although popular sentiment didn't align with Dan Schmidt, neither did it care for the interests of Cara. It favored, instead, the adoptive parents. A CNN–USA Today Gallup poll found that eight out of ten people felt that Baby Jessica should have been left with the couple who had raised her "practically from birth" and not her biological parents. The fact that the birth mother, Cara Schmidt, had changed her mind within a couple of weeks of the adoption was not seen as significant or as deserving of consideration.

In the last part of this chapter I want to focus on birth mothers precisely because they seem to have little voice in either the legal decisions or the popular arena. The suppression of the birth mother's narrative is also evidence of the primacy of a narrative of the paternal, even though it is depicted in seemingly gender-neutral terms. I argue that the liberal and tolerant nuclear family of contemporary popular discourse is not gender-hierarchy-neutral. In fact, if it was previously a patriarchally governed unit, it is now a paternally governed one. The fact that the news media, talk-show hosts, and the public at large were fascinated by these cases, then, is not insignificant. It isn't just that people feed off human misery or that everyone loves a scandal. Rather, these three cases offered the public an opportunity to engage in a debate that epitomizes these "new times," times that Stuart Hall has described as marked by the pervasion of mass-communications technology (Hall 1989, p. 129).

In each of the three cases the "natural" is reclaimed and stabilized, paradoxically, as the cultural. As I described in the first part of my chapter, in the Baby Jessica case the adoptive parents explicitly undertook to colonize the "natural." There I quoted Roberta DeBoer's comments on *Larry King Live*, that she and her husband were Jessica's "natural" parents despite the lack of a biological connection. The "proof" of this lay in Jessica's ability to sing her ABCs, indicating a certain level of intellectual development, and her identification of Roberta and Jan DeBoer as her parents. In the case of Kimberly Mays, the judge refused to rule that Kimberly was the biological child of the Twiggs. The attorney for the Mays interpreted the judge's refusal to do so as a declaration that Robert Mays is and was Kimberly's legal father and, therefore, that it was both unnecessary and legally impossible for him to adopt her (Ginsberg 1993). In other words, Mays could not adopt Kimberly because he, by court ruling, was the natural father and had displaced all others. I would suggest that in refusing to accord the Twiggs the presumption of the natural, the judge in effect enabled Robert Mays to take up that natural position as emanating from the cultural connection.

In the Susan Chamberlain case what is most significant is not that the cultural was made natural but that the biological was made unnatural. Susan was held out to be a heartless, troublesome, immoral, bad, and therefore unnatural mother. On *Geraldo* she was jeered at until she broke down into tears (Chamberlain 1993b), but perhaps the most telling example of the anxiety she produced in others is evident in the following quote from *Newsday:* "As a videotape feed of Susan Chamberlain played yesterday, one of the army of television technicians at the child custody trial in Central Islip urged the woman on the monitor: "Come on, cry, damn it" (Smith and Horwitz 1993). And she did.

These cases unsettle one of the basic structures of our culture and its patriarchal underpinnings—the family that is based on a father, a mother, and biologically related children. What I hope I have done by looking at these cases and their media representation is to show how the crisis of patriarchy is managed through television and how new settlements are made in the realm of the paternal. As I said in part 1, when the traditional "natural" family comes under spectacular challenge, it becomes a site of popular trauma. That trauma is then mediated through its TV representation and both problematized and resolved as social knowledge.

In recent years, the Right has touted the importance of "family values," but not just *any* family values. These are code words that record the anxiety generated as a result of a feminist agenda that has destabilized the foundational status of the "naturalness" of patriarchy, heterosexuality, and white supremacy. Appearing sometime after the moment of family-values rhetoric, these cases register the seismic after-effects of this new reckoning. Connected to the "deracinating grid of being in the world," as Avital Ronell puts it, people in their homes watching TV could not avoid participating in a "virtual" debate about these issues staged in the news, talk shows, Court TV, and docudramas.

One way in which this debate is structured is through the recirculation of certain key sentences and images. For instance, the description of the trauma of Baby Jessica was frequently phrased in the following terms: "Jessica is being forced to leave the only home *she has ever known*" (my emphasis). Kimberly's desires were inscribed as her wanting to stay with the only father "*she has ever known*" (my emphasis). In December 1993 the program *48 Hours* aired a special on adoption and used this phrase in the context of another child as if this were now a kind of official description. These words "the only . . . she has ever known" articulate trauma by offering us an imaginary access to a child's incoherent memory and understanding, which then acts as a screen onto which we can project fantasies of familial stability. These descriptions offer what is perhaps one of the few remaining sites where absolutely sincere evocations of family life as a kind of enchanted stability can be circulated. As I argued at the outset of this chapter, like Dan Quayle's notion of family values, some accounts of the incorruptible family seem representable only in the moment of their violation.

As key phrases were deployed in different cases, so too were key images. The image of Baby Jessica being taken screaming from the arms of her adoptive mother was recycled in the Court TV trial story of the Susan Chamberlain case and again on the 48 Hours program, to name just two instances. This compelling image works to confirm our suspicions about the State acting heartlessly, upholding the rule of law, acting patriarchally. In this way I think the image becomes separable from its justifications. This is the State refusing to listen to a child's screams. According to the DeBoers' attorney, they were screams that actually voiced "I want my dad"; the attorney, at least, clearly evoked the protective and paternal sphere as the sphere being violated. That act of paternal ventriloquism reveals another use of the child as screen. It is one of those privileged moments of private trauma captured publicly. We keep watching it because it images something we haven't otherwise recognized visually. Our insistent perverse rewatching of the event, its perfect replication in the docudrama about the case, signal our own need to read it, to interpret it, and to settle it. The effect of this recirculation of images and language (and I have only picked out a few examples) is that each successive time we see the image or hear the language, the narrative writes itself. Where there is no language and no image, no narrative gets written. This is the case with birth mothers, and unless you actively listen for their voices you will not hear their story at all. The remaining disembodied account of mothering enables its colonization by the paternal sphere.

The 48 Hours program mentioned above did attempt to show the sad stories of a few birth mothers who were clearly subject to coercion by adoption agencies run by the right to life organizations. But these were not birth mothers who, like Cara Schmidt, had had a change of heart. Sympathetic narratives offered about women like Cara were rare. What can we say about mothers who change their minds? The narrative written for the mother is one that is politically immobilizing. This is evidenced by an attorney's recent remarks on CNN: "How do we define parent? Do we define a parent by the fact that you were present at conception or present at giving birth?" (Victor 1993) The first problem with this description is its liberal commitment to the gender-neutral language of parent. As a result of this language, both the mother's and the father's roles at birth have to be contained within a single generalizing statement. The inevitable consequence is a phrase "present at giving birth," which speaks only to the masculine role. The effect is the suppression of any alternative narrative that would speak to the agency and bodily significance of the woman actually giving birth. Women don't just attend the birth of their child like a spectator; they aren't just "present" in a kind of passive but concerned way. Women actually *give* birth!

I have written elsewhere about the anxiety with which the court, doctors, and the public at large deal with the woman's connectedness to the fetus, and then the baby, in cases of drug-addiction and prenatal care (Karpin 1994; Karpin 1992). Just as the law attempts to mark off the boundaries between a woman and her fetus by policing and criminalizing boundary transgression in the case of drug-addicted mothers, so too the failure to speak of a birth mother's embodied relation to her child works to suppress the significance of that connection. The failure to offer an embodied account of being the birth mother, the insistence that it be scientized in terms of the merely biological, all speak to this anxiety. I argue that the question of how we as women assert our significance is crucially linked to an insistence on an embodied account of subjectivity. We are effectively denied significance when we are made actors outside or against our bodies. When, for instance, giving birth is described as "being present" at birth, the detachment of the woman from the process is insisted upon. It is precisely this failure to enunciate a narrative for birth mothers that enables the horrific treatment of women such as Susan Chamberlain. Why was she savaged on *Geraldo*? Because a positive narrative of her pregnant embodiment was not available. Instead, she was only embodied as a sexually deviant and unstable woman (one of the very few narratives that are allowed to be developed on television for women) who could not get her life together and stick by her decision in a moral fashion.

I have been arguing that TV operates simultaneously to reinscribe and resist traditional rhetorics. I am not simply saying that TV is both good and bad or that it works for the dominant group as well as against them. What I am postulating is that it registers and constitutes shifts in the dominant ideology and, in the moment it does so, works to naturalize those shifts. Here I have suggested that the move is from the patriarchal to the paternal. Liberal feminism has offered a liberalized version of the family—one in which the importance of biological ties, heterosexuality, and the legal formality of marriage is diminished and where the family as a "cultural production" is emphasized. Families are constituted in this view through the social and psychological bonding of their members. However, doing away with the importance of the biological has tended to disable women's claim to an embodied experience of the family. The result seems to be that in this new, more liberal version of the family, the paternal is emphasized no less than was the patriarchal in the previous version. The paternal nuclear family is perceived as by definition a family that is caring, benign, responsible, and ethical. This is in stark contrast to the single-mother family, which is classically characterized as an unavoidable bad (Fineman 1991b; D. Roberts 1991). Giving voice to the experiences of birth mothers offers a way out of the patriarchal-versus-paternal construct. It is possible that TV can offer a space where these alternative narratives can be figured.

On July 8, 1993, the *Larry King Live* program featured a segment on the Baby Jessica case. Frank Sesno, standing in for Larry King, interviewed first the DeBoers, then Dan Schmidt (by telephone), and then two experts: William Pierce from the National Council for Adoption and Jon Ryan from the National Organization for Birth Fathers and Adoption Reform. What is interesting about this debate is that it is framed in terms of the rights of the adoptive parents (a liberal, gender-neutral construction) as opposed to the rights of the father. There is no room within this dialectic for the narrative of the birth mother. For example, in Sesno's interview with Dan Schmidt, Schmidt said:

I am the natural father—the father, period. That's just the way it is. And I did not give up my rights. And this country has to stop abusing fathers and taking their rights away and not giving them any say-so about their children. . . . Fathers need to stand up. And I hope this is what I'm showing, that fathers can get their children instead of thinking they don't stand a chance. (Schmidt 1993)

Soon after this appeal from Dan Schmidt, Frank Sesno introduced Jon Ryan, who began by saying, "The father's rights are paramount, and they must be first."

Before going to a commercial, we were shown a clip of the Schmidt's attorney, Marian Faupel, speaking to the press after the Schmidts had won their final victory: "It's a tremendous victory for fathers, I think, but it's a victory for the American family. I think this is a victory for every biologically related family in this country that's not unfit and has a right to be free from government interference." The other side of the debate was represented by Pierce and the DeBoers, who made several appeals to the heart and emotions. Pierce said, "I hope that everybody watching this program will send their petitions and their letters to convince the court of listening to the heart and letting children grow up where they should be—with the people who have raised them." The DeBoers, too, spoke for the rights of the "bonded unit." No narrative offered an account of the birth mothers' feelings or rights.

In another forum, presided over by Barbara Walters, the birth-mother position was finally the subject of discussion. However, her focus was the outlaw status of the actions of certain birth mothers and their rarity. Discussing both the Baby Jessica case and the Kimberly Mays case (Walters 1993b), Walters began the interview by saying, "Despite the ambiguity of the underlying issue—what constitutes a family—the legal issue has been clearly decided." She then goes on to describe how the group that Cara Schmidt turned to after she changed her mind, a group called Concerned United Birth Parents, are often called the "adoption terrorists." Mary Beth Seader, for the National Council for Adoption, then noted how many birth parents were furious that they were being portrayed so negatively. Walters's show thus continued the work of radio talk-show host Nicki Reed, quoted at the beginning of part 2 of this chapter. The message that both Seader and Reed wanted to get out about birth moms was that most birth mothers are "good," meaning they didn't change their minds.

I want to end with an instance in which the techniques of television enabled a rupture. This rupture occurred on CNN's issues program *Crossfire*. *Crossfire* positions itself as a bipartisan political drama. It is headed up by Pat Buchanan on the far right and Mike Kinsley on the so-called left. On August 3, 1993, the program focused on parental custody rights and the Baby Jessica case. Interestingly, in this case the narrative of the birth mother actually squeezed in physically between Buchanan as a kind of old-style, largely discredited patriarch and Kinsley as the product of reconstructed liberalism (what I have been calling the paternal). However briefly, the program not only gave voice to the birth mother's narrative but also offered a kind of spatial political map of how irruptive this discourse might be and where it is politically located between these two poles. But at the moment it's only an occasional interruption, a few words caught in the *Crossfire*. Nevertheless, it is a significant and hopeful intervention. Listen to invited guest Neyrs Patterson, sociologist, attempt to replace the image of Jessica being taken away with a narrative that hasn't otherwise been uttered—that is, the birth mother's narrative.

KINSLEY: Miss Patterson, we all saw on TV these terrible scenes of Baby Jessica being ripped away from the only parents she'd ever known and handed over to these strangers. People wonder, how can that possibly be the right thing to do. How can it?

PATTERSON: It wasn't the right thing to do. The situation should never have arisen in the first place. I think when Cara Schmidt changed her mind, which she did at a very early point in the whole procedure, her change of mind should have been respected. She made it during a period when most women who have just given birth are emotionally very vulnerable.

This may seem definitive. Yet at a later stage we hear, in perhaps more realistic tones, how the debate frays and progresses.

We take up the debate at the point in which Buchanan had just insisted that at an early stage the natural parents had to take precedence:

PATTERSON: Well I quite agree with you. Where our conversation got sort of, I think, sidetracked is when it was brought to our attention by yourself, Mr. Kinsley, that the whole custom of father's rights involves delay, because of the complications of establishing paternity through blood tests. Delay is against the interests of the child, especially when it is extensive delay, as it was in this case—

BUCHANAN: Do you think they should have given back the child right away, then?

PATTERSON: All right. Listen—

BUCHANAN: At one month or two months?

PATTERSON: Yes, what I think should be the case is that the relationship between the biological mother and child ought to be protected and that the relationship between the biological father and the child should be viewed somewhat separately and later.

KINSLEY: OK. Hold on. We've got to—Mr. Victor, I'll let you back in after a little break here, and we're also going to talk about the other case of the fourteen-year-old girl who wants to divorce her parents, after she got switched at the hospital, in just a moment.

Notes

This chapter would not have been possible without the support of the Australian Federation of University Women, Freda Bage Fellowship. I would especially like to thank David Ellison for his thoughtful comments and rare editing skills. I would also like to thank Martha Fineman for her support and the opportunity to give this paper an airing. Others who provided invaluable assistance reading and editing include Phyllis Perlstone, Max Deutscher, and the other editor of this volume, Martha McCluskey.

This paper was written in partial fulfillment of the requirements of the degree of Doctor of the Science of Law in the Faculty of Law, Columbia University.

1. Consider the popular-music magazine *Juice*'s annual attempt to sum up the year and the decade: "Every generation has its issues. In the legendary '60's it was Vietnam, and later disarmament and ecology. The buzz word now is dysfunction and the dysfunctional family." Fittingly, the "poster children" of this new era were none other than Kurt Cobain of the rock group Nirvana (who had committed suicide not long before); Courtney Love, his rock-star wife; and their baby, Frances Bean ("Special Issue" 1995).

2. I am referring here to the Baby Jessica case. Although I am calling Jessica an adopted child, the ac-

tual adoption was invalidated by the courts. I will discuss the implications of this case later in this chapter.

3. Here I am referring to the case of Kimberly Mays, who will be discussed later in this chapter.

4. This case was the Chamberlain/Kaplan case and is discussed in detail later in this chapter.

5. Although the legal issues in each of the three cases that I discuss did not necessarily turn on the maternal rights, I am deliberately describing them as about maternal rights because it is those rights that tend to get suppressed or effaced.

6. While the term "birth mother" refers most commonly to a woman who has a baby and then turns it over for adoption, including those women who do so under surrogacy agreements, it is clear that a woman who gives birth to a child and then retains custody of that child could also be called a birth mother. However, it is important to note that any time a qualifying term is added to the word "mother," it is usually used as a way of indicating the possibility of other kinds of mothers. Generally a woman who keeps her baby is simply called a "mother."

7. Some examples: *NYPD Blue, Rescue 911, L.A. Law,* Court TV; in Australia, *Janus* and *Police Rescue,* to name just two.

8. Perhaps the most best-known restriction on testimony evidence is the rule against hearsay, which prohibits a person from testifying about what somebody told them unless certain conditions are met. Generally witnesses are only allowed to testify to things they themselves witnessed.

9. This is a paraphrasing of the actual comment, to the best of my recollection.

10. Lawrence Friedman (1989, p. 1579) argues that trials are " 'boundary-maintaining' devices; they help cement social solidarity by redefining and proclaiming norms. . . . Of course the boundaries defined, the norms proclaimed, the values affirmed at trials are almost necessarily the norms of the dominant culture."

11. Although in another paper it would be valuable to look at the way the media representation of the issues was different from the legal representation, I am convinced that it would constitute too much of a di-

version to do so here. The law report in itself is a text that would need analyzing. Therefore, I have quarantined myself from reading those reports until this paper is written.

12. By my count it's five, but perhaps the husband of the adult daughter gains access to the title through his role as supportive nonfertilizing mate.

13. Network TV has also explored its interest in family forms through the parafictional mode of the docudrama. Commenting on TV's foray into this genre, one reporter writes, "The supercollider of network TV is bombarding the nuclear family with movies this season about adoption, surrogacy, custody disputes, baby snatching, baby selling and even infanticide" (B. Mills 1993, p. A1).

14. The legal decision also turned on the existence of rights in the biological father. However, I do not view that as an explanation for the failure of the media to articulate Cara Schmidt's sense of loss and deprivation. It is rare that the media will remain within the limits of the legal issues; instead, the moral and ethical issues are viewed as the boundaries. One feels compelled to ask why then, it was so hard to find any lengthy and thoughtful discussion of Cara's claims.

15. In March 1994 Kimberly Mays had a change of heart, and her case was again mentioned in the TV news. The story was announced as follows: "Michael Williams reports on Kimberly Mays, the fourteen-year-old girl who was switched at birth and later divorced her biological parents only to recently return to the home of her natural parents in Sebring" (M. Williams 1994). The report was accompanied by a sound bite in which a friend of the Twigg family said, "[A]fter the meanness died down and she thought about it, these are her parents and this is her flesh and blood." I mention this here to emphasize that the valorization of nonbiological families is a function of popular liberal ideology and tends to flatten out the complex social and political effects of discourses of the biological and nonbiological in its lived effects. Kimberly Mays clearly was torn between the two discourses, and attempts to posit one as more rational than the other led to her obvious distress.

12

Law and Racial Reelism

Black Women as Celluloid "Legal" Heroines

MARGARET M. RUSSELL

Black women occupy a role both central and peripheral, pervasive and invisible, in Hollywood's cinematic history. From the earliest days of film, black women's bodies have been a vehicle through which movieland sexual fantasies and fears have been transmogrified and black women's historical circumstances have been used as fodder for the cinematic trivialization of their oppression. Generations of viewers have grown up with predominant (and sometimes exclusive) imagery of black women as alternately subhuman and superhuman: The animalistic Jezebel (Painter 1992, pp. 209–10), the fleshy and jovial mammy (Bogle 1992), the stern and aggressive matriarch (Gilkes 1983, pp. 288–300), and even the doomed "tragic mulatto" (Bogle 1992, p. 5) are meant to suggest that black women are— quite literally—a "breed apart" from the rest of humanity. The unifying theme underlying all of these stereotypes is one of deviance and worthlessness; whether sycophantic or strong, black women are deemed both powerless and somehow responsible for their own sorry fates. Even the image of the long-suffering, "Rock of Gibraltar" matriarch is laced with assumptions of inferiority

and with the message that black women deserve their subordinated status. What Jacquelyn Grant has observed with respect to black women's historic role in the church also rings true of black women's place in popular culture: "[I]t is often said that women are the 'backbone.' . . . On the surface, this may appear to be a compliment . . . [but] most . . . who use this term are referring to location rather than function. What they really mean is that women are in the 'background' and should be kept there" (1982, p. 141).

Patricia Hill Collins has identified four overarching stereotypes emblematic of the racial/sexual oppression of black women: the docile, domesticated mammy; the emasculating matriarch; the irresponsibly fertile welfare mother; and the sexually aggressive Jezebel/whore. She notes the critical role of the latter stereotype, as well as dominant cultural attempts to define and control black female sexuality, in the formation of all four images:

Each image transmits clear messages about the proper links among female sexuality, fertility, and black women's roles in the political economy.

. . . The mammy represents the clearest example of the split between sexuality and motherhood present in Eurocentric masculinist thought. In contrast, both the matriarch and the welfare mother are sexual beings. But their sexuality is linked to their fertility, and this link forms one fundamental reason they are negative images. The matriarch represents the sexually aggressive woman, one who emasculates black men because she will not permit them to assume roles as Black patriarchs. She refuses to be passive and thus is stigmatized. Similarly, the welfare mother represents a woman of low morals and uncontrolled sexuality, factors identified as the cause of her impoverished state. (1990, p. 78)

The connection between these images and disparaging depictions of black women in popular media is strong and direct.[1] Hollywood movies and television, in particular, have served as the primary medium for the replication and reinforcement of the mammy, matriarch, welfare mother, and whore stereotypes; throughout eight-plus decades of cinema and nearly four decades of television, black women have been relentlessly relegated to these categories of identity.[2] Myriad examples exist; among the earliest and most powerful impressions were etched by the subservient maids of *Gone with the Wind*, the self-hating "mulatta" daughter in *Imitation of Life*, and the harshly nagging Sapphire of *Amos 'n' Andy*. More recently, these images have been softened but not supplanted by the saintly maid of *Fried Green Tomatoes*; the outspoken housekeeper of *Maude* (and, later, *Good Times*); the suffering mixed-race wife in *Jungle Fever*; the feisty matriarchs and back-talking women of *The Jeffersons*, *Family Matters*, and *Living Single*. Despite their otherwise rebellious and iconoclastic intentions, even contemporary films such as *She's Gotta Have It*, *School Daze*, *Straight Out of Brooklyn*, and *Waiting to Exhale* transmit their own share of stereotypical baggage about black female sexuality and self-destructiveness. Certainly, there have been occasional departures from the otherwise incessant parade of insulting characters and plots. Indeed, black actresses have long struggled to resist and transcend the suffocating boundaries of such stereotypes, often with subtle and fascinating results; repeated viewings of even the most embarrassing scenes (for example, those in *Gone with the Wind*) reveal the buried layers of dignity

and irony these women brought to their portrayals of otherwise degrading characters. But these exceptions are nearly eclipsed in the dauntingly ubiquitous context of negative depiction, which disparages black female identity as aberrant and laughable.

This oppressive cultural legacy fosters in the black female viewer a diversity of reactions: stoic detachment, awkward ambivalence, derisive laughter, deep embarrassment, stunning rage. Underlying all of these broad-ranging responses is an overwhelming desire to distance oneself from the detestable image on the screen—and, in turn, to erase the image from the screen as well. For example, bell hooks writes of her childhood reaction to the character of Sapphire in *Amos 'n' Andy*:

> She was there as man in drag, as castrating bitch, as someone to be lied to, someone to be tricked, someone the white and black audience could hate. Scapegoated on all sides. *She was not us.* We laughed with the black men, with the white people. We laughed at this black woman who was not us. And we did not even long to be there on the screen. How could we long to be there when our image, visually constructed, was so ugly. We did not long to be there. We did not long for her. We did not want our construction to be this hated black female thing—foil, backdrop. Her black female image was not the body of desire. There was nothing to see. She was not us. (1992, p. 120)

These reactions—the repudiation of "this hated black female thing" and the concomitant realization that "[t]here was nothing to see" in its stead—capture well the dilemma of the black female viewer. Faced with the empty choices of degrading imagery or outright erasure, black women realize that they must—as an act of self-preservation—contest and resist conventional media representations of their experiences. bell hooks terms this resistance "talking back,"[3] or engaging in the "oppositional gaze": "Subordinates in relations of power learn experientially that there is a critical gaze, one that 'looks' to document, one that is oppositional. In resistance struggle, the power of the dominated to assert agency by claiming and cultivating 'awareness' politicizes 'looking' relations—one learns to look a certain way in order to resist" (hooks 1992, p. 116).

The subordinating nature of black female imagery—and the importance of "talking back" to its powerful sway—are critical themes in legal as well as popular cinematic culture. Legal texts, like popular cultural texts such as films, resonate with interpretive significance far beyond their "four corners." Specifically, with regard to issues of race and gender, media-driven stereotypes play a key role in both reflecting and constructing the social reality that law serves to regulate. In recent years, the proliferation of televised media coverage of legal events has heightened this phenomenon to a notable degree. The Clarence Thomas/ Anita Hill confrontation in October 1991, for example, starkly conveyed the resonance of historic stereotypes about black men and black women in the public imagination; these racial/ sexual myths in turn strongly affected the outcome of the quasi-legal proceedings surrounding Thomas's U.S. Supreme Court nomination.[4] Perhaps the most salient contemporary example of the symbiotic relationship between legal and popular media culture in this regard is the infamous O. J. Simpson criminal trial. Notwithstanding the celebrity of the defendant and the incessant presence of cameras in the courtroom, public impressions of the trial were most dramatically affected by the interracial nature of the crimes alleged to have been committed by Simpson and by the race and gender stereotypes evoked by such allegations. Unquestionably, the public's (including the jury's) interpretations of the Simpson legal drama were filtered through a maze of stereotypes about black/white and male/ female relations. Even though black women lacked a visibly prominent place during the criminal proceedings, they were critically important as jurors who decided Simpson's fate. The Simpson trial has already been scrutinized as a legal text with much to reveal about popular cultural attitudes about race and gender; it is also a kind of cinematic text, the dramatic power of which depends on popular cultural attitudes about the law.

This essay examines several ways in which Hollywood films serve as texts reflecting popular conceptions and concerns about law, lawyers, and justice, particularly with regard to issues of race and gender; specifically, it focuses on the treatment (and mistreatment) of black women as celluloid "legal" heroines as reflective of their subor-dinate status in the law. In the next section, I discuss the concept of films as "legal" texts and the possibilities of using black feminist methods such as the "oppositional gaze" as legal interpretive tools. In the third section, I examine three aspects of the treatment of black women as celluloid "legal" heroines: the problem of the missing black female lawyer; the erasure of black women's experiences in "law films" such as Disclosure; and the distortion present in contemporary films (such as Boyz N the Hood and Losing Isaiah) that attempt to provide realistic depictions of black women's lives within the legal system.

The Popular Film as Legal Text

Legal, Racial, and Gender Reelism

A central theme of both postmodern legal and cultural studies is the power of the text as a source of domination and influence. In legal studies, Robert Cover described this phenomenon as the "violence" of the legal word; he noted that "[l]egal interpretation takes place in a field of pain and death"[5] because of the law's literal and figurative potential to destroy lives. In cultural studies, textual power is often discussed in terms of the hegemonic influence of images, myths, and stereotypes; cultural violence and destruction are wrought not through concrete notions of regulation and punishment, as in the legal system, but through subtler forms of behavioral modification and identity formation.

Popular films may be viewed as legal texts in a number of respects. On the most literal level are films explicitly about lawyers and the law; such movies reflect the public's absorption and even obsession with glamorized notions of what lawyers do and of what trials are all about. The history of Hollywood film is rich with examples of this genre: From To Kill a Mockingbird to Philadelphia, the courtroom trial has served as the focus for many a cinematic morality tale. These movies utilize the dramatic device of the trial not so much to teach the spectator about legal procedures and concepts as to construct a social world in which legal procedure is inevitable and self-justifying.

On a second level, many popular films are law-oriented in their preoccupation with concepts of social order and justice, even if they do not focus explicitly or primarily on lawyers and trials. Classic examples of this genre include *The Man Who Shot Liberty Valence, Bonnie and Clyde, Badlands,* and *Thelma and Louise,* as well as tongue-in-cheek futuristic tales such as *Demolition Man* and *Judge Dredd.* In these films, both characters and plot are heavily laced with assumptions about the necessary—and necessarily oppressive—function of the law as a means of social regulation. Perhaps the epitome of this approach is the comic-book-inspired *Judge Dredd,* in which an America of the future dispenses with the ordinary, everyday trial in favor of a swifter justice system in which "street judges" serve as police, prosecutors, and jury, instantaneously pronouncing guilt and imposing sentences on the spot.

Finally, and most broadly, movies can be read as legal texts because of the influence of their imagery in constructing the social world, which is in turn regulated by law. It is in this sense that race-based, gender-based, and other forms of stereotypes perpetuated by the media can have the most profound influence on the law. As constant consumers—willing or unwilling—of popular culture, the public develops from such imagery indelible impressions of what it means to be black or white, male or female, gay or straight. These conceptions of identity heavily influence all aspects of the legal system. They affect the values and assumptions of legislators, judges, lawyers, clients, and jurors. They find expression in the writing of laws, judicial opinions, and legal scholarship. In a sense, they *become* the legal system itself. Thus, when black women are trapped in a cinematic tradition of negative depictions, the implications are serious and far-reaching; the suffocating nature of such imagery operates to constrict black women's options in life and in law as well as in the "reel" world of movieland fantasy.

Resisting the "Dominant Gaze" as Feminist Method

Popular cultural constructions of black womanhood are filtered through a "dominant gaze"[6] of race and gender subordination, which operates to reinforce the belief that black women are the quintessential, objectified "other" on whom societal expectations may be easily and guiltlessly imposed. The "dominant gaze" in cinema supports the assumption that celluloid black women cannot escape the confining categories of mammy, matriarch, welfare mother, and whore; it also encourages real-world black women to join other spectators in ridiculing the "hated black female thing" on the silver screen. Similarly, a "dominant gaze" of sorts operates in this nation's legal system when concepts of neutrality and objectivity mask underlying ignorance of the harsh impact of the law on black women's lives. Black feminist scholars in various disciplines challenge the orthodoxy of the "dominant gaze" by engaging in what bell hooks terms "talking back" to the text. This method assumes a radically different subject-position for the black female spectator of popular culture, a stance of interrogation and resistance to conventional representations. The critical gaze posited by hooks, Collins, and others is premised on neither complete detachment nor complete identification; it urges neither full rejection nor full embrace of black female screen imagery. Rather, it contests the presumption that black women can be categorically defined as screen personas *or* as viewers, and it stakes a claim for black female spectators to respond to celluloid icons as complexly and ambivalently as they choose.

In so doing, the concept of the critical, "oppositional" gaze suggests that "talking back" to the text should result in multiple interpretive possibilities. With these thoughts in mind, I turn to an examination of the problems of absence, erasure, and distortion faced by black women in Hollywood "law films."

"It's Only a Movie": The Ostensibly Trivial Problem of Images of Black Women in Hollywood "Law Films"

An old parody of a hoary, cliched, quintessentially sappy love song is titled, "How Can I Miss You If You Won't Go Away?" With regard to the inauthentic representation of black women in Hollywood "law movies," one might cynically ask, "How Can We Miss You If You Were Never Here?" While it is certainly true that no one of any color or gender should *expect* from the silver screen anything but a highly contorted version of the vagaries of human existence—that, some would say, is part of the *fun* of films—the patterns and subtleties of such distortions are significant in what they reveal about real-world values and power relations. As already discussed, the effects of media representations on our conceptions of self and society are both seductive and insidious; Patricia Hill Collins has referred to these representations as "controlling images"—ideology-laden depictions "designed to make racism, sexism, and poverty appear to be natural, normal, and an inevitable part of everyday life" (1990, p. 68). With respect to representations of black women, Hollywood "law" films are characterized not only by the use of controlling negative images but also by the outright absence of depiction; both tendencies suggest to black women that their experiences are inevitably inferior and unworthy of serious attention.

The Female Lawyer Film: A Monochromatic Pop Subgenre

With few exceptions (for example, Katharine Hepburn in *Adam's Rib*), the genre of lawyer-as-hero films in Hollywood history has until very recently been a male phenomenon. The ethical conflicts, moral intensity, intellectual acumen, and other razzle-dazzle associated with courtroom dramas have almost exclusively involved the image of the (white) powerful male lawyer who triumphs over the forces of mendacity and corruption by asserting the primacy of law, order, and integrity.[7] *Inherit the Wind* and *Twelve Angry Men* are but a few examples of this cinematic archetype in earlier, pre-1960s film history; present-day analogues include such movies as *The Verdict*, *True Believer*, and *The Firm*. Presumably—or so went the typical line of such arguments, if anyone ever even thought of raising issues of race and gender—the paucity of male nonwhite lawyers, as well as female lawyers of any race, in Hollywood movies was attributable to their scarcity in "the real world" and the concomitant unlikelihood that viewers would find such characters credible, compelling, or sympathetic. But such reasoning tends to be circular, of course; given the influence of visible role models, including celluloid ones, on common visions of what it means to be a lawyer in contemporary society, the cultural stereotype of the fictional heroic lawyer as white and male has quite likely contributed to the perpetuation of a similar stereotype in perceptions of the legal profession overall. These stereotypes, in turn, can influence the demographics of the profession itself—and the exclusionary cycle begins anew.

In the past decade or so, however, perhaps to capitalize on the emergence of significant numbers of female professionals, Hollywood has produced a distinct subgenre of "female lawyer" films, the most famous of which include *Jagged Edge, Suspect, Class Action, Presumed Innocent,* and *The Pelican Brief*. At least superficially, these dramas are premised upon the same lawyer-as-hero model as their male-dominated predecessors; the female lawyer also investigates and litigates, risks her license and her life so that justice will win the day. The female lawyer of these films, however, also bears the burden of serving as a kind of postfeminist/Hollywood sexpot fantasy: smart (but usually still in need of male rescuers); independent (but often foolish in her sexual, emotional, and professional choices); and, of course, conventionally attractive (tellingly, Hollywood moviemakers seem to like even their women lawyers to be mini-skirted and "Virginia Slims" slim). In fact, in comparison with her usually more complexly drawn male celluloid counterparts, the female lawyer seems not so much a legal hero as just a "girl lawyer": good heart, great legs.

Certainly, in comparison with the standard-issue legal eagles of Hollywood's yesteryear, the movie diva lawyers of the 1980s and 1990s provide a fun and refreshing antidotal fantasy—to a certain extent. Even if we savvy spectators know that glamo-heroines like Glenn Close, Cher, Julia Roberts, and Susan Sarandon are not, of course, anything like *real-life* women lawyers, at least their presence (however splashy and superficial) in the lawyer-as-hero genre energizes the stagnant cinematic imagery of the righteous lawyer as always male. In short, the female lawyer subgenre lays claim to its own small piece of territory in pop culture and in the process reminds its audience that women occupy significant space in the real-world legal profession as well.

But what of black women's roles in this movieland legal arena? Can they claim such Hollywood imagery as their own, not as a realistic reflection of their professional lives but rather as the tacit "compliment" (however problematic, ironic, and arguably backhanded) that their lives are worthy of recognition? If the first decade or so of female lawyer films is any indication, the answer is most decidedly no. Aside from the occasional and peripheral legal character (Rae Dawn Chong as law student/love interest in *Soul Man*, Anna Deavere Smith as Tom Hanks's paralegal associate in *Philadelphia*, La Tanya Richardson as Jessica Lange's child custody lawyer in *Losing Isaiah*), black women lawyers are nowhere to be found as celluloid heroines. As far as Hollywood seems to be concerned, the most salable depiction of women in the legal profession is rooted in a fantasy of white, safely (hetero)sexualized pseudo-feminism.

Why are black women so conspicuously absent from the female lawyer pop subgenre? I suspect that there are several intertwined features at work, having to do with peculiar constructions of black and white womanhood as well as with the marginality of black women in real-life legal contexts. One explanation is related to the reasons that black women receive such scarce representation generally as the subjects of mainstream films; the common assumption is that black women are simply not "bankable" subjects for mainstream movies. With the rare exception of films like *The Color Purple* (which enjoyed enhanced marketability because of the broad commercial appeal of its director, Steven Spielberg, rather than the literary fame of its creator, Alice Walker), *Lady Sings the Blues*, and *What's Love Got to Do with It?* (the latter two of which relied primarily on the "Hollywood bio-pic" mode), black women's experiences are generally absent from the silver screen. This widespread indifference toward depicting black women's lives seems unlikely to change unless and until a critical mass of black women exists in film production, direction, screenwriting, and other creative capacities; at present, only a handful of women (e.g., Oprah Winfrey, Whoopi Goldberg, and Suzanne de Passe of Motown Productions) hold such clout.

But aside from the overall dearth of black women as central characters of *any* cinematic story, the specific absence of black women in female lawyer movies implicitly both reflects and reinforces a prevalent assumption that women lawyers are white. The plethora of white female lawyer movies and the corresponding lack of films presenting images of black women lawyers underscore a similar invisibility of representation in the legal profession. Black women (as well as other women of color) certainly *do* exist in substantial numbers as lawyers, judges, and law students; however, the "controlling image" of the female lawyer is still a monochromatic one. Consequently, cinematic space is reserved almost exclusively for constructions of female legal professionalism as a white phenomenon.

The silver-screen female lawyer prototype, while to a certain extent valorized, is of course by no means free of its own contorted notions of gender, power, and feminism. Consider, for example, the hypersexualized nature of the lawyer-heroines of *Jagged Edge* (Glenn Close) and *Suspect* (Cher): two seemingly competent, high-powered attorneys who nevertheless lack the common sense (as well as the professional ethics) to avoid romantic entanglements with, respectively, a client and a juror. In each film, the underlying fantasy seems to be that professional women are somehow fated to give life to the book title *Smart Women, Foolish Choices*, and are all too willing to risk their careers to pursue their fatal attractions. The legal lives of the various women of *Presumed Innocent* are similarly dominated by scenarios of libidinous self-destruction. In a less overtly sexual but similarly sycophantic vein, the law-student ingenue of *The Pelican Brief* (Julia Roberts) initially pursues the dangerous puzzle providing the film's title just to please her law professor mentor, with whom she happens to be having a secret affair; after his mysterious murder, she then seeks the protection of a dashing journalist, who helps whisk her away from danger. Even the tough independence of the courageous defense lawyer in *The Client* (Susan Sarandon), it turns out, is born of the loneliness of a woman who has lost custody of her children because of her alcoholism. Without a doubt, these celluloid lawyer-heroines are saddled with their own stereotypical baggage; at best, they reflect only an ambivalent admiration toward female professionals. But my point is not to argue for a kind of "equal opportunity" cinematic ideal for women; Hollywood movies are, after all, the stuff of which idiosyncratic (and market-driven) fantasies are made. Rather, I emphasize this unspoken monoracial norm to explain why black women's absence is all the more telling; if black women's portrayals as mammies and matriarchs convey a message of inferiority, their utter absence signifies that they are ciphers—not even worthy of depiction.

Erasing Black Women's Experiences: The Decolorization of Sexual Harassment in *Disclosure*

Sometimes, even when their legal stories have reached some measure of visibility and recognition, black women are erased in contemporary popular films that appropriate their experiences to tell a different tale—usually a tale devoid of the race and gender discrimination faced by black women in the real world. This retelling results in a type of absence different from that discussed earlier with respect to black female lawyers; rather than suggesting that black women simply do not exist in a certain realm (as the female lawyer movies do), this second category of films ignores the racial dimensions of particular legal issues the contours of which black women's experiences have played an instrumental role in shaping. Examples of such erasure in the earliest decades of Hollywood cinema include many epics about the postbellum South, such as *The Birth of a Nation* and *Gone with the Wind*, in which black women characters are nonexistent or of dubious significance; more recent examples include the well-intended *Mississippi Burning*, which focuses largely on white male heroism in the civil rights era. These films, like the female lawyer movies, perpetuate black women's invisibility not so much through negative depiction as through negation itself; in a sense, they "decolorize"—as well as "degender"—issues, events, and story lines that integrally involve race and gender.

A recent example of this type of cinematic negation is the treatment of sexual harassment in the 1994 blockbuster *Disclosure* (from the Michael Crichton novel of the same name). *Disclosure*, marketed as a sexy, anti-"PC" twist on so-called conventional wisdom about sexual harassment, spins out a scenario of a hapless male who is seduced, manipulated, and then wrongly accused of sexual harassment by his unfairly promoted, provocatively clad, venal boss (Demi Moore). Notwithstanding its overwrought, hyperbolic presentation, *Disclosure*'s plot has been defended (by author Crichton and others) as at least a skeletally truthful depiction of male victimization and trumped-up sexual harassment complaints; the message conveyed is that *women*, not men, are the primary purveyors of sexual domination and job hierarchy in the workplace. In addition, consistent with the current climate of anti-affirmative-action animus, the film depicts the female character's promotion as an illogical preference accorded to an incompetent female over a talented and innocent white male. Thus, *Disclosure* captures quite well the ire, resentment, and backlash of its antifeminist era; it portrays (and sexualizes) a work world in which women have the upper hand in matters of professional advancement, leaving men to suffer as powerless victims.

Unsurprisingly, *Disclosure* has enjoyed tremendous box-office success. It smugly subverts so-called "politically correct" assumptions in an ostensibly innocuous and apolitical fashion: Real-life problems of male dominance become movie-land fantasies of female dominance; sexual harassment is depicted as the torrid but coercive seduction of a happily married man by an aggressive, single, emotionally warped career woman. Consistent with the film's flashy, cartoonlike conception of sexual harassment is its campy depiction of the female-boss-as-wicked-temptress; one would never guess from *Disclosure*'s world that women suffer workplace discrimination at all.

However, *Disclosure*'s cavalier treatment of sexual harassment as an issue of male victimization is not its only or even its most problematic distortion. On a subtler level, it also recharacterizes sexual harassment grievances as an unfortunate side effect of the professional elite's "war between the sexes"—that is, the war between white professional men and white professional women. This myth implicitly negates the experiences of black women in an arena in which they have been instrumental both in heightening public awareness and in defining new legal frontiers. Without saying a word about black women—in fact, by deliberately not saying a word about the racial dimensions of sexual harassment—*Disclosure* reinforces the presumption that sexual harassment is a feminist concern of white women. There is simply no room (and no need) in *Disclosure*'s fantasy world for the concerns of black women (or black men, for that matter).

This "decolorization" of sexual harassment is at best ironic, given the significance of black women's contributions to heightened societal awareness of sexual harassment. For example, Anita Hill's charges against Clarence Thomas—the nation's most famous sexual harassment controversy and one that contributed enormously to the high visibility of the issue so baldly exploited in *Disclosure*—did much to underscore sexual harassment as a black feminist issue and involved complex questions of gender *and* race. On a less-publicized but equally significant note, the landmark decision of *Meritor Savings Bank v. Vinson* (1986), in which the U.S. Supreme Court first recognized sexual harassment as a violation of Title VII of the Civil Rights Act of 1964, was based on the grievance of a black woman as well. By treating sexual harassment as just so much melodramatic fodder in an otherwise conventional, steamy Hollywood thriller, *Disclosure* does more than simply implement a random choice of plot and characters. In the process, it contributes to a long-standing cinematic tradition of ignoring the complexities that black women's experiences would lend to the picture.

Other Controlling Images: Black Women as Pathological Dependents

Given the virtual absence of black women as silver-screen lawyer-heroines and their similar erasure from plots that might reasonably draw upon (or at least acknowledge the existence of) black women's lives, what representations of black women *do* emerge from an examination of popular films with law-related themes? Unfortunately, black women still suffer distortion of image as much through what is presented as through what is omitted; whereas yesteryear's controlling images were (and sometimes still are) of the mammy and matriarch variety, today's controlling images emphasize the black woman as self-destructive victim—usually of drugs, domestic abuse, and/or a general lack of self-discipline and fortitude. Notwithstanding the benign intentions of many contemporary films of this mold—for example, "urban realism"-oriented films of the early 1990s such as *Straight Out of Brooklyn, Boyz N the Hood, Jungle Fever*, and *Losing Isaiah*—the overwhelming effect of such representations is quite depressing for black women; they are, by and large, trapped in a cycle of dependency, with few admirable qualities and even fewer opportunities to express them. Legal

themes in such films emerge, usually indirectly, in the context of black women's weakness and hopelessness: At best, they struggle ineffectually to preserve their families amid such oppressive forces as an unresponsive welfare system, brutal police, and rapacious drug dealers (e.g., *Straight Out of Brooklyn, Boyz N the Hood*); at worst, they themselves cause ruination through their self-loathing, drug addiction, and/or poor mothering (e.g., *Boyz 'n' the Hood, Jungle Fever*).

Almost never is a black woman presented in a central, independent role with respect to the legal system; relegation to the role of victim and supplicant is far more common. A 1994 film, *Losing Isaiah*, is on its surface a seeming exception to this trend. Its major characters are two women, one black (Halle Berry) and one white (Jessica Lange), who fight for legal custody of a black child who had been abandoned in a garbage heap by the black mother at a time in her life when she had been addicted to drugs. After a period of confinement in a drug recovery program, during which she learns that her child is still alive, she tries to reclaim him, only to discover that he has been adopted by a white social worker and her family. A courtroom battle over the child ensues, pitting the black mother (represented by a black male lawyer) against the white mother (represented by that cinematic rarity, a black female lawyer). The black mother, fully rehabilitated from crack addiction and prostitution, fights not only to establish her fitness as a parent but also to correct the tragic error of her son's placement with a white family; the white mother responds that her care for the child for several years in a loving, stable, and financially secure family setting should be enough to merit continued custody of him. Ultimately, the black mother regains her son, only to learn that he has formed an unbreakable bond with his adoptive mother and is distraught without her. The film ends on an awkward, quasi-Solomonic note, with the black mother agreeing to share the boy with the mother to whom he is more attached.

In many ways, *Losing Isaiah* presents a basic plot of birth mother versus adoptive mother to which its transracial framework makes little difference. In most such custody fights, regardless of racial differences, birth parents are likely to argue that they are the "real" biological parents and that therefore only they can provide the child with authenticity of familial background; adoptive or foster parents reply that their love and stable custodial care has earned them the right to be the child's "real" parents. Moreover, biological parents who win such battles most likely must confront the pain caused by their rupture of the child's previous family ties. In these respects, *Losing Isaiah* is a rather conventional tearjerker, modernized with the "hot-button issue" patina of transracial adoption concerns.

However, given the paucity of black female roles in such legal dramas, the film's plot takes on added dimensions because of its explicit focus on racial concerns and its implicit statements about black female competence. Interestingly, the character of the black mother—notwithstanding her miraculous recovery from a life of drugs and destitution—remains at best in the position of dependent, disbelieved supplicant. She is in fact discredited by *both* sides. Her own attorney, a black man, is motivated to take her case not because he believes in her competence but, rather, because he wants to remove the child from the white family. The opposing counsel, a black woman, attacks her capabilities head-on. Despite the film's obvious intention to set up a balanced portrayal of each mother's attributes and drawbacks, the viewer is left with the impression that the black mother's main arguments for custody are based not on her strength, survival skills, and love but on less sympathetically presented arguments of race and biology, which shed little light on her individual depth of character. In this light, it is particularly unrealistic but unsurprising that she relents at the movie's end and invites the white adoptive mother's participation in caring for the child. One might interpret this clumsy attempt at an even-handed denouement not so much as an acknowledgement of the complexity of the issue as a way to avoid taking a definitive stand on the merits of the custody decision in favor of the black mother. She has won—but not earned—the right to be the child's mother. She is controlled by, rather than in control of, the power of a defining image.

Conclusion

In assessing evolving images of women in film in the 1970s and 1980s, movie critic Molly Haskell sanguinely commented:

For every stereotype there's a counter-stereotype and the story of women can no longer be reduced to a recitation of evils. As a younger, less hidebound and less conflicted generation emerges, it becomes easier for all of us to speak with our own voices and just assume that someone will be listening, to go against the grain of male desires and definitions, to be strange, loud, impolite, enigmatic, baroque, beautiful, ugly, vengeful, funny. We want nothing less, on or off the screen, than the wide variety and dazzling diversity of male options. (1987, p. 402)

Unfortunately, black women still cannot include themselves in this blissful vision of a new generation of diverse female images. The absence, erasure, and distortion of black women in the growing genre of law films is just one category of such exclusion, but it is a telling one, given black women's role in shaping the legal profession and the law itself. In cinema as in law, black women are recognized as individuals of dignity and complexity only when they resist the degradation of the "dominant gaze" with the power of an oppositional one. As a feminist method, the "oppositional gaze" provides black women with an opportunity to imagine themselves as legal and cinematic subjects with their own histories, values, and ideals.

Black legal heroines (both lawyers and non-lawyers) might exist, *should* exist on screen, as they certainly should and do in real life. That they do not speaks volumes about the difficulty of "talking back" in legal and cinematic frameworks, in which black women are often voiceless and listeners are usually scarce.

Notes

Several themes in this essay were developed in conjunction with my 1996 essay, "Rewriting History with Lightning: Race, Myth, and Hollywood in the Legal Pantheon," see Denvir 1996.

1. For further examination of the role of racial stereotypes in popular culture, see J. H. Franklin 1979; O'Connor 1980; Silk and Silk 1990; Takaki 1979.
2. For explicit focus on the gendered dimensions of mainstream media stereotypes, see de Lauretis 1987; Gamman and Marshment 1989; Haskell 1987; Kuhn 1985.

Notable among the few explorations of black female representation in popular culture are Collins 1990; hooks 1992; hooks 1990; hooks 1989b.

3. "Back talk" is "speaking as an equal to an authority figure" (hooks 1989b, p. 5).

4. See Allen and Chrisman 1992; T. Morrison 1992b.

5. Cover 1986. See also Cover 1993; C. West 1993.

6. See M. Russell 1991, pp. 243, 244–45.

7. For varied perspectives on the relationship between Hollywood law films and popular cultural attitudes about the law, see Denvir 1996; Russell 1996.

13

Women on Trial

The Female Lawyer in the Hollywood Courtroom

CYNTHIA LUCIA

Introduction: The Female Lawyer Film and America of the 1980s and Early 1990s

In the 1949 film, *Adam's Rib*, often classified as a screwball comedy, Spencer Tracy plays Assistant D.A. Adam Bonner, married to attorney Amanda Bonner (Katharine Hepburn), whom he suddenly finds opposing him in the courtroom. Defending a woman accused of assaulting her unfaithful husband, Hepburn attempts to reread and reshape the law to reflect progressive values. Lecturing his wife, Tracy's character clearly sees her action as an assault upon law, a challenge to the patriarchal foundations of the law, and by extension, a personal challenge to himself, as a man and as her husband: "Contempt for the law, that's what you've got. It's a disease, a spreading disease. . . . The law is the law. . . . You start with one law then pretty soon it's all laws, pretty soon it's everything; then it's me."

Simply by virtue of her status as a New Woman in post–World War II America, Hepburn's character poses a threat that filters beyond the public arena and into the private sphere (a dichotomy strongly inscribed in American legal discourse and ideology since the Constitution and only lately challenged). Taking center stage against her husband in the space traditionally designated as *his*, Hepburn is responsible for the temporary break-up of her own marriage. Threatening her husband's potency both in the courtroom and at home, Hepburn's designated space within the private sphere is thus destabilized.

The danger Hepburn poses *is* ultimately contained. Although she challenges the court to rethink gender roles—asking the jury to imagine the accused woman as a man defending his home and the husband as an unfaithful wife whose actions threaten family stability (in the film, these words are accompanied by visual images of the characters in reversed gender roles)—she nevertheless argues in terms of traditional family ideology: "An unwritten law stands back of a man who fights to defend his home. Apply this same law to this maltreated wife and neglected woman—we ask you no more—equality." Hepburn's argument clearly forces the jury and the film audience to question basic assumptions about justice and gender. Yet, after winning in court, Hepburn comes to recognize and regret her miscalculation within her own marriage. She and her husband reconcile during a meeting with their accountant to divide their taxable receipts, the family thus reconstituted under the power of property and tax law. To a large extent, the female threat has been contained—Hepburn's courtroom argument has been nullified by a comic scene in which her jealous husband tricks her into admitting the ethical fallacy upon which her logical courtroom argument was constructed. Her sense of accomplishment in winning a courtroom victory is tempered, as well, by nagging guilt resulting from the husband's defeat. She now has learned only to *joke* about opposing him in the election for county court judgeship.

The threat has been contained, but with a difference. *Adams Rib* not only reflects anxieties about the non-traditional role of the post–World War II New Woman, it also educates its audience, on some level, into an acceptance, though a highly uneasy acceptance, of this new state of affairs. The film spectator is encouraged to agree with Tracy when he pronounces Hepburn a threat to the law and by extension to their marriage, yet we are allowed to recognize, if only for a moment, the validity of her courtroom argument. In contemporary films representing female lawyers, the case has become somewhat more complicated.

Within the past decade, Hollywood has produced some fifteen films featuring female lawyers as central characters.[1] While contemporary Hollywood has represented women in a variety of professional roles, these roles—the female doctor, journalist, or business executive, for example— have not appeared with nearly the regularity nor with such consistent codes of representation as have films about female lawyers. Nor have other female professionals been featured consistently as protagonists, as has happened in the case of female lawyers. Even infrequent film goers can recite titles of at least several "female lawyer" films, although they are hard-pressed to name even one or two titles of recent "female doctor" or "female businesswoman" films.

Why has Hollywood chosen law, almost exclusively, as the field for its contemporary female professionals? Perhaps as the most overtly patriarchal of our institutions, law potentially can perpetuate or weaken the phallocentric structures of other political, cultural, and social institutions. The very profession of the female lawyer paradoxically gives her access to such power yet places *her* at the service and under the thumb of the male power structure. Whatever potency she possesses is derived from the patriarchal system. At the same time, however, she *potentially* gains the power to change the law, to revise readings of the law and thus redefine the power base within our culture. Given the interplay of such powerful polarities, the female lawyer film, consciously or not, has gathered up the tensions, anxieties, and contradictions deeply embedded within our culture and history concerning shifting gender roles and demands for rereadings of the law.

In light of Hollywood's almost obsessive production of films about female lawyers, I will examine characteristics common to many of the films, exploring their significance and asking how aesthetics, politics, and the historical moment intersect, to shape the content and stimulate the production of so many films about female lawyers. In attempting to sort out the political significance of the female lawyer film, as reflected through various elements at work in these films, I will call on feminist film theories that examine the place of women within classical Hollywood narrative structure, as well as theories concerning the representation of women in film noir, a group of post–World War II films (appearing from about 1945 to 1958) in which powerful female characters elicit great anxiety. As "phallic women," these film noir females often threaten male power and identity in much the same way, I will argue, as the female lawyer in contemporary film. To further develop this argument, I will very briefly examine Jacques Lacan's notion of phallocentric power and its relationship to language and to law.

Appearing with regularity since 1985, at least one female lawyer film has been released every year, with three films in 1991 and 1993. It seems no coincidence that the bulk of these films either were made or were in the works during the Reagan-Bush administrations, which established an agenda of "containment" around feminist issues, devoting much lip service to women's rights while undermining women through legislative activity and attitudes touting "family values." The New Right agenda revealed a decided discomfort, at best, or "backlash" thinking, at worst, with regard to women abandoning traditional roles. The consistent production of so many films, beginning in the mid-1980s, when the Reagan New Right had firmly established itself, suggests much more than a Hollywood need to satisfy demands for politically correct representations of women in powerful, professional roles. If anything, this group of films reflects the New Right approach to women's and minority issues— a superficial proclaiming of support, sometimes even touting rare individual success stories to validate a "forward thinking" position on such issues, while forging policies to undermine any real empowerment of such groups.

Appearing approximately a decade after feminism's Second Wave, contemporary female lawyer films, at first glance, seem in tune with a feminist agenda. In the films, the women lawyers appear to play central and powerful roles. Reflecting the New Right approach to "political correctness," however, the female lawyer film, on the one hand, is really a form of tokenism, a glossing-over of reactionary impulses. A subtle misogyny emerges in the positioning of female lawyers within the narrative framework and in the representation of these female protagonists as dangerously ambitious yet professionally and personally deficient. Beneath the veneer of liberalism, the films seem dedicated to restoring the law and, by extension, patriarchy to their formerly uncontested positing. On the other hand, odd narrative fissures do exist within the female lawyer film, complication the possibility of achieving complete and uncontested closure, despite the films' most overdetermined efforts to do so. Although it remains a bit premature to claim genre or subgenre status for the female lawyer film, these films consistently share a number of characteristics[2] which, along with the very structure of their narratives, reveal complex and conflicting political undercurrents at work.

Produced in rather rapid succession, female lawyer films are simple in narrative form, encouraging critics, on first viewing, to disregard them as Hollywood fluff or formula, in much the way B-movies and melodramas of the past were dismissed as inferior productions or "weepies," respectively, by their contemporary critics. Underlying the simple form of the female lawyer film, however, is a complicated set of assumptions and contradictions that register a troubled and uneasy acceptance of women in law yet reveal some difficulty in resolving the "problem" of women in law.

To fully appreciate these undercurrents of anxiety operating in the female lawyer film, it may be useful to examine similar anxieties expressed in post–World War II American film noir. Dominant American culture of the 1980s and early 1990s found its activist feminism fading and post-Watergate, post-Vietnam traumas successfully suppressed by Reaganomics and a new nationalism, often reflected in corporate advertising slogans and political campaign strategies. This period was not entirely unlike America of the late 1940s and early 1950s, in which post-Holocaust, A-bomb, and Cold War traumas, along with anxiety concerning changing roles of women, were cloaked in a mantle of cultural entitlement, woven from desires for postwar normalcy, prosperity, and national pride. These unacknowledged tensions, especially concerning the role of women, found indirect expression in countless films noir, many of which characterize women as a source of mystery, confusion, corruption, and death.

Subjected to heavy-handed, guilt-tripping propaganda, which instilled fears of broken marriages and the juvenile delinquency of neglected children, many working women of the day were strongly and successfully encouraged to retreat to the security and normalcy of the clean, sunlit kitchen. Elaine Tyler May, however, points out the ironies of the period: "The female labor force expanded in the postwar years, providing a potential alternative to early marriage and child rearing. . . . Yet . . . the continuing anxiety surrounding women's changing sexual and economic roles helps explain the unprecedented rush into family life and the baby boom of the postwar era" (E. T. May 1989, pp. 155, 167). This anxiety surrounding working women was in part connected to Cold War ideology, according to May, "since an essential ingredient in winning the cold war was presumably the rearing of strong and able offspring" (E. T. May 1989, p. 157). Less overt film noir messages of caution convey guilt and fear with regard to dangerous "independent" women, who occupy dimly lit city streets, unsavory bars, and casinos. Such women became a particular source of tension, according to May, since it was thought that "outside the home, they would yield a dangerous, destructive force" (E. T. May 1989, p. 165).

Despite some harrowing contemporary film portraits of dangerous professional women gone berserk, *Fatal Attraction*–style, professional and working women of the 1980s and 1990s have not been retreating to the kitchen in great numbers, yet our culture greatly pressures them to uphold "family values"—to live heterosexual child-centered lives when they return home from a day at the office—instilling more than a little guilt should they fail to do so. (One need only examine the child custody case, initiated during the O. J. Simpson trial by the ex-husband of Simpson prosecutor Marcia Clark, citing Clark's intense professional commitments to deem her an unfit mother.) Such guilt is fed by the media, particularly women's magazines, which have constructed and valorized the "superwoman," as well as by films that subtly demean female professionals few of whom attain superwoman status. The messages transmitted are an extension of those expressed in a 1972 government civil defense pamphlet, which May cites: "In this vision of the atomic age family, women were the focus of concern: recognize their increasing sexual and economic emancipation but focus those energies within the family" (E. T. May 1989, p. 165).

Beyond confronting media images that subtly communicate anxieties of inadequacy, contemporary working women often confront the frustration of a firmly fixed glass ceiling that keeps many of them from attaining the top positions of power within government and corporations or from attaining partnerships in high-powered law firms. The statistics are numerous, but several examples concerning women in law tell the story. *Barrister Magazine* reports that "[w]omen lawyers are far less likely to be promoted, get paid less, and express more dissatisfaction with their jobs than men" (Rutledge 1991, p. 31), with a study of young lawyers showing that 45 percent of the men make partner, while only 18 percent of the women do (Rutledge 1991). This two-part study, conducted in 1984 and again in 1990, "found that the percentage of all lawyers dissatisfied with their work has increased significantly from 1984 to 1990. In fact, the percentage of dissatisfied men in private firms and corporate counsel doubled. Interestingly, the most sudden increase in dissatisfaction came from women partners" (Rutledge 1991, p. 31). A 1995 study conducted by a panel of the American Bar Association published results that indicate a further decline in opportu-

nities for female lawyers, with promotion and salary rates that lag far behind their male counterparts, prompting one female attorney to remark that the statistics suggest " '. . . not a glass ceiling at the end, but a process that begins right off the bat . . . ' " (Bernstein 1996, p. 9).

Another study, conducted in 1991–92 of career and salary advancement of New York metropolitan area lawyers, reveals how the legal establishment uses inaccurate perceptions of women with children to justify gender bias in earnings: Male lawyers with children, perceived as more stable than men without children, are rewarded with increased earnings, whereas female lawyers with children are perceived as less stable and are therefore penalized by a decrease in earnings (Dixon and Seron 1992). The same study finds that "in reality the allocation of work effort by women with children equals that of men with children" (Dixon and Seron 1992, p. 28). In the 1995 American Bar Association study, it is noted that "In the private sector . . . very few lawyers—1 to 4 percent—dare to take advantage of the 'family friendly' policies adopted by most law firms in the last decade. Those who do are tarred as not seriously committed to the law . . ." (Bernstein 1996, p. 9), leading many female lawyers to feel ". . . less willing to make extreme personal sacrifices to adapt to a work culture defined by white men . . . (Bernstein 1996, p. 9). Beyond such overt discrimination, many female lawyers observe more subtle forms of exclusion ". . . from male networks [which] reinforces the belief that women are less effective as 'rain makers,' lawyers who can bring in business" (Bernstein 1996, p. 9) extending back to law schools in which ". . . women are effectively silenced by male law students who heckle them as 'femiNazis' and overwhelmingly male faculty who ignore them" (Bernstein 1996, p. 9).

Such conditions have led Cynthia Fuchs Epstein to conclude:

The structure of the profession and the cultural views about the nature of men and women often prevent women from becoming fully integrated into the legal profession. While most men can make their lives as lawyers mesh with their private lives, their values, their styles of behavior, few women escape the contradictory pressures and expectations within the profession and outside it. These pressures and contradictions—the products of ambivalence on the part of male gatekeepers and other men and women who do not believe that women belong in the law—create ambivalence in the minds of women. (Epstein 1993, p. 265)

The female lawyer film both reflects this state of affairs and perhaps contributes to it through its contradictory, confused, and demeaning representations of the female lawyer. In fact, after hearing my thesis, a high-powered medical malpractice attorney, who employs *one* female lawyer in his firm, wondered whether films and television shows about female lawyers[3] would undermine the effectiveness of *his* female attorney in the minds of jurors. Such representations not only reflect our deepest anxieties but also create them, it seems.

Politics, Patriarchy, and the Female Lawyer Film

In her 1994 book, *Women Lawyers: Rewriting the Rules*, Mona Harrington further frames the highly charged issue of women in law within the current debate around multiculturalism and conservative resistance to multicultural demands. Conservatives understand that such demands potentially will erode the traditional base of phallocentric power:

[T]he conflicts that lie beneath the whole range of multicultural claims form the fundamental drama of American politics at the end of the twentieth century. Although sometimes coded and disguised, these conflicts have dominated every presidential election since 1960—with the possible exception of the Watergate-driven campaign of 1976. And they came into particularly bitter prominence in 1992, when speakers at the Republican National Convention openly declared a cultural war on groups seeking social change—feminists, homosexuals, single parents, working mothers, and obstreperous racial minorities.

It is within this large context that the old rules defining the power relations between men and women are breaking and re-forming. The premise of the relation inherited from past centuries was unequal power, without any question. Men were supposed to make the rules. They were supposed to govern the political, economic,

and cultural affairs of the world, to rule as father of the family at home. (Harrington 1994, pp. 4–5)

Similar tensions inform the majority of female lawyer films, which carefully construct liberal facades to camouflage underlying reactionary attitudes. At points where the facade wears thin, the conservative frame reveals itself. (As if the organizers of the 1996 Republican National Convention had seen a few too many female lawyer films, all energies were poured into constructing a liberal "ceremonial" facade to hide a decidedly reactionary platform, particularly in regard to women's and racial issues, welfare, and immigration.) In their need to adopt a superficially liberal stance, the female lawyer films reflect deeply rooted contradictions within the politics of patriarchy and its response to feminism—contradictions evident not only within Republican "New Right," as represented by Reagan and Bush, but also within liberal politics and some branches of feminism.

Zillah Eisenstein explores the limitations of liberalism with regard to feminist demands, often the very same ideological limitations evident in many female lawyer films. For instance, Eisenstein reads President Carter's 1979 firing of Bella Abzug as cochair of the National Advisory Committee on Women as his attempt "to demobilize the radical faction of the liberal feminist movement, those who sought to change the everyday conditions of the majority of women by focusing on women's sexual-class identity across economic class and racial lines" (Eisenstein 1984, p. 24). Eisenstein further suggests that "Abzug's dismissal was an effort by Carter to further legitimize the narrow legalistic interpretation of the ERA, rather than the broader view that connects women's rights to questions of the economy, abortion, and homosexuality" (Eisenstein 1984, p. 25).

Likewise, President Clinton's abrupt withdrawal of Lani Guinier, nominated in 1994 to head the Civil Rights Division of the Justice Department, further testifies to the limitations of liberalism (particularly in relationship to female lawyers, in this case a minority female lawyer). While Clinton's response may or may not have been motivated by political pressure from conservatives, who perceived Guinier as especially dangerous to the white male power structure, particularly in terms of her academic writings advocating the "radical" notion of proportional representation, Clinton nonetheless did respond. Clearly, the already shaky liberal commitment to multiculturalism collapsed under the pressure, either real or perceived, of feminist and minority demands for empowerment. Not only does such limited liberalism express itself within the female lawyer film; the apparent liberal ideology adopted by many of the films often itself becomes a tool for discrediting the female protagonists.

In her analysis that oddly resonates within the Clinton administration, Zillah Eisenstein, writing during Reagan's Republican presidency, posits the failure of the Equal Rights Amendment as likewise symptomatic of a political atmosphere that attempts to both profit from and undermine feminist issues:

> Whereas the Carter administration endorsed the ERA (although it did nothing to aid its ratification), the Reagan administration's position is "against the amendment but for equal rights." Reagan has tried to walk this tightrope; he supports the New Right position against the Equal Rights Amendment and yet he tries to appear supportive of equal rights for women. This particular position adopts the neo-conservative position that supports equality of opportunity, but not equality of conditions. In this sense Reagan's position on the ERA straddles both neo-conservative and New Right politics.
>
> Reagan argues that the amendment would be harmful to women because it will treat men and women as though they were the same (equal?). On the other hand, the appointment of [Sandra Day] O'Connor was supposed to prove that a woman is free to be anything she wants to be. All women need is freedom of choice—not equality. (Eisenstein 1984, pp. 131–32)

Eisenstein's reading suggests an atmosphere ripe for the emergence of the female lawyer film and in many ways illustrates the underlying political thrust of the films. Ironically, Reagan also uses O'Connor, a female lawyer, to advance his conservative agenda, which maintains the patriarchal structure, yet in so doing, he *appears* to support women's rights. Quite coincidentally, in 1981, the year of O'Connor's nomination to the Court, *First Monday in October* was released. In this film, the first female nominee to the Supreme Court (Jill Clayburgh) is grilled about her

identity as a woman, a childless woman at that, and about her identity as defined by her deceased husband, also her law partner. Both factors seem to overshadow her record as a lawyer in the minds of the male senators who interrogate her. This obsession with the lawyer as woman is a trope that has firmly taken hold in cinematic representations of female lawyers.

Numerous examples such as Eisenstein's and Harrington's exist, illustrating a patriarchal, phallocentric power structure on the defensive, clinging to its power, whether from a liberal or conservative ideological base. Yet the very definition of patriarchy itself becomes problematic when we attempt to examine its role and its expression within the female lawyer film. While the term "patriarchy" implies a monolithic cultural force, patriarchy does, as we have seen, exist within and support such divergent ideologies as capitalism, Marxism, socialism, fascism, and various religious ideologies, to name but a few. For the purposes of sorting out its influence within the Hollywood female lawyer film, however, I will limit my scope of study to patriarchy as it expresses itself within liberalism and conservatism as defined generally within American politics. Perhaps it is possible to guard against a monolithic understanding of patriarchy by imagining it as a kind of root system, functioning underground and only occasionally surfacing within the operation of established, powerful, phallocentric institutions, as roots sometimes surface near the trunks of particularly sturdy old trees. As the means through which phallocentrism expresses itself, this patriarchal network supports a variety of cultural, political, and social institutions and, most important, both nourishes and is nourished by the law. The roots of patriarchy continue to grow laterally as they grow deeper, at times getting tangled, choking certain parts of the varied systems they form, though generally to the benefit and continued survival of the system as a whole.

Intentionally or not, the female lawyer film has tapped into a serious contemporary concern about the continued survival and strengthening of the patriarchal network, with law as the locus of concern. It is law that defines and establishes the parameters of power for governmental and corporate institutions, as well as defining the position of women and minorities within those institutions. Law defines marriage and the family, as well as parental and reproductive rights and responsibilities. As if to remind us that patriarchy and law are inseparable, almost all female lawyer films include patriarchal figures, such as district attorneys, judges, police or private investigators, and/or male superiors, many of whom initiate the female lawyer within the power structure of the law or deny her access.

Music Box (1990) and *Class Action* (1991) are examples of two female lawyer films that reinforce the connections between law and patriarchy through a decidedly Oedipal subtext. In both of these films, the lawyers' biological fathers become focal points of their legal efforts. A somewhat more bizarre Oedipal subtext operates within *The Client* (1994), based on the John Grisham novel. Barely eking out an identity of her own, the female lawyer here embodies two figures of the Oedipal drama in relationship to the young boy who becomes her client. On discovering the female lawyer's past history of alcohol and drug abuse, her young client identifies her with the father he has rejected. At the same time, however, he sees her as a maternal figure, with whom he ventures to flirt, precociously, if innocently. He alternately rejects and embraces the female lawyer, ultimately guiding *her* along the complicated pathways of a criminal investigation and corresponding legal action, asserting *his* entitlement to the law simply by virtue of being male. He ultimately returns to his biological mother, whom it is clear *he* must guide and care for. But he does so only after asserting his love for his incredibly self-effacing female lawyer. Amazingly, this female lawyer assumes three identities: the rejected but reformed father, with whom the boy happily now can identify; the surrogate mother, whose lack he disdains yet overrides by calling upon his own masculine power, thus constructing his true identity as male; and the potential love object, further securing his newfound masculine identity and potency.

In many other films, most notably *The Big Easy* (1987), *Suspect* (1987), *Physical Evidence* (1988), and *A Few Good Men* (1992), the female lawyer's (potential) lover assumes a patriarchal role in the relationship. Because they lack the required education and legal experience, these male lovers are far less qualified to negotiate the complexities of the law than is the female lawyer, yet neither the men nor the female protagonists (nor the audience, for that matter) seem to recognize these limitations. The films imply that simply by virtue of being male, these characters can "think like . . . lawyer[s]," which David Kairys explains "often seems to involve abandonment of progressive values and the hope of social action" (Kairys 1990, p. 4). In contrast to these confident men, the female lawyers appear inadequate and, at times, incompetent.

Achieving the goal of "thinking like . . . lawyer[s]," which seems so natural to the male characters, requires the female lawyers to invest extraordinary effort, often at the expense of their personal happiness. Many of the women lawyers spend long hours and sleepless nights at their work, in contrast to the relative ease with which men both in and outside of the profession operate. Moreover, in *Suspect* (1987), *Defenseless* (1991), *Love Crimes* (1992), *Guilty as Sin* (1993), and *The Client* (1994), the female lawyers must transgress the boundaries of the law or of ethical conduct in order to advance their cases or protect themselves. Clearly, these women cannot be viewed without ambivalence. Their inability to "think" or "function" innately "like lawyers" (in other words, like men) results in levels of deception and incompetence, which shake the very foundations of the legal process.

The Verdict (1982), a film that revolves primarily around a male lawyer and appeared a few years before the main body of female lawyer films, can be seen as an interesting precursor to the female lawyer film. In it Laura Fischer (Charlotte Rampling) is a lawyer *granted* her place within the law by a powerful corporate attorney, referred to as the "prince of darkness." In this exchange, the Eve-like Laura must gain the trust of down-and-out attorney Frank Galvin (Paul Newman) in order to gather information ensuring his courtroom defeat. Lecturing Laura about the price a woman must pay for a place within the patriarchal system, her serpentlike boss explains, "We're paid to win the case. You finished your marriage. You wanted to come back to practice the law. You wanted to come back into the world." Patriarchy is, indeed, "the world," as defined by these films. Through its own questionable logic, *The Verdict* sees Laura's reentry into that world as destructive and destabilizing yet sees Frank's attempt to reestablish himself as righteous and ennobling.

On a subtextual level the female lawyer film takes its cue from *The Verdict* in adopting a sort of perverse politics of "difference," an ostensibly feminist stance that simultaneously enables the films to reestablish the power of patriarchy. Zillah Eisenstein argues against "difference" on the basis that it supports the patriarchal structure: "Patriarchy is the process of politically differentiating the female from the male, as woman from man. Patriarchy in this sense is the politics of transforming biological sex to politicized gender, which prioritizes the man while making the woman different (unequal), less than, or 'other'" (Eisenstein 1984, p. 90). Repeatedly asserting the female lawyer's difference, the films most certainly establish their protagonists as "unequal" and "other." This position finds its most obvious expression in A Few Good Men (1992). The film uses phallocentric male dominance within the military and legal systems, together, to discount the female lawyer (Demi Moore), whose feminine "difference" inspires recurrent ridicule and contempt until she effaces her own knowledge, power, and identity. Deferring to her male counterparts, the female lawyer masochistically recognizes and accepts her own inferior position, enacting a role of self-imposed silence, thus enabling the legal and narrative processes to move forward and function effectively. The film's promotional ad, displaying a photograph of the key players and the film's title, is curiously revealing. Tom Cruise, Jack Nicholson, and Demi Moore, all in military uniform, are lined up in profile and photographed in medium close-up. Moore, with hair hidden tightly beneath her military cap, looks like a man—one of the "few good men," as the title proclaims. On seeing the film, of course, we find that Nicholson is not at all a "good" man; but the ad and the film together imply that in order to earn a position within the military court of law, the female lawyer must submerge her identity as a woman and thus become a "good man," or, more accurately, become an "absent," silent woman.

The equation of "thinking like a lawyer" with "thinking like a man" is further expressed in The Accused (1989), when the male district attorney threatens to fire his assistant D.A. (Kelly McGillis) if she attempts to prosecute male spectators who cheered, aiding and abetting, as a gang of rapists brutalized a woman in a roadside bar. He articulates the no-win position of a female working within the phallocentric legal structure: "What happens if you lose? You'll look like an incompetent. If you win, you'll look like a vengeful bitch." Along with similar scenes in various other female lawyer films, this moment in The Accused echoes that pivotal scene in the 1949 screwball comedy Adam's Rib, in which Spencer Tracy feels compelled to lecture his wife on the repercussions of her courtroom "performance."

In Adam's Rib on the most obvious narrative level we are asked to judge the guilt or innocence of Doris Attinger (Judy Holiday), accused of attempting to murder her husband. On a more ethical level, we are asked to consider the validity of the legal system in its treatment of women. Amanda claims that "there's lots of things a man can do, and in society's eyes it's all hunky-dory"; whereas, when a woman "does the same thing . . . she's an outcast. . . ."; moreover, "this deplorable situation [has] seep[ed] into our courts of law where women are supposed to be equal." Adam claims that "The law is the law, whether it's good or bad. If it's bad the thing to do is change it, not to bust it wide open." In presenting viewers with these overarching issues, the film goes on to pose the several legalistic and cultural debates that follow: it raises the question of difference in terms that are almost as thorny and contradictory as such questions have become in actual legal decisions and the theoretical critiques to follow those decisions. The film raises the subsequent issue of whether equality before the law is best achieved through equal treatment or through treatment that takes difference and/or disadvantage into account. Adam argues that "[M]ostly, I think females get advantages"; whereas, Amanda asserts that "[W]e don't want advantages. And we don't want prejudices." And finally, Adam's Rib raises one of the key issues concerning post-war America: whether women can occupy the public sphere of profession and career while maintaining stability and happiness within the private sphere of the home

Although the film goes much further than Hollywood films of its own or recent times, it nonetheless fails to acknowledge the full practice or ramifications of the public/private dichotomy, as it falls along gender lines. While traditionally the law has interfered in the family to support male power, it has also failed to protect women and children from male abuse.[4] The very crime at the center of the narrative—a woman's alleged attempt to murder her husband who is having an affair—provides the core around which the various other issues revolve. Amanda cites the "unwritten law" that allows a man to take violent action in order to keep his home intact, while acknowledging that a woman taking similar action is not protected by the same unwritten law. In her historical overview of legal issues involving gender, Deborah L. Rhode cites actual instances, occurring as recently as 1969, of such inequality before the law, in which several jurisdictions recognized a complete defense to murder or manslaughter for men but not women who stumbled on their spouses having sexual intercourse with someone else" (Rhode 1989, p. 47). According to Adam, in the argument constructed by the film, "Crime should be punished, not condoned," to which Amanda adds, "If a woman commits it . . .," with Adam countering, "If anyone commits it." Notions about femininity, masculinity, and difference, with law as mediating force, unfold in all their sticky complexity within the film, anticipating many of the issues currently debated by legal theorists.

The film, then, stakes its initial claim concerning women and culture/law on the overlapping issues of difference and the public/private dichotomy, as both have been used traditionally to define gender roles. In his lecture, Adam openly articulates the anxieties that tend to lie more insidiously below the surface in many contemporary female lawyer films. We witness the moment of Adam's walking out the door on Amanda, but by the time the contemporary female lawyer film arrives on the scene, men have long since exited the lives of these "competitors" or have failed to gain entry in the first place, defining the private lives of these female lawyers as empty and lacking. It is as though the exit line, delivered by Adam while slamming the door—"You want be a big he-woman? Then go ahead and be it but not with me"—has resounded over the course of four decades to inform representations of Amanda's less light-hearted contemporary counterparts. These films continually reassert that winning in the public arena of the courtroom, as Amanda has, results in serious losses in the private world of home and family. But, of course, Adam's Rib is a comedy, and as such, Amanda will not share the fate of unrelenting professional and personal anxiety experienced by her contemporary counterparts or by contemporary audiences, for that matter, who are invited

to ease the anxiety by objectifying the female lawyer in one way or another. Appropriately enough, in Adam's Rib it is the contractual aspect of marriage that seems to prompt reconciliation.

The threat embodied by the contemporary female lawyer, while intensified, is not always so comfortably contained, despite the more extreme narrative efforts to do so. Playing out her repressed, personal anger in the public arena of the courtroom, the female lawyer in Class Action (1991), for instance, opposes her father, also an attorney. Not only are her motives shown to be confused; the film also suggests that by opposing her father, the female lawyer is at least partially responsible for the death of her mother, who collapses on the courthouse steps moments after the first formal bout between father and daughter. Oedipal implications abound.

Further heightening the sense of danger and instability embodied by the female lawyer in film, visual representation is often inflected by film noir stylistics. In The Verdict (1982), though it is not a female lawyer film per se, the duplicitous female lawyer is shot in the deep space of the frame, which defines her as menacing and untrustworthy, a visual trope evident in several female lawyer films. Lighting and shot composition intensify anxiety surrounding the female lawyer's often confused and unclear motives, suggesting that she is unpredictable and unknowable in some fundamental way. Numerous scenes place female lawyers in darkly lit spaces, often with sidelighting, suggesting a split or duplicitous identity.

Perhaps these recent films reflect the more serious crisis posed by the contemporary New Woman, who emerged after feminism's Second Wave, when the public/private dichotomy began to disintegrate further, in more far-reaching ways than in post–World War II America. Economic necessity, single-parent households, and increased numbers of women in somewhat more powerful, professional positions have permanently weakened the boundaries and intensified the anxieties. While modest feminist legal reforms address such issues as sexual harassment, job security, and maternity benefits, as well as reproductive freedom, the law often simultaneously provides and denies women equal treatment. To uncover the anxieties and ambivalence surrounding women's roles and rights in our culture and within our legal system, one need only examine the heated debates surrounding such reforms, as well as case studies showing how these reforms have sometimes been used against women.

Reflecting this ambivalence, female lawyer films tend to cast actresses known for their independence and strength; these women are chosen, it seems, to evoke our admiration and sympathy: Jill Clayburgh, Glenn Close, Debra Winger, Cher, Kelly McGillis, Jessica Lange, Barbara Hershey, Emma Thompson, and Susan Sarandon—women we can root for. At the same time, however, the films often practice an overt misogyny, threatening or inflicting violence on these women, placing them in physical danger. As the women travel through noiresque settings—dark, deserted garages, office buildings, or city streets—we are positioned voyeuristically, watching and waiting, anticipating the attack.

Music Box and Class Action: Case Studies in Patriarchy and Phallocentrism within the Law

Just as Adam lectures his wife on the law in *Adam's Rib*, the contemporary female lawyer film registers its distrust of women lawyers in scenes in which women are instructed in the law. By implying limited knowledge on the part of these women, such scenes attempt to recuperate the power of patriarchy through the power of the law, both of which have been challenged by the very presence of the female lawyer. In addition to these scenes of literal instruction delivered by male colleagues or superiors, images in which the female lawyer confronts stacks of government evidence, as in *Music Box* (1990)—and leather-bound legal volumes or imposing law libraries in many other films—all evoke the patriarchal authority under which the female lawyer operates. The classic design and frequent long-shot framing of imposing, cavernous courtrooms inscribe the law's immovable permanence. Coupled with camera movements along a vertical axis, the mise-en-scène asserts phallocentric dominance. Although the female lawyer is a professional, because she is female her knowledge and access to power are restricted and often negotiated by the men surrounding her—men who, the films suggest, rightfully "own" the true power of language and the law, in Lacanian terms.

A brief look at the work of Jacques Lacan will be instructive in understanding how power relationships are constructed within the law, therefore providing a key to understanding the issue of power within the female lawyer film. As a psycholinguist who rereads Freud in terms of linguistics, Lacan suggests that conceptual thinking is dependent on the child's moving out of a stage he calls the Imaginary and into a stage he calls the Symbolic. The Imaginary is a stage in which difference does not yet structure experience, a stage in which the child exists as one with the mother. With the arrival of the "third term," the father or the law of the father, the child is introduced to difference and thus gains the ability to acquire language and knowledge. The "name of the father" therefore establishes perception of sexual difference, consequently establishing law and the conceptual framework necessary to the construction of law. In the Symbolic, the child perceives and accepts the "law of the father," the structure created by rules, within which he is allowed operate. I use the term "he" deliberately, for to some extent Lacan, like Freud, sees the experience of the male child as privileged in its relationship to the recognition of difference from the mother.[5]

What sexual difference comes to mean in society, then, is the very means by which the phallus is given power. According to Lacan, however, the phallus obtains cultural power only when it is veiled—when male subjectivity is hidden, conferring a false objectivity upon the phallus. Lacan problematizes the Freudian notion of castration anxiety in the Oedipal phase and beyond through this notion of the phallus as a *signifier* (a "suggestion" of potency, power, language, and law), which can operate only when "veiled:" "[T]he phallus can only play its role as veiled, that is, as in itself the sign of latency" (Lacan 1982, p. 82).

Lacan's notion of cultural power, as derived from the veiled phallus, finds expression within the idealized understanding of the law that our culture historically has accepted. Just as feminist theory has questioned both Lacan and Freud in their conception of subjectivity and, more often than not, the denial of a female subjectivity, feminist legal theory has questioned the idealized, almost mythic vision of law upheld and perpetuated by the legal establishment. Such a conception of law traditionally has provided little space for alternative readings of any kind, including feminist readings, as David Kairys points out:

> Basic to the popular perception of the judicial process is the notion of government by law, not people. Law is depicted as separate from—and "above"—politics, economics, culture, and the values or preferences of judges [the veiled phallus, in a sense]. This separation is supposedly accomplished and ensured by a number of perceived attributes of the decision-making process, including judicial subservience to a Constitution, statutes, and precedent; the quasi-scientific objective nature of legal analysis; and the technical expertise of judges and lawyers. (Kairys 1990, p. 1)

These "perceived attributes" of the legal process veil the political, economic, and cultural influences within the law, conferring upon the law an indisputable power and authority, much as the phallus becomes a signifier of power only when veiled—when acting as signifier only. Feminist film theorist Mary Ann Doane explicates Lacan's notion of the phallus, suggesting how the cultural power of the veiled phallus is linked with the notion of truth:

> [T]he phallus—in a perpetual demonstration of the inadequacy of language with respect to meaning—plays its role only when veiled. Neither the woman nor the phallus seems to be capable of completely escaping the problematic of truth, even in its very inaccessibility, in its resistance to the purely visible, or as belonging to the order of language. Whether or not the phallus is feminized, truth, in the Lacanian text, insofar as it concerns a question of veiling is usurped for the phallus. (Doane 1991, p. 65)

The patriarch/female lawyer relationship, as represented in the films, tends to play out tensions implicit within Kairys's idea of the traditional, idealized notion of law. That monolithic vision of law is destabilized and implicitly critiqued through the very presence of the female lawyer, who has thrown politics in the way of language and the law. Doane's assertion that truth ultimately resides within the phallocentric discourse is correct insofar as the female lawyer film is concerned. Yet by her presence alone, the female lawyer (a figure who clearly has moved into the realm of the Symbolic) has lifted the veil from

the phallus (itself defined as the intersection of language and the law) and has weakened the mythic notion of an idealized legal process that somehow stands above politics and cultural influences.

Although the political content may exist only through the female lawyer's presence in some films, other films are far more explicit in their introduction of politics as a factor in the law, particularly *Hannah K.* (1983), *The Big Easy* (1987), *Suspect* (1987), *The Accused* (1989), *Music Box* (1990), *Class Action* (1991), *The Pelican Brief* (1993), and *In the Name of the Father* (1993). In these films the female lawyer (or female law student, in *The Pelican Brief*) is represented as persistently attempting to remove the veil from the phallocentric moorings of the law. While many traditional courtroom dramas, featuring male lawyers as protagonists, uphold the idealized position of law and unquestionable expertise of lawyers and judges, the female lawyer film destabilizes that assumption to some extent. This is especially true when we consider the presence of a "bad father" figure in several of these films. In *Music Box* (1990), Ann's father is a former Nazi police guard, and her former father-in-law is a Nazi sympathizer who tells his grandson that the Holocaust never happened, that "it was all an exaggeration, all made-up." In *Class Action* (1991) and *The Verdict* (1982) the Machiavellian "bad father" figures transgress ethics and the law in order to win at any price. In *Suspect* (1987) the judge himself is a murderous patriarch. Irish director Jim Sheridan's *In the Name of the Father* (1993) indicts the ethics of the entire British justice system, one in which male dominance exists on all levels. Although it is not a female lawyer film per se, this Hollywood-financed film, closely following mainstream Hollywood aesthetics, positions a female lawyer as a key player in a legal system clearly corrupted by political interests. The basic contradiction of the female lawyer film is expressed, as *In the Name of the Father*, when the women lawyers defeat these men, who are often old enough to be their biological fathers, but only by means of the very system these patriarchs govern and uphold.

Further building contradictions, the films typically trap the female lawyer between the word of the "good father" and the word of the "bad father," both of whom compete to influence her. These films show the female lawyer mistakenly following the "bad father," often associated with reactionary politics, and temporarily rejecting the "good father," generally associated with the liberal politics the films themselves superficially adopt. The competing influence of the good and bad father figures often reveals the female lawyer to be self-involved, short-sighted, deficient, and dangerous, not unlike the independent, "castrating" females of film noir. Yet the simplistic polarities of "good" and "bad," as marked by the male patriarchs within the films, line up too neatly behind the equally simplistic categories of "liberal" and "conservative," respectively.

While many female lawyer films adopt an ostensibly liberal stance, they often do so as a means of undermining the female lawyer, whose politics don't "measure up." Like the liberalism of Carter and Clinton in respect to feminist issues, the liberalism of the films collapses under its own weight, as shown through its positioning of the female lawyer within the narrative structure. In effect, the films reveal deeply conservative underpinnings in the treatment of their female characters, not unlike the woman-as-token brand of conservative politics practiced by Reagan and Bush. The good or bad fathers of the films grant female lawyers a place within the system, ultimately, as a means of containing their power. Overt examples are *Music Box* (1990) and *Class Action* (1991),[6] in which attorneys Ann Talbot (Jessica Lange) and Maggie Warde (Mary Elizabeth Mastrantonio) fall prey to the influence of "bad father" figures, whom the films define as fascist. Both films thus contain the power of the female lawyers, in part by showing how their politics fail to measure up to the morally and ethically "correct" liberalism the films seem to adopt.

Incapable of constructing her father's defense and recognizing his guilt, Ann, in *Music Box*, enlists her ex-father-in-law, attorney Harry Talbot (Donald Moffat), to help maneuver the dismissal of charges against her father, who is accused of Nazi war crimes. On one level, *Music Box* asks whether it is at all possible to look at the gentle, loving father of so many years and recognize the Nazi criminal who brutalized, raped, and murdered his victims nearly fifty years earlier. Truly, he is both good and bad father in the distinctly private and public spheres in which he has operated. The film also flirts on the very brink of asking whether his past should matter now. Here, the politics of the film turn insidiously against

the female lawyer. When Ann mails off incriminating photos to the federal prosecutor after charges against her father have been dropped, the film simultaneously applauds and castigates her, implying a certain heartlessness in her ethics and morality. At the same time, however, the film assumes a strong antifascist, liberal stance which, ironically, takes a rather reactionary view of Ann, who only by accident discovers the photos that *force* her to acknowledge the truth. The film quietly implies that Ann's emotional blind spot threatens to subvert the ideological underpinnings of justice. As in so many other films, the female lawyer is pulled between the film's political and ideological polarities. In this case, Ann's adherence to liberal principles over personal loyalties defines her as heartless, yet her initial tendency to believe her father, to give in to emotional, personal ties, defines her as a potential danger within the public, male-dominated sphere. Within these subtle contradictions set up by the film, we are allowed to identify and sympathize with Ann, yet we are also made to feel vaguely uneasy about her, as she, herself, seems to feel.

Throughout the film, mirrors and other reflective surfaces serve as a trope to advance Ann's uneasy acceptance of her own identity, thus problematizing, on a visual level, the relationship between Ann and the spectator. Early in the narrative, just before telling her father she will accept his case, Ann sits on the stairs facing a mirror, outside her son's bedroom. As she listens to her father gently answer his grandson's questions concerning the charges against him, Ann parts her bathrobe. She ponders the reflection of her legs, but after a few moments closes the robe with an air of tired resignation. To what aspect of her identity has she become reluctantly resigned? Her role as attorney, as mother, as daughter, as an unmarried woman whose age places her on the brink of losing the sexual attraction and attractiveness so central to gender construction in our culture? The film remains ambiguous in answering these questions, constructing Ann's identity out of an acknowledged interdependence of these various roles but, unfortunately, refusing to analyze the subsequent implications. Clearly, to Ann this interdependence is troubling.

When Ann first reads the government's evidence against her father, we see another key example of this visual trope. Her face reflected in an office windowpane against a dark night sky, Ann again must confront her identity not only as lawyer—her father's defender—but, more important, as daughter of a man who allegedly performed acts that can define him only as brutal, sadistic, and perhaps even evil. To what extent does she, as daughter, share in this identity? As both his daughter and his defense attorney, does she indirectly act in complicity? Does her defense of her father and her denial of his identity as war criminal become a denial of her own subjectivity?

Such moments within the film stand in relief against a potentially complex discourse on the issue of State power that the film unfortunately never fully develops. Ann challenges the federal prosecutor, also her courtroom opponent, about the ease with which the state constructs the identity of her father as war criminal on the basis of circumstantial evidence, much of it now more than forty years old. The State uses its power to manufacture a false identity, she claims, but ultimately Ann is proven wrong. The trope of split identity as constructed by the State thus extends from her father, both the good and bad father, to Ann herself, who must come to terms with the State's version of her father's identity. Only in accepting the State as the "true" patriarch—as the source of truth—is Ann able to reclaim a subject-position and her identity as attorney working in the cause of truth. Ironically, as in many female lawyer films, when Ann adopts a subject-position by acting independently and sending off the photos that prove her father's guilt, the narrative simultaneously denies her a subject-position because she does so in service to the State. In *Music Box*, as in other female lawyer films, the subject actions or narrative agency of the female lawyer ironically works to erase her as a subject or legitimate agent, primarily because the films fail to develop narratives that acknowledge discontinuities between justice and the law. In consistently equating the law with truth and justice, these films provide no space within which the female lawyer can stake out a coherent subject position.

Likewise trapped within the confused liberal ideology of another narrative, the female lawyer in *Class Action* (1991) works for a conservative corporate law firm and initially denies her "good," liberal father, enacting a heartless professionalism untempered by human understanding. The father/daughter relationship in *Class Action*,

like that in *Music Box*, emphasizes the daughter's ideological limitations. Like Ann Talbot, the young corporate attorney Maggie Warde feels truly divided in her identity, her motives and beliefs. Maggie's career as a lawyer seems driven by unresolved conflicts and resentments in her relationship with her father, Jed (Gene Hackman), an attorney who champions liberal causes for the "common man" and whose legal activism in the 1960s earned him a *Newsweek* cover photo. Maggie defiantly defends wealthy corporate clients, opposing her father "where he doesn't make the rules—in a court of law, in front of a judge," she proclaims, without intentional irony. In her courtroom battle with Jed, defined as the "good father" within the liberal political context of the film, Maggie is guided by Fred Quinn (Donald Moffat), the "bad father," who is the controlling partner of her firm—a "fascist" law firm, as Jed likes to call it. Again, the film's conflation of simplistic archetypes with equally simplistic political polarities undermines the female lawyer.

Maggie's ambiguous subjectivity, unfolds just after her mother's death, in a highly charged, paradoxical scene, in which Maggie effectively challenges her father's command of the law and his "practice" of liberalism. She accuses him of using legal activism as a means of self-advancement, at the expense of the "common people," who helped build his cases, and at the expense of his wife and family, who endured his long absences and extramarital affairs. The film is strongest and the narrative most open when Maggie and Jed debate this issue of conflicting social and personal responsibilities. Ironically, however, even here, the film's liberalism cannot fully support Maggie, who strains to bridge the public/private dichotomy by suggesting that Jed should have limited his activities in the public (male) sphere in order to attend to his responsibilities in the private (female) sphere. Because Maggie's mother has been shown to love and support her husband in spite of his past absence and infidelity, Maggie's (feminist) position seems short-sighted and motivated by insecurity and her own self-interest. In its need to reestablish patriarchal dominance and efface its own uneasy politics, from this point on, the narrative closes off such interrogation of Jed in favor of interrogating Maggie, very much in keeping with similar patterns in a number of other female lawyer films. The film encourages us to choose Jed's (and its own) liberalism by forcing us to recognize Maggie's misguided rightist leanings, as defined by her work in corporate law.

Fred Quinn, the "bad" father figure, orders Maggie to "neutralize" Jed's client in defense of an automobile manufacturer that knowingly markets a defective model (based heavily on the Ford Pinto litigation of the 1970s). During a deposition, Maggie hammers away at Jed's already vulnerable client and reduces him to tears, shattering his masculinity. With a clinical demeanor she displays photos of an accident that killed his family, strongly implying his guilt. As Quinn's instrument, Maggie turns into a castrating female, potentially dangerous to all men and the laws they create. Frequent reaction shots of Jed and his associate Nick define Maggie's actions as despicable and force us to share the moral revulsion, fear, and disbelief of these men who apprehend the perverse potency of the castrating female. Even when she finally joins forces with her "good father," at a much later point in the narrative, Maggie behaves deceptively—this time misleading Quinn and her lover in Quinn's firm, both of whom are guilty of suppressing evidence. But the film keeps us guessing about Maggie's loyalties and motives until the very last moments of a climactic courtroom sequence, thus implying her basic instability and forcing us to fear her unruly power. Although we want to like Maggie, we can neither fully trust her nor identify with her because we sense that she may be too unpredictable and, consequently, too dangerous. Maggie pushes against the grain of or our expectations so aggressively that the film exploits our anxieties entirely at her expense.

Class Action constructs a potent, castrating female while at the same time acknowledging her lack of genuine power within the law, a condition best illustrated in Quinn's response to Maggie's aggressive courtroom tactics: "The jury accepts this kind of thing much better from a woman." On later discovering that Maggie has shared the firm's suppressed evidence with her father, Quinn calls for Maggie's disbarment in a meeting with Jed and the trial judge, a meeting that excludes Maggie herself. The film thus divests Maggie of language and the power of self-assertion, making clear, once again, that men wield the real power.

While the central concerns of *Philadelphia* (1993) are not with a female lawyer, the apparently lone female (Mary Steenburgen) in *Phila-*

delphia's homophobic firm occupies a position similar to Maggie's in *Class Action*. The very negative glimpse we are given of the female lawyer is fueled by the film's apparent yet limited liberalism, which constructs itself around the body, not of the female, but of the homosexual male who cannot conform to phallocentrism, as defined within the tradition of the white, heterosexual male. The film positions us to sympathize with this young man (Tom Hanks), dismissed from his firm when his colleagues learn that he suffers from AIDS. However, we sympathize with him largely at the expense of the heartless, clinical female lawyer, who is shown to be nothing more than an instrument without will, ethics, or power of her own when she whispers, "I hate this case," on returning to her seat after an especially brutal cross-examination.

The liberalism of *Philadelphia* reveals parallel limitations in dealing with its gay male protagonist. Despite narrative strategies that evoke our sympathy, he, like the female lawyer, is defined by the film as "other," as one who cannot and should not truly gain power within this world of white heterosexual males. Although the men of the firm are unappealing and unsympathetic, the film fails to argue coherently against their entitlement within this closed system of power. A boyish figure first accepted then cast out by the powerful "fathers," Hanks's character is shown to be merely a pitiable, nice guy. Although we are told that he's the new whiz-kid of the firm, nothing in the identity he assumes suggests a powerful figure whose career promises legal activism or reform. In fact, he quite happily would have chosen to "pass," were it not for his disease forcing him out of the closet. Furthermore, the film cleverly positions Hanks's African American attorney (Denzel Washington) as the legal instrument "exposing" Hanks's body, literally unveiling his lesions and figuratively unveiling the gay phallus, in Lacanian terms. With the image of Hanks removing his shirt on the witness stand, the film implies that the "sick" gay body is drained of all authority and potency necessary to the practice of law, consequently exploiting the homophobia of mainstream American audiences and exposing its own homophobia, while appearing to do much the opposite.

At the same time, however, Washington's tactics meet with stunned silence in the courtroom and in the movie theater, suggesting that he, along with the female and gay male lawyers, cannot exist as a stable, powerful force within the white phallocentrism of the law. Here, Washington occupies the same complex and contradictory position of protagonists in the female lawyer films. He, like the female lawyers in those films, is our point of identification, yet he is simultaneously defined as "other." In *Philadelphia*, it seems, the "otherness" of the Washington and Steenburgen characters are developed vis-à-vis each other. In fact, the strategies used in many female lawyer films to undermine the potency of women in law are applied in *Philadelphia* to all three marginal figures—the white female, the gay white male, and the African American male—who "intrude" on the terrain of white heterosexual dominance.

Within a dynamic of "otherness" set in motion by the film, viewers are perhaps led to dis-identify with the female lawyer as a means of more closely identifying with the African American lawyer and, to a lesser extent, with the gay male.[7] All three characters are represented as "other". The African American male attorney, through his own homophobia, initially fails to "measure up" to the film's apparent liberalism. The gay male attorney's identity as "gay" is clearly marked as "other" through images of his own unstable body, as well as images of his waltzing, with IV stand in tow, to strains of a Maria Callas aria, and through images of a gay porn theater depicted as a dark den of iniquity. Narrative strategies that force us to identify with his suffering mother, as she watches her son deteriorate, further define Hanks's character as "other" in his capacity to visit such "senseless" pain upon the loving, supportive microcosm of the nuclear family. And, of course, the female lawyer, through her heartless but puppetlike performance in court, a figure drained of sympathy and of any real potency, cannot be seen as anything but "other," in her gross failure to measure up to the film's confused and superficial liberalism.

Desperate, Deficient, and Dangerous

Just as the gay male lawyer is presented as the object of interrogation in *Philadelphia*, so, too, many elements within female lawyer films position their protagonists as objects of viewer interrogation, unveiling their weaknesses and deficiencies in order to reveal fully the threat they

pose to patriarchal and legal authority. The films further attempt to retrieve a more stabilized position for phallocentric power within the law by suggesting that the female lawyer has transgressed, having abandoned the private for the public sphere, where consequently she finds personal pain, not fulfillment. Represented as professionally inadequate and personally unfulfilled—frequently unhappy, unmarried, and without children—the female lawyer threatens the very stability of phallocentric power, the legal system, and the culture. With lives so dangerously out of balance, female lawyers are defined as interlopers who cannot truly belong in the legal arena.

When at home in her apartment, for example, the unmarried female lawyer (Barbara Hershey) in *Defenseless* (1991) constantly paces and mutters to herself, a testimony to her instability, loneliness, and isolation. The unmarried assistant district attorneys in *The Big Easy* (1987) (Ellen Barkin) and *Love Crimes* (1992) (Sean Young) are cold and repressed, greatly afraid of their own sexuality until the men they investigate force them to acknowledge submerged sexual desires. While some female lawyers suppress their sexuality, others aggressively act on their desires, thus compromising their effective practice of law, as in *Defenseless, Jagged Edge* (1985), and *Guilty as Sin* (1993). The female lawyers' unhappy, unresolved personal lives often expose professional vulnerabilities. Carrying on sometimes unethical and often dangerous affairs with their clients or with the men they investigate, the female lawyers are represented as unstable figures within the proper functioning of the law. Though not a female lawyer film per se, *Presumed Innocent* (1990) even attempts to implicate a female lawyer in her own murder by suggesting that unfettered professional ambitions resulted in promiscuity as a strategy for career advancement—a strategy that led her further into unethical behavior. While *Hannah K.* (1983) (an American-French coproduction) initially sees the female lawyer's role in career and family from a surprisingly radical position, the film ultimately confirms the more reactionary underpinnings of the Hollywood female lawyer film. The romantic interests and fierce independence of Hannah (Jill Clayburgh), a Jewish-American lawyer working in Israel, ultimately compromise her judgment and her defense of a Palestinian client accused of terrorist acts. Emotion often clouds the female lawyer's ability to reason, implying by the very stereotypes associated with women and men that women are not suited to practice law.

Though not duplicitous in exactly the sense of the film noir female, the female lawyer is nevertheless divided, in Lacanian terms, between the Imaginary (as represented by a vaguely undifferentiated identity) and the Symbolic (as represented by the law and its demands on her). This divided, uneasy self, evident in *Music Box* and *Class Action* (as I noted earlier), is sometimes represented in other films through androgynous women who destabilize but never challenge the validity of fixed gender roles, as in the poster shot and ad for *A Few Good Men* (1992). In *Love Crimes* (1992), as in *A Few Good Men*, sexual ambiguity is inscribed through the lawyer's androgynous dress and appearance. Similarly, the androgynous or masculinized names of female lawyers in this and other movies further imply destabilized gender roles, thus producing anxiety: Teddy in *Jagged Edge* (1985), T. K. in *Defenseless* (1991), Grey in *Curly Sue* (1991), Dana in *Love Crimes,* Darby in *The Pelican Brief* (1993), and Reggie in *The Client* (1994). Susan Sarandon's character in *The Client*, in fact, is "Reggie Love," a conflation of two major points of anxiety in the female lawyer film—the woman's adopting a masculine professional role, but often at the expense of maternal and/or romantic love, thus denying herself emotional security and personal fulfillment.

Costuming in many of the films reflects a basic incongruity as well. The viewer cannot help but feel some trepidation on noticing the prominent, razor-edged pin gleaming like an instrument of clinical torture (castration?), rather than appearing as a harmless fashion accessory on the jacket worn by Theresa Russell in *Physical Evidence* (1988). Although many female lawyers don the neat, buttoned-down apparel of law, their costuming inevitably is too tight, too out-of-date, or too severe, drawing immediate attention to the female lawyer's body and her failure to "fit properly" into her professional role with grace, comfort, and ease. Visual incongruities arise from long-shot framings of some female lawyers standing in court and wearing clothing that accentuates their sexuality—most notably, Glenn Close in *Jagged Edge* (1985) and Rebecca DeMornay in *Guilty as Sin* (1993). By virtue of her very presence in the courtroom, then, the female lawyer becomes a disruptive force within the cinematic frame.

Such disruption and incongruity likewise produce anxiety within real courtrooms, as evident in an incident that occurred during jury selection in the O. J. Simpson case, when a potential female juror remarked that prosecutor Marcia Clark was wearing her skirts a bit too short. Even more disturbing than the potential juror's observation, however, was Judge Lance Ito's demeaning, deadpan reply: "I was wondering when someone was going to mention that." Clark, it seems, felt obliged to counter the accusation by displaying herself to the court when she "stepped back from the prosecution table and revealed a knee-length dress" (Demma 1994, p. A2). Incongruous, as it seems to be perceived within the courtroom, the authoritative female body is the subject of much anxiety and misreading.

Perhaps cinematic images not only reflect but actually incite misreadings and misperceptions of female lawyers, such as those described in the "Gender Bias Study of the Supreme Judicial Court, Commonwealth of Massachusetts," in which judges reported:

> instances in which gender affected the relationship between opposing counsel, including belittling remarks made to female attorneys, improper address by first name or terms of endearment, and not allowing female attorneys to speak. . . . According to those judges, the observed conduct resulted in drawing attention away from the issues, placing counsel in unequal standing, interfering with female counsel's presentation, delaying the trial, or demeaning the professional atmosphere of the court. (Frug 1992, p. 5)

As in the Hollywood female lawyer films, all but one of which was directed by men, male-driven as well as female-driven anxieties are projected onto the body and the presence of women who occupy positions of power and authority within the courtroom. While the Massachusetts study records the disruptive behavior of males in the presence of female lawyers, that anxiety is displaced and transposed within the female lawyer film, which tends to focus on female disruption, either subtle or overt.

Pam Cook's analysis of *Mildred Pierce*, a 1945 film noir, seems equally relevant to understanding the "disruptive" presence of the female lawyer in contempray film: "[T]he evasion of patriarchal law [and/or the *invasion* of patriarchal law in the female lawyer film] produces a situation in which nothing is stable" (Cook 1978, p. 78). The "problem" with the female lawyer is very much like the problem of film noir women, whose ambitions and sexuality, neither molded nor restrained by marriage or children, "become(s) increasingly threatening, encouraging the spectator to take up a defensive position and to wish for the resolution of the [sexual] ambiguity, to put an end to the feelings of anxiety" (Cook 1978, p. 78).

Only three female lawyers in the films have children, and in all cases these children are products of a "broken home." The young sons, in *Jagged Edge* (1985) and *Music Box* (1990), openly resent their mothers' work and divided attention, indirectly playing into the notions of single motherhood as deviant.[8] The ex-husband/father in both films is nurturing and supportive, not only toward his children but also toward his ex-wife. In fact, one wonders why a divorce has occurred at all, and only one reason is implied— the ambitious female lawyer's career. *The Client* (1994) provides an especially interesting case, in which Reggie's past alcohol and drug abuse resulted in her having lost custody of her children, scarring her with a deep, lingering sadness. Her young client becomes a kind of surrogate child, who seems to instruct *her* in the legal process by surprisingly invoking the Fifth Amendment during a hearing. Reggie performs competently only when calling on her maternal, protective instinct rather than on rational legal skill, leading critic Terrence Rafferty to praise the film without recognizing the compromising position which the woman, as professional, occupies: "When we look at Sarandon, we see Reggie's maternal heroism as a force of nature not merely a force of circumstance" (Rafferty 1994, p. 76).

Many of the films reinstate a stable order when the female lawyer discovers the love of a good man who has the power to neutralize her ambitions. The weary, unhappy lawyer in *Suspect* (1987) spends long, dark winter evenings in her office until an attractive juror gallantly, if unethically, rescues her and enfolds her in his arms. In the romantic comedies *Legal Eagles* (1986) and *Curly Sue* (1991), a good man and his precocious child arouse maternal instincts and show the female lawyers what they've really been missing in life. Instead of pursuing the lost phallus (in Freudian terms) through careers, the women,

these films coyly suggest, should make themselves whole (and wholesome) through husband and child. In *Curly Sue*, particularly, a child transforms the female lawyer from an icy, unpleasant professional into an approachable human being with whom we are eager to identify.

The films encourage us to applaud when, in the end, the women "go quality-of-life," as Grey's boss in *Curly Sue* expresses it. This phrase itself seems designed as a cautionary message for young professional women and as an epitaph of regret for the stereotypical disillusioned professional who has spent the best years of her life contending with glass-ceiling politics. Rather than entreat such women to organize and adopt an activist role in order to change the conditions of their professional lives, this film, among others, encourages women to retreat and relax a little. The closing image of *The Big Easy* (1987) could not be more explicit: As her groom (a police investigator and former target of *her* investigation) whisks her over the threshold, the assistant district attorney, bedecked in white lace and having accepted the power of the phallus, no longer seems uneasy with herself or threatening to patriarchal legal institution.

Even more disturbing are the real-life tensions surrounding female lawyers, into which the films have so successfully tapped. Nowhere are these anxieties more evident than, again, in the case of O. J. Simpson prosecutor Marcia Clark, who, according to the *New York Times*, had undergone a transformation to make her more juror- and media-friendly. The "packaging" of Marcia Clark by jury consultants included their advice that she speak about "domestic themes" to the press— "themes like grocery shopping and children . . . crucial tools in the makeover and motherization of Marcia Clark" (Margolick 1994, p. A10), which one consultant felt was necessary, "since both male and female jurors are put off by tough female lawyers" (Margolick 1994, p. A10). Another consultant said of Clark that "she took to heart what the research has shown: that she's coming across as too hard[,] too cold" (Margolick 1994, A10). The result of Clark's "remaking" involved not only her "scripted" comments to the press, which seemed designed to erase any trace of gender-role ambiguity, but also her successful performance of gender. By adopting the gestures and behaviors defined by our culture as unambiguously feminine and "girlish," Clark had become less threatening to the phallocentric institutions of law and the media. Rather than appearing "grim, humorless, even angry[,] . . . [s]he smiled often, and incandescently. She laughed, even giggled, repeatedly. She rolled her eyes, cocked her head and shrugged her shoulders" (Margolick 1994, p. A10). The male journalist writing this article certainly notices the minute details of gender performance, but in his failure to notice, let alone analyze, the source of public anxieties shaping the "Remaking of the Simpson Prosecutor," as the title proclaims, the journalist tacitly implies that Clark is, thankfully, now on track.

Phallocentrism, both in the narrative and legal discourses, *apparently* is restored in most female lawyer films, as well, when truth emerges. Often, at that moment, the female lawyer simultaneously is absorbed into the dual patriarchal structures of law and the family. In *Class Action* (1991), Maggie and her father dance together in reconciliation as the film ends, and in *Music Box* (1990), Ann walks off with her son, presumably explaining the guilt of his Nazi grandfather and reclaiming the centrality of her role as mother. On some level, however, this final image in *Music Box* supports a mild disruption of the patriarchal order, since both grandfathers have been rejected by the film as legitimate patriarchs.

In dramatic contrast to the Hollywood female lawyer film stands the Dutch film, *A Question of Silence* (1983), a feminist project directed by Marleen Gorris. Rather than comply with the panel of solemn male justices, the female court psychiatrist, in this case, exits the courtroom and in so doing understands that she is also exiting her marriage. She defiantly removes herself from a phallocentric system, within which it is clear that neither the female legal/psychiatric authority nor the female defendants can truly be heard, understood, or empowered.

Women at the Margins: The Conventional Narrative and Legal Systems

But dominant politics demands the restoration of the patriarchal order, which involves "establishing truth without a doubt" (Cook 1978, p. 75) in both cinematic and legal terms. Pam Cook clearly elucidates this tendency in her analysis of *Mildred Pierce* (1945). The conflation of film noir stylistics with elements of the maternal melodrama is designed to contain the transgressive ambitions of Mildred Pierce, a successful businesswoman:

> In the face of impending chaos and confusion the patriarchal order is called upon to reassert itself and take the Law back into its own hands, divesting women completely of any power they may have gained while the patriarchal order was temporarily impaired. This involves establishing the truth without a doubt, restoring "normal" sexual relationships and reconstituting the family unit, in spite of the pain and suffering which such repressive action must cause. (Cook 1978, p. 75)

Truth, as closure, is the driving aim of both the legal process and the conventional narrative film. Whether in the form of a verdict or in the resolution of plot questions, both legal and narrative closure involve the proclamation of truth in some form. In both the narrative and legal systems, that truth is constructed for the audience or for the judge and jury through (re)presentation of visual/physical evidence and through stories or testimony that builds strong cause-and-effect relationships between events. Such cause-and-effect relationships are dependent on the chronological ordering of events—in film, within the narrative structure, and in law, within witness accounts or testimony in which *versions* of events, or stories, are retold and retold.[9]

In the female lawyer film, the discovery of truth often complicates the position of the woman lawyer. When it is she who discovers "the truth" (though often ineptly and purely by accident), she becomes an instrument of the conventional (hierarchical) narrative system and of the patriarchal legal system. By insisting that there is only one acceptable version of truth and that this one version is discoverable, both the classical narrative and legal structures reflect and reinforce each other, effectively neutralizing the female lawyer, since the truth she advances must be the *approved* version of both systems. *A Question of Silence* (1983) once again stands in contrast to this tendency of marginalizing the female lawyer who ultimately "serves" both systems. In that film the female court psychiatrist gradually gains an understanding of her complicity within the system and ultimately refuses to serve that system further. The unconventional narrative structure of the film allows for the dismantling of cause-and-effect relationships. While male justices insist that insanity can be the only causal explanation for the murder of a male shopkeeper by several women who had never met before the moment of that murder, the film's structure, which breaks with chronology and cause-and-effect narrative chains, reveals how shallow that thinking is in its tenacious need to defend and maintain phallocentrism. Through disjunctive movements in time and in space, the film radically questions the notion of a single, apprehensible version of truth and in so doing provides a subject-position for the female. The female court psychiatrist is empowered when she refuses to deliver *the* version of truth already formulated by the intimidating panel of male judges sitting before her. While her action clearly is subversive, this unconventional narrative applauds subversion of both the legal and classical narrative systems in which women are alienated and marginalized. (While this is not specifically a film about a female *lawyer*, it is interesting to note that it and *Love Crimes* (1992) are the only films of the group that were directed by women. In the case of *Love Crimes*, however, Hollywood pressure transformed director Lizzie Borden's original feminist project into something quite the opposite. See Lucia 1992a.)

In their efforts to serve patriarchy by advancing its single version of truth, the women in Hollywood's female lawyer films often suffer a serious loss (a symbolic form of castration). Divided between love and hatred of her own father, Ann Talbot in *Music Box* (1990) ultimately must deny him in the service of truth. In their final scenes the female protagonists in *Jagged Edge* (1985) and *Love Crimes* (1992) lie prostrate and hysterical, reduced to almost infantile states of fear and helplessness, after physically attacking the men who have misled them. In both these films, the female lawyers' insecurities and personal vulnerabilities have led them into danger. Teddy in *Jagged Edge* is drawn into an affair with her client, accused of killing his wife, and Dana in *Love Crimes* is drawn to a potential rapist who kidnaps her yet enables her to recognize and acknowledge her repressed sexual desires. Both women must admit their mistaken judgments during climactic scenes in which these men break into their homes to attack or murder them. Both degrading

and misogynist, the scenes turn the tables on the female lawyers. Now men invade the designated "private" space of these women, completely stripping them of potency, security, and self-respect.

The crimes typical of most female lawyer films further exemplify this ironic reversal. Reflecting male angst in the two bastions of patriarchy—the family and the legal system itself—these crimes involve spousal murders, rape, and other sex-related crimes, all of which threaten the foundation of marriage and the family, or the crime of corruption, implicating various branches of the law or of corporate institutions. In resolving these crimes, the female lawyer restores power to the temporarily impaired patriarchy. In this sense the female lawyer film enacts a more subtle misogyny (in addition to the overt misogyny present in many of the films) in its need to destroy female potency, a misogyny reinforced by conventional or classical narrative structure, as Kaja Silverman points out: "Often the entire narrative is organized around a demonstration and an interrogation of the female character's castrated condition, a demonstration and an interrogation which have as their ultimate aim the recovery of a sense of potency and wholeness for both the male character and the male viewer" (Silverman 1986, p. 229).

Within the female lawyer film, the legal and narrative systems further act in complicity to push women to the margins. Despite the female lawyer's ostensibly central status as protagonist, more often than not it is male characters who conduct investigations and discover truth long before the female can recognize it, as in *Jagged Edge* (1985), *Suspect* (1987), *Physical Evidence* (1988), *Defenseless* (1991), and *The Client* (1994). Despite the warnings of their gruff but kindly private investigators (also "good father" figures), Teddy Barnes in *Jagged Edge* and Jennifer Haynes in *Guilty as Sin* (1993), for instance, initially cannot recognize the truth about their clients, although Jennifer comes to realize it much earlier than Teddy does. Teddy uncovers key evidence, only by accident, after winning her client's acquittal. After spending the night with her client to celebrate, Teddy reaches for fresh bed linens only to discover a hidden, incriminating piece of evidence. While female lawyers are sometimes allowed to tag along, as are Debra Winger, in *Legal Eagles* (1986), and Ellen Barkin in *The Big Easy* (1987), more often than not their male cohort is the one on the move, the one who commandeers the camera once the task of interlocking cause with effect gets fully under way; this is especially true of *Suspect* and *Physical Evidence*. In *Defenseless*, the camera lingers on in admiration as the insightful detective (Sam Shepard) sits pensively, piecing together the crime puzzle, which seriously implicates the female lawyer herself.

Word and image mesh with the legal process of testifying in *The Accused* (1989) to reveal that the full impact and power of truth reside with the male. Although the rape victim (Jodi Foster) testifies in court, only the testimony of a young male witness can validate her words, in terms of both the legal process and the narrative discourse, which privileges his testimony with flashbacks to the actual event. The outcome of the trial and closure of the narrative depend entirely on this male witness speaking, rather than upon the voice of the victim or the efforts of the female attorney.

Conclusion: Uncontested Closure Denied

Despite the determined efforts of female lawyer films to denude the female lawyer of power and thus expose her masquerade, such attempts to recuperate the power of patriarchal structures do not result in an entirely untroubled resolution. The predictability of outcome alone—the reassertion of patriarchal authority—is an interesting and complicated issue in the female lawyer film, especially in terms of how that predictability intersects with viewers' knowledge of contemporary lived experience. Can such knowledge modify or alter readings of the films? Perhaps viewers' very *consciousness* of the inevitably predictable (desirable) outcome creates something of a countercurrent pushing against the films' underlying reactionary impulses. On the other hand, predictability is part and parcel of the function of genre as myth, since it is this very factor which reassures viewers that idealized values or even an idealized notion of the status quo remains intact—that "normalcy" can indeed be restored.

The insistent need for such reassurance itself reveals a fundamental tension expressed through and within the films. In giving themselves over to the mythic function of genre films and to their own desire for the uncomplicated closure such films often provide, viewers on some level are acknowledging that the narratives are indeed mythic, that a permanent rupture has occurred. Questions then arise concerning the appeal of the female lawyer film to male viewers, as well as to female and minority viewers. Do male and female minority viewers find a site of entry or identification within these films, which represent serious, though failed, challenges to white phallocentric dominance of law in terms only of the white heterosexual female? Do female viewers feel empowered through identification with the female lawyer, or do they participate in the films' underlying masochism, which, sadly, reaffirms and expiates unconscious fears of female inadequacy? These fears, it seems, are as deeply ingrained within our culture as they are within our law—reflected most notably, perhaps, by the intense debates and difficulties that resulted in the ultimate defeat of the proposed Equal Rights Amendment. Perhaps some female viewers respond to the films as cautionary tales: Aggressively pursue career goals and you may end up unbalanced, undesirable, isolated and alone.

Do male viewers, on the other hand, participate in sadistic, voyeuristic backlash pleasure, or do they likewise engage in a more subtle form of masochism, arising from the crisis in phallocentric/patriarchal dominance registered within the films? Perhaps male viewers feel the pleasure of empowerment restored, once the law and patriarchy are reestablished as stabilizing cultural forces. Or perhaps a double pleasure or reassurance is derived through the positioning of the female lawyer, who upholds the status quo and serves the patriarchal structure, working as its servant. Unlike the women of film noir, who display their bodies for the pleasure and interrogation of the male gaze, the women of female lawyer films expose their intellect and emotional stability to the scrutiny of the male (and female) consciousness. The discovery of their inadequacy arouses anxiety perhaps only to provide the pleasure of reassurance. Within the context of the conventional narrative and patriarchal legal systems, is the female lawyer herself on trial and found lacking?

The simplicity of the films' resolutions, on the other hand, belies the complexity of the historical moment in which these films have been produced and in which they situate themselves—a moment when competing ideologies require at least a serious recognition of the feminist agenda. In the films, resolutions are so predictably neat and so over determined in their negation of the female lawyer that a fissure does result, perhaps reflecting the gap between the experience of the audience (regardless of how conservative the audience may be) and experience as filtered through the narrative structure. To consider possible reasons for such narrative fissures, it may be useful to examine Chris Straayer's essay "The She-Man: Bi-Sexed Performance in Film and Video," in which she considers the potency that resides in femininity for the male performer, "whose sexual power depends not on the ostensibly stable male body but on embraced incongruity" (Straayer 1992, p. 213). While the incongruity of the female lawyer as represented within the films' patriarchal legal context is not necessarily an "embraced incongruity," it nonetheless results in a destabilizing effect that the narrative cannot entirely absorb. Drawing on Lacan, Straayer examines conventional representations of masculine power and dominance in cinema:

> The historic absence of the penis from cinema's view has allowed the male body an independence from anatomical verification according to sex and has situated the male costume simply to reflect a heroic (phallic) narrative purpose. It is his charging about that has identified a male film character as male, yet it is his penis that has invested man with the cultural right to charge about—the signifier in absentia. . . . In actuality, the penis (man's hidden "nature") cannot compare to the phallus (man's cultural power). Male sexuality, as a representational system, depends on displacing the penis with the phallus. In mainstream cinema, the female costume delivers sexual anatomy, whereas the male costume abandons it. Sex is "present" in both the masquerade of femininity and the female body, doubly absent for the male. (Straayer 1992, p. 203)

Disrupted by the presence of the female lawyer—whether she is androgynous, masculinized, or feminized in excess—neither legal nor narrative systems can be solidly restored, even though the films themselves suggest that an uncomplicated restoration is possible. Once the veil has been lifted through the very presence of the female lawyer, the cultural power of the phallus, as expressed through law, is exposed and somewhat neutralized. The attempts by female lawyer narra-

tives to reposition the veil and thus recuperate the phallocentric discourse of both the legal and classical narrative systems do not entirely succeed. The very fact that there exists a group of films about female lawyers, most of which conform, in one way or another, to similar patterns of representation (or perhaps to tropes of an emerging subgenre), suggests a cultural need for "stories," for a mythology to confirm privately held values or beliefs which, to greater or lesser degrees, run counter to lived experience. This need for a mythology about women in law suggests the difficulty, as Straayer suggests, of reconfiguring the phallus once a disruption has occurred.

Though the reactionary-masquerading-as-liberal politics of female lawyer films (unlike *A Question of Silence*) do not consciously represent or make any attempt to analyze the potential subversive power of the female presence in the courtroom, in male territory, her very presence does disrupt. Although the films build viewer anxiety around this disruption, the presence of that anxiety in itself suggests that the phallus has to some extent been destabilized or unveiled, in Lacanian terms. When applied on a less literal level to the female lawyer film, Straayer's observations provide an unusual key for attempting to understand the failure of these narratives to reach complete, uncontested closure.

Notes

1. The films included in this group and their directors are as follows: *First Monday in October* (1981), Ronald Neame; *Hannah K.* (1983), Constantin Costa-Gavras; *Jagged Edge* (1985), Richard Marquand; *Legal Eagles* (1986), Ivan Reitman; *The Big Easy* (1987), Jim McBride; *Suspect* (1987), Peter Yates; *Physical Evidence* (1988), Michael Crichton; *The Accused* (1989), Jonathan Kaplan; *Music Box* (1990), Constantin Costa-Gavras; *Class Action* (1991), Michael Apted; *Defenseless* (1991), Martin Campbell; *Curly Sue* (1991), John Hughes; *Love Crimes* (1992), Lizzie Borden; *Guilty as Sin* (1993), Sidney Lumet; *The Pelican Brief* (1993), Alan J. Pakula; *The Client* (1994), Joel Schumacher; *Fair Game* (1994); *Primal Fear* (1996), Gregory Hoblit.

Other films that feature female lawyers as significant, though not necessarily central, characters include: *The Verdict* (1982), Sidney Lumet; *Presumed Innocent* (1990), Alan J. Pakula; *Defending Your Life* (1991), Albert Brooks; *Other People's Money* (1991), Norman Jewison; *A Few Good Men* (1992), Rob Reiner; *In the Name of the Father* (1993), Jim Sheridan;

Philadelphia (1993), Jonathan Demme; *Disclosure* (1995), Barry Levinson.

2. The discussion of elements shared by the various female lawyer films draws on my article on the female lawyer film (Lucia 1992b).

3. Because the film industry is itself more patriarchal in structure than television, with many fewer women in positions of power, it tends to be the more conservative medium. Furthermore, film is under no requirement to serve the public interest as television is, and identifiable sponsors do not announce themselves and thus associate themselves with a given vision or representation in film as they do in television. Consequently, film is under less pressure to conform to politically correct representations, and perhaps because the financial stakes are far higher in movies, film tends to play into viewers' subconscious fears and desires, unsavory as they may be, more powerfully than television does. For this reason, I will confine my discussion to representations of female lawyers in film, even though television, too, has its share of female lawyers. Television representations vary more widely than filmic representations do, for the reasons outlined above, and perhaps because marketing efforts in film are more exclusively aimed at a youthful male audience.

In her 1994 book, *Women Lawyers: Rewriting the Rules*, Mona Harrington devotes a chapter to representations of female lawyers in film and television. While her discussion is somewhat limited in terms of cinematic concerns, her examination of the political and cultural influences acting on real female lawyers is a useful, accessible summary of writings in feminist legal theory.

4. Much credit and thanks to Martha McCluskey for this thought and for extremely valuable editorial suggestions throughout.

5. I am deeply indebted to Chris Straayer, New York University, Cinema Studies Department, for her help and editorial suggestions, which not only clarified Lacan for me but which also helped to clarify the essence of Lacan necessary to a coherent argument within this chapter.

6. The discussion of *Class Action* draws on my review of the film published in *Cineaste* (Lucia 1991).

7. I am deeply indebted to *Cineaste* co-editor and New York University doctoral colleague Roy Grundmann for sharing his insights on *Philadelphia* during our long conversations and in his *Cineaste* review (vol. xx, No. 3).

8. The common cultural demon, of course, is the welfare mother, who has shouldered the blame in New Right accusations concerning the decline of the family and the enormous problems within the welfare system. This view of the welfare mother was articulated overtly by Supreme Court Justice Clarence Thomas in reference to his sister, during his Senate confirmation hearings. Although the female lawyer is not represented as a "drain" on the economy as the welfare mother is, her professional ambitions are seen as a factor in the disintegration of the "normal," "happy" family and the conservative values established therein. See also Fineman 1991b.

9. I am very much indebted to David Alan Black, who, in his seminar on courtroom drama at New York University in 1991, presented his work on reflexivity in the courtroom drama, which greatly influenced my thinking about the parallel systems of law and conventional narrative.

ESSENTIALIZING GENDER

Introduction

JOYCE DAVIS

While reading a *New York Times* article dealing with a subject that might appear far removed from the issues in this section—the March 1995 nerve gas poisoning on a Tokyo subway—I came across a sentence that stopped me cold because it so epitomized the media's tendency to objectify women. The article profiled Shoko Asahara, the leader of a religious sect which the police suspected of deploying the poison gas, and it included a seemingly routine background sentence: "[I]n 1978, . . . he met a college student, Tomoko Ishii, and married her" (Kristof 1995). That is, "He married her," as in "He [subject] married [verb] her [object]." Ishii is cast as an object, rather than as an acting subject. He is the actor, she the passive recipient of his action. This sentence, these three words, exemplify what I see as the underlying theme of the essays in this section: The media's continued denial of full personhood and autonomy to women. For the most part, the media participates as a player with the law and other societal institutions to maintain women as Woman[1] and to punish those who step outside their traditional roles, positions, or im-

ages and attempt to assert their autonomy and independence.

Discussing the power of language to control and create reality, Sarah Hoagland explains that "the concept of woman is not based on a bedrock of female behavior, rather [it] determines what counts as normal female behavior" (Hoagland 1988, p. 15). Instead of describing what women actually are and do, the concept creates an image of what Woman is and is expected to be. That image has been used to control and restrict women to certain activities, places, and behaviors. When women (or members of any other marginalized group) begin to reject that definition and create their own, they are seen as out of control, and it becomes necessary to reassert the traditional definition and restore order.

The first three chapters in this section directly confront this issue. They explore what happens to women who repudiate their predetermined role when they spurn the ideal established for them, when they seek to define themselves. The fourth chapter comes at the question more obliquely, focusing on how women out of control become a society out of control. If the essays are read in the order presented, they suggest a progression: Women begin to assert themselves, to claim their sexuality and attempt to control their reproductive choices; then one "bad" mother in a group is deemed to define all the women in the group, and finally control and order collapse, leaving society and us at the mercy of violence and disorder.

Locating these issues historically helps to clarify this progression. For a significant part of United States history, African American women held in slavery were subject to the control of their owners, their masters/mistresses. Other Western women who were not enslaved were in fact generally subject to control by husbands or fathers. In both instances, this control was reinforced and maintained by religion, culture, economic pressures, and the law. Throughout much of U.S. history, married women had no legal identity apart from their husbands, and women in slavery were chattel under the law. Single women retained a legal identity, but they were (usually) economically and politically powerless—that is, they remained subject to the control of men.

This system defined women by their sexuality and reproductive role. They were good or bad, depending on whether their sexuality was controlled within the bonds of marriage. Good women were innocent—wives, mothers, moral pillars of society. Bad women were those who controlled their own sexuality, who to some extent defined for themselves how, when, and with whom they would be sexual—for example, prostitutes, courtesans, "adulteresses." The appellations "Mrs." and "Miss" told us two things: the marital state of the woman and, perhaps more important, whether or not she was (properly) sexual. This undercurrent of meaning in the "naming" of females appears in other cultures as well. In some cultures, for example, it is an insult to call an unmarried female a "woman," because "woman" implies sexual knowledge.

Given this background, one might speculate that "Ms." represents significant change, and indeed, change has occurred. Nonetheless, women still are frequently not accepted as fully autonomous persons, as agents, as subjects. Nowhere is this more clearly demonstrated than in the realm of sexuality and reproduction. Women's attempts to take control of their sexual and reproductive

lives is met with resistance at many levels, and this resistance manifests itself in many ways. One of these is the manner in which women who do not contain their sexuality and reproductive choices within a traditional or acceptable frame are depicted in the media. In this century, the media has become one of the primary mechanisms of power for (re)asserting control and (re)imposing the traditional, essentialistic definition of Woman.

The essays in this section show how the media reflects and perpetuates many of the historical social constructs of women and how women who deviate from these constructs are "punished." They demonstrate how the media continually reiterates these traditional constructs, such as bad girls/women/mothers; good girls/women/mothers; youth-innocence/youth-sexuality; good/bad class; and good/bad race. They demonstrate the power of media to reinvest these constructs with meaning in a current context, and to perpetuate them in a way that continues to define women in traditional, understandable and desirable terms, as wives, mothers, spinsters—that is, as Woman, object, defined in relation to Man, subject.

Tracy E. Higgins and Deborah L. Tolman explore some of these issues within the context of adolescent female sexuality. In chapter 15, "Law, Cultural Media[tion], and Desire in the Lives of Adolescent Girls," they provide a media account of sexual young women, out of control, "obsessed" with sex, "bizarre," "frighten[ing]" and "bewilder[ing]" their male counterparts. It is this out-of-control sexuality that is, according to Charles Murray, responsible for the decline of the Western world.[2] Why is the behavior of these young women such a problem? Simply put, the pronouns are wrong. These young women are behaving toward young men the way (young) men have traditionally behaved toward (young) women: calling them, leaving them notes, asking them out, and sometimes even propositioning them. "She" is acting like a "he." "He" is being treated like a "she." In other words, these young women are behaving as if they were fully autonomous beings, as if they were agents. They are behaving as subjects, attempting to define for themselves a sexual identity and role different from the societal construct of young, innocent girls.

Their overt sexuality is inconsistent with society's (purported) view of young adolescent females. Adolescence represents a transitory state between the innocence of youth, that childhood purity and wonder that many, on some level, miss and long for, and the adult world. This purity perhaps never existed; still, it captures our imagination with great power. We encourage young men to move into the adult world, but we want to keep these women innocent, controlled, sexless. We want to slow down, to stop their transition into adulthood, to protect them from sexual knowledge.

While we loudly deplore this (female) adolescent sexuality, we simultaneously send a contradictory message. Youth is sexy and is promoted as such. Images of teenagers, preteens, and even young children (especially girls) provocatively dressed, made up, and posed permeate the media. Young girls pout dreamily or gaze seductively at the camera—heads tilted downward, eyes lifted, a trace of a smile on their lips. Grown women are pictured in "little girl" dresses, innocence reborn.

It is true that the media is not primarily responsible for creating these images. Most often they are presented in the form of advertisements, but because of the symbiotic relationship between the media and advertising, the media becomes significantly responsible for the dissemination of these images. The media is the dispenser, the exhibitor, the purveyor; the media makes these contradictory images available and facilitates their incorporation into the minds of many young women, and into ours.

By looking and by listening carefully to the words of young women, Higgins and Tolman have given us a story of the intermingling nature of the conflicts created by the different versions of adolescent female sexuality and by the denial, to these young women, of their sexual agency. These conflicting messages make it extremely hard for young women to recognize, name, or claim their own desire, and because they cannot do this, Higgins and Tolman argue, they cannot make informed choices with regard to sex. Because a "good girl" is not supposed to feel sexual desire, a young woman cannot acknowledge what she is feeling and finds it difficult to know and, if she knows, to admit what she wants. Thus, she can define neither what she wants nor what she does not want. Denying girls/women the right to acknowledge their sexual desire denies them full personhood, denies them agency. In effect, they remain controlled by the desire of the young man, compelled psychologically and emotionally, if not physically, to accede to his desire, which, by contrast, is clearly and acceptably defined.

The rationale for the construction of good girls/bad girls presents an intriguing question: Whose sexuality is the real focus of concern? Perhaps it is male sexuality that is so volatile, that we fear will get out of control. Perhaps the creation of the good girl/bad girl dichotomy was an acknowledgment that men cannot or will not control their own sexuality. Thus, "bad girls" may be quite useful to society by allowing boys/men to be sexual without taking responsibility for their own behavior—particularly if "bad" girls are limited to a certain group. This idea is surprisingly reflected in one of Charles Murray's conceptions. Murray deplores the rise in out-of-wedlock births, arguing that "illegitimacy" is what underlies all other societal problems—for example, crime and drugs. Significantly, Murray believes that so long as such deviant behavior remained "a black story, [it was] however dismaying, old news. . . . But, the brutal truth is that American society as a whole could survive when illegitimacy became epidemic within a comparatively small ethnic minority. It cannot survive the same epidemic among whites" (Murray 1993). Young women who have children out-of-wedlock are "bad girls"; that is, they are violating traditional societal norms, and at least some of them are consciously deciding to do so. Murray may be correct that a societal loss of control over female (adolescent) sexuality poses a threat to the established order. However, such a threat is neither necessarily nor wholly negative. Should all, or at least a critical mass, of girls/women become "bad" girls by rejecting societal definitions and begin to define and act on their desire, there will indeed be change. Women, young and old, will have greater control of their own sexuality and their lives, and men will be forced to be more responsible with regard to their own sexuality.

Those girls who are labeled "bad" because they express their sexuality may not necessarily be acting out of a full understanding of their desire and with full agency. Nonetheless, Paulina, one of the young women discussed by Higgins and Tolman, provides an encouraging example. Paulina was able to articulate a critical understanding of her sexuality and of the cultural and social constructs within which she operates. It would be interesting to explore further why it was that Paulina, unlike her peers, was able to reject the good girl/bad girl image and to express her own sense of sexual desire and autonomy.

E. Ann Kaplan, in chapter 16, "The Politics of Surrogacy Narratives," presents us with another version of women out of control—acting in a way that is inconsistent with cultural perceptions of Woman as Mother. Kaplan analyzes the Janus-like way in which the media depicts women who choose to have a baby for someone else. According to Kaplan, when these women make their initial decision, they are often pictured as doing a good thing, as contributing to another's happiness, as making it possible for someone else to experience the joys of motherhood. This image is acceptable to us because it is completely consistent with our traditional view of Woman/Mother as unselfish, self-sacrificing. But wait. How can we reconcile these two views—mother, loving, sacrificing and a mother voluntarily giving up her child? This elective separation, induced not by economic pressures or for the child's sake, is simply outside the realm of our conception of a "good" mother, especially if it is part of a commercial transaction. These two ideas create a conflict most of us have difficulty reconciling, perhaps because it taps into our own deep fears of abandonment and separation from Mother.

If we who are merely spectators find ourselves troubled by these simultaneous and conflicting images, it is certainly not unrealistic to imagine that the woman herself feels troubled and may decide to change her mind and rescind the contract. When she does, rather than portray the complexity of this dilemma and depict the mother in a sympathetic manner consistent with the ideal of Mother, the media capitalizes on the resulting conflict between the two mothers—a conflict created, at least in part, because Woman/Mother has attempted to assert herself, to act as agent, to use her reproductive capacity outside prescribed, approved parameters.

In an ABC-TV presentation of the most famous of these stories, that of Mary Beth Whitehead, the story focused on the guilt and pain of both women associated with the potential loss of the child. Like women who choose abortion, Mary Beth was assumed to feel (be?) guilty. This assumption denies that she or any woman can rationally and without guilt make a reproductive decision contrary to societal expectations, that she can act as a subject. Mary Beth's

"unnatural" voluntary relinquishment of her own child, and the threatened forced loss of the child to Betsy (herself "unnatural" because she could not conceive), extended the idea of women out of control. The popular media portrayal of their out-of-controlness repeated class-based stereotypes (though Kaplan suggests that the ABC presentation may have "unconsciously colluded" in a critique of middle-class "uptightness"). Mary Beth (lower-class) was "hysterical, wild and unreasonable," Betsy (upper-middle-class) "more and more despondent, depressed, silent, tortured." This "raw female emotion," out of control, had to be contained. Enter the "Father, the Law." Mary Beth is appropriately punished, and control is restored.

In chapter 17, Maria Ashe's " 'Bad Mothers' and Welfare Reform in Massachusetts: The Case of Claribel Ventura," Claribel Ventura is another woman out of control. Her behavior in neglecting or abusing her children is shockingly inconsistent with our cultural constructs of Mother, so shocking that the judge almost lost his self-control.

Although the media and the public figures involved readily admitted that Ventura was not typical of welfare mothers, either in her behavior or in the number of children she had, she quickly became a metaphor for welfare out of control. She became an indictment of welfare—not of the system itself but of mothers on welfare. The media and various public officials created a syllogism which, though clearly faulty, was accepted and promoted:

> Claribel Ventura is a welfare mother.
> Claribel Ventura is a bad mother.
> Therefore, welfare mothers are bad mothers.

As in the Mary Beth Whitehead story, the authorities were required to step in to restore control. Ventura was eventually sent to prison, her children were placed in foster care, and Massachusetts passed an extremely punitive welfare reform bill.

Ashe builds her narrative around the media's focus on hands, which can be seen as a metaphor for control. Ventura's hands are described as "spindly" and as shaking "so badly" that "the rattling of the documents she held" could be heard "from across the courtroom." Her brother's hands tremble so badly that he is unable to work (and receives welfare, SSI); and her child's hands are burned and then bandaged so that they are useless. Hands out of control. In contrast, the hands of the policeman who is seen entertaining or feeding the child in the hospital, and those of the EMT and another "visitor," are strong, quiet, composed, representing stability, safety, control. For Ashe, the policeman's hands represent the State: the State replacing the out-of-control mother.

Stories like these of Woman out of control have become, for many, symbolic of a world out of control. This sense of a society, a world, a civilization out of control is captured by Kristin Bumiller in chapter 18, "Spectacles of the Strange: Envisioning Violence in the Central Park Jogger Trial."

This perception of civilization slipping out of control is a projection of our sense of the loss of control over our own lives. We often find ourselves living in a world we don't understand. Many feel that the things we believed in, the things we cherished, the things by which we defined our lives, all are disappearing. In this view, life has lost all predictability; it cannot be understood, it is beyond explanation, the rules that structured our lives no longer apply. Nothing is what it is supposed to be; no one behaves as expected. People in marginalized groups, especially women (both of color and white), men of color, gays and lesbians, assert themselves; they make demands; they want personhood; they want autonomy. For many, this means that stability, control, assurance, comfort are all slipping out of our grasp. Crime, widespread and terrifying, evinces our sense that life is out of control, and the Central Park jogger story becomes the archetypical crime. The assault on the jogger and the trial of the young defendants become a metaphor for turf, for control of the "urban landscape" and ultimately of our lives.

Using the body of the Central Park jogger as text, Bumiller shows how the trial and media reports created for us a story of urban terror, a nightmare city out of control—violence beyond our comprehension, merging with rampant, animalistic sexuality; civilization reverting to savagery. Three young men of color, hyperbolically described as a "roving band" or "the pack," attack the single, lone, vulnerable white woman. Whiteness, safety, stability, solidity, is overtaken by blackness, evil, violence, fear, terror. The jog-

ger's white body is buried in mud and dirt. She is the mud, dark; the mud is her. Her identifying characteristics are lost: Her sexuality is indeterminate, out of control; she is neither male nor female, neither of color nor Caucasian. She is indistinguishable from the turf; the terrain, mud, blood intermingle to deny her personhood. She is unrecognizable as a human being.

We cannot comprehend this crime; it is horrific: such violence, such brutality cannot exist. To restore some sense of control to life, to comprehend the "strangeness," we must distance ourselves from the participants—from the victim as well as from the defendants. The victim cannot be us. She has been desexualized, deracialized; she is not real. Nor can the young men be us; they are a "roving pack," animalized, dehumanized, like the victim, out of control. They are blackness, they are fear, they are wildness itself. Supporters of the defendants did not feel comfortable with the wildness represented by this crime. They, too, created a different reality. Just as the prosecution dehumanized the defendants, their supporters dehumanized the victim. Her initial otherness was enhanced by her miraculous recovery so that she never existed, either as an injured, almost-dead person or as a recovering one.

Individually, we may restore some sense of order through this distancing process, but it is not enough. Control must be restored in a collective sense, and our individual distancing, our construction of both the victim and the defendant as "other," must be countered by the prosecution if it is to restore order through a conviction. The victim must be reconstructed resexualized, reracialized as a human being so that we can identify with her. Her identity as a white Woman must be restored, and her connection to us reinstated; at the same time, our distance from the defendants must be maintained and exaggerated. The defendants must be recast as the only "other." We must be led to believe that control can be restored—that one more conviction, one more person of color sent to prison, one more teenager off the street, will restore order and control. Violence, the young men, the "wild," must be tamed.

The prosecutor understands that we are simultaneously repulsed, terrified, and fascinated by this crime. She manipulates these contradictory feelings by recreating the crime, emphasizing its racial and sexual aspects. The "roving pack," unseen by anyone, stalks the vulnerable prey through the "vast" and "dark" woods. They are mysterious, unknowable, strange—glimpsed, perhaps, but never seen; present, yet never fully perceived. The defendants are reconstructed as "evil forces . . . that overwhelm their victims by their size and strength."

To reconstruct the violence, to reracialize and resexualize the victim and thereby the defendants, the prosecutor repeatedly plays videotapes of the young men's confessions. These confessions reenact the crime, describing the participation of the young men, at times as voyeurs, at times as actors. Because we too have become voyeurs, the prosecution must emphasize the role of young men as actors: their sexual excitement; the enhanced eroticism of violating a white woman.

Finally, in a marvelous Judeo-Christian metaphor, the woman is re-created and resurrected: Out of the mud, the dirt, the clay, she is (re)created; out of (near) death, she arises. She and we (whiteness and familiarity) triumph; wildness (blackness and strangeness) is subdued. Violence is punished, and order and control are restored.

As these stories indicate, the media is a major player in the process by which Woman is created and maintained. It is crucial that we understand the power of the media and its ability to sustain a pervasive influence over what we know and how we think, even about ourselves. We must begin, as suggested by these authors, to create our own stories, to define ourselves and our reality. Step by step, we must learn and relearn who we are, what we want, what we feel. We will then be able to tell our own individual and collective stories and to insist that our diversity and complexity be acknowledged, accepted, and celebrated.

Notes

1. I am adopting Martha Fineman's convention of capitalizing a common noun to indicate its metaphoric qualities (e.g., Woman, Mother). See Fineman 1995.

2. See Fineman 1995, p. 114, nn. 4 and 49, chapter 5 (discussing Murray's—and others'—demonization of single mothers as responsible for practically every evil in the world).

15

Law, Cultural Media[tion], and Desire in the Lives of Adolescent Girls

TRACY E. HIGGINS & DEBORAH L. TOLMAN

In order to perpetuate itself, every oppression must corrupt or distort those various sources of power within the culture of the oppressed that can provide energy for change. For women, this has meant suppression of the erotic as a considered source of power and information within our lives.

—Audre Lorde, *Sister Outsider*

Sexual Stories in the Media and in Law

Sexually assertive girls are making the news. A disturbed mother of a teenage boy wrote to Ann Landers, to complain of the behavior of teenage girls who had telephoned him, leaving sexually suggestive messages. After publishing the letter, Ann Landers received twenty thousand responses and noted, "[I]f I'm hearing about it from so many places, then I worry about what's going on out there. . . . What this says to me is that a good many young girls really are out of control. Their hormones are raging and they have not had adequate supervision" (Yoffe 1991). What were these girls doing? Calling boys, asking them out, threatening to buy them gifts and to "make love to [them] all night." A *Newsweek* story entitled "Girls Who Go Too Far" described the Ann Landers column and referred to the girls as "obsessed," "confused," "emotionally disturbed," "bizarre," "abused," and "troubled" (Yoffe 1991). Parents described the girls' behavior as "bewilder-[ing]" or even "frighten[ing]" to boys. A similar, more recent story in the *Orlando Sentinel* noted

that "girls today have few qualms about asking a boy out—and they have no qualms about calling a boy on the telephone" (Shrieves 1993). Describing late-night telephone calls from girls to their teenage sons, the adults interviewed characterized the situation as "frustrating" and "shocking" and suggested that "parents should be paying more attention to what their daughters are doing." The girls' behavior, including "suggestive notes stuck to a boy's locker or even outright propositions," was described as "obsessive" (Shrieves 1993).

In contrast, media accounts of boys' sexuality tend to reflect what Wendy Hollway has called the "discourse of male sexual drive" (Hollway 1984, p. 63), wherein male sexuality is portrayed as natural, relentless, and demanding attention, an urge that boys and men cannot help or control. Media coverage of the so-called Spur Posse in Lakewood, California, reflects this discourse. Members of the Spur Posse, a group of popular, white high school boys in a middle-class California suburb competed with one another using a point system for their sexual "conquests" (Smolowe 1993; Gross 1993). When girls eventually complained, several boys were charged with crimes ranging from sexual molestation to rape. Although many criticized the incident as an example of adolescent sexuality out of control, others excused or even defended the boys' behavior. One father explained, "Nothing my boy did was anything any red-blooded American boy wouldn't do at his age." A mother commented, "What can you do? It's a testosterone thing" (Smolowe 1993).

These media stories reflect the dominant cultural accounts of distinctly gendered sexuality. The cultural story of women's sexuality is bimodal, positing women either as sexual objects, passive and resisting, or, when women act as sexual agents, expressing their own sexual desire rather than serving as the objects of men's desire, as threatening, deviant, and bad. Missing is any affirmative account of women's sexual desire or agency. In contrast, men's sexuality is defined as natural, urgent, and aggressive and is bounded, both in law and in culture, by the limits of women's consent (Fine 1988; Smart 1989). Thus, even while women's sexuality is denied or problematized, the culture (and the law) tend to assign to women the responsibility for regulating heterosexual sex by resisting male aggression. When women fail in their responsibility to define the boundaries of sexual behavior, including limiting or denying their own sexual desire, they are marginalized or vilified.

Translating this cultural story into the language of moral and legal responsibility, Lynne Henderson has described it as the story of "male innocence and female guilt" (Henderson 1992, p. 131). She suggests that according to this story, men are not morally responsible for their heterosexual conduct because their sexual desire is presumed natural and perhaps impossible to control. Women, in contrast, are held responsible for both their own conduct and the conduct of men. Complementing and reinforcing this presumption of male aggression and female passivity is the problematization of women's and girls' desire. In contrast to the natural dynamic of male aggression and female resistance, the expression of desire on the part of women (and certainly girls) is quickly deemed deviant, an uncontrollable and dangerous lust against which men must defend themselves.

As the Ann Landers column suggests, the cultural anxiety precipitated by unbounded female sexuality is perhaps most apparent with regard to adolescent girls. Coming under scrutiny from across the political spectrum, girls' sexuality has been deemed threatening either to girls themselves (rape, sexually transmitted diseases, unwanted pregnancy) or to society (single motherhood, welfare dependency). Although these issues are not limited to teenage girls, they frequently arise in that context because of society's sense of entitlement, or indeed obligation, to regulate teen sexuality.[1] Accordingly, the cultural and legal sanctions on teenage girls' sexuality convey a simple message: Good girls are not sexual; sexual girls are either bad girls or good girls who have been victimized.

A comparison of the different boundaries of acceptable sexual behavior for girls and boys in these media accounts of adolescent sexuality illustrates the force of the cultural assumption of female passivity and male aggression. Although the Spur Posse incident was covered as a troubling example of unchecked male sexuality, the point at which adolescent sexual aggression becomes suspect is strikingly different for girls and boys. For girls, it's phone calls; for boys, it's rape. The girls' suggestive phone-calling is described as shocking to the parents and even threatening to the sons, not because the desire expressed was unusual in the realm of teen sexuality but because the agents were girls and the objects were boys. It seems unlikely that Ann Landers would suggest that boys who asked girls for dates, bought them gifts, or even propositioned them were "out of control" or lacked "adequate supervision." In contrast, in the Spur Posse incident, the degrading and coercive behavior of the boys, while criticized by many, was defended by some in the community as natural or inevitable, "a testosterone thing." Indeed, when the boys returned to school pending the investigation, they received a hero's welcome (Gross 1993).

The media coverage of the Spur Posse incident reveals not only a contrast between divergent norms of male and female sexual behavior but also the consequences for girls of the intersection of these cultural norms. For many observers of the Spur Posse, the boys' culpability depended on an assessment of the conduct of the *girls* involved. If the girls were shown to have expressed any sexual agency, their desire excused or justified the boys' treatment of them as objects, points to be collected. As one mother put it, "Those girls are trash" (Smolowe 1993). The possibility of girls' sexual agency or desire shifted responsibility from the boys' aggression to the girls' failure to resist. The girls were held responsible for their failure to control the boys' behavior and, as a result, lost their entitlement to protection from male sexual aggression.

The power of the cultural norm of female passivity, or the absence of female desire, to mediate interpretations of teen sexuality is perhaps most vividly revealed in the comments of those who defended the behavior of "aggressive" girls. They did so uniformly by denying the girls' sexual agency or desire. For example, teenage girls interviewed in the *Sentinel* story explained their peers' behavior in terms of girls giving boys what the boys wanted. One suggested that "sometimes girls, in order to get certain guys, will do anything the guy wants. And that includes sex." That would include propositioning a boy "if that's what she thinks *he wants*" (Shrieves 1993). The girl's actions are reinterpreted in terms of satisfying the boy's desire rather than her own. Explaining away the possibility of the girls' sexual desire, a counselor suggested that the girls may not really be "sex-crazed." Rather, they are probably simply "desperate for a relationship" (Shrieves 1993). Describing the girls as trading sex for relationships, the counselor again reinterprets their actions in a manner that is consistent with the cultural story of male aggression and female responsibility. The girl gives the boy what he (inevitably or naturally) wants, negotiating her need for relationship by managing his drive for sexual pleasure. The possibility of her desire is left out altogether, and the bad girl is thereby restored to good-girl status.

Through this cultural story, girls are simultaneously taught that they are valued in terms of their sexual desirability and that their own desire makes them vulnerable. If they are economically privileged and white, they become vulnerable because desiring (read "bad") girls lose credibility and protection from male aggression. If they are poor and/or of color, or bisexual or lesbian, they are simply assumed to be bad; the racism, classism, and homophobia embedded in the cultural story simply deny these girls good-girl status and the protection accompanying it. (Tolman 1996). While in some communities girls' and women's sexuality is acknowledged and more fully accepted (Omolade 1983), the force of the dominant culture presses on all girls. This constant pressure can inflame the desire of marginalized

girls to be considered good, moral, and normal, a status denied them by mainstream standards. Moreover, all girls' vulnerability is compounded by the extraordinary license given to adolescent boys regarding the urgency of their sexuality. Perhaps more than any other group of men, teenage boys are assumed to lack complete control of their sexuality. The responsibility for making sexual choices therefore falls to their partners, usually teenage girls. Those girls, in turn, are constantly at risk of becoming bad girls if they fail to regulate their own sexual behavior and that of their partners.

The cultural messages encoded in the media coverage of "troubling" teen sexuality are consistent with the messages conveyed in rape law and media coverage of rape trials. Premised on the notion of male sexual aggression and irresponsibility, the law of rape incorporates norms that place on the woman the burden of regulating sexual activity and at the same time penalize her for acting as a sexual subject. In so doing, the law of rape implicitly conditions a woman's legal protection on the absence of her desire—the cultural standard defining the good girl.

In cases of acquaintance rape, rape trials frequently hinge on whether nonconsent to sexual intercourse is established—a standard which, as feminists have noted, takes little account of women's sexuality. As Carol Smart has argued, the consent/nonconsent dyad fails to capture the complexity of a woman's experience (Smart 1989). A woman may seek and initiate intimacy as an expression of her own sexual desire while not consenting to intercourse. Nevertheless, by imposing the consent/nonconsent interpretive framework, rape law renders a woman's expression of desire immediately suspect. Expression of desire that leads to intimacy and ultimately submission to unwanted sex falls on the side of consent. As the "trashy" girls who were the victims of the Spur Posse illustrate, to want anything is to consent to everything. By the expression of her own sexual desire, the woman has in effect sacrificed her right to refuse intercourse. Or, more precisely, the expression of her desire undermines the credibility of her refusal. Indeed, evidence that the rape victim initiated sexual interaction at any level operates to undermine her story at every stage of the process: Police disbelieve her account, prosecutors refuse to press the case, and juries refuse to convict. At trial, the issue of consent may be indistinguishable from the question of whether the woman experienced pleasure (Smart 1989). Thus, within rape law, a woman's behavior as sexual subject shifts power to the aggressor, thereby maintaining the power hierarchy of the traditional story—male aggression, female submission. As in pulp romance, to desire is to surrender.

The centrality of the absence of female desire to the definition of rape cuts across racial lines, albeit in complicated ways. As African American feminists have pointed out, rape and race are historically interwoven in a way that divides the experiences of women of color from those of white women (e.g., Collins 1990; A. Harris 1990). Nevertheless, whatever the woman's race, the absence of female desire stands as a prerequisite to the identification of a sexual act as rape. The difference emerges as a product of the interlocking elements of the cultural story about women's sexuality, a story that segregates white women and women of color. For example, a key feature of the cultural story is that African American women are sexually voracious, thereby unrapeable (A. Davis 1981; A. Harris 1990). The absence-of-desire standard is still applied to women of color, but unlike for white women, the presumption is that it cannot be met. Conversely, when white women accuse African American men of raping them, absence of female desire is simply assumed.[2]

If, under ordinary rape law, expression of female sexual desire takes women and girls outside of the protection of the law, rendering them unrapeable, statutory rape law defines female sexuality as outside the law in a different way. By criminalizing all intercourse with minors, statutory rape laws literally outlaw girls' expression of their own sexuality.[3] In terms of female sexual desire, statutory rape represents a complete mirroring of rape law regulating male access to adult women—with statutory rape, absence of female desire is presumed. Instead of rendering a woman unrapeable or fully accessible to men, young women's expression of sexual desire is simply made illegal.

By making women's legal protection from sexual violence contingent upon the absence of sexual desire, the law thus reflects and reinforces broader cultural penalties on women's sexual agency. This problematizing of women's desire is further heightened when the application of these legal standards is refracted through the lens of

the media in the coverage of rape trials.[4] Her sexuality, rather than his, becomes the focus of media scrutiny, and she is frequently cast in one of two clearly defined roles: innocent or desiring, good girl or bad. For example, during the Mike Tyson rape trial, the media repeatedly referred to the fact that Desiree Washington taught Sunday school, as though that fact were necessary to rebut the possibility that she invited the attack by acting on her own sexual desire. In response, the defense deployed a racist strategy premised on the intersection of cultural accounts of the sexuality of African American women and men. Tyson's lawyers emphasized his predatory reputation to suggest that Washington must have wanted whatever treatment she received at his hands.[5]

In an even more extreme case, the adolescent girl with a mental disability who was raped by a group of teenage boys in her Glen Ridge, New Jersey, neighborhood was portrayed both by her lawyers and by the media as largely asexual. To establish nonconsent, the prosecution argued explicitly that she was incapable of knowing or expressing her sexuality (Houppert 1993).[6] Although she was not sexually inexperienced, this strategy was designed to render her sexually innocent by establishing an absence of desire. The defense, on the other hand, attempted to prove that she was in fact a *bad girl*, the sexual aggressor in the case, a Lolita (e.g., Lefkowitz 1992; Hanley 1992). The jury's task, then, was to resolve the question of the boys' guilt by determining in which category she belonged.

In another highly publicized rape trial at the time, that of William Kennedy Smith, the media revealed not only the victim's name but her sexual history and her driving record. Much was made in the press of the victim's sexual promiscuity and her apparent willingness to accompany Smith home that night. By engaging in flirtation and foreplay, she undermined the credibility of her alleged refusal of intercourse. Smith was acquitted.

As illustrated by these examples of media coverage of rape trials, cultural and legal norms interact to normalize male aggression and female passivity, reinforcing the good girl/bad girl distinction. Through the suffusion of this story in our culture, girls and women come to understand the norms of acceptable sexual behavior. Good girls are those who are sexually innocent, meaning without sexual *desire*, although not necessarily without sexual *experience*. These girls are sexual objects, not subjects, charged with defending the boundaries of their own sexual activity by resisting male aggression. Like Desiree Washington and the Glen Ridge rape victim, they are entitled to invoke the law's protection, and rape law, as it exists, most effectively protects these girls. In contrast, bad girls are girls who express their desire, acting as sexual subjects. They are assertive girls, "girls who go too far," girls who engage in foreplay and flirtation as an expression of their own sexuality. Vilified by the media, and the culture more broadly, as deviant and threatening, these girls are far less likely to be able to invoke the protection of rape law and are thus made doubly vulnerable.

Sexual Stories in Feminism: Of Method and Credibility

What significance do these pervasive cultural messages have for women's and girls' sexuality? We argue that they are building blocks in the social construction of sexuality, creating, defining, and limiting individuals' sexual experiences and gender identity. Building on Foucault, the premise that sexuality is socially constructed rejects the notion of a natural, autonomous sexual drive that is universal, innate, and transhistorical (Foucault 1978; Diamond and Quinby 1988; Bordo 1993a). Rather, it posits that culture regulates and mediates sexuality in particular ways by defining the scope of normal sexual behavior. To claim that the media and the law participate in the definition of sexual experience is not to suggest that sexuality is unconnected to human biology[7] but to acknowledge that sexuality is not comprehensible in purely biological terms (Rubin 1984). Sexuality's current meanings, content, and boundaries are products not of nature but of culture, including popular culture, the media, and law.

The thesis that sexuality is a product of social construction suggests that sexuality is a locus for the exercise of power (Foucault 1978; Bartky 1990). The cultural regulation of sexuality occurs both directly, at the level of the law, and indirectly, through cultural images of sexuality, popular morality, and social sanction. Media accounts of sexuality and sexual violence both reflect and reinforce cultural norms of appropriate sexual conduct for men and women. Thus, the Ann Landers and Spur Posse stories are evidence of a cultural norm of female passivity and male aggression and reflect the cultural milieu in which teenage girls interpret their own sexual feelings. They also frame the process of interpretation directly, serving as a source from which girls learn about what it means to become a woman in the culture.

The premise that the sex-gender system is substantially a product of culture rather than biology is central to a feminist critique in that it renders sexuality potentially malleable and thus a site of political struggle. It is important, therefore, for feminists concerned with women's sexuality and sexual violence to explore the operation of cultural accounts of male and female sexuality in the lives of girls and women. How do girls and women interpret these accounts? To what extent are their sexual experiences and choices structured by varied and often conflicting cultural norms? In part III, we begin to explore these questions by turning to the voices of girls themselves as they report their experiences of sexual pleasure and danger. Yet listening to girls' stories as a means of examining the social construction of sexuality raises a difficult (and familiar) methodological question within feminism: How can feminists criticize the oppression of women through the internalization of sexual norms while respecting women's claims of sexual pleasure? Or, in this context, if cultural accounts of female sexuality construct girls' experiences of desire (or the absence of desire), how should we interpret those experiences? Should they be privileged as expressing an affirmative female sexuality or discounted as a product of patriarchy? In other words, to what extent does a theory of social construction allow for individual agency?

Feminists have answered these questions in various ways. For example, Catharine MacKinnon has argued that "the substantive principle governing the authentic politics of women's personal lives is pervasive powerlessness to men, expressed and reconstituted daily as sexuality" (MacKinnon 1989, p. 120). MacKinnon asserts that women's sexuality is entirely a product of male power, completely overdetermined. As she explains, " '[W]oman' is defined by what male desire requires for arousal and satisfaction and is socially tautologous with 'female sexuality' and 'the female sex' " (p. 131). This position leads Mac-

Kinnon to dismiss women's reports of sexual pleasure and to argue that those experiences are not exempt from the constructing force of male power. Although attentive to reports of sexual harm, she has been far less interested in analyzing how women's sexual pleasure is constructed or might be reconstructed from a feminist standpoint.

If MacKinnon has been quick to dismiss accounts of pleasure, some of her critics have responded by denying women's accounts of harm. For example, in her recent, highly publicized book,[8] *The Morning After: Sex, Fear, and Feminism*, Katie Roiphe (1993b) criticizes campus date-rape educators for creating a "rape crisis" for political ends. Rejecting the statistics on date rape as wildly exaggerated, Roiphe argues that "this is the true crisis: that there are a not insignificant number of young women walking around out there with this alarming belief. This hyperbole contains within it a state of perpetual fear" (Roiphe 1993b, p. 58). Thus, for Roiphe the problem lies in the feminist construction of the status quo as one that victimizes women. She warns that "it is the passive sexual role that threatens us still, and it is the denial of female sexual agency that threatens to propel us backward" (p. 84).

In contrast to MacKinnon, Roiphe seems to assume that women do (or at least could) exercise complete agency in their sexual choices, and she identifies feminism, not sexism, as the force undermining that agency. She blames feminism for women's sense of victimhood, criticizing feminists for positing women as weak and vulnerable to verbal or emotional coercion. It is not cultural sanctions on female desire but feminists themselves who have created "their own version of the desexualized woman" (Roiphe 1993b, p. 84). Having asserted the constructing (and distorting) force of feminism, Roiphe discounts women's claims of sexual violence as generated by feminist paranoia.

MacKinnon and Roiphe both tend to ignore the difficult issues raised by their conflicting assumptions about women's agency. Discounting women's accounts of sexual pleasure, MacKinnon suggests that it is pointless (or even antifeminist) to theorize about women's sexuality under patriarchy, postponing such consideration until women are free (or freer) from male oppression (MacKinnon 1989). Discounting women's ac-

counts of sexual violence, Roiphe emphasizes repression rather than oppression and suggests that for women to realize their sexuality they need only be freed from the bind of the sexual double standard (Roiphe 1993b). Neither of these positions takes seriously the possibility that women's (and men's) sexuality under patriarchy is neither fully determined nor fully free. Yet capturing the complexity of women's sexuality requires feminism to interpret women's accounts of their own sexual pleasure as well as their accounts of sexual violence and oppression, a task that both Roiphe and MacKinnon decline to undertake fully.

A theory of social construction of sexuality precludes both MacKinnon's claim that women's sexuality is impossibly distorted by patriarchy or Roiphe's claim that it is realizable fully under conditions of individual freedom or autonomy. Rather, women's sexuality is constituted by social conditions and does not exist apart from those conditions. Attempting to address those conditions, both the risk of sexual violence and the potential for sexual pleasure, some feminists have attempted to evaluate women's accounts of sexuality without ignoring the inequality under which women make sexual choices (e.g., Dimen 1989; Holland et al. 1994). These scholars have suggested that feminists have tended to theorize women's sexuality prematurely, before developing a detailed documentation of the diversity of that sexuality under current conditions (Vance and Snitow 1984; Vance 1992). Undertaking this task of examination and reconstruction, these feminists have emphasized a reliance on women's reports of their own experiences of sexuality, reports that include both vulnerability and agency, movement from sexual subject to sexual object, and explorations of power and powerlessness in the context of relationships that are not necessarily egalitarian. The goal has been to explicate the more complicated ways that women's understanding of themselves as sexual objects, as preservers of relationship, and as potential victims of violence interrupts, undermines, or coexists with their experiences of themselves as sexual subjects.

This feminist position, sometimes misleadingly labeled "pro-sex" feminism (Snitow, Stansell, and Thompson 1983a; Vance and Snitow 1984), has been criticized by others, including MacKinnon, as validating sexual experiences that simply reflect and reinforce women's oppression (MacKinnon 1989). However, if we take seriously an acknowledgment that sexuality is socially constructed, our method must include a critical examination of women's actual experiences rather than condemnation or valorization of an imagined womanhood. Indeed, to postpone any consideration of women's sexual desire and pleasure is to put one's faith in a postpatriarchal, essential woman—an assumption that is inconsistent with a premise of social construction. Women's sexuality as it exists is not a distortion of an underlying, true sexuality, nor is it a reflection of a natural sexuality that must merely be unleashed. Rather, it is simply what women experience under current conditions.

This commitment to understanding women's sexuality under conditions of inequality carries with it methodological implications for both psychology and legal theory. Feminist methodologies in both disciplines have been grounded in a belief in the significance of women's voices speaking from their marginalized perspectives (e.g., Fine 1992; Bartlett 1991). Yet as feminists, we begin with the dual goal of both supporting women as they exist and criticizing the category of woman as it has been created under patriarchy. Returning to our original methodological question, how then do we interpret what women, inescapably gendered, say about their experiences as women?

This dilemma is illustrated in the following colloquy between Carol Gilligan and Catharine MacKinnon:

GILLIGAN: Your definition of power is his definition.

MACKINNON: That is because the society is that way, it operates on his definition, and I am trying to change it.

GILLIGAN: To have her definition come in?

MACKINNON: That would be part of it, but more to have a definition that she would articulate that she cannot now, because his foot is on her throat.

GILLIGAN: She's saying it.
(Dubois et al. 1985)

The question raised is this: What do we do with the fact that "she's saying it"?

Beginning from a premise of social construction, we suggest that feminists may neither fully accept nor fully reject women's reports of pleasure and coercion. Feminists need not theorize women's sexuality as either fully free or fully determined.[9] Instead, we must examine the complicated and sometimes conflicting cultural texts of women's desire within a social setting that includes sexual danger. Although feminist legal theorists have generally acknowledged the need to include a range of women's perspectives in policy-making, they have struggled to reconcile the diversity of women's lives revealed through feminist methodology with the need to articulate a specific and coherent basis for lawmaking. Law's intolerance of "multiple stories" and the imperatives of identity politics have in some cases led to the discounting of certain accounts as "false consciousness." Most feminist legal theorists have rejected this move in theory, although not always in practice (e.g., MacKinnon 1989), because it ignores diversity among women and undercuts the integrity of feminist legal method (Minow 1988; Matsuda 1989b). An alternative for feminist legal theorists is a methodology that is informed more fully by feminist psychology.

Addressing the question of how to listen to women's voices, one group of feminist psychologists has developed a method for interpreting girls' and women's narratives about their own experiences.[10] Based in an epistemology that centers on multiple interpretations rather than a routing out of "truth," this method is framed by two key concepts. First, rather than a move to accusations of false consciousness, the method draws on the psychodynamic notion of the layered psyche to offer an understanding of internalized oppression as a shaping force of experience. In addition, this approach utilizes the concepts of psychological (unconscious) and political (conscious) resistance to oppressive norms in building interpretations. By considering several different perspectives or voices from which to understand a single narrative, the method demands rich description rather than objective assessment and can hold the complexity of contradictions that do not smooth out into a single, logical truth. Thus, this complex listening process moves beyond the simple construction that what a woman *says* is what women's experience *is* to consider other features of a woman's narrative: how she speaks, what she omits, nonverbal markers of her experience. It also takes into account how a woman's position in society or individual relationship history may contribute to an understanding of what she says, where she falters, or when she is silent.

Second, by obligating the interpreter to consider how power differences embedded in a brief research relationship may circulate through the narrative, this method subverts the tendency in psychology to offer an authoritative expert "voice-over" of a girl's or woman's words. Thus, using this method means creating a dialectic between one girl's or woman's words and another woman's understanding of those words from a distinctly feminist point of view. Maintaining a dialectic between women's accounts of their experience and the conditions of women's oppression, this methodology strives to maintain the contradiction between privileging women's voices and recognizing that women are constructed by gender. Choosing among contradicting accounts becomes less important than exploring what the contradictions reveal about women's oppression and women's agency.[11] In turn, understanding the ways in which women live in those contradictions is essential to feminist legal theorists' task of developing effective legal means of protecting women from sexual violence.

Adolescent Girls and the Dilemma of Desire

In this section, we turn to the voices of adolescent girls speaking about their experiences, using the feminist method outlined above to illustrate how the multifaceted cultural story about girls' sexuality may create vulnerability for girls rather than protect them from it. We have chosen three case studies for this analysis. Two are drawn from a psychological study of adolescent girls' experience of desire conducted by Tolman (Tolman 1994a, 1994b); one comes from the legal literature. The cases from Tolman's study were selected because each of the girls chose to speak about a sexual experience with a boy who was not her boyfriend. Although each associated the experience with sexual violence, the two girls differed profoundly in their understanding of these experiences and also in their critical perspective on gender relations, cultural stories about male and female sexuality, and the good girl/bad girl dichotomy. In Jenny's case, a lack of a critical perspective on these issues seems to dis-

able her from feeling outraged or empowered to act on her own behalf. For Paulina, such a perspective appears to enhance her sense of entitlement and her ability to resist. Finally, we selected the case of Sharon from the legal literature to underscore our point that denying desire can diminish girls' ability to garner protection under the law.

The stories of Jenny, Sharon, and Paulina reveal some of the many ways in which cultural norms of women's sexuality operate in girls' lives, limiting and defining the scope of their sexual experiences and creating the framework in which they make decisions about their sexuality. Although these norms have a powerful regulatory force, the girls are not the passive products of socialization. Rather, they participate actively in the construction of their identities and relationships, both following and resisting the dominant culture. In describing sexual experiences that involved coercion and resistance, each assesses her own sexual feelings and attempts to reconcile the presence or absence of desire with cultural stories that make desiring girls vulnerable.

In the context of cultural norms that penalize the expression of female sexual desire, it is not surprising that identifying, describing, and acting on sexual desire is deeply problematic for many girls. One-third of the thirty girls in Tolman's study, regardless of race or class, said that they did not experience sexual desire or that they were confused about whether or not they had experienced it. Although the remaining two-thirds of these girls said that they experienced sexual desire, in their narratives most expressed a lack of entitlement either to have or to act on their own feelings. Sexual agency rooted in their own desire was often elusive. For instance, Emily, who could describe her own feelings of sexual desire, explained, "I don't like to think of myself as feeling really sexual. . . . I don't like to think of myself as being like, someone who needs to have their desires fulfilled."

At the same time that girls expressed such difficulties with their own desire, most of them had had encounters or relationships in which they were sexually involved, including kissing, touching, oral sex, and/or sexual intercourse. Indeed, despite the difficulty many felt in expressing desire or agency, most experienced significant peer pressure to be both sexually desirable and sexually active. These girls' stories reveal a common psychological struggle to align their sexual actions with their own sexual feelings and cultural norms. Just as the counselor in the *Sentinel* story explained girls' sexually aggressive behavior as about relationship rather than desire, many girls in the study were reluctant to act, in Emily's terms, as one "who needs to have their desires fulfilled." The girls characterized the possibility of responding to their own feelings of desire as a failure to control themselves. Their own sexual feelings are left out of the equation, whether or not they choose to participate in sexual activity.

Jenny: When Bad Things Happen to Good Girls

Sixteen-year-old Jenny is the image of the quintessential "good girl." White, suburban, and middle-class, Jenny has long, straight, blond hair framing a lightly freckled, fair face. She is slim, dressed fashionably yet unassumingly. She sits with her legs tensely crossed; she is polite and smiles often. Throughout the interview, Jenny describes how she lives her life by trying to stay carefully within the boundaries of being a "good" girl. She and her mother are "very close," and it is important to her to be "nice" and a "good friend"—even if it means silencing her own displeasure or dissent in relationships (Brown and Gilligan 1992; Jack 1991). Jenny explains that she has never experienced feelings she calls sexual desire: "I actually really don't think I've ever like, wanted anything, like sexually that bad. I mean I don't think I've ever been like sexually deprived or like saying, oh I need sex now or anything. I've never really felt that way before, so, I don't know. I don't really think that there's anything that I would, I mean want. Given Jenny's concern with being a "good girl" in other domains of her life, it is not surprising that she does not report feeling desire. Having a "silent body" is one way of coping with the belief that good girls are not sexual (Tolman 1994a).

The vulnerability that this silence creates in her life is palpable in the narrative she tells about the first time she had sexual intercourse, just prior to her interview. This experience was not what she had hoped it would be:

We got alone together, and we started just basically fooling around and not doing many things. And then he asked me if I would have sex with

him, and I said, well I didn't think I, I mean I said I wanted to wait, 'cause I didn't want to, I mean I like him, but I don't *like* him so, and I mean he sorta pushed it on me, but it wasn't like I absolutely said "no, don't," I—it was sort of a weird experience. I just, I sort of let it happen to me and never like really said no, I don't want to do this. I mean I said no, but I never, I mean I never stopped him from doing anything. . . .

I guess maybe I wanted to get it over with, I guess. You can say, 'cause all my friends basically have had sex and I was one of the only ones who haven't. And I wanted to get it over with, although I wanted it to be special the first time. I thought like, it's with a friend and it's not, I, I don't know but this is scary, he told me he was wearing a condom and, he wasn't, and so I was very scared [laughing]. For about a week I thought I was pregnant [laughing]. . . . So that's another reason I'd, I'm sort of, I was really upset too because, he lied to me and, told me, and, so, I don't know. . . .

I don't know, I, I just, I mean I could've said "no," I guess, and I could've pushed him off or whatever 'cause he, I mean, he wasn't, he's not the type of person who would like rape me or whatever. I mean, well, I don't think he's that way at all. . . . I was always like, well I want to wait, and I want to be in a relationship with someone who I really like, and I want it to be a special moment and everything, and then it just sort of like happened so quickly, and it happened with someone who I didn't like and who I didn't want a relationship with and who didn't want a relationship with me, and it was just sort of, I don't, I don't know, I regret it. . . . I wish I had just, said no. I mean I could've, and I did for once but then I just let it go. And I wish that I had stood up for myself and really just like stood up and said "No, I don't want to do this. I'm not ready, or I want it to be a different experience." I mean I could've told him exactly how I felt. I don't know why I didn't.

In this story, Jenny is unsure about how to understand her first experience with sexual intercourse. In listening to her, we too are unsure. When she begins this story, Jenny knows that she did not want to have sex with this boy, although she did want to "fool[ ] around." She in fact said no when the boy asked her if she would have sex with him. There is a clarity to her "no" that she substantiates with a set of compelling reasons for not wanting to have sex with this boy: She "wanted to wait"; she didn't "like him" or "want a relationship with him." After the fact, she is again clear that she did not want to have sex with this boy. She "regrets it." But we notice that this clarity gives way to a sense of confusion that gains momentum as her narrative, itself an interplay of description and assessment, unfolds. Cleaving to the convention that girls are ultimately responsible for boys' sexual behavior, she attempts to make sense of the fact that this boy behaved as though she had not said no. Assuming responsibility, Jenny suggests that she "never stopped him from doing anything," implying, perhaps, that she had not meant the "no" that she had said.

Jenny's suggestion that she might have said no and meant yes raises a troubling issue for feminists, who have rallied around the claim that "no means no." Although "no means no" is effective as an educational or political slogan or perhaps even as a legal norm, such norms do not protect girls who are caught in a cultural story that denies their sexual agency. Within the broader context of adolescent sexuality, girls' "no" must be credible both to girls and to their partners. Yet the cultural story that good girls do not have sexual desire undermines the credibility of their "no" not only to others but also to themselves. When girls cannot say yes, no (or silence) is their only alternative and must express the range of their choices. The simple answer to this problem offered by Roiphe and others is for girls to take responsibility for communicating their desire. This answer is incomplete, however, in that it fails to account for the cultural sanctions on girls' expression of their sexuality. Leaving those sanctions unaddressed, so-called power feminists reinforce the assignment of responsibility to girls for sexual decision-making without criticizing the constraints under which those decisions are made.

Jenny struggles within those constraints as she attempts to take seriously the possibility that she may have wanted to have sex with the boy despite having said no—the possibility that her "no" meant "yes." Yet her reflection "I guess maybe I wanted to get it over with, I guess" is literally buttressed by doubt. This statement stands as a potential explanation of why she had sex even though she said no and reflects the significance in Jenny's social context of sexual experience and sexual desirability. Yet Jenny herself does not sound convinced. The explanation sounds even less plausible when compared to the clarity of her elaborated and unambiguous statements about why she did not want to have sex. She explains, "I want to be in a relationship with someone who I really like, and I want it to be a special moment and everything."

As her story progresses, we hear Jenny's confusion about what she wanted intensify. This confusion seems to undermine Jenny's knowledge that she had actually said no to this boy. Eventually, Jenny seems to forget that she ever said no at all. Despite having just explained that she had not wanted to have sex with this boy and had told him so, Jenny starts to speak as if she had not said no. "I said no" becomes "I sort of let it happen to me and never like, *really* said no, I don't want to do this." She proceeds to undo her knowledge that she articulated her wish not to have sex. "I mean I could've said no, I guess, and I could've pushed him off or whatever" finally becomes "I wish I had just said no." Thus, when this boy behaved as though Jenny had not said no, Jenny loses track of her knowledge and her voice, becoming confused not only about what she wanted but also about what she said.

The conditions Jenny gives for an appropriate sexual encounter—"a special relationship," someone she "really like[s]"—resonate with the cultural story that girls' sexuality is about relationships and not desire. Because the encounter she describes did not meet these conditions, she decided that she did not want to have sex and told the boy no. Indeed, she is clearest about her entitlement to say no when she reports that he had not worn a condom. The availability of contraception provided a potentially clearer basis for her decision than did her own desire. Nevertheless, under the circumstances Jenny lacked an adequate framework either to make a clear decision and insist that it be respected or, if it was not respected, to identify the incident as one of violation. In this context, it is significant that Jenny makes no reference to her own sexual desire. It is only later in the interview, in response to a direct question, that Jenny reports that she "hadn't felt desire for the person I was with." She notes, however, that this absence of desire does not distinguish this encounter from any other: "I've never like had sexual feelings to want to do something or anything." We wonder whether, in the moment, Jenny was not able to hold on to her knowledge that she did not want to have sex because her own desire has never been available as a guide to her choices. Had Jenny been permitted to attend to her own sexual feelings, free from the constraints of the cultural story of female sexual passivity, her lack of sexual desire in this situation might have operated as a clear signal to her, perhaps leaving her less vulnerable to such confusion.

The consequences of Jenny's confusion include physical and psychological vulnerability. Her inability to maintain the clarity of her "no" and insist that her word be respected leaves her physically vulnerable to sexual encounters that she does not want. By discounting her own thoughts and feelings, she risks becoming dissociated from her own experience and from reality, thereby impairing her psychological integrity. Such dissociation makes it difficult for Jenny to know and name sexual exploitation. Accustomed to being the object of someone else's sexual desire and not considering that her own sexual desire might be relevant or significant, Jenny pastes over the complexity of what did in fact happen with the phrase "it just sort of like happened." This "cover story" reflects and sustains Jenny's vulnerability in a culture that leaves her sexual desire out of the narrative.

By omitting or penalizing girls' desire, the cultural story of girls' sexuality places them in a double bind. On the one hand, Jenny's inability to look to her own desire as a guide to her actions leaves her vulnerable to coercion. On the other hand, as the media coverage of teen sexuality illustrates, expression of desire on Jenny's part also would have rendered her vulnerable by undermining the credibility of her resistance to unwanted sex. In Lakewood, girls who were attracted to the members of the Spur Posse—girls who dated them, who sought their physical attention—were regarded as "trash." By expressing their desire, they lost the approval and protection of the community. Understanding these norms, Jenny's choices are "no," silence, or perhaps "yes" under some circumstances, but not a more complicated expression of what she does or does not want and why.

Jenny's suggestion that "it just sorta happened" also keeps another story at bay, a story of a girl whose spoken wish was not heeded, who was coerced. Was Jenny raped? Jenny herself

brings the word "rape" into her story: "I mean I could've said no, I guess and I could've pushed him off or whatever 'cause he, I mean, he's not the type of person who would like rape me, or whatever. I mean, well, I don't think he's that way at all." She seems to wonder whether this experience might somehow be connected to rape. She may associate this experience with rape because the word signifies something about how it felt for her, a violation. Although she stopped saying no and apparently assented to the act nonverbally, this sexual experience was not related to any feeling of "yes" on Jenny's part. Jenny's experience, of having consented and having been violated, suggests the disjuncture between consent and desire in the legal definition of rape, a disjuncture that heightens Jenny's confusion over how to interpret what happened to her. Such confusion prevents Jenny first from speaking clearly about her desire and later from interpreting what happened in a way that acknowledges her own resistance.

Sharon: Claiming and Losing Good-Girl Status

The legal vulnerability created when girls become confused about desire is illustrated by the testimony of Sharon, the victim in the Supreme Court's statutory rape case *Michael M. v. Sonoma County*.[12] In the portion of the trial transcript reproduced in the Supreme Court's opinion, Sharon, who like Jenny is sixteen and white, is being questioned by the defendant's lawyer about whether she wanted to have sex with the defendant, a boy who was not her boyfriend. Unlike ordinary rape law, the statutory rape prosecution does not require that Sharon make a clear claim that she did not want to have sex with the defendant. Nevertheless, the defense uses the confusion that emerges as Sharon testifies to call into question the legitimacy of the gender-specific statutory rape law by suggesting that Sharon shared responsibility for the sexual encounter.

The lawyer's questions about Sharon's desire subtly garner the good girl/bad girl dynamic as part of a strategy to undermine the credibility of her claim that she did not want to have sexual intercourse. In the face of these questions, Sharon seems unable to maintain clarity about the exact parameters of her desire:

Q: Now, after you met the defendant, what happened?

A: We walked down to the railroad tracks.

Q: What happened at the railroad tracks?

A: We were drinking at the railroad tracks and we walked over to this bus and he started kissing me and stuff, and I was kissing him back, too, at first. Then I was telling him to stop—

Q: Yes.

A: —and I was telling him to slow down and stop. He said, "OK, OK." But then he just kept doing it. He just kept doing it and then my sister and two other guys came over to where we were and my sister told me to get up and come home. And then I didn't . . . We were laying there and we were kissing each other, and then he asked me if I wanted to walk with him over to the park. We walked over to the park, and then we sat down on a bench, and then he started kissing me again, and we were laying on the bench. And he told me to take my pants off. I said "No," and I was trying to get up and he hit me back down on the bench, and then I just said to myself, "Forget it," and I let him do what he wanted to do and he took my pants off and he was telling me to put my legs around him and stuff—

Q: Did you have sexual intercourse with the defendant?

A: Yeah. . . .

Q: Did you go off with [the defendant] away from the others?

A: Yeah.

Q: Why did you do that?

A: I don't know. I guess I wanted to.

Sharon begins by speaking clearly about what she did and did not want to do with the boy. She wanted to kiss him back, she wanted him to slow down and stop, and she also wanted to walk over to the park with him. However, when the sexual interaction turned from kissing or "fooling around" to "tak[ing] off [her] pants," she said no, unequivocally and clearly, and "tri[ed] to get up." We hear that her desire had specific limits: While she had wanted to "fool around," she did not want to have sex. Nevertheless, like Jenny, she stopped saying no and "let him do what he wanted to do." In so doing, she may have given

her consent legally, although not emotionally or psychologically.

Initially Sharon maintains clarity about the limits of her desire. Confusion creeps into Sharon's previously straightforward account, however, as she is asked about her motives for having gone to the park with the defendant. Implicit in the lawyer's question "[Why] did you go off with [the defendant] away from the others?" is the conditional phrase "unless you wanted to have sexual intercourse with him?"—the unspoken condemnation of the actions of a bad girl. So understood, the question is really about Sharon's desire. Having been asked to speak about her own desire, Sharon loses the clarity of her earlier explanation. She seems to suspect (along with the lawyer) that there is an inconsistency between having wanted to go to the park with Michael and not having wanted to have sex with him.

Confronted with the threat of bad-girl status, Sharon retreats from her earlier articulation of her desire. Following on the heels of an unequivocal account that portrays the parameters of her desire, Sharon's statement of ambivalence makes her seem confused and uncertain. By responding that she does not know what she wanted, Sharon undermines the credibility of her previous testimony. Yet reiterating her desire to go to the park with Michael undermines the credibility of her claim that she was coerced. As a witness, Sharon becomes trapped within the good girl/bad girl dichotomy. Having relinquished good-girl status by confessing her desire for sexual interaction, she is unable to rehabilitate her testimony. Like the victim in the William Kennedy Smith case, she cannot be credible once she has admitted her willing participation in flirtation and foreplay.

Together Jenny's and Sharon's narratives illustrate the kinds of legal and psychological vulnerability created by cultural norms that condition a girl's right to protection on the absence of her sexual desire. As girls mature within this culture and internalize this story, they employ various strategies for making sense of their experience within the cultural framework. Rather than developing a sense of entitlement to their own sexual choices, both Sharon and Jenny have learned that their desire is dangerous or unimportant. As a result, they are denied adequate tools for making and defending their choices. This response to the cultural norms penalizing girls' desire is not inevitable, however. By developing a critical perspective on these norms and the social sanctions imposed on those who violate them, girls may become better equipped to resist the confusion such norms can create, to be more effective in making and defending their own sexual choices.

Jenny's own description of the good girl/bad girl dichotomy illustrates the importance of this critical perspective. Jenny is a good observer of the social landscape of adolescent heterosexual relationships. She identifies some imbalances in how girls and boys behave and in how they are treated by others in response to their behavior. She notes that "whenever like a girl and a guy do something and people find out, it's always the girl that messed up or, I mean, maybe the guy messed up but, the guys like get praise for it [laughing] and the girl's sort of like called, either a slut or something, or just like has a bad reputation. Which is sort of [laughing] awful." Jenny believes that "it is just as much the guy's fault as it is the girl's fault. . . . [I]t's just like the guys and girls make fun of the girls but no one makes fun of the guys [laughing]." What Jenny needs is an analytic framework that links the inequities she observes to cultural stories about sexuality. She suspects, but does not know, that these stories operate in a way that creates gendered power differences. Identifying the good girl/bad girl divide, Jenny tries without success to make sense of the contradiction she observes—that both girls and guys may be at "fault" in sexual situations like hers, but only girls are chastised. We notice that she does not say what *she* thinks about this contradiction. When asked directly, her confusion about gender relations is audible: "I really don't know."

Paulina: The Power of Desire

A counterpoint to Jenny's experience can be found in the stories Paulina tells. A white girl living in an urban environment, seventeen-year-old Paulina looks like the other adolescent girls in this study: Long, dark hair frames her pretty, open face, stylish jeans and sweater clothe a slim figure. Despite her appearance, though, Paulina does not sound like the other girls: Having immigrated from Eastern Europe several years prior to the interview, Paulina speaks with a strong accent. It is the content of her narrative, however, that most distinguishes her from the other study participants. Like Jenny, Paulina is also a compe-

tent consumer of the cultural story about girls and sexuality and can recite it without a moment's hesitation:

> They expect the woman to be pure, I mean, she has to be holy and everything, and it's okay for a guy to have any feelings or anything, and the girl has to be this little virgin who is obedient to the men. . . . Usually a guy makes the first move, not the girl, or the girl's not supposed to do it, the girl's supposed to sit there going, no, no you can't. I can't do that. . . . . I mean the guy expects the girl to be a sweet little virgin when he marries her, and then he can be running around with ten other women, but when he's getting married to her, she's not supposed to have any relationship with anybody else.

Paulina echoes Jenny's observation about how the label "slut" is—and is not—used: "Guys, they just like to brag about girls. Oh she does this, and she's a slut because she slept with this guy, and with this guy, but they don't say that about guys. It's okay for them to do it, but when a girl sleeps with two guys its wrong, she shouldn't do that, she automatically becomes a slut."

In contrast to Jenny's ambivalence and uncertainty, Paulina has strong opinions about the sexual double standard: "I just don't agree with it . . . I just don't think so." A sense of entitlement, accompanied by outrage, suffuses her well-articulated view of female sexual agency: "Women can do whatever they want to, why shouldn't they? . . . I think that women have the same feelings as men do, I mean, I think it's okay to express them too. . . . I mean, they have the same feelings, they're human, why should they like keep away from them?" While Jenny seems unable to make sense of this inequity, Paulina grounds her critique in an analysis that links gender and power: "I think males are kind of dominant, and they feel that they have the power to do whatever they want, that the woman should give in to them."

Paulina also parts from Jenny in her detailed knowledge about her own sexual desire. Perhaps not coincidentally, Paulina speaks of this embodied experience with an ease that reflects and underscores her belief that girls' sexual desire is normal or, in her words, "natural": "I feel really hot, like, my temperature is really hot . . . I felt like a rush of blood like pumping to my heart, my heart would really beat fast, and it's just, every-thing are combined, you're extremely aware of every, every touch, and everything, everything together . . . you have all those feelings of want." Paulina is clear that this desire can guide her choices and that it should be respected: "[T]o me if you have like a partner that you're close to, then it's okay. And if you feel comfortable with it, cause if you don't, then you shouldn't do it. You just don't want to." Thus, Paulina grounds her sexual decisions in her own feelings and be-liefs—she can identify and account for the pres-ence and absence of her own desire. As a result, Paulina seems less vulnerable to confusion about what she feels and what she has said.

Like Jenny, Paulina has had a "bad" sexual ex-perience with a boy whom she had thought of as a friend. In the interview, she describes a time when this male friend tried to force her to have sex with him:

There was one experience, the guy wanted to have sexual intercourse and I didn't. . . . I didn't have sex with him. He, he like pulled me over to the couch, and I just kept on fighting. . . . I was just like begging him to like not to do anything, and like, I really did not have like much choice. Because I had my hands behind me. And he just like kept on touching me, and I was just like, just get off me. He goes, you know that you want to, and I said no I don't. Get off me, I hate you. . . . So he's like, well I'll let you go if you're gonna kiss me. So I kissed him, and I'm like well I can go now. And he was like no. But um, the phone rang later on, I said I have to answer this, it's my mother . . . So he let me answer the phone. So. And it was my friend and I just said, oh can you come over? And, since I'm Russian I spoke Russian, so I'm like oh just come over, come over as soon as you can.

Ultimately, when her friend arrived, she was able to convince the boy to leave.

Paulina's assailant attacked her both physi-cally and psychologically, telling her, "You know that you want to." However, because she had a clear understanding of her own sexual feelings, Paulina was able to speak clearly about not feel-ing sexual desire. In response to his coaxing, Pau-lina's retort is direct and unequivocal: "No, I don't. Get off me. I hate you." Unlike Jenny and

Sharon, Paulina is correspondingly clear in her narrative of the encounter. She has no doubt in her mind about the parameters of her own sexual feelings: She did not want any sexual interaction with this young man. Her sense of entitlement to her feelings empowered her to identify the expe-rience as a violation, to resist the attack.

It must be emphasized that Paulina was very lucky in this situation. She was able to think clearly and take advantage of an opportunity—her friend's phone call—to protect herself from being raped. The critical point is not that she was able to avoid assault in this case but that she had a clear understanding of the threat of vio-lence. Had Paulina not escaped attack, it seems likely that she would have maintained her clarity about her own actions and desires, a clarity that would better enable her to claim the protection the law offers.

Conclusion

As reflected in the media and the law, the cul-tural story of human sexuality is one that penal-izes the desire of girls and women while naturaliz-ing the desire of boys and men. Using feminist method to listen to girls describe their experi-ences with their own sexuality and sexual vio-lence, we have argued that this cultural story, meant to protect "good" girls and punish "bad" girls, in fact creates vulnerability for all girls. Le-gally, the story effects a shifting or blurring of responsibility by simultaneously excusing boys' aggression and placing on girls the burden of reg-ulating sexual behavior. According to the cul-tural plot, the rapist can be understood as suc-cumbing to his natural inclinations toward aggressive sexuality and the victim as failing to meet her responsibility in controlling that behav-ior. Psychologically, the cultural story denies girls the full range of sexual choices and feelings by pathologizing female desire. The legal and psy-chological factors interact to render girls less able to invoke legal protections or identify and report sexual coercion.

Defying the conventions of the cultural story, our analysis suggests that sexual desire can be a source of power and strength for women and girls. Paulina's ability to know both her desire and its absence, in contrast to Jenny's "silent body" and Sharon's confusion, is linked to her critical consciousness of the good girl/bad girl dichotomy. Because she rejects a cultural story about her sexuality that makes her own desire dangerous, we think Paulina is less vulnerable to confusion about the boundaries of her responsibility and the contours of her experience. She is better able to know and to speak with clarity about her sexual interactions and the social landscape of gendered relationships. Without a critical perspective, Jenny and Sharon attempt to live the cultural story of female sexual passivity. Although they can identify the good girl/bad girl dichotomy, they do not have a way to escape its conflicting implications for their lives. Denying desire leaves them vulnerable to violence and coercion.

If a sense of entitlement to sexual desire coupled with a critical perspective on the cultural story can empower girls, feminists must include sexual pleasure and agency as part of the struggle against violence. We must make clear that women's and girls' sexual autonomy is not antithetical but *central* to the goal of protecting them from sexual violence, both legally and psychologically. Reversing the emphasis of the cultural story, feminists must focus on girls' entitlement to feelings of sexual desire and boys' responsibility for acting on their feelings of sexual desire. Feminist critiques of the cultural story must be about pleasure as well as protection and responsibility.

The premise of social construction renders sexuality a site of political contest. Having identified it as such, feminists can and must consider how to effect its transformation in a way that is empowering for women and girls. Linking feminist method across disciplines, feminist collaboration can not only reveal the way the debilitating cultural story pervades the media, the law, social institutions, and individual lives but can also suggest potential forms of resistance to that story. In addition to identifying and criticizing oppressive cultural norms, feminists must be active in the process of reconstructing or retelling the cultural story. An affirmative discourse of adolescent girls' sexual desire would be an important part of that retelling (Fine 1988). Such a discourse would recognize, reveal, and then reject the good girl/bad girl categories which organize female sexuality as a patriarchal strategy that disempowers girls and women. This feminist retelling must move beyond the safe bounds of academic journals to the much more contested realm of the mainstream media. It is to the accounts of sexuality and desire circulating in this realm that women and girls most readily turn, and it is therefore a realm of opportunity for a feminist politics of transformation.

Notes

1. The legal regulation of teenage sexuality extends well beyond the constitutional limits on the regulation of adult sexuality. For example, restrictions on teenage access to abortion have been upheld by the Supreme Court. See *Bellotti v. Baird*, 443 U.S. 622 (1979), and *Planned Parenthood v. Ashcroft*, 462 U.S. 476 (1983) (approving parental consent requirements for minors seeking abortion if the statute provides for an alternative procedure). Moreover, statutory rape laws criminalize sexual intercourse with minors whether or not it is consensual. Gender-specific statutory rape laws have been upheld against an equal protection challenge; see *Michael M. v. Sonoma County*, 450 U.S. 464 (1981). The Court was divided on the question of whether such regulation might violate the due process rights of minors; see *Michael M.*, 450 U.S. at 474 n. 8; 450 U.S. at 491 n. 5 (Brennan dissenting).

2. African American feminists have also exposed the way the myth of white women's sexual purity has been used as a weapon against African American men, an issue that has further divided white and African American women over the issue of sexual violence. See, for example, A. Harris 1990.

3. Although the modern reinterpretation of the purpose of statutory rape laws is that such legislation is designed to prevent teen pregnancy, the historical justification was the protection of female virtue. For example, in 1895 the California Supreme Court explained: "The obvious purpose of [the statutory rape law] is the protection of society by protecting from violation the virtue of young and unsophisticated girls. . . . It is the insidious approach and vile tampering with their persons that primarily undermines the virtue of young girls, and eventually destroys it; and the prevention of this, as much as the principal act, must undoubtedly have been the intent of the legislature" (*People v. Verdegreen*, 106 Cal. 211, 214–15, 39 P. 607, 608–9 [1895]). In 1964, the same court explained that "an unwise disposition of her sexual favor is deemed to do harm both to herself and the social mores by which the community's conduct patterns are established. Hence the law of statutory rape intervenes in an effort to avoid such a disposition" (*People v. Hernandez*, 61 Cal. 2d at 531, 393 P. 2d at 674 [1964]).

As Fran Olsen has argued, although the boy's conduct is punished by criminal sanction, it is the girl who is denied the capacity to consent. Under gender-specific statutory rape laws, the boy may legally have intercourse with women who are over the age of consent (see Olsen 1984).

4. For an excellent discussion of media coverage of rape trials, see Benedict 1992.

5. For an exploration of the use of racial stereotypes in the Mike Tyson rape trial, see K. Brown 1992; Burrell 1993.

6. The prosecution's strategy to portray the victim as asexual was not uncontroversial among advocates for people with mental disabilities. See Houppert 1993 (citing Leslie Walker-Hirsch, president of the American Association on Mental Retardation's special interest group on sexual and social concerns).

7. Foucault himself raised the question of the significance of the body, asking whether "the analysis of sexuality necessarily impl[ies] the elision of the body, anatomy, the biological, the functional" (Foucault 1978). He explains: "To this question, I think we can reply in the negative. In any case, the purpose of the present study is in fact to show how deployments of power are directly connected to the body—to bodies, functions, physiological processes, sensations, and pleasures; far from the body having to be effaced, what is needed is to make it visible through an analysis in which the biological and the historical are not consecutive to one another" (Foucault 1978).

8. Even before Roiphe's book was published, the *New York Times* published Roiphe on its op-ed page as well as an excerpt of the book in its weekly magazine. See K. Roiphe 1991; K. Roiphe 1993a. After publication, the book was reviewed in scores of newspapers, including the *Times,* and countless articles commented on the controversy it had created within feminist circles.

9. For a discussion of the problem of sexual agency in feminist theory, see Abrams 1995 (arguing for a theory of partial agency); see also J. Williams 1991; Boyle 1991.

10. This method is called The Listening Guide. It was developed by Lyn Mikel Brown, Carol Gilligan, and colleagues to build interpretations of adolescent girls' narratives of conflict and moral choice (L. M. Brown et al. 1991). The method involves a series of separate readings of a single narrative from different perspectives or for different voices. This process enables an interpretation that takes into account multiple ways of making sense of a girl's words, recognizing that the same words can convey distinct meanings from various points of view. Each perspective is underlined with an individual color, creating a visual map of the multiple realities embedded in the narrative. This map is then used to build an interpretation of the narrative that remains careful to distinguish the voice of the girl from the voice of the reader or interpreter. The challenges of using this method across race and class differences have been elaborated by Jill Taylor and Deborah Tolman (Taylor and Tolman 1992).

11. See Littleton 1989, p. 27, which suggests that feminists "use as a working hypothesis the assumption that women's descriptions of our experience are accurate, reasonable and potentially understandable *given the conditions under which we live*" (emphasis in original).

12. 450 U.S. 464 (1981).

16

The Politics of Surrogacy Narratives

E. ANN KAPLAN

In their narratives, surrogate mothers (SMs) often announce their motive for becoming such mothers as sisterly desire to help infertile women. Yet in practice, surrogacy becomes the terrain for incredible, even unprecedented, hostility and violence between women. It is this discrepancy between sisterly motives and unsisterly practice that I begin to explore here. Since narratives are always discursively formed, my ultimate aim is to understand what discourses produce the women's stories narrated in popular journals: What audiences do they address? What effect does the context of their publication have on the form of the stories? What economic, political, and other social factors enter in? Important for my purposes is how the melodrama form oversimplifies the actual psychological, political, social, and economic contexts of surrogacy. Women need to find more subtle narrative forms—ones that enable multiple perspectives, ambiguities, contradictions—the yes/but and the no/and/yes possibilities that are crucial as feminisms in the 1990s grapple with difference on new levels.

In section I of this chapter, I first lay bare some of the common structures and repeated themes in women's stories as they illuminate the paradox between sisterly motives and unsisterly practice. Section II provides a detailed analysis of a TV movie and a feminist video about the Mary Beth Whitehead surrogacy case.

I

Sisterly motives abound in popular narratives about surrogacy,[1] and there is a surprising uniformity in the basics of the story, even in the language used. Surrogate mothers discuss their pleasure in giving birth for another woman; they express sympathy for infertile women—wanting to give the gift of a child (Kane 1988, pp. 20–22; Whitehead 1989, p. 7; Markoutsas 1981, pp. 71–72). Some discuss their feeling of fulfillment in having their own children and their desire for other couples to share the same joy. "I felt I was made for having babies" is one formulation. For example, Mary Beth Whitehead represents herself as a woman devoted to being a mother and wanting nothing else in life than bearing and nurturing children. "Being a mother was always how I defined myself," she says. "Surrogacy was a way for me to help someone less fortunate" (Whitehead 1989, p. 89). In this story, surrogate mothering is represented as "a positive, multivocal symbol, pointing to previous barrenness and promised fertility" (Deegan 1987, p. 93). The baby born of a surrogate is seen as both of the flesh and of the law—a member, by contract and law, in a gift-relationship (Turner 1969)—rather than the object of baby-selling on a shameful market, as in some narratives noted later in this chapter. It is seen as a special celebration of birth itself.

Surrogacy, unlike many other reproductive technologies, is an old technology and does not require medical sophistication. This may be part of its appeal: The historical and biblical precedent of Abraham, Sarah, and Hagar, Sarah's handmaiden, is sometimes quoted (e.g., Lacayo and Svoboda 1986; Butzel 1987, p. 7; Neff 1987), especially in stories dealing with women who give birth to a sister's baby. Actual sisters acting as surrogates and adoptive mothers is, significantly, often the most positive context for surrogacy in these narratives. Accompanying one such story are images of the sisters hugging, kissing and crying (King 1986, p. 34). The surrogacy in this case is seen as a "family project" (King 1986, p. 35). When the sister miscarries, it is a trauma. The family accept the loss within the framework, "God never meant me to have a child" (King 1986, p. 36). One sister conceptualizes her surrogacy as "I loaned my sister my body for her baby to grow in—I was merely baby sitting for 9 months" (King 1986, p. 38). The baby is called "my little passenger." In a similar story, the sisterly surrogacy is seen as paying the sister back for all her love and support (Karen Mills 1985, pp. 20–22).

In this story, the stress is on surrogacy as a community and family process, not in the hands of expert services and professionals: All members involved in the process meet and eat ritual foods, even if only coffee and cake, to set the tone for its celebratory aspects. In some cases the artificial insemination is done with a turkey baster, to signify links with Thanksgiving rituals. Insemina-

tion, in other words, becomes another festive occasion, part of the "family album" series of festivities, like Christmas, Grandma's birthday, the Fourth of July.

In another narrative it is literally Thanksgiving Day, and the surrogate mother gives birth alone in the delivery room before the father and adoptive mother arrive (Richards 1989, p. 22). The event is presented as happy, not sad, the surrogate mother as content, grateful. In another case the woman has been a surrogate mother four times and is yearning to be pregnant again. Her own story follows, as if to explain her situation: When sixteen years old, she got pregnant and married, then had two children; when her husband joined a motorcycle gang, she gave the children up for adoption. In this narrative the woman has shown her ability to give up her children and is thus supposedly a good surrogate. Bearing other people's children makes up for the loss of her own.

In yet another story the SM is quoted as saying, "I'll never find a cure for cancer, but I'll always know I've done something important" (Gupta 1989, p. 141). A surrogate husband, a rare voice in these narratives and about whom I would like to know a lot more, says, "I rationalized that it was a medical experiment." ZIFT surrogacy (zygote intrafallopian transfer), in which the baby has no genetic claim to the surrogate mother, is said in the same story to be made possible by God and thus acceptable.[2] In the more complex and still more unusual situation of gamete intrafallopian transfer (GIFT), one woman is described as gloating over her twelve eggs. "She [the recipient] and I were cycling at the same time—it's like being in a war together" (a telling metaphor that in itself betrays the unconscious tension between the women involved). The woman undergoing the transfer is quoted as saying, "I almost didn't care if I had a baby—I just wanted to know what having life inside would feel like."

My second set of popular narratives—those I call "negative"—reveal antitechnology sentiments and dwell on the "unsisterly practices" I already noted. SMs whose experiences turned negative adopt narratives circulating elsewhere in North American culture (often originating in religious or right-wing contexts). One set of negative concepts about surrogacy label it "baby-selling on a shameful market." Other negative surrogacy narratives often conjure up Orwell's *1984* to indicate the negative response. Surrogate reproduction is seen as cold and sterile because it is separated from love and family life (De La Fuente 1989, pp. 118–120). Babies born from frozen embryos are said to be cold the rest of their lives. Typical headlines for these stories are "Brave New Baby" or "Tales from the Baby Factory" (Hopkins 1992). "Baby Farming" is conjured up, especially in relation to Third World women, and the figure of the surrogate mom as human incubator predominates (e.g., J. Murphy 1984; Stanworth 1990).

The language used in these stories reveals an implicit negative judgement, as in the term "womb rental fees." Financial arrangements are highlighted in negative narratives and repressed in the positive ones. Mary Beth Whitehead's $10,000 contract is frequently quoted. Indeed, Mary Beth's 1989 book gathers together negative motifs in earlier stories and sets the stage for more to come: "I have learned," she says, "that the rental of a woman's body for the sale of the child she bears is wrong. It violates the core of what a woman is" (Whitehead 1989, pp. xiv–xv). The practice is often labeled "commercial trading in flesh," and articles assert that governments should outlaw surrogacy and the use of fetuses for medical purposes. If surrogacy is regularized, a class of breeder women would be created (Clapp 1989; J. Murphy 1984)—such as Margaret Atwood envisaged in *A Handmaid's Tale* (Kaplan 1992)—women valued only for their unnatural ability to reject their own flesh and blood. Articles here suggest that childless couples could abandon technological alternatives to give love to troubled young people or could adopt "unadoptable" children of mixed race or those who are older, disabled, or deeply disadvantaged (see diverse perspectives in Montgomery 1988).

Quite often, religious figures are quoted decrying surrogacy: A typical pronouncement is that "[t]he practice is morally unjustifiable, because a third party is introduced into the marriage of two who have become one flesh" (McCormick in Markoutsas 1981, p. 72). Another priest says, "Procreation should not be divorced from the context of marital intimacy by involving a third party." Yet another is quoted as saying to an adoptive surrogacy mother, "Your children have not sinned, but you have. You've used Michael's sperm in another woman's body" (Markoutsas 1981, p. 74)—this despite the biblical precedent regarding Sarah and Hagar noted earlier. That precedent is viewed as the medieval church's tolerance of concubinage to regulate the transmission of property, a practice that is not applicable today (Neff 1987, p. 14).

Unsisterly practices emerge in different narratives or later on in the same narratives, at the point where sisterliness changes to "women at odds." The drama of "women at odds" in the cases where surrogates do not want to keep to the adoption contract dominates the negative surrogacy stories. Such drama was spelled out graphically in Elizabeth Kane's book *Birth Mother* (1988). Kane makes a vivid plea against surrogate motherhood on the grounds of the birth mother's inevitable biological bonding with the baby she carries.

Following Kane and popularized psychological studies, stories in commercial magazines assume automatic bonding of mother and child. Writers stress the wrenching separation of the couple ("Elizabeth" 1983) and dwell on negative psychological results (Grogan 1989, pp. 36–41). Surrogacy is discussed as symbolic adultery, and the jealous competition between surrogate and adoptive mothers is emphasized. Authors lament effects of the process on other children in either family, along with the awesome psychological implications of signing a contract to give a child away.

A case is often made that the surrogate child is different from the adopted child, whose mother wanted it but could not keep it. In surrogacy, the mother goes into the birth process intending to give the child up. Stories highlight how, indeed, some surrogates are making up for past acts, like having an abortion or giving a child up for adoption. (Research shows that 35 percent of a sample of women applying to become surrogate mothers at one time either gave children up for adoption [9 percent] or had had abortions [26 percent] [Guinzburg 1983].[3]) From the perspective of the recipient couple, stories dwell on the psychologically painful, heart-wrenching ordeal of couples who, by "hiring" a surrogate birth mother, are trying to have a child partly sharing their genetic inheritance. Narratives stress the "torture" such couples endure while waiting for their surrogate to be pregnant and the tension suffered during the period of the pregnancy. Legal and ethical issues are sometimes noted in popular stories (e.g., Mingay 1982; McKay 1983; Thom 1988; Malcolm 1988; Chesler 1988), although such issues are largely reserved for formidable, specifically legal literature (e.g., Pateman 1988).

II. Commentary, Discourses

I have always been suspicious of the sisterly pronouncements in my first set of narratives and equally troubled by the polemical, self-righteous tone of the negative narratives. One of the things that makes me suspicious in both kinds of narrative is their lack of attention to the jealousy and competition between the women involved. The positive story is invested in showing only love, sharing, generosity, and self-renunciation between the two women involved. And the negative story, instead of dwelling heavily on the "women at odds" aspect, displaces these emotions into the loftier generalized ones to do with shameful baby-selling or "going against nature."

Clearly, the two kinds of narratives set up a false binary that is inadequate for dealing with the actual psychological, political, scientific, economic, and racial aspects of the increasing surrogacy phenomenon. The multiplicity of positions is lost in the polemical arguments being made in both sets of stories. The amazing *similarity* among the popular stories—the repetition of motifs of the gift, of doing something for infertile couples, of frustration, pain, ultimate joy to the adoptive parents, and so on—from as early as 1983 through 1989 is troubling. It demonstrates one of my points—namely, the limiting impact of narratives and conventions, already culturally in place, on what can be said, and perhaps on what can be experienced in the first place. The surrogacy story—itself heavily reliant on prior mother-constructs—gradually acquires the status of myth, with fixed characters, set verbal exchanges, and similar language and tone. It seems that Mary Beth Whitehead's 1989 book, *A Mother's Story*, articulated the full mythic account, so that more cases did not need citing.

In commenting briefly, let me begin with the glaring *absence* of reference to the economic, class, and race issues in positive surrogacy narratives, since this absence is clearly an important

structuring element. The very fact that money is rarely mentioned in these narratives might lead one to suppose that financial gain (usually $10,000 and all medical and other expenses paid for the surrogate) is the real, repressed motive. When the fee is mentioned, it is as enabling the SM to buy needed things or to pay bills when a husband is laid off; these comments are accompanied by statements that claim the main motive is "to make infertile couples happy" (Gelman and Shapiro 1985). The financial surrogate arrangement may account for the class difference between surrogate and adoptive mothers, so why can this not be more readily mentioned? Presumably, the women need to show higher motives for their surrogacy than financial ones; and perhaps this is a need produced through religious or community values. Once again, Mary Beth Whitehead's story provides the prototype for such feelings and values: "I have always been religious, . . . and I certainly prayed that if I did this for another childless couple, God would reward me by giving my sister a baby" (Whitehead 1989, p. 8). Although the women rarely mention the financial part of the contract, I do not assume conscious duplicity. My future research will aim to discover, through interviews and other strategies, what prevents women from mentioning finances.

Something more complex, psychologically and socially, is at stake than emerges from either women's stories or my cynical questions. First, it is important that most of the surrogate mothers seem to be white and lower-middle-class, adoptive ones *apparently* white and middle-class, with the rare exception of Anna Johnson, a black surrogate mother involved in a custodial suit with the white biological parents ("Psychiatrist Testifies" 1990; "Surrogate Mother Sues" 1990). Research on profiles of surrogate mothers is difficult because such profiles are hard to obtain, although in future research I will find what demographies I can. Few narratives talk about either class or race, but the surrogate or recipient mothers touted in the media are rarely minority women.[4]

Also intriguing in narratives is why SMs do not anticipate their heart-wrenching separation from the child or realize that they may desire to keep the child, despite their having had other children. Why does the adoptive mother also not anticipate such a struggle on the SM's part? Increasing desire to keep the child produces the unsisterly practices—the hostility and the violence on both women's parts. Surrogates suddenly, and violently, declare they want to keep the child they have just birthed, while the adoptive mother—having anticipated having the child for nine months—equally violently demands that the child be handed over. It is as if the surrogates and adoptive mothers have started a story whose ending they have forgotten, or as if they step into positions of women-fighting-women so common in film melodrama and TV soaps, as I will suggest later in this chapter. Clearly, neither woman is self-consciously aware of the discursive forces shaping their experiences and of how their stories are linked. Indeed, the SM's violent desire to *keep* the child may be provoked precisely by the adoptive mother's urgent desire to *claim* the child. A symbiotic process may be at work.

I have wondered at my skepticism about the sisterly narratives I began with: Is it really so impossible for one woman to want to do something as disruptive of her own life as bearing and giving birth to a baby for another woman? What does sisterliness of these dimensions really mean? Perhaps I am missing something about what childbirth actually means to many women and simply do not understand the discursive frameworks within which surrogate mothers live: After all, having children is the main or only identity and/or life preoccupation for many women. It is possible that really being able to contribute in a way conceived of as analogous to making scientific discoveries (as one narrator suggested) could motivate women.

But it is also possible that the decision to become surrogates is partly produced through media stories still stressing the self-sacrificial mother; such stories image self-sacrifice as what mothering is all about! The idealized self-sacrifice function has become harder and harder to fulfill, given modern household devices and the new entry of fathers into domestic chores and even child-rearing, so women are possibly reaching for ways to perform it. But desire for this function wills into existence its binary opposite: the jealous, competitive mother, who wants to possess the child. Surrogacy provides a unique situation where these two mothers merge—or where each woman finds herself alternately the "angelic" mother and the evil "witch" mother. The visual fictions to be discussed in the next section will, I hope, make clear how "sisterly motives" quickly turn into "unsisterly practice."

III. The Miniseries and Rosler's *Born to Be Sold*

The traditional angel/witch mother figures in Western culture are obviously reworked in the metaphors and allusions in some stories I have already outlined. But one can isolate two main, linked strands through which this discursive mother-formation arrives back in surrogacy narratives. A possible religious formation for the sisterliness (the angelic paradigm) may be found in the way some narrators refer to "God"; others imply religious discourse by referring to the "gift" or by generating rituals as part of the surrogacy project. Is it possible that select forms of Christian fundamentalism partly produce the sisterly discourse and apparent genuine emotions that go with it? Could the biblical precedent put surrogacy in an entirely different category than other technologies?

The second formation, which has implications for the "women at odds" paradigm, seems more obvious to me: Many of the stories I have already outlined are close to the material of melodrama and soap opera, as I noted earlier and as Linda Gordon once pointed out.[5] In order to explore this formation, I discuss two divergent, deliberately fictional (as against apparently autobiographical) examples of the best-known surrogacy narrative, that of Mary Beth Whitehead, to see how the melodrama "genre" may be differently constitutive in both cases. I may then be in a position to return to the opening supposedly "factual" narratives in order to assess how far they too have been shaped by prior nineteenth- and twentieth-century literary narratives long in popular circulation through fiction, film, and television.

The ABC commercial narrative represented in the TV mini-series *Baby* M focuses most on the problem of *giving up the child*, which causes rivalry between the mothers: "Women at odds," then, forms the traumatic theme of the surrogacy story. It is here that the story links up with nineteenth-century stage, and then film, melodrama. The adulterous mother in such nineteenth-century narratives is punished by having to give up her children. Such narratives (Wood, *East Lynne* 1984/1861 is a well-known model; see Kaplan 1992) dwell on the painful separation from the children—the years-long yearnings for them in exile, the tears over their loss, the poverty the mother succumbs to, her guilt. This convention regarding mothers and children seems to be what the surrogacy situation evokes in the commercial stories.

The miniseries follows the old classical Hollywood melodrama realism that TV soaps have adopted. It claims to be a window on the world, on reality, and conceals its processes of selecting which images to show and which to ignore and the illusory constructions at play. The series attempts to get viewers to identify with the characters as with historical people, and even, in the *Baby M* case, names the characters by those of their real-life equivalents. What is of interest in this connection is exactly what identifications the miniseries solicits and what repressed perspectives are able to emerge unaware.

As I already noted, the TV miniseries genre is always ultimately *melodrama:* That is, it is a film about the domestic sphere, dealing with families, children, and conflicts within this terrain. The genre potentially has both liberatory and regressive aspects; some of the latter include limits on what can be said and what is excluded. But unconscious desires are often at work, and the genre may provide a space for articulation of what cannot be *said*, what has to be repressed but is conveyed implicitly in the drama (Gledhill 1987b).

The first episode of the *Baby M* miniseries opens with revealing title shots taken from the whole series. These isolate the most dramatic parts of the narrative—the most sensational— and they stress the fictional Bill Stern's bonding to the child. Arguably, the title shots show what is *self-consciously* at stake for the makers of the series, which is not the same as what ultimately is communicated.

The women at odds (or the women-to-be-at-odds) are established in deliberately contrasting ways in the opening sequences through careful selection of clothes, body language, physical location—signs that convey culturally loaded meanings. Betsy Stern (*Dr.* Stern, as well, professionally) is represented as stiff, proper, professional, well-dressed, and in control of her emotions. Early scenes assert that Dr. Stern could not have a child, and, despite her emotional control, make clear how upset she is about this inability.

Second, the motivation for Bill Stern's desire for a biological, not adopted, child is stressed by focus on the loss of his mother and his being "all alone." Stern's Jewishness is focused on at some length, perhaps to underscore his need for heritage. Male figures are usually remote authorities or lovers in the melodrama convention, but in this case both males show the impact of 1970s women's movements and see themselves as quite involved with domestic life. But this is especially so for the middle-class Mr. Stern.

The first image of Mary Beth Whitehead contrasts loudly with that of Betsy Stern. Again, stereotypical class signs predominate: Mary Beth is shown in an unattractive manner lying in bed, eating chocolates (sign of decadence, boredom?), watching TV in the afternoon. It is while watching TV that she hears about a surrogacy case, and this gives her the idea of becoming a surrogate— something mentioned frequently in the women's popularized narratives. The following scene, in which she persuades her husband, is the only one in which money is mentioned (and then it's the last thing, an aside). Her main weapon is sex, and again this seems to be a class sign: Betsy's "virgin" to Mary Beth's "whore," in a return to melodrama's weary female types.

Indications of Mary Beth's unreliability—the whore is always unreliable!—mesh with her sexual seductiveness. Mary Beth wears the wrong color suit to the restaurant (she changes her mind at the last moment, prefiguring her change of mind about the baby); and she is seen to be inappropriate in bringing her child, Tuesday, to an insemination session. The film seems to favor Bill's response that this is not right. In the car, Mary Beth has loud rock music playing, and the structure of the scene invites the spectator to identify with Bill Stern's dislike and disapproval of this music.

The miniseries, then, all but puts Betsy and MaryBeth into the old, classic virgin/whore binary in terms of body types and emotional valence. Mary Beth is flirtatious with William Stern, fun-loving, and emotional, while Betsy is stiff, unsexy, and emotionally controlled. Betsy has fair hair, Mary Beth dark black hair. Mary Beth is plump and well-contoured, Betsy thin and plain.

Narratively, Mary Beth becomes the witch when she is frustrated and when she wants her own way. Within dominant gender codes, violent emotion in women still connotes inability to function in the public sphere—irresponsibility, unreliability. Within the miniseries discourse, where motherhood is now part of a legal contract, a hired job, this turns into unreliability as wife and mother. The discourse assumes old notions—namely, that the mother is to be the calm, transcendent presence over the emotional turmoils of the children and then to succor and nurture her husband on his return from the brutal battles of the public sphere. But in neither case is she herself allowed to be emotionally out of control.

Paradoxically, then, Betsy, the career woman, also exemplifies the best emotional life for motherhood. She wins in terms of both class and emotional timbre. Presumably because William Stern is such a devoted father, Betsy's career is not seen to render her an inadequate mother. Indeed, given that she is a pediatrician, it may actually help!

But while the miniseries apparently upholds Betsy as the best mother, some aspects of Mary Beth's own account reappear in the somewhat ambivalent depiction of Betsy. In telling her own story in the ghostwritten book, Mary Beth depicted Betsy as cold, unfeeling, and selfish—the 1950s Hollywood stereotype of the career woman. Does the miniseries unconsciously collude in a sort of critique of the yuppie Stern couple? Certainly, the scene when Betsy finds Mary Beth's dog distasteful could be cited as one critiquing middle-class uptightness and inability to let go and have fun, in contrast to the loose, pleasure-loving working-class family. William's middle-classness is stressed at the beginning in the scenes of his Jewish father's funeral, which highlight his being the last male in his family: Interestingly, however, there seems something too pretty about William from the start, something too stereotypically WASP about Betsy Stern. A subtle critique underlies their representations.

The high-strung emotionality of women at odds predominates in the mini-series once the baby is born and it is clear that Mary Beth will not relinquish her. Mary Beth becomes more and more hysterical, wild and unreasonable, Betsy more and more despondent, depressed, silent, tortured. Their intense rivalry, competition, and even hatred overrides any consideration for each other, let alone for the child. William Stern, and to some degree Rick, Mary Beth's husband, show a degree of ability to distance themselves, but for the most part the series portrays the two women as locked in an intense competition to win the

baby from each other. The baby is reduced to a "thing," standing in for all loss, absence, desire—the breast, the phallus. At some point, this raw female emotion gets out of control and the authorities move in: the police, social agencies, and finally the Father, the law. Hysteria and jealous rivalry are now mitigated through, or displaced into, the series of institutions the women have to move through in order to win each one's desire: the baby-breast-phallus.

While I have put psychoanalytic labels on the women's desire in an effort to understand its intensity, the text itself, of course, does not produce concepts for understanding the intensity of the jealous female rivalry over the baby. Such jealous rivalry in traditional melodramas is usually over the male lover: Think of Bette Davis in *Jezebel*, Vivien Leigh in *Gone with the Wind*, or Olivia de Havilland in *The Heiress*, competing to the death for their man. The similarities in the structure of the jealous competition in stories about male lovers and now about babies is significant and invites psychoanalytic explanations.[6]

Ultimately, the miniseries is more complex than some of the surface details—the surface semiotics—I have noted might make it seem. In line with feminist film critics' theorizing that melodrama is a form that can permit articulation of complex emotional dilemmas and of conflicts culture does not want to address, the miniseries does represent a range of positionalities vis-à-vis surrogacy: It allows viewers to experience the kinds of complications that arise within a given culture, like that of contemporary America. While one can read the images of Betsy and Mary Beth as falling into conventional witch/angel polarities, the narrative does not automatically favor one of the women over the other, as traditional melodramas may do. The varying depictions of the women, and the varying positions spectators are invited to occupy throughout the drama, enable the kind of complexity that results from multiple perspectives.

Ironically, such complexity is less evident in Martha Rosler's *Born to Be Sold: Martha Rosler Reads the Strange Case of Baby S/M*. The video is produced in the alternate sphere, outside the obvious constraints of commercial institutions like Hollywood and commercial TV. Nevertheless, its genre and context of production offer different kinds of constraint: The video is asked to be explicitly didactic, since that is the mission of

Paper Tiger TV. In these videos an expert typically "reads" a media text from a specific, polemical position.

In this case, Rosler "reads" the Mary Beth miniseries. And in so doing she in a way puts herself under yet another constraint—namely, that of responding within the forms that the miniseries first set forth. Rosler's unconventional aesthetic form is determined by the desire to break the conventional realist codes of the commercial series. She does this by inserting herself as speaker in the text, first by reading a paper on camera and then by using her own body, in various dress-up disguises, to image forth the various characters of the melodrama she is deconstructing—Mary Beth, Melissa/Sara, Betsy Stern, William Stern's sperm, doctors, the judge in the case, and so on. She also uses a familiar "collage" technique, inserting clips from Hollywood films and TV news programs to make her polemical points.

For instance, she stages scenes from a Hollywood film about adoption, *Lucky Junior*, which would fit into my first set of "positive" surrogacy stories even though the baby was not "commissioned" or genetically linked. It is used by Rosler to bolster her point that dominant culture demands that lower-class women serve middle-class ones by producing babies for them.

But most of the time, Rosler comments on the TV miniseries. Hers is not a video *about the actual case*, as was suggested in at least one reading (Turim 1991). The figures Rosler acts out are meant to mimic not the historical people but the miniseries versions of those people. The specificities of the clothes and hairstyles mimic those in the miniseries, not the historical figures.

As in agit-prop street theater, Rosler acts out the various key moments in the miniseries melodrama using minimal props and comic, deliberate exaggeration.[7] With no attempt at verisimilitude, Rosler's body, dressed as a character, is usually sitting in a room with wall paintings behind it. Rosler presents a didactic (classical) class analysis of the case and critiques the media as "bourgeois" for supporting the middle-class Sterns all along. ABC miniseries images are repeated in the background in order to prove the case about dominant media that Rosler is making. This direct camera address by the filmmaker avoids any attempt to hide the video's production or its producer.

In this way Rosler's piece breaks the realist illusion of commercial melodramas and makes impossible a viewer's identification with any of the characters as such. In place of the multiple and alternating identifications of the miniseries, the spectator is lectured to even more deliberately than in most Brecht plays. Basically, Rosler's is a radical feminist reading of the case. Turim points out that there is no discussion of the baby as baby anywhere in the video. And while this is true, it may miss the point that Rosler was reading a particular representation of the Whitehead case (the miniseries), not the case itself or the historical figures. The miniseries also ignored the baby and thus did not open a space for attention to this.

There is more strength in Turim's second point—namely, that while the video means to mark feminist consciousness regarding the solidarity of women, it in fact reinforces separation in its simplistic class denunciation of Betsy Stern. For Turim, Rosler wants to show solidarity with the working-class Mary Beth, but at the expense of differently positioned women. The only good women are the lower-class women, Turim notes.

One thing this comment ignores is the power differential between the Sterns and Mary Beth, which Rosler emphasizes. It also ignores Rosler's important focus on the coercive force of capitalist institutions. Turim infers that there can be "solidarity" between women despite the imbalances of class and race, which is doubtful. I am sympathetic to Rosler's class analysis but concerned that the video makes the infertile woman the brunt of ridicule in a simplistic reduction of the complexity of things—a complexity that, ironically, *is* indicated in the commercial text via its use of the melodrama form. As I already noted, the melodrama form leaves space for what cannot normally be said, for expression of emotions male culture normally excludes.

The difference, then, is not surprising: In a polemical critique of the miniseries, Rosler's video reverses the stereotypes and does not attempt to move beyond them. It corrects the commercial fiction's inability to critique class relations and its reduction of all to the level of the individual. But the video in turn repeats the anti-career-woman stance evident in Mary Beth's account (Kaplan 1992), which is, paradoxically, close to right-wing positions.

Further, in inserting the *Lucky Junior* clips, is Rosler using antiadoption arguments to make the case against surrogacy? This is certainly how Cassidy, Mary Beth Whitehead's lawyer, presented the case against the Sterns; she argued for the harmful effects of adoption on the adoptee. As much as the miniseries, the video ironically sides with the stance that the birth mother will "naturally" want to keep her baby, as if biological urges are paramount and cannot be transcended. As Turim points out, prohibition of either surrogacy or abortion relies on a repressive idea of the pregnant woman's body and on legitimating state control over these bodies (Turim 1991).

Finally, the video runs the danger of reflecting antimedicine perspectives that too easily degenerate into antitechnology stances. Such stances assume there is an unmediated "nature," that "biology" is discursively neutral. The antimelodrama narrative is, in these ways, still constituted by melodrama forms.

Rosler's video does make important points about class privilege and the imbalance between those able to buy surrogacy and those willing to provide it. Such discussions are completely avoided in popular and commercial materials. But a major problem in the video is the concept of the central speaking subject—Rosler herself—on which the video relies and which is not problematized or questioned at all. In this sense, Born to Be Sold is a modernist work, not a postmodernist work. It does not argue for the plurality of voices that feminists are currently looking for and that some feminist texts try to produce. However, postmodernism may function at the expense of a class analysis that is needed and too often lacking.

IV. Conclusions

The two films I discussed were both made shortly after the Mary Beth Whitehead case and in direct relation to that case. I offer them as diverse examples of how the Whitehead case was used to make imaginary productions and how it figured in different kinds of imaginations, different fiction-making processes. The different meanings the different textual strategies produce are significant: Martha Rosler's deliberately provocative, didactic video on the miniseries and other media treatments of the case, made from a classical Marxist perspective, critiques dominant media treatment of the case. It does this by focusing

on representations of Mary Beth versus the Sterns from a theory of working-class versus bourgeois relations. It also usefully critiques the medical establishment, though sometimes in ways now quite predictable and problematic.

Meanwhile, the realist, illusionist style of the TV miniseries represses attention to class or values of any kind, while in fact adhering to dominant discourses about class, race, and "family values" that are still central in U.S. culture. These in turn structure how surrogate mothering is conceptualized. The unavoidable genre of melodrama that constructs the Baby M commercial production in turn governs how the two women are categorized and the type of drama that is shown.

Nevertheless, paradoxically, it is the melodrama genre that permits expression of the emotions of jealousy, envy, hate, spite, and even violence and aggression between women that often dominate people's daily lives. These are passions that childbirth and mothering elicit for many women and that rarely find public expression or validation. Such emotions then press for release in sensationalized melodrama modes. However, there is a complex circular process at work, such that *the traditions of the melodrama, brought into existence by the repression of violence between women in the culture, then paradoxically construct or shape the form that women's stories take, including sisterliness becoming unsisterly.* The genre may be constitutive of the experience as much as the reverse, as I noted at the outset. Women need to produce narrative forms that will make possible the writing of different stories and a different experiencing of their lives, their characters, and the characters of other women. Such a plurality of stories, positions, personalities will open up more complex, nuanced, nonbinary possibilities— possibilities that are crucial as feminisms enter the 1990s and attempt to grapple with difference on new levels.

Notes

This chapter is a revised version of my essay in *Feminist Nightmares: Women at Odds: Feminism and the Problem of Sisterhood,* edited by Susan Ostrov Weisser and Jennifer Fleishner (New York University Press, 1994).

1. Research is still in progress, and the results of what I have been able to do are therefore tentative. I selected popular articles listed under the heading "Sur-

rogacy" in the Reader's Guide to Periodical Literature throughout the 1980s. Materials quoted came from many magazines, including *Redbook, Good Housekeeping, Women's World*, and so on. In addition, I looked at about twenty books about surrogacy, ranging from those aimed at quite a broad market to those more highly specialized, addressing legal or medical experts.

2. In future work I will want to explore both the framing contexts of "medicine" and "God" that speakers construct to legitimize surrogacy. The equivalence or nonequivalence of these frames themselves is an important question.

3. The correlation of self-selection for surrogacy if a woman has had an abortion or given up a child for adoption is significant and will be pursued in my future research about surrogacy.

4. Indeed, minority women and reproductive technologies seem a taboo subject; this is why the film *Made in America* was so interesting. The heroine of this film, played by Whoopi Goldberg, has conceived her daughter by artificial insemination. The plot relies on the consequences of the daughter finding out that she was conceived through AI, and that her father was apparently white, for its comic effects.

5. However, Gordon was complaining about what she called "the soap-opera approach to surrogacy" and to the fact that this approach has obscured the politics and the litigation. I believe she had in mind more the media accounts than the SMs' actual narratives. Here I am more interested in how the availability of a form like melodrama in itself conditions the forms in which women think their lives and tell their stories. The genre may be constitutive of the experience as much as the other way around.

It is also hard to determine how far the end products in the media accounts were themselves the products of editors and reporters, who may themselves have turned what women said into familiar melodrama forms for marketing reasons. One would need to do extensive interviewing to see how women articulate experiences, but even the process of "telling to another" (the interviewer) may automatically stimulate women to "perform" the melodrama; that is, a woman may become a self-conscious "actor" in the process of the "telling" situation.

6. A full exploration of the similar structures of these "women at odds" jealousies will be taken up in the longer project.

7. I was most reminded of the agit-prop techniques in a little-known early British feminist film, *The Amazing Equal Pay Show*, which Rosler may well have had in mind. This film, however, did mimic actual historical political figures and was not a reading of a commercial text, as Rosler's piece is.

17

"Bad Mothers" and Welfare Reform in Massachusetts

The Case of Claribel Ventura

MARIE ASHE

In February 1994, in Boston, six young children were removed, by police action, from the custody of their mother, Claribel Ventura. Their removal and the apparent circumstances of their lives immediately became the subject of intensive media coverage.

While the past two decades have been marked by increased public awareness of what is called "child abuse" (Ashe and Cahn 1993; L. Gordon 1988), most legal cases concerning that reality do not receive intensive media coverage. Some do. Claribel Ventura's is one such case. The story of Claribel Ventura—the public story—began to be told on February 13, 1994. On that date, *The Boston Globe* reported the previous day's visit, by members of the Boston Police Department, to the apartment in the publicly subsidized housing project in Boston's Mission Hill section in which Claribel Ventura and her children had at that time been residing for approximately three weeks. The early newspaper accounts reported a police description of the condition of Ventura's home as "trash-filled" (Hutchinson 1994a), its floors

"strewn with human feces" (Vaznis 1994a) and "littered" with beer bottles (Vaznis 1994b).

The February 12 police visit was made in response to a request of Department of Social Services (DSS) workers who had themselves visited the apartment in response to an anonymous call. In complex intertextuality, the *Globe* account of February 14, 1994, provided a preliminary location of Claribel Ventura, siting her by reference to a contemporaneously reported social reality. The *Globe* quoted police officers as reporting that their "findings" in the apartment "reminded them" of (media reports of) a situation that Chicago police had several days earlier reported discovering in the course of investigating a West Side Chicago housing project in which nineteen children had been found "living in squalor" (McMahon and Kuczka 1994).

The *Globe* characterized or identified Ventura herself as a twenty-six-year-old "single mother" of six children; as four months pregnant with her seventh child; as having borne children by four different men; as expecting a child by perhaps an additional different man; and as likely addicted to crack (Sennott and Grunwald 1994). Each of these attributes marked her as clearly "excessive" (Fineman 1991b; Fineman 1995; D. Roberts 1991). Each of them, irrespective of the wellness or illness of her children, marked Claribel Ventura as a woman whose privacy and family life were properly more subject to state regulation than are those of more mainstream women and of men (Fineman 1991b, 1995).

Beyond that, the first *Globe* stories, like the first stories in the *Boston Herald,* summoned a response of horror by their accounts of what might be called failures of "abjection"—failures to maintain proper boundaries between what should be perceived as properly human and what should not.[1] The conditions of the Ventura home were defined by the news accounts as beyond the margins of what might be considered humanly habitable. In the language of the news media, the human bodily markers of abjection—identified as "human feces," as "urine," and as "blood"—were reported to have been present in uncertain quantity and in vaguely defined but clearly improper locations within the home.[2]

References to these body products would recur in later and developing accounts of the Ventura story. The most consistent figure in the stories, however, one that presented itself in the first reports and persistently recurred, was that of a powerfully significant body part—an image of human hands. The initial news reports recited that what police officers found most shocking was the condition of the hands of Claribel Ventura's four-year-old son, Ernesto. The child's hands were described as burned "almost 'to the bone'" (Vaznis 1994b). Ernesto was described as having been discovered "wincing in pain," "behind a locked bedroom door," "nursing scalded hands" (Hutchinson 1994a).

Police arrested Claribel Ventura and transported Ernesto to Boston's Children's Hospital, where he was admitted for treatment of his hands. Police also transported Claribel Ventura's other five children, aged nine months to seven years, to the hospital. Those children underwent medical examination at Children's Hospital and were then entrusted to the state's Department of Human Services (Vaznis 1994a, 1994b).[3]

Authorities of the Boston Police Department and of DSS, the news media reported, believed that the burns on Ernesto's hands had been in-

tentionally inflicted by his mother. They believed that two or more weeks prior to her arrest, Claribel Ventura had gotten angry with her son and punished him by dunking his hands into boiling water. "We're sure it wasn't self-inflicted," said one Boston police sergeant. "It took a second party to take this child's hands, plunge them into this liquid, and hold them there. He is virtually burned down to the bone" (Hutchinson 1994a). "To burn a child to this extent and then lock them in a room without care for two or three weeks, it's beyond comprehension," said one police officer (Hutchinson 1994a). Like the condition of her home, the nature of Claribel Ventura's alleged act was defined as "beyond."

Immediately following her arrest, police reported that Claribel Ventura would be arraigned in the Roxbury District Court on February 14, 1994, on charges of child abuse, mayhem, and assault with a deadly weapon—a boiling liquid (Vaznis 1994b).

Claribel Ventura's own public appearance occurred in court on February 14, and her photograph was featured in both Boston newspapers on the following day. She is pictured on the *Herald*'s front page in a black-and-white close-up shot. Foregrounded in the photo is Claribel Ventura's balled-up left hand, against which she has rested her chin. Part of her mouth and the lower section of her face are concealed behind that hand. The hand punctuates a place at which two wooden planes meet with an upright, defining a corner of what must be a courtroom bench or bar giving depth and dimension to the photo. In its folded attitude that hand marks a transitional area between the hard, straight solidity of wooden surfaces and the curve of Ventura's forearm, the complexity of the differently lined portion of her face which we are able to see: the heavy eyelids, the dark brow, the lashes matted by mascara or by tears. Tracings (of flowers, perhaps) pattern the visible sections of the blouse or dress covering her shoulders. The photo caption notes: "Mission Hill mom Clarabel [*sic*] Ventura trembles as she stares out at the proceedings. . . . Ventura pleaded innocent" ("Welfare Gone Wrong" 1994, p. 1).

Reporter Margery Eagan opened her *Herald* account of the arraignment with a focus on Claribel Ventura's hands. In her first sentence, appearing just beneath the photo, she characterizes them as "spindly." The word invites our eyes to

FIGURE 1. Clarabel Ventura. Photograph © George Martell/*Boston Herald*. Reprinted with permission of the *Boston Herald*.

return to the photo, invites us to imagine how the depicted hand might look if it were opened up. "Claribel Ventura's spindly hands shook so badly yesterday," wrote Eagan (1994a), "you could hear from across the courtroom the rattling of the documents she held before her, or tried to." Eagan's story, like others appearing in the same issue of the *Herald*, reiterated the account of the police findings, the story of Ernesto's hands. They referred to Claribel Ventura, variously, as a woman accused of "boiling her four-year old-son's hands" (Hutchinson 1994b) or as a woman accused of "boiling her child" (Eagan 1994a). The stories reiterated the earlier characterizations of Claribel Ventura as a kind of absolute "other," an extreme manifestation of the already-other figure of the "bad mother," an incomprehensibly sadistic woman.

The stories of the arraignment recorded the response of the legal system to Claribel Ventura through the performance of the district court judge. They characterized the judge as properly maintaining decorum while at the same time demonstrating understandably extreme emotion

that threatened to break through his surface of moderation. The stories note that the judge "barely concealed his anger" while Ventura "wept and trembled" before him (Sennott 1994a). They reported the judge's instruction and admonition to Ventura: "You are to have no contact with any of your children. . . . And you are to stay 200 yards away from each of these children. Do you know how long 200 yards is? It is two football fields. That means that in the city you cannot see a person that far away. That means if any of your children can see you, you have violated the order and you could be locked up for sixty days" (Sennott 1994a).

Reports noted other facts: that there had been no finding suggesting any abuse of Ventura's children other than Ernesto; that those children had been placed into foster care; and that Ventura's lawyer described her as a "loving mother." "We pled not guilty," said the attorney. "That should tell you what we think of the charges" (Sennott 1994a).

While the news accounts initially represented Claribel Ventura through the reported perceptions of police and judicial representatives of the law, they constructed her as a kind of ahistoric manifestation of the "bad mother."[4] Immediately thereafter, however, the press media began to construct its own particularly historicized figure of Claribel Ventura as a certain kind of Everywoman—specifically, as every mother on welfare. Thus, the stories of Claribel Ventura's arraignment were topped by a prominent headline that read "Welfare Gone Wrong" ("Welfare Gone Wrong" 1994, p. 1). The construction of a strong relationship between the injury to Ernesto and Claribel Ventura's welfare status was accomplished through statements by representatives of the state's human services agencies and by state government officials.

The initial reporting about Claribel Ventura's situation immediately evoked a response from the State of Massachusetts's Department of Human Services assuring the public that the department bore no responsibility for the injuries to the child because supervision of Claribel Ventura's family had been made the task of a private agency, La Alianza Hispana, with which DSS had contracted for the delivery of services to Spanish-speaking clients (Armstrong 1994a). Officers of the Department of Human Services indicated that they would immediately seek to sever their contract with Alianza Hispana because of its failure to prevent the injuries that had occurred (Wong and Armstrong 1994; Estes and Hutchinson 1994a). Spokespersons for Alianza Hispana quickly responded, asserting that they had properly handled the Ventura matter and that they would contest any effort to sever their contract with the State of Massachusetts (Armstrong 1994b; Estes and Hutchinson 1994b).

The reporting of the Ventura situation evoked responses from state executive and legislative officials as well as from the agencies involved with supervising "child welfare." Massachusetts's Republican governor, William Weld, called for specific reforms to the state's welfare programs, urging "a more coercive, rather than a less coercive government attitude" (Aucoin 1994), recommending a very strict "workfare" plan and suggesting that had that reform been in place it would have prevented the occurrence of the injuries to Claribel Ventura's young child (Aucoin 1994).[5] At the same time, leaders of the state Democratic Party called for a different welfare reform—a variation of the "workfare" proposal—

which, they insisted, would have prevented the harm (Aucoin 1994).[6] Taken for granted by representatives of both political parties was the reality of a relationship between the child's injuries and his mother's welfare status. All asserted that welfare reform plans, had they been implemented, might have kept Claribel Ventura from abusing her child by "breaking the cycle of intergenerational welfare dependency into which she had fallen" (Aucoin 1994). One state legislator said, regarding Claribel Ventura, "She is a result of a failed system" (Aucoin 1994).[7]

On Sunday, February 20, 1994, after both the governor and the legislators had already spoken of Claribel Ventura, the *Boston Globe* featured a three-page story, commencing on page 1, which reported on the lives and the status with regard to "public benefits" of each member of Claribel Ventura's "three-generations-on-Welfare" family (Sennott 1994c).

The article reported that Claribel Ventura's mother, Eulalia Rivera, had come from Puerto Rico to Boston in 1968; that she had raised seventeen children on welfare; and that fourteen of those seventeen were presently either welfare recipients or recipients of other public benefits programs. Reporters recounted interviews with various siblings of Claribel Ventura. The strong theme of the report (echoing an old principle of Justice Holmes, perhaps) was that "three generations are enough."[8] The implication of the story was not only that being part of a three-generation welfare family is bad for the family members but also that it is bad for "us." "I think people are just fed up," one legislator was reported to have said, explaining his support of a legislative move that would "cut off welfare benefits to most recipients after two years" (Sennott 1994c).[9] Reporters calculated the monies disbursed to Eulalia Rivera's family members from public coffers during the period from 1969, when she first received welfare benefits, to the present. Of the payments of AFDC benefits, the article suggested that "people" are angry about the cost of welfare because AFDC is paid to women to permit their taking care of children, and people don't like "the way these children are being raised" (Sennott 1994c). The article suggested that not only is the public not getting its money's worth in high-quality child care from welfare mothers; it is also being simply bilked. In this regard, the reporter focused on the hands of Claribel Ventura's brother, Juan, reporting that Juan had demonstrated his trembling hands as an indicator of the "nervous condition" that enabled him to receive SSI benefits (Sennott 1994c). The clear implication of the story was that Juan was a malingerer and that the anger of people concerned about "bad mothers" receiving AFDC benefits ought to flow as well toward obviously fraudulent Social Security disability benefits claimants, each category strikingly represented in the Ventura/Rivera families.

In little more than a week's time, the Claribel Ventura story had developed from one about a single, extraordinarily aberrant "bad mother" to one about welfare dependency. This development occurred despite the fact that the state Department of Social Services reported to the *Boston Globe* staff that an examination of its files relating to the *entire* Rivera family (including Claribel Ventura's mother and all her siblings) disclosed "no other instances of child abuse or active investigations into abuse allegations" (Sennott 1994c).

As conservative critics of welfare have frequently pointed out, the system of providing benefits to families through the AFDC program was a Great Society measure intended to assure that the poor should receive (from "us") "a hand and not a handout" (Murray 1984, pp. 22–23; Murray 1988). This theme was quickly developed in Massachusetts by legislators speaking immediately after the appearance of the February 20 Sunday *Globe* account. Within a few days Governor Weld spoke again about the Claribel Ventura matter, indicating that he intended to send copies of the *Globe* story to all Massachusetts state lawmakers. If the ordinary reader's horror was evoked by the details of squalor in the lives of the Ventura children, Weld's horror attached to something more abstract. Demonstrating the attachment of the "power of abjection" to the abstract as well as to the bodily, it was the "pattern of welfare dependency outlined in the [Sunday *Globe*] story" that the governor found "absolutely horrifying" (Aucoin and Lehigh 1994). Weld commented on Claribel Ventura's brother-with-the-trembling-hands: "And the nervous condition, that's very bad business" (Aucoin and Lehigh 1994).

Weld was reported to have acknowledged that the Riveras are "not a typical family." He was reported to have indicated his belief that a "typi-cal family" would be "a single white woman with less than two kids with a short stay on welfare" (Aucoin and Lehigh 1994).[10] In spite of apparently recognizing that the Rivera family represented a "statistical aberration" (Aucoin and Lehigh 1994; Sennott 1994c), Weld noted that the Rivera family presented "an absolutely horrifying statistic" (Aucoin and Lehigh 1994). Despite the nonrepresentative nature of the family, Weld predicted that national columnists may "grab hold" of the Rivera story. Indeed, he indicated that in spite of his own recognition that the Rivera situation was not representative, he had himself discussed the Sunday *Globe* story with William Bennett on the day after it first appeared. And irrespective of his own recognition and, presumably, William Bennett's recognition that the situation was unrepresentative, Weld commented: "Bennett started to foam at the mouth, because it's exactly what he's talking about" (Aucoin and Lehigh 1994).

The media coverage reported only very briefly on Claribel Ventura's own account of the events that culminated in her son's injuries. No direct interview of Claribel Ventura was reported in either the *Globe* or the *Herald*. A brief, hearsay account was offered on the day of Ventura's arrest; it noted that she had told police that the injuries to the child were caused by hot water while he was washing his hands (Vaznis 1994b). The brevity of reports on Claribel Ventura's self-accounts was paralleled by the brevity of reports on her child's explanation. The *Globe* reported; "Authorities said that while being transported by ambulance to the hospital Sunday night from the Mission Hill Extension Housing Development, Ernesto told the attendants that his mother had burned his hands because she was mad at him" (Vaznis 1994b).

While Claribel Ventura did not make use of the media for any form of direct self-disclosure, many others spoke about her, claiming to know not only the truth concerning her actions but also the motivations and circumstances that would account for those actions.

Media accounts in the days following her arrest included reports by various of Ventura's former neighbors. Some comments suggested that Ventura was addicted to crack cocaine; others suggested that she had been the victim of a violent live-in boyfriend (Sennott and Grunwald 1994). Like the stories of news reporters, the stories of neighbors were offered as objective accounts about currently recognizable figures: the "crack addict" and the "battered woman." Each of these figures has become highly codified in the media and in the public consciousness in recent years. Attachment of either code-identification to an individual woman entails the attachment of particular implications concerning her past and expectations concerning her future.[11]

Another kind of report—one claiming less "objectivity" but no less generality—appeared in the remarks of Angela Paris reported in the *Boston Herald* on February 17, 1994. Angela Paris is depicted in that issue in a news photo accompanying an interview-story by Margery Eagan. She is shown sitting in the company of her three children. She appears to be distributing food to two of the children; a third somersaults in the background, under her indulgent eye. Eagan's story supporting workfare reforms is interspersed with the first-person narrative of Angela Paris. In her narrative Paris expresses a knowledge, a recognition of Claribel Ventura, based on her reading of the news accounts of the Ventura story. Eagan reports Paris as saying, "That could've been me. . . . I was there once. I know what she went through."

Asserting a recognition of Claribel Ventura based on her likeness, on a commonality of experience, Angela Paris speaks, according to Eagan, of her experiences with her own children: "I've hit my kids and locked them in the bedroom and told them to 'get outta' here! When I was on crack, trying to get high, they'd come to me every five minutes, 'Mommy this,' 'Mommy that,'" said Paris, going on to describe the neglect of her children that accompanied her addiction to crack cocaine. Speaking positively in support of Eagan's workfare recommendations, Angela Paris describes her own rehabilitation from drug addiction and her residency in a family shelter located in Cambridge, Massachusetts. Paris concludes: "People read about that Ventura woman. They say, 'how can a mother do that?' I know how. I remember" (Eagan 1994b).

Angela Paris, a more-nearly-representative-than-Claribel-Ventura "welfare mom,"[12] claims, in her telling, a kind of privileged location from which she is able to speak for Claribel Ventura as well as for herself. While her account is "subjective" in that it is openly attached to her own

experience, it nonetheless claims a kind of generality. Paris shifts from first person to second person in her account, as reported by Eagan. "I was so paranoid," she observes, on the one hand. "You don't want to be bothered [with children]," she comments, on the other. In the alternation between first- and second-person voices, she occupies a position of "generality" from which she seems to claim to speak not only for herself, not only for others who may have given self-accounts that she can recognize, but also for people like Claribel Ventura—*with reference to whom* texts have been produced. Accepting as "truth" the representations of those texts concerning Claribel Ventura, Angela Paris speaks to express ways in which she recognizes herself therein. Through this statement of recognition, incorporated into her own "recovery" story, Paris contributes her support to the "truth" or "reference" claims of the various Ventura stories. By her self-disclosures Angela Paris contributes her support to our acceptance of the Ventura stories. She tells us that the stories could have been true of her (of Paris) and thereby leads us to consider that if that is the case, they may well indeed be true of Claribel Ventura. It should be noted that Paris's account in fact supports the credibility of stories of *neglect*, while saying nothing of the credibility of stories of active *abuse*—that is, of the kind of intentional act Ventura is alleged to have performed. Nonetheless, while eliding the distinction between neglect and abuse, Paris's contribution works to historicize and specify the nature of Claribel Ventura's "badness," supporting the construction of Claribel Ventura's identity as part of a presently disturbing collectivity of bad mothers—specifically, of bad "welfare moms" who are addicted to drugs and especially to crack cocaine. Angela Paris supports the reality that a level of parental neglect that might otherwise seem unthinkable becomes understandable by reference to the effects of drug addiction (D. Roberts 1991).

Eagan acknowledges that Angela Paris is no more truly representative of "welfare mothers" than Claribel Ventura is. Even though Angela Paris may look more nearly representative, the "vast majority" of welfare mothers, as Eagan notes, "are raising their children and going to school or job training. They're not crack addicts, either. But many are, and many young mothers, like Angela Paris, are wallowing in their addictions, alone with their babies in welfare motels or projects or in dirty, filthy apartments of fellow junkies with neglected and abused babies of their own" (Eagan 1994b).

The intermingled stories of Paris and Eagan express a rather more sympathetic reading of Claribel Ventura than do the earlier reported perceptions of her by police, by judge, by legislators, by the governor, and by neighbors. But like all the preceding stories, they uncritically accept as "true" the construction of Claribel Ventura as a woman who intentionally performed an act of extraordinary cruelty. While the accounts of Eagan and Paris work toward making that cruelty intelligible by reference to a possibility of drug addiction, the effect of the bolstering of intelligibility is a simultaneous bolstering of the "truth" of the cruelty.

A variant account of the experience of Claribel Ventura and her children—and the one that received the least press coverage—was offered by Eulalia Rivera,[13] Claribel Ventura's mother, described in various news accounts as the "matriarch" of the Rivera family. Eulalia Rivera, according to the Boston Globe of February 17, 1994, offered an account of the incidents that preceded and followed Ernesto's injuries, tracking some of the consistently told stories and including some significant variations. Eulalia Rivera corroborated the family's move into the Mission Hill housing project. She stated that on the day of their move into the apartment, the drain to the bathtub in the apartment was clogged, so Claribel Ventura prepared a mixture of hot water and Drano, which she intended to use to unclog the drain. Eulalia Rivera said that Claribel Ventura left the pot on the toilet seat in the bathroom in order to attend to some cooking in the kitchen. She said that while Claribel was preoccupied in the kitchen, Ernesto entered the bathroom and put his hands into the Drano-hot water mixture, badly burning them (Sennott 1994b).

Eulalia Rivera reported visiting her daughter and grandchildren in Mission Hill sometime after Ernesto had been burned. She said that she observed the condition of Ernesto's hands at that time and asked Claribel why she had not obtained medical treatment for Ernesto. She reported that Claribel indicated that she had been afraid to call for medical assistance because she had been afraid that medical personnel would not believe that Ernesto's injuries had been caused accidentally and because she feared that her children would be removed from her.

Eulalia reported that she insisted to Claribel that it was necessary to obtain medical care for Ernesto and that Claribel insisted that she could not do so because of the likelihood that the children would be removed from her. Eulalia said that when Claribel made it clear that she would not obtain medical care for Ernesto, Eulalia herself called the Department of Human Services to request their investigation and thus assure proper treatment for Ernesto. By way of explaining her daughter's behavior, Eulalia commented, "Claribel was not thinking right. She was just so afraid!" (Sennott 1994b).

After Eulalia Rivera told this story, officials of the Department of Human Services released the apparently confirmatory information that in fact it had been a report by a relative of Claribel Ventura that had triggered the DSS and police investigations at the Mission Hill home (Sennott 1994b).

The story told by Eulalia Rivera is not one of sadistic cruelty. She does not purport to shed light on why a mother would have committed the "incomprehensible" act of intentionally burning her child's hands. She does not offer the by-now-familiar story of the battered woman abusing her children. She does not suggest, as did some early news reports, that Claribel Ventura burned her child's hands in some reenactment of her own victimization, her own experience of having herself been burned by an abusive man. She does not suggest that Claribel intentionally reproduced upon her child's body an injury of precisely the kind she had herself received. She does not tell the now readily recognizable story of the bad mother/crack addict. She offers instead a very old story—a story of accident. Of what the law calls "negligence." Of what the law calls "neglect" only when the "negligence" affects the particularly vulnerable—the young, the old, the sick. The story of the burned hands, as told by Eulalia Rivera, is a story that every person who has ever cared for small children or other dependent persons can recognize and understand. Even those of us who have never left a pot of Drano and hot water unattended probably have some memory or memories of near misses, of close calls; I would say every one of us has some memory of this sort. There is nothing like the responsibility of caring for children to remind parents of our limitations, to make us aware than even generally attentive care is never fully adequate to the threats to children.

One might be inclined to imagine that acceptance of Eulalia Rivera's story of Claribel Ventura and Ernesto might make a significant difference, might have some consequences for the law's response to her. But perhaps not. Said Lorraine Carli, spokesperson for DSS: "The cause of the burns, whether accidental or intentional, don't [sic] change the allegation of neglect. Clearly there was a situation where these kids had to be removed" (Sennott 1994b).

The story of the refusal to obtain medical care to treat the child's injuries is perhaps less readily comprehensible than the circumstances that may have given rise to the injuries. That story is told as an account of "fear." Of what or whom could Claribel Ventura have been fearful? Can "we" find it believable that she feared the human services professionals, the police officers, the court, the likelihood of separation from her children? What could it mean when a woman fails to obtain medical care for an injured child? Shall we read that act—or omission—as cruelty or as fear of cruelty; as perpetration of cruelty or as expectation of cruelty; or as all of those?

Before the installation of enormous state and national bureaucracies charged with supervision of "child welfare," the identification of family violence and of child abuse was accomplished through nongovernmental agencies. Prominent among these in the nineteenth century in Massachusetts was the Society for the Prevention of Cruelty to Children. Linda Gordon has written of the habits of the Irish tenement dwellers in Boston during that period: When they observed the recognizable figure of an SPCC worker, they would cry out to their neighbors the warning, rooted in fear, "Here comes the Cruelty!" (L. Gordon 1990, pp. 184–85). The ostensibly beneficent society was perceived as cruel to the degree that it represented an intrusion of members of privileged classes threatening to disrupt and destroy family relationships. Poor people have long had reason to recognize in the coming of such emissaries—as they still do in their contacts with representatives of the "helping professions"—threats of cruelty and occasions of fear:

contacts that offer policing, judgment, and blame and that work to remind them of the gaps between themselves and those who prosper; that remind them of the control and the threat to family relationships that, however we may recognize them as "dysfunctional," remain of enormous significance even to people other than powerful, other than mainstream, and other than well-adapted to the demands of contemporary life. Writers have begun to document the well-founded fears of "professionals" experienced by mothers who live in poverty (N. Ehrenreich 1993). Their work supports the likelihood that women in situations such as Claribel Ventura's may well anticipate contact with "professionals"—of the law, of medicine, of psychology, of social work, or of the news media—with the expectation, "Here comes the Cruelty!"

In reflecting on the reports of Claribel Ventura and her children, I have felt most haunted by two photographs of the child Ernesto in his hospital room. Those pictures, which appeared in the *Boston Herald*, had a powerful impact on many people who saw them. In talking with friends and acquaintances I have repeatedly discovered strong expressions of horror in response to the Claribel Ventura case. That horror has repeatedly been explained to me by people's noting—conclusively—that they've "seen the pictures."

In wondering why those photos so remain with me, it has occurred to me that they are to some degree extremely familiar. Each is reminiscent of the kind of picture we have seen many times. They are paradigm shots—the kind of shot we see of the hero posing with the recovering child whom he has drawn from the river; the firefighter posing with the child whom he has carried from the three-decker clapboard house. Such is the first picture, a shot of Ernesto Laro visited by the Boston police officer who removed him from his home.

The child lies in his bed in a lightly flowered hospital johnny. In the news photo, the pattern of the gown looks like a miniature version of the one in which his mother appears in the Roxbury courtroom. At one side, smiling down at a beaming Ernesto, is the police officer. The officer's hands are concealed. He holds in each hand an object that is not fully identifiable; they appear to be Muppet-like fabrications, perhaps two hand puppets conversing with one another for Ernesto's amusement. The officer is smiling; Ernesto appears to be laughing. The caption notes that they are joking. At the other side of the bed the EMT who transported Ernesto is standing. He is a witness. A stethoscope identifies his profession. He watches the officer and the child with a look of benevolence.

Lying on his back, Ernesto reflects the officer. Like the police officer, Ernesto holds up hands invisible in their wrappings. Perhaps the officer is not conducting a puppet performance at all. Perhaps he has invited Ernesto to adopt the gesture of a boxer. Perhaps Ernesto has done so. The bandages encasing his hands, like boxers' gloves, display no trace of fingers or thumbs. I am reminded of his mother's curled fist on the courtroom bar. I am led to wonder, as I wondered in seeing her fist, what I would see if Ernesto's wrappings were gently undone.

In the year since Claribel Ventura was arrested in Massachusetts, much has occurred.

Ernesto has undergone major surgery to restore function to his hands. Doctors predict that Ernesto's hands will be restored to normal functioning, though they will remain "badly scarred" (Polochanin 1994). Ernesto has been placed in foster care.

Juvenile Court proceedings to terminate Claribel Ventura's parental rights relative to her children have commenced (Ellement and Sennott 1994; Weber 1994).

Following her first court appearance in Roxbury District Court on February 14, 1994, Claribel Ventura was arraigned in Suffolk Superior Court on March 23, 1994. At that time the court set a $10,000 cash bail. The bail was posted by family members on the following day. On April 8, Claribel Ventura failed to appear in court for a pretrial conference. The court issued a warrant for her arrest (Ellement and Sennott 1994; Weber 1994). On April 28, 1994, when she had still failed to appear, her bond was forfeited.

The Boston media continued its investigation and reporting of the Ventura case. In September 1994 a *Globe* story reported from the town of Bani, in the Dominican Republic, that Claribel Ventura was living there and that she had recently given birth to a child whom she had named Jose Pena, after his father—her former boyfriend, Reyson Jose Pena. The *Globe* reporter opined that there was a direct route from Bani to Boston whereby immigrants came to Massachu-

setts and took advantage of the state's welfare benefits (Sennott 1994e).

Shortly thereafter the newspapers reported Claribel Ventura's surrender to FBI agents in Puerto Rico. Held in a women's jail in Vega Alta, outside of San Juan, Claribel Ventura was interviewed by television reporter Uma Pemmaraju. At that time Ventura stated that the injuries to Ernesto had been inflicted by her former boyfriend, Reyson Jose Pena, who had been angry when Ernesto took some food that Pena had wanted for himself. On October 4, 1994, Reyson Jose Pena was indicted with mayhem, assault and battery with a dangerous weapon, and assault and battery. The district attorney characterized the injuries as a "joint venture" of Ventura and Pena (Hutchinson 1994c).

News accounts on the day following Ventura's television interview reported the statement of a "Commonwealth Corrections Administration official in Puerto Rico" who said that "prisoners appalled by Ventura's alleged crimes beat her up inside the women's jail in Vega Alta" (Grunwald 1994).

DSS spokesperson Lorraine Carli in October 1994 cheerfully—if unconvincingly—characterized Ernesto as "thriving" in his foster placement (Hutchinson 1994c).

During the summer of 1994, the Massachusetts legislature passed a welfare reform plan characterized by one state legislator as the most punitive of its kind.[14] Governor Weld vetoed that plan in the expectation of moving the legislature toward an even more stringent program. In February 1995, just a year after the first appearance of Claribel Ventura in the public eye, the legislature has passed and Governor Weld has signed that more stringent welfare reform legislation, widely characterized as the "toughest in the nation."

At the time of Claribel Ventura's return to Boston to await trial, and during the discussion of welfare reform proposals, the news media republished the hospital photos of Ernesto taken some months previously. On January 1, 1995, the *Boston Globe* cited the story of the Ventura matter as one of the "top ten" stories of 1994. There can be little doubt that the effectiveness of the story is related to the "meanings" communicated through the frequently published photos.

In one of these photos, Ernesto is shown in a sitting position. His bandaged hands rest on a

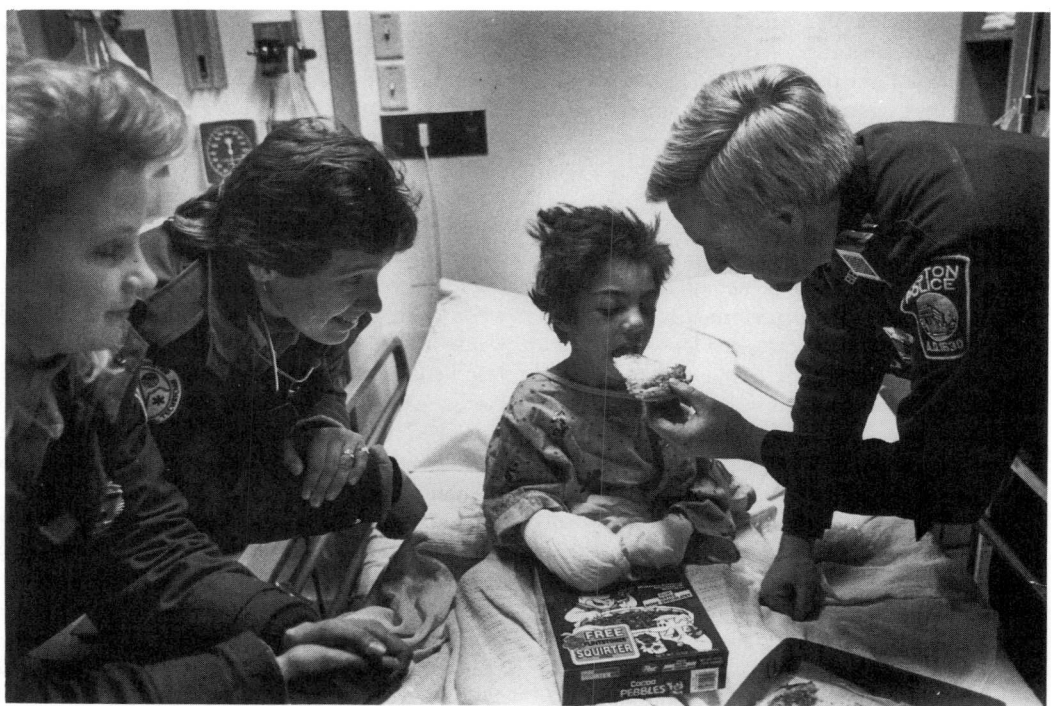

FIGURE 2. Photograph © Curtis Ackerman/*Boston Herald*. Reprinted with permission of the *Boston Herald*.

box of Cocoa Pebbles. His disheveled curls stand upright. His mouth is wide open. He resembles an infant child in the kind of cotton nightie that newborns used to wear, with cuffs that cover their fingers. His look is serious, earnest—even solemn. His most expressive feature is his open mouth. Like an infant's, it leads his body as he inclines forward in some combination of vulnerability and desire, of defenselessness and trust. The intimacy of the setting is striking. It might lead us to wonder who permitted the camera's entry into Ernesto's room, the photographic representation of the transactions occurring there, and the subsequent publication of the wounded child's image to all the world.

The photo can be read as a representation of several sets of hands. Here the police officer has put down or not yet taken up the puppets that we saw in the other photo. He leans toward Ernesto. Visible close to his collar is a diamond-shaped pattern, a logo that identifies his official status. Below it there is a triangular area of light

formed by his left arm reaching in front of his right. The officer's right hand has formed a fist, positioned on Ernesto's bedclothes. In his left hand, the officer extends toward Ernesto's mouth a triangular object—a piece of pizza from the box, its triangular corner visible, that lies at the foot of Ernesto's bed. The gesture is kindly. Two EMTs are visible in this picture—a woman and a man. Their lower bodies cannot be seen. It is not clear whether they stand, sit, or kneel beside Ernesto's bed, positioned like two communicants at an altar rail. Their faces manifest how they are touched—as are we—by the exchange between Ernesto and the man who is feeding him. The woman is smiling peacefully; her hands are clasped together in a kind of prayerful attitude along the side rails of Ernesto's bed. Indeed, there is something sacramental about the setting, something reminiscent of the child taking a first communion in the upward tilt of Ernesto's chin, the trusting openness of his mouth. The other medic, the one we recognize from the first photo, is smiling now, too. His left hand is visible against the right sleeve of his jacket as he inclines slightly toward Ernesto.

Readers of photographic texts, like those of literary texts, have explored what might be called "protocols of reading," reference points from which, even in a postmodernist world of shifting referents, we do not entirely escape. Robert Scholes has discussed one such reference point that has relevance for our reading of the photos of Ernesto. Scholes has examined in detail a photograph that is reproduced in his *Protocols of Reading* (1989, p. 23).[15] The photo represents a woman tending, in a bath, a child whose face and limbs appear severely deformed. The relationship between the woman and the child appears to be one of extraordinary harmony and tenderness. The face of the woman appears to express—like the faces of the "witnesses" in Ernesto's photos—an attitude of reverence for the child, the kind of religious reverence evident in Western art in nativity scenes and in pietàs. Indeed, Scholes detects a continuity or persistence of profoundly deep (if not foundational) expectations operating and determining our response to the photo, expectations concerning the power of mother-love even in the face of what might seem "horrifying." The photo examined by Scholes, like the nativities and the pietàs, both depends upon and contributes to the construction of a cultural conviction about what mothering should be.

In the traditional images—the nativities, the pietàs, the *Life* photo—the mother is made present in the image. In the photos of Ernesto, the mother—Claribel Ventura—is absent. Or, more precisely, she is displaced. For the hospital photos of Ernesto are not simply variations of the familiar ones of child-and-rescuer or of police-officer-as-friend. They are in fact depictions of a new model—of police officer as mother. They contribute to construction of the figure of state as mother.

This is a troubling and worrisome construction because of course the police officer is not the mother and cannot be the mother. Nor can the state be. Nor can the EMTs. Nor the social workers. Nor the judge or lawyers. Like the rest of us, who find it not too difficult to love other people's children from some distance and for a while, the adults within the photo frame will shortly leave Ernesto, retreating to their professional places in the world, places remote from the direct care of the children whose parents we police and judge.

Roland Barthes, in his readings of photographs, has distinguished two aspects of depictions. The first of these is what he calls the *studium*—the subject matter depicted in the photo without any seeming reference to realities outside the frame (Barthes 1981).[16] The second is what Barthes calls the *punctum*, the element of a photo that in some sense pierces through the frame to locate both the *studium* and the viewer in some specific history. Often this *punctum* consists of a small detail. In examining Ernesto's photos, I have found such a detail that speaks to me.

In the photo of Ernesto's feeding, the mother-absent photo, several sets of hands are apparent. I have noted the bandaged hands of the child, the offering hand of the officer, the prayerful hands of the woman. The hands of the second EMT, the one who transported Ernesto, are also visible. His right hand and arm incline in relaxation across the rail of the hospital bed. His left hand rests against the right-hand sleeve of his uniform, its fingers curving across the dark fabric of his jacket. It is not in any of these four pairs of hands, however, but in another that I find what is for me the *punctum* of the photo. I see on the left ring-finger of the EMT a pattern which, living in Boston, I recognize. Its shape and glint are clear and light against the darker tints of the photo.

In Boston, people often wear what are called Claddagh rings. (Teaching at Boston College in 1991–92, I noted that four of the ten students with whom I worked that year wore such rings.) These rings incorporate a pattern with which I have been familiar as long as I can recall. My Irish-born mother habitually wore a silver pin with such a design, which she had loved from her own childhood. The pattern is one of two clasped hands about a heart. This is the pattern I find in Ernesto's photo, on the hand of the EMT. This, for me, is the *punctum*.

The Claddagh design is now commonly crafted into a variety of adornments—rings, pins, earrings, tie clasps, necklaces, bracelets, barrettes, neckties, pendants, stickers, and Christmas tree ornaments. The particular configuration of hands and heart that make up the design has become popular in the broadest sense. Nonetheless, the design continues to carry, at least in Boston, some trace of the ethnic and class signification that attached to its origins: a bearing witness to ethnicity that commenced when, in Boston, being Irish meant being outside the mainstream.

Claddagh rings now are worn by representatives of the mainstream, representatives of the middle classes, representatives of the professions, representatives of the law. As the extra set of hands, excessive somehow, in Ernesto's photo, the Claddagh ring marks the EMT-witness with whom we, the viewers, identify in considering Claribel Ventura and her child. The ring evokes both a recollection of outsider status and a present reality of insider status of the "professionals" involved in the case of Claribel Ventura. The Claddagh ring marks, for many who wear it, a class transition involving movement from having feared the "cruelty" to having somehow *become* the "cruelty." Does it also mark, I wonder, a forgetting? Does the photograph represent, in part, a forgetting, by those who no longer experience the deepest injuries of "class," that others continue to feel those injuries (Sennett and Cobb 1972) and that sometimes those injuries are delivered from the hands of forgetters?

These considerations are, of course, not irrelevant to the urgent questions the photos raise: What will happen? What will happen when the balloons have been deflated, the puppets put away, the pizza eaten, the bandages removed, and the photo opportunity dismantled? Who then will care for Ernesto? That question cannot be adequately addressed without remembering that the "cruelty" perceived and feared today by Claribel Ventura, the cruelty embodied in the "helping professionals" who purport to ally with her son and to act in his "best interests," may well be felt as cruelty tomorrow—or in ten years—by Ernesto himself. Every lawyer who has represented children recognizes that when Ernesto is no longer Claribel Ventura's beautiful little child—when he is fourteen, for example—the police, the judge, and the other professionals—like "us"—will find him, as well as his mother, "other." Not sympathetic. Not appealing. To be feared, to be policed, to be controlled. The child, like his mother, will find us uncaring, inadequate, cruel.

In the face of what has begun to be perceived as a crisis in "child welfare," recommendations abound. Prominent among these are calls for easier and earlier termination of parental rights, for readier placement of children away from their families to foster care and to adoption. But the inadequacy of such recommendations should be evident in the exposure, which began to be developed more than twenty years ago (Mnookin 1973) and which has continued to be developed,[17] of the problems experienced by children in foster care. Indeed, a return to placement of children in institutions, in orphanages, has begun to be proposed in recent years as an alternative to foster care (Aring 1991).[18] Perhaps it has been forgotten that the institutionalization experiment has been tried and that only decades ago it was conclusively determined to have failed (Bowlby 1969).[19] Whatever we are to do, if we want to generate intergenerational stories different from the ones with which we are familiar, we must respect the connectedness of Claribel Ventura and of her child, and the connection of families to larger social structures. We must not abandon but must deepen our understanding that the problems of families are not merely individual or private. And we must especially respect the connectedness of Claribel Ventura to "us."

The calls for reform of "child welfare" have been accompanied by calls for "welfare reform," and the two "reformist" movements have been coupled, as has been evident in the story of Claribel Ventura. Stories such as Claribel Ventura's are consciously and unconsciously utilized to justify societal refusals to support mothers as well as children. Generally ignored in public discussion of welfare is the reality that we indeed "know" very little about its history and its present effects (L. Gordon 1994). The misogynistic impulses that contributed to the shaping of welfare in its earliest forms and that remain influential have been largely overlooked (L. Gordon 1994). Perhaps even more overlooked is our lack of knowledge about the realities of "bad mothers" and their children.

It is urgent that we begin to "know" much more about "bad mothers" and about injured children, as well as about the conditions of life available to people like Claribel Ventura. While feeling urgently the critical need to protect children from injury, we must not forget that existing models of foster care and other professional services will not suffice to provide the care necessary for children's well-being. We must remember that it will be impossible to take care of children like Ernesto and his siblings except by taking care of their mothers—and their fathers.

When we construct the "bad mother" as "other" through the person of Claribel Ventura, we make the mistake of those whose histories should have led us to know better. When we construct any "bad mother" as "other," we falsely imagine that we have some substitute for her, some replacement, some better model. We commit the mistake of imagining that we can ever serve the "best interests" of children without supporting the well-being of their parents.

Notes

1. Julia Kristeva, in *Powers of Horror: An Essay in Abjection* (1982), provides a study of the processes by which human beings name what is abject and to be despised. Kristeva regards as continuous the processes by which certain bodily markers are defined as separate from the "proper" self and the processes by which individuals or groups are characterized as profoundly "other."

2. "Feces" were reported as "strewn" in the room in which Ventura's children were "kept," and as "scattered" in "piles" (Vaznis 1994a, p. 30). In a February 14, 1994, account, it was reported that the mattress of one of Ventura's children was "soaked" with "his own blood, urine and human feces" (Vaznis 1994b, p. 17). "Feces" were reported as "splattered" in the Ventura apartment (Heaney 1994, p. 6). Feces, blood, and urine were reported to have "stained" the bed of Claribel Ventura's son Ernesto (Hutchinson 1994b, pp. 1, 7).

3. The February 13 *Globe* story (Vaznis 1994a) reported that the children were being treated at Children's Hospital for malnutrition. However, the February 14 story indicated that the children had only "initially" been "believed to be suffering from malnutrition." The February 14 story reported the statement of Lorraine Carli, a spokesperson for DSS, who stated that the five children "seemed in good health" and that "there was no evidence that they had been abused" (Vaznis 1994b).

4. For discussion of the persistence of the "bad mother" figure in law and in the larger culture, see Ashe 1992.

5. As reported by the *Boston Globe*, Weld's plan, which on Sunday, February 13, 1994, had been rejected by the Massachusetts Senate, "would have required able-bodied recipients to either find a job or perform community service, also called 'workfare,' after 60 days on welfare. It would have replaced cash grants to 50,000 recipients with day care and health care" (Aucoin 1994).

6. As described by the *Globe*, the Democratic proposal would increase "child care and other support services to unmarried teenage mothers on welfare, who are considered most at risk of chronic welfare dependency. It would turn grants into paychecks by subsidizing employers who hire welfare recipients" (Aucoin 1994).

7. This statement was attributed to Massachusetts state senator Therese Murray, a major proponent of the Democratic reform plan.

8. See *Buck v. Bell*, 274 U.S. 200 (1927), in which Justice Holmes, writing for the Court, noted with regard to the apparent persistence of the problem of "imbecility": "It is better for all the world, if instead of waiting to execute degenerate offspring for crime, or to let them starve for their imbecility, society can prevent those who are manifestly unfit from continuing their kind. [three] generations of imbeciles are enough." See also Gould 1986, pp. 127–41.

9. This statement was attributed to Massachusetts state senator John O'Brien.

10. This characterization corresponds to comments of Joseph V. Gallant, who was reported in the *Boston Globe* to have viewed Claribel Ventura and the Rivera family as "statistical aberrations." According to Gallant, "The average person [on welfare] is not addicted to crack, doesn't abuse their kids and doesn't have that large a family. . . . In fact, the statistical average is a white woman without a high school diploma, without job experience, and less than two kids." At the same time, Gallant spoke in favor of a general "overhaul" of "the system," noting that "dependency" over generations—as manifested in the Ventura/Rivera family—is "increasingly becoming the norm" (quoted in Sennott 1994c).

11. For discussion problematizing each of these simple constructs, see (concerning "crack addict") D. Roberts 1991; (concerning "battered woman") M. Mahoney 1991; Schneider 1986.

12. Paris is more typical in terms of the number of children.

13. In news accounts, Claribel Ventura's mother has been referred to, variously, as "Eulalia Rivera" and as "Eulalia Rodriguez."

14. It was so characterized by Massachusetts state senator Dianne Wilkerson in remarks at Suffolk University Law School, Advanced Legal Studies Program, April 23, 1994.

15. The photograph Scholes writes about is W. Eugene Smith, "Tomoko in the Bath."

16. Barthes, of course, works to expose the social and political forces that operate to determine the viewer/reader's active reading of the photo.

17. Some of the widely recognized problems relating to the lack of supportive relationship and the lack of stability often suffered by children in foster care are illuminated in the legislative history of federal law directed at reform of foster care services. See 42 *United States Code* Sections 670–75 (1983 and Supp. 1985) as well as the legislative history of P.L. 96–272, at 1980 *United States Code Congressional and Administrative News* 1448.

18. Since the November 1994 elections, the recommendations of Speaker of the House Newt Gingrich favoring the reinstitution of orphanages have been widely reported.

19. See also Hasci 1994 (urging wariness about perceiving orphanages as a "panacea," tracing the history of orphanages, and identifying the reasons why communities turned away from the institutionalization of young children).

18

Spectacles of the Strange

Envisioning Violence in the Central Park Jogger Trial

KRISTIN BUMILLER

How do rape trials become spectacles of erotic pleasure? How is our viewing organized to produce a geography of racial transgression and sexual danger? What are the pleasures of viewing violence? These are the questions I pose as I write as an observer of spectacles of interracial gang rape and, in particular, the 1991 Central Park Jogger trial, in which one black and two Hispanic teenage boys were charged with the sexual and physical assault of a young professional woman in Central Park. In this trial the prosecution argued that while jogging in Central Park, a young white professional woman was raped by a roving band of black and Hispanic teenagers. Because the jogger had no memory of the night of the incident when she testified at the trial, the prosecution's case relied on forensic photography of the jogger's body and the written and videotaped confessions of the defendants. The viewing of both the jogger's body and the defendants' confessions produced a spectacle in the courtroom which was reproduced by the media for a larger public audience.

The analysis that follows focuses on my own observations in the courtroom. I describe my own consciousness of viewing and interpret how this spectacle inscribed fears of racial violence and sexual violation in the modern urban scene. It is my contention that the power of trials to confer meaning in everyday life is analyzable through the consciousness of the spectator; through that consciousness we can see the ways rape trials provide the opportunities to subdue and excite the erotic fantasies of a mass audience. I want to notice the unseen fields of violence and desire, because without taking notice we can see ourselves neither as looking, nor as being looked at, in a frame of vision that obfuscates the brutalities of existence for woman and racial "others".

In this chapter I also show how the representation of rape in this trial reproduces images of racial and sexual fears on an urban landscape. This in turn fuels the media's cultural productions of rape images and markets violence in predictable and sensationalized ways. I suggest how these images of rape that become the subject of mass consumption generate rationales for the regulation of the eroticized bodies of women and racial "others."

I begin my exploration of viewing in the Central Park Jogger trial with the first sighting of the "victim" by a Hispanic man named Vanico. Vanico began his testimony by recounting his journey through Central Park on the night of April 19, 1989. He explained that he was talking and drinking beer with his friend Carlos while walking home through the park by way of 100th Street and Central Park West and that he was startled by the sounds of "someone" moaning. He looked in the direction of the moans, he said; he recalled; that "I knew it was a body, I don't know if it was a man or woman." His report of the first sighting of the body became a moment for the rather unexpected release of tension, as spectators in the courtroom burst into spontaneous laughter as Vanico mimicked the sounds of her moaning ("mum, mum, mum") and then enacted a complex gender and racial evasion: "I don't know who it was; I don't know who she is; I knew it was a body hurt, a human being; and I thought she was a man." When later asked by a defense attorney, "Did you see the race?" he answered, "No, I couldn't tell, all that mud was on top of her."

Through a series of questions designed to document the condition and placement of the discovered body, the spectators get their first glance at her nearly dead body. The manifest pleasure of the spectator arises in response to the seeming absurdity of Vanico's claim to know, without seeing: He looked and heard but, he nervously asserted, he couldn't have seen her as alive, as white, or as a woman. Vanico's expression of fear and excitement in witnessing, both at the moment of discovery and during the trial, reminds us of the image of spectatorship as socially dangerous. Looking involves the risk of being seen (and marked as criminal) by authorities, or subjected to the viewing of whoever had done this to her. A defense attorney foreshadows the danger of being caught looking by asking Vanico, "Did they take body sample or tissue samples [from you]?" Yet in another sense, Vanico as a "witness" lends his subjectivity to secure the belief that an act of violence, both real and imagined, has occurred.

As we simply go on looking at the body Vanico has placed into our field of vision, we become observers of reenacted violence—a reproduction according to the narrative structures of the law. This reenactment creates its own textual body, produced at the site of "desire that nearly shatters us" and replicating the violence intrinsically within its narrative structure. By seeing the trial as a site of erotic repetitions, I want to examine how it performs in order to seduce its audience: How does the narrative succeed or fail in its project of simulating and domesticating sexuality and violence? How does the textual body constitute desire and create its own pleasures as a text? How does the narrative mimic a Sadian aesthetics?

I want to suggest that the encounter with the "specter" of the "nearly dead white woman's body," which is reproduced in the trial, simulates the experience of "uncanny strangeness." It is the sight of the "other" (she who shocks me, he who crushes me, and the I whom I reject and with whom I identify) that arouses images of blackness and that loosens boundaries between reality and imagination. The trial and its hyperbolic significance as a cultural metaphor for racial danger appear as the defense, so to speak, against the strange, which we can barely know and which we cannot contain. The visual spectacle of the Central Park Jogger trial and other events, such as the replaying of the videotape of the Rodney King beating, are vehicles for structuring in the dominant vision of how race "can be seen" and for locating, in the collective unconsciousness, the destructive forces, the barbarity, on an urban landscape.

The trial is a repetition, a compulsion driven by the sight of woman and death, that projects the fantasies of blackness. And the pleasures of the text, the legal narrative of the Central Park Jogger trial, are found in its replication of these fantasies of racial transgression and sexual danger. In my viewing of this erotic narrative I want to bring into frame the ways in which images of race are figured in the text and to reveal the narrative's projection of an alien otherness onto bodies, or simply its marking of bodies. More directly, I suggest how racism depends on fantasies of sexual horror to thrive, and how it is attached to what I call the sadistic realism of the trial. I claim not that the trial narrative completely achieves the sadistic form but, rather, that its narration struggles with a sadistic view of pleasure best suited for its realistic representational techniques.

As I look at the trial I note what Roland Barthes describes as two different realisms: The first is the "real," "what is demonstrated but not seen," while the second speaks "reality," "what is seen but not demonstrated" (Barthes 1975, p. 46). The real, in my terms, is a reference to the "real" in the representational systems that defines it, whether the legal concept of evidence, the laws of the physical universe, or the psychoanalytic impossibility of fully being oneself. And "reality," or "the realistic," refers to systems of representation that are read through the "real." I challenge the assumption, made in legal discourse, for example, that the visible real is a truth-effect for the representational real—that real evidence exists unframed by dominant versions of reality.

My argument is developed in two parts. First, I demonstrate how visions of the real contain blackness on urban landscapes. Second, I describe how the realistic version of the trial employs the sadistic appeal of racism.

Toni Morrison, in *Playing in the Dark*, suggests that race has assumed a complex metaphorical life embedded in daily discourses. Images of blackness hold ambivalences, she writes: "[They] can be evil *and* protective, rebellious *and* forgiving, fearful *and* desirable" (T. Morrison 1992a, p. 59). "Whiteness alone," she goes on to suggest, "is mute, meaningless, unfathomable, pointless, frozen, veiled, curtained, dreaded, senseless, implacable" (T. Morrison 1992a, p. 59). While Morrison locates these metaphors in the textual body of "classic" American literature, I want to locate blackness and whiteness in the textual body of the trial, which in turn is located in the urban geography that it replicates. The trial is played out on a landscape, both real and imagined; it is narrated so that blackness is seen as movement, or the residues of a fleeting presence, and whiteness is given a geography, its existence constituted as part of the landscape that represents it.

In the Central Park Jogger trial the prosecutor played a primary role as a scenographer; she created narrative structure by making arrangements and placements of objects, persons, and events within her landscaped vision. She orchestrated a vision of violence by locating all visual points of relevance, such that, for example, each of the statements made by the police who responded to the reports of roving bands of teenage boys was tied to a geographic reference, charted for the jury on maps and aerial photographs. In this way, Central Park operates as a reference point seemingly "outside" the text. As a reference point, it gives the text its sociological realism—it locates the attack of a white woman by black and Hispanic teenage boys in a space of contested urban geography. The park is the focus for the clash over the ownership of public space between a woman who represents the hopes of a new professional class and teenage boys who represent young lives wasted by the forces of racism and poverty. The overlay of buildings and streets outside of the boundaries of the park, as markers for the places within, also structure realistic images of proximity and distance between social classes and races; the closeness of sharing recreational space and the distance between the Schumburg Housing project, where the defendants lived, and the jogger's East Side apartment. For commentator Joan Didion, the perceived social distance between the victim and the assailants produces a crime story that precisely "conflat[es] victim and city" and "personal woe with public distress" (Didion 1992, p. 260). Thus, in the context of the sociological realism of the trial, racial transgression and sexual danger in the park became a site for playing out who owns the city.

If Central Park is seen as the textual landscape, however, the contest arises over the manageability of space according to human designs, or rather the taming of the wild in a contained environment. The park enters the text as the material real, in its soil and debris, leaves, foliage, and rocks, and it enters as a landscape, a terrain that is viewed as a product of its creation under conscious human cultivation.

The connection between the "raped" jogger and the "ravaged" city is managed in the narrative through "real" evidence of bodies and landscapes. When we see her, the Central Park Jogger, figured in the legal text of the trial, her body becomes part of the contested landscape that gives structure and form to our understanding of a racially divided urban geography.

Thus, the victim's body is sighted as part of the terrain. A paramedic who was asked to describe "what she saw" in a ravine illuminated by police car headlights said, "It was heavily wooded, yet as I approached, I saw her in a spasmatic state, moving around." She said she didn't touch the body but "did a visual examination of her wounds." Here she makes way for the re-presentation of a field of vision in which seeing the wounds is a way of seeing the violence itself. The paramedic also reports that she didn't cut a cloth wrapped around the woman's neck even though it was obstructing her breathing because "it was a crime scene." But the paramedic noted her positioning: "[H]er chest was in the water and her head in an easterly direction." This visual inspection showed "mud and blood all over her."

After the body was stabilized and transported to the hospital, the police supervisor in charge testified, he decided to "hold the scene." Since in the supervisor's mind the area was too vast and dark "to do properly," he put police officers at 102nd Street and the bottom of the ravine and told them, "[D]on't let anybody into the area." He kept the shirt that was taken off the body and treated it as an artifact holding the place of the body on the terrain; "it was a blood soaked shirt, turned inside out, a twisted shirt with a hole above the right breast."

The second step in the containment of the scene was to "note areas of blood" and then photograph them. The police officers' vision of the crime scene was, in fact, subsequently reproduced in the trial by this series of photographs. In them, we are shown the marks of her blood on the terrain: "Drag marks toward the tree; significant amount of the blood in the area; paths of blood, disturbed by dirt; tree roots covered in blood." The photographs depict her clothes strewn throughout the wooded area: "[A] shoe and instep in an area of blood; a right shoe and jogging tight 92 feet east off the lower path; and left sneaker down the ravine closer to the stream."

As if to complete the picture, the rest of the landscape was made visible on the victim's body, tagged unknown white woman, by photographs taken as she lay unconscious in the hospital. When these photographs were later displayed as evidence, the marks of the landscape were seen and inscribed on her body. Referring to a photograph showing the backs of her legs, the forensic pathologist, testifying for the state, said, "Here is a multitude of scratches and bruises that run in different directions, consistent with roots, twigs, branches, and the ground cover of the area." On the quarter view, left frontal aspect, of her head, we are shown "a crushing, tearing injury, that is

consistent with a rock," "rough enough to break the skin, and heavy enough" to cause the injury. In some of his testimony, this expert spoke of her body itself as a terrain: He spoke of "abrasions that show horizontal impact left to right and right to left" and "intervening regions of uninjured skin."

The body is repeatedly made visible in the trial as a figure in the terrain. Her body and clothes, blood and hair specimens are all placed in a field on which visual inspection reveals her inundation by mud and blood and her defilement by abrasions and blows. She "exists" and is recognizable only within the landscape of her injuries. She is unrecognizable elsewhere; thus, a friend who looks at her body in the hospital the next morning finds her unidentifiable except for a ring on her finger.

The presence of the teenage boys is also shown through marks on the terrain of the body. Physical contact between the teenage boys and the woman, the image which is left outside of our vision, is verified through the marks on her body and the terrain. The marks are traces, the remains left from the assailants' touching and bludgeoning the body. These disturbances on the body become markers of the "real" in that they preserve the reality of physical contact and sexual union. In this way an unmarked woman, a white woman, is marked by the violence of the "other." The marks on her body signify the violence—the penetration of foreign substance on the white woman's body. These traces are indistinguishable from the violence itself. Their meaning is racialized at the level of pure materiality—the foreign, the dirt, and the forceful objects make racial transgression visible. There is no need to "see" the presence of her attackers to demonstrate the presence of something inhuman.

In contrast, the defendants' bodies, once brought into police captivity, are sampled rather than visually inspected. Their muddy clothing is shown to the jury so they might take notice of the "cuttings"—the holes of fabric where samples have been removed and sent to the lab. Their bodies are desegregated, made subject to techniques of microscopic viewing, in which the real is seen only through its most minute pieces. Thus, in an exchange about Clarence Thomas, one of the defendants (no relation to the Supreme Court Justice), a detective was asked:

Prosecutor: Did you remove anything from Clarence Thomas.

Detective: No, he indicated he washed his hands.

Prosecutor: Are you not interested in whether he washed the rest of his body?

Detective: No, [I am] only [interested] in fingernail scrapings.

Here the detective explains how the visually marked body of the black teenage boy has evidentiary relevance only for the possibility of what could be extracted from its unclean reservoirs. The image of the defendants, in contrast to the display of the victim's body, is a kind of photographic negative to be looked at for distinguishable evidence in a blackened scene.

Blood in the Central Park Jogger trial signified both the mixing of bodily fluids and connection and transgression. The victim's body, when it was discovered, had lost almost all of its blood, which according to the doctor's testimony made it a "medical miracle" that the jogger survived. But the draining of her blood also created a phantasm of racially transgressive violence: the possibility of white blood; that she could be living without her blood, full of innocence and purity, beyond life and death.

In the trial, the victim's spilled blood is seen as literally mixed with the landscape. Samples of her blood are taken from all parts of the terrain, from rocks, leaves, twigs, soil, clothes, and the pavement. This mixing of blood and landscape was reproduced in the courtroom by photographs and physical specimens (held in the prosecutor's latex-gloved hands) as part of visual reenactments of the scenario by which the body was moved across the scene. Yet her blood was never found on the defendants' clothes or in any other sample removed from their person.

Thus the defendants seemed to carry away nothing of her. Forensic tests failed to definitely link the body traces of the defendants with the victim, except for traces of mud which could have gotten on their clothing from any location within the park. For those who sought to contest the reality constructed in the trial, particularly supporters of the defendants who voiced their disbelief in the courthouse hallways, this missing link fueled their sense of the jogger as a ghost— a white person's paranoid fantasy, an apparition on the urban landscape. Here we see the mystery of the "real" engage its audience with the phantasmic.

When the moment came for the woman known as the Central Park Jogger to enter the physical space of the courtroom, she somehow appeared "out of frame." A defense attorney stated, "[W]e all applaud the efforts of the female jogger and her recovery, yet her presence [here, in the courtroom] raises more questions than if she had not been called [to the witness stand] at all." The vision of her as "whole" and "alive" was dissonant with the visual dismemberment and landscaping of her body that had taken place, here, in her absence. The prosecutor, however, aware that for a realistic representation of the jogger as a victim it was necessary to reconstitute her as a whole being, used her short presence on the scene to reconfigure her body. In a series of questions, she asks the jogger as witness, in essence, to lay claim to parts of her body, as follows:

PROSECUTOR: Did you see #33 in evidence?

WITNESS: Yes.

PROSECUTOR: Do you recognize it?

WITNESS: This is the shirt I used to wear.

PROSECUTOR: Prior to April 19, 1989, what color was it?

WITNESS: It was white.

PROSECUTOR: Were there holes there?

WITNESS: No.

PROSECUTOR: Will you examine these tights?

WITNESS: I recognize those as the tights I go running in.

PROSECUTOR: Do you recognize People's exhibit 13a and 6?

WITNESS: Those are my running shoes.

PROSECUTOR: Do you recognize People's 115 and 117?

WITNESS: Those look like my socks.

After this exchange the defense attorneys choose not to cross-examine her. The decision not to engage in the assaultive cross-examination that typifies defense attorney strategy in rape trials enhanced her appearance as a ghost, or a "supraobject" capable of countering deadly violence.

Her presence as a ghostlike figure provided more opportunities for spectators in the courtroom to fixate on her falseness. In the hallways, supporters of the defendants made charges that expressed disbelief about whether a "subject" of violence was really there. They claimed that the witness was an actress, that she was too sophisticated and educated to enable us to see the truth about her, and that she was a whore and would sleep with "anybody."

In the textual body of the trial, the woman and the defendants are never seen at the scene of the crime; they both escape vision except as part of the landscape. Even the prosecutor's attempt to place the defendants in the ravine at the estimated time of the attack operates in the narrative outside of the realm of seeing. Given the number of police in the area that night, it may seem inexplicable that no one saw the "roving band" near the place where her body was discovered, but the fact that the defendants were unseen is also essential to the narrative about their actions in the darkness. An erotic reality depends on the staging of appearance as disappearance; thus, the defendants' presence in the landscape is made real by their seeming ability to slip away into the park or to stay out of view even when the officers coordinated their locations in efforts to "head off the pack." The officers who testified could only speak of radio "transmissions" about roving bands of black and Hispanic teenagers in the north end of the park or report glimpses from a distance as the pack "jumped over a wall and started to separate." Yet to see the prosecution's inability to place the defendants at the scene of the crime as a "problem" for the state in making its case is to miss the power in the narrative of their "unseen" presence at the site. This evidentiary problem in the legal narrative is also a marker of an imaginary "real," in that the attack appears to be all the more inhuman because these teenage boys escape without a trace.

Yet the "unseen racial transgression" is a site of instability in the legal text. The prosecution's story about the motivations of the defendants depends on this "unseen" spectacle becoming a site of erotic imaginings. In the second part of this chapter I will suggest that this "unseen racial transgression" was the focus of a narrative dilemma for the prosecution, in that it forced the prosecution to confirm the reality of the unseen violence by viewing the sadistic pleasure of the defendants. The resolution of this dilemma, therefore, required the prosecution to create a narrative that engaged in its own form of sadistic satisfaction.

The prosecutor is the author of a story about the crime that has the explicit purpose of making the case for the guilt of the defendants. My interpretation of the trial, however, focuses on how prosecutors produce stories that do more than satisfy "love of justice." Indeed, the narrative must also satisfy the fantasies that make the sexual transgression real in the larger cultural narrative of the trial. From my perspective the "pleasure of the text" does not arise from gratuitous sensationalism of the sexual aspects of the crime but, rather, is the process by which the reality of the violence is affirmed in legal narrative constructed by prosecutors.

In the Central Park Jogger trial the prosecutor, Elizabeth Lederer, sought to "secure the vision" of racial transgression and sexual danger in the narrative. Her efforts were encumbered by the ways in which the defendants appeared to escape from actual physical and the textual landscape of the crime scene. The prosecutor "recaptures" the defendants at the scene in two ways: first, by focusing on the defendants videotaped confessions, in which they recount their own viewing of the attack; and second, by asserting that the teenage boys were motivated by the sexual pleasure of assaulting and raping the jogger. As I will soon explain, these strategies require a re-visioning of the rape scene in which the prosecutor replays the movement of sexual action around the jogger's body.

Who is engaging in the pleasure of looking at the sexual spectacle? Answering this was the prosecutor's, Elizabeth Lederer's, narrative dilemma. When she entreated her audience, particularly in her summation, to understand the defendants' brutality through the visual and representational techniques of realism, she risked the chance of making noticeable the prosecution's participation in the pleasures of watching. Thus, the process of making the events in Central Park realistic relies on a theory of sadistic pleasure of spectators, yet it hopes to confine the dangers of looking to the actions of the defendants.

In the summation, the prosecutor tells the story in a way which suggests that the defendants have marked the jogger as the chosen victim. She portrays the defendants as evil forces that arrive on the scene. She emphasizes that the defendants overwhelm their victims by their size and strength. In the prosecutor's version, the Central Park Jogger is "picked" as the victim; as she runs North on East Drive, she becomes "illuminated for the defendants and others to see." The boys took "positions" behind trees and ambushed her; she fell to the ground (leaving her "first trace") and then was dragged into the woods and darkness off the roadway. Here a racial image is evoked: The defendants assume the status of rational monsters, stalking, choosing, and seizing a particular and unknown white woman.

The pleasure of looking at the violence is replicated for the purposes of the Central Park Jogger trial not only by Lededer's reproduction of the scenario in two videotaped confessions by the defendants but also through numerous replays of these videos during the trial, which was over a month long. The prosecutor invited the jury to fully visualize the violence enacted on her body—the beating, the rape and sodomy. In the videotaped confessions we see the boys cornered in a small room, answering a series of questions about their own and others' participation in the rape. We are told that the first boy gripped her shirt and started to feel her. Steven Lopez covered her mouth when she started screaming, "smashed her," and said, "shut up you bitch," yet she keep on screaming and he "just kept smashing her and hitting her with a brick." The defendant explained: "She was like shocked, she just stood there and didn't do anything." In Anton McCray's videotape he described himself watching the other boys hitting her and removing her clothing; he later placed himself, with his pants down, on top of her, "so it would look like we were having sex. I was just doing it so everyone knew I did it." We also hear him say, "I didn't do nothing to her, I didn't put my penis in her."

The prosecutor described this defendant's account of his participation not for what it is, not as an account of the pleasures of viewing or being viewed, but as his futile effort to minimize his culpability. In doing so, she denied the partici-

pants' own version of the sexual scene, a version motivated by a homoerotic dynamic of performance and driven by watching rather than acting in the burying of a white woman in mud and blood. Lededer insisted that the boys experienced the attack as pleasurable in her own erotic terms. She explained that Raymond Santana came to the park "ready" to rob and beat people and "was not about to stand by and not be involved with the woman." In her erotic imaginings, Lededer asks us to visualize the scene, lasting only ten to twenty minutes, in which each boy is waiting to take a turn. She suggests, in an effort to deal with the absence of body traces, "[I]t is not difficult to imagine each person could not remain inside her to climax, they ejaculated before they could ever penetrate her." The dominant story, so to speak, that the prosecutor needs to project in order to tie together the real with the realistic makes pleasure a function of acting rather than viewing, sexuality a heterosexual performance rather than a visual erotics. And it also envisions dark-skinned men seeking out their unmarked target rather than packs of boys roving in the night. At one point Lededer used the defendant Yusef Salaam to validate her link between the "real" and this version of reality. Here she claimed that Yusef was prompted to make his statement not because of police pressure but because he believed the police officers when they told him that they "could get fingerprints off her breasts." In her summation Lededer brings us full circle in the process of nervous spectatorship. As the white, middle-class agent of the law, she climaxes her case with graphic imaginings of the sexual excitement experienced by these teenage boys.

In this chapter I have viewed the Central Park Jogger trial as what it is—a replication of violence, a textual landscape on which marks on bodies and terrain demonstrate the "real" presence of racial transgression, and on which seemingly apparitional visions are focused by realistic reenactments of pleasure. The Central Park Jogger trial as a spectacle is a negative cultural achievement, even a triumph for the dominant fiction, in its narrative ability to locate real and imagined pleasures on highly recognizable terrain of urban geography. The representational practices of the trial make racism seem more threatening, concrete, and embedded in the risks to daily existence. This spectacle, in fact, enables observers' unconscious desires and fears of racial "others" to be narrativized as the dominant perception of "what is seen" as racial transgression on the street, in the park, and other public spaces in urban life.

The link between racial and sexual imagery in the narrative is signified by the "strangeness" of the other. Strangeness is projected as part of the narrative's claim to realism. Because the Central Park Jogger is made familiar—she is the woman driven by the regularity of her work hours, jogging at the same time every day, socializing with friends of the same class and interests, and using a park where she has carefully planned jogging routes—the attack can only be an encounter with the strange: the unforeseen forces of racial violence, so unimaginable it shattered her conscious memory of that night.

The play of strangeness was also highlighted in media accounts of the trial, in which the "real" is sold in predictable and marketable forms

of shock and horror. Moreover, the motif of strangeness is particularly useful in reinforcing a frame of viewing in which we are not conscious of ourselves looking. Thus, the narrative protects the viewers from projecting the strangeness within. As Julia Kristeva argues, we can protect ourselves from encountering the "other" and facing our cosmopolitanism by locating the "other" outside of the familiar. In her words, we can "perceive its existence by means of sight . . . but we do not frame it within our consciousness" (Kristeva 1991, p. 187). Thus, the effect of the trial is to locate the "strange" outside of the familiar and to even seem to "prove" that virtual contact with the racial "other" is catastrophic. Racism, as a way of seeing, invades, and is protected within, unconscious sexual desire, through the projection of scenes that enlarge our capacity to keep fantasies (of ghosts, roving bands of animals, and violence as really pleasurable) alive in spectacles of the alien "other."

MEDIA
IMAGES OF
VIOLENCE

Introduction

The Seens and Unseens of
Popular Cultural Representation

LYNN S. CHANCER

"One of the areas where the media are most likely to be successful in mobilising public opinion within the dominant framework of ideas is on issues about crime and its threat to society," wrote Stuart Hall and several colleagues from the Birmingham Centre for Cultural Studies in 1978. "What debate there is tends to take place almost exclusively *within the terms of reference* of the controllers," they continued, "and this tends to repress any play between dominant and alternative definitions." Those viewpoints which challenge dominant perspectives, Hall and his colleagues argued, seldom shine in the spotlight of contemporary mass culture (Hall et al. 1978).

This is why the four chapters in part IV make an especially important contribution. For the authors would almost certainly agree with the above analysis, each having sought in her own way to criticize mainstream images of crime in the media in order to present alternative perspectives. The images that concern these writers have largely to do with gender. But dominant media representations concerning gender are also bound up—inextricably, in a sense—with other forms of

ongoing discrimination: with biases reflective of a homophobia that continues to be deeply entrenched in patriarchal culture, with still-virulent racist/anti-ethnic sentiments, with the still largely hidden injuries of class. Let me become more specific about these authors' shared presumptions, then, by way of introducing their interesting essays. I will then suggest some equally interesting differences of relative emphasis within this group of writings overall. In the course of such commentary, perhaps this short essay can add something of its own concerning the insights to which we are treated in the work of Kathleen Daly and Amy Chasteen, Ann Russo, Helen Benedict, and Lisa Ikemoto.

"Representations matter," state Daly and Chasteen toward the end of chapter 20, on the other side of the Atlantic from Hall yet in a kindred spirit almost twenty years later. "Whether in news stories, advertisements for safety products, police safety advice to women, or academic discourse on celebrated cases, these representations impinge on women's everyday lives in ways that circumscribe women's movement and discourage independence and strength." Of course, ideological representations not only incubate under conditions of imbalanced power relations but go on to reshape the external world. As has by now been often observed, mediated ideology creates effects in its turn, operating both with a noticeable degree of autonomy and amid ample degrees of constraint. In the feminist sense, personal as well as political life is affected by media; in the sense of social movements, dominant imagery can increase or diminish the likelihood of eventual politicization. Thus, these four essays clearly manifest an affinity with the Birmingham School tradition of devoting serious study to how popular culture encourages or inhibits social change. Not surprisingly, other related intellectual strains are also discernible in the backdrop of this section. In the theoretical background can also be sensed an Althusserian interest in understanding the workings of ideological apparatuses of the state and a Gramsci-esque concern about which interpretations of the social world come to be dominant and why. Applicable to these essays is the Gramscian concept that ideological consent—hegemony—is an achievement that depends on a particular social "reality" coming to appear as though seamless and created freely, as though eternally true even if really historically contingent. The talent of mass-mediated ideology, its quite special sleight of hand, entails a capacity to convince us that appearances are everything: What we see is all we come to believe exists or is possible.

It is precisely with this question of how hegemonic ideas come to be achieved and maintained that a common thread can be traced through the four ensuing essays. Each is, in its own way, a case study on the insidiousness of believing that what we see is all that exists or is possible. Yet perhaps even more germane than the recent intellectual history they share with Gramsci, Althusser, and the cultural studies legacy of the Birmingham School, these essays are inconceivable outside the context of a world profoundly affected by feminism. This is likely an even more important influence, insofar as the articles take up both gender biases and the overlapping of sexist attitudes with other prejudicial beliefs about sexual preference, race, ethnicity, and/or class.

So far, the common denominators this characterization has stated are fairly obvious. But in addition to these concerns about media and gender,

perhaps a subtler theme that also binds the essays together is that all four demonstrate relationships between what could be called the "seens and unseens" of popular cultural representation. Recurrent in these articles is an attempt to trace not only what becomes visible about gender through media but also what is thus rendered hidden; the authors discuss not only what is brought into the light but also that which thereby becomes obscured: Thus, studying mass-media imagery is simultaneously a sociological exploration in the genealogy of this distinction. The connection is illustrated through the essays in three ways. The first involves the fact that the very existence of high-profile crime cases—increasingly of interest not only to people working in media but to scholars as well—means, by implication, that a host of other incidents go ignored. Which cases come to be highlighted and why, the essays implicitly ask, and what does that process of selectivity reveal about American society and its attitudes toward gender, sexual preference, race, and class?

Second, media coverage of gender and crime often foregrounds certain elements of the social world while backgrounding other factors by extension: How does this happen at all, and why at particular moments in time rather than others? For example, if gender is downplayed in media treatments of specific crimes, important implications may result from other interpretations, thereby coming to take on relatively greater explanatory significance.

Third, the essays broach the issue of particular aspects of the social world presented to us in either/or fashion, as though necessarily in competition: Divisions may be underlined, while unifying potentials are relatively deemphasized. Even if gender, race, and class components can be shown to have been involved in a particular high-profile crime, for instance, consequent complexities are frequently reduced to apparently only two-sided proportions. It may be gender that will appear in media as though repetitively in opposition with race (see chapter 22), or one racialized group as though inevitably in opposition with another (see chapter 23). How each side often overlaps with the other, or seeming antagonisms effectively distract our attention from *other* common concerns (say, for example, class inequities in American society), are viewpoints rather predictably played down. Or it may be the good woman/

bad woman, madonna/whore divide that becomes media-magnified, not the forms of oppression that women face in common. Lesbians and/or sex workers can face stigmatization through representation, for instance, compared with other women whose class status can mitigate (though not at all necessarily eliminate) such mediated expressions of gender-related hostility. Common to all three issues taken from the chapters to follow, then, are observations about this relation between the "seen and unseen." The writers analyze how it comes to pass that media images encourage only the glimpsing of some perspectives, while others—and likely, as Hall suggested, those most challenging of dominant ideological beliefs—are relegated out of focus, outside our customary range of vision.

Let me become progressively more concrete now about how the following chapters illustrate these three points. First, a major query of Daly and Chasteen's thought-provoking essay is whether a variety of scholars have become overly concerned with studying the same high-profile cases that attract the media for reasons as uninformed as they may be prejudicial. According to Daly and Chasteen, focusing differential attention on celebrated cases that involved stranger-to-stranger crimes—such as the 1989 Central Park Jogger case they mention in chapter 20 (this case is also the main subject of chapters 18 and 22)—obscures far more typical cases of violence against women committed by acquaintances or family members. The coauthors cite statistics showing decreases in crime overall, so that high-profile cases may serve to make women more fearful of crime than is warranted and not wary *enough* about situations taken for granted to be relatively safe. Thus, patriarchal controls emerge as in part sustained by media-generated fears of crime. For Daly and Chasteen, feelings of insecurity are only reinforced by images of atypical high-profile crimes, which distract attention from criticisms of the nuclear family and the violence that is much more typically prevalent in (rather than outside) its walls.

Continuing this theme of how the seen-as-opposed-to-unseen shapes the content of high-profile crime cases (and the sorts of situations that come to be highlighted or ignored by mass media): Given that certain cases *do* become high-profile crime instances, whether or not we approve, who are the women and/or men toward whom our attentions are directed? Usually, cases are promoted to high-profile visibility because of the perceived respectability of victim or perpetrator, or because of comparative status differences between them. On the opposite side of this coin, other cases and types of cases are thereby *demoted* in the direction of invisibility because of the exact opposite relation—the perceived *disrespectability* of victim or perpetrator, or the differences between them. Chapter 21 is wonderfully instructive with regard to this question. The Central Park Jogger case presented a woman less likely to be doubly stigmatized after bringing rape charges because of her comparatively well-recognized social status (white and an investment banker); co-relatively, a woman who is a sex worker/prostitute, who may be a lesbian, who may be a person of color, or who may be poor will more likely face additional social disapproval simply for having chosen to prosecute violence. Moreover, crimes against lesbians and/or sex workers may not be investigated, let alone prosecuted, by a state still pervaded by patriarchal practices and structures of thought. As Russo points out, the fundamentally sexist bad woman/ good woman dichotomy may be so well ingrained in societal consciousness that people may not even believe sex workers *can* be raped, as though the very notion is a contradiction in terms.[1]

On the other hand, Russo also calls attention to how, even *within* this comparative invisibility of particular women relative to others, some cases nevertheless rise to individual high-profile notice. The case of Aileen Wuornos, widely depicted by journalists as a lesbian "serial killer" who also worked as a prostitute in Florida, showed the media's willingness to make an exception to its usual lack of interest in the conditions of sex workers' lives. Both sensationalistically and rather didactically, Wuornos was presented as the quintessential "bad woman." But given the dangers involved in her work as a prostitute (a reality worsened not only by stigmatization but by the interrelated effects of criminalization), it would not be at all surprising if Wuornos acted in self-defense in at least some of the incidents of which she stood accused. Because such women are seen only through a bad-woman lens, though, the actual threats Wuornos and her colleagues regularly face in prostitution and their much more typical *invisibility* was hidden, presented only in terms of Wuornos having victimized others (rather than in terms of having been exposed to possible victimization herself). An interview conducted for a book I am writing on high-profile crimes verified the existence of this good woman/bad woman dichotomy and its implications for which cases may be taken seriously, or ignored, by police and media. In yet another reference to the Central Park Jogger attack, which took place on April 19, 1989, a New York City detective commented in an interview that certainly an attack on a "black prostitute" would not have gotten so much attention (and, in fact, there were over twenty rapes that same week which went unnoticed by the press); the case of a (white) academic, he added as though presumably a comforting thought, would be dealt with much more soberly by cops and media.[2]

Another illustration of how this seen-as-opposed-to-unseen affects popular cultural representations of gender and crime emerges from chapter 22, by Helen Benedict. One of Benedict's main points is that *even* in the Central Park Jogger case (where the victim seemed to be benefiting from discrimination *in favor* of her class and race, and from media coverage as positive toward her as it was negatively stigmatizing of the teenagers accused of her assault), certain explanatory frameworks used by media nonetheless contributed toward producing gender-biased ideological effects. Drawing on extensive research from her book *Virgin or Vamp: How the Press Covers Sex Crimes*, Benedict shows that the most obvious framework for understanding the Central Park Jogger case—that is, as an instance of misogyny, which pervades sexist societies *across* class and race—was almost entirely omitted from media coverage of this incident. Race, poverty, the problems of teenage youth (or so-called wilding, as the term was speciously misnamed by police who did not understand a Tone-Loc rap reference to "the wild thing"), racist references to "wolfpack language," drugs, violence in inner cities, capital punishment, the need for more education or better family values: a litany of valid or invalid, more and less familiar sociological diagnoses were presented, while gender was conspicuous mostly for the glaring fact of its absence from discussion.

I would suggest, in agreement with Benedict, that the effects of ignoring the pervasiveness of gender bias in this kind of high-profile case can be insidious indeed: Instead of an occasion for calling attention to patriarchal violence's existence across race and class, the incident became an occasion for the media to reveal its own additional race and class-biased tendencies. The absence of gender showed one problematic aspect of "how the press covers sex crimes"; the corollary presence of unexamined assumptions about race and class factors brought other social stereotypes to the surface. In the process, gender certainly did come to be played against race, to the detriment of all involved. This foregrounding of race and class prejudices as subjects of social and media discussion (or "discourse") about the case, and the backgrounding of gender which went along with it, meant that the fact of sexism existing *within* young men of all races and classes could be overlooked in favor of speciously making *these* young men appear as though unique (picked out for high-profile treatment because of their race and class, when, in gender terms, they may have been, if anything, *too* typical).

Simultaneously, it is not surprising that as the Central Park Jogger case went to trial, increased victim-blaming of the young woman tended to unfold *despite* her race and class advantages. On the one hand, because of the media's display of its own race and class biases in this incident, the gendered dimension of violence committed against her was overshadowed by the race and class privileges the jogger possessed: Why is violence committed against poor women and women of color so regularly ignored by media, while this particular incident was catapulted to high-profile consciousness? On the other hand, and in another sense, this same counterposing of gender against race (both in the media and through law) paradoxically mitigated against this atypicality of the jogger's social position, rendering her increasingly vulnerable to exactly the same sort of victim-blaming that is frequently encountered by women in rape cases *across* race and class due to the pervasiveness of patriarchal suppositions.

Through this second foregrounding/backgrounding issue, then, the third respect in which these essays show a connection between the seens and unseens of popular culture comes to be anticipated: namely, the appearance of false social dichotomies as though inevitable, or the setting up of false competitions between certain dimensions of the social world—say, gender versus race. For chapter 22 evidences both the second as well as this third point—as does chapter 23. Like Benedict's, Lisa Ikemoto's essay disturbingly suggests how the factor of gender was missing from media accounts of events leading up to and following the Rodney King verdict in Los Angeles. In a fascinating account, Ikemoto describes the emergence of racial identity as the dominant framework for most of the media's understanding of the L.A. riots/rebellion: The primary conflict presented appeared to be one between Korean Americans versus African Americans. In the process, and at the same time, the terms of debate which unfolded took for granted that this foregrounded racial dimension was fundamentally a dispute *between men*. As Ikemoto points out, a well-known incident that preceded the Rodney King verdict was the Soon Ja Du/Latasha Harlins incident, in which a Korean grocer shot and killed an African American teenager presumed to be a robber; Soon Ja Du was sentenced merely to probation after a Compton jury's conviction, a fact that slowly but surely contributed to rising anger felt by many people in Los Angeles's African American community even before the Simi Valley acquittals were announced. Yet, once again, note the relation between what is seen and not seen in this case: The Soon Ja Du/Latasha Harlins incident was quite indisputably one *between women*. Had this aspect of the story been highlighted in media rather than deemphasized, it might have been more difficult to frame the incident predominantly in terms of a Korean American/African American conflict.

But again—and harkening back to Benedict's chapter as well—Ikemoto's account makes clear that the "Korean versus African American" racial framing has decidedly political/depoliticizing ramifications, whether or not they are consciously intended. For divisions between people come to appear far more important than bridges potentially buildable: In the media, antagonisms are usually taken to be "sexier" than the remarking of similarities. But commonalities are there, were we (or the media) to care to look for them: in (say) similar class positions across race and ethnicity; in (say) common vulnerabilities to bias or false expectations about life in America faced by women as well as men and, of course,

between groups that are new and groups that have lived in this country for generations; or in (say) gender-based common stigmas faced by women despite and within also-important race and class forms of stratification. From a political perspective, then, this sort of post–Rodney King playing of ethnicity/race versus race—and a concomitant failure to emphasize the sense of dispossession and subordination people experience *in common*—can have a self-reproducing effect by nourishing the very resentments, and obscuring the conditions and problems, that influenced the unfolding of events in the first place. This sows seeds of discord rather than potential collective strength, of course, and feeds depoliticization as one of its corollary effects. Still another time, media accounts are presented in far too simplified a manner to adequately encompass the complicated social world such accounts purport to describe—and, in the media's general belief system, purport to describe "objectively".

Gender versus race in Benedict, race versus ethnicity in Ikemoto, the highlighting in media of either/or oppositions, and a downplaying of commonalities between people by extension . . . How, more precisely, might the presentation of such factors as though necessarily oppositional inhibit the likelihood of broader social transformations, theoretically and practically? In researching high-profile crime cases on my own, I have also noticed a gender-versus-race pattern recurring like a variation on the larger theme of American media tending to direct attention toward divisions rather than commonalities. This pattern was certainly exemplified in the 1989 Central Park Jogger case but has continued through a number of even more recent high-profile incidents. For example, it seems peculiar indeed that the three most symbolically celebrated examples of prosecutions for distinctly feminist-oriented crimes in the last decade have been cases brought against well-known African American men from 1991 to the present. Think back: The most successful high-profile presentation of a man for rape was that of Mike Tyson in 1991 (not William Kennedy Smith, whose acquittal is also well-known); also in 1991, the best-publicized case of sexual harassment to date emerged in the figure of Clarence Thomas, not (as might have been possible) Bob Packwood or even Bill Clinton; the criminal trial of O. J.

Simpson for homicide brought more public attention to the problem of domestic violence than any other case in recent times.

The point on which I wish now to focus attention is that there are decidedly political implications of the mass media's having highlighted *these* cases as opposed to others which might have become widely publicized instead. (Since we know that rape, sexual harassment, and domestic violence take place across class and race lines, surely there must have been a few well-to-do white men who might have become the subject of high-profile media treatments?) A troubling ramification of this pattern may be to speciously make feminist concerns seem as though *necessarily* opposed to an equally thorough awareness about ongoing realities of race- and class-based discriminations in American society. In and through the race-patterned highlighting of the Tyson, Thomas, and Simpson cases, feminism's past negative associations with mostly white and middle-class women's concerns—with a "white" feminism that historically did not sufficiently encompass both commonalities *and* differences between women by race, class, and/or sexual preferences—appears to still be ongoing, to be a fear still seemingly well-founded as now reinforced in the media. At the same time, concerns about race (quite real concerns, not only in the Central Park case but in the other cases as well—for why do we focus differentially only on certain victims, and on certain defendants as well?) appear as though themselves antagonistic to sensitivity about *gender*-based concerns—which *do*, of course, apply to women of color, including to the concerns of Desiree Washington and Anita Hill in these very cases. Moreover, last but not least, the counterposing of gender versus race as a repetitive pattern in and through the Tyson/Thomas/Simpson cases contributes to class receding ever more subtly into the background. The relative downplaying of class, a social factor that rarely appears as the focus or at the center of media debates about American culture and politics, may serve only to further solidify the playing of gender against race by dint of its own only apparent insignificance.

Perhaps this analysis can be illuminated more forcefully with a hypothetical example. Imagine a situation in which it was *not* Tyson, Thomas, and Simpson who became symbolic and mass-mediated exemplars of distinctively feminist concerns about the frequency of violence against women—rape, sexual harassment, domestic violence—in the United States. Instead, imagine that it was Donald Trump who was accused of rape (and then by a woman who was poor or working-class, and perhaps a woman of color); Newt Gingrich or Robert Dole who was accused of sexual harrassment; and Clint Eastwood or Sylvester Stallone who was accused of domestic violence and/or homicide. Suddenly we go from one actual situation to another hypothetical one, and in so doing we greatly alter the sociological configurations involved (as in Configurations I and II below: I have put the race, gender, and class characteristics of the accused defendants on the left-hand side, and those of the person on whose behalf charges are being prosecuted on the right):

Configuration I: Tyson/Thomas/Simpson

Characteristics of Defendants:	*Characteristics of Victims/ Accusers:*
Minority	Minority/white
Male	Female
Well-to-do	Middle-class professional/well-to-do

In this first (the actual) configuration, note that it is the factor of *gender* which most clearly differentiates the two "sides," sides that result from media accounts reflecting a "defendant" versus "complainant" structure of court cases. At the same time, race and class seem to be neutralized by virtue of the fact that in all of the cases, class statuses are similar on the opposite sides. In two of the cases, race can be held as though constant (two of the women bringing charges were, of course, themselves African American, though observers tended to focus more on their gender than their race, a differential highlighting that likely results in part from the gender-versus-race effects I am analyzing). Thus, it may be a gender-based difference which will come to seem most responsible for each of the three cases posing a threat to the success of a well-known African American *man* who has risen in class status (while what is alleged to have happened to an *African American* woman thereby recedes from focus in the mediated view). If Tyson is convicted, Thomas not confirmed, Simpson found guilty, then black men's symbolic successes are simultaneously placed in jeopardy. What is interesting in this configuration is that gender emerges as seemingly most to blame for bringing about this diminution in race/class/gender status of male defendants—and *not* the ongoing realities of class and race discrimination in America. Relatively speaking, class and race *appear* to be *ir*relevant social factors (and capable of being cancelled out) because of their similar presence on both "sides" of the legal equation.

Now imagine a second scenario, this time entirely hypothetical:

Configuration II:
Trump/Gingrich/Dole Eastwood/Stallone

Characteristics of Imagined Defendants:	*Characteristics of Imagined Victims/Accusers:*
White	Minority/Male
Male	Female
Well-to-do	Working-class/poor

This time, in and through this imaginary media scenario, gender can no longer be played against race and class as forms of bias because now race and class do *not* appear as though irrelevant: Class and race do *not* seem as though they can be cancelled out, or neutralized, on both sides of a legalistic equation. Rather than being on opposite sides of legal court cases that come to high-profile attention, race and class are in this hypothetical *aligned* with gender, insofar as I have conceived of the defendants as women who might have been poor and/or of color. Now, suddenly, the sociological characteristics of imagined "accusers" reflect the possibility that they have experienced multiple and overlapping forms of *powerlessness,* just as these imagined "accuseds" in all probability possess multiple and mutually overlapping forms of *power.* Consequently, and by extension, power relations that become *apparent* in media suddenly coincide with what we know to be true about *actual* (and statistically demonstrable) socioeconomic stratification as it much more realistically exists in the United States.

I propose this imaginary scenario not only for purposes of political critique but also to provide a sharper illustration of how a world might look if the four authors' observations about the seens-as-opposed-to-unseens of popular culture were to be treated with due importance. Not only would representations matter, as Daly and Chasteen argue, but what is *not represented would also matter.* Consequences almost certainly would arise from commonalities' becoming easier to glimpse through alternative images and from insights' stemming out of alternative theoretical/political work. Suddenly, we can turn our attentions toward the actually existing structures of power all around us rather than dwelling only on media representations of legal cases that are actually quite delimiting of our social imaginations.

But I would like to end these introductory comments with some observations about differences, too, about several interesting points of divergence that are found amid these essays in addition to their common unveiling of hidden assumptions and false dichotomies within media representations. Two issues strike me as especially worthy of note. The first has to do with an internal debate that is easy to see if the articles are juxtaposed with one another. Daly and Chasteen question precisely the focus on high-profile crime cases that is the subject of other essays in this section (Benedict's and Ikemoto's essays and to some extent Russo's), of other essays in this book (for instance, Bumiller's), of my own research into high-profile crime cases (mentioned in passing in this introductory essay). Are Daly and Chasteen right to be concerned about the wisdom of directing so much energy toward examining high-profile cases, thereby potentially losing sight of much more typical and everyday crime incidents that affect diverse women's lives in quite diverse ways? Or, on the other hand, would ignoring high-profile crime cases be rather silly—in a cultural sense its own way analogous to the futility of Luddites' having tried to throw out machines rather than accept the irreversibility of the Industrial Revolution and technological changes? Are these celebrated cases part of our culture, whether we like it or not? If so, then perhaps Bumiller's earlier article has critical importance, insofar as it explores in depth—and beneath the surface at potentially deeper levels of our social psyches—*why* it is that high-profile crime cases attract us, possibly providing unconscious pleasure in spectatorship by also "playing" with generally unacknowledged mythological fantasies about gender and/or race. If Bumiller is right that such unconscious feelings about eroticized violence are tapped through high-profile cases (and perhaps the attraction of media *and* publics are commonly linked through these incidents), then attempting to supplant them with more "typical" cases may not be successful because new cases can also become framed so as to meet these deeply felt and often unconscious desires—desires that profoundly relate to how our social psyches have in large part been socially influenced and constructed.

A second noticeable, and related, debate among these essays has to do with whether or not there "really" is the amount of crime in American society that the media (and high-profile cases emphasized within media) would lead us to believe. There is a growing literature, both in British sociology and criminology and currently burgeoning in the United States as well, about "fear of crime" being nurtured through the media at the same time that crime rates have been going down. According to Daly and Chasteen, it is important to call attention to fear of crime. Yet from some of the other essays (notably, Russo's and Benedict's), one comes away with a sense that violence against women—and especially against women who find themselves in relatively demeaned socioeconomic positions—is not being taken seriously *enough* and that patriarchal violence continues to be underemphasized or underreported. How can these two viewpoints be reconciled, if at all?

Perhaps readers will agree (or perhaps not) that just as gender need not be counterposed competitively against race, nor one racial group against another (even if they have been thus aligned, antagonistically, by the media up until now), so these two sets of positions need not be posed as either/or polarities. It may be true *both* that attention to high-profile cases needs to be analyzed with a grain of salt, within the context of critical distance (in order not to confuse media appearances with social existence, and allowing attention to also be directed toward the more typical situations that media images frequently *mis*represent). *And* it may be true, at the same time, that there is value in analyzing high-profile crime cases per se since we cannot alter media predilections overnight any more than we can immediately change deeply embedded psychic needs on which these cases quite likely play. It may be true *both* that crime in American society has diminished in certain categories and that

within those categories certain types and victims of crime (including violence against women, and then violence against some women more than others) are still not given sufficiently intelligent recognition and analysis by the press, nor adequate recognition within the criminal justice system. Rather than a adopting "fear of crime" perspective that strengthens a Katie Roiphe–style assertion that violence against women is vastly exaggerated, perhaps we do need to give precise and specific thought to where and how violence is occurring both in and beyond the institutions of media. How has it come to pass in the twenty years since radical Second Wave feminism that criticisms of the nuclear family (and domestic violence, including rape, agreed to be common within it) have themselves been often overlooked or forgotten? How can we begin to alter misogyny throughout a variety of social spheres and institutions, in the process calling attention to problems faced by *all* women—not only middle-class and white women but also women who are poor, or who happen to be lesbian, or who are treated as though of second-class minority backgrounds, or who may work at great risk in the still patriarchally oriented political economy of sex work?

This essay itself tried to demonstrate some of the seens and unseens and specious either/ors of mass-media images of gender and crime, as glimpsed through this set of chapters. But more important, I urge the reader to discover for herself/himself how "representations matter" in and outside the essays that follow.

Notes

1. I discussed the double standard surrounding the criminalization of prostitution in a recent article entitled "Prostitution, Feminist Theory, and Ambivalence: Notes from the Sociological Underground" (Chancer 1994).

2. I refer to an interview conducted with a member of the New York City Police Department as research for the book *Provoking Assaults* (Chancer 1996). Second, according to Terry 1989, there were twenty-eight other first-degree rapes or attempted rapes during the week of April 19, 1989, the same week when the Central Park Jogger assault took place.

20

Crime News, Crime Fear, and Women's Everyday Lives

KATHLEEN DALY & AMY L. CHASTEEN

On any given day when we pick up a newspaper, listen to the radio, or watch television, the crime and justice stories we read and hear about bear little relationship to the "reality" of crime. While the content of crime stories can vary by medium and market, crime news focuses disproportionately on violent offenses and atypical cases. The most serious types of crimes—whether forms of street crime, intimate violence, or elite crime—receive the greatest media coverage. The crimes considered "newsworthy" are "ingenious, vicious, audacious" acts (Katz 1987, p. 50); they feature unusual, dramatic, or whimsical circumstances and famous or high-status people (Roshier 1973). The most sensational crimes—what we term celebrated cases—combine several newsworthy elements. For several decades, scholars have noted a disjuncture between what crimes "make the news" and the wider world of crime from studies and statistics (Barak 1994a; Ericson, Baranek, and Chan 1989; Fishman 1978; Surette 1992; Warr 1991). Scholars are less sure, however, about how crime in the news (or in television drama) affects people's attitudes and beliefs about

crime or the formation of public policy toward crime.

Joined with the *crime-news disjuncture* is a *crime-fear disjuncture*. A recent poll of U.S. adults shows substantial gender differences in crime fear: Far more women (55 percent) than men (26 percent) report that they are afraid to walk alone at night in their own neighborhood—a gender gap of about 30 percentage points. That gap in crime fear has been even larger in previous years: on the order of 35 to 40 percentage points (Maguire and Pastore 1994, pp. 188–89, Table 2.39).[1]

At the same time, surveys of people's experiences of victimization show that men are more likely to be victims of crime, especially violent crime, than women. As calculated from the National Crime Victimization Survey (NCVS), the estimated annual rate of men's violent crime victimization is about 40 per 1,000; that for women is 25 per 1,000 (Bachman 1994, p. 2).[2] There are well-known problems with the NCVS interview methodology in gathering accurate data on violent victimization, especially for rape and intimate or family violence. Specifically, those interviewed were never directly asked if they had been raped (Bachman 1994, p. 14; Eigenberg 1991) or if they had been victimized by someone they know (Bachman 1994, p. 13; Bachman and Taylor 1994); thus, women's violent crime victimization rates, as estimated from the NCVS through 1991, have been underestimated.[3] But even if we assume that women's violent victimization rate were as high as men's, we would need to explain why women's generalized fear of crime is so much greater than men's. What explains the disjuncture between women's fear of crime and their likelihood of being victims of crime?

Feminist scholars suggest that women's greater fear is not "irrational" but reflects the different dangers men and women face in their daily lives.[4] For example, Stanko (1990) argues that while victimization surveys measure "public crime" (typically understood as "stranger danger"), crime-fear surveys are also tapping women's experiences with "private danger" (violent victimization from intimates). Further, Stanko (1985, 1990) and others (Gardner 1988; Gordon and Riger 1989; Hanmer and Maynard 1987) point out that while men may worry about assault, women's fears center more on rape. Complicating the matter is that women's fears of violent victimization are most likely to be concentrated on stranger rape, for which their chances of victimization are relatively low, whereas they are less likely to fear intimate violence or rape, for which their chances of victimization are higher. The NCVS data for 1987 to 1991 show that for violent victimizations (rape, robbery, and assault), the composition of victim-offender relations for women victims was as follows: intimates and relatives 33 percent, acquaintances 35 percent, and strangers 31 percent.[5] By comparison, for men victims, the composition was intimates and relatives 5 percent, acquaintances 50 percent, and strangers 44 percent (Bachman 1994, p. 6; in 1 percent of men's and women's victimizations, the relationship was unknown).

Might women's greater fear of crime be related to media-generated images of likely crimes and victims? How do media-generated images of crime affect the ways that, in Stanko's terms (1990, p. 6), women "negotiate the daily threat and experience of danger"? Like most scholars (e.g., Ericson 1991; Ericson, Baranek, and Chan 1989; Schlesinger et al. 1992; Surette 1992), we

acknowledge the difficulty of claiming any specific media "effects" on audiences. "The media" and "audiences" are highly varied in the way stories are told, received, and read.[6] However, we wish to contribute to a small but growing sociological literature on women's experiences with violence, women's fear of crime, and media-generated stories about crime.

In our analysis of the crime news and crime fear disjunctures, we want to consider a third component: disciplinary and methodological differences in analyzing images of crime in the media. We compare what is termed "cultural studies" with social science[7] approaches to analyzing media. With due regard for diverse work that may fall under a cultural studies umbrella, we are concerned with a tendency by those taking a cultural studies approach to focus on celebrated crime cases. Thus, the same problems we see in media-generated stories about crime are repeated in critical analyses of cases, which without a wider appreciation of crime patterns produce a scholarly version of crime sensationalism.

Our chapter is organized in four sections. First, we consider the varied disciplinary and methodological approaches to analyzing culture, of which the media images of crime are just one part. Second, we review the literature on crime news and what's wrong with crime news. We are interested in the regular media conventions used in telling stories about crime and how these may foster increased anxieties or fears of crime. We then turn to two research studies that analyze women's fear of crime, their experiences of victimization, the role of the media in shaping crime fear, and how and why single women routinely make decisions with safety uppermost in their minds. The final section sums up our argument and considers implications for scholars, journalists, and feminist advocates.

Cultural Studies and Social Science Approaches to Culture

Over the last several decades, an interest in culture has burgeoned within and across disciplines in the humanities and social sciences (Agger 1992; Dirks, Eley, and Ortner 1994; Nelson and Grossberg 1988). That interest has spawned academic inquiry into popular culture and diverse forms of mass media (Baudrillard 1983; Fiske

1989; Hall 1981; Hebdige 1988; Kellner 1990; Mukerji and Schudson 1991; Radway 1984; R. Williams 1974, 1977). News stories are one product of media institutions; thus, an analysis of news suggests the need to consider what culture is and how it can be analyzed. We compare two analytic orientations: cultural studies and social science approaches.

A basic difference in these two ways of analyzing culture lies in their locations. With a social science approach, a sociological or anthropological analysis of culture is located within a particular discipline. Culture is one of many relatively fixed objects of study on which one can focus with a sociological or anthropological lens. It is an entity, historically conceived of as a unified set of phenomena to be observed, identified, and scientifically analyzed. Traditional anthropological notions of culture, for example, defined culture as "shared" and as a "system of symbols" (Dirks, Eley, and Ortner 1994). As such, culture may be viewed from the outside by a scientific observer and analyzed with a particular disciplinary lens.

Cultural studies is not located in a discipline or focused on a single, unified culture. Rather, cultural studies uses a broader definition of culture that includes popular culture or forms of low culture that had previously been ignored (Agger 1992; Bourdieu and Wacquant 1992; Hall 1988; Hebdige 1988). From an enlarged view of what constitutes culture, questions are raised about what has traditionally been conceived as culture in sociology, anthropology, or other social sciences. For example, when we speak of culture as "shared," we may now ask, shared by whom and in what ways? (Dirks, Eley, and Ortner 1994). From a cultural studies perspective, the cultural field is about power and about conflict over socially legitimate practices and meanings (Agger 1992). Culture is not simply a neutral system of symbols, shared and reproduced, but, rather, a power struggle over meaning.

With a cultural studies orientation, power is not something held by some to be exercised over others. Rather, power may flow through institutions and individuals: It cannot be possessed, only produced and resisted (Foucault 1984, 1986). Cultural studies scholars argue that culture can function as a form of resistance (Bourdieu and Wacquant 1992; Hall 1981; Hebdige 1979). Thus, culture is not simply an object to

be observed, but a potentially counterhegemonic practice of rebellion (Agger 1992; Dirks, Eley, and Ortner 1994; Gramsci 1971). Viewing culture in this way reconfigures the position of the researcher or scholar from that of observer to that of participant. It also reconfigures the role of the audience members from that of passive recipients to that of active readers. Thus, no external reference point exists from which to describe or measure culture: It is an active and dynamic process of creation and interpretation. Or as Agger suggests, "[R]eading writes" (1992, p. 105).

Cultural studies practitioners, and especially those taking a postmodern bent (e.g., Baudrillard), have been criticized for analyses that seem nihilistic or useless. Our concern with cultural studies is not with its premises about power and representation but, rather, with the methodological tools and assumptions used to analyze culture. The typical approach is sustained attention to a selective set of illustrative or interesting cases (Hall 1988; Hebdige 1979, 1988). Two recent examples are Garber, Matlock, and Walkowitz's *Media Spectacles* (1993) and Fiske's *Media Matters* (1994). The authors of the first volume focus on celebrated cases (also termed "media spectacles" or "atrocity tales") such as the William Kennedy Smith rape trial, the Jeffrey Dahmer case, coverage of the Gulf War, and the assassination of John F. Kennedy. Likewise, Fiske (1994) draws from events such as the O. J. Simpson trial and the Hill Thomas hearings. He argues that through public discussion and debate about these events, previously unheard voices of women and racial/ethnic minorities emerged in various media domains.

We grant that high-profile cases are part of culture and, as such, they are appropriate subjects for analysis. But in the area of crime and justice, to focus on such cases to the exclusion of a broader understanding of crime patterns and justice system practices is to replicate the media's organizational practices in the selection of crime stories. Many scholars now seem to be taking the same approach as journalists and news editors who choose stories on the basis of their newsworthy elements. We are aware, of course, that neither scholars nor media personnel can hold a mirror to a culture in depicting some reality of crime. Yet it is important that empirical studies of media and crime be conducted in a systematic way, one not driven by a celebrated case-based focus. We should investigate how people's understandings of crime are shaped by celebrated crime and justice cases. We should probe citizens' perceptions of "the crime problem," how crime and danger are managed in our lives, and how fear of crime and victimization are experienced along the multiple axes of class, race, gender, and other factors. As long as media and scholarly practices attend to celebrated cases, without an appreciation of variation or sociohistorical grounding, citizens' knowledge about crime and justice system practices will be based on an impoverished (if dramatic) diet of extreme cases. What may be newsworthy or illustrative from a journalistic or cultural studies point of view may satisfy readers on many levels of emotional pleasure. It may also exact a cost in amplified fears of crime for some groups and decreased understanding of the broader problem of crime for all.

Crime in the News

In reviewing research on crime in the news, we have several observations. First, we know a good deal about the crime-news disjuncture—that is, the difference between what is known about crime from official statistics and what is reported about crime in the media. We also know that news outputs vary by the medium used, be it television, radio, or print. Second, we know less (or studies conflict) about the effect of crime news on citizens' attitudes toward crime or preferred policies toward crime. Third, we know very little about *variation* in the impact of crime news for members of different class, racial, or gender groups. With some exceptions, this chapter focuses on analyses of crime stories in the news rather than crime in television or film drama, in the television tabloids, or in "reality-based" programming. All these sources of crime news are important in understanding how citizens make sense of crime and danger, but we wished to simplify our task by focusing on "the news" as one major source of information about crime.[8]

Crimes That Make the News

Crimes that occur least often are the most likely to be reported in the news. The Uniform Crime Reports (UCR) index of the seven violent and property crimes reported to the police shows that the violent crimes (murder and non-negligent manslaughter, rape, robbery, and aggravated assault) represent about 12 percent of crimes reported by citizens and recorded by the police. *Of these violent offenses,* 1 percent are of murder and non-negligent manslaughter; 6 percent, rape; and 36 percent, robbery. Overall, then, murder and rape are a tiny fraction (.2 and .7 percent, respectively) and robbery a small fraction (5 percent) of the seven index crimes reported to the police.[9] Crime news tells a different story about crime. As reviewed by Warr (1991, p. 15), newspapers and especially television are likely to report criminal homicide: Of crimes reported in the news, murder comprised 12 to 26 percent of stories in New Orleans and Chicago newspapers and 45 to 50 percent of stories on three New Orleans television stations. Robbery was the next most likely violent crime reported in the newspapers and on television (about one-third of the stories), and rape accounted for 3 to 6 percent of stories. Violent or dramatic offenses and those involving famous or high-status people are the crimes that make the news (Bortner 1984; Katz 1987; Roshier 1973). There is no relationship between the coverage of crime stories in the news and increases and decreases in selected crimes reported to the police.[10] For example, the number of homicides reported to the police decreased somewhat from 1992 to 1993, but the number of homicide news stories reported in the three major networks' evening news broadcasts tripled during the same period of time (Center for Media and Public Affairs 1994, p. 2).

Estimates vary on the frequency with which crime news appears on television and in newspapers. Researchers may define "crime news" differently or use a different population of total stories. Comparing research on newspapers, the percent of crime news stories ranges from a low of 11 to 16 percent (Chermak 1994, pp. 102–3; Jerin and Fields 1994, p. 190), to 22 to 28 percent (Jerin and Fields 1994, p. 190, referencing their study and that by Graber 1979), to a high of 45 to 47 percent (Ericson, Baranek, and Chan 1989, p. 241). Crime news is the third largest category in newspapers (Chermak 1994, p. 101, citing Sherizen 1978; see also Graber 1979), following news of government and politics and economic and social issues. While crime news is a staple of news reporting, it is also used as filler. For example, on a slow news day, column space or television air time may be filled in with crime stories, whereas on a day when other stories are breaking, crime news stories may be edited out.

Gleaning the major images from television and newspapers, we find two distinctive types of lawbreakers: "a high status person gone berserk with greed" (Surette 1992, p. 35) and "the violent, predatory criminal . . . who preys upon unsuspecting victims" (Surette 1994, pp. 150, 136). Bortner's review of research on crime news conducted during the 1960s and 1970s concludes that the typical criminal portrayed was older, of higher social status, and white, compared to the profile of those arrested for crime (1984, p. 17). She finds, however, that media images and official statistics were consistent in representing men as lawbreakers. We have not found research that has analyzed the profiles of either victims or victim-offender relations in crime-news stories. However, studies of crime entertainment drama during the 1970s and 1980s show that crime victims are depicted as helpless and passive; compared to official victimization data, victims in television crime entertainment are more likely to be white and to be young women (Surette 1992, p. 35).

The most comprehensive analysis of the content of crime news to date has been conducted by Ericson, Baranek, and Chan (1989).[11] The authors analyzed the content of crime news in two newspapers, two television stations, and two radio stations during a thirty-three-day period in the summer of 1983 in Toronto. They selected a popular and quality outlet for two media (newspaper and radio); both television stations had a popular-market orientation. Although they did not explore how gender or race and so on featured in the content of news stories of crime and victimization, their study is important in showing similarities and differences across media and market orientations. Compared to previous scholars (Fishman 1978; Hall et al. 1978; Tuchman 1978a, 1978b), they offer a more pluralistic reading of "what's in the news" and why. Some of their findings are highlighted as follows.

1. Reported stories varied by medium and market. Interpersonal conflict, especially individual acts of violent crime, dominated in the popular newspaper, the popular radio station, and both

television stations. Economic deviance was more frequent in the quality newspaper and, to a lesser extent, in the quality radio station (p. 353).

2. Journalists and government officials were the most frequently cited source types. They were so dominant that the authors conclude that "the news is primarily a public conversation among journalists and government officials with others allowed to make only occasional utterances and to eavesdrop" (p. 349).

3. In almost all crime stories (90 percent) sources offered no evidence to support their claims. Depending on the medium, research studies or official statistics were cited by a very small proportion (1 to 3 percent) of news sources (p. 351).

4. Sources of all types were called upon to provide "primary factual understanding." Explanations, however, were infrequent. When given, they were low-level accounts without consideration of social structure or process (pp. 350–51).

5. News and legal discourse share common ways of representing order. Both are event-oriented, examine conflict on a case-by-case basis, deal with moral principles through individualization and personalization, emphasize procedure, and try to package information as naturalized—"like it is"—in the mode of realism (p. 8).

Feminist legal and cultural studies scholars need to be especially aware of this last item, the affinity of news and legal discourse. It reminds us that a case-based approach, so prevalent in legal thinking, also features in newsmaking discourse. And as we already noted, a case-based approach is the norm for cultural studies approaches to crime and media. A critical-analytical stance toward mediated images, including those about crime and justice, may require a discursive leap from the seduction and drama of individual cases.

Impact of Crime News

Recent commentary on "effects research" suggests a good deal of uncertainty about the impact of crime news on viewers and readers. Despite that uncertainty, some patterns emerge from Surette's review of the literature (1992, pp. 95–96):

1. Newspapers may affect people's understanding of the factual knowledge about crime more than television, which is more often related to attitudes such as fear of crime.

2. Media effects may be most powerful for subject areas further removed from a person's experience.

3. Some individuals are more susceptible to media influences than others; for example, "hypermasculine males" are more affected by sexually violent material, and socially isolated individuals' beliefs are more affected by media-generated crime news.

4. Heavy television viewing may be associated with a "mean world view," inaccurate beliefs about high crime and victimizations levels, and support for particular crime-control policies such as increased spending for the police.

Surette's findings on the role of television in producing factual misperceptions about crime is confirmed in Best's (1990) analysis of public opinion and concern over the social problem of "missing children" in the 1980s. He finds that those who expressed the greatest concern about threats to children were more likely to exaggerate the frequency of stranger-abductions and to believe that press coverage of the problem was accurate; they said their main source of information was television. The groups most concerned with the problem of missing children—women and those with fewer years of education—are also those with higher levels of crime fear.

A general problem with the body of television-effects research is that we cannot be sure what part of the effect comes from the impact of viewing television, and perhaps many hours of television, and what part comes from the worldviews already held by heavy television viewers. There are other problems, as well, with any simple reading of television effects. Some shows may influence viewers more than others, and depending on viewers' experiences with crime, some viewers may be more profoundly affected by what they see. Viewers are not passive receptacles but take a more active role; this produces "polysemic" (varied, multiple) readings of television shows.

What's Wrong with Crime News?

Crime news has been criticized on three grounds (Barak 1994a; Bortner 1984; Ericson et al. 1991; Surette 1992):

1. It distorts the broader picture of crime by focusing on individual acts of violence and on the bizarre and exceptional.

2. It portrays crime of all types—common, corporate, political—as an individual rather than social phenomenon.

3. Explanations of crime are not related to political-economic conditions, to social inequality, or to broader processes of social control. The criminal justice system is not examined with regard to crime control as an industry.

While some journalists call for greater professionalism in crime-news reporting (e.g., Benedict 1990), others suggest that "professionalism isn't the solution to our journalism problem, it is our journalism problem" (Weaver 1994, p. 195, Weaver's emphasis added). In particular, Weaver castigates the legacy of Joseph Pulitzer, a nineteenth-century New York City newspaper owner who revolutionized the news by dramatizing it. Weaver suggests that the press "put the dysfunctional heritage of Joseph Pulitzer behind" by redefining the news (p. 197). That would mean cutting back on coverage of disasters and crises: "[T]he gluttonous binging and gorging at the crisis-and-scandal table has got to stop" (p. 199).

As sociologists, we are concerned about how a worst-case scenario is used to make a generalization. The patching together of a celebrated case or two, which somehow adds up to a "crime trend," is a common, though troubling, feature of crime-news practices. This practice was evident in the media coverage of crack-using pregnant women (Maher 1990; Reeves and Campbell 1994) and of "missing children," especially those believed to be abducted by strangers (Best 1990).

In analyzing a sample of about a hundred television news stories on "threats to children" (including child abuse, missing children), Best (1990, pp. 91–111) identified the following "framework of conventions" used in the stories. The story opens with particular individuals to "grab" the viewers' attention and personalize the issue. The problem is "typified" by reference to the most serious cases, but the impression given is that the problem exists throughout the society. Statistics are given which may lead one to think that the most serious cases are typical. The explanations offered are overly simplified: Deviants are cast as flawed individuals; rarely are they described as affected by broader social forces.

The framework of conventions used by social scientists or criminologists differs from that of journalists. Criminological knowledge about patterns, shifts over time, or broader social conditions do not fit into the journalist's crime story, its structure, substance, and angle. The desired crime-news story often centers on why crime is increasing, why things are getting worse, or why certain "evil" individuals are preying on innocent citizens.

Impact of Crime-News Practices

Although we have noted the difficulties in positing effects of crime news on viewers, we can say something about the effects of crime-news practices and conventions. We would hypothesize that a focus on the most serious crimes and on the more violent and unusual crimes, coupled with attention to selected new crimes (e.g., "elderly victimization" in Fishman 1978; "mugging" in Hall et al. 1978; "threatened children" in Best 1990), creates a generalized public anxiety about crime, with varied effects on population subgroups.

Our hypothesis requires empirical investigation, but recent research by the Center for Media and Public Affairs shows how media practices can affect the public's imagination about crime. Scholars associated with the center studied crime stories on the three national television networks in 1992 and 1993. In 1992, 830 crime stories were aired; this number doubled to about 1,700 stories in 1993. Crime was the number one news story on television in 1993; the next most frequent was economic news, with 1,457 stories. The number of murder stories tripled from 1992 to 1993, rising from 104 stories to 329. Violent crime coverage doubled over the year. In the first part of 1993 (January through July), "violent crime coverage was 66 stories per month," but from August to the end of the year, "violent crime coverage was 111 stories per month" (Center for Media and Public Affairs 1994, p. 2).

Might this media crime wave have affected public opinion? For many years, pollsters have asked citizens what they consider the "most important problem" facing the country. The two most commonly named "most important" problems have been the economy and foreign policy; crime is ranked lower, with 4 to 5 percent of those polled naming it the most important problem. Thus in 1993, 5 percent of those polled named crime the most important problem. But in January 1994, 31 percent did (Center for Media

and Public Affairs 1994, p. 1). This shift was seen in other polls, and it is a major one of about 20 to 25 percentage points (T. Smith 1994).[12]

Commentators assume that the crime issue has come to seem of greater importance because there are no major foreign policy crises and because the economy appears to be improving (for some segments, at least). In addition, we suspect that the increased stories about crime, the tripling of stories about murder, and an escalation in violent crime coverage in the latter part of 1993 had an impact. A general backdrop of citizen anxiety is formed by news practices that focus on "newsworthy" cases. This backdrop is punctuated by celebrated cases—whether the kidnapping and murder of Polly Klaas, the Long Island train shooting, or various media-generated "crime waves" (such as the tourist murders in Florida, carjackings, sexual predators, murders by children and parents)—that create new terrors for some citizens.[13] Surely journalists have a role in reporting these stories. At issue is whether crime news can be reported in more informed and measured terms, as, for example, reports of economic news or foreign policy are.

Media, Crime Fear, Women's Experiences with Violence, and Women's Everyday Lives

We return to the two questions posed at the outset of this chapter. Might women's greater fear of crime be related to media-generated images of likely crimes and victims? How do media-generated images of crime affect the ways that women "negotiate danger"? We find partial and provisional answers to these questions by reporting from two studies in some detail.

Media, Crime Fear, and Women's Experiences with Violence

Schlesinger, Dobash, Dobash, and Weaver (1992) conducted research on women's responses to viewing television violence; they took seriously the notion of an "active audience," although within circumscribed limits. They were interested in learning whether women's responses to crime stories varied according to whether they had suffered violent victimization themselves. Earlier research by Kelly (1988) suggested that some women who had experienced violence found it difficult to watch or even to read about violence. The study by Schlesinger and colleagues (1992) is the first to systematically explore this question. A total of ninety-one women participated in the study; about half had been previously victimized, typically by a male partner. The women were from Scotland and England; the researchers recruited them with the aim of analyzing variation by nationality, class, and ethnicity.[14]

A background survey of the women explored the relationships between victimization, crime fear, and media influences. The researchers learned that women who had been victims of violence expressed a greater sense of vulnerability and crime fear than women who had not experienced violence (p. 38). "Private danger" spilled into perceptions of "public crime" in that women victimized by intimate violence were more likely to feel vulnerable to crime in public places. Most of the women in both groups said that certain types of media tended to increase their anxieties about crime: television news, television dramas and documentaries, television films, and the tabloid press. Other media formats or outlets (radio and quality newspapers) were rarely mentioned. While media influences seemed to increase crime fear, they played no role in decreasing it. Most women thought that there should be greater controls on media portrayals of women, especially in television and video; these beliefs were most strongly expressed by the Afro-Caribbean and Asian women.

From this study we learn that the sharpest distinctions among the women were based on whether they had experienced violence. Those who had experienced violence were "more sensitive to televised violence, more subtle and complex in their readings, more concerned about possible effects, and more demanding in their expectations of the producers of such content" (Schlesinger et al. 1992, p. 165). While noting these differences, the authors found that women were similar in expressing fear of rape. That is, women need not have experienced rape "to fear it, to condemn it out of hand, or to imagine its consequences" (p. 166). In attempting to explain the crime-fear disjuncture, the authors propose that rape fear be distinguished from domestic violence fear: "[R]ape . . . is more likely to be a matter of *universal* concern to women . . . while

domestic violence is less likely to engender fear *except for those who have actually had such experience*" (Schlesinger et al. 1992, p. 167, emphasis in original).[15] The question begs itself: Why is stranger rape so worrisome to women? Schlesinger and his colleagues reply, "popular cultural beliefs," including lessons learned at an early age "about not walking alone in dark places and the dangers of specific places and people" (p. 167). From this study we find that televised violence may have a similar effect on women when viewing some crimes such as stranger rape, but it may have different effects when women view other crimes. Reactions will vary by how much viewers identify with the characters or circumstances in the drama.

From this study we also learn that media-generated images of crime, including those on television news, can serve to increase women's fear of crime. The particular types of stories that increased women's fear were pornographic magazines, sensationalist forms of reporting, and the "reality-based" reenactments of crimes (p. 39). While this research suggests a link between media representations of crime and women's crime fear, we require more study of the kinds of victim-offender relations reported in crime news (or crime dramas) and the circumstances surrounding the violence.

Socialized Fear Perspective and Concerns for Safety

The second study draws from in-depth interviews[16] one of us conducted in 1991 with twenty-five single women[17] about their decisions concerning housing, transportation, and leisure activities (Chasteen 1994). The purpose was to learn what major factors influenced the women's decisions in choice of housing, modes of transport, and leisure-time activities. The women lived in a midsized city in the South (Knoxville, Tennessee) and were recruited by a snowball sample.[18] Their ages ranged from twenty-seven to fifty-four years; over two-thirds had been married before, almost all were white (two were African American), and two were openly lesbian.

We find that three factors influenced these women's decisions: affordability, convenience, and safety. Of these, safety emerged as the most important. In moving through the environment, the women carried what we term a *socialized fear perspective* on the world, others, and themselves. Confirming previous research (Gardner 1988, 1990; Gordon and Riger 1989; Stanko 1987; Warr 1985), the women had a nascent fear of assault from unknown men. This fear, which pervaded their everyday decisions and routine self-presentation, is thought to be "part of the contemporary experience of being a woman in the U.S." (Gordon and Riger 1989, p. 2).

Housing. For housing, the women typically considered a variety of safety-related factors, such as a neighborhood's reputation regarding crime, proximity of the house or apartment to street lighting, amount of foliage near windows, number of windows and doors, and closeness and degree of familiarity with neighbors. The majority (68 percent) altered their housing in some way to increase their sense of safety, typically by adding locks or storm windows. Those who did not alter their housing commented on how the security features they needed (e.g., storm windows) were already present. The layout and location of housing and its relationship to neighbors were all significant factors influencing women's housing choices.

Transportation. Concerns with transportation repeatedly emerged in three areas: perceptions of safety when biking or walking (especially at night), driving routes and level of alertness when driving alone, and the impact of the presence of others on women's fear. Virtually all the women said they did not walk, ride a bike, or drive through dangerous parts of the city after dark. About half reported that they either limited their driving to daylight hours or changed driving routes after dark to use better-lit or familiar roads. Those women who had to drive in the evening for occupational or other reasons described the tense alertness they maintained: They locked all the car doors and were attentive to their surroundings. Such precautions decreased when a woman had a companion, whether a man or a woman.

The women felt especially safe with male companions. Men seemed to offer symbolic protection: The women felt that they looked less "noticeable" or that they presented an image of not "asking" for anything. The advantage of a male companion was that because a woman was assumed to be "with" him, another man (or group of men) would be less likely to make advances or bother her.

Leisure activities. When asked about their leisure activities, the women immediately distinguished between activities they did with others and those they did alone. When they were with others, few limited themselves. For those who limited their activities, it was when they were in the company of women. When the women were alone, however, almost all avoided numerous activities. The two places most often mentioned were hiking trails, because of the isolation, and bars, because of the perceived likeihood of being seen as "looking for something." Other activities or places that women avoided while alone were movie theaters, restaurants, malls, laundromats, and bank machines.

In decisions about housing, transportation, and leisure activities, the women in this study clearly saw the world through a socialized fear perspective. This fear should not be understood as a constant state of anxiety. Rather, it was a diffuse, taken-for-granted level of fear that the women perceived as normal and reasonable.

During the interviews, many women initially said they were "not afraid at all," but they would then go on to describe relatively elaborate safety measures they had taken, such as nailing doors or windows shut, or they would mention particularly heightened levels of sensitivity. For example, Donna[19] said she was never afraid, but later she described an incident that belied her initial claim. While sleeping, she heard a car break down on the road near her house, and she awoke; she immediately called her brother-in-law and brother to come to her house in case a man was driving the car and came to her house for help. The fact that she was aware of a car breaking down outside, despite being asleep, and that she reasoned that the "natural" thing to do was to call two men to come over is testimony to the taken-for-granted and embedded nature of women's fears. From Donna's point of view, her action seemed a normal response, not a fearful one.

Understanding Women's Fear: Social Relationships and the Media

The women in this study, as in other studies, exemplified a relatively high level of ingrained fear that was central to the way they oriented themselves to the world. There was variation among them, however. For some, the fear was uppermost in their thoughts, strongly influencing their movements and decisions. For others, the fear perspective was more latent, surfacing in particular contexts (e.g., a dark street).

Despite this variation, virtually all the women connected their fear perspective to two beliefs. The first was that they were responsible for averting the results they feared, primarily through image manipulation and restricting their movements. The second was that the presence of men could reduce their chances of being a victim of crime, especially assault. These beliefs, though distinct, are related and reinforce one another. They reflect media depictions of "typical victims"—that is, those victimizing contexts that women have responsibility for averting—and they are rooted in the irony of a patriarchal protection racket, wherein women view their male friends, family members, and the police as sources of protection.

Averting victimhood. It is important to consider the origin of the victim-image women want to avert. For the women in this study, their understanding of the "typical victim" came largely from media depictions. To avoid assault, women tried not to look "like a victim": They preferred the company of others (especially at night), they stayed home in the evenings, or they sought help from men they knew. The "victim" women avoid looking like was the media victim of the stranger-offender, not the more probable offender in women's violent victimizations: intimates and relatives. Celebrated cases such the Central Park Jogger help, in part, to fuel such fears. But celebrated cases are not the only fuel. As Stanko (forthcoming, p. 13) observes for Britain, fear also results from the routine "newsworthy" case of violence against women that contains "a random attack [and] an innocent victim grateful for her sympathetic treatment [by] the police."[20] Stanko argues that embedded in both news stories and police advice literature is an expectation of "the responsible woman," who, if she takes the necessary precautions, can avoid men's violence (p. 14). Even if women know that the chances of violent victimization by a "faceless stranger" are less likely than victimization by intimates and relatives, it is, as Stanko (1990, p. 11) suggests, the "confrontation with the stranger that is the curiously controlled feature of managing danger."

Patriarchal protection racket. Women's fear perspective mandates fear of strangers, and it en-

courages women to seek husbands, male friends, or other known men for protection. The irony is that women's fear perspective encourages them to avoid being a victim by seeking help from those likely to do them harm. In other words, while women avoid walking alone and going out alone at night to avoid assault, they will also call a male friend, family member, or boyfriend to stay with them or stop by when they are scared. Known men thus come to be seen as vital symbolic protectors.[21]

Illustrative of the perceived symbolic value of a man's presence is "Safe-T-Man," which is sold by Service Merchandise, a chain store, and Safe-T-Zone, a mail-order business.[22] This doll is a life-size male dummy that a woman can place in her car or house to give the impression that she is protected by a man. It costs about $100 (not including the tote bag), comes in several racial varieties, is easily portable (weighs only four pounds), and has detachable legs. Clothing is not included; buyers are invited to dress him according to their preferences. Safe-T-Man is a vivid reminder of the way in which women's fear perspective and the corresponding male protection racket is exploited by media depictions, corporate marketing, and police advice to women. While a dummy may prove to be a safer form of protection than a real man, we worry that its presence may do more damage than good by escalating women's fear level and not necessarily reducing their chances of victimization.

The male protection racket was apparent in the comments women made in this study (discussed later in this chapter and in Chasteen 1994). They relayed many stories of admonitions given to them by male family members and friends as they were growing up and in their current lives. They were repeatedly warned against going out alone or without a man, and they were often told that living as a single woman was dangerous. In the messages they received through socialization and in their current social relationships, being "female" meant being reserved, cautious, and fearful of strange men.

As women learn fear, men learn to expect fear from women and to internalize a complementary view of themselves as protectors of women they know. A corollary is that women unattached to men are "fair game." Gordon and Riger (1989) find, for example, that when women and men are asked to estimate risks posed *to women* in a variety of environments, the men's estimates are consistently higher than the women's. Men's perceptions of women's safety can then be "used to justify men's insistence that their wives, mothers, . . . are unsafe out alone and should therefore go out only in the company of men" (p. 39).

Gordon and Riger's finding was evident in the women interviewed in this study. Katie, thirty-four years old, described her ex-husband's attitude this way: "When I was married, my husband was concerned that I was out a lot. He said that there was a problem with men on interstates finding single girls, pretending to be cops or something, and raping them. He used to mention that all the time." This story and other "urban legends"[23] of women raped or murdered when they were out alone were told to the women by their male friends and family members. In fact, the most important factor influencing women's level of fear was marital history. Women who had never been married were the least fearful, while those who were recently divorced or widowed were the most fearful and cautious. Women who were long divorced usually had relatively low levels of fear but typically described an earlier time in their lives when they had been more cautious. These women described a process of unlearning fear in which they gradually engaged in more activities alone and, as a consequence, were able to dispel some of their fears.

Nonetheless, virtually all the women in this study described a level of habitual caution in their daily lives, which was shaped by stories told to them by male coworkers or family members. For example, Lisa, twenty-seven years old, quit hiking alone. She said that doing it "never used to bother me, but my boyfriend and dad [told] me I shouldn't go," so she stopped. Likewise, Heather, forty-one years old, explained that she still did things alone sometimes but that when she did, she avoided telling her coworkers because they "often don't think single women should go out [alone]."

Women's fear perspective is encouraged by media attention to particular stories of violence against women and a variety of urban legends told and retold mostly by male friends and family members. These media stories and urban legends are, as Stanko (forthcoming) suggests, recycled in police advice literature to women. The irony of the patriarchal protection racket is that women learn to depend on the police or men they know as sources of protection, but these sources of protection heighten women's fears and maintain women's sense of vulnerability.

We are not suggesting that the "female fear" is groundless nor that women are passive dupes of media sensationalism or a patriarchal protection racket. Our claim is more modest: Representations matter. Whether in news stories, advertisements for safety products, police safety advice to women, or academic discourse on celebrated cases, these representations impinge on women's everyday lives in ways that can circumscribe women's movements and discourage independence and strength.

Discussion and Implications

Katz (1987, p. 60) argues that "the public does not read crime news in a naive search for the empirical truth about crime." Rather, crime news interests readers because it offers "resources to work out sensibilities routinely made problematic in everyday modern urban life" (p. 48). He suggests further that "[crime news] serves a purpose similar to the morning shower or routine physical exercise: a ritual, non-rational value of experience that is . . . shocking and uncomfortable . . . [but] taken up by adults in acknowledgement of their personal burden for sustaining faith in an ordered social world" (Katz 1987, p. 72). Katz's analysis reveals the *pleasures* of experiencing cycles of anxiety and reassurance that may come from reading crime news. We have proposed that crime news generates a misinformed *public anxiety* about crime with its focus on violent, stranger-danger, and atypical cases. What news organizations define as "newsworthy" is repeated in academic work. Scholars should reflect on how their practices act to reinforce mediated images of crime and to foster citizen misperceptions about the wider world of crime and cases prosecuted in criminal court. The critical posture of cultural studies is easily undermined when attention is directed solely to the dramatic, the unusual, the sensational. Better, we think, to attend to the mundane and routine crimes and typical court cases. Better also, we think, that scholars appreciate how atypical celebrated cases are and what this implies for analyses of culture and social relations. The dailiness, not just the drama, of crime and justice needs to be understood and analyzed.

We are especially critical of media organizations, editors, and journalists whose words and commentary reach huge audiences. The commodification of crime and stories of greed and misery is not new. What is new is the explosion of magazine news formats, crime reenactment dramas, and infotainment shows that give audience members the sense that they are learning more about the "reality" of crime, policing, and the justice system when they are not. Responsible newsmaking must shift from commodifying crime and fear to educating citizens about crime as a moral, political, and economic problem.

Such a shift is crucial because representations of crime and violence matter: They filter into public understandings of dangers posed in everyday life. We have argued that heightened coverage of extreme examples of crimes against women may lead to undue restrictions of women's movement. Feminists, in particular, should be especially concerned that the nature of crime in women's lives is described with care and accuracy.

Some have criticized feminist advocates for exaggerating the "facts" about women's victimization with the intention of convincing young women that they live in constant danger from the threat of violent men (e.g., Sommers 1994a; Paglia 1994b; K. Roiphe 1993b). We agree with these critics that a misleading use of "facts" on crime and justice delegitimates the feminist enterprise. And we concur that sensational stories of stranger danger and unusual cases of intimate violence bolster "the female fear" and maintain images of men as monsters. This is not good for women, or fair to men, or effective as feminist strategy. We do not subscribe, however, to the assumptions of Paglia and others that a conspiracy of sorts exists in which feminists are "brainwashing" young women in order to convert them to the fold.

We are saying something quite different: Inaccurate or exaggerated "facts" are not the result of an intentional conspiracy but rather a consequence of three factors. First, some feminist advocates may not be knowledgeable about or take the requisite care in using and interpreting statistical data. Second, like journalists and some academics, feminist advocates may focus on the unusual or dramatic cases without considering the broader picture of crime. Third, as in any movement defining a social problem, feminist advocates as claims-makers will attempt to persuade the public of the seriousness of women's victimization by selective attention to the worst cases (see Best 1990).

We have argued that a systematic social science (or sociohistorical) approach, which offers historical perspective and a broader picture of variation, is crucial to building more responsible depictions of crime and justice. It offers an antidote to the commodification of crime and a dramatic-case-based focus, which commonly features in crime news and in some quarters of academic scholarship and feminist advocacy.

Although we do not assume that feminist advocates seek to create fearful lives for women, we are concerned that some interventions against men's violence can ironically fuel what we term a male protection racket. For example, on many college campuses, escorts are provided to walk women home or to their cars. Such safety programs may give some students (and their parents) peace of mind and provide a measure of safety. But they are a cosmetic gloss and come at a price. Whether explicitly or by implication, the message conveyed is that women should avoid going out alone and should instead seek help from males for protection. Such strategies serve to solidify the male protection racket, and as a consequence, they pose little threat to male power. Men will continue to play the role of dominant, strong safekeeper, and women as the "weaker sex" will continue to be seen as in need of male protection.

Notes

1. What is termed as the "general fear question" is posed this way: "Is there any area near where you live—that is, within a mile—where you would be afraid to walk alone at night?" There are race and age differences in those polled. Blacks report being more fearful than whites (58 and 40 percent, respectively, 1993 data); in the last two decades, the race gap in crime fear has ranged between 15 and 20 percentage points. Older people (50 years or older) report being more fearful than younger people (18 to 20 years) (51 and 31 percent, respectively, 1993 data). The age gap in crime fear has varied over time: In some years the

gap is nil, whereas in other years it ranges between 5 and 20 percentage points (See Maguire and Pastore 1994, pp. 188–89, Table 2.39).

2. Gender differences in violent crime victimization are evident within race and ethnic groups (Maguire and Pastore 1994, p. 264, Table 3.19):

Rate per 1,000

	MEN	WOMEN
black	56	32
Hispanic	50	29
white	39	24
other(Asian/ Native American)	39	23
non-Hispanic	40	24

3. The NCVS interview changed during the 1990s; the NCVS now asks a series of direct questions about rape victimization and has developed a more sensitive interview protocol for intimate or family violence. As a consequence (in part) of introducing new questions concerning rape, the estimated number of rapes and attempted rapes jumped from 133,000 in 1991 to 310,000 in 1993 (see "Survey Question Changed" 1995). *New York Times.* August 17.

4. Gender differences in crime fear start young. A poll taken of fifth-graders in the mid-1980s showed that "girls were significantly more likely than boys to be worried about becoming a missing child, to perceive themselves as susceptible to becoming a missing child, and to think more often about becoming a missing child." Another poll of "youth" (age not given) showed that a higher percent of girls (84 percent) than boys (69 percent) were very concerned about kidnapping (Best 1990, p. 154).

5. We can expect that this composition of victim-offender relations will change and show an even *smaller* share of stranger offenders with the redesigned NCVS interview format, which asks respondents more directly about being victimized by someone they know. In addition to the *content* of the interview questions, critics have been concerned with interview *context*— for example, the fact that women are asked about violent victimization with their husband (or partners) present in the room (see D. Russell 1984 for an early critique). Bachman and Taylor (1994, pp. 508–10) discuss these contextual problems and the steps taken to rectify them in the redesigned NCVS protocol.

6. Press (1991, pp. 19–26, n. 1, p. 197) provides a sketch of the influential role that the Birmingham School (or British) cultural studies tradition has had on studies of media audiences in the United States and elsewhere. Their assumption of an "active and resistant audience" challenged earlier views of a largely passive audience and a single meaning from an audiovisual text (see also Schlesinger et al. 1992, pp. 4–8).

7. Another way to contrast these approaches is by terming them "cultural studies" and "sociology of culture". However, works that fall under a sociology of culture rubric may take a cultural studies approach. We are interested in comparing how crime stories might be better analyzed using the methods of social science rather than those in the humanities.

8. Surette (1992, pp. 62–63) suggests that crime news and crime entertainment drama do not differ that much. That is, both tend to focus on violence and explain crime in individualist or pathological terms. For an analysis of crime in television drama, see Sparks (1992) and Surette (1992, chap. 2); for an analysis of crime in "reality-based" programming shows, see Cavender and Bond-Maupin (1993).

9. It is well-known that UCR counts of rape reported to the police are likely to be the most underreported of the violent offenses.

10. In light of what we term the "crime-news disjuncture", coupled with problems of interpreting crime rates (like rape), we worry that journalists, even those who are critical of crime reporting, may not appreciate these problems. For example, Benedict reports, "In the summer of 1990, the FBI released crime statistics showing that rape is the fastest rising crime in America—rape has been rising four times faster than the overall crime rate for the past decade. Rape will therefore be a story that every news reporter will have to cover with increasing frequency" (1992, p. 11) Because of the crime-news disjuncture, commentators should not assume that news reports of crime reflect actual crime reporting patterns. Moreover, one cannot interpret increases (or decreases) in UCR rates of reported crime as reflecting increases or decreases in the "actual" amount of crime. For rape, increases may reflect changes in reporting practices by victims and recording practices by police, as much as shifts (if any) in the numbers of rapes that have occurred.

11. This is the third in a trilogy of works by Ericson and his colleagues. Ericson (1987) analyzes the organization and culture of news production, and Ericson, Baranek, and Chan (1989) analyze the relationships between journalists and news sources.

12. Print and radio media mistakenly reported this poll as suggesting that Americans were more fearful of crime than ever before. Specifically, a *Newsweek* article reported that "the public's fear of crime is now at record highs" (Marin 1994, p. 71). Data from several polls show that the media got it wrong. In response to the general fear question (see n. 1), about one-third of those polled in the 1960s said yes. But from 1972 to the present, the percent saying yes has oscillated between 40 and 45 percent (this is the population average; the percent varies by subgroup). Our most recent data is for 1993, where 43 percent responded yes to the general fear question. While this latest poll suggests that fear is high, it is no higher than two decades ago.

13. Recent examples include the cover of *U.S. News & World Report* for September 19, 1994, which

was entitled "Sexual Predators: Can They Be Stopped?" In the wake of the arrest of Susan Smith for killing her two children, *Newsweek*'s cover for November 14, 1994, was captioned "Sins of the Mother." Television talk shows also focused on these subjects.

14. Women who had been victims of sexual assault or domestic violence were actively recruited through Women's Aid and other victim support groups in England and Scotland. Those who had not experienced such victimization were recruited by a market research organization, which used street recruiters to choose women at random on the basis of selected study criteria (Schlesinger et al. 1992, pp. 25–26).

15. The authors' distinction in fact seems to be between stranger rape and intimate violence (which we assume included rape), not rape and domestic violence per se.

16. The interview used broad, open-ended questions (e.g., "What are some things you consider when looking for a place to live?"). The women's answers were probed further to elicit more detailed discussions and explanation of their decisions. The interview material was coded and analyzed using a qualitative data analysis program, Ethnograph. See Chasteen (1994) for a detailed presentation of the methods and findings.

17. "Single" included those women who were never married and those who were divorced or widowed. Those married or currently living with a male or female partner were not included. Despite divergent life paths, the women shared a similar social status as unmarried at the time of the research.

18. Snowball sampling is a method in which a pool of respondents is located; in this case, respondents volunteered after seeing a public posting or hearing about the project at a community group meeting. After each interview the respondent is asked for the name and telephone number of someone they know who might be willing to participate in the study. Although it is useful for reaching people who would otherwise not volunteer, the snowball method has well-known limitations, particularly regarding generalizability. Because the sample was not randomly chosen, the findings must be viewed as exploratory and provisional.

19. All names are pseudonyms.

20. Stanko (forthcoming, p. 6) notes that the British police literature uses "women police as a public relations tool" in depictions of female officers helping and interviewing victimized women and children.

21. Our argument does not consider variation for younger and older women in violent victimization, victim-offender relations, and perceptions of fear and vulnerability. We have in mind the largest "population at risk" for violent victimization, which is younger women (see Bureau of Justice Statistics 1994 age-based comparisons).

22. In talking with Safe-T-Zone's vice-president, Melanie Franklin, we learned that Safe-T-Man was created, in part, in response to carjackings. It was first advertised in a 1993 Christmas catalogue; an estimated 2,000 to 3,000 were sold that year. Ms. Franklin says that older women are the main market but that men also buy the dummy for their wives. At the Service Merchandise store, one of us (Chasteen) sat next to the dummy to observe shoppers' reactions to him. Most of the women seemed to think it was interesting, a bit strange, but a good idea. Most of the men didn't notice it or didn't say anything. One man said he thought it would be good to have in order to drive in the carpool lane during rush hour.

23. Best (1990, pp. 137–38) defines "urban legends" as "contemporary, orally transmitted tales that . . . describe criminal attacks, contaminated consumer goods, and other risks of modern life. . . . Whether a legend begins with a real incident or as a fictional tale, it is told and retold, often evolving as it spreads." See Brunvand (1981, 1985) for some early examples.

21

Lesbians, Prostitutes, and Murder

Media Constructs Violence Constructs Power

ANN RUSSO

What is the value of a woman's life? This question haunts me daily. In the United States social, historical, and cultural context, the question has no simple answer. It depends on race, class, sexual identity, and marital status, as well as on the politics of the situation, the interests being served by the valuation, the life being protected or incriminated. In this chapter, I explore the social construction of violence, murder, and power in the news media when victims or perpetrators are identified as either lesbians or women working in prostitution.[1] I am interested in how media constructions inform and shape social value hierarchies that reinforce gender, race, sexual, and class inequalities in this society.

Violence against lesbians and women working in prostitution in this country—police brutality, psychiatric stigma and consequent punishment, and daily harassment and violence—has a history of being legitimized and condoned. Both lesbians and women working in prostitution have been labeled and treated as criminals and "deviants" for not living within or representing a normatively defined femininity; prostitution in this country is illegal, and while lesbianism is more accepted in some urban areas of the country, both lesbians and prostitutes continue to be the targets of assault, battery, and murder. Joan Nestle's essay "Lesbians and Prostitutes: An Historical Sisterhood" makes the connection between the two group identities historical and material. She writes, "Whores, like queers, are a society's dirty joke" (Nestle 1987, p. 158). Nestle links the lives of lesbians and prostitutes concretely when she describes how in the "bars of the late fifties and early sixties where I learned my Lesbian ways, whores were part of our world. We sat on barstools next to each other, we partied together, and we made love together. The vice squad . . . controlled our world, and we knew clearly that whore and queer made little difference when a raid was on" (p. 158).

Given the heightened awareness of violence against women in this society, many scholars, activists, and concerned citizens criticize the mass media for glorifying, sensationalizing, and/or eroticizing violence against women as entertainment. They argue that the media encourages and incites individual men to do violence against women; in other words, media violence produces criminals who are increasingly uncontrollable in their attacks on women. Others, however, argue that the problem is not simply the capacity for such media to incite individuals to violence but the way in which the media reinforces social power hierarchies and control through its construction of violence. From this perspective, one must consider which violence is socially constructed as legitimate and which as illegitimate, which violence is condoned and which is punished. George Gerbner argues, "The power to define violence and project its lessons, including stigmatization, demonization and the selective labeling of terror and terrorists, is the chief cultural requirement for social control. . . . Media violence is a political scenario[;] . . . it is a demonstration of power: of who has it, who uses it, and who loses it" (1992, p. 98). The main social function of media is to "maintain, reinforce, and exploit rather than to undermine or alter conventional conceptions, beliefs and behaviors" (Gerbner and Gross 1976, p. 181).

In this essay I argue that the media marginalizes most lesbians and women working in prostitution through neglect and indifference with regard to the violence they experience, especially when they are poor, working-class, and/or women of color. A privileged race and/or class identity seems to increase the value the media accords a woman's life. This constructs a context of social apathy in response to endemic violence against some women, as opposed to compassion and concern for socially privileged women. It reinforces the idea that lesbians and/or women working in prostitution, particularly those who are poor and/or women of color, are less valued and thus expendable. By defining lesbians and women working in prostitution as social outcasts, the media constructs them as legitimate targets of violence, which in turn reinforces social hierarchies.

Simultaneously, the media reinforces the social power of white men by legitimating their violence against women in general, but particularly against "deviant" women, like lesbians and women working in prostitution. Race and class clearly figure into this construction of "deviance": Not only are poor women of color often portrayed as women in prostitution, but they are also portrayed as expendable (Crenshaw 1992a; Collins 1990). While the news media portray the mostly white men who serially murder women as individually deviant, they also lend a sympathetic eye to the killers' motives and background, particularly in terms of how women in their lives have mistreated them (Caputi 1987; Cameron and Frazer 1987). It is significant to note that violence against women perpetrated by men who do not have race and/or class privilege are *not* given the same social legitimacy, most particularly if that violence is directed against white middle-class women (A. Davis 1981; Russo 1991; Crenshaw 1992a). Mostly the media neglects or registers indifference with regard to intraracial violence against women within communities of color, although when such violence is reported, racial, class, and/or cultural stereotypes and bias become the explanatory frameworks; the men and women are not given the benefit of individualist explanations for the violence. In significant contrast, media reports consistently sensationalize interracial violence perpetrated by men of color against white women. Witness the media's response to the killing of Carol Stuart when her husband, the actual murderer, initially implicated an African American male, or how the media racially constructed the young men involved in the Central Park Jogger rape (P. Williams 1991; Russo 1990, 1991; Crenshaw 1992a). In these cases the media constructs interracial violence against white, especially middle-class, women as brutal atrocities. The violence is attributed to the racial and/or class backgrounds of the perpetrators, and the media response calls for swift and urgent action. This construction is in sharp contrast to how the media constructs the violence perpetrated by white middle-class men. The perpetrators here are constructed as individuals with personal histories and identities; their violence is often made "understandable" in media constructions. Witness the media's response to the St. John's University rapists, who sexually assaulted a black West Indian woman. The media constructed the white middle-class athletes as up-and-coming young men and tended to characterize the incident within a very "boys will be boys" framework, which is mostly reserved for white middle-class men (Russo 1991; Crenshaw 1992a). Thus, it is important to recognize that the media does not construct violence against women in a generic way. In fact, the media is fairly predictable in its differential construction of both victims and perpetrators, and legitimate and illegitimate violence, in terms of its reinforcement of existing race, gender, and class hierarchies.

When lesbians and/or women working in prostitution cross the lines of power and control by using violence against men, their deviance is confirmed, they are sensationalized and vilified in the media, and the need for social control is reestablished. The media's sensational treatment of Aileen Wuornos—a lesbian and prostitute convicted for the murder of six middle-aged white men—initially compelled me to consider the similarities in how the media socially constructs violence when the perpetrators are identified as lesbians and/or women working in prostitution. News stories used Wuornos's lifelong history of abuse and her involvement in prostitution to frame her story as one of "revenge" against men, and they used her lesbian identification to say she was a "man-hater" out to kill men. Labeled as lesbian, as prostitute, Wuornos became, for "the establishment," a symbol of fear and terror. I was curious as to how these two "deviant" identities were constructed as explanatory frameworks for Wuornos's "unwomanly" actions. The media sensationalism in response to Wuornos stands in stark contrast to the mediated social apathy regarding the large numbers of women who are disappeared and murdered across the country, an apathy perpetuated by way of labeling the women involved as "prostitutes."

To Be Valued, One Must First Be Visible as a Human Being

I think it's very plausible that Aileen Wuornos was fighting her own disappearance.
—Leslie Ernst,
"Forum I: Women Who Kill"

I put prostitutes and gays at about the same level, and I'd be hard put to give somebody life for killing a prostitute.
—Jack Hampton,
a Texas state district
court judge, in 1988[2]

Lesbians and women working in prostitution are often invisible in the media. While 1993 was deemed a media success for lesbians, with a few stories about the lifestyles of some contemporary lesbians—k. d. lang on the cover of Vanity Fair,

a Newsweek cover story about lesbian life and culture (June 21, 1993)—this visibility was very limited in its selection of lesbian life, and it was not sustained. The stories highlighted "successful," professional, and mostly middle-class women, active in politics, who were not portrayed as challenging the norms of white middle-class femininity by their existence. Media stories about women working in prostitution in the United States tend to fluctuate between constructions of the "happy hooker with a heart of gold" who loves her work and is loved by her customers and constructions of prostitution as a "social problem" that threatens the so-called moral fabric of society. Interestingly, I found most of the articles featuring individual "successful" women who worked as "call girls" in Cosmopolitan, a magazine with a primary female readership, while in mainstream news media, the focus was on street prostitutes, whose existence was said to constitute a "social problem."

Gregory Herek argues, "Through cultural heterosexism, homosexuality is largely hidden in American society and, when publicly recognized, is usually condemned or stigmatized" (Herek and Berrill 1992, p. 90). Consequently, reports of harassment, assault, and murder of lesbians are mostly absent from mainstream news. I had great difficulty, for instance, obtaining news stories about the murder of lesbians, let alone harassment or assault of lesbians. The New York Times Index doesn't even have a category specific to lesbians; it says, "See Homosexuality," and under "homosexuality and homicide," almost all of the articles are about violence against gay men. Part of the reason for this is that when women are harassed, assaulted, or murdered, news stories may not discuss the fact that the victims are lesbians, or the lesbianism is muted, despite its potential relevance to the incidents. For instance, the initial news reports about Debra Reid, a battered lesbian who killed her lesbian lover in self-defense, fluctuated between describing their relationship as one between roommates, friends, or lovers. Some articles which referred to the women as lovers had headlines using the word "friends." It was not until she sought commutation of her prison sentence, on the grounds of being a battered lesbian several years later, did the case become a *lesbian* case. Once her case became defined as a *lesbian* case, Reid became a "lesbian slayer" in at least one news report.

In the 1988 case of two white middle-class lesbians who were murdered while on vacation on a Caribbean island, the first three *Boston Globe* articles construct the women as professional and well-known psychotherapists in the Boston area, who "shared their lives as a couple" (S. Murphy 1988; Hernandez 1988; "Scotland Yard" 1988). Their identities as professional white American tourists in the Caribbean is what gave their deaths importance. The implications for tourism and the issue of anti-American or antiwhite motivation in the killing were central to the stories. The word "lesbian" was not highlighted until the fourth article, which focused on the mourning and fear the deaths had generated in the lesbian community, which was then defined as "a Boston subculture largely obscure to straight society" (Longcope 1988). It is in this article that the possibility of homophobia as a motive in the murders is raised and then quickly dismissed with quotes from island authorities. While the article dismisses homophobia as a motive, it implies that lesbian visibility may be a cause. It reads, "Many lesbians, unlike the two whose stabbed and bludgeoned bodies were found last week[,] . . . tend to mask their sexual orientation, [and] embrace private, quiet, home-centered lifestyles" (Longcope 1988). Nevertheless, neither the issue of homophobia nor that of sexism is ever given serious consideration. Thus, the issue of antilesbian violence is never central to the story or to later reports on violence against women or lesbians and gay men.

In many of the serial murder cases I researched, I suspect that some of the women murdered were lesbians, but such information remains obscure in the accounts. In the "true crime" book *The Search for the Green River Killer*, the possibility of lesbian existence is mentioned. Here the writers, who were journalists for the case, mention offhandedly the lesbian relationships of women who knew the murdered women, but they never discuss this aspect of the women's identities and its potential connection to their murders (Smith and Guillen 1991). In sum, information about antilesbian violence is difficult to find.

The gay and lesbian movement has put antigay violence on the social and political map of this society. "Sexual orientation" is included as an official category in the 1990 version of the Hate Crimes Statistics Act (Herek and Berrill 1992). In media reports about antigay hate crimes and violence, however, specifics about lesbians are rare. The term "gay bashing" continues to call up images of mostly white middle-class men being bashed by young heterosexual men. While the word "lesbian" is included in the general statements made about the increasing level of violence against the gay and lesbian communities, the examples and the analysis are predominantly based on white middle-class men. For instance, the *Boston Globe* carried an article about a national study on gay victims of murder in 1994 (Auerbach 1994). While the article mentions that the study focuses on "lesbians and gay men," its content presumes that men are the primary victims of antigay killings. They report that in 95 percent of the cases, the victims are male. This statistic, however, may be due to the way that crimes are reported and classified; activists and reporters alike assume that antigay violence is mostly perpetrated against men, not women, and that violence against lesbians has more to do with sexism than homophobia. Victoria Brownworth, in an article on the invisibility of antilesbian violence that appears in an issue of *The Advocate* devoted to antigay violence, reports on several antilesbian assaults which were not classified as homophobic despite the fact that the "assailants allegedly cited the women's sexual orientation as the reason for the assault" (Brownworth 1991, p. 50). The other articles in the issue, however, barely mention violence against lesbians. The invisibility and marginality of lesbians reinforces the idea that violence targeting lesbians is less pervasive than that against gay men. Racial exclusion underlies this social construction as well. While large-scale studies of antigay violence reveal that lesbians and gay men of color are more vulnerable to violence, most of the national reports on violence are based on sample populations consisting of predominantly white, mostly middle- to upper-middle-class gay men (Herek and Berrill 1992; Russo 1992). But this limitation is never mentioned in the media reports, thus reinforcing the construction of the problem as one exclusively affecting only one part of gay and lesbian communities.

The harassment, rape, and murder of women working in prostitution is also either socially invisible or conceptualized as "just life." Pimps, johns, and the police often harass, assault, rape, and batter women working in prostitution, but those few media stories discussing this violence seem to assume it is "consensual" because the woman involved *is presumed to be* a prostitute. For instance, with regard to a woman's report of rape by a Boston police officer, the first news story in the *Boston Globe* (Locy and McGrory 1994) used the word "rape" at the beginning of the article. The remainder of the article, however, used the term "sex" or "sex acts" to describe encounters in which police coerced women into sex with threats of arrest if they did not comply. Thus, the claim of rape—the alleged focus of the story—is essentially erased by the end of the article. Moreover, the incident would never have made it into the media had the woman not been approached immediately after she exited the police car by two journalists from the *Boston Herald* who happened to be doing a story on prostitution. Violence is a daily reality facing women involved in street prostitution. A group in Minneapolis, Minnesota, called Women Hurt in Systems of Prostitution Engaged in Revolt (WHISPER) has an ongoing oral history project focused on women's lives in prostitution; they have found that 76 percent of the women report being beaten by their pimps; 50 percent report being kidnapped by pimps; 79 percent report being beaten by a customer; and 50 percent report being raped by customers ("Statement of WHISPER Action Group Members" 1992, p. 3).

When women working in prostitution are murdered, it is often because they are targeted as prostitutes (Caputi 1987; Cameron and Frazer 1987). As Margaret Baldwin writes, "To be a 'prostitute' is to be rapable, beatable, killable, and *why* women are (righteously to noncontroversially) raped, beaten and killed" (Baldwin 1992, pp. 87–88). Men who rape and murder women working in prostitution often justify their violence by saying they are punishing the women, that the women ask for it or consent to it by the fact that they are engaged in prostitution. Moreover, it is very difficult to estimate the number of women murdered, especially those involved in prostitution, not only because the FBI does not have a category that would indicate this information but also because of the " 'disappeared' status of women and girls involved in the practice" (Baldwin 1992, p. 86).[3] "Disappeared" refers to the many women who are reported missing every year; the police often assume that the women are involved in prostitution or drugs and have therefore "disappeared" by "choice," so they do not follow up on the reported disappearances. As Phyllis Chesler suggests, "Serial killers may be responsible for the daily, and permanent, disappearance of thousands of prostituted and nonprostituted women, each and every year, all across the United States. . . . [And they] are rarely ever found or convicted" (Chesler 1993, p. 946). Baldwin gives us a listing of just some of the numbers: "Up to thirty-one women murdered in Miami over a three year period, most of them prostitutes; fourteen in Denver; twenty-nine in Los Angeles; seven in Oakland. Forty-three in San Diego; fourteen in Rochester; eight in Arlington, Virginia; nine in New Bedford, Massachusetts; seventeen in Alaska; ten in Tampa," and so on (1992, p. 88). According to Jane Caputi, "police officials [in the mid-1980s] say that there are somewhere around four thousand serial murders annually in this country, most of them murders of women, although exact sex ratios are not given" (Caputi 1987, p. 117).

The media response to the disappearance and murder of women involved, or assumed to be involved, in prostitution is overwhelmingly one of indifference. As the Combahee River Collective points out about the murders of twelve black women in Boston in 1979: "At first there was hardly any attention paid to the deaths. . . . When articles and television coverage began to appear more frequently, the victims were universally described as runaways, prostitutes, or drug addicts who 'deserved' to die because of how they had lived" (Combahee River Collective 1981, p. 68). This was clear in the media treatment of the serial killings being discovered in New Bedford, Massachusetts, in 1988. When the bodies were first discovered but not yet identified, the women were always referred to as women who frequented an area of New Bedford "known for prostitution and illegal drug activity." As the identities of the women became known, their lives were consistently constructed by way of reference to this presumed location and presumed set of activities, even when family members or others were quoted as telling a different story about the women. In San Diego, California, the police attached the label "NHI" to their so-called investigation into the murders of forty-five women that took place between 1985 and 1992. "NHI" is evidently a police term that translates to "No Humans Involved." This phrase is frightening for its overt banality and hatred. According to one officer, "These were misdemeanor murders, biker women and hookers." Another police officer, responding to a feminist oppositional art exhibit called *More Women Involved*, offered that "he had been trained to disregard the humanity of victims from the 'darker side' of life" (Sisco 1993, p. 43). In the Green River murders, many of the women eventually found and identified had been reported missing for months. The police routinely ignored these missing person reports, despite pressure from friends and family, who were met with anger and resentment for taking up valuable police time (Smith and Guillen 1991).

What we learn from the police is that they often have the same attitudes toward the women as the killers do, attitudes which the media legitimates and the general public comes to accept; as Caputi writes, "we learn [from official statements about such murders] that it is normal to hate prostitutes. The killer is even assured of solidarity in this emotion. . . . The logical inference is that the prostitutes are already guilty and thus deserving of the punishments meted out to them by self-appointed avengers, or 'streetcleaners' as the convicted murderer Peter Sutcliffe later referred to himself" (1987, p. 94). In the media reports that focused on the individual women murdered in the New Bedford, Massachusetts, area, the stories were constructed to show how the women's life choices *led* them to their deaths; there was little discussion about the social conditions that would *lead* a man or group of men to serial-kill women, whether the women work in prostitution or not.

And yet, before this picture begins to be too simplistically organized by gender, it is important to recognize that the murder of women is not *always* tolerated and excused. Some serial-murder victims are given the status of "innocent victims" and their deaths are deemed significantly tragic. Not surprisingly, in a racist and classist society this "innocence" is inevitably related to the race and class identification of the women; women of color and working-class or poor women are not afforded the same value as white and middle-class women. A woman's involvement in prostitution, drugs, lesbianism, and other so-called deviant activities seemingly diminish her value. For instance, Elizabeth Sisco contrasts the media response to the murders of women who the San Diego police identified as involved in prostitution with the response to a male intruder who

entered "bedrooms in a quiet, middle-class neighborhood" and brutally sexually assaulted and murdered five women. The response to the latter case? "The largest manhunt in San Diego Police Force history stopped him. Police held daily press briefings from a special command post set up in the neighborhood and a city councilman went door-to-door warning residents to take extra precaution." The murdered women in this case represented the "good-woman victim"; one, for instance, was "a college student who worked at a sporting goods store." In constructing a valued victim, the police and media "de-emphasized the fact that [this same college student] also worked part-time as a nude dancer. Nude dancing was not an occupation that fit this particular victim profile" (Sisco 1993, p. 44).

In contrast, in the Green River murders, as in the serial murders of women identified as "prostitutes" around the country, the media response is apathetic at best, unless activist groups press for action. Again the differential treatment can be found in the words of a police investigator of the Green River murders, who offers, "There was public attention in the Ted [Bundy] case . . . because the victims resembled everyone's daughter. . . . But not everyone relates to prostitution on the Pacific Highway" (quoted in Baldwin 1992, p. 87). Here the women in prostitution are not even accorded human status as individuals; instead they are collectively referred to as "prostitution." And the normative assumptions in the term "everyone's daughters" erase the daughters of working-class or poor communities and/or communities of color. By routinely referring to the serial murders of women as "prostitute murders," Elizabeth Sisco aptly says, the police and media encourage "us" "to believe that violence and death are known occupational hazards for sex workers, [so] we respond to their demise with apathy or a resigned willingness to blame the victim, to accept the murder of a prostitute as one of life's harsh realities. At the same time, we are relieved that such brutality could never be visited upon those of us who comply with societal mores" (1993, p. 42).

In many of these murder cases, the police claim the need to control information released to the media in order to more efficiently investigate the case. They justify holding back information on the grounds that more information might provoke copycat murders and/or give the murderer the opportunity to hide evidence and leave town.

However, the level of media involvement is often connected to the race and class status of the victims. For instance, the Boston news media handled two murder cases very differently. In one case, a young African American woman was brutally gang-raped and murdered by a group of young men in her neighborhood. A brief article mentioned the murder in early November 1990, but nothing else was reported until November 20, when several young men were arrested (Ellement and Hernandez 1990). At this point, community activists demanded that the media and the police explain why the neighborhood and the larger community had not been alerted (Ellement et al. 1990). While the media was forced to address the incident in more detail after community protests, the articles tended to focus on the difficulties in the young woman's life that led up to her brutal death, as if she herself set the scenario up (Jacobs 1990). In stark contrast, when an upper-middle-class law school professor was murdered in April 1991, less than a year later, the Boston newspapers carried major news articles immediately following the incident (see, e.g., Reid et al. 1991; Flint 1991). The neighborhood was alerted, and special networks for women's safety were put into place (D. Smith 1991). In this case, the news reports focused on the woman's important and established career, and on the tragedy involved in losing such a valued member of the community to murder (Brelis and Flint 1991).

The Wuornos case provides another illustration of the strongly contrasting way the media and police respond to different murders. As Munster, one of the investigators in the Wuornos case, reports: "We don't normally go to the press, but we felt we had a responsibility to warn the public of the danger in picking up female hitchhikers or females posing as women in distress. . . . If we hadn't gone to the media when we did, there would have been a good possibility of additional victims, and I don't believe [the alleged murderer] would be in custody today" (quoted in John Bankston 1991, p. 50). In grave contrast, a New York Times journalist, asked to attend a press conference concerning the murder of the black women in Boston in 1979, responded: "Twelve Black Women murdered. That's not news. I could call any city in this country and get that statistic" (quoted in Combahee River Collective 1981, p. 68). In another serial murder case in South Central Los Angeles, a predominantly black community where at least seventeen women were killed over a three-year period, the police didn't even notify the media until after the tenth women was found (Rachel West 1988, p. 284).

The label "prostitute" or "lesbian," or the association of a woman with a negative stereotype of an entire neighborhood (usually attached to racial or class stereotypes), can be a way to diminish the value of a woman's life and, therefore, the necessity for an urgent social response to the violence against her. I find this diminishment even among students in the courses I teach on violence against women; in discussing media and/or police indifference to violence against poor women who are identified as or assumed to be involved in prostitution, at least one student will inevitably excuse this response on the grounds that "people don't care" about "these" women. In this construction, the women who are killed and their community of family, friends, acquaintances are erased from the category of "people." It is very difficult to challenge this construction, so "naturalized" in mainstream media. But it is imperative that those of us who are educators, writers, or activists do so.

"Respectability" and the Politics of Visibility

"As I was being raped, I was called a dyke and a cunt. The rapist used those terms as if they were interchangeable. And as I talk to other women who have been raped—straight and gay—I hear similar stories. Was my attack antilesbian? Or was it antiwoman? I think the facts are simple. I was raped because as a woman I'm considered rapeable and, as a lesbian I'm considered a threat. How can you separate those two things?"
—Victoria Brownworth, quoted in "An Unreported Crisis"

"[L]esbian invisibility compounds anti-lesbian violence."
—Suzanne Pharr, quoted in Victoria Brownworth, "An Unreported Crisis"

Since the 1960s, the feminist and gay and lesbian rights movements have drawn attention to gender or sexually motivated harassment, assault, rape, and murder. Many activists recognize that in order to stop the endemic violence, people must recognize and value the humanity of all people—regardless of gender, race, class, or sexual identification. One way to do this is to make the violence a public issue in the media, to demand that the media cover crimes against all women in a way that frames the violence in the larger context of a white supremacist, male-dominant, capitalistic society. However, in so doing, these movements, especially as they have become more institutionalized in this society, often reinforce value distinctions between women grounded in differences of class, race, and sexual orientation. This has resulted in the invisibility or diminishment of lesbians and women working in prostitution, whose lives and identities do not fit a narrow and normatively defined white middle-class heterosexual femininity.

The feminist construction of the issue—violence against women—has often erased and distorted the differences and divisions between women. For instance, the impulse of the predominantly white, middle-class women's movement against violence is to explicitly downplay, deny, ignore, or resist socially constructed differences and divisions between women. While claiming that the movement is for all women, they implicitly construct valued "innocent" victims—those supposedly *most* harmed by harassment, assault, and murder. Given the predominantly white middle-class heterosexual orientation of the movement, the valued victims are inevitably white, middle-class, and/or heterosexual women. This value hierarchy is apparent when some feminists, in an effort to socially legitimate the public concern about violence against women, insist that the violence is "not just" a problem for poor women or women of color but that it affects middle- and upper-middle-class white women *as well* and therefore is socially significant. Thus, the importance attached to the issue becomes dependent on whether it affects those socially constructed as the "valued victims" (see also Crenshaw 1994).

Since mainstream media historically have undermined feminist challenges to the status quo by associating feminism with "lesbian man-haters," feminists (heterosexual and lesbian) have not consistently insisted on *lesbian visibility* in public representations of the movement.[4] Many movement organizations disassociate themselves from lesbians in order to gain legitimacy, credibility, and respectability in the "larger" society. As Suzanne Pharr writes, "The word *lesbian* is instilled

with the power to halt our work and control our lives. And we give it its power with our fear" (Pharr 1988, p. 25). Despite the leadership of lesbian feminists in the creation of crisis lines, shelters, safe houses, and speak-outs on gender violence, many of these organizations erase this participation in their public representation. Given homophobia within and outside of the movement, and the fear it instills, feminists have tended to define, analyze, and respond to violence as strictly a gender issue, one that affects women similarly across all lines of division between women—race, sexual orientation, class, ethnicity. Violence *against lesbians as lesbians*, or violence against African, Asian, Latina, Native American women *as women of color*, or violence *against women working in prostitution* remains mostly invisible, undocumented, unknown. The centrality of race, class, and/or sexual orientation differences in determining the social constructions, interpretations and responses to specific incidents of violence is minimized or ignored (Crenshaw 1994). The overriding assumption, unspoken but present, is that the women under discussion, the "valued victims," are for the most part *not* lesbians, *not* women of color, *not* poor women, *not* women working in prostitution. Reports in the media are not different from the mainstream white middle-class definition of the issue, thus perpetuating a social hierarchy of value and worth accorded to different groups of women.

The specific mandate to keep lesbians and women who work in prostitution invisible and to keep poor or working-class women and women of color on the margins constructs a context where the public does not visualize women of color, lesbians, women working in prostitution, working-class women, poor women as valued victims and survivors of violence and therefore as those needing or deserving services. In most cases, when victims/survivors of violence are identified in the media as lesbians or as women working in prostitution, especially when they are poor women and/or women of color, the social importance of the crimes involved is diminished. The violence is not recorded as an aberration or reason for outrage but, rather, as routine daily life. The feminist movement against violence participates in this construction by not demanding public recognition and response to violence specifically directed against women as lesbians, as members of racial and ethnic minorities, or as prostitutes and raising public awareness about their heightened vulnerability to violence.

In the past twenty years, feminists have sought to put men's violence against women on the public agenda as a social rather than a personal issue. And the media has slowly begun to acknowledge the social aspects of the crimes against women occurring in the context of intimate relationships. However, the construction of the problem tends to retain an exclusive assumption of heterosexuality. Feminist activists and service providers themselves often presume that violence against women is done by men, not other women. Lesbian battering by lesbians, or violence against lesbians by heterosexual women, remains mostly unthinkable. It is uncommon to see materials, programs, support groups, newsletters, or shelters that address violence against lesbians, lesbian battering, lesbian survival (although this is changing). In part this is due to the desire to construct women as "innocent" and passive victims of male aggression in order to enlist empathy. As a result, for media events, the focus remains on men's violence against women in intimate, monogamous, noncontractual heterosexual relationships. Lesbians and women working in prostitution remain invisible or, at best, on the margins of this public discourse.

Over the years, lesbian-specific organizations like the Boston-based Network for Battered Lesbians have diligently and persistently fought the invisibility. It has been mostly battered lesbians in the battered women's movement who have brought these issues out into the open. But feminist activists against violence and service providers in battered women's shelters remain reluctant to insist on lesbian visibility in media coverage both as victims and perpetrators of violence. In 1989, Debra Reid, a lesbian in prison for the killing of her female lover, joined forces with her legal team and the Network for Battered Lesbians in seeking to gain public and legal recognition of lesbian battering (Russo 1992a). Debra Reid was the *only lesbian* in the group of incarcerated women seeking commutation of their prison sentences. She faced consistent denial and resistance to her identification as a battered woman, from the group of incarcerated women to the media accounts of "the Framingham Eight," to the Advisory Board of Pardons, who eventually decided not to commute her sentence.

The resistance to her story had to do with a refusal to recognize the specific victimization of

lesbian battery and to recognize how homophobia contributed to that victimization (in the battery as well as in the original trial). Some media reports quote David LaFontaine from the Coalition for Lesbian and Gay Civil Rights, who dismissed the significance of Reid's case, stating, "Obviously, there are going to be individual cases of abuse, but my experience of gay people is I think as a whole they're a very nonviolent group of people." The gay and lesbian community's fear of increasing homophobic bigotry underlies the persistent refusal to recognize battering as a serious social issue. While this fear is a legitimate one, the realities of intimate violence continue and will only continue to disempower the communities if not addressed (Lobel 1986). The existence of lesbian battering also contradicts the feminist rhetoric which has tended to maintain that men are always the perpetrators of violence and women are always the victims of violence. The denial about women's use and abuse of violence contributes to the construction of the valued and "innocent" victim, who passively endures violence and certainly never uses violence. In Reid's case, the need to recognize the realities of violence involving women as both perpetrators and victims, and the inability to construct victims and perpetrators solely along the lines of gender or sexual orientation, were seen as potential liabilities to the accepted and exclusive frameworks of sexist or homophobic violence. The resolution of the Advisory Board of Pardons, and subsequently the media, was to construct a story of "mutual abuse," where both Reid and her partner were equally responsible for the violence in their relationship. Reid's claim of self-defense in response to being attacked by her lover was thus erased. The construction of violence among lesbians becomes one of mutuality—lesbians beat each other up, and it is hard to distinguish one from the other. So the need for social concern and response to lesbian battering are diminished, and at best, lesbians are once again relegated to the margins of discourse on battering.

As I noted earlier, most of the public media attention to antigay violence focuses on gay male victims of violence, mostly white gay men. One of the myths perpetrated in the movement is that lesbians are not vulnerable to attack *as lesbians* but, rather, simply as women. For instance, Beatrice von Schulthess (1992), in the only essay on antilesbian violence in the anthology *Hate Crimes: Violence against Lesbians and Gay Men*

(Herek and Berrill 1992), opts for misogyny as *the* primary explanation for antilesbian violence. She writes, "I no longer frame the issue of violence against lesbians only in terms of sexual orientation. Instead, I conceptualize lesbianism as an extension of gender and conceptualize antilesbian violence as an extension of misogynistic violence." Based on her survey, the harassment and violence lesbians experience falls "along a continuum ranging from exclusively antiwoman at one end to exclusively antilesbian at the other" (p. 71). But she notes that most of the violence begins as antiwoman and escalates to antilesbian. Those surveyed also report that most of the harassment was verbal rather than physical. However, on closer inspection, we find that the lesbians of color surveyed reported more physical violence, but since they are not adequately represented in the sample, their experience does not inform the conclusions. It may be that the lesbians in her sample were also primarily middle-class. Thus her analysis is based on the experience of a very limited group of women. It would be important to know, for instance, whether the women interviewed are able to pass on the street as heterosexual. If so, this might explain their experience of being targeted first as women and only later as lesbians. Ultimately, von Schultess contributes to the nonrecognition of explicitly antilesbian violence experienced by lesbians who do not pass. The stories of lesbians documented in Nestle's edited anthology, *A Persistent Desire* (1992), and in Leslie Feinberg's semiautobiographical novel, *Stone Butch Blues* (1993), stand out in stark contrast to the conclusions offered in von Schulthess's study. In the stories illuminated in these books, lesbians were targeted for abuse and violence because they were identified *as lesbians* by the police and by men on the street. It was the identification of them as "gender outlaws," rather than simply as women, that made them more vulnerable to the violence. When I first began to think about antilesbian violence, I too saw it as primarily antiwoman, but that was grounded in my own experience as a white, middle-class lesbian who is often assumed to be heterosexual. But on reflection, the stories of my lesbian friends who do *not* pass as heterosexual and who have been harassed and assaulted *as lesbians* came to the surface. As activists, we must begin to recognize and publicize the specificity of this violence and its victims. Otherwise, lesbian,

gay, and feminist activists participate by exclusion in accepting the violence against some lesbians as "just life."

Similarly, feminist media campaigns in general do not highlight the abuse and violence perpetrated against women working in prostitution. Those few feminists who focus on violence against women working in prostitution have met with virulent criticism and hostility on the grounds that this focus somehow erases women's agency in choosing prostitution as an arena for work. The U.S. feminist debate over prostitution rages on, and meanwhile, a significant number of women working in prostitution continue to disappear. The life realities of women working in prostitution often are not on the anti-rape and battered women's movement agenda. Emanating from the tendency to construct "innocent victims" for the purposes of gaining public support and establishing social legitimacy, in combination with class, race, and sexual prejudices, activists and service providers may distance themselves from women who do not fulfill the requirements of the "innocent victim." This results in the systematic invisibility of women working in prostitution, who are relegated to the margins of discourse and practice. As with lesbians, feminists tend toward the "It's not me" response with prostitutes. As Baldwin writes, "The fate of a woman's claims on justice, we all seem to know somewhere, crucially depends on her success in proving that she is not, and never has been, a prostitute" (1992, p. 81). She goes on to quote Dworkin, who says, "The woman's effort to stay innocent, her efforts to prove innocence, her effort to prove that she was used against her will is always and unequivocally an effort to prove she is not a whore." Baldwin argues that much feminist legal work has sought to distinguish "with great delicacy and equal urgency between 'prostitutes' and 'other women.' The political rescue of 'real womanhood' from conditions of prostitution, within the spheres of life believed occupied by 'normal women' has been the mainstream feminist tactic advanced within many of our campaigns" (p. 67).

This disassociation can only be labeled appalling in the face of evidence which suggests that women working in prostitution and lesbians, who are poor and women of color, may be the most vulnerable to violence and murder. The way to change the socially constructed value hierarchy among women who are victims of assault and murder is for activists to recognize the humanity of all women, to challenge the socially constructed differences between women, and to make visible and central to our campaigns against violence the women who are most vulnerable to violence and who currently are on the margins of media discourse. In other words, activists must refuse to participate in the construction of a value hierarchy in an effort to establish social legitimacy and concern about violence. The media will not change without public pressure and activism; the responsibility for forcing the issue is ours. Otherwise, our rhetoric should be more honest and specific about what violence and victims we are talking about.

Lesbians, Prostitutes, and Man-Haters

"A woman, by definition, is not violent, and if violent, a female is not a woman."
—Jeffner Allen,
quoted in Lynda Hart,
Fatal Women

While lesbian existence is mostly absent from, or at best marginal in, mainstream social constructions of violence, the hegemonic culture associates lesbians with the perpetuation of violence and hatred; lesbians and man-hating seem to be intricately intertwined in the popular imagination. In some ways the threat of lesbianism seems to have more to do with lesbian autonomy from men—translated simultaneously into lesbian hatred of men, or overidentification with men—than with lesbian sexual activities (images of which are consumed in mainstream heterosexual pornography). The angry and indignant response to lesbians seems connected to those lesbians who are perceived as assuming and/or usurping the rights to male behaviors and actions, including violence. In turn, lesbians are said to have an intense animosity toward men, presumably because lesbians challenge men's exclusive claim to a "masculinized" authority or power. There seems to be a fear that because we are assumed to be autonomous from men's control, lesbians might not experience as much constraint in using violence as a weapon, one historically reserved for men (at least in public

discourse). The discourse of deviance about lesbians, however, applies mostly to those perceived to be crossing gender boundaries. The threat to the social order, it seems, is the "butch" lesbian, not the "femme," and the working-class lesbian, not the middle-class one. For instance, in the working-class bars of the 1940s and 1950s, the police singled out and assaulted lesbians who dressed and looked "like men" more frequently than those perceived as "real" women (Feinberg 1993; Nestle 1992; Kennedy and Davis 1993).

Since women are, by definition, not supposed to be violent, then women who are violent must be labeled as not real women—unfeminine, malelike. Lynda Hart insightfully argues that lesbian identity has served as "a site where women's aggression has been displaced. . . . [T]he female invert's *aggressiveness* was what marked her as deviant and therefore dangerous, *not* her object choice" (Hart 1994, p. 9). Hart shows how the construction of the "female offender" in criminology and the "invert" in sexology at the turn of the century were one and the same discourse. In summarizing the early criminologist Lombroso's construction of the "female offender," Hart (1994) draws out the linkages:

Her propensity is to approximate the dress, behavior, appearance, and eroticism of the male. She is marked by an absence of maternal affection, indicating further that she is more like a man, even a normal man, than she is like a normal woman. She retains the sex of a female but acquires the gender attributes of masculinity. She is tyrannical, selfish; she wants only to satisfy her own passions. Love is replaced in her by an "insatiable egotism." She is incapable of resignation and sacrifice, and her desire results in acts of tyranny. . . She is, in fact, remarkably like Ellis's congenital invert. . . . The congenital invert and the born female offender marked the limits of cultural femininity. And they did so as a couple, not separately, but together. (p. 12)

This construction of lesbians as "not women" and as aggressive and manhating can be seen operating in the explanations offered for Aileen Wuornos's behavior. After Wuornos was arrested, descriptions such as the following inundated the media reports: "America's first female serial killer is a man-hating lesbian who posed as a prostitute to lure at least seven men into her web of death" (quoted in Ernst, Greenblatt, and McWhinney 1993, p. 53).

Despite Wuornos's claims to self-defense, *the* major question in the media was whether Wuornos could be classified a "female serial killer." Robert Ressler, a former FBI agent and expert on serial killers, was quoted widely. He distinguishes Wuornos from both male serial murderers and women who murder more than one person. He defines a "true serial killer" as "a predator, one who for his own motives is hunting down people with murder in mind." Sexual issues are central, according to Ressler: "Serial murders stem from a man's inability to deal with women on a sexual basis, or from unresolved sexual problems and inadequacies." He says that Wuornos is "an enigma."

Historically, women who kill more than one person have not been classified as "serial killers"; murder by women is interpreted as categorically different. According to the traditional framework for murder by women, the assumption is that women kill people they are in close association with—children, husbands, patients under their care in hospitals. Skrapec suggests that women who kill more than one person are considered *aberrant women* but still within the confines of femininity—individual, isolated, and needing of explanation; they are "[t]ypically presented as case studies and summarily typecast as 'black widows' (women who kill a series of husbands, their children, and other relatives), 'angels of death' or 'mercy killers' (women who kill patients in their care), and the like" (Skrapec 1994, pp. 243–44). Thus, Wuornos is supposedly different. Dr. Kathy Morall, a forensic psychiatrist, labels Wuornos an *aberrant* female killer, rather than a representative one, "[b]ecause of the confusion in sexual identity—you have a person making an effort to put herself in the place of a male, physically and mentally." She says, "There's nothing to prevent Miss Prissy in a prom dress from going around and shooting forty people, but historically we haven't seen it" (quoted in Edmiston 1991, p. 325). Ressler offers, "If Wuornos is seen to be a serial killer, we have to rewrite the rules. With women the base may be hatred, mental disorder, even monetary reasons—there could be a number of possibilities" (Edmiston 1991, p. 324). James Alan Fox, another expert on murder, also distinguishes between Wuornos and other female serial killers; he says that women "generally kill people they know. They kill for particular reasons, such as jealousy or revenge. My guess is that the motive in this case was actually control, power, dominance. It could be that these men were trying to take control, and submission, perhaps, is not something she was into. This may have been some attempt to get back at men" (in Kunen et al. 1991, p. 46). In fact, Wuornos's difference seems to be her unwillingness to accept women's subordination and powerlessness in relation to men's use and abuse.

The media mapped this difference onto Wuornos lesbian identity, which was used to explain her aggressiveness, hatred, and indifference to men, and therefore her motivation to kill. Despite the fact that Wuornos has only been in two lesbian relationships in her life and does not identify herself as a lesbian, the media persistently defines her as both a lesbian and a man-hater (see Brownworth 1995). Ressler says, for instance, "There may be an intrinsic hatred of males here, as well as an identification with male violence which helped push her across the line into what has been considered a 'male' crime" (quoted in Edmiston 1991, p. 325). The comments of one of Wuornos's childhood friends were enlisted to construct the connection further; she is quoted as saying, "I know she hated men. . . . She had no dates, no major crushes. If she was with a boy, it was always for the money. She had no close friends. And not a single adult ever helped her, absolutely not one" (quoted in MacNamara 1991, p. 96). A worker at a convenience store Wuornos frequented says, "She struck me as a very aggressive person. . . . The way she carried herself, the way she flexed her muscles. Whenever a nice-looking male customer would come in—I mean, I looked, Ty[ria Moore, Wuornos's lover at the time of the killings] looked, but Lee [Aileen] didn't look. Or if she did, she snarled" (quoted in MacNamara 1991, p. 100). Wuornos's motives are most often ascribed to hatred and revenge arising from her sexual identification and her abusive past, not from the circumstances surrounding the crimes.

Neither sexist attitudes nor misogyny are called on to explain the serial killings of women by men, despite the fact that most perpetrators of serial murder are male and most victims female. Instead, the murders are conceptualized as arising from the perpetrator's individual pathology, not his masculinity nor his gender identification. For instance, the journalists who wrote the "true crime" book on the Green River killer, in line with the experts' profile of the killer, write that the killer "does not [have], nor has he ever [had,] an aversion toward women." This is in stark contrast to descriptions of Wuornos, whose violence the media consistently links to man-hating. The Green River killer's motives are nonetheless connected to gender, but they are not labeled as such. Rather, the motives seem only "natural" within the social reality of contemporary gender relations. The experts say that the killer must be someone who "has felt that he has been 'burned' or 'lied' to and fooled by women one too many times. In his way of thinking, women are no good and cannot be trusted and he feels women will prostitute themselves for whatever reason and when he seeks women openly prostituting themselves, this makes his blood boil" (Smith and Guillen 1991, p. 118). Wuornos, on the other hand, despite the recognition that she experienced years of sexual and physical abuse as well as poverty and prostitution, is characterized as a deviant "man-hater" who kills without cause. There is no "natural" explanation. In the language of the prosecution, she is "a remorseless, diabolical killer" who was a "candidate for the electric chair if ever there was one" (quoted in Lavin 1992). According to Phyllis Chesler, the prosecutor portrayed Wuornos as a "predatory prostitute" whose " 'appetite for lust and control had taken a lethal turn;' and 'had been exercising control for years over men' and who 'killed for power, for full and ultimate control.' " She points out that the prosecutor was the same man—a born-again Christian—who, as Ted Bundy's "minister" on death row, "tried to delay Bundy's execution" (Chesler 1992, pp. 30–31).

Yet in a strange way, media stories characterized Wuornos's actual lesbian relationship in terms of love and friendship. They portray Tyria Moore, Wuornos's lover at the time of the killings, as an innocent and feminine lover, the "wife" of Wuornos, who, according to most of the stories, Wuornos loved. No stories suggest that Wuornos was violent toward Moore, though they report that Moore was increasingly afraid of Wuornos, given her suspicions about the killings.[5] Again, the crime of lesbianism in the stories is not about the relationship between the women but about the autonomy, anger, and seeming rejection of men. The problematic "sex-ual identity" that makes her unfeminine and hateful toward men is then linked to her inherent propensity to murder. At the same time, the sexual aspect of their relationship is downplayed. In one made-for-TV movie, for instance, Wuornos and Moore are portrayed as friends, not lovers.[6]

Both the media and the police, their primary source of information, seem to fluctuate in their identification of Wuornos as a prostitute. Sometimes they minimized her work in prostitution; instead painting Wuornos as someone who targeted the men for murder in the tradition of serial killers. They minimize the context of prostitution in making sense of the relationship between Wuornos and the men she killed. The men are, for the most part, constructed as completely innocent victims. A New York Times article (Smothers 1991) describes the victims as middle-aged men who "traveled in their jobs and were frequently on the roads." In this story, Wuornos lured the men to remote areas in order to kill them. Major Henry, one of the investigators, is quoted as if he was asking an open-ended question: "What was it that led him and others to let their guard down? We think there may have been some offer of sex involved." Another account reads, "They said they believed that some of the men were killed after picking up, or stopping to help, their assailant on the highway." In one article an investigator named Munster claimed that Wuornos was not working as a prostitute at the time of the murders and that she was killing in order to rob the victims of money. In this report she is characterized as having "sought out expensive cars, sometimes stopping them by throwing herself in their path so the driver was forced to brake." He also claimed that after "the first killing she began ordering the victims to take off their clothes. Why? It's physical evidence" (quoted in Edmiston 1991, p. 324). Evidence for these claims is never offered, and they contradict other statements by Sergeant Munster and other investigators. The stories attribute complete innocence to the men and premeditation and lethal intent on the part of Wuornos, despite her claims of rape, attempted rape, and assault.

Some stories did raise the possibility of self-defense in response to the violence or the threat of violence that Wuornos may have encountered, but the stories retain contradictions that undermine Wuornos's claim. For instance, Munster says that "[Wuornos] was often described to us as obnoxious, aggressive, not sexy. . . . Most men put her out without any money at all. So that may have been part of it. . . . But really she was just a female predator who needed money" (quoted in MacNamara 1991, p. 98). The refusal of "most men" to pay for sexual services is passed over without comment. Horpeza, another investigator for the case, said that "Wuornos tried to turn eight or 10 tricks a night." According to him, Wuornos said, "All I wanted was to get my money for sex. If I could do it clean, no problem. When somebody gave me a problem, that's when the incident happened" (quoted in Kunen et al. 1991, p. 46). The mistreatment and economic exploitation of women in prostitution is never addressed as a problem *for the woman involved in prostitution,* and as such, as a possible motive for Wuornos's behavior. The allusions to the men's violence in the articles is never addressed as cause; it serves as background, but not one that might explain the killings. When raised it is often countered with a discussion of Wuornos's desire for power and control over men in general, which is defined as unnatural, illegitimate, and arising from unjustified hatred.

Neither the media nor Wuornos's defense team sought out information about the men who were murdered. Phyllis Chesler points out that Richard Mallory, the first man killed by Wuornos, had a history of violence, according to his former girlfriend. This woman told one of the investigators that Mallory "had served ten years in prison for burglary, suffered from severe mood swings, drank too much, was violent to women, enjoyed the strip bars, was 'into' pornography, and had undergone therapy for some kind of sexual dysfunction" (Chesler 1993, p. 956). Chesler's own investigation found that Mallory had "done many years in Patuxent Prison, in Maryland, as a sex offender. In [his] criminal record he was described as an 'impulsive and explosive individual who will get into serious difficulty, most likely of a sexual nature. . . . Because of his emotional disturbance and his poor control of his sexual impulses, he could present a potential danger to his environment in the future'" (Chesler 1993, p. 958). This information would have helped support Wuornos's claim of self-defense, but her own defense team never followed up these leads. Moreover, the judge would not allow information about Mallory's past behavior into the trial. Wu-

ornos's defense team also did not draw on experts who could speak to the high level of violence and threat of violence that many street prostitutes face on a daily basis, testimony that could have bolstered Wuornos's claim of self-defense (Chesler 1993). Instead, her defense team tended to characterize her as "a terribly deprived victim," "a damaged, primitive child" who warranted mercy rather than hatred (Lavin 1992). None of the mainstream media articles developed the self-defense claims. Instead, they relied on the police investigators speculations. The mainstream media articles did not address the endemic violence women working in prostitution experience at the hands of pimps, johns, and/or the police; nor did they seek out experts on rape or abuse trauma, or feminist legal experts familiar with women's self-defense cases.

The story of Wuornos—a woman who worked in prostitution for many years, who faced the possibility of abuse and violence as part of her job—is severely minimized in the reports. Wuornos's claims of self-defense were mostly absent from the media stories. As described by Candice Skrapec (1994), Wuornos "asserted that Mallory [the first male killed] had raped, tortured, and threatened to kill her, and that she had used the handgun in her purse, which she carried for protection, to save her life" (p. 242). Wuornos claimed that she killed the other men under similar circumstances.

The Framing of Women Who Murder

Passion and/or pathology have been the key historical constructs for explaining, and containing, women's aggression. Women like Aileen Wuornos are not supposed to exist.

—Lynda Hart,
Fatal Women

As long as we insist on maintaining our innocence, we lock ourselves into helplessness. In this way we become complicit with our oppression.

—Melanie Kaye/Kantrowitz,
The Issue Is Power

"When 'violence' appears *against* 'oppression,' it is a *negation of institutionalized* violence. Such acts are *acts of bravery.* . . . It is a betrayal of humanity, and of hope, to represent such acts as shameful, or regrettable."

—Ti-Grace Atkinson,
quoted in Melanie Kaye/Kantrowitz,
The Issue Is Power

It seems very rare in this social landscape for the claim of self-defense against rapists, batterers, abusers, and potential killers to get a hearing in the media. Mainstream media stories that seem sympathetic instead obscure the claims to self-defense by highlighting the psychology of victimized and abused women. Those empathetic to women who kill sidestep the issue of self-defense by focusing on past histories of abuse and trauma, presumably to gain public sympathy for the woman as a victim. The psychology of the victim is then used to explain why she resorted to violence; violence is assumed to be behavior uncharacteristic, unnatural, and unreasonable for women. Phyllis Murphy, cochair of Florida's chapter of the Gay and Lesbian Alliance against Defamation, criticized the media treatment of Wuornos for the way they "sensationalized her lesbianism rather than her abusive childhood. There are a lot of abused children who grow up to do violence, both homosexual and heterosexual. The prosecutors are playing up her hatred of men" (quoted in Bankston 1991, pp. 50–51). Donald Suggs offered abuse as the explanatory narrative, in contrast to the homophobic explanations of "criminal experts": "Ressler [former FBI agent] sees in Wuornos's lesbianism an 'intrinsic hatred of males,' which he apparently considers to be more of a motivating factor in the killings she has been accused of committing than her lifetime as a victim of violence and sexual abuse" (1992, p. 98). Absent from both discussions is Wuornos's own explanation of self-defense against violent men.

Caught between competing explanations and defenses of Wuornos, Suggs concludes, "While it would be difficult not to feel queasy about Wuornos's actions, the bigoted assumptions underlying the media coverage of the case are also a sordid proposition. Whether or not Wuornos is ultimately found to be a serial killer[,] . . . lesbians and gays must neither apologize for the way many women are forced to defend themselves nor allow the actions of one troubled lesbian to become a pretext for attacking an entire community" (1992, p. 98). Suggs seems caught in the dilemma

of whether to recognize that Wuornos may have legitimately killed the men in self-defense or to define her actions as those of a "troubled individual." The past history of abuse and trauma are used to explain Wuornos in psychological terms as a victim-turned-perpetrator, rather than to recognize abuse and violence as legitimate causes for Wuornos to fight back in defense of her life. The anger attributed to Wuornos is defined as unreasonable or unusual.[7] Wuornos is constructed as a woman whose victimization has made her judgment and behavior aberrant and pathological. This construction of pathology undermines and dismisses, without further investigation, Wuornos's own argument of self-defense. It shifts the focus from the violence and threat of violence that Wuornos faced, on a daily basis and in these particular circumstances, to her personality and perception of reality.

Using past history of abuse as an explanatory framework in cases of self-defense deflects attention away from the circumstances surrounding the killings, and it pathologizes the women fighting to defend their lives. As Lynda Hart says, "The appeal [to past trauma] will rest on the very pathology that reproduces the social conditions in which Aileen Wuornos performed her desperate actions" (1994, p. 151).[8] Hart points out that Wuornos herself refuses this narrative:

> Aileen Wuornos is "guilty" under the law; but she refuses to enact the "guilt" that secures the fiction of law's justice. She confesses to the acts but is still unrepentant. And although we might find her incredible when she insists that her "past" has nothing to do with the crimes she has committed, there is something fascinating, and unnerving, in her implacable self-defense, her disregard for a linear narrative of a life's trajectory that begins with victimization and ends in retaliation. . . . By refusing to accede to the narrative of her "traumatic past," Aileen Wuornos repudiates not just a personal history but also the story of "vengeance," with its ever-threatening promise of repetition. (1994, p. 152)

Nonetheless, Hart (1994), like Chesler (1992), recognizes that constructing such a story of abuse and trauma might have been Wuornos's only chance of not being given the death sentence, which she inevitably received.[9] But in so doing, it dismantles Wuornos claim of self-defense—it "even more powerfully asserts that

Wuornos's perception of a 'clear and present danger' was not *real*."[10]

Wuornos claimed in interviews with the media that she committed each of the six killings in self-defense. She argued that as someone who worked in prostitution, she was in contact with many men every day whom she did not kill. She claimed, then, that she killed *these particular* men because they raped her, attempted to rape her, or in some way threatened her life. Wuornos testified that she killed the first victim, Richard Mallory, in self-defense after he raped and sexually abused her. Her story is as follows:

So we go into the woods. He's huggin' and kissin' on me. He starts pushin' me down. And I said, wait a minute, you know, get cool. You don't have to get rough, you know. Let's have fun. . . . I said I would not [have sex with him]. He said, yes, you are, bitch. You're going to do everything I tell you. If you don't I'm going to kill you and [have sex with you] after you're dead, just like the other sluts. It doesn't matter, your body will still be warm. He tied my wrists to the steering wheel, and screwed me in the ass. Afterwards, he got a Visine bottle filled with rubbing alcohol out of the trunk. He said the Visine bottle was one of my surprises. He emptied it into my rectum. It really hurt bad because he tore me up a lot. He got dressed, got a radio, sat on the hood for what seemed like an hour. . . . Eventually he untied me, put a stereo wire around my neck and tried to rape me again. . . . Then I thought, well, this dirty bastard deserves to die because of what he was tryin' to do to me. We struggled. I reached for my gun. I shot him. I scrambled to cover the shooting because I didn't think the police would believe I killed him in self-defense. . . . I have to say it. I killed them all because they got violent with me and I decided to defend myself. (Quoted in Chesler 1992, p. 31)

As Hart (1994) describes, media commentators continually questioned Wuornos on her version of reality. They would suggest to Wuornos that the public does not believe that prostitutes can be raped because they are paid to engage in sexual relations. Wuornos would unapologetically insist that women working in prostitution know the difference between sex and rape, that they *can* be raped and that *she* was raped. She often offered graphic details of the rapes she experi-

enced. When an interviewer suggests that the killings were evidence that she was out of control, Wuornos responds: "Those men are out of control. I'm sick and tired of those men out there thinking they can control us and do whatever they damn well please with our bodies and think they can get away with it" (quoted in Hart 1994, p. 141). Wuornos herself refuses the story of the completely victimized and insane woman turned killer. Instead, she forthrightly presents herself as someone who was trying to save her own life. Although neither the media nor her defense team took the threat to her life seriously, Wuornos had no choice. In her narrative, Wuornos refers to Mallory's reference to the destiny of other women's refusal—"You're going to do everything I tell you. If you don't, I'm going to kill you and [have sex with you] after you're dead, just like the other sluts." Given prostitutes' high rate of vulnerability to serial murder, as delineated earlier in this essay, and the specific cases in the state of Florida, Wuornos had every reason to believe she was in serious danger of being killed. But in this society, which tends to demonize lesbians, pathologize women, and stigmatize women working in prostitution, Wuornos is unnatural, her narrative unbelievable, and her claim of self-defense socially illegitimate.

The tendency to resort to individual psychology as an explanation of women's use of violence in self-defense seeps into feminist analyses as well. For instance, in the spring of 1994 a local group of feminists created an exhibit on Debra Reid's case for their art show on feminist activism. On the night of the opening, I was shocked to find an exhibit that characterized Reid as a "battered woman" with sole reference to the childhood abuse she experienced in her family. Absent from the exhibit was a description of how Reid's lover had systematically battered her—physically, emotionally, sexually, verbally, and economically—for most of their five-year relationship. Despite the fact that her commutation petition was grounded in a self-defense claim, the events that led up to the killing were not described. It was as if her history of child abuse explained the killing, rather than the actual events of the night in question and the history of the couple's relationship.

The challenge for activists is to make the claim of self-defense for women without pathologizing them. Rather than solely emphasizing a woman's psychological state as an explanation for her actions, arguments must be made for a woman's right to self-defense in response to real violence and threats to her life. As Susan Madden writes, "For a woman to fight back means that she values her self enough to fight for it. And for society to support her in that fight would mean a recognition of her innate human value, her right to live unmolested and without fear, and her freedom from intimate captivity" (1981, p. 146). This is a very different argument from one that talks about the psychological state that induces a woman to resort to violence.

In *Fight Back! Feminist Resistance to Male Violence*, Melanie Kaye challenges us to think about the possibilities: *"[I]magine: every day in the paper, instead of a story about a woman who was attacked, raped, beaten, tortured and/or murdered—information which certainly has its effects on us—there was a story about a rapist or batterer who was beaten, shot, stabbed—even public humiliation would be better than nothing"* (1981, p. 163).

In a very provocative article, "Imagined Violence/Queer Violence," Judith Halberstam (1993) suggests "imagined violence" as a strategy for disrupting the power-and-violence equation that the media socially constructs. Halberstam defines "imagined violence" as "the fantasy of unsanctioned eruptions of aggression" emanating from those who June Jordan describes as the socially constructed *legitimate* victims of violence—"the wrong people, of the wrong skin, the wrong sexuality, the wrong gender." Rather than shying away from exploring the capacity for violence among the oppressed, Halberstam argues that "our violence needs to be imaginable because the power of fantasy is not to represent but to destabilize the real. . . . Imagined violence does not advocate lesbian or female aggression but it might complicate an assumed relationship between women and passivity or feminism and pacifism" (Halberstam 1993, p. 199).

Similarly, rather than seeking to disassociate from women who fight back against violence to defend their own lives or the lives of others, and rather than pathologizing women's life histories to neutralize their actions, the real challenge to the social value hierarchy would be to recognize, support, and socially validate such women's actions and behaviors. To disassociate from and/or pathologize "deviant" women who are fighting for their/our lives is not a strategy toward fundamen-

tal change in the social order. It might help a few women out, but in the meantime it accepts and perpetuates the dehumanization and marginalization of many women. In "Poem about My Rights," June Jordan (1980) eloquently refuses the construction of legitimate violence. She writes:

I am not wrong: Wrong is not my name

My name is my own my own my own
and I can't tell you who the hell set things up like this
but I can tell you that from now on my resistance
my simple and daily and nightly self-determination
may very well cost you your life.

The argument that I have been making in this essay is that the mainstream media indifferently accepts violence against women who are identified as lesbians and/or women working in prostitution. This makes the violence "legitimate" and "understandable" in the current social reality. Moreover, the media demonizes and pathologizes lesbians and/or women working in prostitution when they become "a problem" or "threat" to the status quo, which creates a context where violence against them becomes socially legitimate and acceptable. A major strategy for disrupting this construction of social power is to persistently challenge the terms on which it is lodged. At the very least this means that as writers, educators, and activists, we must insist that we ourselves as well as the media make visible and socially significant the violence against all lesbians and all women working in prostitution, as well as violence against poor, working-class women of color, who are the most vulnerable to violence. We must persistently refuse the construction of "deserving victims" whose disappearances and deaths are unworthy of social urgency and outrage. And we must publicly defend the right of women, all women, to defend our lives, not as pathological responses of "troubled" women but as reasonable responses to vicious, brutal, and life-threatening attacks.

Notes

1. In this essay I use the phrase "women working in prostitution" rather than "prostitutes" whenever possible because I do not want to participate in the

objectification process that I observe in mass-media accounts of "prostitutes," which renders the women themselves invisible and does not necessarily reflect how the women define themselves.

2. Jack Hampton, a Texas state district court judge, who gave "a killer of two gay men a 30 year sentence instead of life in prison after remarking that the men wouldn't have been killed 'if they hadn't been cruising the streets picking up teenage boys' " (Boulard 1994).

3. Caputi quotes Jack Levin and James Alan Fox in the discussion of a particular serial killer and the number of women he killed: "We will never know for certain, because the majority of them would have been prostitutes whose disappearance may not have been reported. Some may have ended up among the many 'Jane Doe' in the Los Angeles County morgue" (Caputi 1987, pp. 100n, 224).

4. In general, the generic term "women" continues to be used to refer to centers, organizations, and projects which are predominantly lesbian. For instance, the "women's" music festivals in Michigan, California, and the East Coast tend to be predominantly lesbian-initiated and organized, but the festivals are not called "lesbian."

5. Moore was never implicated in any of the killings, presumably because she helped get Wuornos to confess to her own involvement. This is despite some evidence that Moore helped Wuornos, at least once, to clean out and abandon a car that belonged to one of the men killed.

6. In this movie, on the other hand, the violence is attributed to her past abuse: The encounters with the men she killed are portrayed as triggering flashbacks to earlier abuse and trauma, which induce her to kill.

7. Again, this stands in stark contrast to men's violence against women; men's violence against women is considered legitimate for the most part, except for violence by men of color against white women. I am struck by the contrast in the understanding granted to men who serially kill women versus that given to women who kill men who have abused them.

8. Hart labels this strategy as the one feminists were using, and while you can see hints of this in Chesler's essays about Wuornos, you can also see a clear defense of Wuornos, as in the concluding line to Chesler's article in On the Issues, where she says that Wuornos is turning the question "Well, [being raped, beaten, robbed, arrested and killed] is part of the job, why doesn't she get out?" around to "'If men don't want to be killed, they should stay away from prostitutes—or at least stop degrading and assaulting them" (Chesler 1992, p. 31).

9. Wuornos has tried to appeal the seven murder convictions against her. The Florida Supreme Court rejected four of these appeals in early October 1994. For more information, contact the defense committee working to support her process of appeal, which is being organized by Iraya Robias and Kate Raphael, 3543 18th Street, Box 30, San Francisco, Calif. 94110.

10. You can see the contradictions in such reasoning in Chesler's own recognition of the problem of an "insanity" defense; she writes, "I am not saying that Wuornos did not kill anyone, nor am I saying she is sane—merely that a strategic use of the insanity plea might have saved her from the death sentence. It is still justifiable—even for a seriously traumatized woman—to kill in self-defense and Wuornos's claim of self-defense against a violent john is plausible" (Chesler 1992, p. 31).

22

Blindfolded

Rape and the Press's Fear of Feminism

HELEN BENEDICT

Feminists are funny—at least that is the attitude I have discovered in my examination of a decade's worth of rape coverage by the American press. Feminists are dogmatic at best, extremist at worst. At any rate, they are not to be consulted about anything as explosive as a rape case. To do so would be to commit biased reporting.

This summarizes the point of view I have found among the majority of editors and reporters in the mainstream magazines and newspapers of this country. Virtually the only time the press mentions feminists or their theories in its coverage of rape is to attack them for exaggeration, for extremism, or for being dogmatically "politically correct." Indeed, the mainstream press is more inclined to make fun of feminists as they monitor trials or demonstrate against rape than it is to consult them for explanations of the crime. Feminist analyses of rape are confined to opinion pages, letters sections, or columns, or to the alternative press, as if they are nothing but unsubstantiated opinion, never fact. Essentially, the mainstream press is so afraid of feminism that it is covering rape without reference to feminist re-search, theory, or to the association between rape and sex roles—in other words, without understanding. As historian Roy Porter wrote in his essay "Rape—Does It Have a Historical Meaning?": "In surveying the history of rape . . . two formulations arising from the writings of feminists do seem fully justified: (a) rape cannot be fully understood in terms of individual rapists, but only in terms of masculine values at large; (b) rape is more an expression of misogyny than of pent-up sexual desire" (R. Porter 1986, pp. 229–30). In short, not every sexist is a rapist, but every rapist is a sexist. No one can understand rape without understanding the workings of sexism in this country.

My first example can be found in the coverage of the Central Park Jogger case of 1989–91, a widely covered New York story about a runner who was raped, horribly beaten, and left for dead in the mud by a gang of teenagers.[1] Throughout the case, even up to the start of the trial, the white and black press in New York kept running articles trying to analyze *why* the youths had committed this heinous crime against the jogger.

They looked for answers in race, drugs, and class, and in the ghetto's "culture of violence." They tried to blame the crime on rap music, on single mothers, on the lack of a death penalty, on Mayor Koch, on television and the movies, on schools, on boredom, on teenage lust, on peer pressure, and even on the full moon (Benedict 1992, pp. 189–249). But even though some of these explanations had partial validity (and many were absurd), they were not complete, for the press never looked at the most glaring reason of all for rape: women's position in society as sexual prey. For example, in 1990 *Newsweek* magazine ran a cover story called "The Mind of the Rapist," inspired by the Central Park Jogger case, which devoted page after page to analyses of why men rape without one single mention of gender relations in our society. Instead, it provided answers in terms of individual pathology and dabbled in the old "rape is sex and motivated by lust" myth. The article pathetically concluded, "No single profile provides an answer to why men rape. Opportunity, emotional illness, lust—it happens for all of those reasons, yet often for none of them" (Gelman 1990, pp. 46–52).

The *New York Times* also ran a background article on the attack by David E. Pitt titled "Gang Attack: Unusual for Its Viciousness." This story offered an analysis of violence among youth groups, but it, too, failed to mention their antifemale attitudes (Pitt 1989, p. B1). Even the sociologists and psychologists interviewed for the article mentioned nothing about attitudes toward women in their discussions of gang rape. Only the *Village Voice* and other such alternative papers touched on the relation between gender issues and rape during this case; as the *Voice* itself proclaimed at the time, "Sexism: The Forbidden Issue" (Bryant et al., 1989, p. 1).

I asked the reporters and editors who covered this case why they had gone out to ask experts and people in the street if they thought racism was at the root of the crime but had neither asked anyone if sexism or gender roles might have played a part nor gone to a single rape expert for their explanations of the rape. Their answers revealed how deeply reluctant they were to discuss gender relations in our society at all.

Mike Pearl, court reporter for the *New York Post*: "You'll have to talk to the *New York Times* about that. Tabloid newspapers aren't going to go into sociological explanations. I just don't think that this is a subject for a tabloid or even for a paper like the *Times*" (Pearl, New York, 1991). Race relations were all right to report on, apparently, but gender relations were not.

Jim Willse, then editor of the *Daily News*: "I can't recall why we had no coverage like that, but if we didn't do it, we didn't do it, and I don't see anything wrong with not doing it" (Willse, New York, 1991).

Hap Hairston, city editor of *Newsday* at the time of the case: "That kind of journalism is thumbsucking journalism. I don't think that kind of reporting is really legitimate. Once you write a piece about rape experts talking about why people do gang rape, there's no follow-up (Hairston, New York, 1991)."

Pat Clark, then court reporter for the *Daily News*: "That sort of explanation is more appropriate on an editorial page" (Clark, New York, 1991).

Michael T. Kaufman, then metropolitan reporter for the *New York Times*: "I can't imagine the range of reaction to the sexual aspect of the crime would be very strong. I may be wrong but I can't think right off-hand what questions one ought to ask about that" (Kaufman, New York, 1991).

Paul Fishleder, an editor at the *New York Times*: "Racism is the big story in New York. Men-women relations, or whatever you want to call them, are not" (Fishleder, New York, 1991).

The basic pattern here is this: The mainstream press refuses to look at societal reasons for rape (except when it can blame the crime on racial tensions) and insists on covering the crime only in terms of individual pathology. Occasionally this pattern will change if the racial roles of victim and assailant are reversed (see discussion of the St. John's University case later on), but such exceptions are rare. The press thus refuses to explain the enormously high rate of rape in this country—a woman is raped every five minutes, according to the FBI[2]—with any reference to media images of women as objects of torture and conquest, to the judicial system's persistent refusal to take rape seriously (only one in a hundred rapists is sentenced to more than a year in prison,[3] and almost a quarter of convicted rapists are released on probation and thus avoid prison altogether[4]), to the historical role of women as sexual property and second-class citizens, or to the continuing inequality of women in pay, positions of power, and so on. According to our press, each one of those rapists who strike every five minutes is simply a nutcase. The crime is covered as if gender inequality and violence toward women—as if sexism itself—do not exist.

The press's insistence on portraying rapists as individual psychopaths takes a willful effort to ignore the nearly three decades of research on rape that has been conducted by feminist sociologists, criminologists, and psychologists. Their research, for example, has found that rapists have more normal psychological profiles than any other criminal; that rapists say they rape to achieve power or revenge, not out of simple lust; that the most common type of rape is committed by someone of the same race and class as the victim, whom she knows;[5] and that "rape culture" tends to go hand-in-hand with patriarchal societies that have male military hierarchies, male dominance in politics, "interpersonal violence in general, an ideology of male toughness, and distant father-child relationships."[6] Yet the press's portrayal of this crime tells us the opposite of these discoveries: that rape is committed by monstrous perverts or by red-blooded males tempted by loose women; that most rapists are strangers to their victims; and that rape is usually the woman's fault.

The press's reluctance to correct these inaccuracies by consulting feminists for rape stories has repeated itself in the recent cases that have been pouring into the papers with depressing regularity. During the spring and summer of 1993, for example, two all-white rape cases generated enormous amounts of copy, virtually none of it enlightened by feminist explanations. The 1993 Glen Ridge, New Jersey, trial of several high school boys who were accused of sodomizing and molesting a mentally retarded girl in a basement was covered with nary a mention of what it is in our society that makes boys like this think they can do such things. (Three of the assailants were convicted of aggravated sexual assault in March 1993 [Lefkowitz 1993]). The only attention paid to feminists in the news sections of the press were articles referring to the two members of NOW attending the trial and to the occasional demonstration. In the mainstream press, those mentions were usually mocking. (Guest editorials and columns were an exception to this tone.)

Likewise, during March 1993 coverage of the Lakewood, California, case, where a group of high school boys who called themselves the "Spur Posse" were accused of raping several girls, some as young as ten, the voice of feminists was also glaringly absent. Jane Gross of the *New York Times* wrote a story reporting the views of the boys and their defenders in the case, who were quoted calling the girls "sluts" and "promiscuous" and saying things like, "These [girls] are not the prettiest, you know[,] . . . so they take whatever they can get," but nowhere in the story did she interview feminists criticizing those comments (Gross 1993). The story was even headlined, "Where 'Boys Will Be Boys,' and Adults Are Befuddled." Perhaps the story was supposed to have an ironic twist, to let the boys hang themselves, but because the girls' side of the story was limited to one quote in a two-page story, many a reader probably missed the irony. The girls' side was never given equal space in the *Times*, and that paper never sought feminist views of the case.

More recently, in April 1994, New York's tabloid press was moved to cover rape at length because a rash of rapes and murders committed against middle-class white women had come to the press's attention (the constantly high numbers of attacks on women of color never seem to provoke such attention in the press) and because a new set of statistics was released showing that although crime in general had been declining in New York, rape alone was rising.[7] In general, this attempt to inform the public about the reality of rape by running a series on the subject was a step in the right direction and a welcome relief from covering each case as an aberrant crime, as was done in the Central Park Jogger case, but the series still neglected the causes of rape. For example, *New York Newsday* chose to cover the story by running a huge front-page headline that read "RAPE: The Crime That Won't Go Away" (1994, p. 1) and including three pages of related stories. These stories described individual cases, reported how the Central Park Jogger was faring, gave statistics on the frequency and types of rapes, and featured acquaintance rapes, but not a single article addressed the causes of rape.

Even more pertinent was a four-part series called "The War on Rape" run by the *Daily News* at the same time. The emphasis of the series was how much women have to fear, as revealed by headlines such as "RAPISTS STRIKE EVERY THREE HOURS" and, "Spring Is the Season to Be Most Fearful" (1994, pp. 4–5). The series covered new statistics, the effects of rape on victims, a profile of a rapist and his individual psychosis, and advice from victims on how women should protect themselves. The series did at least consult a few feminist sources, although both *Newsday* and the *Daily News* relied primarily on sources in the legal justice system for their information, but none of the stories addressed the causes of rape or why the numbers were going up. One reporter did tell me she had prepared a piece about just that but it was never run, presumably because it was considered the least important of all the stories on rape.

The result of coverage like that of the *Daily News* and *Newsday* is that it spreads fear without offering recourse, and it lays all the emphasis on women—the potential victims—and none on rapists, the men who are perpetuating the terror. This emphasis on the victim instead of the perpetrator is also typical of the media's approach to covering rape, and again, it is a result of avoiding feminists. By turning to the police all the time for sources, the press cannot find out much about perpetrators, because the police want to prevent the press from derailing their investigations, so the press must turn to the one part of the story that is concrete—the victim. (The rare exception to this focus on the victim is when she is portrayed as innocently virginal and the perpetrators as monsters, which happened in the Central Park Jogger case. I discuss this case further later in the chapter.) Yet by constantly covering rape as something women can and should prevent, the press is perpetuating the old myth that men rape because women tempt them beyond endurance and is yet again blaming the victims for the crime; in short, this sort of coverage assumes that rape is the responsibility of women, not men. This approach is not only inaccurate and unjust but also useless, for covering rape by focusing on the victim actually tells us nothing about the crime, because the victim neither committed nor caused the rape. Journalists should instead be asking, who is the accused? What is he like? Why did he do it? Why is rape so prevalent in our society? What is wrong with us that our men attack women so often? Those are the great unasked questions in this field: the story the press is not getting.

The American press has not always so thoroughly ignored societal causes of rape. According to Margaret T. Gordon and Stephanie Riger, authors of *The Female Fear*, the press underwent a major shift in its approach to rape coverage in the 1970s as a result of the women's movement (1989, p. 67). During that time, these authors say, the press reported many more rape stories than ever before, and for the first time it printed articles on the aftereffects of rape, on how victims can be helped, and on the anger of survivors. Above all, it looked at rape as a societal rather than an individual problem. Unfortunately, the 1980s, and now the 1990s, have seen widespread regression to the ill-informed coverage of the 1950s and 1960s.

There have been some modern-day exceptions to the press's habit of ignoring feminist explications of rape, however, and of focusing on the victim as if she holds the explanation of the crime. Every now and then the press feels moved to include an article about why professional athletes tend to assault women, for example, or why sexual assault is so prevalent in male bastions such as the military (i.e., in the stories about the Tailhook scandal)—although even in these stories, reporters tend to go to psychologists rather than to feminists for answers. I examined some of this coverage, too, to see what might have compelled the press to be more responsible, and I found a consistent pattern: When the accused rapist fits the criminal stereotype of being dark-skinned or poor, especially if the victim is white, the press blames the crime on the ghetto's "culture of violence" or on racial hatred. The Central Park Jogger case was a perfect illustration of this tendency. When the accused does *not* fit the criminal stereotype (i.e., is white and/or upper-middle-class), the press tends to blame the woman in the case, painting her as a sexually loose tramp who tempted the perpetrator beyond endurance. If, however, circumstances make it an impossible stretch to blame the woman, only then will the press look to societal mores (and feminist theories) for explanations. Allow me to illustrate with a case that happened around the same time as the Central Park Jogger rape mentioned earlier, at St. John's University, a Catholic college in New York.

The St. John's case was also a gang attack, only this time the accused were white and upper-middle-class and the victim was black and foreign-born. The story of the case was as follows: The alleged victim, a student at St. John's University, accepted a ride home from a fellow student in one of her classes. The student told her he needed to drop by his fraternity house to get money for gas and invited her in. She accepted. He offered her a drink and, in some accounts, forced alcohol on her until she was barely conscious. (She was from a religious family and did not drink, according to trial testimony, but said she felt compelled out of politeness and some fear to accept the punch laced with vodka.) While she slipped in and out of consciousness as a result of drinking too much, he and five other men taunted her, forced her to engage in repeated oral sex, and molested her sexually.

Once the woman escaped from the house, she did not report the assault for some time, which is usual for traumatized victims of sex crimes. But eventually, with the support of counselors, she did report it. Six students were arrested and charged with sodomy and other sexual abuses. They pleaded not guilty to all charges and were set free without bail. They were not allowed to return to college. The trial was not held until June 1991, when three of the defendants were acquitted. Two others pleaded guilty to reduced charges, and the sixth took a plea bargain but confessed to the substance of the charge: that he had taken her to his house, had made her drunk, and had forced her to engage in oral sex (Fried 1992).

During the pretrial coverage of this case, the press, especially *Newsday* and the *Times*, suddenly decided to use the case as a chance to discuss gang rape, sexual assault by athletes, and abuse of women by fraternities and other college male groups.[8] In other words, the press was giving the kind of background information to explain this crime that had been so sorely missing in the Central Park Jogger case. The fact that the press was willing to examine gang rape and violence against women in this case, where the assailants were white, but not in the Central Park case, where the assailants were black, revealed the racism inherent in sex-crime coverage: When the assailants are white, the press is occasionally willing to explain gang rape in terms of the male ethos (unless, as I already said, they can simply blame the woman). When the assailants are black, the press looks instead to stereotypes of the violent black underclass.[9]

These exceptions aside, the mainstream press on the whole covers rape after rape without any context. When I interviewed major reporters and editors in New York about their rape coverage, I heard several of them express surprise at my suggestion that they contact a rape crisis center or look up "rape" in the library index to get some perspective on the crime. I also found that only one of the thirty or so reporters I interviewed in my research had ever read a book about rape, yet they were all covering it regularly.

Meanwhile, at the same time that the press has been reluctant to consult feminists about rape, it has recently been giving a good deal of attention to those writers who say that rape statistics are exaggerated or fabricated. In March 1993, for example, *New York* magazine ran an article called, "Crying Rape: The Politics of Date Rape on Campus" (Hellman 1993), attacking student feminists for exaggerating the rape issue on Columbia University's campus. A few months later, in June 1993, the *New York Times* ran a cover article by Katie Roiphe titled "Rape Hype Betrays Feminism," a preamble to her book *The Morning After* (1993b). Roiphe also accused "campus feminists" of exaggerating the rate and dangers of rape and claimed that feminists are advocating a regression to the 1950s image of women as frigid and passive. Roiphe received a great deal of attention for her views (indeed, the *New York Times* ran no less than five large features in 1993 either about or by Roiphe before they ran a single rebuttal of her ideas[10]), which were under-researched and ill-informed, while the real story of rape—why it is so prevalent and so persistent in our society—went, and still goes, untold.

The latest FBI Uniform Crime Report records 292 rapes a day—and that is only those rapes that are reported to the police.[11] The government's 1991 National Crime Victimization Survey counts a rape every three and a half minutes.[12] The same survey estimates that attacks during the last twenty years must have left over twelve million women rape survivors in the United States (Report of the Majority Staff of the Senate Judiciary Committee 1993, pp. 7–10). The prevalence of rape is so extreme, and the danger of that prevalence so grave, that the press should be constantly monitoring why men rape and how they can be stopped. Rape is not only commonplace; it is a terrifying and crippling bias crime against women—an extreme expression of sexism. Not only does the crime cause horrible fears and phobias in its victims—psychologists have likened the aftereffects of rape to the post-traumatic stress disorder experienced by soldiers after combat—but the fear of rape cripples women's freedom everywhere. Covering rape without reference to sexism—that is, to societal attitudes toward women—is as absurd as covering lynching without mentioning attitudes toward blacks. Yet that is what the mainstream press in this country is doing every day.

I would like to conclude this bleak analysis of the U.S. press coverage of rape with a suggestion. The press has a lot to learn from the rapes of Bosnian women in the war over former Yugoslavia. As much as anyone might criticize the press for sensationalizing or capitalizing on those rapes, one thing was clear: The rapes of the Bosnian women were covered as acts of torture, committed as war crimes. If we took a leaf from the books of war reporters and covered rape as torture, not merely as unwanted sex, significant improvements could be made in the press's coverage of this crime. Stories of torture don't describe the looks of the victim or how she was dressed, as do so many rape stories. Stories of torture don't blame the victim for the crime because of her "vivacious," "pert," or "flirtatious" behavior, as do so many rape stories.[13] And stories of torture do describe, with reservations of taste, what exactly was done to the victim to get across the horror and inhumanity of the act. That should be the press's model in rape coverage. If the U.S. press covered rape as an act of torture, the *right* questions would come up, and the press would finally get the story it is at the moment ignoring: Who was the torturer, what did he do, why did he do it, and how can he be stopped?

Notes

Some of this article is based on material from *Virgin or Vamp: How the Press Covers Sex Crimes*, by Helen Benedict. Copyright © 1992 by Helen Benedict. Used by permission of Oxford University Press, Inc.

1. See chapter 6 in Benedict 1992.
2. Federal Bureau of Investigation 1992a, pp. 14, 17, 24, 58, Table 1 ("Index of Crimes, United States, 1972–1991").
3. Report of the Majority Staff of the Senate Judiciary Committee 1993, pp. 11, 25–60. In Buchwald, Fletcher, and Roth 1993.
4. Ibid.
5. For a roundup of this research, see Benedict 1992 and Benedict 1994.
6. Hood 1989.
7. Rape rose by .1 percent from 1992 to 1993, while the six other categories of major crimes dropped, according to the New York Police Department (Tyre and Parente 1994).
8. Eskenazi 1990; W. Douglas 1990.
9. This pattern was seen again in the 1991 rape case against William Kennedy Smith. As a result of the accusation by a woman he had met in a bar that he raped her, articles abounded about "date" or "acquaintance" rape. Once again, a rape cases involving a white man revealed a press willing to explain rape in terms of the male ethos rather than in terms of stereotypes. One example was Gross 1991. Another was a cover story in *Time*, N. Gibbs 1991.
10. K. Roiphe 1993a; Lehmann-Haupt 1993b; Kaminer 1993a; Noble (interview with Roiphe's mother about her daughter's success); K. Roiphe 1993c.
11. Federal Bureau of Investigation 1992a.
12. Crime Victimization Survey Report 1992, pp. 72–75, 79, 148–49.
13. These words, along with "hysterical," "bubbly," "pretty," "attractive," "bubbly," and "prudish," were all words I found used to describe rape or sex-murder victims in the past decade. These words are never used for men.

23

Race Under Construction

The Master Narrative of White Supremacy in the Media Representation of African American/Korean American Conflict

LISA C. IKEMOTO

In the mass of words and pictures arising from the civil unrest that took place in Los Angeles in 1992, the notion of Korean American/African American conflict emerged as an explanation for the violence that occurred. And "Los Angeles" became both metaphor and prophecy for race relations in late-twentieth-century United States society. Without denying that a conflict occurred or exists, my aim is to examine the way we interpreted and gave meaning to race and racial identity during five specific days when what happened on the streets and what happened in the media became apparently inseparable.

Because Los Angeles is not an island, in geographic or political terms, the descriptions of civil unrest reflected and merged into an ongoing discourse about race. Many have accused the mainstream media of creating the conflict to increase the market value of the events of 1992. There is probably truth in this, but the mainstream media is not separate from the dominant discourse on race. It is both instrument of and instrumental in that discourse. I focus largely on the words and images the print media published

during and immediately after the period between April 29 and May 3, 1992, but it seems to me that the television news coverage during those same days influenced the print media and shapes my own reading of what appeared in print.[1] In examining the descriptions of conflict set forth by reporters and those they reported on, I have found influential traces of the dominant discourse on race—a master narrative of white supremacy.

In particular, in the media depiction of conflict and violence, race was the key component of individual and group identity. Race determines identity, according to the media stories. Moreover, the dominant discourse on race, as traced through the media coverage, is flat, narrow, and constraining. It provides little room for its objects to be perceived as having depth or complexity. It subsumes other categories, such as gender, and makes maleness an aspect of racial identity. The racialized images of African Americans and Korean Americans were masculine. So the role of women in the conflict, the effect of violence on African American and Korean American women, the voices and experience of women of color, were not seen or heard. The master narra-tive links white supremacy and patriarchy and makes them interdependent.[2]

Constructed Conflict

Korean American/African American conflict be-came a media focal point during the days of street violence. Journalists reported the conflict as both phenomena and explanation for the civil unrest. Questioning the stories of conflict reveals that Korean Americans, African Americans, and others used concepts of race and identity in ways that described conflict as inevitable. Additional interrogation of the stories suggests that despite the absence of obvious whiteness in a conflict de-scribed as intergroup, culturally embedded white supremacy (racism)[3] provided the operative dy-namic. I use "master narrative"[4] to refer to a so-cial/political/legal discourse that simultaneously legitimates and masks white supremacy.[5] In the media events I examine, the master narrative has prescribed exclusionary concepts of race and privilege that act to maintain intergroup conflict and limit the possibility of building better under-standings between these communities.

In my analysis I work from the premise that these concepts are socially constructed. Further, I note that there is no single, consistent construct of race and racial identity operating at any one time. Some identities or aspects of them result from conscious or unconscious racism (Lawrence 1987, p. 316; Matsuda 1989a, pp. 2320, 2327). That is, they are formed from the norms of white supremacy, within the master narrative. The con-structs of race and identity used to describe Ko-rean American/African American conflict were not newly and originally formed in 1992. They emerged from a historically rooted, ongoing dis-course premised on white supremacy. Some iden-tities or aspects of them result from acts of resis-tance to the master narrative. Different understandings of race and racial identity pre-dominate at different times, hiding other possible understandings in their shadow. Too often, those in the shadow are the ones that offer alternatives to white supremacy. This analysis examines the constructs that formed, and shadowed others, in the spring of 1992.

Racism is so much a part of our experience that we cannot always recognize those moments in which we participate.[6] Nor can we easily set the constructs aside. On the other hand, we must try. In the words of Audre Lorde, we must learn "how to take our differences and make them strengths. For the master's tools will never dis-mantle the master's house" (Lorde 1984, p. 112). I am trying to expose how the current constructs of difference make us weak and hide our strengths.

I do not aim to provide a complete descrip-tion of the master narrative, if indeed that were possible. Rather, I try here to give my sense of a dynamic that lies beneath the surface of the sto-ries that were told. I do not assume a unilateral or conscious "master hand" at work, although at times I may use that image to evoke a sense of control that is felt but not seen and a sense of a social reality in which what we are told about the other shapes our experience with the other. When I assert that I write with the goal of re-vealing the hand of the master narrative in social discourse, I mean that I will point to traces of white supremacy as evidence of that narrative.

In telling of a master narrative, I may take the role of narrator and impose my own hand. In fact, I start right here. One point of contention in describing the events of April 29 to May 3, 1992, has been what to call those events. The terms "rebellion," "civil unrest," "uprising," "riot," and "sa-i-ku" (Kim 1993, p. 216) have all been used. Many Korean Americans and others who were harmed reject "rebellion" as a glorifi-cation of the violence that took place and the harm that they suffered. Many African Ameri-cans and others prefer "rebellion" to signify that the anger that erupted was based on real, long-standing, race-based inequities and harms. Many simply refer to those days and their aftermath as "Los Angeles." I choose "uprising" to express hope that the effects of April 29 through May 3, 1992, will be a "from the bottom up" change (Matsuda 1987, p. 323; Matsuda 1989a, p. 2320). I also use "civil unrest," "violence," and "protest" in their more simple descriptive sense, and to shade my discussion with their positive and nega-tive connotations. I acknowledge Paul Gilroy's point that my own understanding of race is so embedded in white supremacy that I/we cannot fully question it (Gilroy 1993, p. 9). Accordingly, I use "we" and "us" to refer both to those who would identify with me as an outsider and to my/our de facto membership in dominant society vis-à-vis the interdependence of otherness and whiteness.

In examining the concepts of race used to describe a Korean American/African American conflict, I note that the master narrative defines racial identities oppositionally. That is, the master narrative has set up Black/African American identity[7] as a counter to Asian/Korean American identity,[8] and vice versa. And the narrative has racialized (Omi and Winant 1994, pp. 53–76) these identities: It selects traits, links them inextricably with color, and gives the resulting flat and narrow race-image the power to limit our understanding of persons as more complicated, powerful, positive, and valuable than the image itself. This strategy subsumes ethnicity, cultural practice, gender, and class into race.[9] It nearly obscures personal belief and practice. With respect to African Americans, the master narrative tells us that Asians are Koreans who are merchants and crime victims. More particularly, Koreans are merchants who sell to Blacks and are the victims of crimes committed by Blacks. The assumption that Asians are rude foreign intruders underlies this description. With respect to Asian Americans, the narrative tells us that African Americans are Blacks who are violent and criminal but who are also victims of immigrant invaders.

Each component of this conflict replicates the dominant society's negative understandings of Blackness and Asianness. This coincidence suggests that the primary oppositional construct is the nonapparent one; that is, these racializations were first forged in opposition to whiteness. These descriptions of Korean Americans and African Americans persuaded audiences as to their truth because they confirmed older stereotypes about these groups—stereotypes first deployed in white/Black or white/Asian conflicts and later altered and repositioned in the widespread media coverage of the 1991 trial and controversial sentencing of Soon Ja Du, a Korean American woman who shot and killed a young African American woman named Latasha Harlins. While the constructs of race and identity are much more complex than I have suggested, they are also malleable and therefore easily adaptable. So the constructed identities adjust to fit into new contexts—for example, when an old story is retold with a new moral. But they continue to evidence their origins in function, if not appearance; they continue the master narrative.

Media Focal Points during the Uprising

In this section I try to identify the components of the constructs of conflict as they appeared in mainstream newspaper stories published between April 29 and May 3, 1992. In tracking these components, I have found that while race dominated the media discourse from the first stories about the uprising, different types of race relations and racial identities predominated at different times.

Prior Events as Constructing Components

Reporters and their sources used several prior events as reference points in describing and explaining the uprising. These events were "events" not simply because they occurred but also because they received widespread media coverage. Note that I do not try to (or cannot) distinguish between the fact that something occurred and the way the media reported it. Nor do I often try to separate the way the journalists described an event from the way those they observed, interviewed, and quoted described an event. I focus instead on the way these stories, as reported, connect with the larger discourse about race.

The most obvious prior event was the one that immediately preceded the uprising—the "not guilty" verdicts in the trial of four Los Angeles Police Department officers who were videotaped beating the now-famous civilian Rodney King. Before the verdict, while the jury was still deliberating, two types of stories predominated. There were many stories about the jury deliberation process. And there were stories about the anticipation of a violent response to the then-unknown verdicts. These stories about anticipated violence seemed to arise from two events. Darryl Gates, who was then the city's police chief, announced that he had set aside one million dollars for extra policing, and Black community leaders warned against the use of police in a way that would provoke or escalate violence. In other words, the stories about anticipated violence directly paralleled the story behind the jury deliberations: Black versus white (police).

Once the media focused on African American/Korean American conflict as the main story in the uprising, "Latasha Harlins" became a key reference point. It appears that some African

American participants in the street violence first used "Latasha Harlins" as a rallying cry. In reporting this fact, the media made the earlier media coverage of Soon Ja Du's shooting of Latasha Harlins a component of this media event. The reference to "Latasha Harlins" was used to make at least two points. Judge Karlin's sentencing of Soon Ja Du to five years' probation, a $500 fine, and 400 hours of community service for killing Latasha Harlins was controversial. In 1992 that sentence became additional evidence that the "not guilty" verdicts for the police beating of Rodney King reflected systemic antiBlack racism. In addition, the death of Latasha Harlins and the fact that a heavier penalty was not imposed were cited as cause for Black anger at Korean Americans. So the death of Latasha Harlins was used to refer to both white/Black and Korean American/African American conflict. The reference implied that with respect to Blacks, Asians were positioned similarly to whites.

As I have noted, Soon Ja Du is a woman. And Latasha Harlins was a teenage girl or young woman. Those who used Latasha Harlins as a rallying cry claimed that she was the victim. Those who defended Soon Ja Du cast *her* as victim. These victim stories juxtaposed race and gender in telling ways. They used gender to describe the victim, and they used race to identify the perpetrator. A Korean merchant shot and killed Latasha Harlins, a young Black teenage girl. Or Soon Ja Du, a Korean woman, shot and killed a Black teenager suspected of shoplifting. So when race alone is used as an identifier, it defaults to the masculine. Unless the feminine is expressly inserted into the story, it has no role to play. Perhaps more telling is that beyond these particular victim claims, the notion of race as masculine predominated in the retelling of Soon Ja Du and Latasha Harlins.

Some who addressed systemic racism against African Americans juxtaposed another event to that of Latasha Harlins's death. After the sentencing of Soon Ja Du and before the "not guilty" verdict for the beating of Rodney King, many compared an earlier story about a man who shot and killed a dog. The man was sentenced to six months in jail. The initial stories of the man's acts and the subsequent trial were not expressly about race. But when juxtaposed with Latasha Harlins, this event became further evidence that in a society as racist as ours, the life of a dog has

more value than the life of an African American teenager.[10]

The media stories about the uprising published during the uprising referred to two more distant events. One was relatively distant geographically. Once the media stories focused on Korean American/African American conflict, comparisons to Korean American/African American conflicts in New York and other major cities emerged. This comparison implied that the conflict was inherent in the racial identities at issue—it had something to do with Blackness and Koreanness.

The other event took place in Los Angeles. The Watts riots, however, were more distant in time—1965. The post-1992 uprising analysis distinguishes 1992 from 1965. In 1965 all the physical violence took place in east Los Angeles. In 1992, the violence spread, not only to Koreatown but also to affluent white neighborhoods. In 1965 the conflict was clearly white versus Black. In 1992 the conflict was multiracial. But in the first stories about 1992, Watts was a point of comparison, not contrast. The fires and other signs of violence alone recalled Watts for reporters and other commentators. This led to the analytical point that neither economic nor political conditions for African Americans had improved since Watts.[11]

Racial Conflict under Construction

Wednesday, April 29, 1992, was the day the Simi Valley jury verdicts were announced: The jury found the four LAPD officers not guilty on ten of eleven counts, and it deadlocked on one count against officer Laurence Powell. That was the day the street violence now called the "L.A. riots" began. But the newsprint media published the stories reporting the response to the verdicts on Thursday, April 30.

Thursday, April 30, 1992 Despite the earlier media attention given to Soon Ja Du and Latasha Harlins, the initial reporting of the uprising did not mention African American/Korean American conflict. The newspaper stories published on April 30, 1992, addressed the verdicts, reported on the street violence that had occurred, and described the physical damage caused by violence. Many of the stories did address race, but not this particular conflict. In addition, the media discourse published on April 30 only expressly described a Black racial identity. The stories only mentioned Asian, Latino, and white, without further description of their racial identities.

In the stories about the verdicts, individuals who were interviewed for their responses to the verdicts pointed to systemic racism against African Americans—white over Black—to explain the verdicts. Many of those quoted were community leaders or politicians. For example, Paul Cobb, an African American activist in Oakland, was quoted as saying, "If Rodney King had been white, he would have gotten a hundred million dollars, or if Rodney King had been white and the police officers had been black, the issue would have been how to prevent them from getting the death penalty. It makes you wonder, what does a person have to do to prove guilt or innocence" ("Reactions to the Rodney King Case" 1992). And Tom Bradley, who was then the city's mayor, was quoted as saying, "To acquit every officer on every count, in my wildest imagination, I could not have imagined . . . . I believe that the issue of the justice system . . . based upon race is something that I would have to say was a factor. I cannot in any other way explain the jury's decision" (Orlov 1992). The print media stories quoted very few whites other than President Bush and the attorneys involved in the case. The stories did include "person on the street"-type reactions. In nearly every case, the story identified the speaker as African American. For example: " 'If the police are going to be unjust and the legal system is going to be unjust, we have to answer back with injustice,' William Moore, 23, a San Jose State University criminal justice major, said at Phi Beta Sigma fraternity, whose members are black" (Gathright and Cassidy 1992).

The stories described many of those quoted in terms that associated the speaker with violence. Most of the quotes from "persons on the street" were made by street protesters. For example: "At 55th Street and Normandie Avenue in the inner city, 31-year-old Tonia Smith, a mother of two, stood screaming about the verdicts. 'It was wrong! Suspended without pay, that's no justice!' she hollered. 'They beat that black man! It's time for us black folks . . . to reunite. It's our turn now. We're tired of being slaves!' " (Wallace and Ferrell 1992). The sentence preceding this passage describes the neighborhood as "near a boil."

After quoting Ms. Smith, the reporters wait two paragraphs before stating that "the mostly black crowd limited its displays of emotion to verbal blasts." So the print stories, taken as a whole, described the problem as white versus black. They created the sense that all African Americans were outraged and potentially violent, that few whites had anything to say, and that no other people of color in Los Angeles could speak to the issues.[12]

Of the journalists and whites who commented about race, many apparently sought to express unity despite race. The speakers also mentioned class, gender, religion, and ethnicity. The speaker and the means of referring to race vary among these comments. But the message is the same— we all feel the same outrage.

> As the *Los Angeles Times* reported, "two African-American officers and one top administrator [race not specified] called a joint press conference to register their displeasure." As quoted in the story, executive assistant police chief, Norman Stamper, stated, "there's shock and disbelief. . . . I have heard the same thing from police officers of all colors within the San Diego Police Department as well." (Gathright and Cassidy 1992)

One story opened with the reporters' words: "[O]utrage and indignation swept through much of the city Wednesday as citizens rich and poor, black and white, struggled to reconcile the acquittals of four Los Angeles police officers with the alarming, violent images captured on a late-night videotape" (Wallace and Ferrell 1992). A story consisting entirely of comments made in telephone calls to the *Los Angeles Times* included the statement [from a caller], "I am a white, middle-class Mormon woman and I am totally outraged at the verdict on the Rodney King beating" ("Angry Callers Flood Times Switchboard" 1992). One story opened with this sentence: "Donald Northcross felt a wave of sadness when he heard the news bulletin Wednesday afternoon while driving in his car." It then identified Northcross as chairman of Sacramento's Black Deputy Sheriff's Association. The story continued, "[A]cross the nation—regardless of race or ethnicity—the response was the same for many" (Hoge, Wong, and Stanton, 1992).

These comments may have been pleas for peace as well as expressions of common outrage.

More significant, though, is that they each used race in the same particular way. They made twin claims that originate from the master narrative. First, the fact that the speaker or reporter expressly referred to race acknowledged the social and political significance of race and signaled the speaker's sensitivity to the problems of racism.[13] Second, the claim to common outrage despite racial and other differences denied the speaker's responsibility for racism. The claim of commonality also minimized the significance of racial difference. It assumed that racism produces temporary emotional effects that can be overcome with sympathy and color-blindness.

These two claims match the traditional liberal approach to color-blind equality (Gotanda 1991). The call to commonality and color-blindness obscures both the real effects of racism and the positive potential of recognizing the value of difference. At the same time, the claim of commonality makes clear that the initial bow to the significance of race really only acknowledged the problems of racism for whites. By reducing the problems of racism to feelings of outrage, the speakers ignored the experience of African Americans and imposed the white experience of racism as the measure of harm. The presentation of the words claiming common outrage simultaneously with descriptions of street violence by Blacks no doubt implied to many that white outrage was more justifiable and reasonable than Black outrage.

One other thread runs through these comments; it parallels the ironic inconsistency between the acknowledgment of difference and the claim of commonality. Each of the comments describes a society that is more complex than Black and white. They admit awareness of other races and ethnicities, as well as gender and class differences. They echo a multicultural sensibility. But the claim of common outrage asserts the value of the universal over the value of difference. Thus, color-blind liberalism subverts the transformative potential of multiculturalism. In this context, "multicultural" refers to all the racial differences we must overcome, rather than all the differences we can define as strengths. Gender, as a difference or a strength, simply disappears. This keeps the door open for using whiteness as the universal.

I mentioned two other types of stories published on April 30, 1992—reports of street vio-

lence and descriptions of physical damage. There was very little recognition yet that the violence was aimed specifically at Korean Americans. The reports depicted African Americans as justifiably angry at an unjust system. The stories that focus on the street violence and the explanations for it, rather than the stories that focus on the verdicts, show the link made between Latasha Harlins and Rodney King. " 'There is no justice for black people in Los Angeles—first Latasha Harlins and now Rodney King,' said Pearl Bell of Los Angeles, who joined the crowd at the First AME Church" (Stone and Orlov 1992). The few stories that noted the arson and other damage in Koreatown mentioned that "[r]elations between Korean merchants and black customers have been tense because of several violent incidents" (Raine, Hull, and Brazil 1992), but they listed these facts as part of a much bigger picture of violence.

Many reports of violence and damage emphasized, sometimes insistently, the multiracial nature of the street violence and its targets:

As many as 300 people, many different races, their faces sweating in the warm night, stood watching the chaos in the 1900 block of Normandie. Occasionally they looted liquor stores, antiques shops and other businesses along the street. (Lambert and Alexander 1992)

Downtown, a racially mixed group of protesters massed outside Parker Center, eventually hurling rocks and setting fire to a small kiosk. (Lacey and Hubler 1992)

Reports from the riot scenes described a multiethnic reaction to the trial verdict, and it was spreading throughout the city and county. (Furillo and Wiegand 1992)

The stories sometimes specified the race of protesters.

As a multistory apartment building burned just a block away, Asian and Latino looters rushed and ransacked several stores in the area. (Raine, Hull, and Brazil 1992)

Just around the corner at Vermont and Third, police no sooner arrested three young Asian men for looting at La Machaca Metro Center than a crowd of 150 people, mostly Latinos, made a rush on JC's Auto Security Store and, within minutes, ignored by police, emptied it. (Raine 1992)

Many of the perpetrators of the attacks were African-Americans; some victims were white and Asian. (Lacey and Hubler 1992)

As this last quote indicates, to the small extent that these stories expressly mentioned whites, they almost always identified whites as victims.[14]

The references to multiracial and multiethnic violence were first and foremost descriptive. They indicated the scope of the violence that began on April 29. But interpreted from within an ongoing discourse about race, and the emerging story of "Los Angeles," the emphasis on multiracial violence acquired several other meanings. When read with the stories about the verdict, this emphasis seemed, in part, to be a component of the effort to claim common outrage. At the same time, "multiracial" shifts the focus from Black/white conflict to everything but white. And as the last sentence indicates, since the master narrative has linked "race" most strongly with "black," the reports of violence and damage were not just about justifiable Black anger or about the number of Blacks who participated. They were also about defining blackness as criminal and violent[15] and whiteness as innocent and victimized.

Friday, May 1, 1992   The media focus shifted on April 30, the second day of unrest. The print media published those stories on May 1. The April 30 reporting, as I already discussed, tended to give the impression that racial tensions were part of the impetus for the unrest but that the violence itself was only partly about race. It was also about frustration with The System, a common source of anger. Or it was described as indiscriminate and apolitical. Many, of course, saw enough to indicate a race riot, but the stories that addressed race seem to assume that the relevant racial issues were the same old ones, whatever those were. Journalists provided little detailed analysis of how race was operating in the street violence, no doubt due largely to lack of information and time for reflection that early in the story. But the dearth of detailed analysis may have also reflected the assumption that we were dealing with familiar issues, so generalities would

suffice to clue readers in about what was involved. The bottom-line assumption was that we all understand race. But on May 1, racial conflict became the focus of the reporting about the unrest, and the story about African American/Korean American conflict began to emerge.

Very generally, on May 1, 1992, the print media reported on two aspects of race in the uprising and used two themes to comment. These stories and themes were not mutually exclusive, and some articles included both stories and both themes. In addition, the reporting began to describe the Korean American racial identity that would be used to define the conflict. The initial sketch of African American racial identity appeared in the first reports of violence. As I mentioned earlier, both identities are derived in part from images of African Americans and blackness, and Korean Americans and Asianness, constructed in earlier chapters of the master narrative. But as this chapter of the master narrative unfolded, the two-way dynamic between constructing conflict and forming identity filled in the details.

One type of story about race in the uprising continued to describe the multiracial character of the participants and victims. The column-one *Los Angeles Times* story linked multiracial violence to one theme—"View of Model Multiethnic City Vanishes in Smoke" (Braun and Dunn, May 1, 1992).[16] It is this theme that continues to resound in the use of "Los Angeles" as a prophetic metaphor for late-twentieth-century racial dystopia. The message here follows from the subversion of multiculturalism: Multiculturalism cannot work.

The other theme is closely linked to the fallen-model-city theme but makes a more general claim about social disorder. Like the fallen-model-city theme, this theme suggests that what happened in Los Angeles is just the beginning. "Social order broke down today across a broad area of the nation's second-largest city as vandals and looters roamed the streets, carloads of young men attacked pedestrians and uncounted fires burned out of control" (Mydans 1992a). Many of the May 1 stories included brief accounts of how Los Angeles came to be multiracial. When joined with the theme of social disorder, the accounts of Asian and Latino immigration became more than background. They became explanations of how immigrants cause social disorder.

The Latino community was among the hardest hit and least mentioned in the media coverage. For example, despite Los Angeles Police Department policy not to turn people over to U.S. immigration authorities, the police arrested at least 1,044 Latinos during the uprising with the intent to turn them over to the Immigration and Naturalization Service. But the Latino presence in print media coverage from April 29 to May 3 peaked on May 1, 1992, and this presence was fleeting.

The reporting on the multiracial character of the unrest often listed Latinos among the participants and among those who suffered damage. The race grouping in these lists is revealing:

black, Latino and white looters (Braun and Dunn 1992)

dazed white and Latino passersby beaten by angry black assailants (Braun and Dunn 1992)

Authorities said most of the looters roaming the streets were black, but whites, Hispanics and Asian Americans also were involved (Cannon and Smith 1992)

the rioters—predominantly blacks, but also including Asians, Hispanics and whites (Drape and Opdyke 1992)

newly realized black and Latino harmony (Dawsey 1992)

The narrative within the reporting rarely grouped African Americans and Asian Americans together. Latinos and whites were paired together, or Latinos and Blacks were paired together. And Latinos were listed with Blacks or Asians, but not both at the same time. It seems that even the reports of multiracial unrest placed African Americans and Asian Americans oppositionally. And while these media stories did not expressly define Latino identity any further than the use of "Latino" or Hispanic," the fact that they paired Latino with Black or white suggests that the racial content of Latino identity was in flux during the uprising. As I will discuss later, Asian American identity also shifted between relative whiteness and color in ways that simultaneously maintained the dominant status of whiteness and the negative status of blackness and Asianness.

The other story about race focused on the targeting of Korean-owned businesses by African Americans. As I mentioned earlier, within this story the master narrative built Korean American and African American identities in opposition to each other so that conflict appeared inherent and inevitable. Both types of stories about race described African Americans as participants in and victims of the damage. So nearly every story associated blackness with violence. Many reports of racial targeting referred to Latasha Harlins. At this point, Latasha Harlins became more than a symbol of systemic racism. She also became an explanation for the racial targeting and a claim that relative to Blacks, Korean Americans are white. However, in the May 1 stories, violence by African Americans appeared more difficult to justify than it had been in the April 29 stories. The April 29 stories tied the violence to the just-announced verdicts, a source of outrage the claims of commonality had deemed acceptable. The May 1 stories focused more on the violence itself and less on the verdicts. That shift in focus and the fact that the impetus for the anger—Latasha Harlins—was more remote in time than the verdicts made violence by Blacks seem inappropriate, but inherent in the race.

The Korean American identity that began to emerge was also violent, but the violence was defensive rather than offensive. More specifically, the violent stance was made in defense of property and therefore appeared appropriate, if not justified. For example, one story described "angry black assailants, frightened Korean merchants guarding their shuttered markets with guns" (Braun and Dunn 1992), and another recounted, "A gunfight broke out this afternoon between Korean merchants and a group of black men" (Mydans 1992a). So from May 1, 1992, all Korean Americans were shopkeepers, and all Korean American shopkeepers toted guns they were willing to use to defend their property, particularly against violent Black wrongdoers (Gotanda 1995; Lee 1992). The nouns used to identify Koreans and African Americans are telling. Koreans are merchants—persons of means and status. African Americans are angry Black assailants or, simply, men. There is certainly nothing derogatory about "men," but placing "men" in opposition to "merchants" implies both that African Americans are lesser men than merchants and that Korean American women and African

American women were either not physically present or significant.

When linked with fallen-model-city and social-disorder themes, the Korean American/African American conflict became more than a particular intergroup problem. It seemed to represent the problems of living in a multiracial society. It told of the potential for all relations among communities of color. In addition, the references to cultural misunderstanding between Korean American merchants and African American customers clearly cast Korean Americans as foreigners and immigrants. As immigrants, Korean Americans were identified as contributors to social disorder. So the constructed Korean American identity included the inference that while Korean Americans may have been victims of Black violence, they may have asked for what they got.

Saturday, May 2, 1992   On May 2, 1992, the Korean American/African American conflict became the print media's primary focus. It became the Race Story of the uprising.

Some of the articles published on May 2 restated and added to stories begun on the previous days of uprising. The stories about the multiracial character of the unrest continued. These stories also contained more information about how population changes in Los Angeles in the years preceding 1992 had affected race relations in Los Angeles. One of the prevailing themes of these background stories was the rapid increase of the Korean American population in recent years and how their presence as storeowners in Black neighborhoods made this conflict inevitable.[17] The estimates of Korean Americans in Los Angeles ranged from 200,000 to 400,000. One article referred to a projection that there would be one million Koreans in Los Angeles by the year 2000 (Zuniga 1992). Reporters used the numbers to give a measure of the pressure level between African Americans and Korean Americans, or to indicate that the conflict will not go away and may get bigger. None of the stories I found estimated the African American population in Los Angeles. In the context of a discourse characterized by xenophobia and immigrant-bashing, the use of Korean American population estimates took on the air of "Did you know there were so many of them here?"

At this point in the description of conflict, the media stories worked first and foremost at defining the racial identities of African Americans and Korean Americans. In other words, the media not only reported that African Americans were targeting Korean American–owned businesses; the media now focused on describing the parties to the conflict in a way that directly linked their characteristics to race. The stories about conflict were very dense with quotes from African Americans and Korean Americans. Using these quotes conveyed some of the raw emotion the events of April 29 to May 2 evoked in the speakers. It also created the sense that the views conveyed by the quotes (in the context of the reporter's words) defined and explained the conflict.

In a notable departure from previous days' reporting, these stories contained few statements or quotes from persons identified as community leaders, activists, or political figures. These were primarily "person on the street" quotes, statements from people whose voices are rarely heard and whose views are rarely solicited. For that reason, these views should have been particularly significant. But the print stories attached only names and labels—labels that became part of the speaker's racialized identity—to the speaker. The stories separated the speakers from how they lived and who they thought they were. Those who were quoted were chosen to air their anger and pain, hostility and bewilderment for the mainstream public's benefit, as if to say, "See how the other half lives?"

The May 2 stories more clearly associated African Americans with criminality. Prior to May 2, the stories emphasized violence. On May 2, criminality became the race-trait du jour. There were more reports of looting, arson, and drive-by shooting than in previous days, presumably because there was more of this activity to report. The stories not only described the looters, arsonists, and drive-by shooters by race—usually as black—but also directly contrasted the race and activity of the persons harmed by these crimes.

The racial identity of Korean Americans had three facets. The Korean Americans described or quoted were nearly always identified as businessmen, entrepreneurs, or merchants. The media continued to valorize the image of Korean American men arming themselves to defend their businesses and property by placing this image against that of Black looters. The word-pictures of Korean Americans became more militaristic on May 2. The stories used descriptive phrases like "pitched gunfights," "the look of a fortress." For many, these images must have recalled earlier ones, from Korean War news coverage, movies, and television shows. The stories also consistently made the point that Korean Americans were foreigners and immigrants.

In the stories printed on May 2, the racialized identities of the parties to the conflict solidified, and those identities were male. The image of blackness as violent and criminal is one we interpret as male, whether or not the word "he" is used. The Korean as merchant and property defender also suggests, based on historically based gendered images that the actors are male. Although the key players in one of the constructing stories—Soon Ja Du and Latasha Harlins—were female, their race rather than their gender became the main constructing element. Women's voices and experiences were also absent in the stories published during the unrest. Of persons quoted on May 2, very few were women. And of the women quoted, most were Korean American, not African American. Cornel West described the events of April 1992 as a "multiracial, transclass, and largely male display of justified social rage" (C. West 1993, p. 255). Even if this is true, it overlooks the particular effects of these events on women. From the media coverage we could only infer that women were present and involved in these two communities.[18]

Sunday, May 3, 1992 On May 2, there was a march in Koreatown to show support for Korean Americans harmed by the violence. The cleanup of damaged property and neighborhoods began in earnest. The May 3 stories featured these events, always identifying, of course, the race of the participants. They also recapped and began to analyze in earnest the events of April 29 through May 2.

In recapping the events, the media identified two types of race stories as the key to the unrest: the multiracial character of the participants and the Korean American/African American conflict. The theme of the fallen model city was raised again. But the theme of social disorder had changed. From April 30 to May 2 the theme was lawlessness. On May 3 the theme was race war. And with respect to racialized identity, the recaps confirmed that the images solidified on May 2

were predominant, nearly monolithic, placing other possible understandings of blackness and Asianness in shadow.

The Presence of Whiteness

As I have mentioned, the first reports of violence targeting Korean Americans described it as shocking, not solely because of the malice and harm involved but also because it seemed to be a new phenomenon. Perhaps because we were so used to having whiteness mediate, we resisted acknowledging a conflict in which whiteness was not apparent. But while whiteness was not obvious in the telling of African American/Korean American conflict, whiteness still defined its terms.

Although the conflict, as constructed in these stories, does not directly speak of dominant white society, it arranges the various racial identities so as to preserve the authority of whiteness and devalue difference. When racial identity is constructed oppositionally, conflict becomes inevitable and coalition becomes unimaginable, and both groups are publicly debilitated and exposed. The assumption that the conflict is only African American/Korean American identifies these two communities and their members as sources of major social disorder. Isolating these communities as the source of disorder enhances the moral and political authority of the one not identified with the conflict—dominant white society. I say "*the one* not identified with the conflict" because in the stories of conflict, there are no others whose views or interests matter.

In the stories of conflict, the master narrative defines the racial categories in terms that limit how the problem of African American/Korean American conflict gets defined. For example, to the extent that Korean Americans are described as violence-prone immigrant shopkeepers and African Americans as gang members and looters, the problem gets defined primarily as one of police control. To the extent that the conflict is cast as one between small-scale foreign entrepreneurs who have unfair economic advantages over members of the American "underclass," who lack entrepreneurial opportunities, the problem becomes one best addressed by corporate America.

The constructed racial identities also limit who gets to speak to the problem. Since Korean

Americans are the all-encompassing Asian for purposes of this conflict, to the extent that we accept this understanding of of race, we assume that non-Korean Asians are already represented or are irrelevant. At the same time, the master narrative has discounted the views of Korean Americans and African Americans by identifying them as the problem, not the solution. Since the issue is race, meaning color and not whiteness, we assumed that Latinos have been represented or are irrelevant. And since the issue is race, we assumed that other categories of difference, such as gender, sexual orientation, and disability, are irrelevant. So any attempt to expand the scope of the discussion about social disorder becomes very difficult.

Myths and Strategies from the Master Narrative

Many of the "person on the street" speakers seemed to be making entitlement claims—statements by which the speaker not only described the points of conflict but also explained why African Americans or Korean Americans were more (or less) deserving than the other in the conflict. The overall theme was about competition for a too-small piece of the economic pie. To support their conclusions about who should get what, the speakers wove fragments of racialized identity with familiar myths about American life. The speakers used the myths as the myths have always been used—to rationalize inequitable outcomes while simultaneously reifying concepts of fairness and merit that, according to the mythology, make America special.

I examine how, in making these entitlement claims, the Korean American and African American speakers used narrative strategies that simultaneously resisted and perpetuated the master narrative.

Claims of Entitlement

The following quotes indicate that many types of entitlement claims were made:

"The pie is only so big, and everybody wants a piece, and they're fighting over it." (Quoted in Mydans 1992b)

"Just twenty-three percent of the blacks said they had more opportunities than recently arrived immigrants. Twice that many whites said they had more opportunities." (Toner 1992)

"People here are out of jobs and yet they allow foreign people to come over and take work away from people born here in America. . . . [T]hey can come over and get loans and open up businesses, but no one will lend any money to us." (Quoted in P. Reeves 1992)

"These businesses belong to people who have exploited, abused and disrespected black people." (Quoted in Dawsey 1992)

"I respect the different cultures . . . but they are here in America now, and they're doing business in our community." (*Nightline,* "Stop the Madness," ABC television broadcast transcript, May 1, 1992)

"We didn't do anything wrong," said [Bona Lee,] who came to Los Angeles from Korea two decades ago. "We worked like slaves here." (Braxton and Newton 1992)

"I left Korea because America is a good country, a free country, and to get rich." (Quoted in Kamen and Castaneda 1992)

"This is not an act of aggression. This is just saying, 'Leave us alone and let us get back to business.' " (Quoted in "Korean-Americans Mount Own Defenses" 1992)

As one can see from these quotes, some people complained that Korean Americans had, in effect, cut in line. The premise was that African Americans have been waiting in line for a longer time and that more recent arrivals must go to the back. This claim is more complex than it first appears. There is the image of the breadline[19] and the use of a first-in-time principle. The breadline image evokes a picture of hierarchy. At issue is whether Korean Americans or African Americans must stand further back in line or lower on the hierarchy. The image also admits that both Korean Americans and African Americans are out-groups dependent on the will and leftovers of a top group. It presupposes deprivation by social and political forces beyond our control. And it assumes that the competition must occur among those forced to stand in line, not between those making the handouts and those who are the objects of the handouts. More significantly, the breadline image and the sense of forced competition it expresses is historically rooted in earlier African American/Chinese American and African American/Japanese American conflicts (Hellwig 1977 and 1979; Johnsen 1980; Shankman 1977 and 1978; Droker 1976). Apparently, the conflict is not so new. It cannot be coincidence that neither group has moved further up in line.

The use of the first-in-time principle echoes traditional property law.[20] One wonders whether the Supreme Court's suggestion in *Johnson v. M'Intosh*[21] that Western European nations were the first to "discover" America despite the presence of fifteen million Native Americans foreshadows this link between race and one's place in line. The invocation of the first-in-time principle to complain about lack of economic access suggests that the process of keeping out-groups in line has commodified status as well as goods (C. Harris 1993). One must purchase a place in line. What one gains by moving up in line is economic opportunity. It is implicit that from economic opportunity follow other choices and freedoms that are not currently available. So while the claim denies a free market, it apparently embraces capitalism. But this version of economic competition also seems like a mutated form of social Darwinism—the line that nineteenth-century (white) industrial capitalists handed to the working poor to justify their exploitation. The coin is not really the dollar; it is relative power. In this version, the object of trade is the production of the other.

A closely related entitlement claim was that Korean American merchants were not giving back to the Black community. African Americans charged Korean merchants with failure to hire Blacks, rudeness to Black customers, and exploitative pricing. "One looter . . . voiced the outrage of many black residents toward some of the immigrant merchants: 'These businesses (we) burned down don't care about us. . . . they just charge high prices and take our money. Now we are taking some back'" (Peterson and Tobar 1992). The claim draws a boundary around the Black community as the in-group, relative to the Korean outsiders who can gain admission only by purchasing it—by giving back value. Jobs and respect are the local currency within this claim.

The claim also elaborates on the breadline image in a telling way. It describes the Black community as the in-group with the authority to set the standards for admission; yet by claiming victimhood status for the Black community, it places the Black community behind Korean Americans in the breadline. This simultaneously excuses the resulting end-of-the-line position of African Americans and delegitimizes the relatively better place of Korean Americans.

At times the claim made was that Korean Americans did not understand the plight of Blacks in America and that if they did, they would wait their turn. This assertion expresses what African American progressive intellectual Jerry G. Watts refers to as a "resilient, naive faith in America" (Watts 1993, pp. 238–39). It is the hope that "all that prevents white America or bourgeois black America [or Korean Americans] from intervening on behalf of the black poor is the 'correct' information" (Watts 1993, p. 239). This hope springs from the myth of liberalism, which says formal equality will address discrimination. This assumes that those doling out the equality will get the information in the first place. Formal equality, however, has done little but mask the fact that the constructs of race and identity created within the master narrative translate the information into reasons for devaluing difference. This, in turn, creates a need for formal equality. So more than forty years after *Brown v. Board of Education*,[22] we are still waiting for those making the handouts to understand our plight. This entitlement claim concedes a lack of agency relative to Korean Americans; it admits that all that African Americans can do is wait in line, while Korean Americans may at least be able to reduce their waiting time. The constant in the Korean American identity construct underlying each of these claims is foreignness. The African Americans and others who define the in-group in opposition to foreign birth and non-Western ancestry use an excluding concept of "American." This claim labels immigrants as foreign or non-American because they are different. It simultaneously reifies the national culture as monolithic (Gilroy 1993, p. 64; Hing 1993a). The claim is both historically rooted and specific to these constructs.

The nativism expressed in this claim recalls the American-born white response to immigrant whites from Southern and Eastern Europe in the late nineteenth and early twentieth centuries. However, the claim more clearly and directly traces to the several periods of anti-Asian fervor—anti-Chinese, anti-Japanese, anti-Filipino, anti-Vietnamese (Chan 1991a; Chan 1991b; Hing 1993b; Takaki 1989). These parts of our nativist history are more clearly and directly linked to this conflict not simply because they were anti-Asian and Koreans are Asian. It is the more complicated point that the constructed Korean American identity is "Asian" in the way that Chinese, Japanese, Filipino, and Vietnamese Americans have been (and continue to be) made "Asian." "Asian," when linked with nativism, refers to racial identity. It is certainly no coincidence that the earlier label, "oriental," means the opposite of "occidental."

What might seem odd is that African Americans should make difference a negative. But the claim apparently is about relevant differences. From a position of blackness in a dominant white society, foreign birth or non-Western ancestry can be distinguished from race. This claim about foreignness states in part that the "foreigner" does not fit in, while Blacks and whites already fit in. Yet in this conflict, those making the claim assert that Blackness has been used to preserve the status of whiteness, and they defend that fit. The real irony is that defining blackness as American by using foreignness as its opposite seems to draw a line between race and culture, but the notion of American culture used to draw that line is so flat and essentializing that it operates like race. That is, it justifies out-group status based on an ascribed, acontextual identity. Excluding Korean Americans from the category of American suggests that Asians are not also subject to racism, while simultaneously racializing Korean American identity.

Korean Americans responded, in part, by casting themselves as actors in the American Dream—immigrants working hard to support their families by starting as small-scale entrepreneurs. The Dream holds out the possibility, uniquely available in the United States, of achieving the good life—economic success, liberty, and happiness. This claim placed Korean Americans squarely within one cultural myth about what is quintessentially "American." The American Dream is one of several stories in which individual hard work, know-how, and sacrifice lead to both personal and national success.

In this context it countered the claims made on behalf of the African American community on several points.

The claims made against Korean Americans were issued as one group to another. The American Dream did make a claim on behalf of all Korean Americans, but it emphasized the value of individual effort and good character. It suggested that one can rise above one's group-based circumstances. It also responded to the use of the first-in-time principle. The claim assumes some economic access. That is, it seemed to deny the complaint implied in the first-in-time principle—that African Americans lack economic access in this land of opportunity and must depend on their place in line.

On the other hand, the picture of Korean Americans within the American Dream may have jarred some. The claim makes apparent the contradictions between the constructed Korean American identity and the whiteness of the "American" the myth describes. The Korean American in the picture is, if nothing else, foreign. The quintessential American is, by definition, anything but foreign. The foreignness of Korean American identity derives not from the possibility that the person in the picture may have been born in Korea, or may speak Korean. It follows from the fact that Korean Americans are Asian. Within the master narrative, Asian identity is a racial construct. "Foreign" refers to color: It means not-white and not-Black. In other words, Asian is really foreign because it is outside the master white/Black paradigm of racial identity. And within the master narrative, Korean American identity includes assumed foreign birth and foreign language as characteristics attributable to race. So when Korean Americans laid claim to the American Dream, they may have only reinforced the conclusion that Asians do not fit into the picture of "American."

Strategies from the Master Narrative

The constructs of race and racial identity in the media stories published during and immediately after the uprising evidence at least three strategies that operate within the master narrative. At this point, I name these strategies and try to suggest how they reinforce the authority of whiteness.

Racial Pairing and Essentialism   One narrative strategy, racial pairing, is a corollary to the fact that the master narrative constructs racial identities oppositionally. So certain aspects of constructed African American identity implicate constructed Korean American identity and vice versa. This racial pairing essentializes Korean American and African American, and it makes conflict the most obvious possible relation between the two groups.

I have already described the oppositional construct and how the stories of conflict racialize the images of African American and Korean American. Racial essentialism is inherent in racial pairing. That point follows obviously from the fact that any identity construct formed as one side of a two-sided racialized image must be reductive. How it happens may be less obvious.

One key is that while the notions of race and identity we saw in 1992 emerged from a historically rooted discourse, those particular images were also both situationally specific and easily adaptable to other situations. That is, they formed to fill a gap or explanatory need at a particular point in time in the master narrative. So it is no coincidence that some African Americans claimed in-group status in opposition to the immigrant status of Korean Americans or that Korean Americans "understood their 'Americanness' as an opposition to the resident black population" (T. Morrison 1992a, p. 47). The Black/immigrant opposition has occurred before. But in 1992 the immigrant was specifically Korean American.

The essentialization of Korean American identity occurs via a syllogism. In the context of nonwhite conflict with African Americans, cultural misunderstanding, and/or economic competition at the bottom, the most strongly associated racial identity is that of the Korean American. The aspect of Korean American identity the master narrative has deemed most relevant to these social problems is foreignness or Asianness. So in association with these social problems, the ethnic-specific label of Korean American really refers to an identity stripped of ethnic and cultural content. It is probably accurate to say that the syllogism concludes that all Asians are Korean in these contexts.[23]

On the other side of the construct, racial pairing also essentializes African American identity in particular ways. I have discussed the criminali-

zation of blackness and the attribution of violence to race. In this construct, these traits also become foreign, in a sense. At various times, blackness has been construed as a foreign presence in the United States, often with reference to the "dark continent." The Korean American claim to the American Dream follows from this history. To the extent that this claim taps into the myth of Asians as the model minority—hardworking, economically successful, entrepreneurial minorities—blackness becomes its opposite, the misfit minority. The traits of laziness and failure get deemed as inherently Black in a similar way that "Asian" signifies inherently foreign.

The explanatory power of this conflict for Los Angeles 1992 goes back, in fact, to earlier stories—New York, Chicago, Detroit, and so on. By 1992, relations between Korean American shopkeepers and African Americans had already become an explanation for urban violence. This does not deny that there are real points of tension and misunderstanding. But earlier stories of conflict set up a series of assumptions—that we know the other and that the difference we perceive in the other is racially inherent exploitativeness or criminality, or whatever the ascribed race-trait is, and that the appropriate response is to oppose the other. After March 1991, when Latasha Harlins died, Dennis Westbrook, director of the Martin Luther King Dispute Resolution Center, noted an increase in the number of consumer merchant disputes involving Korean Americans and African Americans. In Westbrook's opinion, many of these complaints may have been an "inappropriate response to the conflict" (George 1992, p. 80). It may also be that once Latasha Harlins's death became a story about Korean American/African American conflict, the ways of understanding each other narrowed for some African Americans and Korean Americans, and opposition became the most apparently appropriate response.

We must also consider the role this construct of conflict will have in future stories of the master narrative. The stories of conflict have given many the sense that they know about Korean Americans and African Americans and relations between these groups. As Walter Ong has written, "[L]ooking fixedly at another person has the effect of reducing him to a surface, a noninterior, and thus to the status of a thing" (Ong 1977, p. 166). The media images fixed our gaze. "Korean

American" and "African American" invoke a whole set of conclusions that follow not from a personal or group history or from present Korean American and African American experience but from the media-deployed images of race in 1992. The construct of conflict not only filters out personal experience, group history, and community-formed culture; it also deems them irrelevant, and in so doing, it eliminates possible bases of understanding and coalition.[24]

Racial Positioning A second narrative strategy arises from the hierarchy suggested by the bread-line image. What becomes clear, on examination, is that the hierarchy is race-based. It is not simply about economic competition. The entitlement claims made by African Americans and Korean Americans reflect some level of awareness that African Americans are lower on the hierarchy and that those handing out the bread are white. In a conflict apparently between African Americans and other nonwhites, the goal is to position one's group as the relative white.

In this context, Korean Americans seemed to have a presumption of relative whiteness. The racialized Asian identity assigned to Korean Americans, and, in particular, the myth of the model minority, raised this presumption. That some Korean Americans invoked the American Dream signaled that they had accepted the model-minority myth. Indeed, many Korean Americans cited the American Dream to explain the depth of their disillusionment. They had believed that if they became hardworking, quiet Americans, they would get their due because white America cared about them. The events of 1992 proved them wrong.

The American Dream also seemed to reinforce Korean Americans' relatively better position by describing them as successful Americans. But relative whiteness did not confer any real advantage. It lumped Korean Americans with other Asian American groups who have, at times, been labeled as model minorities. And "Korean American" picked up not only that label but also the inherited resentment of the status it implies and the assumptions of success and greed attached to it (Cho 1993, p. 197). Here, African Americans used the assumptions underlying the model-minority myth as whites have used them—to deny that Asians are subject to racism, even while making them objects of race.

African Americans who invoked the first-in-time principle positioned themselves as relative whites by defining themselves as more American. Historically, dominant society has usually defined the real American as white. The American hero images of the western explorer, the cowboy, and the yeoman farmer are wholly white in myth, despite the fact that "[b]lacks contributed to every phase of western development, as trappers, explorers, soldiers, settlers and city laborers" (Hine 1973, p. 205). African Americans used the dominant white notion of "American"—western pioneers—in the same way that whites used it, to claim higher status. It may be that the real positioning here was white over Black, with Korean Americans as the retaining wall.

Racial Distancing Many responded to the stories of conflict and the identity constructs by expressing, in various ways, a desire for distance. African Americans, Korean Americans, and those who were constructed as outside the conflict used racial distancing. But the result in each case was the same—to limit the definition of the problem to Korean Americans and African Americans and to deny that any other part of society had responsibility.

Some explained the conflict as a class issue and denied that it was about race. Race and class were inseparable in the racialized identities of Korean Americans and African Americans. The model-minority myth, for example, says that Asian Americans are potentially middle-class or explains middle-class Asian Americans by casting them as models. The images of blackness that dominated the media discourse from April 29 to May 3 were of inner-city poor Blacks, despite the text which read that participation in the street violence was transclass. These images attributed poverty, greed, and lawlessness to some notion of cultural poverty that the master narrative has deemed inherent in the race. Those who denied that race was the issue were not simply disingenuous; they were wary of the consequences of defining a problem as one of race. Within the master narrative, race problems are intractable and stigmatizing; race-neutral class problems are "cleaner" (they lack the "taint" of race) and potentially solvable.

Another type of racial distancing accepted race as a relevant point of conflict but used some form of class to pull rank. Some Blacks and non-

Korean Asian Americans felt compelled to distance themselves from "those Blacks" and "those Asians" within the conflict. The fact that African Americans and Asian Americans had to work to make the point that not all were looters or shopkeepers indicates just how monolithic the racial identities were. African Americans who distanced themselves used class and/or geography by restating the predominant story that the violence and criminality came from South Central residents, now constructed as the prototypical permanently poverty-ridden, inner-city, gang-member population that plagues the United States.

Asian Americans who used racial distancing did so by subtly or pointedly identifying themselves as Chinese American, Japanese American, or simply not Korean American. This may have reflected a fear of reviving old anti-Asian hostilities and a reluctance to go through them yet again. But the expression of fear in this instance also revived old techniques for isolating the current out-group.[25] The claim of belonging to a different Asian group invoked a class claim, to the extent that Chinese and Japanese Americans are more closely identified as the upwardly mobile model minority, thus twisting that myth yet again. And denial of Koreanness reinforced Korean American identity as foreign relative to more established Asian American communities.

A third important type of racial distancing operated through the theme of social disorder. The theme of social disorder makes Korean American/African American conflict symbolic of the problems of a multiracial (multicultural)[26] society. The theme of social disorder says that such a society is doomed to conflict. Since "multiracial" means everything but white, non-white racial conflict displaces white supremacy as the central race issue. That displacement, in turn, strengthens the distinction and furthers the distance between whiteness and race. Whiteness becomes order, and race becomes disorder.

Conclusion

It is no coincidence that the main issues in the current California political scene are crime and immigration. These issues resounded strongly in 1992. Nor is it coincidence that at both points

in time, crime and immigration are inextricably linked with race and social disorder. The constructs that dominated the news between April 29 and May 3, 1992, had deep roots in the ongoing discourse on race and have cast long shadows in the newest chapter of the master narrative.

Questioning the constructs of race and identity is only a first step toward dismantling the master's house. The constructs as presented in the media stories suggest that there were (and are) several opportunities for resisting the master narrative. In the first two days, the stories of race and the racial identities were multiple and fluid. In addition, the racial identities of Latinos and Asian Americans were in flux and less fixed than those of African Americans. These moments of flux may be opportunities to intervene, to challenge the telling of the story so far, to complicate it with anti-essentializing detail and thus change the course of the narrative. It may also be possible to subvert the narrative strategies during these moments (and perhaps others) by valuing difference as strength, rather than as points of opposition, and by looking beyond oppositions to points of possible juncture. We can look into our pasts for examples of how to make these abstract goals concrete, and in the process we may create new ways to resist the master narrative.

Notes

This paper develops ideas that I initially sketched in "Traces of the Master Narrative in the Story of African American/Korean American Conflict: How We Constructed "Los Angeles," in 66 *Southern California Law Review* 1581 (1993). I would like to thank Camille Loya, Richard Delgado, Robert Chang, Neil Gotanda, and Jayne Lee for their support and ideas.

1. Media images, especially television news images, gave viewers the sense that we saw and experienced the street violence in person. That we presume the media to be objective reinforced the notion that we saw the truth of what happened in Los Angeles. But the images we saw were removed not just from the streets but also from their larger social, historical, and legal contexts.

2. For a more explicit illustration of the link between white supremacy and patriarchy, see Blee 1991.

3. For further elaboration on this definition of racism, see hooks 1989a, p. 112.

4. Paul Gilroy contrasts the master narrative with the possibility of a transcending discourse: "There are,

for example, grounds on which we can defend the vitality and richness of what might be called webbed accounts in contrast with the static and arid state of historiography's master narratives (Gilroy 1993, p. 70). See also Lowe 1991, p. 26.

5. I am trying to follow David Papke's point that we "should unmask, demystify, and demonstrate the way the master narrative embodies false consciousness and legitimates dominant power structures" (Papke 1990, p. 154).

6. I find Joel Kovel's term "metaracism" useful: "Metaracism is a distinct and very peculiar modern phenomenon. Racial degradation continues on a different plane, and through a different agency: those who participate in it are not racists—that is, they are not racially prejudiced—but metaracists, because they acquiesce in the larger cultural order which continues the work of racism" (Kovel 1984, pp. 211–212).

7. I use "Black/African American" as a reminder that while "Black" refers to the identity claimed by African American, it has also to some extent become a racial category defined and imposed by the dominant culture and, as such, has been used in a homogenizing, culture-erasing way. Hence, I also use Black/African American to invoke the possibility of understanding identity as founded in African American culture, and as dynamic and rich with the possibility of liberation. See Gotanda 1991, pp. 4–5.

8. I use "Asian/Korean American" as a reminder that while dominant culture has used "Asian" to refer to race, or to posit a monolithic culture, "Asian American" includes the experience of persons who have immigrated or whose ancestors have immigrated from China, Japan, Korea, the Indian subcontinent, the Philippines, Thailand, Vietnam, Laos, and Kampuchea, and does not exclude others. To the extent that Asian Americans are assumed to be Korean Americans, the experience of other Asian Americans is erased. And to the extent that Korean Americans are assumed to be part of a monolithic group of Asian Americans, the experience and consciousness of Korean Americans is erased.

9. Compare the conflict constructed from the Clarence Thomas confirmation hearings. The fact that both Clarence Thomas and Anita Hill are African American had the effect of submerging race to gender in dominant culture's account of the conflict. This reinforces the point that existing categories inadequately describe the experience of oppression. See Crenshaw 1992b, p. 402.

10. See "Sentence Ends in Question" 1992 ("Consider, for example, the six-month jail sentence imposed by another judge two years ago on a Pacoima postal worker who shot a dog. Considering the disparity between the two sentences, might it not be reasonable for many to conclude that the life of a dog is worth more than the life of a black teenager?"); G. T. Gibbs 1991.

11. See, for example, Boyarsky 1992.

12. See Rosenthal 1992. Apparently, the television media shaped the story in a similar way. Rosenthal's critique of the television coverage includes this comment: "[T]he overwhelming sense you got from channel hopping was that all minorities were incensed and most whites—save for those connected to the case, such as police, relatives and lawyers—couldn't be bothered to care since they largely were unseen and unheard from."

13. These are prime examples of the "empathic fallacy," the belief that "[w]e can, in short, think, talk, read, and write our way out of bigotry and narrowmindedness, out of our limitations of experience and perspective." (Delgado and Stefancic 1992, pp. 1261, 1281).

14. The attack on white truck driver Reginald Denny is one among many accounts of specific acts and harms. On April 30, 1992, he was not yet the symbolic Innocent Victim of Racial Violence.

15. See, for example, Reiner 1992. That study reports that "the police have identified almost half of all Black men in Los Angeles County between the ages of 21 and 24 as gang members" (p. iv). The fact that the police made these identifications should raise questions about the finding. The report itself admits that the "number is so far out of line with other ethnic groups that careful, professional examination is needed to determine whether police procedures may be systematically over-identifying Black youths as gang members" (p. iv). See also Braun and Dunn 1992: "Each new graphic televised image—. . . angry black assailants, frightened Korean merchants guarding their shuttered markets with guns—threatened to reinforce the long-held fears and prejudices gnawing at the city's populace, worried community leaders and race relations experts said Thursday."

16. See also Abcarian 1992.

17. For a more accurate discussion of Korean American immigrant life in Los Angeles, see Cho 1993, p. 196.

18. Between April 29 and May 1, 1992, the Asian Women's Shelter in San Francisco received twice as many crisis calls as usual (Masaki 1992).

19. In a slightly different take, Mike Davis described the uprising, in part, as a "major postmodern bread riot—an uprising of not just poor people but particularly of those strata of poor in Southern California who've been most savagely affected by the recession" (M. Davis 1993, p. 142).

20. See "Time, Property Rights and the Common Law" 1986 for a recent evaluation of this principle.

21. 21 U.S. (8 Wheat.) 543 (1823).

22. 347 U.S. 483 (1954).

23. Other contexts raise other identity presumptions. For purposes of economic competition at the top, all Asians are Japanese (not Japanese American). Or more generally, Asian is more likely to mean Japanese if the context includes trade or labor issues. The Detroit murder of Vincent Chin, a Chinese American,

by two white auto workers who called him "Jap" and blamed him for the loss of jobs in the auto industry, tragically illustrates this point.

24. For an example of how the media actively participates in this conflict constructing process, consider the issue of rebuilding liquor stores in South Central Los Angeles. This issue became a flashpoint between Korean Americans and African Americans during the late summer and early fall of 1992. In October 1992, Asian Pacific Americans for a New L.A. (APANLA) adopted a position supporting community control, the reduction of liquor stores in South Central, compensation for liquor licenses, and assistance for store owners to relocate or convert to other types of business (Asian Pacific Americans for a New L.A. 1992). The position

paper expressed a spirit of coalition and inclusiveness. The *Los Angeles Times* story, however, emphasized potential points of racial divide and distorted the nature of the statement. See Sengupta 1992, p. B1.

25. When the U.S. government and mainstream society expressed its anti-Japanese sentiment against Japanese Americans (because they were, according to the master narrative, all of the same "enemy race"), other Asians, such as Chinese Americans, identified themselves as not-Japanese.

26. Stuart Alan Clarke makes the point that some have racialized "multiculturalism." "In this context, it is unsurprising that the 'multicultural threat' is pictured most compellingly in the public imagination as a black threat" (Clarke 1992, pp. 40–41).

References

Abcarian, Robin. 1992. "Reality Collides with L.A.'s Image." *Los Angeles Times*. May 1:E1.

Abner, Allison. 1994. "Gangsta Girls: Gang Membership among Young Black Girls Is Rising." *Essence*. July:64.

Abrams, Kathryn. 1989. "Gender Discrimination and the Transformation of Workplace Norms." *Vanderbilt Law Review*. 42:11.

———. 1991. "Hearing the Call of Stories." *California Law Review*. 79:971.

———. 1994. "Songs of Innocence and Experience: Dominance Feminism in the University." Review of *The Morning After*, by Katie Roiphe. *Yale Law Journal*. 103:1533.

———. 1995. "Sex Wars Redux: Agency and Coercion in Feminist Legal Theory." *Columbia Law Review*. 95:304.

The Accused. 1989. Directed by Jonathan Kaplan. Paramount Pictures.

Adams, Jacqueline. 1994. "The White Wife." *New York Times Magazine*. September 18:36.

Adam's Rib. 1949. Directed by George Cukor. Metro-Goldwin-Mayer.

Adler, Jerry, and Lauren Picker. 1990. "Advise and Consent at Dartmouth." *Newsweek*. August 6:68.

Agger, Ben. 1992. *Cultural Studies as Critical Theory*. Washington: Falmer Press.

Allen, Robert C. 1985. *Speaking of Soap Operas*. Chapel Hill: University of North Carolina Press.

Allen, Robert L., and Robert Chrisman, eds. 1992. *Court of Appeal: The Black Community Speaks Out on the Racial and Sexual Politics of Thomas v. Hill*. New York: Ballantine Books.

Als, Hilton. 1995. "Quoth Quivers." *New Yorker*. April 17:35.

Alter, Jonathan, and Pat Wingert. 1995. "The Return of Shame." *Newsweek*. February 6:21.

Amiel, Barbara. 1993. "America, Anita and the Feminine Thought Police." *Sunday Times* (London). May 2 (section 2):6.

Amos 'n' Andy. 1928–53. CBS radio and television series.

Andersen, Kurt. 1993. "Big Mouths: Populist and Popular, Radio's Right-Wing Pundit and Gross-Out Wild Man Have New Mega-Best Sellers." *Time*. November 1:60.

Anderson, Judith. 1994. "Viewpoint: Why Aren't Eating Disorders a National Health Priority?" *Glamour*. March:139.

Ang, Ien. 1985. *Watching Dallas: Soap Opera and the Melodramatic Imagination*. Translated by Della Couling. New York: Methuen.

Angier, Nathalie. 1993. "About the Search for a Breast Cancer Gene: Interview with Mary-Claire King." *Glamour*. December:182.

"Angry Callers Flood Times Switchboard." 1992. *Los Angeles Times*. April 30:A23.

Aring, Charles D. 1991. "In Defense of Orphanages." *American Scholar*. 60:575.

Aris, Brenda. 1994. "Battered Women Who Kill: The Law Still Denies Us a Fair Hearing." *Glamour*. April:160.

Armstrong, David. 1994a. "DSS Said to Have Flagged Woes with Agency Overseeing Family." *Boston Globe*. February 16:18.

———. 1994b. "Agency Rapped in Scalding Case Demands State Restore Contract." *Boston Globe*. February 18:25.

Ashe, Marie. 1992. "The 'Bad Mother' in Law and Literature: A Problem of Representation." *Hastings Law Journal*. 43:1017.

Ashe, Marie, and Naomi R. Cahn. 1994. "Child Abuse: A Problem for Feminist Theory." In Fineman and Mykitiuk, eds. First published in *Texas Journal of Women and the Law, 2* (1993):75.

Asian Pacific Americans for a New L.A. (APANLA). 1992. "Statement of Position on Liquor Stores in South Central Los Angeles." Vol. 4 *Asian Pacific Planning Council*. Los Angeles: Appcon/Pacific Asian Resource Coordination Committee.

Aucoin, Don. 1994. "Roxbury Case Cited in Welfare Debate; Democrats, Republicans Say Their Reform Plans Would Have Prevented Abuse." *Boston Globe*. February 16:19.

Aucoin, Don, and Scott Lehigh. 1994. "Weld Using Story on Welfare Family to Aid His Case on Need for Reform." *Boston Globe*. February 25:14.

Auerbach, Jon. 1994. "Study: Killings of Gays More Brutal." *Boston Globe*. December 21:18.

Auletta, Ken. 1993. Review of *Street Soldiers* (radio program). *New Yorker*. November 8:68.

Baby M. 1988. Directed by James Steven Sadwith. ABC Circle Films. ABC, May 22 and May 23.

Bachman, Ronet. 1994. "Violence against Women." Washington: U.S. Department of Justice, Bureau of Justice Statistics.

Bachman, Ronet, and Bruce M. Taylor. 1994. "The Measurement of Family Violence and Rape by the Redesigned National Crime Victimization Survey." *Justice Quarterly*. 11:499.

Badlands. 1973. Directed by Terrence Malich. Warner Brothers and Edward R. Pressman Film Corporations.

Baer, Donald. 1993. "The Trials of Lani Guinier." *U.S. News & World Report*. June 7:38.

Baldwin, Margaret A. 1992. "Split at the Roof: Prostitution and Feminist Discourses of Law Reform." *Yale Journal of Law and Feminism*. 5:47.

Ball, Aimee Lee. 1994. "Rolemodels—Ballbusters: Success Secrets of Six Pushy Women." *Marie Claire*. September/October:58.

Ballenger, Josephine. 1992. "Uncovering Abortion." *Columbia Journalism Review*. March/April:16.

Bankston, John. 1991. "Florida Shocked by Case of Lesbian Accused of Serial Murders." *The Advocate*. May 21:50.

Barak, Gregg. 1994a. "Media, Society, and Criminology". In Barak, ed.

———, ed. 1994b. *Media, Process, and the Social Construction of Crime: Studies in Newsmaking Criminology*. New York: Garland.

Barnouw, Erik. 1975. *Tube of Plenty*. New York: Oxford University Press.

Barthes, Roland. 1975. *The Pleasure of the Text*. Translated by Richard Miller. New York: Hill and Wang.

———. 1981. *Camera Lucida: Reflections on Photography*. Translated by Richard Howard. New York: Hill and Wang.

Bartky, Sandra Lee. 1990. *Femininity and Domination: Studies in the Phenomenology of Oppression*. New York: Routledge.

Bartlett, Katharine T. 1991. "Feminist Legal Methods." In *Feminist Legal Theory*, edited by Katherine T. Bartlett and Rosanne Kennedy. Boulder, Colo.: Westview Press. First published in *Harvard Law Review, 103* (1990):829.

Bastian, George. 1924. *Editing the Day's News*. New York: Macmillan.

Baudrillard, Jean. 1983. *Simulations*. Translated by Paul Foss, Paul Patton, and Philip Batchman. New York: Semiotext(e).

Beasley, Maurine H., and Sheila J. Gibbons, eds. 1993. *Taking Their Place: A Documentary History of Women and Journalism*. Washington: American University Press.

Behrens, David. 1993. "The Date Rape Debate." *Newsday*. October 13:58.

Bell, Derek. 1993. Telephone interview with author Laurel Leff, July.

Benderly, Beryl Lieff. 1994. "The Testosterone Excuse." *Glamour.* March:184.

Benedict, Helen. 1992. *Virgin or Vamp: How the Press Covers Sex Crimes.* New York: Oxford University Press.

———. 1994. *Recovery: How to Survive Sexual Assault.* New York: Columbia University Press.

———. 1997. "Blindfolded: Covering Rape without Feminism." In Fineman and McCluskey, eds.

Bennett, W. Lance. 1988. *News: The Politics of Illusion.* New York: Longman.

Benshoof, Janet. 1995. "Ever Had a Pregnancy Scare?" *Glamour.* May:121.

Bernstein, Nina. 1996. "Equal Opportunity Recedes for Most Female Lawyers," *New York Times.* January 8:A9.

Best, Joel. 1990. *Threatened Children: Rhetoric and Concern about Child-Victims.* Chicago: University of Chicago Press.

The Big Easy. 1987. Directed by Jim McBride. Columbia Pictures.

Birch, Helen, ed. 1994. *Moving Targets: Women, Murder, and Representation.* Berkeley: University of California Press.

"Birth Mothers, Pro and Con." 1993. Letters to the Editor. *San Francisco Chronicle.* August 17:A18.

Birth of a Nation. 1915. Directed by D. W. Griffith. Epoch.

Blee, Kathleen M. 1991. *Women of the Klan: Racism and Gender in the 1920s.* Berkeley: University of California Press.

Blumenfeld, Laura. 1994. "Ultimate Feminist: Hillary Rodham Clinton." *Cosmopolitan.* May:212.

Bly, Robert. 1990. *Iron John: A Book about Men.* Reading, Mass.: Addison-Wesley.

Bogle, Donald. 1992. *Toms, Coons, Mulattoes, Mammies, and Bucks: An Interpretive History of Blacks in American Films.* New York: Continuum.

Bolick, Clint. 1993. "Clinton's Quota Queens." *Wall Street Journal.* April 30:A12.

Bollinger, Lee C. 1991. *Images of a Free Press.* Chicago: University of Chicago Press.

Bolotin, Susan. 1993. "The Good News about Rape." *Elle.* August:88.

Bonnie and Clyde. 1967. Directed by Arthur Penn. Warner Brothers.

Boot, Max. 1994. "Wild Bronco Chase: Pundits Squeeze O.J." *Wall Street Journal.* June 24:A9.

Boot, William. 1992. "The Clarence Thomas Hearings." *Columbia Journalism Review.* January/February:25.

Bordo, Susan. 1993a. "Feminism, Foucault, and the Politics of the Body." In *Up against Foucault:*

Explorations of Some Tensions between Foucault and Feminism, edited by Caroline Ramazanoglu. New York: Routledge.

———. 1993b. *Unbearable Weight: Feminism, Western Culture, and the Body.* Berkeley: University of California Press.

Bordwell, David, Janet Staiger, and Kristin Thompson. 1985. *The Classical Hollywood Cinema: Film Style and Mode of Production to 1960.* New York: Columbia University Press.

Born to Be Sold: Martha Rosler Reads the Strange Case of Baby S/M. 1988. Paper Tiger Video and Video Data Bank. Videorecording.

Bortner, M. A. 1984. "Media Images and Public Attitudes toward Crime and Justice." In *Justice and the Media,* edited by Ray Surette. Springfield, Ill.: C. C. Thomas.

Boulard, Garry. 1994. "The Anti-Twinkie Defense." *The Advocate.* June 14:33.

Bourdieu, Pierre, and Loic J. D. Wacquant. 1992. *An Invitation to Reflexive Sociology.* Chicago: University of Chicago Press.

Bowlby, John. 1969. *Attachment and Loss.* New York: Basic Books.

Bowman, James. 1993. "The Leader of the Opposition: Political commentator Rush Limbaugh." *National Review.* September 6:44.

Boyarsky, Bill. 1992. "The Challenge of Holding the City Together." *Los Angeles Times.* April 30:B2.

Boyer, Peter J. 1995. Interview by *Frontline. Frontline,* transcript #1311. PBS, February 28.

Boyle, James. 1991. "Is Subjectivity Possible?: The Postmodern Subject in Legal Theory." *University of Colorado Law Review.* 62:489.

Boyz N the Hood. 1990. Directed by John Singleton. New Deal and Columbia Pictures.

Braun, Stephen, and Ashley Dunn. 1992. "View of Model Multiethnic City Vanishes in Smoke." *Los Angeles Times.* May 1:A1.

Braxton, Greg, and Jim Newton. 1992. "Looting and Fires Ravage L.A." *Los Angeles Times.* May 1:A1.

Brelis, Matthew, and Anthony Flint. 1991. "An Accomplished Life, a Brutal Death." *Boston Globe.* April 14:1.

Brenner, Elsa. 1993. "Crime in County Falls for Second Time in Two Years." *New York Times.* May 9 (Section 13, Westchester County):1.

Bridge, M. Junior. 1993. "The News: Looking Like America? Not Yet . . . ." Los Angeles: Center for Women, Men, and the Media.

Britt, Donna. 1993. "Carol Moseley-Braun Talks about Her First Year in the Senate." *Glamour.* November:117.

Brock, David. 1992. "The Real Anita Hill." *American Spectator*. March:18.

———. 1993a. *The Real Anita Hill*. New York: Free Press.

———. 1993b. *The Real Anita Hill*. Excerpts. *Wall Street Journal*. April 9:A10.

———. 1993c. "Jane and Jill and Anita Hill: At the *New Yorker*, They Don't Know Jack." *American Spectator*. August:24.

Broder, John M. 1993. "White House Seeks to Save Rights Nominee." *Los Angeles Times*. May 27:A18.

Brooks, Dianne L. Forthcoming. *The Law of Daytime: Soap Operas, Issue Plots, and Law Narratives*. Durham, N.C.: Duke University Press.

Brott, Armin A. 1993. "When Women Abuse Men: It's Far More Widespread Than People Think." *Washington Post*. December 28:C5.

Brown, Kevin. 1992. "The Social Construction of a Rape Victim: Stories of African American Males about the Rape of Desiree Washington." *University of Illinois Law Review*. 1992:997.

Brown, Lyn Mikel, and Carol Gilligan. 1992. *Meeting at the Crossroads: Women's Psychology and Girls' Development*. Cambridge: Harvard University Press.

Brown, Lyn Mikel, Elizabeth Debold, M. Tappan, and Carol Gilligan. 1991. "Reading Narratives of Conflict and Choice for Self and Moral Voices: A Relational Method." In *Handbook of Moral Behavior and Development: Theory, Research, and Application*, edited by William Kurtines and Jacob Gewirtz. Hillsdale, N.J.: Lawrence Erlbaum.

Brown, Mary Ellen. 1987. "The Politics of Soaps: Pleasure and Feminine Empowerment." *Australian Journal of Cultural Studies*. 4:1.

Brownstein, Ronald. 1993. "Nomination May Add Race Issue to Democrats' Schism." *Los Angeles Times*. May 26:A1.

Brownworth, Victoria. 1991. "An Unreported Crisis." *The Advocate*. November 5:50.

———. 1995. "Crime and Punishment: Are the Rules of Law Different for Lesbians Charged with Crimes?" *Deneuve*. February.

Brunvand, Jan Harold. 1981. *The Vanishing Hitchhiker: American Urban Legends and Their Meaning*. New York: Norton.

———. 1985. "Urban Legends in the Making." *Whole Earth Review*. 48:124.

Bryant, Linda Goode, Cathy Campbell, Barry Michael Cooper, Nelson George, Andrea Kannapell, Lisa Kennedy, Joan Morgan, and Greg Tate. 1989. "Sexism: The Forbidden Issue." In "The Voices Not Heard: Black and Women Writers on the Central Park Rape." *Village Voice*. May 9:1.

Buchanan, Patrick, and Michael Kinsley. 1993. "The Ties That Bind." *Crossfire*, transcript #890. CNN, August 3.

Buchwald, Emilie, Pamela R. Feltcher, and Martha Roth eds. 1993. *Transforming a Rape Culture*. Minneapolis: Milkweed.

Buckley, William F., Jr. 1993. "Book Presents the Case for Judge Thomas, Viewpoints." *Buffalo News*. May 5:3.

Bureau of Justice Statistics. 1994. "Elderly Crime Victims." Washington: U.S. Department of Justice, Office of Justice Programs.

Burnham, Margaret. 1992. "The Supreme Court Appointment Process and the Politics of Race and Sex." In Morrison, ed.

The Burning Bed. 1984. Directed by Robert Greenwald. Tisch-Avnet Productions, Inc. NBC, October 8.

Burrell, Darci E. 1993. "Myth, Stereotype, and the Rape of Black Women." *U.C.L.A. Women's Law Journal*. 4:87.

Butler, Judith, and Joan W. Scott, eds. 1992. *Feminists Theorize the Political*. New York: Routledge.

Butzel, Henry M. 1987. "The Essential Facts of the Baby M Case." In H. Richardson, ed.

Cahn, Naomi R. 1994. "Family Issue(s)." Review of *Family Bonds: Adoption and the Politics of Parenting*, by Elizabeth Bartholet. *University of Chicago Law Review*. 61:325.

Cain, Joy Duckett. 1994. "We Wear the Pants." *Essence*. March:92.

Cameron, Deborah, and Elizabeth Frazer. 1987. *The Lust to Kill: A Feminist Investigation of Sexual Murder*. New York: New York University Press.

Campbell, Linda. 1993. Telephone interview with author Laurel Leff, July.

Campbell, Linda, and Michael Tackett. 1993. "Race Issue, Not Radicalism, Scuttled Guiner Selection." *Chicago Tribune*. June 6:1C

Campbell, Sue. 1994. "Women Right Now . . . The Girl Revolution." *Glamour*. April:112.

Cancian, Francesca M., and Bonnie L. Ross. 1981. "Mass Media and the Women's Movement: 1900–1977." *Journal of Applied Behavioral Sciences*. 17:9.

Cannon, Lou, and Leef Smith. 1992. "24 Dead, 900 Injured in L.A. Rioting." *Washington Post*. May 1:A1.

Caputi, Jane. 1987. *The Age of Sex Crime*. Bowling Green, KY.: Bowling Green State University Popular Press.

Carlson, John. 1994. "Goldwater Would Be Proud

of the New Republicans." *Seattle Times*. December 13:B4.

Carmody, Deirdre. 1992. "Editor's Story: 25 Years of Creating Glamour." *New York Times*. June 22:D8.

———. 1995. "An Enduring Voice for Black Women." *New York Times*. January 23:D1.

Carmody, John. 1993. "Women, Minorities Still Shut Out, Survey Reports." *Washington Post*. June 16:B1.

Carroll, E. Jean. 1994. "The Future of American Womanhood." *Esquire*. February:58.

Carroll, Ginny, Eleanor Clift, Howard Fineman, and Tom Morgenthau. 1992. "Will Hillary Hurt or Help." *Newsweek*. March 30:30.

Carton, Barbara. 1994. "A Rebel in the Sisterhood: Author Christina Sommers Wants to Rescue Feminism from Its 'Hijackers.'" *Boston Globe*. June 16:69.

Cassata, Mary B., and Thomas Skill, eds. 1983. *Life on Daytime Television: Tuning-in American Serial Drama*. Norwood, N.J.: Ablex Publishing Corp.

Cavender, Gray, and Lisa Bond-Maupin. 1993. "Fear and Loathing on Reality Television: An Analysis of 'America's Most Wanted' and 'Unsolved Mysteries.'" *Sociological Inquiry*. 63:305.

CBS News. 1993. Anchored by Dan Rather. November 8.

Ceulemans, Mieke, and Guido Fauconnier. 1979. *Mass Media: The Image, Role, and Social Conditions of Women: A Collection and Analysis of Research Materials*. Reports and Papers on Mass Communications. Paris: UNESCO.

Chamberlain, Susan. 1993a. Interview by Sally Jessy Raphael. "I'm a Surrogate and Had Sex to Get Pregnant." *The Sally Jessy Raphael Show*. NBC, May 4.

———. 1993b. Interview by Geraldo Rivera. "Bizarre and Controversial Stories of Surrogacy." *Geraldo*. CBS, September 23.

Chan, Sucheng. 1991a. *Asian Americans: An Interpretive History*. Boston: Twayne.

———, ed. 1991b. *Entry Denied: Exclusion and the Chinese Community in America, 1882–1943*. Philadelphia: Temple University Press.

Chancer, Lynn S. 1993. "Prostitution, Feminist Theory, and Ambivalence: Notes from the Sociological Underground." *Social Text*. (Winter 1994):143.

———. 1996. *Provoking Assaults*. Berkeley: University of California Press.

Charen, Mona. 1994. "Gender Feminism." *Baltimore Sun*. May 31:9A.

Chase, Anthony. 1986. "Toward a Legal Theory of Popular Culture." *Wisconsin Law Review*. 1986:527.

Chasteen, Amy L. 1994. "'The World around Me': The Environment and Single Women." *Sex Roles*. 31:309.

Chermak, Steven. 1994. "Crime in the News Media: A Refined Understanding of How Crimes Become News." In Barak, ed.

Chesler, Phyllis. 1988. *Sacred Bond: The Legacy of Baby M*. New York: Simon.

———. 1992. "Sex, Death and the Double Standard: Wuornos on Trial." *On the Issues*. Summer:28.

———. 1993. "A Woman's Right to Self-Defense: The Case of Aileen Carol Wuornos." *St. John's Law Review*. 66:933.

A Child Too Many: The Patty Nowakowski Story. 1993. Directed by Jorge Montesi. New World Entertainment and O'Hara-Horowitz Productions. NBC, October 11.

Cho, Sumi K. 1993. "Korean Americans vs. African Americans: Conflict and Construction." In Gooding-Williams, ed.

Christiano, Donna. 1994. "Where Is RU 486?" *Glamour*. March:102.

Chunn, Louise. 1993. "Date Rape Puts a Damper on College Mating Game." *Ottawa Citizen*. November 14:B3.

Clark, Pat. 1991. Telephone interview with author Helen Benedict.

Clarke, Stewart Alan. 1992. "Fear of a Black Planet: Race, Identity Politics, and Common Sense." *Socialist Review*. 21:37.

Class Action. 1991. Directed by Michael Apted. Interscope Communications and Twentieth-Century Fox.

The Client. 1994. Directed by Joel Schumacher. Regency Enterprises, Alcor Films, and Warner Brothers.

"Clinton's Reproductive Rights Report Card: 1992–1994." 1994. Editorial. *Glamour*. December:91.

Cohn, Bob. 1993a. "Crowning a 'Quota Queen?'" *Newsweek*. May 24:67.

———. 1993b. "So Long, Lani." *Newsweek*. June 14:26.

———. 1993c. Telephone interview with author Laurel Leff, July.

Coker, Cheo H. 1994. "A Hip-Hop Nation Divided: Who's Gonna Take the Weight?" *Essence*. August:63.

"Colby Defends Crackdown on Underground Fraternities." 1991. *Portland (Maine) Press Herald*. May 2:1D.

Colker, Ruth. 1986. "Anti-Subordination above

All: Sex, Race, and Equal Protection." *New York Law Review.* 61:1003.

Collins, Patricia Hill. 1990. *Black Feminist Thought: Knowledge, Consciousness, and the Politics of Empowerment.* New York: Routledge.

The Color Purple. Directed by Steven Spielberg. Amblin Entertainment, Guber-Peters Company, and Warner Brothers.

Combahee River Collective. 1981. "Twelve Black Women: Why Did They Die?" In Delacoste and Newman, eds.

Committee of the Judiciary, United States Senate. 1993. *The Response to Rape: Detours on the Road to Equal Justice: A Majority Staff Report Prepared for the Use of the Committee of the Judiciary, United States Senate, One Hundred Third Congress, First Session.* Washington: United States Government Printing Office.

Cook, Pam. 1978. "Duplicity in *Mildred Pierce.*" In *Women in Film Noir,* edited by E. Ann Kaplan. London: British Film Institute.

Coombs, Mary I. 1993. "Telling the Victim's Story." *Texas Journal of Women and the Law.* 2:277.

Corbin, Beth. 1994. "The Media Is the Message." *National NOW Times.* April:15.

Corliss, Richard. 1994. "Hurricane Camille Blows Again." *Time.* December 12:90.

Cover, Robert M. 1986. "Violence and the Word." *Yale Law Journal.* 95:1601.

———. 1993. *Narrative, Violence, and the Law: The Essays of Robert Cover.* Edited by Martha Minow, Michael Ryan, and Austin Sarat. Ann Arbor: University of Michigan Press.

Crenshaw, Kimberlé Williams. 1992a. "Race, Gender, and Sexual Harassment." *Southern California Law Review.* 65:1467.

———. 1992b. "Whose Story Is It Anyway? Feminist and Antiracist Appropriations of Anita Hill." In Morrison, ed.

———. 1994. "Mapping the Margins: Intersectionality, Identity Politics, and Violence against Women of Color." In Fineman and Mykitiuk, eds.

———. 1995. Interview by Lori S. Robinson. In "A Feminist Vision." *Emerge: Black America's Newsmagazine.* 6 (March):20.

Crichton, Sarah. 1993. "Sexual Correctness: Has It Gone Too Far?" *Newsweek.* October 25:52.

Crime Victimization Survey Report. 1992. "Criminal Victimization in the United States, 1991." *Bureau of the Census for the Bureau of Justice Statistics.* December (NCJ-139563):72.

Cunningham, Amy. 1994. "Who Are the Women Who Are Pro-Life?" *Glamour.* February:154.

Curly Sue. 1991. Directed by John Hughes. Warner Brothers.

Danielsen, Dan, and Karen Engle, eds. 1995. *After Identity: A Reader in Law and Culture.* New York: Routledge.

"Date Rape 101." 1993. *Washington Times.* October 31:D2.

Davis, Adrienne D., and Stephanie M. Wildman. 1992. "The Legacy of Doubt: Treatment of Sex and Race in the Hill-Thomas Hearings." *Southern California Law Review.* 65:1367.

Davis, Angela Y. 1981. *Women, Race, and Class.* New York: Random House.

Davis, Flora. 1991. *Moving the Mountain: The Women's Movement in America since 1960.* New York: Simon & Schuster.

Davis, Mike. 1993. "Uprising and Repression in L.A.: Interview by the *CovertAction* Information Bulletin." In Gooding-Williams, ed.

Dawsey, Darrell. 1992. "Much L.A. Looting Selective." Quoting Jamil Shabazz, co-owner of Crenshaw Cafe. *Detroit News.* May 1, Gannett News Service.

A Deadly Silence. 1989. Directed by John Patterson. Robert Greenwald Productions. ABC, April 16.

DeBoer, Roberta. 1993. Interview by Frank Sesno. *Larry King Live,* July 8.

DeCrow, Karen. 1993. "Women Are 'Victims' Again." *USA Today.* October 5:11A.

Deegan, Mary Jo. 1987. "The Gift Mother: A Proposed Ritual for the Integration of Surrogacy into Society." In H. Richardson, ed.

Defending Your Life. 1991. Directed by Albert Brooks. Geffen and Warner Brothers.

Defenseless. 1991. Directed by Martin Campbell. Seven Arts and New Line Cinema.

Delacoste, Frédérique, and Felice Newman, eds. 1981. *Fight Back!: Feminist Resistance to Male Violence.* Minneapolis: Cleis Press.

De Lauretis, Teresa. 1984. *Alice Doesn't: Feminism, Semiotics, Cinema.* Bloomington: Indiana University Press.

———. 1987. *Technologies of Gender: Essays on Theory, Film, and Fiction.* Bloomington: Indiana University Press.

Delgado, Richard, and Jean Stefancic. 1992. "Images of the Outsider in American Law and Culture: Can Free Expression Remedy Systemic Social Ills?" *Cornell Law Review.* 77:1258.

De La Fuente, Pat. 1989. "Beyond Baby M: The Controversy Over Surrogate Motherhood." *UTNE Reader.* May/June: 118–23.

DeMarco, Rene. 1994. Interview by Mary Tillotson, December 1.

Demma, Joseph. 1994. "Potential Juror: O.J. Is 'a Hunk.'" *New York Newsday*. October 29:A2.

Demolition Man. 1993. Directed by Mario Brambilla. Warner Brothers and Silver Pictures.

Denvir, John, ed. 1996. *Legal Reelism: Movies as Legal Text*. Urbana and Chicago: University of Illinois Press.

Devitt, Tiffany. 1992. "Abortion Coverage Leaves Women out of the Picture." Fairness and Accuracy in Reporting, *Extra!* Special Issue:18.

De Witt, Karen. 1994. "Teen Moms Who Beat the Odds: Determination Helped These Women Get Their Lives Back on Track." *Essence*. August:53.

Diamond, Irene, and Lee Quinby, eds. 1988. *Feminism and Foucault: Reflections on Resistance*. Boston: Northeastern University Press.

Didion, Joan. 1992. "New York: Sentimental Journeys." In *After Henry*. New York: Simon & Schuster.

Dimen, Muriel. 1989. "Power, Sexuality and Intimacy." In *Gender/Body/Knowledge: Feminist Reconstructions of Being and Knowing*, edited by Alison M. Jaggar and Susan Bordo. New Brunswick, N.J.: Rutgers University Press.

Dirks, Nicholas B., Geoff Eley, and Sherry B. Ortner. 1994. Introduction to *Culture/Power/History: A Reader in Contemporary Social Theory*, edited by Nicholas B. Dirks, Geoff Eley, and Sherry B. Ortner. Princeton: Princeton University Press.

Disclosure. 1994. Directed by Barry Levinson. Baltimore Pictures/constant c.

Dixon, Jo, and Caroll Seron. 1992. "Lawyers in Love: The Effects of Human Capital and Family Status on Income Attainment of Males and Females in Various Occupation Sectors of the Legal Profession." National Science Foundation.

Doane, Mary Ann. 1991. *Femmes Fatales: Feminism, Film Theory, Psychoanalysis*. New York: Routledge.

Dobbs, Michael. 1987. "Master of Radio Invective Eyes Official Soapbox." *Washington Post*. April 11:A3.

Dominus, Susan. 1994. "A Job Victory for Women." *Glamour*. March:98.

———. 1995. "Your Body Image: Does Race Make a Difference?" *Glamour*. February:92.

Doner, Kalia. 1993. "Women's Magazines: Slouching towards Feminism." *Social Policy*. Summer:37.

Doten, Patti. 1993. "Clare Dalton Looks Back in Anger." *Boston Globe*. October 25:36.

Douglas, Susan J. 1992. "Missing Voices: Women and the U.S. News Media." Fairness and Accuracy in Reporting, *Extra!* Special Issue:4.

———. 1994. *Where the Girls Are: Growing Up Female with the Mass Media*. New York: Random House/Times Books.

Douglas, William. 1990. "Disturbing Pattern Seen in Gang Rapes." *Newsday*. May 13:2.

Douglass, Victoria. 1993. "Prisoners of Thin: The Whole Country Has an Eating Disorder." *Mademoiselle*. December:134.

Dowd, Maureen. 1992. "Hillary Clinton as Aspiring First Lady: Role Model or a 'Hall Monitor' Type?" *New York Times*. May 18:A15.

———. 1993. "Hillary Rodham Clinton Strikes a New Pose and Multiplies Her Images." *New York Times*. December 12:E3.

———. 1994a. "On Washington; The First Lady's New Clothes." *New York Times Magazine*. July 10:16.

———. 1994b. "Senate Approves a 4-star Rank for Admiral in Tailhook Affair." *New York Times*. April 20:1.

Drape, Joe, and Tom Opdyke. 1992. "Guard Sent In as Terror Grips L.A. for a Second Night." *Atlanta Constitution*. May 1:A1.

Draper, Robert. 1994. "What Can Be Done to Stop Repeat Sex Offenders?" *Glamour*. April:260.

Drexler, Madeline. 1995. "What Can You Do about Endometriosis?" *Self*. January:122.

Dreyfous, Leslie. 1993. "Assault-Case Jury Finds 'Crime' in Moral Vacuum." *Maine Sunday Telegram*. March 21:5A.

Driscoll, Margarette. 1993. "Have We Gone Too Far?" *Sunday Times* (London). October 24:14.

Droker, Howard A. 1976. "Seattle Race Relations during the Second World War." *Pacific Northwest Quarterly*. 67:163.

D'Souza, Dinesh. 1991. *Illiberal Education: The Politics of Race and Sex on Campus*. New York: Free Press.

Dubois, Ellen, Mary Dunlap, Carol Gilligan, Catharine MacKinnon, and Carrie Menkel-Meadow. 1985. "Feminist Discourse, Moral Values, and the Law—A Conversation." *Buffalo Law Review*. 34:11.

Dunn, Katherine. 1994. "The Fists Swing Both Ways in Cases of Spousal Assault." *Rocky Mountain News*. July 24:A8.

Dutka, Elaine. 1990. "Women and Hollywood: It's Still a Lousy Relationship." *Los Angeles Times*. November 11 (Calendar):8.

Eagan, Margery. 1992. "America Is Not Ready for a His and Hers Presidency from the Clintons." *Boston Herald*. March 19:8.

———. 1994a. "It's Time to Demand Workfare." *Boston Herald*. February 15:1.

———. 1994b. "Recovering Addict and Welfare Mom Thankful for a Second Chance." *Boston Herald*. February 17:7.

Eaton, Mary. 1994. "Abuse by Any Other Name: Feminism, Difference, and Intralesbian Violence." In Fineman and Mykitiuk, eds.

"The Editorialists." 1994. San Francisco Examiner. June 24:A23.

Edmiston, Susan. 1991. "The First Woman Serial Killer?" *Glamour*. September:302.

Edwards, Audrey. 1993. "From Aunt Jemima to Anita Hill: Media's Split Image of Black Women." *Media Studies Journal*. 7:214.

Ehrenreich, Barbara. 1981. "The Women's Movements: Feminist and Antifeminist." *Radical America*. 93 (Spring):97.

Ehrenreich, Nancy S. 1990. "Pluralist Myths and Powerless Men: The Ideology of Reasonableness in Sexual Harassment Law." *Yale Law Journal*. 99:1177.

———. 1993. "The Colonization of the Womb." *Duke Law Journal*. 43:492.

Eigenberg, Helen M. 1991. "The National Crime Survey and Rape: The Case of the Missing Question." *Justice Quarterly*. 7:655.

Eisenstein, Zillah. 1984. *Feminism and Sexual Equality: Crisis in Liberal America*. New York: Monthly Review Press.

"Elizabeth." 1983. "A Surrogate's Story of Loving and Losing." *U.S. News & World Report*. June 6:77.

Ellement, John, and Efrain Hernandez Jr. 1990. "8 Teen-Agers Charged in Rape, Killing of Dorchester Woman." *Boston Globe*. November 20:1.

Ellement, John, Sean P. Murphy, Adrian Walker, and Michael Rezendes. 1990. "Police Defend Low-Profile Handling of Franklin Field Murder; Critics Say Community Should Have Been Warned." *Boston Globe*. November 21:1.

Ellement, John, and Charles M. Sennott. 1994. "Mother Charged in Scalding Fails to Appear in Court." *Boston Globe*. April 9:18.

Ellis, Bret Easton. 1994. *Informers*. New York: Knopf.

English, Dierdre. 1993. "Un-Telling the Story." Review of *The Real Anita Hill*, by David Brock. *The Nation*. June 28:910.

Epstein, Cynthia Fuchs. 1993. *Women in Law*. 2d ed. Urbana: University of Illinois Press.

Ericson, Richard V. 1987. *Visualizing Deviance: A Study of News Organization*. Toronto: University of Toronto Press.

———. 1991. *Representing Order: Crime, Law, and Justice in the News Media*. Toronto: University of Toronto Press.

Ericson, Richard V., Patricia M. Baranek, and Janet B. L. Chan. 1989. *Negotiating Control: A Study of News Sources*. Toronto: University of Toronto Press.

Ernst, Leslie. 1993. "Forum I: Women Who Kill." In Scholder, ed.

Ernst, Leslie, Cathy Greenblatt, and Susan McWhinney. 1993. "(Ain't) Natural History." In Scholder, ed.

Eskenazi, Gerald. 1990. "Athletic Aggression and Sexual Assault." *New York Times*. June 3 (Section 8, Sports):1.

Estes, Andrea, and Bill Hutchinson. 1994a. "State Cuts Agency's DSS Pact." *Boston Herald*. February 17:1.

———. 1994b. "Embattled DSS Agency Cries Foul in Contract Losses." *Boston Herald*. February 18:14.

Estrich, Susan. 1987. *Real Rape*. Cambridge: Harvard University Press.

———. 1994. "The Last Victim." *New York Times*. December 18:54.

"Even in Prison, Men Get Better Treatment Than Women." 1994. Editorial. *Glamour*. March:80.

Faludi, Susan. 1991. *Backlash: The Undeclared War against American Women*. New York: Crown.

———. 1993. "Whose Hype?" *Newsweek*. October 25:61.

———. 1995. "I'm Not a Feminist, But I Play One on TV." *Ms.* March/April:31.

Family Matters. 1989 to present. ABC television series.

Farney, Dennis. 1994. "Elite Theory: Have Liberals Ignored 'Have Less' Whites at Their Own Peril?" *Arizona Republic*. December 18:F1.

Farrell, Warren. 1993a. *The Myth of Male Power*. New York: Simon & Schuster.

———. 1993b. "The Myth of Male Power." *Playboy*. 40 (July):112.

———. 1994. "Spouse Abuse: A Two-Way Street." *USA Today*. June 29:A15.

Federal Bureau of Investigation. 1984. *Manual of Law Enforcement Records: Uniform Crime Reports*. Washington: United States Department of Justice, Federal Bureau of Investigation.

————. 1992a. "Crime in the United States, 1991." August 30.

————. 1992b. *Uniform Crime Reports in the United States, 1991.* United States Department of Justice, August 30.

Feinberg, Leslie. 1993. *Stone Butch Blues.* Ithaca, N.Y.: Firebrand Books.

"The Feminist Mistake." 1994. *Marie Claire.* September/October:126.

Ferrato, Donna. 1991. *Living with the Enemy.* New York: Aperture.

Feuer, Jane. 1983. "The Concept of Live Television: Ontology as Ideology." In *Regarding Television: Critical Approaches,* edited by E. Ann Kaplan. Frederick, Md.: University Publications of America.

A Few Good Men. 1992. Directed by Rob Reiner. Castle Dock Entertainment and Columbia Pictures.

Fields, Suzanne. 1994. Interview by Mary Tillotson, December 1.

Fine, Michelle. 1988. "Sexuality, Schooling and Adolescent Females: The Missing Discourse of Desire." *Harvard Educational Review.* 58:29.

————. 1992. *Disruptive Voices: The Possibilities of Feminist Research.* Ann Arbor: University of Michigan Press.

Fineman, Martha Albertson. 1991a. *The Illusion of Equality: The Rhetoric and Reality of Divorce Reform.* Chicago: University of Chicago Press.

————. 1991b. "Images of Mothers in Poverty Discourse." *Duke Law Journal.* 1991:274. Also in Fineman and Karpin, eds.

————. 1992. "The Neutered Mother." *University of Miami Law Review.* 46:653.

————. 1995. *The Neutered Mother, the Sexual Family and Other Twentieth Century Tragedies.* New York: Routledge.

Fineman, Martha Albertson, and Isabel Karpin, eds. 1995. *Mothers in Law: Feminist Theory and the Legal Regulation of Motherhood.* New York: Columbia University Press.

Fineman, Martha Albertson, and Martha T. McCluskey, eds. 1997. *Feminism, Media, and the Law.* New York: Oxford University Press.

Fineman, Martha Albertson, and Roxanne Mykitiuk, eds. 1994. *The Public Nature of Private Violence.* New York: Routledge.

Finkel, David. 1990. "The Last Housewife in America." *Esquire.* June:102.

Finley, Lucinda M. 1986. "Transcending Equality Theory: A Way Out of the Maternity and the Workplace Debate." *Columbia Law Review.* 86:1118.

First Monday in October. 1981. Directed by Ronald Neame. Paramount Pictures.

Fischer, Arlene. 1986. "I Want to Stay Home—Where I Belong." *Redbook.* April:96.

Fischl, Richard Michael. 1987. "Some Realism about Critical Legal Studies." *University of Miami Law Review.* 41:505.

Fishleder, Paul. 1991. Telephone interview with author Helen Benedict.

Fishman, Mark. 1978. "Crime Waves as Ideology." *Social Problems.* 25:530.

Fiske, John. 1986. "Television: Polysemy and Popularity." *Critical Studies in Mass Communication.* 3:391.

————. 1987. *Television Culture.* New York: Methuen.

————. 1989. *Understanding Popular Culture.* New York: Routledge.

————. 1994. *Media Matters: Everyday Culture and Political Change.* Minneapolis: University of Minnesota.

Flint, Anthony. 1991. "Motive Still Unknown in Law Professor's Slaying." *Boston Globe.* April 8:19.

48 Hours. 1993. "Custody Battles." Anchored by Dan Rather. CBS, December 1.

Fosburgh, Lacey. 1970. "Traditional Groups Prefer to Ignore Women's Lib." *New York Times.* August 26:44.

Foucault, Michel. 1978. *The History of Sexuality: An Introduction,* volume 1 New York: Pantheon

Foucault, Michel. 1984. *The Foucault Reader.* Edited by Paul Rabinow. New York: Pantheon.

————. 1986. *The History of Sexuality,* vol. 1, *An Introduction.* Translated by Robert Hurley. New York: Pantheon.

France, Kim. 1993. "The *Ism* That Dare Not Speak Its Name: Not since Gloria Steinem Has Feminism Had Such a Media-Friendly Face. But Can Naomi Wolf Make the *F*-Word Palatable Again?" *Elle.* November:74.

Franklin, John Hope. 1979. " 'Birth of a Nation'— Propaganda as History." *Massachusetts Review.* 20:417.

Franklin, Melanie, vice-president of Safe-T-Zone. Interview with authors Kathleen Daly and Amy L. Chasteen.

Fraser, Nancy. 1991. "Rethinking the Public Sphere." *Social Text.* 8:56.

Freedman, Estelle. 1992. "The Manipulation of History at the Clarence Thomas Hearings." *Southern California Law Review.* 65:1361.

Freeman, Jo. 1993. "The Politics of Women's Liberation." In Beasley and Gibbons, eds.

Fried, Joseph P. 1992. "St. John's Sex Abuse Case Ends with Plea Bargain." *New York Times*. February 12:B3.

Friedan, Betty. 1974. *The Feminine Mystique*. 10th anniversary ed. New York: Norton.

———. 1981. "Feminism's Next Step." *New York Times Magazine*. July 5:14.

Fried Green Tomatoes. 1991. Directed by Jon Avnet. Universal Pictures.

Friedman, Lawrence M. 1989. "Popular Legal Culture: Law, Lawyers and Popular Culture." *Yale Law Journal*. 98:1579.

Friedman, Leon, and Burt Neuborne. 1993. "Attack on Civil Rights Nominee Is Unfair." Letter to the Editor. *New York Times*. June 3:A22.

Friend, Tad. 1994. "Yes." *Esquire*. February:48.

Frug, Mary Joe, ed. 1992. *Women and the Law*. University Casebook Series. Westbury, N.Y.: The Foundation Press.

Furillo, Andy, and Steve Wiegand. 1992. "Cops Acquitted; L.A. Erupts; 3 Dead, 108 Injured; Wilson Calls in Guard." *Sacramento Bee*. April 30:A1.

Gamman, Lorraine, and Margaret Marshment. 1989. *The Female Gaze: Women as Viewers of Popular Culture*. Seattle: Real Comet Press.

Gans, Herbert J. 1979. *Deciding What's News: A Study of CBS Evening News, NBC Nightly News, Newsweek, and Time*. New York: Pantheon.

Garber, Marjorie, Jann Matlock, and Rebecca L. Walkowitz, eds. 1993. *Media Spectacles*. New York: Routledge.

Gardner, Carol Brooks. 1988. "Access Information: Public Lies and Private Peril." *Social Problems*. 35:384.

———. 1990. "Safe Conduct: Women, Crime, and Self in Public Places." *Social Problems*. 37:311.

Garrow, David. 1986. *Bearing the Cross: Martin Luther King, Jr. and the Southern Christian Leadership Conference*. New York: W. Morrow.

———. 1993. "How Anita Hill's Charges Became Political Grist." *Newsday*. May 4:58.

Gathright, Alan, and Mike Cassidy. 1992. "Bay Area Residents Say Public Trust Is a Victim of Verdict." *San Jose Mercury News*. April 30:A18.

Gelman, David. 1990. "The Mind of the Rapist." *Newsweek*. July 23:46.

Gelman, David, and Daniel Shapiro. 1985. "Infertility: Babies by Contract." *Newsweek*. November 4:74.

George, Lynell. 1992. *No Crystal Stair: African-Americans in the City of Angels*. New York: Verso.

Gerbner, George. 1978. "The Dynamics of Cultural Resistance." In Tuchman, Daniels, and Benet, eds.

———. 1992. "Violence and Terror in and by the Media." In *Media, Crisis and Democracy: Mass Communication and the Disruption of Social Order*, edited by Marc Raboy and Bernard Dagenais. Newbury Park, Calif.: Sage.

Gerbner, George, and Larry Gross. 1976. "Living with Television: The Violence Profile." *Journal of Communication*. 26:17.

Gibbs, Geoffrey Taylor. 1991. "Can African-Americans Now Truly Believe in Judicial Fairness?" Opinion. *Los Angeles Times*. November 24:M6.

Gibbs, Nancy. 1991. "When Is It Rape?" *Time*. June 3:48.

Gigot, Paul. 1993. "Hillary's Choice on Civil Rights: Back to the Future." *Wall Street Journal*. May 7:A14.

Gilkes, Cheryl Townsend. 1983. "From Slavery to Social Welfare: Racism and the Control of Black Women." In *Class, Race, and Sex: The Dynamic of Control*, edited by Amy Swerdlow and Hanna Lessinger. Boston: G. K. Hall.

Gillers, Stephen. 1989. "Taking L.A. Law More Seriously." *Yale Law Journal*. 98:1607.

Gilroy, Paul. 1993. *Small Acts: Thoughts on the Politics of Black Cultures*. New York: Serpent's Tail.

Ginsberg, Art. 1993. Interview by Sonya Friedman. *Sonya Live*, transcript #361. CNN, August 18.

Gitlin, Todd. 1980. *The Whole World Is Watching: Mass Media in the Making and Unmaking of the New Left*. Berkeley: University of California Press.

———. 1983. *Inside Prime Time*. New York: Pantheon.

Given, John L. 1907. *Making a Newspaper*. New York: Henry Holt & Co.

Glasser, Theodore I. 1992. "Objectivity and News Bias." In *Philosophical Issues in Journalism*, edited by E. D. Cohen. New York: Oxford University Press.

Glasser, Theodore I., and James S. Ethena. 1989. "Investigative Journalism and the Moral Order." *Critical Studies in Mass Communications*. 6:1.

Gledhill, Christine. 1987a. "The Melodramatic Field: An Investigation." In Gledhill, ed.

———, ed. 1987b. *Home Is Where the Heart Is: Studies in Melodrama and the Woman's Film*. London: British Film Institute.

Goffman, Erving. 1974. *Frame Analysis: An Essay on the Organization of Experience*. New York: Harper and Row.

Goldstein, Marilyn. 1994. "Now Gorgeous Is Good Enough." *Newsday*. December 12:A8.

Goldstein, Richard. 1995. "Save the Males: The Making of the Butch Backlash." *Village Voice*. March 7:25.

Gone with the Wind. 1939. Directed by Victor Fleming. Metro-Goldwin-Mayer.

Gooding-Williams, Robert, ed. 1993. *Reading Rodney King/Reading Urban Uprising*. New York: Routledge.

Goodman, Ellen. 1992. "Women's Movement Misses . . . Movement." *St. Louis Post-Dispatch*. February 25:3D.

———. 1994a. "What This Poll Proves about Women (and about Men)." *Esquire*. February:67.

———. 1994b. "O.J. Isn't Dead; Nicole Is." *San Jose Mercury News*. June 22:11B.

Goodrich, Chris. 1993. "A Battle of Politics, Not Principles." Review of *The Real Anita Hill*, by David Brock. *Los Angeles Times Book Review*. May 9:9.

Good Times. 1974–79. CBS television series.

Goodwin, Jan. 1994. "From the Valley of the Chador." *Mirabella*. April:106.

Gordon, Linda. 1987. "Some Policy Proposals: Reproductive Rights for Today." *The Nation*. September 12:230.

———. 1988. *Heroes of Their Own Lives: The Politics and History of Family Violence*. New York: Viking.

———. 1990. "Family Violence, Feminism and Social Control." In *Women, The State, and Welfare*, edited by Linda Gordon. Madison: University of Wisconsin Press.

———. 1994. *Pitied But Not Entitled: Single Mothers and the History of Welfare*. New York: Free Press.

Gordon, Margaret T., and Stephanie Riger. 1989. *The Female Fear: The Social Cost of Rape*. Urbana: University of Illinois Press.

Gordon, Robert W. 1984. "Critical Legal Histories." *Stanford Law Review*. 36:57.

Gotanda, Neil. 1991. "A Critique of 'Our Constitution Is Color-Blind.'" *Stanford Law Review*. 44:1.

———. 1995. "Reproducing the Model Minority Stereotype: Judge Joyce Karlin's Sentencing Colloquy in *People v. Soon Ja Du*." In *Re-Visioning Asian America: Locating Diversity*, edited by Wendy L. Ng. Seattle: University of Washington Press.

Gould, Stephen Jay. 1986. "Carrie Buck's Daughter." In Joseph Goldstein, Anna Freud, Albert J. Solnit, and Sonja Goldstein, *In the Best Interests of the Child*, Appendix 1. New York: Free Press.

Graber, Doris A. 1979. "Is Crime News Excessive?" *Journal of Communication*. 29:81.

Gramsci, Antonio. 1971. *Selections from the Prison Notebooks of Antonio Gramsci*. Edited and translated by Quintin Hoare and Geoffrey Nowell Smith. New York: International Publishers.

Grant, Jacqueline. 1982. "Black Women and the Church." In *All the Women Are White, All the Blacks Are Men, But Some of Us Are Brave: Black Women's Studies*, edited by Gloria T. Hull, Patricia Bell Scott, and Barbara Smith. Old Westbury, N.Y.: Feminist Press.

Greenwald, Robert. 1988. Interview with author Elayne Rapping, August.

Gregory, Deborah. 1994. "Heavy Judgment: A Sister Explores the Pain of 'Living Large.'" *Essence*. August:57.

Gregory, Deborah, and Patricia Jacobs. 1993. "The Ugly Side of the Modeling Business." *Essence*. September:89.

Grogan, D. 1989. "Little Girl, Big Trouble: A Surrogate Birth, a Divorce and a Tangled Custory Fight Mean an Uncertain Future for a Child Known Only as Tessa." *People*. February 20:36.

Groll, Christina. 1994. "Gender Bias in the Media Treatment of John and Lorena Bobbitt." Unpublished manuscript, Stanford Law School.

Groner, Jonathan. 1991. *Hilary's Trial: The Elizabeth Morgan Case: A Child's Ordeal in America's Legal System*. New York: American Lawyer Books/Simon & Schuster.

———. 1993. "The Thomas-Hill Debate: A Revisionist's View." Review of *The Real Anita Hill*, by David Brock. *Washington Post Book Review*. May 3:C1.

Gross, Jane. 1991. "Even the Victim Can Be Slow to Recognize Rape." *New York Times*. May 28:A8.

———. 1993. "Where 'Boys Will Be Boys,' and Adults Are Befuddled." *New York Times*. March 29:A1.

Grossberg, Lawrence. 1984. "I'd Rather Feel Bad Than Not Feel Anything at All." *Enclitic*. 8:95.

———. 1992. *We Gotta Get Out of This Place: Popular Conservatism and Postmodern Culture*. New York: Routledge.

Grunwald, Michael. 1994. "Ventura's Former Boyfriend Indicted in Child's Scalding." *Boston Globe*. October 5:1.

Guddiero, Josephine A., and Louise C. Weston. 1985. "Work Options for Women in Women's

Magazines: The Medium and the Message." *Sex Roles*. 12:535.

Guilty as Sin. 1993. Directed by Sidney Lumet. Hollywood Pictures and Buena Vista.

Guinier, Lani. 1989. "Keeping the Faith: Black Voter in the Post-Reagan Era." *Harvard Civil Rights-Civil Liberties Law Review*. 24:393.

———. 1991a. "No Two Seats: The Elusive Quest for Political Equality." *Virginia Law Review*. 77:1413.

———. 1991b. "The Triumph of Tokenism: The Voting Rights Act and the Theory of Black Electoral Success." *Michigan Law Review*. 89:1077.

Guinzburg, Suzanne. 1983. "Surrogate Mothers' Rationale." *Psychology Today*. April:79.

Gupta, Nelly Edmondson with Frank Feldinger. 1989. "Brave New Baby." *Ladies' Home Journal* 106. October:140–41.

Hackett, Robert A. 1984. "Decline of a Paradigm? Bias and Objectivity in New Media Studies." *Critical Studies in Mass Communication*. 1:229.

Haines, Janine. 1993. "The Front Page vs. the Female Pol." *Ms*. January/February:84.

Halberstam, Judith. 1993. "Imagined Violence/Queer Violence." *Social Text*. (Winter):187.

Hairston, Hap. 1991. Telephone interview with author Helen Benedict.

Hall, Stuart. 1977. "Culture, Media, and the Ideological Effect." In *Mass Communication and Society*, edited by James Curran, Michael Gurevitch, and Janet Woollacott. London: Edward Arnold.

———. 1981. "Notes on Deconstructing 'the Popular.'" In *People's History and Socialist Theory*, edited by Raphael Samuel. Boston: Routledge and Kegan Paul.

———. 1988. "The Toad in the Garden: Thatcher among the Theorists." In Nelson and Grossberg, eds.

———. 1989. "The Meaning of the New Times." In *New Times: The Changing Face of Politics in the 1990s*, edited by Stuart Hall and Marin Jacques. London: Lawrence and Wishart.

Hall, Stuart, Chas Chritcher, Tony Jefferson, John Clarke, and Brian Roberts. 1978. *Policing the Crisis: Mugging, the State, and Law and Order*. New York: Holmes & Meier.

Hallin, Daniel C. 1992a. "The Passing of the High Modernism of American Journalism." *Journal of Communications*. 42:14.

———. 1992b. "Sound Bite News: Television Coverage of Elections: 1968–1988." *Journal of Communications*. 42:5.

Hanley, Robert. 1992. "Defense Lawyers in Glen Ridge Abuse Case Say Woman Was Aggressor." *New York Times*. October 17:A31.

Hanmer, Jalna, and Mary Maynard, eds. 1987. *Women, Violence and Social Control*. Atlantic Highlands, N.J.: Humanities Press International.

Hannah K. 1983. Directed by Constantin Costa-Gavras. K.G. Productions/Gaumont/Films AZ and Universal Pictures.

Hanrahan, Tom. 1990. "The Surreal State of Colby Football." *Central Maine Morning Sentinel*. April 24:13.

Harding, Sandra. 1991. *Whose Science? Whose Knowledge?: Thinking from Women's Lives*. Ithaca: Cornell University Press.

Hariman, Robert. 1990. Introduction to *Popular Trials: Rhetoric, Mass Media and the Law*, edited by Robert Hariman. Tuscaloosa: University of Alabama Press.

Harrington, Mona. 1994. *Women Lawyers: Rewriting the Rules*. New York: Knopf.

Harris, Angela P. 1990. "Race and Essentialism in Feminist Legal Theory." *Stanford Law Review*. 42:581.

Harris, Cheryl I. 1993. "Whiteness as Property." *Harvard Law Review*. 106:1710.

Hart, Lynda. 1994. *Fatal Women: Lesbian Sexuality and the Mark of Aggression*. Princeton: Princeton University Press.

Hasci, Tim. 1994. "Are Orphanages the Answer?" *Chicago Tribune*. March 16 (Perspective Section):27.

Haskell, Molly. 1987. *From Reverence to Rape: The Treatment of Women in the Movies*. Chicago: University of Chicago Press.

Heaney, Joe. 1994. "Mother Accused of Scalding Son." *Boston Herald*. February 13:6.

Hebdige, Dick. 1979. *Subculture: The Meaning of Style*. London: Methuen.

———. 1988. *Hiding in the Light: Images and Things*. New York: Routledge.

Hellman, Peter. 1993. "Crying Rape: The Politics of Date Rape on Campus." *New York Magazine*. March 8:32.

Hellwig, David J. 1977. "Afro-American Reactions to the Japanese and the Anti-Japanese Movement, 1906–1924." *Phylon*. 38:93.

———. 1979. "Black Reactions to Chinese Immigration and the Anti-Chinese Movement: 1850–1910." *Amerasia*. 6:25.

Henderson, Lynne. 1992. "Rape and Responsibility." *Law and Philosophy*. 11:127.

Herek, Gregory, and Kevin Berrill, eds. 1992. *Hate*

Crimes: Confronting Violence against Lesbians and Gay Men. Newbury Park, Calif.: Sage.

Hernandez, Peggy. 1988. "Youth Held in Island Killing Reportedly Suspect in Thefts." *Boston Globe.* December 2:44.

Herrnstein, Richard J., and Charles Murray. 1994. *The Bell Curve: Intelligence and Class Structure in American Life.* New York: Free Press.

Hess, Stephen. 1981. *The Washington Reporters.* Washington: Brookings Institution.

Higgins, Lynn A., and Brenda R. Silver, eds. 1991. *Rape and Representation.* New York: Columbia University Press.

Higgins, Tracy E., and Deborah L. Tolman. 1997. "Law, Cultural Media[tion], and the Missing Discourse of Desire." In Fineman and McCluskey, eds.

"Hillary Pillory!" 1994. *People.* June 20:42.

Hinds, Mary Hancock. 1993. "Putting a New Face on Feminism: Fed-Up Women Giving Mainstream a Voice." *Washington Times.* December 16:C8.

Hine, Robert V. 1973. *The American West: An Interpretive History.* Boston: Little, Brown.

Hing, Bill Ong. 1993a. "Beyond the Rhetoric of Assimilation and Cultural Pluralism: Addressing the Tension of Separatism and Conflict in an Immigration-Driven Multiracial Society." *California Law Review.* 81:863.

———. 1993b. *Making and Remaking Asian America through Immigration Policy, 1850–1990.* Stanford: Stanford University Press.

Hinton, Diane (as told to Danelle Morton). 1994. "First Person—I Survived Ovarian Cancer." *Marie Claire.* September/October:111.

Hirsch, Marianne, and Evelyn Fox Keller, eds. 1990. *Conflicts in Feminism.* New York: Routledge.

Hiscock, John. 1994. "'Perfect' Models Make Women Sick with Envy." *Daily Telegraph.* January 6:3.

Hitchens, Christopher. 1994. Interview by Charlie Rose. Transcript #1022. WNET Educational Broadcasting Co., January 3.

Hoagland, Sarah. 1988. *Lesbian Ethics: Towards New Value.* Palo Alto, Calif.: Institute of Lesbian Studies.

Hodge, Shelby. 1992. "*Mirabella* Takes Lead in Politics." *Houston Chronicle.* August 15:4.

Hoge, Patrick, Jeannie Wong, and Sam Stanton. 1992. "Many in Capital Expressed Bitterness; 'There Is No Justice,' King's Aunt Says." *Sacramento Bee.* April 30:A22.

Holland, Janet, Caroline Ramazanoglu, Sue Sharpe, and Rachel Thomson. 1994. "Power and Desire: The Embodiment of Female Sexuality." *Feminist Review.* 46 (Spring):21.

Hollway, Wendy. 1984. "Women's Power in Heterosexual Sex." *Women's Studies International Forum.* 7:63.

Hood, Jane C. 1989. "Why Our Society Is Rape-Prone." Letter to the Editor. *New York Times.* May 16:A23.

hooks, bell. 1984. *Feminist Theory: From Margin to Center.* Boston: South End Press.

———. 1989a. "Overcoming White Supremacy: A Comment." In her *Talking Back: Thinking Feminist, Thinking Black.*

———. 1989b. *Talking Back: Thinking Feminist, Thinking Black.* Boston: South End Press.

———. 1990. *Yearning: Race, Gender, and Cultural Politics.* Boston: South End Press.

———. 1992. *Black Looks: Race and Representation.* Boston: South End Press.

———. 1993. "Color Roiphe Privileged, Says Black Feminist." *Newsday.* October 27:57.

———. 1994. *Outlaw Culture: Resisting Representations.* New York: Routledge.

Hopkins, Ellen. 1992. "Tales from the Baby Factory." *The New York Times Magazine.* March 15:40–41, 80–83.

Houppert, Karen. 1993. "Baseball Bats and Broomsticks: The Glen Ridge Rape Trial Draws to a Close." *Village Voice.* March 16:29.

"House Approves Smaller Spending Bill." 1993. *USA Today.* May 27:4A.

Howard, Manny. 1993. "Public Laws for Private Lives: A Coast-to-Coast Guide to How Your State Handles All Kinds of Laws from Drugs to Guns to Nonmissionary Sex." *Mademoiselle.* December:154.

Howell, Sharon. 1990. *Reflections of Ourselves: The Mass Media and the Women's Movement, 1963 to the Present.* New York: Peter Lang.

Howkins, Mary Ann. 1994. "How to Avoid Pesticide Residues in Fruits and Vegetables." *Glamour.* April:56.

Hurt, Harry, III. 1995. "Women Who Kill Men: Is the Justice System Biased against Women?" *Self.* January:119.

Hutchinson, Bill. 1994a. "Mother Unfazed by Tot's Terror." *Boston Herald.* February 14:7.

———. 1994b. "Agency Let Boy's Family Slip through the Cracks." *Boston Herald.* February 15:1.

———. 1994c. "Claribel's Boyfriend Faces Abuse Charge; DA Connects Hub Man with Vicious Scalding of 5-Year-Old." *Boston Herald.* October 5:1.

Ifill, Gwen. 1993. "The Guinier Battle: Anatomy of the Failure to Confirm a Nominee." *New York Times*. June 5:9.

Ikemoto, Lisa C. 1993. "Traces of the Master Narrative in the Story of African American/Korean American Conflict: How We Constructed 'Los Angeles.'" *Southern California Law Review*. 66:1581.

Imitation of Life. 1959. Directed by Douglas Sirk. Universal Pictures.

Inherit the Wind. 1960. Directed by Stanley Kramer. United Artists.

Institute for Women's Policy Research. 1993. "Trends in Women's Labor Force Participation: Fact Sheet." Washington: Institute for Women's Policy Research.

In the Name of the Father. 1993. Directed by Jim Sheridan. Hell's Kitchen and Universal Pictures.

Isikoff, Michael. 1993a. "Confirmation Battle Looms over Guinier." *Washington Post*. May 21:A23.

———. 1993b. "White House Affirms Support of Guinier." *Washington Post*. May 28:A4.

———. 1993c. "Power behind the Thrown Nominee: Activist with Score to Settle." *Washington Post*. June 6:A11.

———. 1993d. Telephone interview with author Laurel Leff, July.

Issacharoff, Samuel. 1993. Telephone interview with author Laurel Leff, July.

Jack, Dana Crowley. 1991. *Silencing the Self: Women and Depression*. Cambridge: Harvard University Press.

Jackson, Cath. 1993. "Trouble and Strife" (cartoon). In Caryl Rivers, "Bandwagons, Women and Cultural Mythology." *Media Studies Journal*. 7:4.

Jacobs, Sally. 1990. "Father of Attack Victim Looks Back in Anguish." *Boston Globe*. November 21:1.

Jacoby, Susan. 1994. "How to Spot and Resist the Rapist You Know." *Glamour*. February:164.

Jagged Edge. 1985. Directed by Richard Marquand. Columbia Pictures.

James, Caryn. 1994. "Film: Tales from the Corner Office." Review of *Disclosure*. *New York Times*. December 11 (section 2, Arts and Leisure):1.

The Jeffersons. 1975–85. CBS television series.

Jerin, Robert A., and Charles B. Fields. 1994. "Murder and Mayhem in *USA Today*." In Barak, ed.

Johnsen, Leigh Dana. 1980. "Equal Rights and the 'Heathen Chinee': Black Activism in San Francisco, 1865–1875." *Western Historical Quarterly*. 11:57.

Johnston, Jill. 1992. "Why Iron John Is No Gift to Women." *New York Times Book Review*. February 13:1.

Jones, Charisse. 1994. "Living Single: Facing the Possibility That We May Never Marry." *Essence*. May:138.

Jordan, Emma Coleman. 1992. "Race, Gender, and Social Class in the Thomas Sexual Harassment Hearings: The Hidden Fault Lines in Political Discourse." *Harvard Women's Law Journal*. 15:1.

Jordan, June. 1980. "Poem about My Rights." In *Passion: New Poems*. Boston: Beacon Press.

Judge Dredd. 1995. Directed by Danny Cannon. Buena Vista Distribution Group, Judge Dredd Productions, and Edward R. Pressman Film Corporation.

Jungle Fever. 1991. Directed by Spike Lee. Fever Films, Forty Acres and a Mule Filmworks, and Universal Pictures.

Kahn, Kim Fridkin, and Edie N. Goldenberg. 1991. "The Media: Obstacle or Ally of Feminists?" *The Annals of the American Academy of Political and Social Sciences*. 515:104.

Kairys, David, ed. 1990. *The Politics of Law: A Progressive Critique*. Rev. ed. New York: Pantheon.

Kakutani, Michiko. 1993. "Critics Notebook: Beyond Iron John? How about Iron Jane?" *New York Times*. August 27:C1.

———. 1994. "Some Familiar Terrain after 'American Psycho.'" Review of *The Informers*, by Bret Easton Ellis. *New York Times*. August 2:C19.

Kamen, Al, and Ruben Castaneda. 1992. "Koreans Bear Arms to Protect Businesses." *Washington Post*. May 2:A1.

Kamen, Paula. 1991. *Feminist Fatale: Voices from the "Twentysomething" Generation Explore the Future of the "Women's Movement."* New York: Donald I. Fine.

Kaminer, Wendy. 1993a. "What Is This Thing Called Rape?" Review of *The Morning After*, by Katie Roiphe, and *Sexual Violence*, by Linda A. Fairstein. *New York Times Book Review*. September 19:1.

———. 1993b. "Feminism's Identity Crisis." *Atlantic Monthly*. 272 (October):51.

———. 1994. "Feminazis? Nous?" *Mirabella*. April:30.

Kammer, Jack. 1994. "Goodwill toward Men; Interviews with Feminists." *Playboy*. 41 (February):46.

Kane, Elizabeth. 1988. *Birth Mother*. New York: Harcourt Brace.

Kaplan, E. Ann. 1992. *Motherhood and Representation: The Mother in Popular Culture and Melodrama*. New York: Routledge.

———. 1994. "The Politics of Surrogacy Narratives: Notes Toward a Research Project." In *Feminist Nightmares: Women at Odds: Feminism and the Problem of Sisterhood*. New York: New York University Press.

Karl, Jonathan. 1992. "Bookshelf: No One's Responsible." *Wall Street Journal*. September 14:A9.

Karpin, Isabel. 1992. "Legislating the Female Body: Reproductive Technology and the Reconstructed Woman." *Columbia Journal of Gender and Law*. 3:325.

———. 1994. "Reimagining Maternal Selfhood: Transgressing Body Boundaries and the Law." *Australian Feminist Law Journal*. 2:36.

Katz, Jack. 1987. "What Makes Crime 'News'?" *Media, Culture and Society*. 9:47.

Kaufman, Michael. 1991. Telephone interview with author Helen Benedict.

Kaye, Melanie. 1981. "Women and Violence." In Delacoste and Newman. 1981. *Fight Back!: Feminist Resistance to Male Violence*. Minneapolis: Cleis Press.

Kaye/Kantrowitz, Melanie. 1992. *The Issue Is Power: Essays on Women, Jews, Violence and Resistance*. San Francisco: Aunt Lute Books.

Keehn, Joel. 1994. "Vaginal Infection? Don't Assume It's Yeast." *Glamour*. February:39.

Keith, Bruce. 1993. *The Herald* (Glasgow). Commentary. July 29:12.

Kellner, Douglas. 1990. *Television and the Crisis of Democracy*. Boulder, Colo.: Westview Press.

Kelly, Liz. 1988. *Surviving Sexual Violence*. Cambridge, Eng.: Polity.

Kennedy, Elizabeth Lapovsky, and Madeline Davis. 1993. *Boots of Leather, Slippers of Gold: The History of a Lesbian Community*. New York: Routledge.

Kilpatrick, James J. 1994. "Chalk One Up for Free Speech." *San Diego Union-Tribune*. October 18:B6.

Kim, Elaine H. 1993. "Home Is Where the Han Is: A Korean-American Perspective on the Los Angeles Upheavals." In Gooding-Williams, ed.

King, Sherry. 1986. "'I Gave Birth to My Sister's Baby.'" Edited by Elaine Fein. *Redbook*. April:34.

Kolbert, Elizabeth. 1994. "Our New Participatory Tabloid Videocracy." *New York Times*. July 17:E3.

"Korean-Americans Mount Own Defenses against Further Violence." 1992. *Agence France Presse*. May 2, newswire (dateline: Los Angeles).

Kovel, Joel. 1984. *White Racism: A Psychohistory*. New York: Columbia University Press.

Kranhold, Kathryn, and Katherine Farrish. 1993. "Anxiety about Sex, Dating, Rape Transforms College Life." *Hartford Courant*. October 10:A1.

Krauthammer, Charles. 1993. "Defining Deviancy Up." *New Republic*. November 22:20.

Kristeva, Julia. 1982. *Powers of Horror: An Essay On Abjection*. Translated by Leon S. Roudiez. New York: Columbia University Press.

———. 1991. *Strangers to Ourselves*. Translated by Leon Roudiez. New York: Columbia University Press.

Kristof, Nicholas D. 1995. "The Seer among the Blind: Japanese Sect Leader's Rise." *New York Times*. March 26:A1.

Kronke, David. 1995. "Four Talk Shows and a Premiere." *Los Angeles Times*, July 15:F4

Krupp, Charla. 1994. "When Will a Woman Host a Late-Night Talk Show?" *Glamour*. April:177.

Kuhn, Annette. 1985. *Power of the Image: Essays on Representation and Sexuality*. Boston: Routledge and Kegan Paul.

Kunen, James S., Meg Grant, Cindy Dampier, and Sara Gay Dammann. 1991. "Florida Cops Say Seven Men Met Death on the Highway When They Picked Up Accused Serial Killer Aileen Wuornos." *People*. February 25:44.

Kurtz, Howard. 1993. "A Revisionist's Nightmare: David Brock Rewrote the Anita Hill Story and Won Praise, Then the Liberals Got a Look." *Washington Post*. June 10:D1.

Lacan, Jacques. 1982. *Feminine Sexuality*. Translated by Jacqueline Rose. Edited by Juliet Mitchell and Jacqueline Rose. New York: Pantheon.

Lacayo, Richard, and Wayne Svoboda. 1986. "Is the Womb a Rentable Space?" *Time*. September 22:86.

Lacey, Marc, and Shawn Hubler. 1992. "Rioters Set Fires, Loot Stores." *Los Angeles Times*. April 30:A1.

Lady Sings the Blues. Directed by Sidney J. Furie. Paramount Pictures.

Laird, Cheryl. 1994. "Morning-After Pill Remains Secret to Many." *Houston Chronicle*. January 23:G1.

Lambert, Marjie, and Amy Alexander. 1992. "L.A.

Erupts in Blood, Rioting, Burning; Frustrations to Riot and Mindless Violence in Los Angeles." *Fresno Bee*. April 30:A1.

Lauter, David. 1993a. "Aides Say Clinton May Drop Rights Nominee." *Los Angeles Times*. June 2:A1.

———. 1993b. "Guinier Nomination All But Dead, Officials Say." *Los Angeles Times*. June 3:A1.

Lauter, David, and Sam Fulwood III. 1993. "Clinton Withdraws Guinier as Nominee for Civil Rights Job." *Los Angeles Times*. June 4:A1.

Laver, Ross. 1994. "Injustice—The Court Took My Children: A Career Mother Punished." *Marie Claire*. September/October:40.

Lavin, Chris. 1992. "Jury Urges Death for Wuornos." *St. Petersburg Times*. January 31:1A.

Law, Sylvia A. 1984. "Rethinking Sex and the Constitution." *University of Pennsylvania Law Review*. 132:955.

Lawrence, Charles R., III. 1987. "The Id, the Ego, and Equal Protection: Reckoning with the Unconscious Racism." *Stanford Law Review*. 39:317.

Lawson, Laurie. 1986. "I Was a Career Junkie." *Working Woman*. June:48.

"Leading Feminist Puts Hairdo before Strike." 1970. *New York Times*. August 27:30.

Lee, Jayne. 1992. "Innocent Victims: The Construction of Korean American Merchants and African American Looters in Los Angeles." Unpublished paper, on file with author Lisa C. Ikemoto.

Leff, Laurel. 1986. *From Mirror to Mirage: The Transformation of American Journalism in the Twentieth Century*. Master's thesis, University of Miami.

———. 1993. "From Legal Scholar to Quota Queen." *Columbia Journalism Review*. September/October:36.

———. 1997. "The Making of a Quota Queen: News Media and the Bias of Objectivity." In Fineman and McCluskey, eds.

Lefkowitz, Bernard. 1992. "Teen Called Sex Obsessed." *New York Newsday*. October 17:74.

———. 1993. "3 Guilty in Jersey Rape." *New York Newsday*. March 17:5.

Legal Eagles. 1986. Directed by Ivan Reitman. Universal Pictures.

"Legalized Prostitution," 1991. *Economist*. Sept. 7:28.

Lehmann-Haupt, Christopher. 1993a. "Books of the Times: Peering behind the Anita Hill-Clarence Thomas Matter." Review of *The Real Anita Hill*, by David Brock. *New York Times*. April 26:C18.

———. 1993b. "Books of the Times: Divergent Views of Rape as Violence and Sex." Review of *The Morning After*, by Katie Roiphe, and *Sexual Violence*, by Linda A. Fairstein. *New York Times*. September 16:C15.

Leibman, Abby J. 1992. "Doubting Thomas." *Southern California Law Review*. 65:1441.

Leive, Cindi. 1994a. "Sarah Brady's Anti-Gun Efforts Pay Off." *Glamour*. February:68.

———. 1994b. "The Latest on . . . Women, AIDS, Condoms and Confidence." *Glamour*. May:180.

Leo, John. 1994. "De-escalating the Gender War." *U.S. News & World Report*. April 18:24.

"Let's Get Real about Feminism: The Backlash, the Myths, the Movement." 1993. *Ms*. September/October:34.

Lever, Janet, and Pepper Schwartz. 1993. "Sex and Health: Did Her Ob-Gyn Abuse Her?" *Glamour*. November:83.

Levi, Lili. 1993. "Challenging the Autonomous Press." *Cornell Law Review*. 78:665.

Lewis, Anthony. 1993. "Abroad at Home: Sleaze with Footnotes." *New York Times*. May 21: A27.

———. 1994. "Where Is the Freedom for Unpleasant Speech?" *Houston Chronicle*. October 23:3.

Lewis, Lisa A. 1990. *Gender Politics and MTV: Voicing the Difference*. Philadelphia: Temple University Press.

Lewis, Neil A. 1993a. "Civil Rights Nominee's Words Make Her a Target." *New York Times*. May 14:B8.

———. 1993b. "Clinton Faces Battle over a Civil Rights Nominee." *New York Times*. May 21:B9.

"Liberating Women." 1970. *Time*. June 15:93.

Limbaugh, Rush. 1994. "The Vicious Attacks of Fearful Liberals on the Run." *San Francisco Examiner*. November 27:A19.

Lipsitz, George. 1990. *Time Passages: Collective Memory and American Popular Culture*. Minneapolis: University of Minnesota Press.

Littleton, Christine A. 1989. "Women's Experience and the Problem of Transition: Perspectives on Male Battering of Women." *University of Chicago Legal Forum*. 1989:23.

Living Single. 1993 to present. Fox television series.

Lobel, Kerry, ed. 1986. *Naming the Violence: Speaking Out about Lesbian Battering*. Seattle: Seal Press.

Locy, Toni, and Brian McGrory. 1994. "Woman Alleges Officer Forced Sex." *Boston Globe*. April 30:1.

Lois Gibbs and the Love Canal. 1987. Directed by Glen Jordan. Moonlight Productions and Filmways. CBS, August 7.

Longcope, Kay. 1988. "Area Lesbians Share Sadness, Fear after Couple's Slaying." *Boston Globe.* December 4:1.

Lorde, Audre. 1984. *Sister Outsider.* Trumansburg, N.Y.: Crossing Press.

Losing Isaiah. 1994. Directed by Stephen Gyllenhaal. The Koch Company and Paramount Pictures.

Lovdal, Lynn T. 1989. "Sex Role Messages in Television Commercials: An Update." *Sex Roles.* 21:715.

Love Crimes. 1992. Directed by Lizzie Borden. Sovereign Pictures and Millimeter Films.

Lowe, Lisa. 1991. "Heterogeneity, Hybridity, Multiplicity: Marking Asian American Differences." *Diaspora.* 1:24.

Lucia, Cynthia. 1991. "Class Action (Film Review)." *Cineaste.* 18:48.

———. 1992a. "Redefining Female Sexuality in the Cinema: An Interview with Lizzie Borden." *Cineaste.* 19:6.

———. 1992b. "Women on Trial: The Female Lawyer in the Hollywood Courtroom." *Cineaste.* 19:32.

Lundy, Sandra E. 1993. "Abuse That Dare Not Speak Its Name: Assisting Victims of Lesbians and Gay Domestic Violence in Massachusetts." *New England Law Review.* 28:273.

Mack, John. 1992. "Stop the Madness." *Nightline.* ABC, May 1.

MacKinnon, Catharine A. 1987. *Feminism Unmodified.* Cambridge: Harvard University Press.

———. 1989. *Toward a Feminist Theory of the State.* Cambridge: Harvard University Press.

———. 1993. *Only Words.* Cambridge: Harvard University Press.

MacNamara, Mark. 1991. "Kiss and Kill." *Vanity Fair.* September:90.

Madden, Susan. 1981. "Fighting Back with Deadly Force: Women Who Kill in Self-Defense." In Delacoste and Newman, eds.

Made in America. 1993. Directed by Richard Benjamin. New Regency Productions and Warner Brothers.

Maguire, Kathleen, and Ann L. Pastore, eds. 1994. *Sourcebook of Criminal Justice Statistics 1993.* Washington: U.S. Department of Justice, Bureau of Justice Statistics.

Maher, Lisa. 1990. "Criminalizing Pregnancy—The Downside of Kinder, Gentler Nation?" *Social Justice.* 17:111.

Mahoney, Martha R. 1991. "Legal Images of Battered Women: Redefining the Issue of Separation." *Michigan Law Review.* 90.

———. 1994. "Victimization or Oppression? Women's Lives, Violence and Agency." In Fineman and Mykitiuk, eds.

Mahoney, Sarah. 1994. "Making Men Listen: If Your Male Coworkers Aren't Paying Attention When You Talk, Here Are Some Strategies for Getting Heard on the Job." *Glamour.* March:226.

Malcolm, Andrew H. 1988. "Steps to Control Surrogate Births Stir Debate Anew." *New York Times.* June 26:1.

Malveaux, Julianne. 1992. "Wise Up Hillary: Women BakeCookies." *San Francisco Examiner.* March 23:A13.

Manegold, Catherine S. 1994. "The Citadel's Lone Wolf: Shannon Faulkner." *New York Times Magazine.* September 11:56.

Manning, Anita. 1993. "Gender Wars on Campus: 'Crisis' Forces the Sexes to Redefine Roles." *USA Today.* September 2:1A.

Manoff, Robert Karl. 1986a. Introduction to *Reading the News.* In Manoff and Schudson, eds.

———. 1986b. "Writing the News (by Telling the 'Story')." In Manoff and Schudson, eds.

Manoff, Robert Karl, and Michael Schudson, eds. 1986. *Reading the News.* New York: Pantheon.

Mansfield, Stephanie. 1985. "Hittin' It Big and Kissin' It Goodbye." *Washington Post.* February 26:C1.

The Man Who Shot Liberty Valance. 1962. Directed by John Ford. Ford Productions and Paramount Pictures.

Marcus, Isabel. 1994. "Reframing 'Domestic Violence': Terrorism in the Home." In Fineman and Mykitiuk, eds.

Margolick, David. 1993. "Musty Academic Speculation or Blueprint for Political Action?" *New York Times.* June 4:A18.

———. 1994. "Remaking of the Simpson Prosecutor." *New York Times.* October 3:A10.

Marill, Alvin H. 1989. *Movies Made for Television 1964–89.* New York: New York Zoetrope.

Marin, Richard T. 1994. "Miami's Crime Time Live." *Newsweek.* March 21:71.

Markoutsas, Elaine. 1981. "Women Who Have Babies for Other Women" (condensed from *Good Housekeeping,* April 1981). *Reader's Digest.* 119 (August):71.

Marmon, Lucretia, and Alissa Rubin. 1995. "Women in Washington: What Have They Done for Us Lately?" *Glamour.* February:92.

Maryles, Daisy. 1994. "The Sky's the Limit." *Publisher's Weekly*. March 7:53.

Marzolf, Marion Tuttle. 1993. "Deciding What's 'Women's News.'" *Media Studies Journal*. 7:32.

Masaki, Beckie. 1992. Telephone interview with author Lisa Ikemoto, November 16.

Matalin, Mary. 1993. "Stop Whining!" *Newsweek*. October 25:62.

Matsuda, Mari J. 1987. "Looking to the Bottom: Critical Legal Studies and Reparations." *Harvard Civil Rights-Civil Liberties Law Review*. 22:323.

———. 1989a. "Public Response to Racist Speech: Considering the Victim's Story." *Michigan Law Review*. 87:2320.

———. 1989b. "When the First Quail Calls: Multiple Consciousness as Jurisprudential Method." *Women's Rights Law Reporter*. 11:7.

Maude. 1972–78. CBS television series.

Mauro, Tony. 1993. "Two Clinton Nominees Face Tough Sledding." *USA Today*. May 4:2A.

May, Clifford D. 1994. "Feminist Questions Familiar Stereotypes." *Rocky Mountain News*. September 21:50A.

May, Elaine Tyler. 1989. "Explosive Issues: Sex, Women, and the Bomb." In *Recasting America: Culture and Politics in the Age of Cold War*, edited by Lary May. Chicago: University of Chicago Press.

Mayer, Jane, and Jill Abramson. 1993. "The Surreal Anita Hill." Review of *The Real Anita Hill*, by David Brock. *New Yorker*. May 24:90.

———. 1994. *Strange Justice: The Selling of Clarence Thomas*. New York: Houghton Mifflin.

Mayne, Judith. 1984. "The Woman at the Keyhole: Women's Cinema and Feminist Film Criticism." In *Re-Vision: Essays in Feminist Film Criticism*, edited by Mary Ann Doane, Patricia Mellencamp, and Linda Williams. Frederick, Md.: University Publications of America.

Mays, Kimberly. 1993. Interview by Barbara Walters (1993a), July 27.

Mays, Robert. 1993. Interview by Barbara Walters (1993a), July 27.

McClary, Susan. 1991. *Feminine Endings: Music, Gender and Sexuality*. Minneapolis: University of Minnesota Press.

McCluskey, Martha T. 1992. "Privileged Violence, Principled Fantasy, and Feminist Method: The Colby Fraternity Case." *Maine Law Review*. 44:261.

———. 1994. "Transforming Victimization." *Tikkun*. March/April:54.

———. 1997. "Fear of Feminism: Media Stories of Feminist Victims and Victims of Feminism on College Campuses." In Fineman and McCluskey, eds.

McCracken, Ellen. 1993. *Decoding Women's Magazines: From Mademoiselle to Ms*. New York: St. Martin's Press.

McKay, Shona. 1983. "A Media Judgment on Surrogate Birth." *Maclean's*. February 14:41.

McMahon, Colin, and Susan Kuczka. 1994. "19 Kids Found in Filth." *Chicago Tribune*. February 2:1.

"Medical Flash!" 1995. *Self*. January:65.

Messner, Michael A., Margaret Carlisle Duncan, and Kerry Jensen. 1993. "Separating the Men from the Girls: The Gendered Language of Televised Sports." *Gender & Society*. 7:121.

Miller, Abraham H. 1990. "Radicalism in Power: The Kafkaesque World of American Higher Education." *The Heritage Lectures*. Heritage Foundation Reports, 13 June.

Miller, Susan. 1993. "Opportunity Squandered—Newspaper's and Women's News." *Media Studies Journal*. 7:167.

Mills, Bart. 1993. "Networks Quell Violence to Explore Family Issues." *Chicago Tribune*. October 10:C3.

Mills, Karen. 1985. "'I Had My Sister's Baby.'" *Ladies' Home Journal*. October:20.

Mills, Kay. 1993. "The Media and the Year of the Woman." *Media Studies Journal*. 7:18.

Mingay, Jane. 1982. "The Furor over Surrogate Motherhood." *Maclean's*. July 5:18.

Minnesota Advisory Committee to the United States Commission on Civil Rights. 1993. *Stereotyping of Minorities by the News Media in Minnesota*. Washington: The United States Commission on Civil Rights.

Minow, Martha. 1988. "Feminist Reason: Getting It and Losing It." *Journal of Legal Education*. 38:47.

———. 1990. *Making All the Difference: Inclusion, Exclusion and American Law*. Ithaca: Cornell University Press.

Mirabella, Grace. 1993a. "A Few Good Minds: The Mirabella Health Symposium." *Mirabella*. August:63.

———. 1993b. "Hillary on Health: From Her Lips to Your Ears." *Mirabella*. August:62.

Mississippi Burning. 1988. Directed by Alan Parker. The Mississippi Company and Orion Pictures.

Mnookin, Robert. 1973. "In Whose Best Interest?" *Harvard Educational Review*. 43:599.

Modleski, Tania. 1982. *Loving with a Vengeance: Mass-Produced Fantasies for Women*. Hamden, Conn.: Archon Books.

Molotch, Harvey L. 1978. "The News of Women

and the Work of Men." In Tuchman, Daniels, and Benet, eds.

Monson, Nancy. 1993. "The Update on Fibroid Tumors: New Treatments Can Preserve a Woman's Fertility." *Glamour*. November:68.

Montgomery, Peter. 1988. "Should Surrogate Motherhood Be Banned?" *Common Cause Magazine*. May/June:36.

Morris, Monica B. 1973. "Newspapers and the New Feminists: Blackout as Social Control." *Journalism Quarterly*. 50:37.

Morrison, Patt. 1992. "Time for a Feminist as First Lady?" *Los Angeles Times*. July 14:A1.

Morrison, Toni. 1992a. *Playing in the Dark: Whiteness and the Literary Imagination*. Cambridge: Harvard University Press.

———, ed. 1992b. *Race-ing Justice, En-gendering Power: Essays on Anita Hill, Clarence Thomas, and the Construction of Social Reality*. New York: Pantheon.

Morrow, Lance. 1994. "Men; Are They Really That Bad?" *Time*. February 14:52.

Mukerji, Chandra, and Michael Schudson, eds. 1991. *Rethinking Popular Culture: Contemporary Perspectives in Cultural Studies*. Berkeley: University of California Press.

Murphy, Julie. 1984. "Egg Farms." In *Test-Tube Women: What Future for Motherhood*, edited by Rita Arditti, Renate Dueilli Klein, and Shelley Minden. London: Pandora Press.

Murphy, Sean P. 1988. "2 Women from Mass. Slain in Caribbean." *Boston Globe*. December 1:1.

Murray, Charles. 1984. *Losing Ground: American Social Policy 1950–1980*. New York: Basic Books.

———. 1988. *In Pursuit of Happiness and Good Government*. New York: Simon & Schuster.

———. 1993. "The Coming White Underclass." *Wall Street Journal*. October 29:A14.

Music Box. 1990. Directed by Constantin Costa-Gavras. Tri-Star Pictures.

Mydans, Seth. 1992a. "Riots in Los Angeles: Overview." Quoting James N. *New York Times*. Late edition. May 1:A1.

———. 1992b. "Separateness Grows in a Scarred Los Angeles." *New York Times*. November 15:A1.

Neff, David. 1987. "How Not to Have a Baby: Surrogate Mothers May Create a New Class of Breeder Women and Further Confuse the Family Unity." *Christianity Today*. April 3:14.

Nelson, Cary, and Lawrence Grossberg, eds. 1988. *Marxism and the Interpretation of Culture*. Urbana: University of Illinois Press.

Nelson, Jill. 1994. "Doing Time: Our Women in Prison." *Essence*. May:83.

Nelson, Vendnita. 1993. "Prostitution: When Racism and Gender Intersect." *Michigan Journal of Gender & Law*, 1:81.

Nestle, Joan. 1987. "Lesbians and Prostitutes: An Historical Sisterhood." In *A Restricted Country*. Ithaca: Firebrand Books.

———, ed. 1992. *The Persistent Desire: A Femme-Butch Reader*. Boston: Alyson Publications.

Nethaway, Rowland. 1995. "Angry White Men, Enough Already!" *San Diego Union-Tribune*. January 2:B5.

Newcomb, Horace. 1991. "On the Dialogic Aspects of Mass Communication." In *Critical Perspectives on Media and Society*, edited by Robert Avery and David Easton. New York: Guilford Press.

Newcomb, Horace, and Paul Hirsch. 1987. "Television as a Cultural Forum." In *Television: The Critical View*, edited by Horace Newcomb. New York: Oxford University Press.

Nixon, Agnes. 1994. Personal interview with author Dianne Brooks, August 21.

Noble, Barbara Presley. 1993. "At Lunch with Katie and Anne Roiphe: One Daughter's Rebellion or Her Mother's Imprint?" *New York Times*. November 10:C1.

Nochimson, Martha. 1992. *No End to Her: Soap Opera and the Female Subject*. Berkeley: University of California.

"No Grounds to Reject This Nominee." 1993. Editorial. *Chicago Tribune*. May 27:30.

Nyhan, David. 1994. "Hello Rush, I'm a He-Man, and I've Had It!" *Boston Globe*. November 9:19.

O'Connor, John E. 1980. *The Hollywood Indian: Stereotypes of Native Americans in Films*. Trenton: New Jersey State Museum.

Olsen, Frances. 1984. "Statutory Rape: A Feminist Critique of Rights Analysis." *Texas Law Review*. 63:387.

Omi, Michael, and Howard Winant. 1994. *Racial Formation in the United States: From the 1960s to the 1990s*. New York: Routledge.

Omodale, Barbara. 1983. "Hearts of Darkness." In Snitow, Stansell, and Thompson, eds.

Ong, Walter. 1977. "I See What You Say: Sense Analogues for the Intellect." In *Interfaces of the Word: Studies in the Evolution of Consciousness and Culture*. Ithaca: Cornell University Press.

O'Reilly, Jane. 1993. "The Lost Girls." *Mirabella*. April:116.

———. 1994. "The Pale Males of Punditry." *Media Studies Journal*. 7:125.

Orlov, Rick. 1992. "Vexed Bradley Asks City Residents to Voice Anger with Restraint." *Daily News of Los Angeles*. April 30:N1.

Other People's Money. 1991. Directed by Norman Jewison. Yorktown Productions and Warner Brothers.

Otto, Jean. 1993. "A Matter of Opinion." *Media Studies Journal*. 7:157.

Page, Clarence. 1991. "New GOP Weapon: The 'Feminist' Threat." *Chicago Tribune*. October 30:C19.

Page, Shelley. 1991. "Look Beyond the Gloss of the Woman's Mag." *Ottawa Citizen*. December 29:D4.

Paglia, Camille. 1994a. Interview by Ben Wattenberg, November 4.

———. 1994b. *Vamps and Tramps*. New York: Random House.

Painter, Nell Irvin. 1992. "Hill, Thomas and the Use of Racial Stereotype." In Morrison, ed.

Papke, David R. 1990. "Discharge as Denouement: Appreciating the Storytelling of Appellate Opinions." *Journal of Legal Education*. 40:145.

Pasternak, Judith Mahoney, and Chris Seymour. 1994. "What the Simpson Case Really Means." *Tikkun*. September/October:25.

Patai, Daphne, and Noretta Koertge. 1994. *Professing Feminism: Cautionary Tales from the Strange World of Women's Studies*. New York: New Republic/Basic Books.

Pateman, Carole. 1988. *The Sexual Contract*. Stanford, CA: Stanford University Press.

Patterson, Neyrs. 1993. Interview by Pat Buchanan and Michael Kinsley, August 3.

Patterson, Orlando. 1991. "Race, Gender, and Liberal Fallacies." *New York Times*. October 20:E15.

Patterson, Sasha. 1994. "Sexual Harassment, the Media and the Message: Anita Hill and the Reasonable Woman." Paper presented at Law & Society Association Annual Meeting, Pheonix, AZ.

Patterson, Thomas E. 1980. *The Mass Media Election: How Americans Choose Their President*. New York: Praeger.

Pearl, Mike. 1991. Telephone interview with author Helen Benedict.

Peirce, Kate. 1990. "A Feminist Theoretical Perspective on the Socialization of Teenage Girls through *Seventeen* Magazine." *Sex Roles*. 23:491.

The Pelican Brief. 1993. Directed by Alan J. Pakula. Warner Brothers.

Pennington, Nancy, and Reid Hastie. 1991. "A Cognitive Theory of Juror Decision Making:

The Story Model." *Cardozo Law Review*. 13:519.

"People: . . . Anna Deveare Smith." 1994. *Essence*. August:40.

Peterson, Jonathan, and Hector Tobar. 1992. "South L.A. Burns and Grieves." *Los Angeles Times*. May 1:A1.

Peyser, Andrea. 1994. "We've Come a Long Way Baby!: Feminism Now!" *Cosmopolitan*. May:198.

Pharr, Suzanne. 1988. *Homophobia: A Weapon of Sexism*. Inverness, Calif.: Chardon Press.

Phelps, Timothy M., and Helen Winternitz. 1992. *Capitol Games*. New York: Hyperion.

Philadelphia. 1993. Directed by Jonathan Demme. Clinica Estetico and Tri-Star Pictures.

Phillips, Leslie. 1993. "President Rethinks Controversial Pick for Civil Rights Job." *USA Today*. June 3:4A.

Physical Evidence (Smoke). 1988. Directed by Michael Crichton. Columbia Pictures.

Picker, Lauren. 1993. "Stop Whining . . ." *Newsday*. October 31:46.

Pinkney, Andrea Davis. 1994. "Winning in the Workplace." *Essence*. March:79.

Pitt, David E. 1989. "Gang Attack: Unusual for Its Viciousness." *New York Times*. April 25:B1.

Pollitt, Katha. 1994a. "Not Just Bad Sex." In *Reasonable Creatures: Essays on Women and Feminism*. New York: Knopf. First published in the *New Yorker*, 1993, October 4:220.

———. 1994b. "Subject to Debate." *The Nation*. October 17:409.

Polochanin, David. 1994. "Scalded Boy Is Reported Faring Well in Foster Care." *Boston Globe*. October 2:33.

Porter, Philip W., and Norval Neil Luxon. 1935. *The Reporter and the News*. New York: D. Appleton-Century Company.

Porter, Roy. 1986. "Rape—Does It Have a Historical Meaning?" In *Rape*, edited by Sylvana Tomaselli and Roy Porter. New York: Blackwell.

Posner, Richard. 1993. Review of *Only Words*, by Catharine MacKinnon. *New Republic*. October 18:31.

Press, Andrea L. 1991. *Women Watching Television: Gender, Class, and Generation in the American Television Experience*. Philadelphia: University of Pennsylvania Press.

Presumed Innocent. 1990. Directed by Alan J. Pakula. Mirage and Warner Brothers.

"Psychiatrist Testifies in Black Surrogate Mom's Favor." 1990. *Jet Magazine*. October 29:9.

A Question of Silence. 1982. Directed by Marleen

Gorris and Conny Brak. Quartet Films Inc.

Quindlen, Anna. 1994. "And Now, Babe Feminism." *New York Times*. January 19:A21.

———. 1992. "The Two Faces of Eve." In her *Thinking Out Loud*. New York: Random House. First published in *New York Times*, 1992, July 15:A21.

———. 1993a. "The Real Anita Hill?" *New York Times*. April 24:E17.

———. 1993b. "Women as Change Makers: Building and Using Political Power." In *The Scholar and the Feminist*, edited by Barnard Conference Paper Series. New York: Barnard Center for Research on Women.

Quinn, Sally. 1992. "Feminists Have Killed Feminism." *Los Angeles Times*. January 23:B7.

Radway, Janice. 1984. *Reading the Romance: Women, Patriarchy, and Popular Literature*. Chapel Hill: University of North Carolina Press.

Raeburn, Paul. 1995. "The Female Condom: It's Now on Drug-Store Shelves. Is It Right for You?" *Glamour*. February:47.

Rafferty, Terrence. 1994. "The Current Cinema." Review of *The Client. New Yorker*. August 1:76.

Raine, George. 1992. "Verdict 'an Excuse to Burn, Break In.'" *San Francisco Examiner*. April 30:A1.

Raine, George, Tupper Hull, and Eric Brazil. 1992. "L.A. under Siege; Looters Hit Downtown Stores; Troops Deployed, Nine Dead, 192 Injured, 300 Fires Set; The Rodney King Case: The Aftermath." *San Francisco Examiner*. April 30:A1.

"Rape: The Crime That Won't Go Away." 1994. *New York Newsday*. April 19:1.

"Rapists Strike Every Three Hours." 1994. (New York) *Daily News*. May 19:4.

Rapping, Elayne. 1987. *The Looking Glass World of Nonfiction TV*. Boston: South End Press.

———. 1992. *The Movie of the Week: Private Stories/Public Events*. Minneapolis: University of Minnesota Press.

———. 1994a. "Gender and Media Theory: A Critique of the 'Backlash Model.'" *Journal of Social Philosophy*. 25 (June):7.

———. 1994b. *Media-tions: Forays into the Culture and Gender Wars*. Boston: South End Press.

———. 1994c. "Women Are from Venus, Men Are from Mars: Women's and Men's Periodicals." *The Progressive*. May:40.

"Reactions to the Rodney King Case: The Aftermath." 1992. *San Francisco Examiner*. April 30:A16.

Reed, Christopher. 1993. "Custody Battle Rivets Americans." *The Gazette* (Montreal). August 4:A7.

Reed, Nicki. 1993. "Radio Show Host Announces Baby's up for Adoption." Interview by Bob Edwards. National Public Radio, September 9.

Reese, Stephen P. 1990. "The News Paradigm and the Ideology of Objectivity." *Critical Studies in Mass Communication*. 7:390.

Reeves, Jimmie L., and Richard Campbell. 1994. *Cracked Coverage: Television News, the Anti-Cocaine Crusade, and the Reagan Legacy*. Durham, N.C.: Duke University Press.

Reeves, Phil. 1992. "Riots in America: Divided Community Settles Old Scores." Quoting Rodney Walker. *The Independent*. May 2:2.

Reid, Alexander, Ray Richard, Peggy Hernandez, and Phyllis Coons. 1991. "Cambridge Police Have a Knife, No Motive in Professor's Murder." *Boston Globe*. April 6:1.

Reidy, Chris. 1993. "Learning the Rules; Taking Date Rape 101 Still Doesn't Mean Men Know the Boundaries." *Boston Globe*. September 26:74.

Reiner, Ira. 1992. *Gangs, Crime and Violence in Los Angeles: Findings and Proposals from the District Attorney's Office*. Los Angeles: Office of the District Attorney, County of Los Angeles.

Report of the Majority Staff of the Senate Judiciary Committee. 1993. "The Response to Rape: Detours on the Road to Equal Justice." In *Transforming a Rape Culture*, edited by Emilie Buchwald, Pamela R. Fletcher, and Martha Roth. Minneapolis: Milkweed Editions.

Rhode, Deborah L. 1983. "Equal Rights in Retrospect." *Law and Inequality Journal*. 1:1.

———. 1989. *Justice and Gender: Sex Discrimination and the Law*. Cambridge: Harvard University Press.

———. 1991. "The 'No-Problem' Problem: Feminist Challenges and Cultural Change." *Yale Law Journal*. 100:1731.

———. 1994. "Feminism and the State." *Harvard Law Review*. 107:1181.

———. 1997. *Speaking of Sex*. Cambridge: Harvard University Press.

Rich, Frank. 1994. "Brock's Strange Journalism." *New York Times*. December 29:A21.

Richards, Louise. 1989. "Giving the Gift of Life." *Ladies' Home Journal*. February:22.

Richardson, Elaine. 1994. "Reading . . ." *Elle*. March:54.

Richardson, Herbert, ed. 1987. *On the Problem of Surrogate Parenthood*. Lewiston, N.Y.: Edwin Mellen Press (Symposium Series 25).

Rivers, Caryl. 1996. Slick Spins and Fractured Facts. New York: Columbia University Press.

Roan, Shari. 1992. "Negative Images? Twentysomethings Say Women's Magazines Can Erode Self-Esteem." Los Angeles Times. August 18:E1.

Roberts, Dorothy. 1991. "Punishing Drug Addicts Who Have Babies: Women of Color, Equality and the Right of Privacy." Harvard Law Review. 104:1419.

Roberts, Steven V. 1993. "America Is Not South Africa." U.S. News & World Report. June 14:20.

Roberts, Steven V., Ted Gest, and Thomas Toch. 1993. "Civil Rights after Guinier." U.S. News & World Report. June 14:45.

Roberts, Tara. 1994. "A Hip-Hop Nation Divided: Dilemma of a Womanist." Essence. August:62.

Robertson, Nan. 1992. The Girls in the Balcony: Women, Men and the New York Times. New York: Random House.

Robinson, Michael, and Margaret A. Sheehan. 1983. Over the Wire and on TV: CBS and UPI in Campaign 1980. New York: Russell Sage Foundation.

Roe v. Wade. 1987. Directed by Hoblit Gregory. Manheim Company and NBC Productions. NBC, May 15.

Rogovin, Wendy M. 1992. "The Regulation of Television in the Public Interest: On Creating a Parallel Universe in Which Minorities Speak and Are Heard." Catholic University Law Review. 42:51.

Rohlena, Jody, ed. 1993. Sounds Like a New Woman. New York: Penguin.

Roiphe, Anne. 1993. "Fear and Feminism: Katie Roiphe Thinks College Women Cry Date Rape Too Often." Mirabella. August:54.

Roiphe, Katie. 1991. "Date Rape Hysteria." New York Times. November 20:A27.

———. 1993a. "Date Rape's Other Victim." New York Times Magazine. June 13:26.

———. 1993b. The Morning After: Sex, Fear, and Feminism on Campus. Boston: Little, Brown.

———. 1993c. "All the Rage." New York Times. November 29:A17.

Romano, Carlin. 1986. "The Grisly Truth about the Bare Facts." In Manoff and Schudson, eds.

———. 1993. Review of Only Words, by Catharine MacKinnon. The Nation. November 15:563.

———. 1994. "Feminism in the Fray: A Break with the Old Guard Renews Debate." Pittsburgh Post-Gazette. August 7:L1.

Ronell, Avital. 1992. "Video/Television/Rodney King: Twelve Steps beyond The Pleasure Princi-

ple." Differences: A Journal of Feminist Cultural Studies. 4 (Summer):1.

Rose, Charlie. 1994. Charlie Rose, transcript #1022. WNET Educational Broadcasting Co., January 3.

Rosenthal, Phil. 1992. "Case Began on Camera, Violence Kept It There." Daily News of Los Angeles. April 30:N14.

Roshco, Bernard. 1975. Newsmaking. Chicago: University of Chicago Press.

Roshier, Bob. 1973. "The Selection of Crime News by the Press." In The Manufacture of News: Social Problems, Deviance, and the Mass Media, edited by Stanley Cohen and Jock Young. Beverly Hills, Calif.: Sage.

Ross, Andrew. 1992. "The Private Parts of Justice." In Morrison, ed.

Ross, Ishbel. 1974. Ladies of the Press. New York: Harper Press.

Ross, Susan Deller. 1992. "Proving Sexual Harassment: The Hurdles." Southern California Law Review. 65:1451.

Rubin, Gayle. 1984. "Thinking Sex: Notes for a Radical Theory of the Politics of Sexuality." In Pleasure and Danger: Exploring Female Sexuality, edited by Carole Vance. Boston: Routledge and Kegan Paul.

Russell, Diana E. H. 1984. Sexual Exploitation: Rape, Child Sexual Abuse, and Workplace Harassment. Beverly Hills, Calif.: Sage.

Russell, Margaret M. 1991. "Race and the Dominant Gaze: Narratives of Law and Inequality in Popular Film." Legal Studies Forum. 15:243.

———. 1996. "Rewriting History with Lightning: Race, Myth and Hollywood in the Legal Pantheon." In Denvir. ed.

Russo, Ann. 1990. "Feminist Thoughts on the Stuart Case." Sojourner. February:16.

———. 1991. "If Not Now, When: Fighting Violence against Women." Part 1. Sojourner. November:7.

———. 1992. "Loving Dangerously." Review of Hate Crimes: Violence against Lesbians and Gay Men, edited by Gregory Herek and Kevin Berrill. Women's Review of Books. October:21.

———. 1992a. "A Battered Lesbian Fights for Recognition." Sojourner 17:9 May:14, 16–17.

———. 1997. "Lesbians, Prostitutes, and Murder: Media Constructs Violence Constructs Power." In Fineman and McCluskey, eds.

Rutledge, Bruce. 1991. "Women Lawyers: A Status Report." Barrister Magazine. Fall:31.

Rutten, Tim. 1992. "Since When Did Working Women Become the Enemy?" Los Angeles Times. August 27:E1.

Ryan, Jon. 1993. Interview by Frank Sesno, July 8.

Sackett, Victoria. 1984. "Color Me Political: Changing Fashions in Women's Magazines." *Public Opinion*. August/September:47.

Safire, William. 1992. "Politics Is Showcasing the New Woman." *San Francisco Chronicle*. January 28:17.

Salholz, Eloise. 1993. "The Power and the Pride." *Newsweek*. June 21:54.

Salholz, Eloise, Renee Michael, Mark Starr, Shawn Doherty, Pamela Abramson, and Pat Wingert. 1986. "Too Late for Prince Charming?" *Newsweek*. June 2:54.

Sanders, Marlene. 1994. "Fashion Mags' Model Women: The Young, The Thin and The White." (New York) *Daily News*. December 23. Copy of article on file with author Julia Hanigsberg.

Sarat, Austin, and Thomas Kearns, eds. 1991. *The Fate of Law*. Ann Arbor: University of Michigan Press.

Savage, David. 1993a. "Paper Trail Could Block Nominee for Justice Post." *Los Angeles Times*. May 22:A1.

———. 1993b. Telephone interview with author Laurel Leff, July.

Scheppele, Kim Lane. 1992. "Just the Facts, Ma'am: Sexualized Violence, Evidentiary Habits, and the Revision of Truth." *New York Law School Law Review*. 37:123.

Schillinger, Liesl. 1994. "The Woman Who Made Harvard Blink." *Glamour*. February:68.

Schlafly, Phyllis. 1994. "Radical Feminists Undercutting Women's Support of President." *Houston Post*. October 26:A33.

Schlesinger, Philip, R. Emerson Dobash, Russell P. Dobash, and C. Kay Weaver. 1992. *Women Viewing Violence*. London: British Film Institute.

Schlosberg, Jeremy. 1992. "Reader Reigns: Reader's Magazines." *Mediaweek*. April 6:17.

Schmidt, Dan. 1993. Interview by Frank Sesno, July 8.

Schneider, Elizabeth M. 1986. "Describing and Changing: Women's Self-Defense Work and the Problem of Expert Testimony on Battering." *Women's Rights Law Reporter*. 9:195.

Scholder, Amy, ed. 1993. *Critical Condition: Women on the Edge of Violence*. San Francisco: City Lights Books.

Scholes, Robert E. 1989. *Protocols of Reading*. New Haven: Yale University Press.

School Daze. 1988. Directed by Spike Lee. Forty Acres and a Mule Filmworks, School Daze Productions, and Columbia Pictures.

Schudson, Michael. 1977. "Origins of the Ideal of Objectivity in the Professions: Studies in the History of American Journalism and American Law 1830–1940." Ph.D. diss., Harvard University.

———. 1978. *Discovering the News*. New York: Basic Books.

———. 1986. "Deadlines, Datelines and History." In Manoff and Schudson, eds.

Schwartz, Karin. 1992. "Lesbian Invisibility in the Media." Fairness and Accuracy in the Media, *Extra!* Special Issue:20.

"Scotland Yard Helps Probe 2 Watertown Women's Deaths." 1988. *Boston Globe*. December 3:30.

Seader, Mary Beth. 1993. Interview by Barbara Walters (1993b), August 3.

Sedgwick, Eve Kosofsky. 1990. *Epistemology of the Closet*. Berkeley: University of California Press.

Sedgwick, John. 1995. "America Is Fat!" *Self*. January:82.

"See, Rush Told You So." 1993. *Economist*. November 6:28 (American edition).

The Seeger Family. 1993. Interview by Phil Donahue. "My Mother Is My Sister, and Dad Is My Grandpa." *The Phil Donahue Show*, show #3830. NBC, October 4.

Sengupta, Somini. 1992. "Incentives to Close Liquor Stores Sought." *Los Angeles Times*. October 15:B1.

Sennett, Richard, and Jonathan Cobb. 1972. *The Hidden Injuries of Class*. New York: Knopf.

Sennott, Charles M. 1994a. "Abuse Case Stirs Alarm; Mother Arraigned; Private Agency Faces Questions." *Boston Globe*. February 15:1.

———. 1994b. "Kin Say Boy's Burn Accident; Insist Child Plunged His Hands into Mix of Hot Water, Drano." *Boston Globe*. February 17:15.

———. 1994c. "Finding 4 Generations Sustained by Welfare; Family of Abuse Suspect Has Dozens on Public Aid." *Boston Globe*. February 20:1.

———. 1994d. "Welfare Program under Fire; Critics Say SSI Troubled by Fraud." *Boston Globe*. February 24:1.

———. 1994e. "Abuse Charge Follows Fugitive to Caribbean; Claribel Ventura Can't Escape Scorn of Dominicans." *Boston Globe*. August 29:1.

Sennott, Charles M., and Michael Grunwald. 1994. "Abuse Suspect Fought Drugs, Other Woes." *Boston Globe*. February 16:1.

"Sentence Ends in Question." 1992. Editorial. *Los Angeles Times*. January 28:B6.

Sesno, Frank. 1993. *Larry King Live,* transcript #866. CNN, July 8.

"Sex and the Super-Groupie." 1971. *Time.* April 12:75.

"The Sexual-Harassment Controversy. Should a Woman Who Sues Have to Prove 'Severe' Psychological Damages? The Supreme Court Will Soon Decide." 1994. Editorial. *Glamour.* November:112.

Shales, Tom. 1993. "The DeBoers' War: Baby Jessica—An Emotional View of an Unfeeling System." *Washington Post.* September 25:B1.

Shankman, Arnold. 1978. "Black on Yellow: Afro-Americans View Chinese Americans, 1850–1935." *Phylon.* 39:1.

Sharpe, Rochelle. 1993. "Losing Ground: In Latest Recession Only Blacks Suffered Net Employment Loss." *Wall Street Journal.* September 14:A1.

Shaw, Donald L. 1967. "New Bias and the Telegraph: A Study of Historical Change." *Journalism Quarterly.* 44 (Spring):3.

Sherizen, Sanford. 1978. "Social Creation of Crime News: All the News Fitted to Print." In *Deviance and Mass Media,* edited by Charles Winick. Newbury Park, Calif.: Sage.

Sherven, Judith, and James Sniechowski. 1994. "Women Are Responsible, Too." *Los Angeles Times.* June 21:B7.

She's Gotta Have It. 1986. Directed by Spike Lee. Forty Acres and a Mule Filmworks and Island Pictures.

Shrieves, Linda. 1993. "The Bold New World of Boy Chasing." *Orlando Sentinel.* December 22:E1.

Sigal, Leon V. 1973. *Reporters and Officials.* Lexington, Mass.: D. C. Heath.

———. 1986. "Sources Make the News." In Manoff and Schudson, eds.

Silk, Catharine, and John Silk. 1990. *Racism and Anti-Racism in American Popular Culture.* Manchester, Can.: Manchester University Press.

Silverman, Kaja. 1986. "Suture." In *Narrative, Apparatus, Ideology: A Film Theory Reader,* edited by Philip Rosen. New York: Columbia University Press.

Simon, Rita J., and Cathy Young. 1994. "Men Too Are the Victims of Domestic Violence." Letter to the Editor. *New York Times.* February 4:A22.

Singer, Joseph. 1984. "The Player and the Cards: Nihilism and Legal Theory." *Yale Law Journal.* 94:1.

Sisco, Elizabeth. 1993. "Forum I: Women Who Kill." In Scholder, ed.

Skrapec, Candice. 1994. "The Female Serial Killer: An Evolving Criminality." In Birch, ed.

Sloan, Louise. 1994. "Do Ask Do Tell: Lesbians Come Out at Work." *Glamour.* May:242.

Smart, Carol. 1989. *Feminism and the Power of the Law.* New York: Routledge.

Smith, Carlton, and Tomas Guillen. 1991. *The Search for the Green River Killer.* New York: Onyx.

Smith, Dolly. 1991. "Cambridge Meeting Addresses Street Crime." *Boston Globe.* April 19:68.

Smith, Estelle Lander, and Paul Horwitz. 1993. "Parenthood Cases Stretch Old Notions." *Newsday.* August 5:29.

Smith, Tom, National Opinion Research Center. 1994. Personal communication with authors Kathleen Daly and Amy L. Chasteen.

Smolowe, Jill. 1993. "Sex with a Scorecard." *Time.* April 5:41.

Smothers, Ronald. 1991. "Woman Is Arrested in a Series of Killings in Florida." *New York Times.* January 18:A16.

Snitow, Anne, Christine Stansell, and Sharon Thompson. 1983a. Introduction. In Snitow, Stansell, and Thompson, eds.

———, eds. 1983b. *Powers of Desire: The Politics of Sexuality.* New York: Monthly Review Press.

Sobchack, Vivian. 1990. "Toward a Phenomenology of Cinematic and Electronic Presence: The Scene of the Screen." *Postscript.* 10:50

———. 1991. "Child/Alien/Father: Patriarchal Crisis and Generic Exchange." In *Close Encounters: Film, Feminism, and Science Fiction,* edited by Constance Penley, Lynn Speigel, and Janet Bergstrom. Minnesota: University of Minnesota Press.

"So Little Leadership." 1994. Editorial. *New York Times.* April 21:A17.

Sommers, Christina Hoff. 1991. "Hardline Feminists Guilty of Ms.-Representation." *Wall Street Journal.* November 7:A14.

———. 1994a. *Who Stole Feminism?: How Women Have Betrayed Women.* New York: Simon & Schuster.

———. 1994b. Interview by Pat Buchanan and Michael Kinsley. *Crossfire,* transcript #1127. CNN, July 4.

———. 1994c. Interview by Ben Wattenberg, November 4.

Soul Man. 1986. Directed by Stephen Miner. Balcor Film Investors and New World.

Sowell, Thomas. 1993a. "New Book Challenges the Image of Anita Hill as a Shy, Demure Victim." *Atlanta Journal and Constitution.* April 16:A10.

————. 1993b. "'Politically Correct' Anointed Don't Want to Be Confused by the Facts." *Atlanta Journal and Constitution.* April 20:A12.

Sparks, Richard. 1992. *Television and the Drama of Crime: Moral Tales and the Place of Crime in Public Life.* Philadelphia: Open University Press.

"Special Issue, 1994 in Review." 1995. *Juice* (Australia). January:95.

Spigel, Lynn. 1992. "The Suburban Home Companion: Television and the Neighborhood Ideal in Postwar America." In *Sexuality and Space,* edited by Beatriz Colomina. New York: Princeton Architectural Press.

Spigel, Lynn, and Denise Mann, eds. 1992. *Private Screenings: Television and the Female Consumer.* Minneapolis: University of Minnesota Press.

"Spring is the Season to Be Most Fearful." 1994. *The Daily News.*

Stanko, Elizabeth A. 1985. *Intimate Intrusions: Women's Experience of Male Violence.* Boston: Routledge and Kegan Paul.

————. 1987. "Typical Violence, Normal Precaution: Men, Women, and Interpersonal Violence in England, Wales, Scotland, and the USA." In Hanmer and Maynard, eds.

————. 1990. *Everyday Violence: How Women and Men Experience Sexual and Physical Danger.* London: Pandora Press.

————. Forthcoming. "Warnings to Women: Police Discourse and Women's Safety." In *Police Discourse,* edited by Andrew Goldsmith.

Stanworth, Michelle. 1990. "Birth Pangs: Conceptive Technologies and the Threat to Motherhood." In Hirsch and Keller, eds.

""Statement of WHISPER Action Group Members." 1992. *WHISPER VI.* (Winter/Spring) :3.

Steinem, Gloria. 1992. *Revolution from Within: A Book of Self-Esteem.* Boston: Little, Brown.

————. 1994. "Sex, Lies and Advertising." In *Moving beyond Words.* New York: Simon & Schuster.

Stern, Ellen. 1993. "1993 Women of the Year." *Glamour.* December:102.

Sternhell, Carol. 1994. "The Proper Study of Womankind." *Women's Review of Books.* December:1.

Stoffman, Judy. 1994. "The Charming Camille Paglia: Not the Amazon Her Work Leads You to Expect." *Toronto Star.* November 8:B6.

Stone, Judith. 1993. "The Good News about Women and Aging." *Glamour.* November:174.

Stone, Keith, and Rick Orlov. 1992. "Rioters Set Fires, Loot—and Kill." *Daily News of Los Angeles.* April 30:N1.

Straayer, Chris. 1992. "The She-Man: Postmodern Bi-Sexed Performance in Film and Video." In *Classical Hollywood Narrative: The Paradigm Wars,* edited by Jane Gaines. Durham, N.C.: Duke University Press.

Straight out of Brooklyn. 1991. Directed by Matty Rich. Blacks N' Progress and Samuel Goldwyn Company.

Streitfeld, David. 1994. "Writers of the Right." *Washington Post.* December 20:B1.

Sturz, James. 1993. "Abortion, Adoption or a Baby." *Glamour.* November:232.

Suggs, Donald. 1992. "Did the Media Exploit the 'Lesbian Serial Killer Story?'" *Advocate.* March 10:98.

Sullivan, Barbara. 1993. "The Victim Trap." *Chicago Tribune.* October 14:1.

Sullivan, Deborah. 1994. "Date Rape Allegation Ignites a Furor at Pomona College." *Los Angeles Times.* May 21:B1.

Sullivan, Kathleen M. 1993. "The Hill Thomas Mystery." *New York Review of Books.* August 12:12.

Surette, Ray. 1992. *Media, Crime, and Criminal Justice.* Pacific Grove, Calif.: Brooks/Cole.

————. 1994. "Predatory Criminals as Media Icons." In Barak, ed.

"Surrogate Mother Sues for Baby's Custody." 1990. *New York Times.* August 15:A22.

Survey Question Changed, F.B.I. Doubles Its Estimates of Rape

Suspect. 1987. Directed by Peter Yates. Tri-Star Pictures.

Swan, Susan. 1993. "Woman on the Verge: Kim Campbell Is a Conservative Who Disrobed for the Camera, a Feminist Who Voted to Recriminalize Abortion. And She's Canada's New Prime Minster, for Now." *Mirabella.* August: 70.

Tackett, Michael, and Linda Campbell. 1993. "Clinton Expected to Withdraw Controversial Civil Rights Choice." *Chicago Tribune.* June 3:10.

Takaki, Ronald T. 1979. *Iron Cages: Race and Culture in Nineteenth-Centure America.* New York: Knopf.

————. 1989. *Strangers from a Different Shore: A History of Asian Americans.* Boston: Little, Brown.

Tannen, Deborah. 1994. "The Triumph of the Yell." Editorial. *New York Times.* January 14:A29.

Tavris, Carol. 1993. "Viewpoint: Do You Menstruate? If So, Psychiatrists Think You Might Be Nuts." *Glamour*. November:172.

Taylor, Jill, and Deborah L. Tolman. 1992. "Relational Contours of Race and Racism: Voices in Research Relationships between White Women and Adolescent Girls of Color." Paper presented at the Jean Piaget Society, Montreal, Canada.

Taylor, Stuart, Jr. 1993a. "DOJ Nominee's 'Authentic' Black Views." *Legal Times*. May 17:23.

———. 1993b. Telephone interview with author Laurel Leff, July.

Terry, Don. 1993. "In the Week of an Infamous Rape, 28 Other Victims Suffer." In *Gender and Public Policy*, edited by Kenneth Winston and Mary Jo Bane. Boulder, Colo.: Westview Press. First published in *New York Times*, 1989, "Week of Rapes: The Jogger and 28 Not in the News." May 29:A25.

Thelma and Louise. 1991. Directed by Ridley Scott. MGM-Pathe and Percy Mann Productions.

"Think of the Real O. J. Simpson." 1994. Editorial. *San Francisco Examiner*. June 24:A23.

Thom, Mary. 1988. "Dilemmas of the New Birth Techologies." *Ms*. May:70.

———. 1993. "The Personal Is Political—Publishable Too." *Media Studies Journal*. 7:223.

Thomas, Cal. 1993. "Clarence Thomas Sees the Light of Vindication." *San Jose Mercury News*. April 18:3C.

Thompson, Anne. 1994. "A Much Better Year for Women in the Movies." *Glamour*. January:97.

Thompson, Olya. 1993. "Motherhood Myopia: Blowing the DeBoer Story." *New York Newsday*. August 11:85.

Tillotson, Mary. 1994. *CNN & Company*, transcript #479. CNN, December 1.

"Time, Property Rights, and the Common Law." 1986. Symposium. *Washington University Law Quarterly*. 64:661.

Todorov, Tzvetan. 1984. *Mikhail Bakhtin: The Dialogical Principle*. Translated by Wlad Godzich. Minneapolis: University of Minnesota Press.

To Kill a Mockingbird. 1962. Directed by Robert Mulligan. Universal.

Tolman, Deborah L. 1994a. "Daring to Desire: Culture and the Bodies of Adolescent Girls." In *Sexual Cultures: Adolescents, Communities and the Construction of Identity*, edited by Janice Irvine. Philadelphia: Temple University Press.

———. 1994b. "Doing Desire: Adolescent Girls' Struggle for/with Sexuality." *Gender & Society*. 8:324.

———. Forthcoming. "Adolescent Girls' Sexuality: Debunking the Myth of the Urban Girl." In *Urban Adolescent Girls: Resisting Stereotypes*, edited by B. Leadbetter and N. Way. New York: New York University Press.

Toner, Robin. 1992. "Los Angeles Riots Are Warning, Americans Fear." *New York Times*. May 11:A1.

Tuchman, Gaye. 1972. "Objectivity as Strategic Ritual: An Examination of Newsmen's Notions of Objectivity." *American Journal of Sociology*. 77:660.

———. 1978a. "Introduction: The Symbolic Annihilation of Women by the Mass Media." In Tuchman, Daniels, and Benet, eds.

———. 1978b. *Making News: A Study in the Construction of Reality*. New York: Free Press.

Tuchman, Gaye, Arlene Kaplan Daniels, and James Benet. 1978. *Hearth and Home: Images of Women in the Mass Media*. New York: Oxford University Press.

Turim, Maureen. 1991. "Viewing/Reading *Born to Be Sold: Martha Rosler Reads the Strange Case of Baby S/M* or Motherhood in the Age of Mechanical Reproduction." *Discourse*. 13:2.

Turner, Victor W. 1969. *The Ritual Process*. Chicago: Aldine.

Twelve Angry Men. 1957. Directed by Sidney Lumet. United Artists.

Twigg, Regina. 1993. Interview by Barbara Walters (1993a), July 27.

Tyre, Peg, and Michele Parente. 1994. "Rape: Still a Secret Crime; Crime Figures Show Rise, But How Many Unreported?" *Newsday*. April 19:A5.

Tyrrell, R. Emmett, Jr. 1993. "Anita Hill Mystique Unraveled." *Washington Times*. April 18:B3.

United States Department of Justice. 1994. *Violence against Women: A National Crime Victimization Survey Report*. Washington: National Criminal Justice Reference Service.

United States Senate Committee on the Judiciary. 1991. *Nomination of Clarence Thomas to Be an Associate Justice of the Supreme Court*. Hearings before the Committee on the Judiciary, 102d Congress, 1st session, October 11–13.

Vance, Carol. 1992. "More Danger, More Pleasure: A Decade after the Barnard Sexuality Conference. Introduction to *Pleasure and Danger: Exploring Female Sexuality*. 2d ed. Edited by Carol Vance. London: Pandora Press.

Vance, Carol, and Anne Barr Snitow. 1984. "Toward a Conversation about Sex in Feminism: A Modest Proposal." *Signs*. 10:126.

Vaznis, James. 1994a. "Six Children Found Living in Filth, Mother Faces Charges." Replate edition. *Boston Globe*. February 13:30.

———. 1994b. "Roxbury Neglect Shakes Officers; Boy's Hands Burned Almost 'to the Bone.'" *Boston Globe*. February 14:17.

The Verdict. 1982. Directed by Sidney Lumet. Twentieth-Century Fox.

Victor, Richard. 1993. Interview by Pat Buchanan and Michael Kinsley. *Crossfire*, August 3.

Von Drehle, David. 1993. "Lani, We Hardly Knew Ye." *Washington Post*. June 4:C1.

von Schulthess, Beatrice. 1992. "Violence in the Streets: Anti-Lesbian Assault and Harassment in San Francisco." In Herek and Berrill, eds.

Waiting to Exhale. 1995. Directed by Forest Whitaker.

Wallace, Amy, and David Ferrell. 1992. "Verdicts Greeted with Outrage and Disbelief." *Los Angeles Times*. April 30:A1.

Wallis, Claudia. 1989. "Onward, Women!" *Time*. December 4:80.

Walsh, Kenneth T. 1993. "Now the First Chief Advocate." *U.S. News & World Report*. January 25:46.

Walt, Vivienne. 1994. "Women of the World— South Africa's Women Heroes and Warriors." *Marie Claire*. September/October:84.

Walters, Barbara. 1993a. "Switched at Birth: Kimberly's Story." *Turning Point*. ABC, July 27.

———. 1993b. "Adoption Law after the Baby Jessica Case." *Nightline*. ABC, August 3.

Ward, Jean. 1993. "Talking (Fairly) about the World—A Reprise on Journalistic Language." *Media Studies Journal*. 7:183.

Warr, Mark. 1985. "Fear of Rape among Urban Women." *Social Problems*. 32:238.

———. 1991. "America's Perceptions of Crime and Punishment." In *Criminology*, edited by Joseph Sheley. Belmont, Calif.: Wadsworth.

Warren, Carl. 1959. *Modern New Reporting*, 3rd ed. New York: Harper Brothers Publishers.

Warren, James. 1993. "Women's Chronicler: Ruth Whitney Keeps Glamour Unfashionably Ahead of the Competition." *Chicago Tribune*. December 5:C2.

Wattenberg, Ben. 1994. *Think Tank with Ben Wattenberg*. Federal News Service, November 4.

Watts, Jerry G. 1993. "Reflections on the Rodney King Verdict and the Paradoxes of the Black Response." In Gooding-Williams, ed.

Weaver, Paul H. 1994. *News and the Culture of Lying: How Journalism Really Works*. New York: Free Press.

Weber, David. 1994. "Mom Misses Court Date." *Boston Herald*. April 9:5.

"Welfare Gone Wrong." 1994. Headline. *Boston Herald*. February 15:1.

West, Cornel. 1993. "Learning to Talk of Race." In Gooding-Williams, ed.

West, Rachel. 1988. "U.S. Prostitutes Collective." In *Sex Work: Writings by Women in the Sex Industry*, edited by Frédérique Delacoste and Priscilla Alexander. San Francisco: Cleis Press.

West, Robin L. 1993. *Narrative, Authority, and Law*. Ann Arbor: University of Michigan Press.

"Westside Neighbors Plan for Gay Center." 1995. *Los Angeles Times*. July 22:B1.

"When It Comes to the New Health-Care System, We Can Help Congress Keep Women's Priorities in Mind." 1994. Editorial. *Glamour*. February:74.

What's Love Got to Do with It? 1993. Directed by Brian Gibson. Touchstone Pictures.

White, Lucie E. 1990. "Subordination, Rhetorical Survival Skills and Sunday Shoes: Notes on the Hearing of Mrs. G." *Buffalo Law Review*. 38:1.

Whitehead, Mary Beth. 1989. *A Mother's Story*. With Loretta Schwartz-Nobel. New York: St. Martin's Press.

Whitesell, Christopher. 1994. Personal interview with author Dianne Brooks, January.

"Who's Come a Long Way, Baby?" 1970. *Time*. August 31:16.

Whose Child Is This: The War for Baby Jessica. 1993. Directed by John Kent Harrison. ABC Production. ABC, September 26.

Wilkins, David B. 1992. "Presumed Crazy: The Structure of Argument in the Hill-Thomas Hearings." *Southern California Law Review*. 65:1517.

Wilkinson, Signe. 1993. "The Case against Anita Hill." *New York Times Book Review*. May 23:11.

Will, George F. 1993a. "Anita Hill's Tangled Web." *Newsweek*. April 19:74.

———. 1993b. "Roiphe's Book Gives Some Feminists the Vapors." *Atlanta Constitution*. October 25:A10.

Williams, Brian. 1993. Report from *The Today Show*. NBC, August 3.

Williams, Carol Traynor. 1992. *"It's Time for my Story": Soap Opera Sources, Structure, and Response*. Westport, Conn.: Praeger.

Williams, Joan. 1991. "Gender Wars: Selfless Women in the Republic of Choice." *New York University Law Review*. 66:1559.

Williams, Michael. 1994. *NBC News*. NBC, March 9.

Williams, Patricia J. 1991. *The Alchemy of Race and Rights*. Cambridge: Harvard University Press.

———. 1994. "Hate Radio." *Ms*. March/April:25.

Williams, Raymond. 1974. *Television: Technology and*

Cultural Form. London: Fontana. Reprinted 1975, New York: Schocken Books.

———. 1977. *Marxism and Literature*. Oxford: Oxford University Press.

Willis, Ellen. 1994. "The Libertine's Lament: There Are at Least Two Faces to Feminism." *Mirabella*. April:34.

Willse, Jim. 1991. Telephone interview with author Helen Benedict.

Witt, Linda, Karen M. Paget, and Glenna Mathews. 1994. *Running as a Woman: Gender and Power in American Politics*. New York: Free Press.

Wolf, Naomi. 1990. *The Beauty Myth*. Toronto: Vintage.

———. 1993a. *Fire with Fire*. New York: Random House.

———. 1993b. "Women as Winners." *Glamour*. November:222.

———. 1993c. "Loving Men." *Glamour*. December:196.

———. 1994. Interview by Charlie Rose, January 3.

Wolff, Jennifer. 1994. "Sex by the Rules." *Glamour*. May:256.

"Women and the Chlamydia Epidemic." 1994. *Glamour*. February:46.

"Women Crime-Fighters in Texas." 1994. *Glamour*. March:98.

Women, Men, and the Media. 1993. "The News, as if All People Mattered." New York: Women, Men, and the Media, New York University.

———. 1994. "Are American Standards of Beauty Obsolete?" New York: Women, Men, and the Media, New York University.

"Women of the Year, 1994." 1994. *Glamour*. December:94.

Women's Action Coalition. 1993. *WAC STATS: The Facts about Women*. New York: New Press.

Women's Institute for Freedom of the Press. 1993. *What's Wrong with Mass Media for the Women Half of the Population—Rebuilding the System*. Washington: Women's Institute for Freedom of the Press.

Wong, Doris Sue, and David Armstrong. 1994. "State Cuts Ties with Agency over Scalding." *Boston Globe*. February 17:1.

Wood, Mrs. Henry. 1984 (1861) *East Lynne*. New Brunswick, NJ: Rutgers University Press.

Worrell, Kris. 1993. "Rethinking Feminism: Broad Definitions of Sexism and Rape Have Cast Women as the Weak Victims of Society, Young Author Argues in Book That's Raising Strong Emotions." *Atlanta Constitution*. September 27:B1.

Wright, Lisa. 1994. "Ms. Editor Opens Lectures." *Toronto Star*. February 20:A2.

Wright, Robert. 1994. "Feminists, Meet Mr. Darwin: The Evolutionary Psychology of the Female Mind." *New Republic*. 211 (November 28):34.

Yoffe, Emily. 1991. "Girls Who Go Too Far." *Newsweek*. July 22:58.

Yost, Barbara. 1994. "Feminists Are Shunned But Not Their Advances." *Phoenix Gazette*. October 21:B8.

Young, Cathy. 1992. "Women, Sex and Rape: Have Some Feminists Exaggerated the Problem?" *Washington Post*. May 31:C1.

———. 1993. "When a Woman Cries Wolf." *New York Newsday*. January 25:34.

———. 1994. "Keeping Women Weak." In *Next: Young American Writers on the New Generation*, edited by Eric Liu. New York: Norton.

Zuniga, Jo Ann. 1992. "The King Verdict: Shock Waves." *Houston Chronicle*. May 2:A13.

Table of Cases